Laos

written and researched by

Jeff Cranmer and Steven Martin

this edition updated by
Kirby Coxon

ROUGH GUIDES

www.roughguides.com

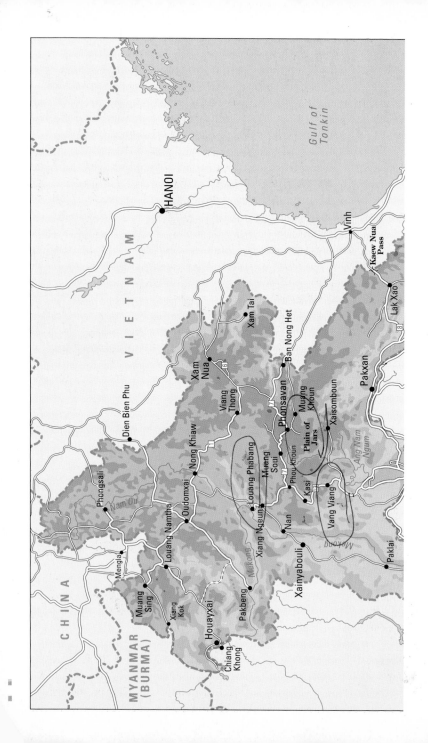

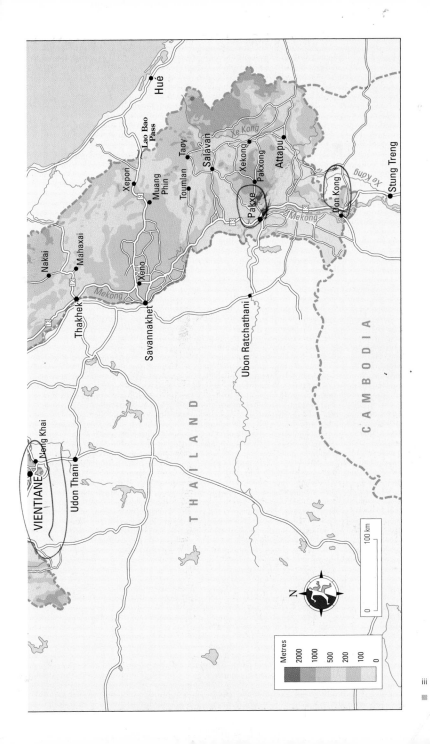

Introduction to
Laos

Less than a decade ago, Laos was more or less unknown to Western travellers. Other than a brief period during the 1960s, when the diminutive Buddhist kingdom became a player in the Vietnam War, it has remained a backwater – a situation that only intensified after the 1975 revolution and the years of xenophobic communist government that ensued, when the former French colony was largely forgotten, at least by the West. However, when the Lao People's Democratic Republic reluctantly reopened its doors to the outside world in the 1990s, after its major source of aid dried up with the collapse of the Soviet Union, a trickle of visitors braved the travel restrictions and exorbitant visa costs to have a look.

What they found was a poverty-stricken country stunted by war and politics and still doing things the old-fashioned way. The mighty Mekong and its tributaries were still the principal conduits for trade and, for much of the population, a pair of legs was the chief means of transport. Only a handful of provinces were wired for electricity, and Vientiane, the capital, was a sleepy town of tree-lined avenues, decaying French villas and a surviving opium den or two. Tourist infrastructure was almost nonexistent, and the very inadequacies that made travel in Laos unique were also causes of exasperation.

In the past few years, however, Laos has become much more accessible. Visa prices have come down and restrictions on travel have been all but lifted. In the major towns and cities there is good-value accommodation and a surprisingly diverse array of cuisines on offer. Conditions in the countryside, however, remain primitive and challenging, but travellers willing to brave difficult roads and basic, candlelit accommodation will be rewarded with sights of a landscape and people not much changed from

Fact file

- The Lao People's Democratic Republic, whose capital is Vientiane, is Southeast Asia's only land-locked country and shares borders with Thailand, Burma (Myanmar), China, Cambodia and Vietnam. One of Asia's least populated countries, modern Laos covers more than 236,000 square kilometres yet has a population of just 5.6 million.

- Lowland Lao (Lao Loum) comprise 68 percent of the population, while upland Lao (Lao Theung) and highland Lao (Lao Soung) make up 22 and 9 percent of the population respectively; within these broad definitions, there are many smaller divisions. Chinese and Vietnamese, mostly merchants, make up a further 1 percent of the population. The national language is Lao, a tonal language closely related to Thai, although the written scripts differ. Most Lao speak Thai as a second language but English is the most popular European language.

- Laos is a predominately Buddhist country and follows the Theravadan school of Buddhism which it shares in common with neighbouring Thailand and Cambodia, but up to 40 percent of the population, particularly in the highlands, follow animistic beliefs.

- A constitutional monarchy until 1976, Laos is today a one-party dictatorship and one of the world's last official communist states. It is one of the world's poorest countries with a primitive infrastructure and a per capita income of just US$300. Heavily reliant on foreign aid, the country is slowly opening up to foreign investment.

those that greeted French explorers a century ago.

Laos's lifeline is the Mekong River, which runs the length of the land-locked country, at times bisecting it and at others serving as a boundary with Thailand. The rugged Annamite Mountains also run much of the country's length and historically have acted as a buffer against Vietnam, with which Laos shares its eastern border. Much of Laos is forested and, despite the ongoing use of the slash-and-burn technique of agriculture, there are still considerable tracts of dense forest inhabited by myriad animal species. Tigers and other majestic cats, all but vanished from neighbouring countries, still stalk the hinterlands of Laos, and new species of large mammals are still being discovered, such as the deer-like soala or spindlehorn. There is even an endangered colony of rare freshwater dolphins inhabiting an isolated stretch of the Mekong.

For such a small country – its population is about 5.6 million – Laos is surprisingly diverse in terms of its people. Colourfully dressed hilltribes populate the higher elevations, while in the lowland river valleys, coconut palms sway over the Buddhist monasteries of the ethnic Lao. Laos also retains some of the French influence it absorbed during colonial days: the familiar smell of freshly baked bread and coffee mingles with exotic local aromas in morning markets. Economic reforms undertaken in the early Nineties gave the green light to Lao entrepreneurs, but recent economic woes have hamstrung the fledgling capitalists. The future is unclear, as the revolutionary old-guard remains firmly at the helm but with little idea of which course to steer. For the visitor using US dollars, there are bargains to be had, and while accommodation and modes of transport are often

The Hmong

The last of the great waves of tribal peoples to drift down from China's Yunnan Plateau, the Hmong are scattered throughout the highland regions of Indochina. Without a country to call their own, Hmong villages can be found in Thailand, Vietnam and even Burma (Myanmar), but are most widespread in Laos, a land rich in ethnic diversity. Travel by road anywhere through the mountains of northern Laos, and you'll be sure to come across numerous Hmong settlements. Precariously perched along the razor-back ridgelines of rugged mountain chains, Hmong villages usually hold around fifty households who eke a living out of the poor mountain soil. Recognizable by their elaborately embroidered tunics and hand-beaten silver jewellery, the Hmong are a tough but easy-going mountain people, delighted to have foreign guests and quick to extend hospitality.

very basic, they give visitors ample opportunity to rub shoulders with the people of Laos: a gentle and fun-loving folk whose patience and resilience continue to help them weather tough times.

Where to go

For many, a journey through Laos consists of a whistlestop tour through the two main towns of Vientiane and Louang Phabang, with perhaps a brief detour to the mysterious Plain of Jars or ancient Wat Phou. Yet, as Laos has relatively few proper tourist sites, you haven't really seen the country unless you've spent some time, slowed to a crawl aboard some ancient jalopy or slow boat, leisurely taking in the rugged natural beauty of the forests, mountains and waterways and witnessing the diverse cultures of the many peoples who make up the country's rich ethnic mosaic. If you want to travel the length of the country with some degree of leisure, seeing something of the northern mountains and the islands of the far south, and have enough time to absorb a little of the serene Lao way of life, you'll really need to be in the country for two to three weeks. With only two weeks at your disposal, you can either do a whirlwind trip up the Mekong River Valley, or perhaps better, focus on one region and enjoy it at an easy pace. If you do want to get a taste of

more than one region, internal flights, while unreliable, can speed up an itinerary substantially and are cheap enough not to break your budget.

For the majority of visitors, **Vientiane** provides a smooth introduction to Laos. Set on a broad curve of the Mekong in the Vientiane Plain, it is perhaps Southeast Asia's most modest capital city. Yet, although Vientiane lacks the commercial buzz of Ho Chi Minh City or Bangkok, the capital has been transformed in the past decade from a desolate city of boarded-up shopfronts into a quaint backwater, with a string of cosmopolitan restaurants and cafés to complement charming rows of pale yellow French-Indochinese shop-houses. Robbed of its more splendid temples long ago in battles with Siam, Vientiane is more a place for adjusting to the low-key pace of Lao life and indulging in herbal saunas and sunset drinks on the banks of the Mekong than one for breakneck tours of monuments and museums. Few tourists passing through the capital miss a chance for a half-day journey out to Xiang Khouan, the riverside meadow filled with mammoth religious statues, one of Laos's most arresting and bizarre sights.

With Vientiane seen off, most tourists venture north, the overwhelming majority making the dash on one of Lao Aviation's one-hour hops to Louang Phabang, though it's worth taking more time and doing the journey by bus. This gives you a chance to take in **Vang Viang**, a town set in a spectacular landscape of glimmering green paddies and sawtoothed karst hills, a popular spot for caving, kayaking, rock climbing and long walks in the countryside. From here the road rollercoasters through some of Laos's most stunning scenery along the mountainous old Royal Road to the north-

Riding the rivers

Situated high above the plains of Thailand and Vietnam, Laos is country of mountains, deep valleys and fast-running rivers. Although the rivers of Laos have for years served as the country's highways, it is only recently that the country's potential for kayaking, rafting, and canoeing has started to be realized.

Most of the action is currently limited to areas where there are whitewater travel companies on the ground, the best developed centres being Vang Viang (see p.119), Louang Phabang (see p.137) and Louang Namtha (see p.218). Most such operators offer a choice of day-trips or multi-day adventures, which usually include all equipment, an experienced guide and meals and lodging. Given the location and the overall quality of such tours, river adventures in Laos are astonishingly good value. Indeed, it could be argued that until you've got out on a river, you haven't really seen Laos at all.

ern capital. The more intrepid can indulge in a road-and-river expedition through Laos's northwestern frontier, catapulting up Southeast Asia's ancient highway, the Mekong River, by speedboat, or at a more measured pace aboard a slow boat, stopping off in the remote outpost of **Xainyabouli**, the right-bank province grudgingly turned over twice to the French by the Thais, and home to a large portion of the country's diminishing elephant population.

Once the heart and soul of the ancient Lao kingdom of Lane Xang, regal **Louang Phabang** is the centre of northern Laos and lies at the confluence of the Mekong and Khan rivers in a dramatic valley ringed by steep mountains. Despite the ravages of time, the gilded temples and weathered French-Indochinese shop-houses of this tiny, cultured city still possess a spellbinding majesty that make this Laos's most enticing destination. You won't want to leave without having taken a few day-trips out of the city, whether it's messing about on the Mekong en route to the sacred **Pak Ou Caves**, two riverside grottoes brimming with thousands of Buddha images, or meandering through hillside ethnic minority villages on the way to **Kouang Si waterfall**.

To the north of Louang Phabang, the wild highlands of the **far north**, part of which falls within the borders of the notorious, opium-rich **Golden Triangle**, aren't the easiest to get around, but this often spectacular, unrelentingly mountainous region is home to a patchwork of upland tribal groups and the setting for two of the country's most invigorating river journeys. The prospect of trekking off into nearby hilltribe villages has put easy-going **Muang Sing** on the map, a Tai-Leu settlement accessible via Louang Namtha and the Chinese-dominated hub of Oudomxai. From Muang Sing, a corkscrew ride through **Akha** country to the Burmese border lands you in **Xiangkok**, a frontier village perched on the banks of the Mekong River. Heading downriver, you'll pass **Houayxai**, an entry point popular with travellers arriving from northern Thailand in search of a slow boat for the leisurely, picturesque journey south to Louang Phabang. Even more scenic is the trip from Louang Phabang up the idyllic **Nam Ou River**, the emerald waterway lined with sandy beaches and craggy limestone hills, and on the banks of which lies the

War relics

The scars of the Second Indochina War, when Laos was used as a pawn by American and Vietnamese forces, continue to define the landscape of the country's rugged eastern frontier. Fly across the Plain of Jars to Xiang Khouang and a moonscape will stretch out below you, craters left from a time when American planes turned Laos into one of the most heavily bombed bits of earth in the world. Elsewhere, more reminders of the country's tumultuous recent history continue to haunt – journeying through the remote south you'll find the rusting skeletons of tanks and helicopters along the arteries of the Ho Chi Minh Trail, while strolling down the streets of downtown Phonsavan you'll stumble across mortar shells and dud bombs stacked against wooden shop-houses. The people of Laos have made the most of their misfortune: merchants from Vientiane carted off scrap metal in exchange for hard-earned kip, while rural villagers have transformed bomb casings into planters for vegetables, fences for country temples and sturdy supports for their homes. De-miners from around the world are still scrambling to clean up the mess, but it's an endless task.

Although there's little risk to the average tourist, travellers heading off the beaten track should keep this danger in mind (see p.65).

breathtaking village of **Nong Khiaw**. Those looking for more of a challenge can venture off the beaten track in Nong Khiaw by continuing upriver to Laos's chilly northernmost province, **Phongsali**, or opt to hop onto one of the rare pick-ups chugging off into the country's isolated **northeast**, towards Viang Thong and the farflung provinces of Xiang Khouang and Houa Phan.

Lost in the misty mountains of the far northeast, **Houa Phan** was the nerve centre of communist Laos during the Second Indochina War and remains well removed from the traditional Mekong River Valley centres of lowland Lao life. If you make it as far as the provincial capital of **Xam Nua**, you'll find it hard to resist the temptation to visit **Viang Xai**, where the Pathet Lao directed their resistance from deep within a vast cave complex. Following Route 6 south from Houa Phan you'll arrive in **Xiang Khouang** province, which was for centuries home to an independent Lao Phuan kingdom and remains the heartland of Laos's **Hmong** population. Layered with a too-often tragic history, Xiang Khouang was one of the

first places where civilization took root in Laos, though years of war have stripped the former Phuan kingdom of its line of kings and its reputedly elegant style of temples, the only remaining example of which lies far to the west, in Louang Phabang. **Phonsavan**, a dusty ramshackle town at the core of Xiang Khouang, is a good base from which to visit the region, in particular the province's premier attraction, the mystical **Plain of Jars**.

To the **south**, the tail of Laos is squeezed between the formidable Annamite Mountains to the east and the Mekong River as it barrels towards the Cambodian border. The vast majority of travellers, with the exception of those heading on to Vietnam, zip down Route 13, stopping off in the three major southern towns, Thakhek, Savannakhet and Pakxe. Independent-minded **Thakhek** is somewhat overshadowed by the other major Mekong towns, but the town distinguishes itself with its crumbling colonial facades and proximity to the jagged sea of limestone hills that shelter the **Mahaxai Caves**, as yet little known, but definitely worth seeing. With an architectural charm second only to Louang Phabang, genial **Savannakhet**, a town that is almost as culturally Vietnamese as it is Lao, is the south's most famous town and offers a pleasant urban retreat for those weary of the road. Downriver, the major market town of **Pakxe** lacks Savannakhet's charm, but good transport links make it a convenient base for trips to the remoter parts of the **far south**. Visitors rarely venture across the fertile Bolaven Plateau, where most of Laos's **coffee** is grown, to visit the three remote provinces of **Salavan**, **Xekong** and **Attapu**, Laos's wild east, preferring to strike south towards the diminutive former royal seat of the Lao principality of **Champasak**, with its red-dirt streets and princely villas. Nearby, the ruins of **Wat Phou**, the greatest of the Khmer temples outside Cambodia, perch on a forested hilltop. Anchoring the tail of Laos, the countless river islands of **Si Phan Don** lie scattered across the immense expanse of the Mekong, swollen to 14km from bank to bank, all the way to the lawless Cambodian border. One of the most significant wetlands in the country, Si Phan Don boasts scores of long-established fishing communities on the islands and on either bank of the Mekong. The area emerged from the years of civil war comparatively unscathed, and the large wooden homes of Si Phan Don's villages, as well as centuries-old lowland-Lao traditions, have been preserved.

When to go

November to January are the most pleasant months to travel in lowland Laos, when daytime temperatures are agreeably warm and evenings are slightly chilly, necessitating a light-weight jacket. However, at higher elevations temperatures are significantly cooler, sometimes dropping to freezing point – a heavy coat is a must. In February, temperatures begin to climb, reaching a peak in April, when the lowlands are baking-hot and humid. During this time, the high-

lands are, for the most part, equally hot if a bit less humid than the lowlands, though there are places, such as Pakxong on the Bolaven Plateau, that have a temperate climate year round. Generally, the rains begin in May and last until September. This is important to keep in mind, as the rainy season affects the condition of Laos's network of unpaved roads, some of which become impassable after the rains begin. On the other hand, rivers which may be too low to navigate during the dry season become important transport routes after the rains have caused water levels to rise.

Average daily maximum temperatures and monthly rainfall

	Jan	Feb	Mar	Apr	May	June	July	Aug	Sept	Oct	Nov	Dec
Louang Phabang												
°C	28	32	34	36	35	34	32	32	33	32	29	27
mm	15	18	31	109	163	155	231	300	165	79	31	13
Vientiane												
°C	28	30	33	34	32	32	31	31	31	31	29	28
mm	5	15	38	99	267	302	267	292	302	109	15	3

things not to miss

It's not possible to see everything that Laos has to offer in one trip – and we don't suggest you try. What follows is a selective and subjective taste of the country's highlights: stunning temples, colourful festivals and great activities. They're arranged in five colour-coded categories to help you find the very best things to see, do, eat and experience. All highlights have a page reference to take you straight into the guide, where you can find out more.

01 **Wat Sisaket** Page **97** • Buddha images nestle in temple walls at Vientiane's oldest temple, the only religious site spared the torch of invading Siamese in the 1800s.

02 Louang Phabang Page **137** • Laos's most enchanting city, centered on its sacred hill.

03 Trekking Page **227** • Rugged mountain forests set the scene for hikers seeking to explore the remote hill villages of the north.

04 Villa Santi Page **146** • Once home to royalty, Louang Phabang's most famous hotel still exudes colonial grandeur.

05 Boat races Page **56** • With roots in ancient planting rituals, boats races are held near the end of the rainy season throughout the country.

06 Kouang Si Falls Page **175** • A dip in the cool blue pools below Louang Phabang province's most picturesque waterfall is a refreshing respite from the tropical heat.

07 Mekong River Page 377 • The lifeline of a landlocked nation, the Mekong figures in every visit to Laos, supplying the fish for dinner, a route to travel along and a stunning array of sunsets.

08 Royal Palace Page 151 • The home of the country's last king provides a glimpse into Laos's fading royal past.

09 Plain of Jars Page 203 • Ancient funerary urns lie scattered across the heart of the northeast, the remnants of a lost civilization.

10 **Colonial shop-houses** Page **153** • French-Indochinese shop-houses add a splash of colour to city streets in Mekong River towns.

11 **Wat Xiang Thong** Page **154** • Spared wars, fires and overzealous restorations, the jewel of temple-rich Louang Phabang is as elegant as it is historic.

12 Markets Page **44** • With fresh greens, pigs' heads and bootlegged DVDs of the latest Hollywood thriller all on offer, the country's markets make for a rich hunting ground for intrepid shoppers.

13 Textiles Page **368** • Weavers plying their craft still work the looms under their homes in the countryside, where each ethnic group is known for having its own style of textiles.

14 Vang Viang Page **119** • A spectacular landscape dotted with sawtoothed karsts, Vang Viang offers a chance to romp in the outdoors, with kayaking, rock climbing and caving all on hand.

15 That Chomsi Page **158** • Stunning panoramas await those who reach the golden crown of Louang Phabang's sacred hill.

16 Herbal healing Page **66** • Rejuvenate yourself with a visit to a traditional Lao sauna, where the herbal remedies in the steam bath and the tea are jealously guarded secrets.

17 **That Louang Festival** Page **56** • Held at Laos's most important religious site, the country's largest temple fair is a weeklong carnival of games, fireworks and alms-offerings.

18 **Up the Nam Ou**
Page **241** •
Whether by speedboat or lazy cruise, a journey along the tropical waterways of the mountainous north is an experience not to be missed.

19 **Wat Phou**
Page **295** • The most evocative Khmer ruin outside of Cambodia, this rambling mountainside complex dates from the sixth to twelfth centuries.

20 **Haw Pha Kaew** Page **98** • Once the king's personal shrine, the Temple of the Emerald Buddha now houses the best collection of Lao art in the country.

21 **Patouxai** Page **99** • The Paris-inspired Victory Arch lends a monumental air to the otherwise low-rise and understated capital.

22 **Buddha Caves** Page **173** • Hundreds of buddhas gaze serenely across the Mekong from their riparian perch.

Contents

Using the Rough Guide

We've tried to make this Rough Guide a good read and easy to use. The book is divided into six main sections, and you should be able to find whatever you want in one of them.

Colour section

The front colour section offers a quick tour of Laos. The **introduction** aims to give you a feel for the place, with suggestions on where to go. We also tell you what the weather is like and include a basic country fact file. Next, our authors round up their favourite aspects of Laos in the **things not to miss** section – whether it's a great festival, amazing sights or a special hotel. Right after this comes a full **contents** list.

Basics

The Basics section covers all the **pre-departure** nitty-gritty to help you plan your trip. This is where to find out which airlines fly to your destination, what paperwork you'll need, what to do about money and insurance, about internet access, food, security, public transport, car rental – in fact just about every piece of **general practical information** you might need.

Guide

This is the heart of the Rough Guide, divided into user-friendly chapters, each of which covers a specific region. Every chapter starts with a list of **highlights** and an **introduction** that helps you to decide where to go, depending on your time and budget. Likewise, introductions to the various towns and smaller regions within each chapter should help you plan your

itinerary. We start most town accounts with information on arrival and accommodation, followed by a tour of the sights, and finally reviews of places to eat and drink, and details of nightlife. Longer accounts also have a directory of practical listings. Each chapter concludes with **public transport** details for that region.

Contexts

Read Contexts to get a deeper understanding of what makes Laos tick. We include a brief history, articles about **religion**, **the arts**, **peoples**, **the environment** and **myth and literature**, and a detailed further reading section that reviews dozens of **books** relating to the country.

Language

The **language** section gives useful guidance for speaking Laos and pulls together all the vocabulary you might need on your trip, including a comprehensive **menu reader**. Here you'll also find a **glossary** of words and terms peculiar to the country.

Index + small print

Apart from a **full index**, which includes maps as well as places, this section covers publishing information, credits and acknowledgements, and also has our contact details in case you want to send in updates and corrections to the book – or suggestions as to how we might improve it.

Chapter list and map

- Colour section
- Contents
- **B** Basics
- **①** Vientiane and the northwest
- **②** Louang Phabang
- **③** The northeast
- **④** The far north
- **⑤** South central Laos
- **⑥** The far south
- **C** Contexts
- **L** Language
- **I** Index

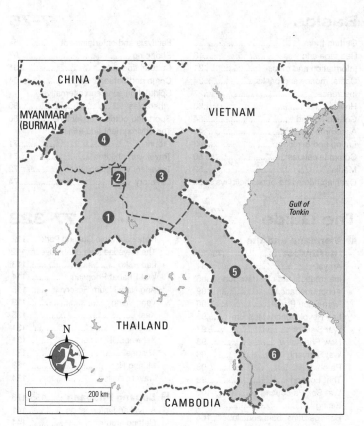

Contents

Contexts

325–390

Language

391–402

Index + small print

403–411

Map symbols

Maps are listed in the full index using coloured text.

- - - -	International boundary		🕌	Mosque
- - -	Chapter division boundary		⊙	Statue/monument
═══	Major road		✈	Airport
══	Minor road		★	Bus/taxi stand
⊞⊞⊞⊞	Steps (town maps)		🛢	Petrol station
━━	Rail line		🕓	Telephone office
— —	Ferry route		@	Internet access
────	River		ⓘ	Tourist information
♦	Point of interest		⊠	Post office
🗻	Mountain range		⊞	Hospital
▲	Mountain peak		⬜	Market
🌊	Waterfall		⬭	Stadium
∴	Ruin		⬛	Building
⌒	Cave		✛	Church/cathedral
⛩	Temple/monastery		▨	Park
⌁	Stupa/that		▨	National Biodiversity Conservation Area (NBCA)
🏮	Chinese temple			

Basics

Basics

Getting there

The quickest and easiest way to get to Laos is to fly. Vientiane is the main gateway into Laos but there are no direct flights from Europe, America or Australasia; instead major airlines fly to Bangkok, from where you can take a daily, hour-long flight to Vientiane with Thai Airways International or Lao Aviation.

Booking a **scheduled ticket** direct with the airline is the most expensive way to fly. Generally, you're best off booking through an established discount agent, which can usually undercut airline prices by a significant amount. Barring special offers, the cheapest of the airlines' published fares is usually an **Apex** ticket, although this will carry certain restrictions: you will most likely have to book – and pay – at least 21 days before departure, spend at least seven days abroad (maximum stay three months), and you tend to get penalized if you change your schedule. There are also **Super Apex** tickets available in winter, slightly cheaper than an ordinary Apex, but limiting your stay to between 7 and 21 days. Some airlines also issue Special Apex tickets to people under the age of 24, often extending the maximum stay to a year. Many airlines offer **youth or student fares** to under-25s, though requirements vary and these tickets are subject to availability and can have eccentric booking conditions. If you qualify, you'll save perhaps eight to ten percent, but you'll need to book as far in advance as you can, as seat availability at these prices is limited. It's worth remembering that many will only give a percentage refund if you need to cancel or alter your journey.

You can normally cut costs by going through a **specialist flight agent** – either a **consolidator** (in North America only), who buys up blocks of tickets from the airlines and sells them at a discount, or a **discount agent**, who in addition to dealing with discounted flights may also offer special **student and youth fares** and a range of other travel-related services such as travel insurance, car rental, tours and the like. Many companies sell tickets on the internet too,

and **online agents** like www.travelocity.com are worth a try. Bear in mind, though, that penalties for changing your plans can be stiff. Don't automatically assume that tickets purchased through a specialist flight agent will be cheapest – once you get a quote, check with the airlines and you may turn up an even better deal.

A further possibility is to see if you can arrange a **courier flight**, although you'll need a flexible schedule, and preferably be travelling alone with very little luggage. In return for shepherding a parcel through customs, you can expect to get a deeply discounted ticket, though you'll probably be restricted in the duration of your stay.

Regardless of where you buy your ticket, **fares** will depend on the season. The most expensive time to fly to Laos is during high season, which on most airlines runs from the beginning of July through to the end of August and also includes most of December. Note also that flying at weekends adds to the fare.

If Laos is only one stop on a longer journey, you might want to consider buying a **Round-the-World (RTW) ticket**. Some travel agents can sell you an "off-the-shelf" RTW ticket that will have you touching down in about half a dozen cities; others will have to assemble one for you, which can be tailored to your needs but is apt to be more expensive.

Online travel agents

Many airlines and discount travel websites offer you the opportunity to book your tickets **online**, cutting out the costs of agents and middlemen. Good deals can often be found through discount or auction sites, as well as through the airlines' own websites.

Online booking agents and general travel sites

ⓦ **www.cheapflights.com** Bookings from the UK and Ireland only. Flight deals, travel agents, plus links to other travel sites.

ⓦ **www.etn.nl/discount.htm** A hub of consolidator and discount agent Web links, maintained by the nonprofit European Travel Network.

ⓦ **www.expedia.com** Discount airfares, all-airline search engine and daily deals.

ⓦ **www.flyaow.com** Online air travel info and reservations site.

ⓦ **www.geocities.com/Thavery2000** Has an extensive list of airline toll-free numbers and websites.

ⓦ **www.hotwire.com** Bookings from the US only. Last-minute savings of up to forty percent on regular published fares. Travellers must be at least 18 and there are no refunds, transfers or changes allowed. Log-in required.

ⓦ **www.lastminute.com** Bookings from the UK only. Offers good last-minute holiday package and flight-only deals.

ⓦ **www.priceline.com** Name-your-own-price website that has deals at around forty percent off standard fares. You cannot specify flight times (although you do specify dates) and the tickets are non-refundable, non-transferable and non-changeable.

ⓦ **www.skyauction.com** Bookings from the US only. Auctions tickets and travel packages using a "second bid" scheme. The best strategy is to bid the maximum you're willing to pay, since if you win you'll pay just enough to beat the runner-up regardless of your maximum bid.

ⓦ **www.smilinjack.com/airlines.htm** Lists an up-to-date compilation of airline website addresses.

ⓦ **www.sydneytravel.com** Sydney-based travel agent, with special offers and discounts for booking on-line.

ⓦ **www.travel.com.au** Web-based travel agent, with special offers and discounts for booking on-line.

ⓦ **www.travelforless.co.nz** Travel agency chain specializing in economy travel.

ⓦ **http://travel.yahoo.com** Incorporates a lot of Rough Guide material in its coverage of destination countries and cities across the world, with information about places to eat, sleep and so on.

ⓦ **www.travelocity.com** Destination guides, hot web fares and the best deals for car hire, accommodation and lodging as well as fares. Provides access to the travel agent system SABRE, the most comprehensive central reservations system in the US.

ⓦ **www.travelshop.com.au** Australian website offering discounted flights, packages, insurance, online bookings.

Flights from Britain and Ireland

As there are **no direct flights** from Europe to Laos, you'll need to fly to Bangkok and then on to Vientiane with Thai Airways International (daily 8.20am) or Lao Aviation (daily 6.25pm). Return fares to Vientiane from Bangkok rarely fluctuate, hovering around $200 on both airlines for the one-hour flight. Discount travel agencies in Bangkok can't offer a better price than the airlines so you may as well book this leg from home.

There are non-stop flights from **London to Bangkok** with Qantas, British Airways, EVA Airways or Thai International – a journey time of about twelve hours. Many scheduled airlines operate indirect flights (ie, flights with one or more connections), which usually take up to four hours longer, but work out significantly cheaper, particularly if you go with Lauda Air via Vienna, or Royal Jordanian Airways via Amman.

There are no non-stop flights to Bangkok from British **regional airports or Ireland**, only from London, therefore you may find it convenient to fly via other European cities, and fares sometimes work out about the same as for indirect flights from London – though in the case of Ireland it may be worthwhile getting a cheap flight or ferry to England, then booking your flight to Bangkok from London.

Generally, you're best off booking through an established **discount agent**, which can usually undercut airline prices by a significant amount. See p.11 for a list of recommended agents, all of which are members of official travel organizations such as ABTA or IATA, which means that you'll get a refund on your fare should the company go bust. Discount agents' adverts in national Sunday papers, London's *Evening Standard* newspaper or *Time Out* magazine, or in major regional newspapers and listings magazines, may give even better deals, but possibly lack ABTA/IATA affiliation. If you are a **student or under 26**, you may be able to get further discounts on flight prices, especially through agents such as STA Travel. However, for this part of the world, there's often little difference between a youth fare and a regular discounted one.

Fares vary with the time of year. During the **high season** (July–August & December), a discounted flight is likely to cost you around £550; flights get booked solid and should be reserved several weeks in advance. Prices drop considerably at other times of the year, when you should be able to find a fare for under £450.

With a long-haul destination such as Laos, it's always worth considering **stopping off** for a few days en route. You'll probably have to go with the associated national airline, for which service there should be no extra charge. Alternatively, you could put together a more extensive **Round-the-World itinerary**, which allows you several stops in Asia or elsewhere. For example, a one-year open ticket from London taking in Bangkok with a side-trip to Vientiane, Bali, Brunei, Brisbane/Melbourne, Auckland and New York starts as low as £750, rising to around £1000 if you add stops in India and the South Pacific.

Finally, if you're interested in getting a **courier flight** contact the International Association of Air Travel Couriers UK (☎0800/0746 481 or 01305/216 920, ⓦwww.aircourier.co.uk), which acts as an agent for lots of companies.

Airlines in Britain with flights to Bangkok

British Airways ☎0845/77 333 77; Republic of Ireland ☎1800/626 747, ⓦwww.britishairways.com. Daily non-stop flights from Heathrow.
Eva Airways ☎020/7380 8300, ⓦwww.evaair.com.tw. Three non-stop flights a week from Heathrow.
Lauda Air ☎0845/601 0948, ⓦwww.laudaair.co.uk. Two flights a week from Gatwick via Vienna. Once a week from Gatwick to Phuket, also via Vienna.
Qantas ☎0845/774 7767, ⓦwww.qantas.com.au. Daily non-stop flights from Heathrow.
Thai International ☎0870/606 0911, ⓦwww.thaiair.com. Daily non-stop flights from Heathrow.

Discount flight agents in Britain and Ireland

Bridge the World UK ☎020/7911 0900; ⓦwww.bridgetheworld.com. Specializing in round-the-world tickets, with good deals aimed at the backpacker market.
Flightbookers UK ☎0870/010 7000, ⓦwww.ebookers.com. Low fares on an extensive selection of scheduled flights.
North South Travel UK ☎ & ☎01245/608 291, ⓦwww.northsouthtravel.co.uk. Friendly, competitive travel agency, offering discounted fares worldwide – profits are used to support projects in the developing world, especially the promotion of sustainable tourism.
STA Travel UK ☎0870/1600 599, ⓦwww.statravel.co.uk. Worldwide specialists in low-cost flights and tours for students and under-26s, though other customers welcome.
Trailfinders UK ☎020/7628 7628, ⓦwww.trailfinders.com. Dublin ☎01/677 7888, ⓦwww.trailfinders.ie. One of the best-informed and most efficient agents for independent travellers; produce a very useful quarterly magazine worth scrutinizing for round-the-world routes.
Travel Bag UK ☎0870/900 1350, ⓦwww.travelbag.co.uk. Discount flights to Australia, New Zealand, USA and the Far East; official Qantas agent.

Packages and organized tours

Inevitably more expensive and less spontaneous than if you travelled independently, **package tours** to Laos are nonetheless worth investigating if you have limited time or a specialist interest. They range from highly specialized tailor-made trips to more wide-ranging tours of Indochina. It's also sometimes possible to use them as a starting point to your holiday, allowing you to get the feel of the place with minimal hassle – just check before booking that you can stay on independently and fly back at a later date. Your local travel agent should be able to book any tour for you at no additional cost.

A large chunk of the holiday price goes on the flight, so anything below £750 for room-only rates is good value; many companies are quoting for five-night trips now, rather than a full week, so be vigilant when reading brochures.

Specialist tour operators in Britain and Ireland

Explore Worldwide 1 Frederick St, Aldershot, Hants GU11 1LQ ☎01252/760 000, ⓦwww.explore.co.uk. Explore Worldwide's epic eighteen-day "Spirit of Laos" tour starts in Bangkok and includes Northern Laos, the Plain of Jars, and the Boloven Plateau.

Guerba Expeditions Wessex House, 40 Station Rd, Westbury, Wiltshire BA13 3JN ☎01373/826611, ⓕ858351, ⓦwww.guerba.co.uk. Guerba run a fifteen-day Bangkok to Hanoi overland tour that takes you down the Mekong to Louang Phabang then to Vientiane and Pak Lao, and across Route 9 to Hanoi. They have a policy of employing local guides and encouraging an open-minded approach to the cultures you encounter.

Magic of the Orient 2 Kingsland Court, Three Bridge Road, Crawley, West Sussex RH10 1HL ☎01293/537 700, ⓦwww.magic-of-the-orient.com. Upmarket tour company offering a wide range of packages, with both comfort and soft adventure covered. Their five-day "Laos Classic" tour concentrates on the ancient capital of Louang Phabang and can be done in conjunction with their Yunnan tour.

Regent Holidays 15 John St, Bristol BS1 2HR ☎0117/921 1711, ⓕ925 4866, ⓦwww.regent-holidays.co.uk. The fourteen-day "Laos in Depth" tour (£1141) features an excursion to the temple ruins at Wat Phou, a trip on the Mekong River, Louang Phabang, Boloven Plateau, and the Plain of Jars; it starts and finishes in Vientiane.

Steppes East Castle Eaton, Cricklade, Wiltshire SN6 6JU ☎01285/810267, ⓕ810693, ⓦwww.steppeseast.co.uk. Tailor-made and exclusive holidays in Indochina. A fourteen-day suggested itinerary for Laos (£1880) covers the 4000 Islands, Boloven Plateau, Wat Phou, Vientiane and Louang Phabang.

Symbiosis 113 Bolingbroke Grove, London SW11 1DA ☎020/7924 5906, ⓕ924 5907, ⓦwww.symbiosis-travel.co.uk. An environmentally aware and exclusive outfit. Organized tours include one centred around the Louang Phabang Boat Race Festival and specialised kayaking tours to the Nam Ou, Nam Xekong, and rivers on the Vientiane Plain. They also arrange tailor-made trips.

Flights from the US and Canada

As there are no direct flights from North America to Laos, you'll need to catch one of the many daily flights from major North American cities to Bangkok and then contin-ue on to Vientiane with Thai Airways International (daily 8.20am) or Lao Aviation (daily 6.25pm). Return fares to Vientiane from Bangkok rarely fluctuate, hovering around $200 on both airlines for the one-hour flight. Discount travel agencies in Bangkok can't offer a better price than the airlines so you may as well book this leg from home.

Direct flights to Bangkok depart from Vancouver, Seattle, San Francisco and Los Angeles on the West Coast, from Detroit in the Midwest and from New York and Newark on the East Coast. Flying time from the West Coast to Bangkok is sixteen to eighteen hours, twenty hours from the New York area and Detroit. Flights from Toronto usually stop in Vancouver before continuing on to Bangkok via East Asia, although it's possible to fly directly from Toronto to Osaka at certain times of the year. The layover time between connecting flights varies from airline to airline and even between different flights belonging to the same carrier, although you won't have to make an overnight stop.

Going to Laos is a great excuse for a **stopover**, as all flights to Bangkok from North America fly via East Asia, with the most common hubs being Tokyo, Hong Kong, Seoul and Taipei. You can also opt for a flight via Europe, a route that takes nineteen hours from New York and a full 24 hours from the West Coast. For those combining a trip to Laos with a visit to one of its neighbours, Vientiane can also be reached by air from southwestern China, Vietnam and Cambodia as well as by a variety of overland routes (for details, see p.17).

Fares to Bangkok vary widely. Count on being able to get a better deal via Asia than on flights via Europe, especially if you're departing from the West Coast. Note also that flying on weekends can add as much as $200 to a round-trip fare. For regular high-season (July–August & December) return fares from the West Coast you can expect to pay $1200–1400, and from the East Coast $1300–1500. For low-season fares from the West Coast reckon on $750–1000 and from the Midwest and the East $850–1200. China Airlines, which flies via Taipei, and Korean Airlines, which flies via Seoul, tend to be the cheapest, although EVA, which flies via

Taipei, is worth considering for its Evergreen Deluxe Class, which offers near-business class comforts for what it would cost to fly economy on some other carriers.

Air Canada has the most convenient service to Bangkok from the largest number of Canadian cities. From Vancouver expect to pay around CDN$2000 in low season (CDN$300 more in high season), from Toronto CDN$2300 (CDN$400 more in high season).

Another option is a **Round-the-World (RTW) ticket**, which allows you several stops in Asia or elsewhere. For example, an itinerary of Los Angeles–Taipei–Shanghai–overland on your own–Hanoi–Vientiane–Bangkok–Delhi–overland on your own–Bombay–Cairo–overland on your own–Paris–San Francisco would cost from $1700, while New York–Hong Kong–Singapore–overland on your own–Bangkok–Delhi–Bombay–London–New York would only cost $1380, but would mean you having to visit Laos as a side trip. You can get RTW tickets tailored to your needs, though this is apt to be more expensive. The Star Alliance, which includes Thai Airways International, Air Canada, Lufthansa, SAS, Varig, United Airlines, Ansett Australia and Air New Zealand, offers a mileage-based RTW fare from $2499, which allows you to take in three to fifteen destinations, with a certain amount of backtracking and a number of side-trips.

Similarly, discount travel agents and some major airlines offer **Circle Pacific** deals that allow you to make a certain number of stopovers, usually on the condition that you travel in an onward direction. Even if Vientiane doesn't actually feature in the deal, Bangkok and Vietnam often do, allowing you to visit Laos as a side trip. A couple of sample itineraries are: San Francisco–Los Angeles–Hong Kong–Bangkok–Hong Kong–San Francisco for $1170 and New York–Hong Kong–Ho Chi Minh City–Vientiane–Bangkok–Jakarta–Bali–Los Angeles–New York for $1910. Some airlines, such as Thai Airways International and Cathay Pacific (usually through its website www.cathay-usa.com), routinely offer promotions that allow you to take in a number of Asian cities for a discounted fare.

Airlines in the USA and Canada

Air Canada Canada ☎1-888/247-2262; US ☎1-800/776-3000; ⓦwww.aircanada.ca. Daily flights from most major Canadian cities via Japan.
Air France US ☎1-800/237-2747; Canada ☎1-800/667-2747; ⓦwww.airfrance.fr. Daily flights to Bangkok via Paris from Los Angeles, Houston, Chicago, Miami, Washington DC, New York, San Francisco, Toronto and Montréal.
Cathay Pacific ☎1-800/233-2742, ⓦwww.cathay-usa.com. Daily flights to Bangkok from New York, Vancouver and Los Angeles via Hong Kong.
China Airlines ☎1-800/227-5118, ⓦwww.china-airlines.com. Daily flights to Bangkok via Taipei from Los Angeles and San Francisco; on Monday, Wednesday and Saturday from New York.
Delta Airlines ☎1-800/241-4141, ⓦwww.delta-air.com. Daily flights to Bangkok via Seoul or Tokyo from most major US cities.
EVA Airlines ☎1-800/695-1188, ⓦwww.evaair.com.tw. Daily flights to Bangkok via Taipei from New York, Seattle and Vancouver.
Japan Air Lines ☎1-800/525-3663, www.japanair.com. Daily flights to Bangkok via Japan from San Francisco, Los Angeles, Chicago, Detroit, Seattle and New York.
Korean Airlines ☎1-800/438-5000, www.koreanair.com. Daily flights to Bangkok via Seoul from New York, Los Angeles and Vancouver.
Northwest/KLM US ☎1-800/447-4747; Canada ☎1-800/361-5073, ⓦwww.klm.com. Daily flights to Bangkok via Japan from most major US cities.
Singapore Airlines ☎1-800/742-3333, www.singaporeair.com. Daily flights to Bangkok via Singapore from New York, Los Angeles, San Francisco and Vancouver.
Swiss US ☎1-800/221-4750; Canada ☎1-800/267-9477, ⓦwww.swiss.com. Daily flights to Bangkok via Zurich from Montréal, New York and Toronto.
Thai Airways International US ☎1-800/426-5204; Canada ☎1-800/668-8103, ⓦwww.thaiairways.com. Daily flights to Bangkok via Japan from Los Angeles.
United Airlines ☎1-800/538-2929, ⓦwww.ual.com. Daily flights to Bangkok via Japan from most major US cities.

Discount travel companies in the USA and Canada

Air Brokers International ☎1-800/883-3273 or 415/397-1383, ⓦwww.airbrokers.com. Consolidator and specialist in RTW and Circle Pacific tickets.

Air Courier Association ☎1-800/282-1202 or 303/278-8810, ⓦwww.aircourier.org. Courier flight broker.

Airtech ☎1-877-247-8324 or 212/219-7000, ⓦwww.airtech.com. Standby seat broker; also deals in consolidator fares and courier flights.

Council Travel ☎1-800/226-8624, Ⓕ617/528-2091, ⓦwww.counciltravel.com. Student/budget travel agency with branches in many US cities.

Educational Travel Center ☎1-800/747-5551 or 608/256-5551, ⓦwww.edtrav.com. Student/youth discount agent.

High Adventure Travel ☎1-800/350-0612 or 415/912-5600, ⓦwww.airtreks.com. Round-the-world and Circle Pacific tickets. The website features an interactive database that lets you build and price your own round-the-world itinerary. Also does Asian overland connections

International Association of Air Travel Couriers ☎352/475-1584, ⓦwww.courier.org. Courier flight broker with membership fee of $45 a year or $80 for two years.

Now Voyager ☎212/431-1616, ⓦwww.nowvoyagertravel.com. Courier flight broker and consolidator.

Skylink US ☎1-800/247-6659 or 212/573-8980; Canada ☎1-800/759-5465; ⓦwww.skylinkus.com. A consolidator with branches in New York, Chicago, Los Angeles, Montréal, Toronto, and Washington DC.

STA Travel ☎1-800/777-0112 or 1-800/781-4040, ⓦwww.sta-travel.com. Worldwide specialists in independent travel; also student IDs, travel insurance, etc.

Travac ☎1-800/872-8800, ⓦwww.thetravelsite.com. Consolidator and charter broker with offices in New York City and Orlando. Worldwide.

Travel Avenue ☎1-800/333-3335, ⓦwww.travelavenue.com. Full-service travel agent that offers discounts in the form of rebates.

Travel Cuts Canada ☎1-800/667-2887, US ☎1-866/246-9762, ⓦwww.travelcuts.com. Canadian student-travel organization.

Travelers Advantage ☎1-877/259-2691, ⓦwww.travelersadvantage.com. Discount travel club; annual membership fee required (currently $1 for 3 months' trial).

Packages and organized tours

An **organized tour** is worth considering if your time is limited or if you have a special-ized interest. By relying on tours you won't be fully immersing yourself in the country and its culture, but a guide and a minivan can cut the trail to some of Laos's far-flung sites and keep you from getting stranded in towns with limited transport.

North American and Canadian package tour operators

Adventure Center 1311 63rd St, Suite 200, Emeryville, CA 94608 ☎1-800/227-8747, ⓦwww.adventurecenter.com. This company offers no less than nine separate trips in Laos lasting between five and twenty-one days. "Laos Trekking Adventure", a seven-day to Louang Phabang and northwestern Laos, includes kayaking or biking and trekking, as well as overnight stays in a hillside Hmong village for $745 excluding airfares. "Spirit of Laos" is an eighteen-day journey that takes in many of Laos's major tourist destinations, including the north, 4000 Islands, the Boloven Plateau, and the Plain of Jars. The latter trip starts from $1770, not including flights.

Adventures Abroad 2148-20800 Westminster Hwy, Richmond, BC V6V 2W3 ☎1-800/665-3998, ⓦwww.adventures-abroad.com. Small-group tour specialists with eight regional tours lasting from 8 days right up to 45 days which include Laos on their itinerary. They also have a seven-day tour just of Laos for CDN$1390.

Far Horizons PO Box 91900, Albuquerque, NM 87199-1900 ☎1-800 552-4575, ⓦwww.farhorizon.com. Specialists in archeological and cultural trips. Their "Discover Angkor Wat and Laos" tour lasts sixteen days and costs $6295 (including flights), with an optional river boat extension which takes in Wat Phou in southern Laos.

Geographic Expeditions 2627 Lombard St, San Francisco, CA 94123, USA. ☎1-415-922-0448 or 1-800-777-8183, ⓦwww.geoex.com. This company offers several Southeast Asian loops which include Laos. Their nine-day Laos tour includes Vientiane, Louang Prabang, the Plain of Jars and the Boloven Plateau for $2335.

Himalayan Travel 110 Prospect St, Stamford, CT 06901 ☎1-800/225-2380 or 203/743-2349, ⓦwww.himalayantravelinc.com. There are four Laos tours avaliable including "Bike Northern Laos" and "Exploring the Middle Mekong". Three-to-eleven-day customized tours to Laos also available.

Journeys 107 Aprill Drive, Suite 3, Ann Arbor MI 46103 ☎1-800/255-8735, ⓦwww.journeys-intl.com. Specialists in small-group nature and culture explorations. "Laos Odyssey" is a six-day river and road journey from $1175; the six-day

"Laos Highlights" tour takes in Louang Phabang and Vientiane and costs from $1175.
Mountain Travel-Sobek 6420 Fairmount Ave, El Cerrito, CA 94530 ☎1-888/687-6235, ⓦ www.mtsobek.com. "Focus on Northern Vietnam and Laos" is an eighteen-day journey visiting historic sites in Laos and ethnic minority villages in northern Vietnam, from $4290 (not including flight).

Flights from Australia and New Zealand

There are no direct flights from Australasia to Laos, so you'll need to fly via an Asian gateway city. Bangkok is your best bet, as Thai Airways International flies from both Australia and New Zealand to Thailand and also between Thailand and Laos. Although Laos is often just one stop on a longer trip, it's rare for round-the-world ticket routings to include Vientiane, and it's more usual to take in Laos as a side-trip from Thailand or Vietnam.

Fares are structured according to seasons and vary between A$1100/NZ$1400 and A$1500/NZ$1800. High season is generally December to mid-January; shoulder season is mid-January to end-February, early to mid-April, end-June to mid-July, mid-September to early October and mid- to end-November. The rest of the year is low season. Several airlines have a set fare from major eastern Australian cities to Bangkok; fares from Perth and Darwin are around A$100–200 cheaper. From Christchurch and Wellington you'll pay NZ$150–300 more than from Auckland.

From Australia, there are frequent **direct flights to Bangkok** from Sydney, Melbourne or Brisbane with Thai Airways International for around A$950 low season and A$1200 high season. Olympic Airways have rock-bottom fares to Bangkok from Sydney at A$800 low season, A$1050 high season. Flying on an airline like Qantas or British Airways will cost slightly more, with fares starting at A$890 in low season. From Perth, the cheapest fares are with Royal Brunei Airlines to Bangkok, at A$850 in low season and A$930 in high season; Thai Airways International is more expensive at A$935–1150. Connecting flights are available from **Bangkok to Vientiane** for A$310 return on Thai Airways International.

From New Zealand, Qantas offers the cheapest direct low season fares (NZ$1100); Thai Airways International flies Auckland to Bangkok for around NZ$1400 low season. Singapore Airlines via Singapore to Bangkok costs around NZ$1250 low season. From Bangkok you can pick up a Thai Airways International flight to Vientiane and back for approximately NZ$420.

If you want to take in Laos as part of a world trip, another option is a **Round-the-World ticket**. Although few itineraries include Vientiane, several offer a stop in Bangkok, from where you can take a side-trip. Of the ever-increasing choices available, Qantas–British Airways' "Global Explorer" and "One World" tickets cost from A$2000/NZ$3090 low season – allow on average six stopovers on three continents. One of the few itineraries that includes Vientiane is offered by the Star Alliance, which includes Thai Airways International, United Airlines, Ansett, Air New Zealand, Air Canada, Lufthansa, SAS and Varig; a fare of A$2799/NZ$3300 allows 25,000 miles of travel on a minimum of four continents.

If you don't want to travel outside of Asia, a better option is a **Circle Asia ticket**. Put together by an alliance of airlines, these tickets allow you to travel via two or more Asian cities en route, but can be a little complicated to arrange as each sector needs to be costed separately and back-tracking isn't allowed.

Airlines in Australia and New Zealand

Air New Zealand Australia ☎13 24 76; New Zealand ☎0800/737 000, ⓦ www.airnz.com.
British Airways Australia ☎02/8904 8800, New Zealand ☎0800/274 847, ⓦ www.britishairways.com. Daily service from Sydney to Bangkok.
Cathay Pacific Australia ☎13 1747; New Zealand ☎09/379 0861, ⓦ www.cathaypacific.com. Daily service from Auckland, Brisbane, Sydney, Melbourne, Adelaide, Cairns and Perth to Bangkok via Hong Kong.
Egypt Air Australia ☎02/9267 6979, ⓦ www.egyptair.com.eg.
Garuda Australia ☎02/9334 9970; New Zealand ☎09/366 1862, ⓦ www.garuda-indonesia.com. Daily service from Auckland, Adelaide, Brisbane, Cairns, Melbourne and Sydney to Bangkok via Denpasar or Jakarta.

Gulf Air Australia ⓣ 02/9244 2199; New Zealand ⓣ 09/308 3366, ⓦ www.gulfairco.com.
Malaysia Airlines Australia ⓣ 13 2627; New Zealand ⓣ 09/373 2741, ⓦ www.mas.com.my. Daily service from Sydney, Melbourne and Auckland to Bangkok via Kuala Lumpur.
Olympic Airways Australia ⓣ 02/9251 2044, ⓦ www.olympic-airways.com.Twice-weekly service to Bangkok from Sydney and Melbourne.
Qantas Australia ⓣ 13 13 13, New Zealand ⓣ 09/661 901, ⓦ www.qantas.com.au. Daily flights from major Australian and New Zealand cities to Bangkok.
Royal Brunei Airlines Australia ⓣ 07/3017 5000, ⓦ www.bruneiair.com.
Singapore Airlines Australia ⓣ 13 10 11, New Zealand ⓣ 09/303 2129, ⓦ www.singaporeair.com. Daily service to Bangkok from Sydney, Adelaide, Melbourne and Auckland via a transfer in Singapore.
Thai Airways International Australia ⓣ 1300/651960; New Zealand ⓣ 09/377 3886, ⓦ www.thaiair.com. Several flights a week to Vientiane from Sydney, Brisbane, Melbourne and Auckland via a transfer in Bangkok.

Discount flight agents in Australia and New Zealand

Anywhere Travel 345 Anzac Parade, Kingsford, Sydney ⓣ 02/9663 0411, anywhere@ozemail .com.au. Bargain airfare retailer.
Budget Travel 16 Fort St, Auckland, plus branches around the city ⓣ 09/366 0061 or 0800/808 040, ⓦ www.budgettravel.co.nz. Cheap flight agent.
Destinations Unlimited 3 Milford Rd, Auckland ⓣ 09/373 4033. Budget fares on major airlines.
Flight Centres Australia ⓣ 13 31 33 or 02/9235 3522, New Zealand ⓣ 09/358 4310, ⓦ www.flightcentre.com.au. Large chain of discount flight specialists.
Northern Gateway Australia ⓣ 08/8941 1394, ⓦ www.northerngateway.com.au.
STA Travel Australia ⓣ 1300/733 035, ⓦ www.statravel.com.au, New Zealand ⓣ 0508/782 872, ⓦ www.statravel.co.nz. Worldwide specialists in "learning travel", with low-cost flights for students and under-26s; other customers also welcome. Over 200 branches overseas.
Student Uni Travel 92 Pitt St, Sydney ⓣ 02/9232 8444, ⓔ australia@backpackers.net, plus branches in Melbourne, Darwin, Perth, Cairns and Brisbane. Specialists in student and backpacker deals.
Trailfinders 8 Spring St, Sydney ⓣ 02/9247 7666. ⓦ www.trailfinders.com.au. Australian branch of large UK-based independent travel specialists.

Packages and organized tours

An **organized tour** is worth considering if you have ambitious sightseeing plans and only a short time to accomplish them. Some of the "adventure" oriented tours can also help you to get to more remote areas and organize activities that may be difficult to arrange yourself, such as trekking and cycling. Most tours don't include airfares from Australasia, so expect to pay between A$1000/NZ$1300 and A$3000/NZ$3300 for the land content only.

Specialist tour operators in Australia and New Zealand

Adventure World Australia ⓣ 02/8913 0755, ⓦ www.adventureworld.com.au, New Zealand ⓣ 09/524 5118, ⓦ www.adventureworld.co.nz. Agents for Orbitours' customized packages for independent travellers including trekking and hilltribe visits.
Asean Travel Australia ⓣ 02/9868 5199, ⓔ msp@jwasean.com.au. Southeast Asia airfares, hotel accommodation in capital cities, and tours.
Asian Travel Centre Australia ⓣ 03/9245 0747, ⓦ www.planit.com.au. Discounted airfares and accommodation packages in Southeast Asia.
Intrepid Travel Pty Ltd 12 Spring St, Fitzroy, Vic ⓣ 1300/360 667, ⓦ www.intrepidtravel. com.au, ⓔ info@intrepidtravel.com.au. Low-impact tours taking in the local customs along the way. Sixteen-day Laos adventure available for A$1560 ex-Bangkok including accommodation, transfers and sightseeing; hilltribes of Laos sixteen-day trip ex-Vientiane also A$1560; fifteen-day Bangkok to Hanoi overland tour, starting in Thailand, going through Laos and ending in Vietnam costs A$1490.
Peregrine Adventures 258 Lonsdale St, Melbourne ⓣ 03/9663 8611, ⓦ www.peregrine.net.au, ⓔ travelcentre@peregrine.net.au, plus offices in Brisbane, Sydney, Adelaide and Perth. Small-group adventure and cultural tours. Trips to Laos available from A$1750 for seven days, land only.
Travel Indochina 403 George St, Sydney ⓣ 1300 365 355, ⓦ www.travelindochina.com.au. Goes beyond the obvious sights and can arrange cross-border visas for Thailand, Laos, Vietnam, China and Cambodia. Offers a fourteen-day Laos–Mekong adventure tour for A$2710 ex-Bangkok; a fifteen-

day Bangkok to Hanoi tour overland via Laos costs A$2795. Also available is a "highlights of Laos" five-day-tour orginating in Vientiane and costing A$865.

Getting there from neighbouring countries

Laos is a short hop by plane from most **Southeast Asian capitals** and is also accessible overland via a number of border crossings with its neighbouring countries. Visas to Laos are easily obtainable from embassies and consulates in all neighbouring countries (see p.18 for further details).

Thailand

The most convenient way to get to Laos from Thailand is by **flying from Bangkok** to Vientiane ($200) with Thai Airways International (daily 8.20am) or Lao Aviation (daily 6.25pm), or from Chiang Mai to either Louang Phabang ($130) or Vientiane ($200) with Lao Aviation. All journeys take about an hour. If cost is a concern, you can fly for roughly half the price of a Bangkok–Vientiane ticket to the northeastern Thai city of Udon Thai, where Thai Airways International provides a van ($3) for the forty-minute drive to the Thai Australian Friendship Bridge near Nong Khai. Although Thai Airways International has a better safety record than Lao Aviation and charges the same price, it only operates on the Bangkok-Vientiane route.

If you're travelling **overland**, there are currently five points along the **Thai border** where it's permissible to cross into Laos: Chiang Khong to Houayxai (see p.234); Nong Khai to Vientiane (The Friendship Bridge, see p.85); Nakhon Phanom to Thakhek (see p.258); Mukdahan to Savannakhet (see p.264); and Chong Mek to Pakse (see p.284). **Crossing overland** allows you ample time to visit Thailand's mountainous north or explore the northeast, an area heavily populated by ethnic Lao. **The Friendship Bridge** is the only overland crossing with **visa-on-arrival** services; if you intend to enter at any of the other four land borders it's best to apply for a visa at the Lao Embassy in Bangkok (see p.19) or at the consulate in Khon Kaen (see p.19). All crossings are accessible by various combi-nations of road, rail and river transport. It is no longer possible to cross from Nong Khai to Thadua by ferry: Western tourists must use the Friendship Bridge, a few kilometres west of Nong Khai town.

Vietnam

Both Vietnam Airlines and Lao Aviation **fly** from **Hanoi** and **Ho Chi Minh City** (Saigon) to Vientiane (1hr). It's also possible to travel **overland** into Laos at either of two border points. Route 8 across the **Kaew Nua Pass** (the Cau Treo/Nam Phao crossing), which links Vinh with Vientiane, is now paved and served by daily direct buses connecting Vientiane to a number of cities on the coast of Vietnam, including Hanoi and Ho Chi Minh City. It is also possible to break this journey up into stages by using local transport. Route 9 across the **Lao Bao Pass** (the Lao Bao/Daen Sawan crossing), links the Vietnamese city of Dong Ha with the Mekong River town of Savannakhet, and is also served by direct buses. However, Route 9 is not paved and is an extremely dusty, hard journey, although enough travellers do it to support rustic guest houses and exchange services on both sides of the border. As with Route 8, it is also possible to travel Route 9 in stages using local transport although, due to delays and guest-house costs, this technique does not necessarily work out cheaper. At least three other additional Lao–Vietnamese border crossings are expected to be open in 2003 (see p.184).

Bear in mind that **Vietnamese officials** are notorious sticklers for paperwork, so be sure that you have the correct port of departure and arrival stamped on your Vietnamese visa. Vietnamese embassy officials have been known to incorrectly stamp exit/entry points in visitors' passports, and changing the form means paying a surcharge, so it's best to check the stamp straight away.

China

From China's southwestern **Yunnan** province, it's possible to travel by road or air into Laos. Lao Aviation operates **flights** from Kunming to Vientiane, a three-hour journey via Louang Phabang. Travelling **by road** you'll pass through the virgin rainforests of

Flights to Vientiane from Southeast Asia

Lao Aviation Bangkok ☎02/236-9822-3; Chiang Mai ☎053/404033; Hanoi ☎4/846-4873; Ho Chi Minh City ☎8/822-6990; Kunming ☎871/3163000; Phnom Penh ☎23/216563; Siem Reap ☎063/963263; Vientiane ☎021/212051-3. Daily flights from Bangkok; flights from Chiang Mai (via Louang Phabang) on Sunday and Thursday; flights from Hanoi daily; flights from Ho Chi Minh City on Wednesday; flights from Phnom Penh daily; flights from Kunming on Sunday; flights from Siem Reap on Tuesday and Friday.

Thai Airways International Bangkok ☎02/280-0060; Vientiane ☎021/216143. Daily flights from Bangkok to Vientiane.

Vietnam Airways Hanoi ☎4/829 8118; Vientiane ☎021/217562. Flights from Hanoi daily except Monday.

Xishuangbanna, a region whose history and peoples have close ties with Laos. There are direct **buses** from Jinghong to Oudomxai and Louang Namtha; from Mengla, it takes ninety minutes by minibus to reach Mo Han, 6km from the border, beyond which lies the Lao town of Boten. The **river route** from China to Laos down the Mekong is currently only open to cargo boats but there is talk of allowing foreign tourists to use this route in the near future.

Myanmar

Western tourists are not officially permitted to cross between **Myanmar** (Burma) and Laos at Muangmom or Xiang Kok, the two official border points between the two coun-tries, although a few foreigners have reportedly slipped through.

Cambodia

Lao Aviation operates direct **flights** from both **Phnom Penh** and **Siem Reap** to Vientiane. The fare is $130 return and the flying time is 3hr 20min.

Although the **border crossing** between Cambodia and Laos is not "officially" open, a steady stream of Western travellers have been getting through in both directions without incident. Travellers attempting this journey should be aware that lawlessness is not uncommon along the Cambodian border in this area, and sometimes spills over into Laos.

Red tape and visas

Visas are required for all non-Thai visitors to Laos. You don't need a visa in advance: fifteen-day visas can be bought on entry to the country. To apply for an advance visa, which is good for longer than fifteen days, you will have to go through a Lao embassy or a tour agency.

Lao officialdom picked up some bad habits from the shoulder-shrugging bureaucracy of the French, but things have improved vastly over the past few years and obtaining a visa has become both cheaper and much more straightforward than it used to be.

All visitors to Laos must have a **passport** that is valid for at least six months from the time of entry into Laos. If you want to stay longer than the fifteen days allotted with the visa-on-arrival scheme you'll have to apply for an advance visa through a Lao embassy or a tour agency. Note that there is no Lao embassy in the UK or Ireland. If you're travelling to other Southeast Asian countries before entering Laos, you'll find it much easier to apply for a visa, say, in Bangkok (same day service, see below) than in the West (up to a month). Wherever you get your visa, it's worth bearing in mind that Lao visa regulations, requirements and prices are subject to frequent change.

Visas on arrival take just a few minutes to process, cost $30, are good for fifteen days, and are available to passengers flying into Wattay Airport in Vientiane, Louang Phabang Airport or crossing into Laos via the Friendship Bridge between Thailand's Nong Khai and Vientiane. Only US dollars are accepted as payment and a passport-size photograph is required. Note that when entering or exiting Laos via the Friendship Bridge, there is an entry/exit fee of less than $1 that can be paid in kip or Thai baht.

Many visitors opt to apply for a Lao visa while staying in Bangkok or Hanoi in order to utilize overland crossings into Laos, which have no visa on arrival facilities. In **Bangkok**, you can obtain visas directly from the **embassy** (Mon–Fri, 8.30am–noon & 1–4pm; see p.20 for the address). Fifteen-day visas cost approximately 750 baht ($21). Thirty-day visas cost 1000 baht ($23) for nationals of Britain, Australia and New Zealand, 1200 baht ($27) for Americans and 1400 baht ($32) for Canadians. Two passport-size photographs are required and processing is done on the same day provided you apply before noon. It's also possible to get more than one visa at a time, that is, two thirty-day visas, for double the price. Note that the Lao embassy in Bangkok only accepts Thai baht for transactions. If you don't fancy the trip out to the embassy, which is on the outskirts of the city, and you're willing to pay a bit extra, you can go through one of the many **travel agents** concentrated on and around Khao San Road. Prices charged by agents start at 750 baht for a fifteen-day visa, up to twice as much for a thirty-day visa depending on nationality. Should you decide to go through a Bangkok travel agency, make sure you actually get the class of visa you have paid for (see the box on p.20). Payment is in Thai baht only and the visa generally takes three working days to process. A Lao consulate in **Khon Kaen** in Thailand's northeast can also issue visas, though the fees being charged and the time taken to process the visa here are somewhat erratic.

The Lao embassy in **Hanoi**, and consulates in **Ho Chi Minh City** and **Da Nang**, can also issue visas but it's important to note that the types of visas issued and the prices charged vary from place to place, and the regulations and conditions change frequently. Lao visas issued in Vietnam are also significantly more expensive than those issued in Thailand.

At the time of writing, one month visitor visas issued in Hanoi cost $50–70 depending on the nationality of the applicant and require three working days. The one-day express service costs an extra $20. In Ho Chi Minh City, you can get a thirty-day visitor visa ($50; same day service) but in Da Nang, you can only get a fifteen-day tourist visa ($50; 2 working days) or a five-day transit visa ($30; 2 working days), which will allow you take Route 9 over to Mukdahan in Thailand. If you are going to cross overland into Laos from Vietnam be sure to **specify the crossing** you intend to use – Lao Bao or Cau Treo – when applying for the visa. The immigration officials on the Vietnam side have been known to refuse exit to travellers whose visa does not specify where they intend to cross, although this could be just another incidence of fishing for bribes.

Transit visas, good for only five days and non-extendable, are offered at the Lao embassy in **Hanoi** and the consulate in **Kunming**, China, for travellers flying to Bangkok who wish to make a short stopover in Vientiane. For this reason, the visa may only be valid for one province. Transit visas are also available in Da Nang for travellers wanting to take Route 9 to Thailand. The price of a transit visa is between $25 and $30, depending on your nationality, and takes three working days to process.

Visitors without visas planning to enter Laos **from Chiang Khong** in Thailand's Chiang Rai province can still obtain visas through resourceful travel agencies in Chiang Khong. The fifteen-day visas take two working days to process and cost the baht equivalent of $27. Thirty-day visas take three working days and cost the baht equivalent of $38. In both cases, the visas are actually issued by the Lao embassy in Bangkok, and the passports are couriered to Bangkok and back, so delays can occur.

Lao visas

Visa on arrival: Fifteen days, extendable for two extra weeks. Only available at Wattay International Airport (Vientiane), Luang Phabang International Airport, and the Friendship Bridge (Vientiane).

Tourist visa (VT): Fifteen days, extendable.

Visitor visa (B3): One-month stay. Extendable for two extra weeks.

Transit visa (VTR): Maximum five days for a stay (one province only).

Business visa (B2): One-month stay. Multiple extensions. Requires a Lao sponsor.

Multiple entry visa: Only issued by the Ministry of Foreign Affairs, Consular Department.

Extending Lao visas

Visa extensions are fairly easy to obtain, but the rules regarding the extensions are far from uniform and so the price of an extension will vary from place to place or day to day. In Vientiane, extensions can be applied for at the immigration office on Hatsady Road. Most people are charged $2 per day, but some people have been able to get an extension for as little as $1 per day. The maximum length of your visa extension is fifteen days but this is up to the official on duty. Officially speaking, only the immigration office in Vientiane can issue visa extensions. However, it is sometimes possible to get a visa extended in other towns; it's certainly worth asking if you are in some remote provincial capital and nearing the end of your visa. Should you accidentally **overstay** your visa, both airport and border immigration offices generally charge $5 per day for overstays.

Lao embassies and consulates abroad

Australia 1 Dalman Crescent, O'Malley, Canberra ☎02/6286 4595, fax 6290 1910.

Cambodia, 15-17 Keomani Rd, Phnom Penh ☎23/26441.

China 11 E 4th St, Sanlitun, Chaoyang, Beijing ☎010/65321224; *Camelia Hotel*, Suite 3226, 154 E Dong Feng Rd, Kunming ☎0871/3176624.

Cuba 7 Ave Calle 36 A, 505 Miramar, Havana ☎(+53 7) 33-1056, 33-1057, 33-1058.

France 74 Avenue Raymond Poincaré, Paris ☎01/45 53 02 98, ℉47 27 57 89.

Germany Bismarckallee 2A, 14193 Berlin ☎49/30 89 06 06 47, ℉30 890 606 48.

Hong Kong Room 1002 Arion Commercial Centre, 2–12 Queen's Road West, Hong Kong ☎852/25441186.

India Panchsheel Park New Delhi-17 ☎(+91 11) 642-7447, ℉ (+91 11) 642-8588.

Indonesia 33 Jalan Kintamani Raya, Kuningan Timur, Jakarta ☎021/520-2673, ℉522-9601).

Japan 3-3-22, Nishi-Azabu, Minato-ku Post Code:106 ☎54112291/2, ℉ 54112293.

Malaysia Jalan Bellamy, 50460 Kuala Lumpur ☎03/248-3895, ℉242-0344.

Mongolia Ikh Toiruu PO BOX 1030, Ulaanbaatar, ☎(+976 1) 326-440, 329-898.

Myanmar (Burma), Diplomatic Headquarters, Taw Win Road, Yangon (Rangoon) ☎01/22482.

New Zealand Contact embassy in Canberra.

Philippines 34 Lapu-Lapu St, Magallanes, Makati, Metro-Manila (☎02/833-5759.

Poland, UL Rejtana 15/26 02-516 Warsaw ☎(+48 22) 484-786, 488-949, ℉(+48 22) 497-122.

Russia Moscow 121069 Ul Katchalov 18 ☎(+7 095) 203-1454, 291-8966, ℉(+7 095) 290-4226.

Singapore 101 Thomson Road, 05–03A, United Sq ☎6/2506044, 2506741; ℉62506014.

Thailand 502/13 Ramkhamhaeng Soi 39, Bangkapi, Bangkok ☎02/539-6668; 19/1-3 Phothisan Rd, Khon Kaen ☎ 043/223-698.

USA, 222 S St NW, Washington DC ☎202/332-6416, ℉332-4923.

Vietnam 40 Quang Trung, Hanoi ☎04/845-3836; 181 Hai Ba Trung; Ho Chi Minh City ☎08/829-7667;12 Tran Quy-Cap, Danang ☎51/21208.

Customs

Lao **customs regulations** limit visitors to 500 cigarettes and one litre of distilled alcohol per person upon entry, but in practice bags are rarely opened unless a suspiciously large amount of luggage is being brought in. A **customs declaration form** must be filled out along with the arrival form, but typically nobody bothers to check that the information is correct. There is no limit on the amount of **foreign currency** you can bring into Laos.

Information and maps

The Lao are still unsure just what it is that draws visitors to Laos, and this is reflected in the scant tourist information there is to be had. The National Tourism Authority of Laos (NATL) operates offices in a few places, including Vientiane, but the organization is, according to a spokesman, "not an information provider for tourists, rather an organization to monitor, control, and promote tourism". Similarly, queries or requests for information posted to Lao embassies abroad will elicit no response. Private tour agencies, guest-house owners, fellow travellers and the internet are much better sources of information.

Tourist offices and information

The occasional government-run **tourist information office** that you may come across will be practically useless, as staff are generally untrained and speak little English, although some offices may have a very limited selection of maps and brochures for sale. Privately owned travel companies, such as **Sodetour** and **Diethelm**, can often provide reliable information in provincial capitals (see "Getting around" section, p.34, for more information on tour companies).

Most travellers, however, get their information **word-of-mouth** from other travellers, and this is often the best source, as conditions in Laos change with astonishing rapidity. No one will better be able to describe the condition of the road between Xiang Kok and Muang Sing than someone who has just traversed it.

Laos online

One of the best ways to find good material on Laos is simply to **surf the web**. The things you'll turn up are simply amazing, from anti-communist sites advocating the violent overthrow of the government to the on-line memoirs of old-time warriors from the "secret war". Although there are many contenders, the mother of all **links pages** is found at ⓦ www.vientianetimes.com. You could spend hours in there. Another incredible site is the Laos WWW Virtual library ⓦ www.global.lao.net/laoVL.html, with good articles and tons of valuable links. At the Asian links site, ⓦ www.search.asiaco.com,

which covers all of Asia, you'll find 87 links on their Lao page. Once you get going on these three sites you'll find there's no end. The following is our selection of useful websites for all-round information on Laos.

General resources

ⓦ **www.laopdr.com** A good jumping-off point, this is an excellent general info site with lots of links.
ⓦ **www.mekongexpress.com** Huge general info site.
ⓦ **www.global.lao.net/laoVLhtml** Lao Net is a good source of facts and information with useful links and a virtual library.
ⓦ **www.city.net/countries/laos** Excite Travel's City Net features geopolitical and tourist information.
ⓦ **www.laoembassy.com** The website of the Lao Embassy to the United States posts visa regulations and an updated list of border crossings, although the information on sites in the country is very thin.
ⓦ **www.roughguides.com** Maintains an interactive site for independent travellers, with forums, bulletin boards, travel tips and features, plus online travel guides.

News and media

There are several good digital **newspapers** on Laos. In fact, it's fair to say you'll find much more news on-line about Laos than you can in the country.
ⓦ **www.vientianetimes.com** The website of the *Vientiane Times* is the best place to start. It contains most of the stories from Laos's only English-language newspaper and related news from other publications around the world.

Ⓦ www.lasoguide.com and Ⓦ www.lan-xang
.com Both are good sources of news and articles.
Ⓦ www.laosnews.net Has articles and extensive
links.
Ⓦ www.muonglao.com An excellent online
magazine with many good articles on Laos.
Ⓦ www.bangkokpost.net The website of
Thailand's leading daily.
Ⓦ www.asiaweek.com General articles on the
region.
Ⓦ www.feer.com. The website of the *Far Eastern
Economic Review*.
Ⓦ www.asiaobserver.com The *Asian Observer*'s
selection of articles on Laos is particularly extensive.

Tourist information

Ⓦ www.visit-laos.com The best all-around
travel site on Laos.
Ⓦ www.laos-travel.itgo.com Another promising
general site for tourist information.
Ⓦ www.savannanet.com A good travel page
with articles and links.
Ⓦ www.theboatlanding.laopdr.com An
excellent site on travel in Northern Laos. Features
information on independent trekking and eco-
tourism, has great links and is visually one of best
Lao websites.
Ⓦ www.wildside-laos.com Gives you a run
down of possible adventure tourism opportunities
in the north.
Ⓦ www.laos-hotels.com Has a fairly complete
list of Lao hotels and other tourist information.

Travel advice

Travel advice is posted on the following
websites, although you should check with a
Western embassy in Vientiane on arrival as
the information can be out of date.
Australian Department of Foreign Affairs
Ⓦ www.dfat.gov.au. Advice and reports on
unstable countries and regions.
British Foreign and Commonwealth Office
Ⓦ www.fco.gov.uk. Constantly updated advice for
travellers on circumstances affecting safety in over
130 countries.
Canadian Foreign Affairs Department
Ⓦ www.dfait-maeci.gc.ca/menu-e.asp. Country-
by-country travel advisories.
US State Department Travel Advisories
Ⓦ http://travel.state.gov/travel_warnings.html.
Website providing "consular information sheets"
detailing the dangers of travelling in most
countries of the world.

Maps

Good commercial **maps** of Laos are difficult
to come by. Many towns and villages have
changed names since the revolution, whole
towns have been moved, and new villages
have sprung up. The country has also
embarked on a significant road-building programme in the last five years. The best traveller's road map of Laos is the *Laos 2002
Guide Map* (1:1,400,000) published by
Golden Triangle Rider and available at book-
stores in Thailand or at Wildside Outdoor
Adventure offices in Laos. Nelles
1:1,500,000 map of Vietnam, Laos and
Cambodia or its Southeast Asia "Road
Atlas" shows the physical topography and is
adequate for orientation but can be mislead-
ing, especially when it comes to trying to
discern the position and condition of inter-
provincial roads or accurately pin-pointing
towns and villages. Likewise, the
Bartholomew 1:2,000,000 Vietnam,
Cambodia and Laos map is attractive but
not always reliable.

Topographical maps can be found at the
Lao National Geographic Service (NGS),
whose office is located just north of the
Patouxai monument in Vientiane. Maps of a
scale from 1:1,000,000 to 1:500,000 are
available, but more detailed maps of a scale
of 1:50,000, suitable for trekking or kayaking, can only be purchased with "special
permission". The NGS has also put out a
series of **city maps** which includes
Vientiane, Louang Phabang, Thakhek,
Savannakhet and Pakxe. They include basic
information about points of interest in the
immediate vicinity. While these maps are
useful, they're not always easy to find. The
NGS office sometimes has city maps in
stock, but photocopies are just as likely to
be on offer at minimarts or souvenir shops
catering to Western visitors in Vientiane and
other Mekong towns.

Map outlets

In the UK and Ireland

Blackwell's Map and Travel Shop 50 Broad St,
Oxford OX1 3BQ ☎ 01865/793 550,
Ⓦ http://maps.blackwell.co.uk/index.html.

Easons Bookshop 40 O'Connell St, Dublin 1
☎01/873 3811, ⓦwww.eason.ie.
Heffers Map and Travel 20 Trinity St, Cambridge
CB2 1TJ ☎01865/333 536, ⓦwww.heffers.co.uk.
Hodges Figgis Bookshop 56–58 Dawson St,
Dublin 2 ☎01/677 4754,
ⓦwww.hodgesfiggis.com.
James Thin Booksellers 53–59 South Bridge
Edinburgh EH1 1YS ☎0131/622 8222,
ⓦwww.jthin.co.uk.
The Map Shop 30a Belvoir St, Leicester LE1 6QH
☎0116/247 1400, ⓦwww.mapshopleicester
.co.uk.
National Map Centre 22–24 Caxton St, London
SW1H 0QU ☎020/7222 2466, ⓦwww.mapsnmc
.co.uk, ⓔinfo@mapsnmc.co.uk.
Newcastle Map Centre 55 Grey St, Newcastle-
upon-Tyne, NE1 6EF ☎0191/261 5622.
Ordnance Survey Ireland Phoenix Park, Dublin 8
☎01/8025 349, ⓦwww.irlgov.ie/osi,
ⓔosni@osni.gov.uk.
Ordnance Survey of Northern Ireland Colby
House, Stranmillis Ct, Belfast BT9 5BJ ☎028/9025
5755, ⓦwww.osni.gov.uk.
Stanfords 12–14 Long Acre, WC2E 9LP
☎020/7836 1321, ⓦwww.stanfords.co.uk,
ⓔsales@stanfords.co.uk. Maps available by mail,
phone order, or email. Other branches within
British Airways offices at 156 Regent St, London
W1R 5TA ☎020/7434 4744, and 29 Corn St,
Bristol BS1 1HT ☎0117/929 9966.
The Travel Bookshop 13–15 Blenheim Crescent,
W11 2EE ☎020/7229 5260,
ⓦwww.thetravelbookshop.co.uk.

In the US and Canada

Adventurous Traveler Bookstore 102 Lake
Street, Burlington, VT 05401 ☎1-800/282-3963,
ⓦwww.adventuroustraveler.com.
Book Passage 51 Tamal Vista Blvd, Corte
Madera, CA 94925 ☎1-800/999-7909,
ⓦwww.bookpassage.com.
Distant Lands 56 S Raymond Ave, Pasadena, CA
91105 ☎1-800/310-3220,
ⓦwww.distantlands.com.

Elliot Bay Book Company 101 S Main St,
Seattle, WA 98104 ☎1-800/962-5311,
ⓦwww.elliotbaybook.com.
Forsyth Travel Library 226 Westchester Ave,
White Plains, NY 10604 ☎1-800/367-7984,
ⓦwww.forsyth.com.
Globe Corner Bookstore 28 Church St,
Cambridge, MA 02138 ☎1-800/358-6013,
ⓦwww.globecorner.com.
GORP Travel ☎1-877/440-4677,
ⓦwww.gorp.com/gorp/books/main.htm.
Map Link 30 S La Patera Lane, Unit 5, Santa
Barbara, CA 93117 ☎805/692-6777,
ⓦwww.maplink.com.
Rand McNally ☎1-800/333-0136,
ⓦwww.randmcnally.com. Around thirty stores
across the US; dial ext 2111 or check the website
for the nearest location.
The Travel Bug Bookstore 2667 W Broadway,
Vancouver V6K 2G2 ☎604/737-1122,
ⓦwww.swifty.com/tbug.
World of Maps 1235 Wellington St, Ottawa,
Ontario K1Y 3A3 ☎1-800/214-8524,
ⓦwww.worldofmaps.com.

Australia and New Zealand

The Map Shop 6–10 Peel St, Adelaide, SA 5000
☎08/8231 2033, ⓦwww.mapshop.net.au.
Mapland 372 Little Bourke St, Melbourne, Victoria
3000, ☎03/9670 4383, ⓦwww.mapland.com.au.
MapWorld 173 Gloucester St, Christchurch, New
Zealand ☎0800/627 967 or 03/374 5399,
ⓦwww.mapworld.co.nz.
Perth Map Centre 1/884 Hay St, Perth, WA 6000,
☎08/9322 5733, ⓦwww.perthmap.com.au.
Specialty Maps 46 Albert St, Auckland 1001
☎09/307 2217, ⓦwww.ubdonline.co.nz/maps.

Online travel bookstores

Adventurous Traveler
ⓦwww.adventuroustraveler.com
Amazon ⓦwww.amazon.com
Bookpages ⓦwww.bookpages.com
Literate Traveler ⓦwww.literatetraveller.com

Costs, money and banks

Laos is one of the world's poorest nations and consequently one of the cheapest Asian countries to travel in. Accommodation and transportation are very Inexpensive though restaurant prices tend to be similar to neighbouring Thailand. For this reason, it's not uncommon to spend as much or more on meals than on accommodation.

Due to the instability of the national currency, the **kip**, American dollars and Thai baht are also widely used. The Asian financial crisis in 1997 badly affected the Lao currency. Between June 1997 and early 1999, the kip, which is not freely convertible, fell more than eighty percent against the dollar – more than any other Southeast Asian currency during that period. Lao banks went broke and inflation was running at over a hundred percent a year. Although **inflation** has since settled to thirty-five percent per annum, many Lao are suffering real hardship, as prices continue to rise while salaries have remained the same. Moreover, the government seems to have no policy to deal with the crisis.

A **black market** in foreign currencies emerged when the government tried to fix the currency rate in mid-1997. Accordingly, the price of foreign goods shot up, a major problem for a country that imports many of its everyday goods from Thailand. By 1998, the discrepancy between the two rates was at times as much as fifteen percent and a black market, or *talat meut*, of illicit currency traders appeared. Today, the initial shock of the Asian financial crisis has abated and the difference between the official and black-market rate is now so small that the once thriving black market in foreign currencies

hardly exists. Although the government urges tourists to use banks and official exchange kiosks, just about every business in Laos is happy to change your currency at a favourable rate. At the time of writing, the official **exchange rate** was 9500 kip to the US dollar, 215 kip to the Thai baht and 12,975 kip to the pound sterling.

Currency

Lao **currency** is available in 5000K, 2000K, and 1000K notes; smaller notes also exist, but you're only likely to see them in a curio shop alongside Pathet Lao notes and French coins. There are no coins in circulation. In addition, the Thai baht and American dollar operate parallel to the kip. In fact, Thai currency makes up an estimated thirty percent of all cash circulating in the Lao capital.

Although a law passed in 1990 technically forbids the use of foreign currencies to pay for goods and services in local markets, many hotels, restaurants and tour operators routinely quote their prices in dollars or baht, and it is perfectly acceptable to pay in either of these currencies, regardless of what the price is quoted in. One exception, however, is the government-owned airline, Lao Aviation, which only accepts payment in American dollars cash.

Carrying large sums of money in **kip** can be cumbersome, even with the addition of the 5000K note in 1998. Indeed, most travellers tend to retain the bulk of their cash in dollars or baht, changing money when they need to. Bear in mind that you cannot convert your kip back into dollars or baht when leaving the country – and that you won't be able to burn up your kip at the duty-free shops, as they only accept dollars and baht.

Kip and dollars

Given the **volatility of the kip**, prices for accommodation, river travel and car hire in the Guide have been given in their more stable dollar equivalents. Indeed, many hotels and guest houses have opted to fix their rates to the dollar, or simply to quote the price in dollars outright, and some restaurants have begun to do the same. Throughout the Guide, prices quoted in kip for transport, museum entrance fees, etc were correct at the time of research and have been retained to give a relative idea of costs, though in practice many of these prices will be higher. The kip stood at a comparatively stable 9,500 to the dollar at the time of writing. **Current rates** as well as a commodities basket reflecting the current prices of various goods and services in kip are published on the *Vientiane Times*' website (®www.vientianetimes.com), and daily rates are posted at all foreign exchange counters in Laos.

Costs

You'll find Laos an extremely **inexpensive** place to travel. By eating at noodle stalls and cheap restaurants, taking local transport and opting for basic accommodation, you can travel in Laos on a **daily budget** of less than $10. The simplest of meals nationwide is *fõe*, the Vietnamese-inspired noodle soup, which costs $0.50 for a large bowl; rice dishes run closer to $1 and there's always the option of eating as the locals do, by going to the market and buying takeaway food. Prices for food and **accommodation** tend to be slightly cheaper outside the capital. While you can find rooms in Louang Phabang for $3 a night, you'll get nothing for less than $7 in Vientiane.

Staying in **upmarket hotels** and resorts and eating in top-notch restaurants can be quite reasonable in Laos; count on spending $40–50 a day, but realize that many Lao towns lack these facilities. **Fast travel** also comes at a premium – flights and speedboats cost many times the price of local bus transport. (The 10hr bus ride from Vientiane to Louang Phabang costs around $5, while the hour-long flight costs $57). **Buses** are basic and cheap, although a few routes out of Vientiane are serviced by express, air-conditioned transport, for which you'll pay a few dollars more.

Price tiering

The lack of a fixed pricing scheme in Laos can take some getting used to. Merchandise almost never has price tags and prices can vary from shop to shop. Official government **price tiering** does exist in Laos, with for-

eigners paying more than locals for some services. The dual system applies for airfares, speedboat tickets and entry fees to museums and famous sites. Frequently, you'll come across bus, sawngthaew, and boat drivers who feel entitled to levy their own foreigner surcharge. Indeed, cases of foreign visitors being overcharged for goods and services have now become fairly common, as anywhere else in the world. But be cautious about causing a scene until you've established the cost of things, and remember prices vary throughout Laos as you enter more remote areas. The best way to avoid being over-charged is simply to know the correct price before you buy or ride.

Bargaining

It's also good to keep your cool while **bargaining**, which is very much a part of life in Laos. While restaurants and some shops have fixed prices, dry goods purchases in a market should always be negotiated, as should the cost of transport for hire (fares on passenger vehicles are not open to bargaining). Hotel and guest-house operators are usually open to bargaining, particularly during off-peak months. Good bargaining is an art form, requiring a delicate balance of humour, patience and tact. It's also important to remain realistic, as vendors will lose interest if you've quoted a price that's way out of line, and to keep a sense of perspective: cut-throat haggling over 1000K only reflects poorly on both buyer and seller. As the Lao in general – with the exception of some tour operators and souvenir/textile sellers in Vientiane and Louang Phabang –

are less out to rip off tourists than their counterparts in Thailand and Vietnam, they start off the haggling by quoting a fairly realistic price and expect to come down only a little. **Tipping** in restaurants isn't a Lao custom, although upmarket Vientiane restaurants expect a gratuity of around ten percent.

Travellers' cheques, cash & cards

The most convenient way to travel in Laos is to arm yourself with an ample supply of American dollars and Thai baht in cash. Although **travellers' cheques** are the safest way to carry your money, you'll have trouble cashing cheques outside Vientiane and major cities such as Louang Phabang, Savannakhet and Pakxe. Sometimes, provincial banks will make an exception, usually when someone needs dollars to buy an airline ticket, and then usually only when presented with a letter from Lao Aviation. Travellers' cheques are available for a small commission from most banks and travel agents – keep the purchase agreement and a record of cheque serial numbers separate from the cheques.

Major **credit cards** – American Express, Visa and Mastercard – are slowly catching on in Vientiane and are accepted at many hotels, upmarket restaurants and shops catering to tourists. **Cash advances** on Visa cards, and less frequently Mastercard, are possible in major urban centres – you can count on this service in Louang Phabang, Vientiane, Savannakhet and Pakxe – but you will most likely be required to withdraw a minimum of $100 in kip at a rate of 2.5 to 3 percent. Cash advances in dollars are possible at a rate of 3.5 percent at BCEL in Vientiane. The American Express representative is Diethelm Travel Laos, based in Vientiane. At present, it's not possible to withdraw cash from **ATMs** in Laos.

Banks and exchange

Banking **hours** are generally 8.30am to 4pm, Monday to Friday nationwide, although some banks in the provinces keep different hours. Exchange kiosks keep longer hours but are rare – with a few operating in downtown Vientiane and others found in provincial post offices, airports and at some border checkpoints. **Exchange rates** tend to be better in Vientiane, decreasing slightly in major urban centres, and slipping again in the satellites of provincial centres. Before travelling into smaller towns, **change enough money** to get you through until the next major town. It's also a good idea to stay atop of the daily fluctuations of the market, so that you don't get an inferior rate.

For a period, the re-emergence of the **black market** in foreign currencies provided some Lao with a means of supplementing their incomes by moonlighting as freelance currency traders. Such traders used to hang around outside the markets in Vientiane and Louang Phabang, but are now rare. In most towns your best bet for a rate more favourable than the bank is to enquire at a gold shop or your guest house.

Wiring money

Having money wired from home using one of the companies listed below is never convenient or cheap, and should be considered a last resort. It's also possible to have money wired directly from a bank in your home country to a bank in Laos, although this is somewhat less reliable because it involves two separate institutions. If you go this route, your home bank will need the address of the branch of the bank where you want to pick up the money and the address and telex number of the capital city head office, which will act as the clearing house; money wired this way normally takes two working days to arrive, and costs around £25/$40 per transaction.

Money-wiring companies

American Express Moneygram US and Canada ☎1-800/926-9400, Australia ☎1800/230 100, New Zealand ☎09/379 8243 or 0800/262 263, UK and Republic of Ireland ☎0800/6663 9472, ⓦwww.moneygram.com.
Thomas Cook US ☎1-800/287-7362, Canada ☎1-888/823-4732, UK ☎01733/318 922, Belfast ☎028/9055 0030, Dublin ☎01/677 1721, ⓦwww.us.thomascook.com.
Western Union US and Canada ☎1-800/325-6000, Australia ☎1800/649 565, New Zealand ☎09/270 0050, UK ☎0800/833 833, Republic of Ireland ☎1800/395 395, ⓦwww.westernunion.com.

Insurance

Most people will find it essential to take out a good travel insurance policy to cover against theft, loss and illness or injury. Before paying for a new policy, however, it's worth checking whether you are already covered. Credit and charge cards (particularly American Express) often have certain levels of medical or other insurance included, and travel insurance may also be included if you use a major credit or charge card to pay for your trip. Similarly, some all-risks home insurance policies may cover your possessions when overseas, and many private medical schemes include cover when abroad.

In Canada, provincial health plans usually provide partial cover for medical mishaps overseas, while holders of official student/teacher/youth cards in Canada and the US are entitled to meagre accident coverage and hospital in-patient benefits. Students will often find that their student health coverage extends during the vacations and for one term beyond the date of last enrollment.

After exhausting the possibilities above, you might want to contact a specialist travel insurance company, or consider the travel insurance deal we offer (see box, below). A typical travel insurance policy usually provides cover for the loss of baggage, tickets and – up to a certain limit – cash or cheques, as well as cancellation or curtailment of your journey. Most of them exclude so-called dangerous sports unless an extra

premium is paid: in Laos this can mean white-water rafting, rock-climbing and trekking, though probably not kayaking or jeep safaris. Many policies can be chopped and changed to exclude coverage you don't need – for example, sickness and accident benefits can often be excluded or included at will. If you do take medical coverage, ascertain whether benefits will be paid as treatment proceeds or only after return home, and whether there is a 24-hour medical emergency number. When securing baggage cover, make sure that the per-article limit – typically under £500 – will cover your most valuable possession. If you need to make a **claim**, you should keep receipts for medicines and medical treatment, and in the event you have anything stolen, you must obtain an official statement from the police.

Rough Guides travel insurance

Rough Guides offers its own travel insurance, customized for our readers by a leading UK broker and backed by a Lloyds underwriter. It's available for anyone, of any nationality and any age, travelling anywhere in the world.

There are two main Rough Guide insurance plans: **Essential**, for basic, no-frills cover; and **Premier** – with more generous and extensive benefits. Alternatively, you can take out annual **multi-trip insurance**, which covers you for any number of trips throughout the year (with a maximum of 60 days for any one trip). Unlike many policies, the Rough Guides schemes are **calculated by the day**, so if you're travelling for 27 days rather than a month, that's all you pay for. If you intend to be away for the whole year, the Adventurer policy will cover you for 365 days. Each plan can be supplemented with a "Hazardous Activities Premium" if you plan to indulge in sports considered dangerous, such as skiing, scuba-diving or trekking.

For a policy quote, call the Rough Guide Insurance Line on UK freefone ☏0800/015 09 06; US freefone ☏1-866/220 5588, or, if you're calling from elsewhere ☏+44 1243/621 046. Alternatively, get an online quote or **buy online** at ⓦwww.roughguides.com/insurance

Health

Laos is the poorest country in Southeast Asia, with an average life expectancy of just over 50. Poor hygiene is largely to blame, and travellers should take special care what they eat to avoid diarrhoea and other intestinal disorders. Malaria and other mosquito-borne diseases are also rife in Laos, and you'll need to take a number of precautions to avoid contracting these, especially if you plan on spending long periods of time in rural regions.

Health care in Laos is so poor as to be virtually non-existent. The nearest medical care of any competence is in neighbouring **Thailand**, and if you find yourself afflicted by anything more serious than travellers' diarrhoea, it's best to head for the closest Thai border crossing and check into a hospital. A clinic attached to the **Australian embassy** in Vientiane is mainly for embassy personnel but can be relied upon in extreme emergencies.

Before you go

Plan on consulting a doctor at least two months before your travel date to discuss which diseases you should receive **immunization** against and which drugs should be prescribed for the journey. Some antimalarials must be taken several days before arrival in a malaria-infested area in order for the drug to be effective. Travelling with **small children** requires special precautions, and a doctor will be able to advise on what over-the-counter drugs to bring. If you are going to be on the road for some time, a dental check-up is also advisable as Laos is no place to have a toothache.

In the **UK**, pick up the Department of Health's free publication, Health Advice for Travellers, a comprehensive booklet available at the post office or by calling the Health Literature Line on ☎0800/555 777. The content of the booklet, which contains immunization advice, is constantly updated on pages 000-000 of CEEFAX. Most general practitioners in the UK can give advice and certain vaccines on prescription, though they may not administer some of the less common immunizations, and only some immunizations are free under the NHS.

Vaccinations

While there are no mandatory **vaccinations** for Laos (except yellow fever if you are coming from an infected area), a few are recommended. Hepatitis A, typhus, tetanus and polio are the most important ones, but you should also consider Hepatitis B, rabies and Japanese encephalitis. All shots should be recorded on an **International Certificate of Vaccination** and carried with your passport when travelling abroad.

For up-to-the-minute information, make an appointment at a travel clinic (see p.29), though immunizations can be costly, as these are private clinics. They also sell travel accessories, including mosquito nets and first-aid kits.

Hepatitis A is contracted via contaminated food and water and can be prevented by the Havrix vaccine which provides protection for up to ten years. Two injections two to four weeks apart are necessary, followed by a booster a year later. The older one-shot vaccine only provides protection for three months.

Hepatitis B is spread via sexual contact (both semen and saliva), transfusions of tainted blood and dirty needles. Vaccination is recommended for travellers who plan on staying for long periods of time (six months or more). Note that the vaccine can take up to six months before it is fully effective.

Rabies, contracted via contact with rabid mammals, can be prevented by a vaccine that consists of two injections over a two-month period with a third a year later and boosters every two to five years. If bitten by a potentially rabid animal, you must still get shots.

Japanese encephalitis, a mosquito-borne disease, is quite rare, but doctors may recommend a vaccination against it. The course of injections consists of two shots at two-week intervals plus a booster, but is not recommended for those with liver, kidney or heart conditions or those with multiple allergies.

Medical resources for travellers

Websites

⊛http://health.yahoo.com Information on specific diseases and conditions, drugs and herbal remedies, as well as advice from health experts.
⊛www.tmvc.com.au Contains a list of all Travellers Medical and Vaccination Centres throughout Australia, New Zealand and Southeast Asia, plus general information on travel health.
⊛www.istm.org The website of the International Society for Travel Medicine, with a full list of clinics specializing in international travel health.
⊛www.tripprep.com Travel Health Online provides an online-only comprehensive database of necessary vaccinations for most countries, as well as destination and medical service provider information.
⊛www.fitfortravel.scot.nhs.uk UK NHS website carrying information about travel-related diseases and how to avoid them.

Travel clinics

UK and Ireland

British Airways Travel Clinics 28 regional clinics (call ☏01276/685 040 for the nearest, or consult ⊛www.britishairways.com), with two in London (Mon–Fri 9.30am–5.15pm, Sat 10am–4pm): 156 Regent St, London W1 (☏020/7439 9584, no appointment necessary); and 101 Cheapside, London EC2 (☏020/7606 2977, appointment required). All clinics offer vaccinations, tailored advice from an online database and a complete range of travel healthcare products.
Communicable Diseases Unit Brownlee Centre, Glasgow G12 0YN ☏0141/211 1062. Travel vaccinations including yellow fever.
Dun Laoghaire Medical Centre 5 Northumberland Ave, Dun Laoghaire Co, Dublin ☏01/280 4996, ℱ280 5603. Advice on medical matters abroad.
Hospital for Tropical Diseases Travel Clinic 2nd floor, Mortimer Market Centre, off Capper St, London WC1E 6AU (Mon–Fri 9am–5pm by appointment only; ☏020/7388 9600; a

consultation costs £15 which is waived if you have your injections here). A recorded Health Line (☏09061/337 733; 50p per min) gives hints on hygiene and illness prevention as well as listing appropriate immunizations.
Liverpool School of Tropical Medicine Pembroke Place, Liverpool L3 5QA ☏0151/708 9393. Walk-in clinic Mon–Fri 1–4pm; appointment required for yellow fever, but not for other jabs.
Malaria Helpline 24-hour recorded message ☏0891/600 350; 60p per minute.
MASTA (Medical Advisory Service for Travellers Abroad) London School of Hygiene and Tropical Medicine. Operates a pre-recorded 24-hour Travellers' Health Line (UK ☏0906/822 4100, 60p per min; Republic of Ireland ☏01560/147 000, 75p per minute), giving written information tailored to your journey by return of post.
Nomad Pharmacy surgeries 40 Bernard St, London, WC1; and 3-4 Wellington Terrace, Turnpike Lane, London N8 (Mon–Fri 9.30am–6pm, ☏020/7833 4114 to book vaccination appointment). They give advice free if you go in person, or their telephone helpline is ☏09068/633 414 (60p per minute). They can give information tailored to your travel needs.
Trailfinders Immunization clinic (no appointment necessary) at 194 Kensington High St, London (Mon–Fri 9am–5pm except Thurs to 6pm, Sat 9.30am–4pm; ☏020/7938 3999).
Travel Health Centre Department of International Health and Tropical Medicine, Royal College of Surgeons in Ireland, Mercers Medical Centre, Stephen's St Lower, Dublin ☏01/402 2337. Expert pre-trip advice and inoculations.
Travel Medicine Services PO Box 254, 16 College St, Belfast 1 ☏028/9031 5220. Offers medical advice before a trip and help afterwards in the event of a tropical disease.
Tropical Medical Bureau Grafton Buildings, 34 Grafton St, Dublin 2, ☏01/671 9200, ⊛http://tmb .exodus.ie, ℮appointments_gs@tmb.ie.

USA and Canada

Canadian Society for International Health 1 Nicholas St, Suite 1105, Ottawa, ON K1N 7B7 ☏613/241-5785, ⊛www.csih.org. Distributes a free pamphlet, "Health Information for Canadian Travellers", containing an extensive list of travel health centres in Canada.
Centers for Disease Control 1600 Clifton Rd NE, Atlanta, GA 30333 ☏1-800/311-3435 or 404/639-3534, ℱ1-888/232-3299, ⊛www.cdc.gov. Publishes outbreak warnings, suggested inoculations, precautions and other background information for travellers. Useful

website plus International Travelers Hotline on ☎1-877/FYI-TRIP.

International Association for Medical Assistance to Travellers (IAMAT) 417 Center St, Lewiston, NY 14092 ☎716/754-4883, ⓦwww.sentex.net/~iamat, and 40 Regal Rd, Guelph, ON N1K 1B5 ☎519/836-0102. A non-profit organization supported by donations, it can provide a list of English-speaking doctors, climate charts and leaflets on various diseases and inoculations.

International SOS Assistance 8 Neshaminy Interplex Suite 207, Trevose, USA 19053-6956 ☎1-800/523-8930, ⓦwww.intsos.com. Members receive pre-trip medical referral info, as well as overseas emergency services designed to complement travel insurance coverage.

MEDJET Assistance ☎1-800/863-3538, ⓦww.medjetassistance.com. Annual membership program for travellers ($175 for individuals, $275 for families) that, in the event of illness or injury, will fly members home or to the hospital of their choice in a medically equipped and staffed jet.

Travel Medicine ☎1-800/872-8633, Ⓕ1-413/584-6656, ⓦwww.travmed.com. Sells first-aid kits, mosquito netting, water filters, reference books and other health-related travel products.

Travelers Medical Center 31 Washington Square West, New York, NY 10011 ☎212/982-1600. Consultation service on immunizations and treatment of diseases for people travelling to developing countries.

Australia and New Zealand

Travellers' Medical and Vaccination Centres 27–29 Gilbert Place, Adelaide, SA 5000 ☎08/8212 7522; 1/170 Queen St, Auckland ☎09/373 3531; 5/247 Adelaide St, Brisbane, Qld 4000 ☎07/3221 9066; 5/8–10 Hobart Place, Canberra, ACT 2600 ☎02/6257 7156; 147 Armagh St, Christchurch ☎03/379 4000; 270 Sandy Bay Rd, Sandy Bay, Hobart, Tas 7005 ☎03/6223 7577; 2/393 Little Bourke St, Melbourne, Vic 3000 ☎03/9602 5788; 45 Stirling Hwy, Nedlands, WA 6009 ☎08/9386 4511; Level 7, Dymocks Bldg, 428 George St,

Sydney, NSW 2000 ☎02/9221 7133; Shop 15, Grand Arcade, 14–16 Willis St, Wellington ☎04/473 0991.

General precautions

The average traveller to Laos has little to worry about as long as they use common sense and exercise a few **precautions**. The change in climate and diet experienced during travel collaborate to lower your resistance, so you need to take special care to maintain a healthy intake of food and water and to try to minimize the effects of heat and humidity on the body. Excessive alcohol consumption should be avoided, as the dehydrating effects of alcohol are amplified by the heat and humidity.

Bacteria thrive in the tropics and the best way to combat them is to keep up standards of **personal hygiene**. Frequent bathing is essential and hands should be washed before eating, especially given that much of the Lao cuisine is traditionally eaten with the hands. Cuts or scratches, no matter how minor, can become infected very easily and should be thoroughly cleaned, disinfected and bandaged to keep dirt out. Most health problems experienced by travellers are a direct result of something they've eaten. Avoid eating uncooked vegetables and fruits that cannot be peeled. Dishes containing raw meat or fish are considered a delicacy in Laos but people who eat them risk ingesting worms and other parasites. **Bottled water** and Chinese **tea** made from boiled water are generally safe, but travellers should shun homemade **ice**. Cooked food that has been sitting out for an undetermined period of time should be treated with suspicion as well. While the communal nature of Lao dining makes it difficult to do so, you should avoid sharing glasses and utensils.

What about the water?

The simple rule while travelling in Laos is **don't drink river or tap water**. Contaminated water is a major cause of sickness due to the presence of pathogenic organisms: bacteria, viruses and cysts. These micro-organisms cause **diseases** such as diarrhoea, gastroenteritis, typhoid, cholera, dysentery, polio, hepatitis A, giardia and bilharzia, and can be present even when water looks clean and safe to drink. Most travellers in Laos need not worry about contracting these diseases from drinking water, as safe **bottled water** is available almost anywhere. When buying water, however, be sure to check that the seal is unbroken as bottles are occasionally refilled from the tap.

Stomach trouble and viruses

According to NGO doctors posted in Laos, the most common fatal disease among the rural Lao is **diarrhoea**. The majority of these victims are infants who actually die from the resulting dehydration. Most travellers experience some form of **stomach trouble** during their visit to Laos, simply because their digestive system is unaccustomed to the local germs and will need time to adapt. If you do experience travellers' diarrhoea, it is usually enough to drink lots of liquids and eat lightly, avoiding spicy or greasy foods in favour of bland noodle soups, until your system has had time to recover. The use of Lomotil or Imodium should be avoided unless long-distance road travel makes it absolutely necessary. Diarrhoea accompanied by severe stomach cramps, nausea or vomiting are an indication of **food poisoning**. As with common diarrhoea, it usually passes after a couple of days. In either case, be sure to increase your liquid intake to make up for lost fluids. It's a good idea to bring **oral rehydration salts** with you from home. Otherwise, you could try a Thai-made athletes' rehydration beverage, which is available at restaurants and drink stands in many parts of Laos, and, when mixed with bottled water, is good for replacing lost salts. If symptoms persist or become worse after a couple of days you should consider seeking medical advice in Thailand.

The presence of blood or mucous in the faeces is an indication of dysentery. There are two types of dysentery and they differ in their symptoms and treatment. **Bacillary dysentery** has an acute onset with severe abdominal pain accompanied by the presence of blood in the diarrhoea. Fever and vomiting may also be symptoms. Bacillary dysentery requires immediate medical attention and antibiotics are usually prescribed. **Amoebic dysentery** is the more serious of the two and the onset is gradual with bloody faeces accompanied by abdominal pain. The symptoms may eventually disappear but the amoebas will still be in the body and will continue to feed on internal organs, causing serious health problems in time. The treatment of amoebic dysentery by a physician should not be delayed. In the case of contracting either type of dysentery, medical advice in Thailand should be sought.

Hepatitis A is a viral infection contracted by eating contaminated food or water and is quite common in Laos. The infection causes the liver to become inflamed and resulting symptoms include nausea, abdominal pains, dark-brown urine and light-brown faeces that may be followed by jaundice (yellowing of the skin and whites of eyes). Vaccination is the best precaution and there is no cure except to get plenty of rest and eat light meals of non-fatty foods.

Another scatological horror is **giardia**, symptoms of which include a bloated stomach, evil-smelling burps and farts, and diarrhoea or floating stools. As with dysentery, treatment by a physician in Thailand should be sought immediately.

Occasional outbreaks of **cholera** occur in Laos. The initial symptoms are a sudden onset of watery, but painless diarrhoea. Later nausea, vomiting and muscle cramps set in. Cholera can be fatal if adequate fluid intake is not maintained. Copious amounts of liquids, including oral rehydration solution, should be consumed and medical treatment in Thailand should be sought immediately.

Like cholera, **typhoid** is also spread in small, localized epidemics. The disease is sometimes difficult to diagnose, as symptoms can vary widely. Generally, they include headaches, fever and constipation, followed by diarrhoea.

Mosquito-borne illnesses

Malaria is rife in much of Laos. While urban Vientiane is said to be malaria-free, visitors to other parts of Laos should take all possible precautions to avoid contracting this sometimes fatal disease. Night-feeding mosquitoes are the carriers, so you'll need to take extra care in the evening, particularly at dawn and dusk: **insect repellent** is a must, while wearing trousers, long-sleeved shirts and socks gives mosquitoes less skin to target. Most accommodation places provide a **mosquito net**, but many newer hotels have replaced nets with screened-in windows, which is fine if the room door remains shut at all times, but unfortunately doors are usually left wide open when maids are tidying up the rooms between guests, and invariably mosquitoes fly in by the dozen. If you don't want to bathe in bug repellent before going to bed, insist on a mosquito net, or better still, bring your own. In addition to these precautions, it's advisable to take **antimalarial tablets** for added insurance against the disease. Though **doxycycline** and **mefloquine** are the most commonly prescribed antimalarials for Laos, malarial mosquitoes have already begun showing a resistance to the latter drug. Some antimalarials can have unpleasant side-effects. Mefloquine in particular can sometimes cause dizziness, extreme fatigue, nausea and nightmares. Pregnant or lactating women are not advised to take mefloquine. While none of these drugs gives a hundred percent guarantee that you will not contract malaria, the risks will be greatly reduced. Malaria's **symptoms** include headaches, fever and chills. If you think you've contracted malaria, you should immediately check into a Thai hospital.

Day-feeding mosquitoes are the carriers of **dengue fever**, a malady once commonly known as "break-bone fever". The disease is common in urban as well as rural areas and outbreaks occur annually during the rainy season. The symptoms are similar to malaria and include fever, chills, aching joints and a red rash that spreads from the torso to the limbs and face. Dengue can be fatal in small children and there is no preventative vaccination or prophylactic. Travellers should use the same precautions as with malaria, using insect repellent, keeping skin covered with loose-fitting clothing and wearing socks. There is no specific treatment for dengue other than rest, lots of liquids and paracetamol for pain and fever. Aspirin should be avoided as it sometimes leads to internal haemorrhaging.

Sun-related maladies

The Lao deal with the hottest hours of the day by getting horizontal in the shade, and for good reason. The Lao **hot season**, roughly March to May, can be brutal, especially in the lowlands. Visitors from temperate climes may not immediately appreciate the dangers that the tropical sun presents. To prevent **sunburn**, fair-skinned people should wear sun block and consider purchasing a wide-brimmed straw hat. Most people find UV protective sunglasses are essential to cut the sun's glare, which can be especially harsh during river journeys. The threat of **dehydration** increases with physical exertion. Even if you do not feel thirsty, force yourself to drink plenty of water. Not having to urinate or passing orange-coloured urine are sure signs that your system is not getting enough liquids. **Heat exhaustion**, signified by headaches, dizziness and nausea, is treated by resting in a cool place and increasing your liquid intake until the symptoms disappear. **Heat-stroke** can be life-threatening if not treated immediately and is indicated by high body temperature, flushed skin and a lack of perspiration. Reducing the body's temperature by immersion in tepid water is an initial treatment but is no substitute for prompt medical attention. Heat and high humidity sometimes cause **prickly heat**, an itchy rash that is easily avoided by wearing loose-fitting cotton clothing. A Thai-made remedy, "St Luke's Prickly Heat Powder", available in Vientiane and towns along the Mekong, provides relief and prevents the rash from recurring.

Critters that bite and sting

In Laos the **bugs** are thick, especially during the rainy season when they swarm round light bulbs and pummel bare skin until you feel like a trampoline at a flea circus. Fortunately, most flying insects pose no threat and are simply looking for a place to land and rest up.

Visitors who spend the night in hilltribe villages where hygiene is poor risk being infected by **scabies**. These microscopic creatures are just as loathsome as their name suggests, causing severe itching by burrowing under the skin and laying eggs. Scabies is most commonly contracted by sleeping on dirty bedclothes or being in prolonged physical contact with someone who is infected. More common are **head lice**, especially among children in rural areas. Like scabies, it takes physical contact, such as sleeping next to an infected person, to contract head lice, though it may also be possible to contract head lice by wearing a hat belonging to someone who is infected.

The variety of **leeches** most commonly

encountered in Laos are about the size and shape of an inchworm, and climb foliage to wait for a suitable "host" to pass by. Travellers are most likely to pick them up while trekking through wooded areas. Take extra care when relieving yourself during breaks on long-distance bus rides. The habit of pushing deep into a bush for privacy gives leeches just enough time to grab hold of your shoes or trousers. Later they will crawl their way beneath clothing and attach themselves to joint areas (ankles, knees, elbows) where veins are near the surface of the skin. An anaesthetic and anticoagulant in the leaches' saliva allows the little vampires to gorge themselves on blood without the host feeling any pain. Usually the victim is not even aware they have been bitten until the bloated leech drops off and blood continues to flow from the small wound. Tucking your trouser-legs into your socks is an easy way to foil leeches. Wounds left by sucking leeches should be washed and bandaged as soon as possible to avoid infection.

Laos has several varieties of **poisonous snakes**, including the king cobra, but the Lao habit of killing every snake they come across, whether venomous or not, keeps areas of human habitation largely snake-free. Travelling in rural areas greatly increases the risk of snakebite, but visitors can lessen the chances of being bitten by not wearing sandals or flip-flops outside of urban areas. While hiking between hilltribe villages especially, trekkers should take the precaution of wearing boots, socks and long pants. If you are bitten, the number one rule is not to panic. Remain still to prevent the venom from being quickly absorbed into the bloodstream. Snakebites should be washed and disinfected and immediate medical attention should be sought. Huge, black **scorpions** the size of large prawns lurk under the shade of fallen leaves and sting reflexively when stepped on, another solid reason to restrict flip-flop-wearing to urban areas. While the sting is very painful, it is not fatal and pain and swelling usually disappear after a few hours.

Animals that are infected with **rabies** can transmit the disease by biting or even by licking an open wound. Dogs are the most common carriers but the disease can also be contracted from the bites of gibbons, bats and other mammals. Travellers should stay clear of all wild animals and resist the urge to pet unfamiliar dogs or cats. If bitten by a suspect animal, wash and disinfect the wound with alcohol or iodine. Seek medical help immediately as the disease is fatal if left untreated.

Sexually transmitted diseases

Prostitution is on the rise in Laos and with it the inevitable scourge of **sexually transmitted diseases** (STDs). Gonorrhoea and syphilis are common but are easily treated with antibiotics. Symptoms of the former include pain or a pus-like discharge when urinating. An open sore on or around the genitals is a symptom of syphilis. In women symptoms are internal and may not be noticed. The number of cases of **AIDS** is also rising in Laos, mostly the result of Lao prostitutes contracting HIV in Thailand. Condoms are the best prevention for all STDs, but they are not a hundred percent safe. Bringing condoms from home is a good idea. Most condoms sold in Laos are imported from Thailand where surveys have found that over ten percent of Thai-made condoms are defective.

A traveller's first-aid kit

Among items you might want to carry with you – especially if you're planning to go trekking – are:

- ❏ Antiseptic cream
- ❏ Anti-fungal cream
- ❏ Insect repellent
- ❏ Plasters/band aids
- ❏ Water sterilization tablets or water purifier
- ❏ Gauze and sealed bandages
- ❏ Knee supports
- ❏ Imodium (Lomotil) for emergency diarrhoea treatment
- ❏ Paracetamol/aspirin (useful for combating the effects of altitude)
- ❏ Multi-vitamin and mineral tablets
- ❏ Rehydration salts
- ❏ Hypodermic needles and sterilized skin wipes (more for the security of knowing you have them, than any fear that a local hospital would fail to observe basic sanitary precautions)

Getting around

Getting around on Laos's transport system is an adventure in itself, what with its barely seaworthy boats, ropey aeroplanes, aged jalopies with hard seats and hot, crowded buses. Don't be fooled by maps and distance charts either; seemingly short rides can take hours or days, as tired vehicles slow to a crawl in their uphill battle against muddy, mountainous roads. Take heart though, in knowing that many visitors have their best encounters with the people of Laos amid the adversity of a bad bus ride.

At long last Laos's **road network**, neglected by the French and bombed by the Americans, is being extensively upgraded. Laos's main thoroughfare is **Route 13**, which stretches from Louang Phabang to the Cambodian border, passing through Vientiane, Savannakhet and Pakxe. Only completed in its entirety in 1998, Route 13, once plagued by bandit attacks between Kasi and Louang Phabang (see p.64), is now safe, and the last unsurfaced 170km stretch between Savannakhet and Pakxe was being paved at the time of writing. Off Route 13, you'll encounter a wide range of road conditions – from freshly paved to bone-rattlingly potholed. Highways not currently under construction are barely maintained and some are only built to last a season, washed away each year by the monsoon. Note also that some roads remain off-limits because of security problems (see p.64–65).

With road conditions improving, **buses** have begun displacing **river travel**, the traditional means of getting around. However, cargo boats still regularly ply the Mekong, Southeast Asia's ancient highway, and small passenger boats are available for hire on Laos's numerous other navigable waterways.

You only need to travel for a week or two in Laos before you realize that **timetables** are irrelevant: planes, buses and boats leave on a whim and estimated times of arrival are pointless. Wherever you go in Laos, the driver does not seem to be in any hurry to arrive.

Inter-town transport

Visitors hoping to see anything of the country can expect hours of arduous, bone-crunching travel on Laos's motley fleet of lumbering jitter-boxes. Improvements in the national highway system have, however, resulted in shorter travel times, more comfortable rides and increased safety, but buses on many routes can be few and far between and link only larger towns, making a number of interesting attractions, such as ruins and waterfalls, difficult to reach. Even when there is transport, you may find that the limited bus timetables will allow you to get to a particular site, but not make a same-day return trip – something of a problem given the dearth of accommodation in farflung spots.

Buses

Buses in Laos range from new, air-con tourist coaches on the Vientiane to Louang Phabang route to rattling wrecks in the outlying provinces. Coming in all shapes and sizes, ordinary buses provide cheap transport between major towns and link provincial hubs with their surrounding districts. Cramped, overloaded and designed for the smaller Lao frame, buses in Laos are profound tests of endurance and patience. Seats have either torn cushions or are nothing more than an inch of foam on a hard plank. Luggage – ranging from roosters, with the runs, to sloshing buckets of fish and the inevitable fifty-kilo sacks of rice – is piled in every conceivable space, filling up the aisle and soaring skywards from the roof. **Breakdowns** are commonplace and often require a lengthy roadside wait as the driver repairs the bus on a lonely stretch of road. In the rainy season, unpaved roads dissolve into rivers of mud, slowing buses to a crawl or swallowing them whole. Even vehicles in reasonably good condition make painfully slow progress, as drivers combat **mountainous roads** and make frequent, and at times, long stops, to pick up passengers, load goods and even haggle for bargains at roadside stalls.

Operating out of Vientiane, a fleet of blue, **government-owned buses** caters mostly to the capital's outlying districts, although it does provide a service to towns as far north as Vang Viang and as far south as Pakxe. While newer than most vehicles in Laos, these Japanese- and Korean-built buses are not air-conditioned and have cramped seats, a situation that worsens as rural passengers pile in. Buses plying **remote routes** tend to be in worse shape: aged jalopies cast off from Thailand or left behind by the Russians, which reach new lows in terms of discomfort and are even more prone to breakdowns. These vehicles range in style from buses in the classic sense of the word to souped-up tourist vans. Converted Russian flat-bed trucks, once the mainstay of travel in Laos, still operate in remote areas.

It's necessary to **buy a ticket** at the station before boarding the bus only in larger towns such as Vientiane, Savannakhet and Louang Phabang. On most routes it's common practice to buy them on board, although some buses do not issue any tickets at all. Lao bus operators are generally honest, although you may find a few drivers that charge foreigners a somewhat higher rate. However, it's not usually more than double the standard fare.

For an idea of frequency and duration of bus services between towns, check the **travel details** at the end of each chapter. Given the poor condition of many roads and buses, as well as the many unscheduled stops en route, all travel times should be taken as rough estimates. **Timetables** only exist in regional hubs like Vientiane, Louang Phabang and Savannakhet; elsewhere it's best to go to the bus station the night before you plan to travel to find out the schedule for the next day. Where there is no information, it's best to get to the bus station as **early in the morning** as possible – between 6 and 7am – as that is when the majority of Lao passengers prefer to travel, especially on long-distance runs. Very few buses leave after midday.

Even though they're scheduled, buses often won't depart if empty; many drivers will sit in the bus station long after their stated departure time, revving their engines in an attempt to lure enough passengers to make the trip worthwhile. Route 13, however, sees a steady flow of bus traffic and it's usually possible to flag down a vehicle during daylight hours provided it's not already full.

Express buses and vans

A handful of **private companies** have recently sprung up to offer air-conditioned **express service** on a few select routes such as between Vientiane and Savannakhet, with stops in Pakxan and Thakhek. There is also a new $10 air-con coach service from Vientiane to Louang Phabang, although this has no fixed schedule and currently only runs a few times a month. Such services leave Vientiane from their own private "stations", and reservations, which can be made through the companies' respective Vientiane offices, are recommended. Additionally, several van and mini-bus services have started up offering services to Vang Viang and even as far afield as Savannakhet. Conditions change rapidly so check with travel agents in Vientiane for the latest information on routes and bookings.

Sawngthaews

In rural areas, away from the Mekong Valley, the bus network is often replaced by **sawngthaews** – converted pick-up trucks – into which drivers stuff as many passengers as they possibly can. Passengers are crammed onto two facing benches in the back ("sawngthaew" means "two rows"); latecomers are left to dangle off the back, with their feet on a running board, an experience that, on a bumpy road, is akin to inland windsurfing.

Sawngthaews also ply routes between larger towns and their satellite villages, a service for which they charge roughly the same amount as buses. They usually depart from the regular bus station, but will only leave when a driver feels he has enough passengers to make the trip worth his while. Some drivers try to sweat extra kip out of passengers by delaying departure. Your fellow passengers may agree to this (this is more likely to happen on routes with few riders), but most often they grudgingly wait. In some situations, you can save yourself a lot of trouble and waiting by getting a few fellow travellers together and flat-out **hiring the driver** to take you where you want to go. In any case the fares are ridiculously low so this is quite affordable. To catch a sawngthaew in between stops simply flag it down from the side of the road and tell the driver where you're headed so he knows when to let you off. The fare is usually paid when you get off or at the end of the ride. Drivers working without fare collectors tend to stop on the outskirts of their final destination to collect the fare in case someone refuses to pay.

City and town transport

With even the capital too small to support a local bus system, transport within Lao towns and cities is left to squadrons of motorized *samlaw* (literally, three wheels) vehicles, more commonly known as **jumbos** and **tuk-tuks**. Painted in primary reds, blues and yellows, the two types of *samlaw* look alike and both function as share taxis, with facing benches in the rear to accommodate four or five passengers. Jumbos are the original Lao vehicle, a homemade three-wheeler consisting of a two-wheeled carriage soldered to the front half of a motorcycle, a process best summed up by the name for the vehicle used in the southern town of Savannakhet – Skylab (pronounced "sakai-laeb"), after the doomed space station that fell to earth, piece by piece, in the late 1980s. Offspring of the three-wheeled taxis known for striking terror in Bangkok pedestrians, tuk-tuks are really just bigger, sturdier jumbos, the unlikely product of some Thai factory, which take their name from their incessantly sputtering engines. Lao tend to refer to these vehicles interchangeably.

Although most northern towns are more than manageable on foot, the Mekong towns tend to sprawl so you'll find tuk-tuks particularly useful for getting into town from

a bus station. **To catch a tuk-tuk**, flag it down as it passes in the street by waving your hand, palm face down and parallel to the ground. Tell the driver where you're going, bargain the price and pay at the end of the ride.

There are also **shared tuk-tuks** which collect people from markets or stations and then do a run into the centre or vice versa. In this case the payment is per person according to the distance travelled and your bargaining skills. Rates vary from town to town and are prone to fluctuate in step with rising petrol prices, but figure on paying around 500K per kilometre. In some towns, tuk-tuks run set routes to the surrounding villages and leave from a stand, usually near the market, once full. Chartering tuk-tuks is also a good way to get to sites within 10 to 15km of a city.

Boats

With the country possessing roughly 4600km of navigable waterways including stretches of the Mekong, Nam Ou, Nam Ngum, Xe Kong and seven other arteries, it's no surprise to learn that **rivers** are the ancient highways of mountainous Laos. Road improvements in recent years, however, have led to the decline of river travel between many towns, with buses and sawngthaews replacing the armada of wooden cigars that once plied regular routes. The main **Mekong routes** that remain link Houayxai to Louang Phabang, Louang Phabang to Vientiane, and Pakxe with Si Phan Don. Since the upgrade of Route 13 in the south, boats only rarely ply the stretch of river between Vientiane and Pakxe. Aside from the larger, so-called, "slow boats" on the Mekong routes, smaller passenger boats still regularly cruise up the wide Nam Ou River, the Nam Tha River, and a few others, provided water levels are high enough.

Slow boats

The diesel-chugging cargo boats that lumber up and down the **Mekong routes** are known as "**slow boats**" (*heua sa*). Hammered together from ill-fitting pieces of wood, and powered by a jury-rigged engine that needs to be coaxed along by an on-board mechanic, these "slow" boats on the Mekong are one of Asia's last great adventures. Built to fit the maximum amount of cargo – from roosters to sacks of rice and, unbelievably, even pick-up trucks – these boats do not have any seats, leaving passengers to grab any spot they can find on the floor or to sit on the roof. Landing involves ramming the boat into the riverbank; a plank is placed at the side to allow passengers to disembark, a process that can be very wet and muddy. On the Houayxai to Louang Phabang run there are daily departures, but on the Louang Prabang to Vientiane leg the schedule is variable: sometimes there's just no boat. Passengers doing the Louang Phabang to Vientiane route must sleep in villages or aboard the boat. This section is well off the tourist track, so it's a good idea to bring extra water and food.

On **smaller rivers**, river travel is by long, narrow **passenger boats** powered by a small outboard engine. Confusingly, these are also known as "slow boats", although, unlike the big Mekong cargo boats, they only hold eight people and never attempt the Mekong, serving instead its smaller tributaries. They never have a fixed schedule and only leave if and when there are enough passengers.

Due to the casual nature of river travel in Laos, the best way to deal with uncertain departures is to simply **show up early** in the morning and head down to the landing and ask around. Be prepared for contradictory answers to questions regarding price, departure and arrival time, and even destination. Given fluctuations in current and water level and the possibility of breakdowns and lengthy stops to load passengers and cargo, no one really knows how long a trip will take. On occasion, boats don't make their final destination during the daytime, forcing passengers to sleep in the nearest village or aboard the boat. Such stops will take you off the tourist track, so if you're travelling alone or were counting on finding a guest house and a fruit shake at the end of the journey, such unannounced stopovers can take you out of your comfort zone. In such instances it helps to link up with fellow foreigners; it's

also a good idea to bring extra water and food.

The **northern river routes** are somewhat better managed, with tickets sold and ports overseen by a local government official, who will generally shepherd you in the right direction. **Tickets** are sold from a wooden booth or office near the landing and you buy your ticket the day you leave. Fares are generally posted but foreigners pay significantly more than locals. Always arrive early in the morning.

Southern routes are more haphazard. Unlike in the north, you won't need to buy a ticket. The downside is that you won't know what the exact fare for the ride is. The crew may try to overcharge you a few thousand kip, but usually never so much as to provoke indignation. The recent completion of Route 13 means that traffic along this route will surely decline in coming years, although the presence of far-flung villages on the right bank and on various islands means that a boat service should continue to Si Phan Don for the foreseeable future.

Travel by slow boat can be dangerous and reports of boats **sinking** are not uncommon. The Mekong has some particularly tricky stretches, with narrow channels threading through rapids and past churning whirlpools. The river can be particularly rough late in the rainy season, when the Mekong swells and uprooted trees and other debris are swept into the river.

Speedboats

On both the Mekong and its tributaries, **speedboats** (*heua wai*) are a costlier but faster alternative to slow boats. Connecting towns along the Nam Ou and the Mekong from Vientiane to the Chinese border, these five-metre-long terrors are usually powered by a 1200cc Toyota car engine and can accommodate up to eight passengers. **Crash helmets** are handed out before journeys: the head gear is meant to spare your hearing from the overpowering screech of the engine – not your head. Although the roar of the engine is less annoying on board than it is from the banks, you should still consider bringing along **ear plugs**. Some drivers also provide life jackets.

Donning a crash helmet and being catapulted up the Mekong River at 50km an hour may not sound like most people's idea of a holiday in Laos, but if you're up for it, speedboats can shave hours or days off a river journey and give you a thrilling spin at the same time. It's by no means safe, of course, although captains swear by their navigational skills. The boats skim the surface of churning whirlpools and slalom through rapids sharp enough to turn the wooden hull into toothpicks. In one particularly nasty accident in 1998, two boats collided head-on, killing all on board.

Speedboats leave from a **separate landing** in Vientiane, Thadua, Paklai, Louang Phabang, Pakbeng and Houayxai, departing when full. Seating is incredibly **cramped**, so you may want to consider paying for the price of two seats. **Tickets** cost as much as two to three times what you might pay to take a slow boat. To give you an idea of costs, the journey from Louang Phabang to Pakbeng is around $12. Speedboats can also be **chartered** for around $50 per hour. To charter a speedboat from Louang Phabang to Phongsali you'll pay around $200, to Houayxai $100.

Cross-river ferries

Clunky metal car **ferries** and **pirogues**, the dug-out wooden skiffs propelled by poles, paddles or tiny engines, are both useful means of fording rivers in the absence of a bridge. Both leave when they have a sufficient number of passengers and usually charge 1000K, unless you're taking a vehicle across, in which case you can expect to pay around 2000–5000K. If you don't want to wait, pirogues are always open for **hire**. In the outback, fishermen can usually be persuaded to ferry you across to the opposite bank for a small sum of money.

Planes

Lao Aviation is the sole carrier servicing the country's **internal flight network**. With demand for domestic flights soaring in recent years, Lao Aviation's tiny, patchwork fleet of Chinese Yun-12 and Yun-7s and its two ATR 72s has come under severe strain

as it struggles to maintain safety standards and keep key flight routes open. Several Western embassies have **travel advisories** warning against flying Lao Aviation. Locals call the Yuns "tuk-tuks with wings". Expatriates familiar with the airline claim that it is safe to fly the ATR, although you can't always be certain which plane you'll get and, as many international organizations will only allow their employees to fly this plane, it can be difficult to get a seat on it. Check with one of the Western embassies in Vientiane for an update on the status of Lao Aviation. For some travellers flying with Lao Aviation is a kind of macho bravado but for most it's not something you want to do if you don't absolutely have to. Signs outside Lao airports read not too reassuringly, "We wish you have a safe flight".

As with other forms of transport in Laos, you'll need to remain flexible. Reliability increases on key routes: Vientiane–Louang Phabang, Vientiane–Pakxe and Vientiane–Phonsavan. Given the popularity of such routes in the peak season it's even wise to **book ahead**. On other routes, you may find it better to reconfirm the departure of your flight by stopping by the Lao Aviation office. When **buying a ticket** keep in mind that Lao Aviation only accepts US dollars cash. In the provinces, if you do not have dollars, you'll need to get a letter from Lao Aviation informing the local bank that you need to exchange a travellers' cheque for dollars. Some banks may be able to give you a cash advance on Visa in dollars. As all this can be somewhat time-consuming, it's advisable to set aside US dollars to buy plane tickets if you plan on flying. Sample one-way fares are: Vientiane to Phonsavan $46; Vientiane to Xam Nua $72; Phonsavan to Louang Phabang $37; Louang Phabang to Vientiane $57; Vientiane to Pakxe $97.

Vehicle rental

Renting a **private vehicle** is expensive, but is sometimes the only way you'll be able to get to certain spots, given the limitations of Laos's transport network. Self-drive is an option, and cars can be rented from a couple of agencies in Vientiane. However, it's usually easier and cheaper to hire a **car and driver**. Tour agencies will rent out air-conditioned vans and 4WD pick-up trucks as well as provide drivers. Inflated by the excessive rates paid by UN organizations, prices can be as much as $80–100 per day, sometimes more if you're hiring a car to head upcountry from Vientiane. When settling on a price, it's important to clarify who is responsible for what: check who pays for the driver's food and lodging, fuel and repairs, and be sure to ask what happens in case of a major breakdown or accident. In Vientiane, one of the better agencies is Asia Vehicle Rental on Lane Xang Road (℡021/217493). A much cheaper alternative for short distances and day-trips is to charter a tuk-tuk or pick-up truck (see pp.35–36).

Motorbikes

One of the best ways to explore the countryside is to rent a **motorbike**. Unfortunately, this is only an option in Vientiane, Vang Viang, Louang Phabang, Thakhek, and Pakxe and even then you'll only be able to find smaller bikes, usually 100cc stepthroughs such as the Honda Dream. Rental prices for the day are generally $6–10, depending on the age and condition of the bike. You'll also be required to leave your passport as a deposit and you may be required to return the bike by dark. A licence is not required. Insurance is not available, so it's a good idea to make sure your travel insurance covers you for any potential accidents. Before zooming off, be sure to **check the bike** thoroughly. Check for any scratches and damaged parts and take it for a test run to make sure the vehicle is running properly. More powerful 125cc **dirt bikes** suitable for cross-country driving are available only in Vientiane and cost $20 a day.

As far as **equipment** goes, a helmet is good protection, although few rental places will have one to offer you. It's not against the law to ride without a helmet, but, if you can get one, it's probably a good idea to wear it. Sunglasses are essential in order to fend off the glare of the tropical sun and keep dust and bugs out of your eyes. Proper shoes, long trousers and a long-sleeved shirt are all worthwhile additions to your biking outfit and will provide a thin layer of protection if you take a spill.

Bicycles

Bicycles are available in most major tourist centres. If you can find one, bikes are an excellent way to beat the heat. Guest houses, souvenir shops and a few tourist-oriented restaurants sometimes keep a small stable of Thai- or Chinese-made bikes – though rarely mountain bikes – which they will rent out for 10,000K per day.

Hitching

Hitching in Laos does not exist in the Western sense, although there is a tradition of people flagging down passing trucks and catching rides in exchange for a small payment. Given the rather limited amount of traffic on Laos's highways, you won't want to count on hitching your way around the country, although you may find yourself flagging down a truck if you miss the last bus or if the one you're already on breaks down. As with hitching anywhere in the world, think twice before hitching solo, especially if you're a woman.

Trains

The skeleton of an engine and a few sections of narrow-gauge rail, installed early in the century on the islands of Don Khon and Don Det by the French, are all that remain of Laos's brief fling with the iron rooster. Plans are in the works to connect Vientiane with the Thai railway system via Nong Khai and eventually connect the Lao capital with the Chinese rail network. Tracks have been laid up to the Thai side of the Friendship Bridge, although there are as yet no other signs of this project moving forward any time soon.

Organized tours

Although less spontaneous and considerably more expensive than independent travel, **organized tours** are worth looking into if you have limited time or prefer to have someone smooth over the many logistical difficulties of travelling in Laos. Such tours can be booked from abroad with international tour operators, or after you arrive in Laos with local travel companies. About a dozen **tour companies** have sprung up in Vientiane, all offering similar tours in roughly the same price range, although it never hurts to shop around and bargain. A typical multi-day package might include a private cruise down the Mekong River on a slow boat operated by the tour company, with guided day-tours around Louang Phabang and other towns. While some tours include accommodation, meals and entry fees, others don't, so check what you're getting before paying.

Another type of tour rapidly gaining popularity in Laos is organised **adventure tours**. These can be single day or multi-day programmes and usually involve hilltribe trekking or river kayaking, or a combination of both. Rafting tours are also available and organized rock-climbing is just starting to take off. The main centres for adventure tours are Vientiane, Vang Viang, Louang Phabang, Louang Namtha, and Muang Sing, but at the current rate of growth it won't be long before these activities are on offer all over the country.

All Vientiane's tour companies are authorized by the National Tourism Authority of Laos, which ensures that you won't be dealing with a fly-by-night organization. Although the government of Laos encourages all travellers to visit Laos through an authorized tour company, tours themselves aren't bogged down in political rhetoric and guides tend to be easygoing and informative. Laos-based tour companies also offer a wider range and

much cheaper tours than packages organised by agencies based in Europe, America or Australia.

Guides are generally flexible about adjusting the itinerary, but if you want more **freedom**, an alternative is to set up your own custom-made tour by gathering a group of people and renting your own vehicle plus driver (see "Vehicle rental", p.39).

Local tour operators

Diethelm Travel Laos Nam Phou Place, PO Box 2657, Vientiane ☏ 021/215920, ℻ 217151. In Bangkok ☏ (662) 255-9150/70, ℻ 256-0248/9, ℮ dietravl@ksc.net.th, ⓦ www.diethelm-travel.com/laos/.

Inter-Lao Tourisme Louang Phabang Road, PO Box 2912, Vientiane ☏ 021/214232 or 214832, ℻ 216306, ⓦ www.interlao.laopdr.com.

Lane Xang Travel Pangkham Rd, PO Box 4452, Vientiane ☏ 021/213198 or 212469, ℻ 215804.

Lao National Tourism Authority ⓦ http://mekongcenter.com/home.htm

Lao Tourism Lane Xang Avenue, PO Box 2511, Vientiane ☏ 021/216671, ℻ 212013.

Lao Travel Service Lane Xang Avenue, PO Box 2553, Vientiane ☏ 021/216603-4, ℻ 216150.

Phudoi Travel Nong Bon Road, PO Box 5796, Vientiane ☏ 021/413639 or 413888, ℻ 413639 or 415578.

SODETOUR 16 Fa Ngum Rd, PO Box 70, Vientiane ☏ 021/216314, ℻ 216313.

Accommodation

Cheap accommodation can be found in larger towns all over Laos: for the most basic double room, prices start at around $2 in the provinces and $8 in Vientiane. At these prices rooms can be pretty shabby, although there are a few diamonds in the rough. Moving up the scale to $20 lands you a cosy room in a restored French villa. The recent influx of foreign visitors has meant a rapid increase in hotels and improved standards in tourist centres, although out in the boondocks change is coming more slowly and comfort can be hard to come by.

Expect to find higher standards of accommodation, as well as the greatest variety, in larger towns. **Vientiane** is slowly becoming cheaper for backpackers, but the number of budget guest houses and hotels is still rather limited. The number and quality of hotels in provincial capitals outside the Mekong Valley is growing in tune with recent increases in tourism. Upcountry towns, with the exception of popular stopovers on backpacker routes, tend to lag far behind, with small towns on well-travelled highways offering at best one or two rather rustic guest houses.

Finding a room is more or less up to you, as few towns have touts or taxi drivers trying to influence your decision. Outside Louang Phabang and the capital, finding a place to stay is a far simpler process than in most Southeast Asian countries – often because there are only one or two places in town and they're often a short walk from one another.

Once you've found a spot, ask to see a number of rooms before opting for one, as standards and room types can vary widely within the same establishment. You'll need to look at the bed arrangement for starters (a

double can be two single beds or one large bed, among other permutations), but also check the water pressure and the air-conditioning unit if you've opted for an air-con room, and make sure that there's a mosquito net (or screens) and a functioning lock on the door. In cities that lack a constant supply of electricity, you should weigh the added cost of an air-con room against the number of hours you'll have power. Some hotels may give you the option of not switching on the air-con and billing you for a fan room. En-suite showers and flush toilets are the norm only in mid-range and top-end hotels; for cheap accommodation it's a mixed bag, ranging from clean, en-suite bathrooms, with hot-water showers and western toilets, to grubby thin-walled rooms with shared facilities, cold water and squat toilets.

When you **check in** at a hotel or guest house in Laos, you are asked to fill in a brief **registration form** and to pay for your first night in advance, although some places don't mind billing you at the end of your stay. Prices throughout the Guide have been listed in US dollars. Establishments that do not already quote their prices in dollars or

Accommodation price codes

Accommodation throughout the Guide has been categorized according to the following price codes:

❶ less than $3	❹ $10–15	❼ $40–60
❷ $3–6	❺ $15–25	❽ $60 and above
❸ $6–10	❻ $25–40	

The prices reflect the minimum you can expect to pay for a **double room**. Where a range of prices is indicated in the text, this means that the establishment offers rooms with varying facilities – as explained in the review. In cases where an establishment charges per bed the price is given in the text rather than indicated by a price code.

baht keep a close eye on the volatile exchange rate and change their prices frequently, keeping the room rate at roughly the same dollar value. **Payment** can generally be made in Lao kip, dollars or Thai baht; count on being able to use credit cards only at higher-end establishments in Louang Phabang and Vientiane. Hotels and guest houses generally have exchange rates close to the official rate.

Most places are open to **negotiation**, especially in the low season, so it's a good idea to try and bargain; your case will be helped if you are staying for several days. You should also establish whether both parties are talking about a per-person or per-room rate before you begin haggling.

Not all accommodation places have **phones**, which is why some listings in this Guide don't have numbers alongside.

Budget accommodation

The distinction between a **guest house** and a **budget hotel** is rather blurry in Laos. Either can denote anything ranging from a bamboo-and-thatch hut to a multi-storey concrete monstrosity. There's very little that's standard from place to place – even rooms within one establishment can vary widely – although in tourist centres the cheapest bet is generally a fan room with shared washing facilities, at best kitted out with a ceiling fan and mosquito net. As you tack on extra dollars, you'll gain the luxury of a private bathroom with a hot-water shower and an air conditioner. In small towns in remote areas you'll find that the facilities are rustic at best – squat toilets and a large jar of water with a plastic scoop with which to shower. The further off the beaten track you go the greater the chances are that you'll be pumping your own water from a well or bathing in a stream.

There are no youth hostels as yet in Laos, though some government-owned flop houses operate as dorms, charging by the bed, and sometimes **dormitory accommodation** is one option among many at guest houses.

In **peak season**, finding a cheap room in Vientiane can be tricky. It helps to check in by noon, just after people begin checking out for that day. Guest houses and budget hotels rarely take advance booking unless they know you already.

Moderate accommodation

Dozens of new, **mid-range hotels** have been opening up in medium-sized towns all over Laos for the last few years, greatly improving the accommodation situation. Most of these hotels are four or five storeys and offer large rooms with tiled floors and en-suite bathrooms with hot-water and western-style toilet for between $3 and $5. The mattresses are usually hard but the sheets and quilts are consistently clean. The bathroom fittings in such hotels are usually brand new but they don't all have hot-water machines. Because the construction is poor and there is no concept of maintaining buildings, such hotels tend to age very quickly.

Upmarket hotels

Once you've crossed the $20 threshold, you enter a whole new level of comfort. In the former French towns on the Mekong this translates into an atmospheric room in a restored colonial villa or accommodation in a recently built establishment where rooms boast some of the trappings of a high-end hotel, such as cable television, fridge, air conditioning and a hot-water shower. In the case of **colonial-era hotels**, however, there are often a limited number of rooms, so you'll want to **book ahead** – well in advance if you plan to visit during the peak months (Dec–Jan). Many of these places are firmly ensconced on the tour-group circuit, so push for a discount if you're travelling independently.

Thanks to foreign investors, a few **top-end hotels** have opened their doors in Vientiane and Louang Phabang. You'll be able to get high quality for upwards of $60 – a third of the price you'd pay for similar accommodation in the West. The best hotels in the capital, such as the *Settha Palace Hotel* and the *Novotel Belvedere*, have international-class facilities, including business centres and gyms. At the moment, there's a glut of high-end hotel accommodation in the capital, so don't hesitate to ask for discounts, especially for longer-term stays.

Staying in villages

The government doesn't encourage foreigners to spend the night at a **villager's house**.

However, should you find yourself stuck in a small town for the night, a victim of the tired machinery of Laos's infrastructure or the yawning distances between villages, villagers are usually kind enough to find space for you in the absence of a local guest house. If there's a local **police station**, you should make yourself known to them, otherwise you should ask for permission to stay from the **village headman**. Don't expect much in the way of luxuries: you'll most likely find yourself bathing at the local well or in the river and going to the bathroom under the stars. Many small towns don't have so much as a noodle shop, so you'll also need to prepare yourself for some very authentic cooking. Before leaving, you should offer to remunerate your host with a small sum of cash.

Eating and drinking

Closely related to Thai cuisine, Lao food is, in fact, more widely consumed than you might think: in addition to the more than two million ethnic Lao in Laos, Lao cuisine is the daily sustenance for roughly a third of the Thai population, while more than a few Lao dishes are commonplace on the menus of Thai restaurants in the West. Although Lao cuisine isn't strongly influenced by that of its other neighbours, Chinese and Vietnamese immigrants have made their mark on the culinary landscape by opening restaurants and noodle stalls throughout the country, while the French introduced bread, paté and pastries.

Fiery and fragrant, with a touch of sour, **Lao food** owes its distinctive taste to fermented fish sauces, lemon grass, coriander leaves, chillies and lime juice. Eaten with the hands along with the staple sticky rice, much of Lao cuisine is roasted over an open fire and served with fresh herbs and vegetables. Pork, chicken, duck and water buffalo all end up in the kitchen, but freshwater fish is the main source of protein in the Lao diet.

Vientiane and **Louang Phabang** are the country's culinary centres, boasting excellent Lao food and international cuisine at fabulous value. Outside the Mekong corridor, however, Laos can be a culinary wasteland where you'll be lucky to find anything more than a simple bowl of noodles.

Hygiene is an important consideration when eating anywhere in Laos but, while it's important to be careful where and what you eat, in some of the smallest towns you

For a **food and drink glossary**, see pp.397–398.

may have no choice. It's also a good idea to go easy on your stomach by avoiding too many chillies and excessive amounts of fresh fruit during your first few days and by always drinking bottled or boiled water. As a general rule, noodle stalls and restaurants that do a brisk business are safe bets, though this is not much of a guide in smaller towns and villages, as so few people eat out. In some remote places, the stall-holder will wait until someone orders food before going to the market to buy the ingredients.

Where to eat

Generally speaking, there are four places from which to choose when getting your food. A step up from the **hawkers** peddling fruit from handcarts and selling roasted bugs on sticks to bus passengers are **markets**, where inexpensive, pre-made takeaways can be purchased, usually starting late in the afternoon. Often in and around the market or on a town's main road, **street stalls** are also inexpensive and offer simple dishes such as spring rolls, baguettes and noodles.

43

Restaurants in Laos come in all shapes and sizes, ranging from unpretentious noodle shops or open-air eateries to fancy French establishments serving quality wine by candelight.

In the smallest of towns you're only likely to find a noodle shop, but many proprietors will be happy to make you a proper meal with rice providing you give them enough advance warning. Bear in mind that, away from the Mekong River valley, the kitchen is often just a shack without proper lighting or even running water, and the cooking is done over an open fire. Furthermore, in many northern towns there is no electricity to run refrigeration. As a rule, sticking to tourist-class restaurants is the safest bet but it is by no means a guarantee of not getting an upset stomach. The Lao have poor knowledge of food preparation, storage, and hygiene and, although the food is much safer than in Nepal or India, you can pretty much expect to get the trots at some point.

Restaurant listings in the Guide do not include telephone numbers, as you won't need to make **reservations** while eating your way through Laos, even at Vientiane's poshest establishments. Although restaurants stay open later in the capital, as a rule the Lao **eat early**: outside the major cities and tourist centres, street stalls and noodle shops rarely stay open beyond 8pm and may close even earlier.

When it comes to **paying**, the normal sign language will be readily understood in most restaurants, or simply say "*khǎw sék dae*" ("the bill, please"). You'll only be able to use major **credit cards** at upscale establishments in Vientiane and high-end hotel restaurants in Louang Phabang.

Markets, street stalls and noodle shops

The **cheapest places** for food are markets, food stalls and noodle shops. Found in most towns throughout Laos, **morning markets** (*talat sâo*) remain open all day despite their name and provide a focal point for noodle shops (*hân khǎi fõe*), coffee vendors, fruit stands and sellers of crusty loaves of French bread. In Louang Phabang and Vientiane, vendors hawking pre-made dishes gather in

evening markets known as *talat láeng* towards late afternoon. Takeaways such as grilled chicken (*pîng kai*), spicy papaya salad (*tam màk hung*) and in some instances a variety of dishes, displayed in trays and ranging from minced pork salad (*làp mu*) to stir-fried vegetables (*khùa phák*), are all available.

While many market vendors offer only takeout food, **noodle shops** and a few other food stalls feature a makeshift kitchen surrounded by a handful of tables and stools, inhabiting a permanent patch of pavement or even an open-air shop-house. Most stalls will specialize in only one general food type, or, in some cases, only one dish, for example a stall with a mortar and pestle, unripe papayas and plastic bags full of pork rinds will only offer spicy papaya salad and variants on that theme. Similarly, a noodle shop will generally only prepare noodles with or without broth – they won't have meat or fish dishes that are usually eaten with rice.

A step up from street stalls and noodle shops are *hân kin deum*, literally "**eat-drink shops**", where you'll find a somewhat greater variety of dishes and be able to quench your thirst with beer and whisky.

Restaurants

Proper **restaurants** (*hân ahǎn*) aren't far ahead of eat-drink shops and noodle shops in terms of comfort; most are open-air establishments of dubious hygiene tucked beneath a thatch or corrugated tin roof. Ethnic **Vietnamese** and **Chinese** dominate the restaurant scene in Laos; indeed it can be downright difficult to find a Lao restaurant in some towns, as many Lao simply don't eat out, preferring the less expensive option of eating their dinner at home. A Lao-food restaurant is identifiable by the *típ khào* (lidded wicker basket for sticky rice) on the tables next to diners. Many of these basic eateries won't have any **menus** – in Lao or English – so it's a good idea to have a few stock dishes on the tip of your tongue when ordering.

Increasingly, restaurants catering more to foreigners have been cropping up in tourist centres. Such establishments, which usually have an English menu, offer a hodge-podge of dishes ranging from fried noodles and fried rice to the occasional sandwich, in addition to a variety of Lao, Chinese and Thai dishes intended to be eaten with steamed rice.

For more relaxed dining, **Vientiane** has a range of more expensive restaurants specializing in gourmet Lao cuisine as well as some of the best and best-value international food in Southeast Asia. The most popular cuisine on offer is **French**, although good Italian, Japanese and Indian are all well represented. The cost of a meal in one of these restaurants is hardly prohibitive – it's unlikely to set you back more than $15 per person, and many offer even less expensive set menus.

How to eat

Most Lao meals are enjoyed with **sticky rice** (*khào niaw*), which is served in a lidded wicker basket and eaten with the hands. Although it can be tricky at first, watching the Lao around you, it's fairly easy to pick up the proper technique. Grab a small chunk of rice from the basket, roll it into a firm ball with your fingertips and then dip the rice ball into one of the dishes. At the end of your meal, it's thought bad luck not to replace the lid of the *típ khào*. Plain steamed **white rice** (*khào jâo*) is eaten with a fork and spoon, with the former held in the left hand and the latter in the right (reverse for southpaws) – the spoon and not the fork is used to deliver the food to your mouth. Chopsticks (*mâi thu*) are reserved for **noodles**, the only exceptions being Chinese-style rice served in bowls (usually encountered at Chinese restaurants where you'll only be given chopsticks) and spicy papaya salad as eaten by the people of Louang Phabang. Attempting to eat sticky rice with chopsticks will only serve to baffle the Lao.

So that a variety of tastes can be enjoyed during the course of a meal, Lao meals are eaten communally, with each dish, including the soup, being served at once, rather than in courses. The dishes are placed in the centre of the table, and each person helps him- or herself to only a little at a time. If you're eating a meal with steamed white rice, only put a small amount of one dish onto your rice at a time. If the meal is accompanied by sticky rice, it's normal to simply dip a ball of

rice into the main servings. When ordering a meal, if there are two of you it's common to order two or three dishes, plus your own individual servings of rice, while three diners would order three or four different dishes.

If you are **dining with a Lao family** as a guest, wait until you are invited to eat by your host before taking your first mouthful and resist the temptation to continue eating after the others at the table have finished. Custom dictates that a little food should be left on your plate at the end of the meal.

What to eat

The staple of Lao meals is **rice**, preferably sticky rice, with **noodles** a common alternative for breakfast or as a snack. Typically, rice will be accompanied by a fish or meat dish and soup, with a plate of fresh vegetables such as string beans, lettuce, basil and mint served on the side. **Freshwater fish** is the mainstay of the Lao diet, although many in rural Laos, especially in the more remote mountainous regions, prefer animals of a wilder sort – mouse deer, wild pigs, rats, birds or whatever else can be caught – much to the dismay of tourists and wildlife conservationists.

In addition to chillies, coriander, lemon grass and lime juice, common ingredients used in Lao food include ginger, coconut milk, galingale, shallots and tamarind pulp. Another vital addition to certain Lao dishes is roasted rice, or *khào khùa*. Made from raw rice, ready to be steamed, *khào khùa* is roasted in a wok until thoroughly browned and then pounded into powder and used to add both a nutty flavour and an agreeably gritty texture to food.

The definitive accent, however, comes from the fermented fish mixtures that are used to salt Lao food. An ingredient in nearly every recipe, *nâm pa*, or **fish sauce**, is made by steeping large quantities of fish in salt in earthen containers for several months and then straining the resulting liquid, which is brown like a peaty water. Good fish sauce, it has been said, should attain the warm, salty smell of the air along a beach on a sunny day. Most Lao use *nâm pa* imported from Thailand. While *nâm pa* is found in cooking across Southeast Asia, a related concoction, *pa dàek*, is specific to Laos and northeastern Thailand. Unlike the bottled and imported *nâm pa*, thicker *pa dàek* retains a homemade feel, resembling fish sauce, but with chunks of fermented fish as well as rice husks, and possessing a scent that the uninitiated usually find foul. Although cherished by the Lao, *pa dàek*, along with the liquid strained from it, carries with it the risk of liver flukes. (*Pa dàek* found in Vientiane and Louang Phabang, however, is considered much safer than that found in rural areas, particularly in the far south).

Use of **monosodium glutamate** (MSG) is also quite common, and sometimes the seasoning, which resembles salt, even appears on tables in noodle shops with various other seasonings. If you'd prefer to avoid MSG, try saying *baw sai phõng sú lot* when ordering your food and hope for the best.

Noodles

When the Lao aren't filling up on glutinous rice, they're busy eating *fõe*, the ubiquitous **noodle soup** that takes its name from the Vietnamese soup *pho*. Although primarily eaten in the morning for breakfast, *fõe* can be enjoyed at any time of day, and, outside of large towns, visitors to Laos often have to fall back on *fõe* for a lot of their meals, owing to the lack of any eating places other than noodle shops. The basic bowl of *fõe* consists of a light broth to which is added thin rice noodles and slices of meat (usually beef, water buffalo or grilled chicken). It is served with a plate of fresh vegetables, usually including lettuce, mint and coriander leaves and bean sprouts. Flavouring the broth is pretty much up to you: containers of chilli, sugar, vinegar and fish sauce (and sometimes lime wedges and MSG) are on the tables of every noodle shop allowing you to find the perfect balance of spicy, sweet, sour and salty. Also on offer at many noodle shops is *mi*, a yellow wheat noodle served in broth with slices of meat and a few vegetables. It's also common to eat *fõe* and *mi* without broth (*hàeng*), and at times fried (*khùa*).

Many other types of noodle soup are dished up at street stalls. *Khào biak sèn* is another soup popular in the morning, consisting of soft, round rice noodles, slices of chicken and fresh ginger and served in a chicken broth, though it's hard to find outside bigger towns. More widely available, and a favourite at family gatherings during festivals, is *khào pûn*, a dish of white flour noodles, onto which is scooped one of any number of sweet, spicy coconut-milk based sauces. These noodles also find their way into several Vietnamese dishes, such as barbecued pork meatballs (*nâm néuang*) and spring rolls (*yáw*), in which they are served cold with several condiments and a sauce. There's also a Lao incarnation of *khào soi*, the spicy noodle curry eaten throughout northern Thailand and the Shan States of Myanmar; found in Louang Phabang and certain northwestern towns, the version common in Laos consists of rice noodles served in almost clear broth and topped with a spicy meat curry.

Lao food

If Laos were to nominate a national dish, a strong contender would be *làp*, a **"salad"** of minced meat or fish mixed with garlic, chillies, shallots, eggplant, galingale, fried rice and fish sauce. Làp is either eaten raw (*díp*) – a culinary experience you may want to avoid – or *súk* (cooked) and served with a side dish of lettuce, which is good for cooling off your mouth after swallowing a chilli. The notion of a "meat salad" is a common concept in Lao food, although in Louang Phabang you'll find Lao salads closer to the Western salad, with many falling into the broad category of *yam*, or "mixture", such as *yam sìn ngúa*, a spicy beef salad.

Another quintessentially Lao dish is *tam màk hung*, a **spicy papaya salad** made with shredded green papaya, garlic, chillies, lime juice, *pa dàek* and, sometimes, dried shrimp and crab juice. One of the most common street-vendor foods, *tam màk hung* is known as *tam sòm* in Vientiane. Stalls producing this treat are identifiable by the vendor pounding away with a mortar and pestle. Each vendor will have their own particular recipe, but it's also completely acceptable to pick out which ingredients – and how many chilli peppers – you'd like when you order. One of several variants on *tam màk hung* is *tam kûay tani*, which replaces shredded papaya with green banana and eggplant.

Usually not too far away from any *tam màk hung* vendor, you'll find someone selling *pîng kai*, basted **grilled chicken**. Hawkers wander onto buses to sell *pîng kai* on a stick, and a few restaurants in Vientiane specialize in the dish, serving up plump, whole chickens along with sticky rice and draught Beer Lao. Fish, *pîng pa*, is another grilled favourite, with whole fish skewered and thrown on the barbecue.

Soup is a common component of Lao meals and is served along with the other main courses during a meal. Fish soups, *kaeng pa*, and fish soups with lemon grass and mushrooms, *tôm yám pa*, frequently appear on menus, as does *kaeng jèut*, a clear, mild soup with vegetables and pork, which can also be ordered with bean curd (*kaeng jèut tâo hû*).

A speciality of southern Laos and Louang Phabang well worth ordering if you can find it is *mók pa* or **fish steamed in banana leaves**. Other variations, including *mók kheuang nai kai* (chicken giblets grilled in banana leaves) and *mók pa fa lai* (the same recipe made with freshwater sting ray) are also worth sampling, although they appear less frequently on restaurant menus.

Restaurants catering to travellers can whip up a variety **stir-fried dishes**, which tend to be a mix of Thai, Lao and Chinese food, and are usually eaten with steamed rice. **Fried rice** is a reliable standby throughout the country, as are dishes such as pork with basil over rice, *mū phát bai holapha*, chicken with ginger, *khùa khing kai*, and mixed vegetables, *khùa phák*.

Vegetarian

Although very few people in Laos are **vegetarian**, it's fairly easy to persuade cooks to put together a vegetable-only rice or vegetable dish. In many places that may be your only option unless you eat fish. If you don't eat fish, keep in mind that most Lao cooking calls for fish sauce so, when ordering for a veggies-only dish, you may want to add "*baw sai nâm pa*" ("without fish sauce"). When in Vientiane and Vang Viang, vegetarians can seek out actual vegetarian restaurants but elsewhere you'll be limited to ordering from the vegetables-only page of the regular menu.

Fruits and sweets

The best way to round off a meal or fill your stomach on a long bus ride is with **fresh fruit** (*màk mâi*), as the country offers a wide variety, from the more commonly known bananas, papayas, mangoes, pineapples, watermelons and green apples imported from China to more exotic options: crisp green guavas; burgundy lychees, with tart, sweet white fruit hidden in a coat of thin leather; wild-haired, red rambutans, milder and cheaper than lychees; dark purple mangosteen, tough-skinned treasures with a velvety smooth inside divided into succulent sweet segments; airy, bell-shaped green rose apples; pomelos, gigantic citruses whose thick rinds yield a grapefruit without the tartness; fuzzy, brown sapodillas, oval in shape and almost honey-sweet; large, spiky durian, notoriously stinky yet divinely creamy; oblong jackfruit, with sweet, yellow flesh possessing the texture of soft leather; and rare Xiang Khouang avocados, three times the size of those in France, with a subtle perfumed flavour. Restaurants occasionally serve fruit to end a meal and, in Vientiane, handcart-pushing hawkers patrol the streets with ready-peeled segments. Elsewhere, track down your fruit directly from stands at the market.

Sweets don't really figure on many restaurant menus, although some Vientiane restaurants will usually have a few desserts featuring **coconut milk** or cream, notably banana in coconut milk (*nâm wăn màk kûay*). Markets often have a food stall specializing in inexpensive coconut-milk desserts, generally called *nâm wăn*. Look for a stall displaying a dozen bowls, containing everything from water chestnuts to corn to fluorescent green and pink jellies, from which one or two items are selected and then added to a sweet mixture of crushed ice, slabs of young coconut meat and coconut milk. Sticky rice, of course, also turns up in a few desserts.

As **mangoes** begin to ripen in March, look for *khào niaw màk muang*, sliced mango splashed with coconut cream served over sticky rice; those who don't mind the smell of durian can try that variant on this dessert. *Khào lăm*, another treat, is cooked in short sticks of bamboo, which is gradually peeled back to reveal a tube of sticky rice and beans joined in coconut cream. Also popular are light Chinese **doughnuts**, fried in a skillet full of oil and known as *khào nõm khu* or *pá thawng ko*, and another fried delight, crispy bananas (*kûay khaek*).

What to drink

The Lao don't drink **water** straight from the tap and nor should you. Plastic bottles of drinking water (*nâm deum*) are sold countrywide for around 1500K, even in smaller towns. Noodle shops and inexpensive restaurants generally serve free pitchers of weak tea or boiled water (*nâm tóm*), which is fine to drink, although perhaps not as foolproof as bottled water. In some cases you'll find that budget hotels will give you complimentary bottles of water, refilled with boiled water, with your room. It's best to drink more water than you think you need, as it's easy to get dehydrated in tropical climates.

Brand-name **soft drinks**, such as 7Up, Pepsi and Fanta, are widely available and sell for around 2000K per bottle (cans are somewhat more expensive). Bottles are returnable so, if you're on the go, you'll have to drink the bottle at the shop. Most vendors will pour the drink into a plastic bag (which is then tied with a string or rubber band and inserted with a straw) for takeaways.

More refreshing are the **fruit shakes** churned out by many restaurants and drink shops in larger towns. These *màk mâi pan* consist of your choice of fruit blended with ice, liquid sugar and sometimes a hint of salt and sweetened condensed milk. Look for a blender stationed next to bowls of fruit. More readily available are freshly squeezed **fruit juices**, such as lemon (*nâm màk nao*) and coconut juice (*nâm màk phao*), which is enjoyed directly from the fruit after it has been dehusked and cut open. Also popular is the exceptionally sweet sugar-cane juice, known in Lao as *nâm oi*.

Given the extraordinarily hot weather in Laos, it can be difficult to resist the temptation to cool off by filling your drink with **ice**. Most ice in Laos is produced in large blocks under hygienic conditions, but it can become less pure in transit or storage, so be wary, or simply avoid it altogether.

Hot drinks

Laos's best **coffee** is grown on the Bolaven Plateau, outside Pakxong in southern Laos, where it was introduced by the French in the early twentieth century. Twenty thousand tonnes of coffee are produced in Laos annually, most of which is hardy robusta, although some arabica is grown as well. Quality, although much improved in recent years, can still vary widely. The Lao drink very strong coffee, or *kafeh hâwn*, which is made by pouring hot water through a sock-like bag filled with ground coffee and then served in a short glass filled with a generous dollop of sweetened condensed milk and a spoonful of sugar. Traditionally, hot coffee is served with a complimentary glass of weak Chinese tea or hot water. If you prefer your coffee black, and without sugar, order by asking for *kafeh dam baw sai nâm tan*. More appropriate for Laos's hot weather is *kafeh yén*, in which the same concoction is mixed and poured into a mug of crushed ice or a plastic bag. Some establishments that are accustomed to foreigners may serve instant coffee (*kafeh net*, after the Lao word for Nescafé, the most common brand); if you prefer locally grown coffee ask for *kafeh Láo* or *kafeh thõng*, literally "bag coffee", after the traditional technique of preparing the coffee. A few bakeries and restaurants catering to foreigners in Vientiane may serve imported coffee, while in more remote areas you may only be able to find instant coffee.

Black and Chinese-style **tea** are both served in Laos. Weak Chinese tea is often found, lukewarm, on tables in restaurants and can be enjoyed free of charge. For stronger Chinese tea (*sá jin*) you'll need to order it. Black tea, grown locally and imported, is available at most coffee vendors and is usually what you get, mixed with sweetened condensed milk and sugar, when you request *sá hâwn*.

Alcoholic drinks

Many foreign **beers**, including Heineken, Singapore's Tiger and ABC Stout,

Vietnamese 333 and Singha from Thailand, are available in Laos, although **Beer Lao** (Bia Lao in Lao), with a 98 percent market share, is by far and away the most popular and the cheapest at just 7000K a bottle. The beer owes its light, distinctive taste to the French investors who founded the company in 1971, although the company was later state-owned, with Czechoslovakian brewmasters training the Lao staff, until it was privatized in the mid-1990s. Nearly all that goes into making Beer Lao is imported, from hops to bottle caps, although locally grown rice is used in place of twenty percent of the malt. Available throughout Laos in 330ml cans and 660ml bottles, Beer Lao contains five percent alcohol. In Vientiane and Louang Phabang, draught Beer Lao known as *bia sót* and sometimes appearing on signs in English as "Fresh Beer", is available at bargain prices by the litre. Often served warm from the keg, the beer is poured over ice, though some establishments serve it chilled. There are dozens of *bia sót* outlets in the capital, most of which are casual outdoor beer gardens with thatch roofs. You can usually get snacks here too, known as "**drinking food**" or *káp kâem*. Typical dishes include spicy papaya salad, fresh spring rolls, Lao-style omelette, fried peanuts (*thua jeun*), shrimp chips (*khào kiap kûng*) and grilled chicken.

Drunk with equal gusto by the Lao is *lào-láo*, a clear **rice alcohol** with the fire of a blinding Mississippi moonshine. Although the government distills its own brand, Sticky Rice, which is sold nationally, most people indulge in local brews, the taste varying from region to region and even town to town. *Lào-láo* is usually sold in whatever bottle the distiller had around at the time (look twice before you buy that bottle of Fanta) and sells at drink shops and general stores for around 1000K per 750ml. You can indulge in some of the best *lào-láo* in Si Phan Don and Phongsali.

Drinking *lào-láo* often takes on the air of a sacred ritual, albeit a rather boisterous one. After or sometimes during a meal, the host of the dinner will bring out a bottle of *lào-láo* to share with his guests. The host begins the proceeds by pouring a shot of *lào-láo* and tossing it onto the ground to appease the house spirit. He then pours himself a measure, raising the glass for all to see before throwing back the drink and emptying the remaining droplets onto to floor, in order to empty the glass for the next drinker. The host then pours a shot for each guest in turn. After the host has completed one circuit, the bottle and the glass are passed along to a guest who serves him or herself first and then the rest of the party, one by one. Guests are expected to drink at least one shot in order not to offend the house spirit and the host, although in such situations there's often pressure, however playful, to drink much more than one shot. One polite escape route is to take a sip of the shot and then dump out the rest on the floor during the "glass emptying" move.

Another rice alcohol, *lào hái*, also inspires a festive, communal drinking experience. Drunk from a large earthenware jar with thin, bamboo straws, *lào hái* is fermented by households or villages in the countryside and is weaker than *lào-láo*, closer to a wine in taste than a backwoods whisky. Drinking *lào hái*, however, can be a bit risky as unboiled water is sometimes added to the jar during the fermentation process. An excellent, and safe, way to sample *lào hái* is at the monthly full moon party at Lao Pako Resort (see p.113).

Several brand-name **rice whiskies**, with a lower alcohol content than *lào-láo*, are available for around $1 at local general stores. Chevreuil d'Or, Mae Khong and Sing Thong all taste similar to Thailand's Mekong whisky and are more enjoyable over ice with Pepsi or soda water than neat. In Vientiane, you can find a selection of **Western spirits** and an excellent selection of **French wines** (for Southeast Asia), sometimes for as little as $2 for a drinkable bottle of table wine. Elsewhere you'll have trouble finding anything other than $1–2 bottles of spirits produced by the Lao Winery Company, but if you look hard enough you'll usually be able to hunt down a bottle of Johnnie Walker Black or Red Label. In the case of foreign brands, check that the cap is properly sealed and the bottle doesn't look used, as fakes sometimes find their way into Laos from Vietnam and Thailand.

Communications

Laos's communications network has improved dramatically in recent years, but many glitches remain, and outside Vientiane and other Mekong towns standards are low. The post is slow, but international direct dialling and the handful of Internet cafés make keeping in touch easier.

Mail services

The Lao **postal system** is reliable, if not exactly fast. Mail takes seven to fourteen days in or out of Laos, depending on where you are. Overseas postal rates are reasonable: a postcard costs around $0.30 and a standard letter runs for under $1. Express Mail Service operates to most Western countries and certain destinations within Laos; the service cuts down on delivery time and automatically registers your letter. Alternatively, several **international couriers**, including DHL and FedEx, have offices in Vientiane. If you're moving to Laos, you'll have to rent a post office box, as there are no household deliveries. Recognizable by their mustard-yellow colour scheme, **post offices** throughout the country are open at least five days a week, normally 8am–noon and 1–4pm – exceptions are noted where relevant in the Guide.

Poste restante services are available in Vientiane and Louang Phabang. Post offices in both towns charge a small fee for letters (postcards are free) and keep mail behind the counter for two or three months. Bring your passport on the off-chance that you're asked to show identification when picking up your mail.

Mail should be addressed: name, GPO, city, Lao PDR, using the country's official name rather than "Laos". To avoid misfiling, your surname should be underlined or capitalized; when checking your mail, it doesn't hurt to check under your first name as well.

When sending **parcels**, leave the package open for inspection. Incoming parcels are also subject to inspection.

Phones

Laos has at last entered the age of satellite telecommunications, but the new network is still shaky at best. International connections are made via satellite to Hong Kong, Japan and Australia, with provincial outposts hooked up to the main telephone exchange in Vientiane. But although IDD is now widely available in Vientiane, the telephone service in many provincial outposts is still in comparatively poor shape.

Outside of your hotel room, the best place to make **international calls** is the Telecom Office (daily 7.30am–10pm) on Setthathilat Road in Vientiane. Most provincial capitals have similar offices that are normally open from 8am until 9pm at night; otherwise, international calls can be placed at the post office. Calls to the UK and North America cost approximately $3 per minute, whereas calling New Zealand is somewhat cheaper at roughly $1.50. Australians travelling around Southeast Asia should wait until they get to Laos before phoning home – the charge for a call to Australia is less than $1 per minute, thanks to the country's assistance in revamping Laos's telecommunications network. It's also quite cheap to call Thailand, although calls to Vietnam and Cambodia will cost you the same as it would to ring Wellington. International calls are charged by the minute. Calling overseas from a hotel invariably results in surcharges.

There's no facility for collect or reverse-charge calls but you can almost always get a "**call back**": ask the operator for the minimum call abroad and get the phone number of the post office you're calling from. You can then be called back directly at the post office for the cost of the initial call plus a small charge for the service. An alternative, particularly good in towns without Internet cafés, is **faxing**. For the price of a brief phone call, you'll find that you can say a great deal and receive a return fax for a small fee. International and domestic fax services are available at upmarket hotels in Vientiane and Louang Phabang and at most provincial post offices.

Public phones are wired for both domestic and international calls and are usually stationed outside post offices in provincial capitals; larger towns have several booths although many seem to be out of service much of the time. Phone cards (*bat tholasap*) for these phones, which are available at shops, post and telephone offices, are sold in units of time rather than money and come in several denominations of units costing between $2.50 and $6.00. Because of high charges for overseas calls and the low amount of time units available, it's difficult to make an overseas call that lasts for more than a few minutes before you're cut off.

Local calls can be made at hotels and guest houses for a small fee. Regional codes are given throughout the Guide: the "0" must be dialled before all long-distance calls. Some hotels have **line numbers** – thus ☏021/221200-5 means that there are six lines and that you can substitute the last digit with any number between 1 and 5.

Dialling codes

To **call Laos from abroad**, dial your international access code, then ☏856 + area code minus first 0 + number.

To **call abroad from Laos**, dial 00 and then the relevant country code:
UK ☏44
USA ☏1
Canada ☏1
Ireland ☏1
Australia ☏61
New Zealand ☏64

Time differences: Laos is 7 hours ahead of London, 15 hours ahead of Vancouver, 12 hours ahead of New York, 3 hours behind Sydney and 5 hours behind Auckland.

Mobile phones

If you want to use your **mobile phone** abroad, you'll need to check with your phone provider as to whether it will work abroad, and what the call charges are. In the **UK**, for all but the very top-of-the-range

packages, you'll have to inform your phone provider before going abroad to get international access switched on. You may get charged extra for this depending on your existing package and where you are travelling to. You are also likely to be charged extra for incoming calls when abroad, as the people calling you will be paying the usual rate. If you want to retrieve messages while you're away, you'll have to ask your provider for a new access code, as your home one is unlikely to work abroad. Most UK mobiles use GSM, which gives access to most places worldwide, except the US. For further information about using your phone abroad, check out ⓦwww.telecomsadvice.org.uk/features/using_your_mobile_abroad.htm.

Unless you have a tri-band phone, it is unlikely that a mobile bought for use in the **USA** will work outside the States, with many only working within the region designated by the area code in the phone number, ie 212, 415 etc. They tend to be very expensive to own in the US, too, as users are billed for both incoming and outgoing calls. For details of which mobiles will work outside the US, contact your mobile service provider.

Most mobiles in **Australia and New Zealand** also use GSM, which works well in Southeast Asia – check with your provider.

Email and the internet

Email is an excellent alternative to post office post restantes, and the added cost is offset by your ability to send and receive mail at the click of a mouse. The emergence of an Internet Service Provider (ISP) in Laos has drastically reduced the price and increased the availability of access to the Web. Currently you'll find email and Internet services at **cybercafés** and **computer shops** in Vientiane, Louang Phabang, Vang Viang, Oudomxai, Houayxai, Thakhek, Savannakhet and Pakxe, although it won't be long before these services spring up in other parts of the country. Charges range from 100K to 1000K per minute, depending on how far you are from the capital, where the lone ISP – Laonet – is based.

If you're thinking of taking a lap-top with you and you intend using your **home-based email account**, make sure you're allowed access to your account via the Internet.

Otherwise, you'll have to dial your Online Service Provider or Internet Service Provider's nearest international access number, and the chances are your ISP won't have a local number for Laos, leaving you dialling long-distance to Bangkok or another regional hub. Despite what your ISP may say, these numbers tend to be unreliable and you'll most likely pay a surcharge to your ISP on top of the long-distance charge for reaching Thailand.

A better alternative is to sign up for a **free email account** through a service such as Yahoo! or Hotmail and get your messages forwarded from your home-based account. If you haven't arranged this before you leave, attendants in Cybercafés in Laos can help you set up an account, or simply plug into ⓦwww.hotmail.com or ⓦwww.yahoo.com and follow the instructions.

Those moving to Laos who are interested in setting up an account with a local ISP can contact GlobeNet (☎021/218841), which shares an office with KPL News Service on the first floor of the *Lao Hotel Plaza*.

Media

Tightly controlled by the communist party since the Pathet Lao came to power in 1975, Laos's miniscule media struggles to compete with flashy Thai TV game shows, the multitude of channels offered by satellite dishes and the English-language news radio broadcasts available via shortwave. With only one tenth the population of neighbouring Thailand, it's very hard for Laos to compete with Thai media.

Lao radio, however, continues to thrive, helped along by the fact that newspapers, including the English-language daily the *Vientiane Times*, rarely find their way outside Vientiane and that the country's two national TV stations are not available to many people in the countryside. One of the oddest sights in Laos is that of rickety bamboo and thatch huts and houses all over the country with huge, modern satellite dishes attached to the roofs.

Newspapers and magazines

Laos has only one **English-language newspaper**, the *Vientiane Times*, established in 1994. Despite being somewhat thin, self-censored and nearly impossible to find outside the capital, it is nonetheless a good window on Laos. Published by the Ministry of Information and Culture, the *Vientiane Times* focuses primarily on business and trade issues, although interesting cultural pieces do slip in from time to time and the occasional column showcasing people's opinion on a selected social topic is a worthwhile read. You'll also find ads for restaurant specials and a brief listings section on the back page.

There are two **Lao-language dailies** and five weeklies. Of the two dailies, *Wieng Mai* and *Pasason*, the latter is more widely read. Both get their international news from KPL, the government news agency, and for the most part, have their own reporters who file domestic news. Neither is known for its independent-minded reportage.

Foreign publications are extremely difficult to find outside Vientiane, and even in the capital there are scant copies. *Newsweek*, *Asiaweek* and *Time* are sold at major hotels, although you'll only find copies of the *Bangkok Post* in hotel lobbies and at *Xang* coffee shop because, legally, it's only available by subscription. You may be able to talk a minimarket into selling you a day-old copy, however. If you're desperate, foreign embassies tend to have a selection of periodicals available.

Television

Lao television's two **government-run channels** broadcast a mix of news, cultural programmes and Western re-runs for several hours a day, but the vast majority of Lao prefer watching Thai television. Reception is poor, however, in rural areas. Many mid-range and top-end hotels provide satellite TV – though these seem rigged to show only a handful of channels – as do a few coffee shops and bakeries in Louang Phabang and Vientiane.

Radio

Laos's main radio station, **Lao National Radio**, can be picked up in the vicinity of Vientiane or on shortwave in roughly seventy percent of the country. LNR gets its international news from a number of sources, including CNN, BBC, Xinhua and KPL, and broadcasts the news in English twice a day. Tuning into LNR will also give you a chance to hear traditional **Lao music**, which you otherwise may only get to hear at festivals. With a **shortwave radio**, you can pick up Voice of America (Ⓦ www.voa.gov), BBC World Service (Ⓦ www.bbc.co.uk/worldservice) and a variety of other international stations in most parts of Laos. Times and wavelengths are updated several times a year, so pick up a recent schedule before beginning your trip; most stations post an up-to-date schedule on their website.

Opening hours and holidays

In 1998, the official working hours of all government offices were adjusted. The two-hour lunch break was shortened to one, and government workers were given Saturday off. Old habits die hard though, and many civil servants have found it difficult to give up the two-hour siesta that was a relic of French rule. This means that while official hours for government offices are 8am–noon and 1–5pm Monday to Friday, very little gets done between 11am and 2pm.

Post offices generally open 8am–5pm Monday to Friday, 8am–4pm on Saturday and 8am–noon on Sunday, though some provincial post offices keep different hours. Long-distance telephone services at post offices are usually open until 11pm. **Banks** are generally open 8.30am–4pm Monday to Friday.

Opening hours for **private businesses** vary but almost all are closed on Sunday. During the heat of the day many shop owners will partly close their doors and snooze to escape the heat. If you need to buy something it is perfectly acceptable to wake them up. Daily **markets** are always best in the morning, the earlier the better, and by mid-afternoon most have all but shut down.

The posted hours on **museums** are not scrupulously followed and on slow days (almost every day) the curators and staff are surely tempted to pack it up and head home. Unless a festival is taking place, **monasteries** should only be visited during daylight hours as monks are very early risers and are usually in bed not long after sunset.

Public holidays

Two decades ago when they were created, most of these **holidays** were celebrated in Vientiane with rallies and speeches. Today, little if anything happens officially, but a holiday is a holiday: government offices and banks are closed. Very infrequently, the Lao government holds **national elections**, which temporarily paralyze the country. Even border crossings are shut down for a few hours.

January 1 New Year's Day	**May 1** International Labour Day
January 6 Pathet Lao Day	**June 1** Children's Day
January 20 Army Day	**August 13** Lao Issara
March 8 Women's Day	**August 23** Liberation Day
March 22 Lao People's Party Day	**October 12** Freedom from France Day
April 15–17 Lao New Year	**December 2** National Day

Festivals and entertainment

During a brief period following the communist take-over in 1975, traditional Lao festivals, most of which are linked to Buddhism, were officially suppressed as being "wasteful". Likewise, certain ancient spirit rites, such as the rocket festival, were denounced by prudish officials who felt that the traditional display of phallic symbols was "an embarrassment". Fortunately, this wet-blanketry was quickly quashed by howls of protest from the fun-loving Lao masses. Participation in festivals has risen again to pre-revolution levels, although the government still ensures that aspects of the festivals that refer to the old monarchy do not resurface.

All major festivals, whether Buddhist or animist in nature, are multi-faceted affairs with parades, games, music and dancing, not to mention the copious consumption of *lào-láo*, a liquor made from sticky rice. Many traditional Lao **sports** are bound up with **ritual**. Long boats are raced on rivers to lure *naga* out of the flooded rice fields and *tikhi*, based on a celestial sport of the gods, is re-enacted at the That Louang festival.

Besides the nationwide festivals listed below, there are numerous **local festivals** (called *bun wat*), centred around a monastery. It's worth enquiring at your guest house when the annual *bun* takes place. If you happen to be in a town or village that is gearing up for a festival, consider altering your plans so that you can attend – unless of course you are a teetotaller, in which case you're advised to clear out immediately. In rural areas especially, a festival can transform an entire village into a wild, week-long party.

The average visitor is most likely to encounter the festivals of the Buddhist lowland Lao who make up the majority of the population in the river valleys of the Mekong and its tributaries. Because the Lao calendar is dictated by both **solar and lunar** rhythms, the dates of festivals change from year to year and even just a few days prior to a parade or boat race, there is sometimes confusion over just which day it will take place. For the Lao this is not really a problem, as the days leading up to and immediately following large lunar festivals are filled with merry-making as well.

On certain **Buddhist holy days**, such as the That Louang Festival, the faithful make merit by walking clockwise around a stupa or a *sim* three times while holding offerings of incense, lotus blossoms and candles in a prayer-like gesture. Visitors are free to take part in this picturesque ritual, called **wian thian** in Lao, and may even be encouraged to do so. **Hilltribe festivals**, such as the Akha swing ceremony in the north and tribal Mon–Khmer buffalo sacrifices in the south, are less open to outsider participation. If, when trekking, you do happen across a tribal festival, watch from a distance and do not interfere unless it is clear that you are being invited to participate.

Major Lao festivals

New Year's Day

Just like the rest of the planet, the Lao celebrate New Year's Eve with parties and midnight mass hysteria. New Year's Day is a time for private *basi* ceremonies (see p.66) and family visits (January 1).

Vietnamese and Chinese New Year

The large ethnic-Vietnamese and Chinese populations of Vientiane, Thakhek, Savannakhet and Pakxe celebrate their lunar new year privately with parties and visits to Mahayana Buddhist pagodas. Most businesses are closed for three days to one week (new moon in late January to mid-February).

Makkha Busa

This **Buddhist holy day** commemorates a legendary sermon given by the Buddha after 1250 of his disciples spontaneously congregated around the enlightened one. People observe the festival by going to **monasteries** to make merit; they walk around the *sim*, bearing offerings, while monks chant inside (full moon in February).

Lao New Year

Called *pi mai lao*, the beginning of the **lunar new year** is fervently celebrated all over Laos, but is most stunningly observed in **Louang Phabang**. There, the town's namesake Buddha image is ritually bathed by townsfolk, a procession led by Pu Nyoe and Nya Nyoe (the guardian spirits of Louang Phabang and the Seven Daughters of Brahma) is held, sand stupas are erected in monastery grounds, and Buddhists make a pilgrimage to nearby **caves** to bathe the Buddha images stored there. In **Vientiane**, a parade takes place, led by a white elephant and its handlers, who wave bunches of bananas before the great, pink beast to coax it along.

In **villages** and small towns, the lunar new year is marked with *basi* ceremonies (see p.66) and merrymaking. If you are in the right place at the right time, you may be ambushed by young people carrying pails of water and

armed with squirt guns. After being forced to down a few shots of *lào-láo* you will be given a thorough drenching followed by a liberal dusting with talcum powder and frenzied smearing with blood-red lipstick (April 15–17).

Wisakha Busa

Commemorating the historic Buddha's birth, enlightenment and passing into Nirvana, this holy day is celebrated by laypeople in much the same way as Makkha Busa (full moon in May).

Bun Bang Fai

Also known as the **rocket festival**, this **rainmaking ritual** predates Buddhism in Laos, and is a madcap combination of fireworks and firewater. Crude rockets are fashioned from stout bamboo poles stuffed with gunpowder and, after being blessed, are propped up on wooden launch platforms that resemble rickety ladders to heaven. As villagers dance and cheer, the rockets are shot skywards. The thundering noise and clouds of smoke reassuringly simulate rainy season conditions, which is in turn supposed to inspire the spirits to produce the real thing. Celebrations in the south can be wonderfully bawdy: men brandishing foot-long, wooden phalli give the local maidens something to giggle about. The rocket festival is also very popular with the ethnic-Lao in northeastern Thailand where it has evolved into more of a sporting event, with participants wagering on what heights the rockets will attain (May).

Lai Heua Fai

A **festival of lights**, this event is most magically celebrated in **Louang Phabang**. In the days leading up to the festival the different neighbourhoods, or *ban*, that make up the city build large floats and festoon them with lights. On the appointed evening, the floats are paraded down to Wat Xiang Thong along Xiang Thong Road where they are judged for aesthetic merit and then carried down to the Mekong and set atop boats for a second procession on the river.

All evening, along the Mekong River road, vendors offer saucer-sized floats made from banana stalks and leaves and containing flowers, incense and a candle. After selecting one, celebrants take the little offerings down to the river and launch them on the current. Lai Heua Fai is celebrated concurrently with **Awk Phansa**, the end of the three-month "rains retreat", a time when laypeople donate new robes and other offerings to Buddhist monasteries (full moon in October).

That Louang Festival

In the days leading up to the festival, the great stupa and national symbol of Laos comes to resemble the centrepiece of a fairground, as vendors hawking everything imaginable set up booths in the open spaces around it. The week-long festival kicks off with a mass **alms-giving** to hundreds of monks and a **procession** from Wat Simuang to That Louang. Over the next few days a series of bands and performances occupy a stage near the stupa, and *tikhi*, a game resembling field hockey in which the ball traditionally symbolizes the skull of a demon, is played. On the last evening the whole city shows up to process with offerings around That Louang (full moon in November).

Suang heua (boat races)

What at first glance may seem to be a mere sporting event is actually rooted in ancient beliefs that predate Buddhism in Laos. To this day, many lowland Lao believe that the Mekong and other local waterways are the abode of *naga*, serpent-like creatures that leave the river during the rainy season and inhabit the flooded paddy fields (see box on p.154). The **boat races**, held near the end of the rainy season, are designed to lure the *naga* out of the fields and back into the rivers, so that ploughing may begin. During the days of the monarchy, the quasi-religious ceremonies involved in building and launching the boats were as important as the races themselves. Sadly, though, these rituals were suppressed after the revolution. Still, the Lao thoroughly enjoy themselves at the races, finding in them yet another reason to imbibe large quantities of *lào-lào* (October to December).

National Day

The birth of the Lao People's Democratic Republic is celebrated with parades, speeches and no end of hammer-and-sickle flags (December 2).

Bun Pha Wet

Commemorating the *jataka* tale of the Buddha's second-to-last incarnation as Pha Wet, or Prince Vessantara, this celebration takes place at the local monastery where a contingent of monks recite the tale as a long chant. In larger towns, entertainment in the form of a live band and dancing takes place (December or January).

Traditional sports

While the Lao can often be seen glued to the television whenever Thailand broadcasts a sporting event, relatively few people play the usual team sports simply because equipment is prohibitively expensive. The honourable exception is **kataw**. Played with a grapefruit-sized woven wicker ball, *kataw* is thought to have originated in the Malay Archipelago, but is also quite popular in Thailand. *Kataw* is something like a no-hands version of volleyball and is played both with and without a net. The acrobatics involved are simply astounding. Games are played just about anywhere, but are commonly seen in schoolyards or in monastery grounds.

As with the rest of Southeast Asia, **cockfighting** is a celebrated diversion in Laos. This should come as no surprise, as the "blood sport" originated in this region. The sport has its national differences and unlike cockfighting in some Southeast Asian countries, knives are not attached to the rooster's legs in Laos, which means that cockfights last much longer and the birds don't usually die in the ring. **Betting** is, of course, the whole point. Cockfights take place on Sundays and the local cockpit can usually be found by wandering around and listening for the exuberant cheers of the spectators.

Another sport that relies on a wager to sharpen excitement is **rhinoceros beetle fighting**. Although it is difficult to say just how far back the tradition of beetle fighting goes, it is known to be popular among ethnic Tai peoples from the Shan States to Northern Vietnam. The walnut-sized beetles hiss alarmingly when angered and it does not require too much goading to get them to do battle. Pincer-like horns are used by the beetles to seize and lift an opponent, and the fight is considered finished when one of the two beetles breaks and runs. "Beetle season" is during the rainy season when the insects breed, and they are sometimes peddled in markets tethered to pieces of sugarcane.

Shopping

One of the pleasures of shopping in an non-industrial country like Laos is the availability of hand-crafted goods. Because items made by hand can only be produced in limited quantities, they are usually sold or bartered in the village in which they were made and seldom get very far afield. Hand-made baskets, bolts of cloth and household utensils are best acquired at the village level, as everything is cheaper at the source, though it's not all that easy for non-Lao-speaking visitors to turn up and make it known what they're after. Provincial markets are the obvious alternative and prices are usually just a bit more than what you would pay were you to buy directly from village artisans. Of course, if village-made objects make it all the way to the boutiques of Vientiane their "value" will have multiplied many times over.

As with the rest of Southeast Asia, merchandise often has no price-tag and the buyer is expected to make a spirited attempt at **haggling** the quoted price down. Even if an item is sporting a price-tag it is still perfectly acceptable to ask for a discount. Bargaining for a price that both the buyer and seller can be happy with takes patience and tact, and knowing what an item is really worth is half the battle. The first price quoted will usually be inflated. If you feel the price is way out of line, it is better to just smile and walk away than to squawk in disbelief and argue that the price is unfair – no matter how loud or valid your protestations, nobody will believe that you cannot afford to buy. On the whole, **Louang Phabang** is better for shopping than Vientiane, as much of what is for sale in Louang Phabang is manufactured nearby.

Textiles

A surprisingly large number of the different ethnic groups that make up the population of Laos produce cloth of their own design.

Traditionally, most textiles stayed within the village where they were woven, but the increasing popularity of Lao textiles with visitors has led urban textile merchants to employ buyers to comb isolated villages for **old textiles** that might be resold at a profit. The result is that many merchants have only a vague idea of where their old textiles are from or which group made them. This doesn't seem to deter foreign buyers, however, and sales are brisk, which has given rise to the practice of boiling new textiles to artificially age them. Some of these so-called antique textiles sell for hundreds of dollars.

These days, though, the vast majority of the textiles for sale are **new textiles** specifically made for the tourist market; if you're after antique textiles you have to ask. To some shopkeepers "old" can mean ten years or so and most will have little idea what the age of a certain piece is, but if you persist in asking, they will often claim an item has been around for a couple of centuries. As textiles are difficult to date, it's best to take such claims with a pinch of salt. All in all, though, it is rare for the local merchants to go to great lengths to deceive customers. Unless you are an expert or have money to burn, it is a good idea to stick to new textiles, which can be had for as little as $2 and are just as pleasing to the eye as the older pieces.

Lao weavers have a long tradition of combining **cotton** and **silk**: a typical piece may have a cotton base with silk details woven into it. Modern pieces of inferior quality substitute synthetic fibres for silk, and some vendors have been known to try to pass off hundred-percent synthetic cloth as silk. If there is any doubt whether or not a piece is genuine silk, a simple test will prove its authenticity: take a thread from the textile in question and hold a flame to it. A silk thread will burn into a ball and emit a smell like that of burning hair. Pinch the ball-shaped ash and it should crush between your fingers. A synthetic thread will also burn into a ball but the ash will be hard – like a ball of plastic – and uncrushable. The thread will also smell of burning plastic when ignited. Lastly, the synthetic dyes used by most weavers are not colourfast, something to bear in mind when laundering newly purchased textiles.

Silver

Although Thai antique dealers have made off with quite a bit of old Lao **silver** (and marketed it in Thailand as old Thai silver) there is still a fair amount of the stuff floating around. Items to look out for are paraphernalia for **betel chewing**: egg-sized round or oval boxes for storing white lime, cone-shaped containers for holding betel leaves and miniature mortars used to pound areca nuts. Larger silver boxes or bowls with human or animal figures hammered into them were once used in religious ceremonies. C-shaped **bracelets** and anklets are found in a variety of styles. Bracelets and anklets of traditional Lao style, as opposed to hilltribe design, have a stylized lotus bud on each end. **Hilltribe silver jewellery** is usually bold and heavy – the better to show off one's wealth. With few exceptions, the hilltribe jewellery being peddled in Laos is the handiwork of the Hmong tribe. Traditionally, silver French piastres were melted down and hammered to make this jewellery. In **Louang Phabang**, the old silversmith families that once supplied the monarchy with ceremonial objects are again practising their trade, and their silver creations represent some of the best-value souvenirs to be found in Laos.

Antiques and reproductions

For the record, Thai merchants regularly scour Laos for **antiques** so there are probably more authentic Lao antiques for sale in the malls of Bangkok and Chiang Mai than anywhere in Laos. Conversely, many of the "antiques" for sale in Laos are actually reproductions made in Thailand or Cambodia. This is particularly true in the case of Buddhist or Hindu figurines made of any kind of metal. As with so many antique shops in Asia, the proprietors will tell you whatever you want to hear about the age and rarity of that patinaed bauble you're dying to be the owner of. Therefore, the best advice to visitors interested in purchasing Lao "antiques" is not to pay more than what you think the item's visual worth is: the days when Laos sold valuable heirlooms for a fraction of their international price are long gone. If looking at it only gives you ten dollars' worth of pleasure, don't pay twenty for it.

Antique wooden **Buddha images** are often genuine, but were most likely pilfered from some temple or shrine. To discourage this practice, visitors should refrain from buying them. Prospective buyers should also be aware that there is an **official ban** on the export of Buddha images from Laos. Although this is aimed primarily at curbing the theft – increasingly common in recent years – of rare Lao bronzes from rural monasteries, small images are also included in the ban. That said, it is highly unlikely that Lao officials will confiscate new Buddhas from foreign visitors.

Antique brass weights, sometimes referred to as "**opium weights**", come in a variety of sizes and shapes. Those cast in zoomorphic figures (stylized birds, elephants, lions, etc) are an established collectable and command high prices, sometimes selling for hundreds of dollars. Weights of simpler design, such as those shaped like miniature stupas, are much more affordable and can be bought for just a few dollars in provincial towns.

Opium pipes come in sundry forms as well. Although very few are genuine antiques, the workmanship is generally quite good. A typical pipe may have a bamboo body, a jade bowl and silver ornamentation. Keep in mind while browsing over these things that anti-drug laws in your home country may give customs officers a reason to confiscate such a purchase.

Banknotes, coins and stamps

While antiques are risky business, old **stamps, coins and banknotes** are excellent value. The iconography and symbolism found on Lao stamps, coins and banknotes speak volumes about the country's history and culture, giving an immediate sense of the values of the government that issued them. And because they are so easy to transport and weigh almost nothing, they make ideal souvenirs.

Banknotes

Pre-revolution **banknotes** are the most easily acquired mementos of the old monarchy. Specimens from the French era were also legal tender in what is now Vietnam and Cambodia and motifs reflect the three main cultures that were encompassed by French Indochina. The denominations were also written out in Lao, Khmer, Vietnamese and Chinese, as well as French.

Banknotes issued soon after independence from France bear colourful portraits of King Sisavang Vong and, despite countless stacks being ceremonially burned by zealous communists after the revolution, small caches are still commonly found in antique shops.

Immediately after the revolution, from 1976 to 1979, the Lao government issued the so-called "**liberation kip**" with illustrations of revolutionary combat themes. Most interesting are the ten-kip note with armed villagers setting booby traps; the two-hundred kip note with porters and elephants traversing the Ho Chi Minh Trail; and the five-hundred kip note, with anti-aircraft guns shooting down American planes over the Plain of Jars.

The series of banknotes currently in circulation was issued to replace the liberation kip

in the late Seventies, but inflation has forced the government to stop printing small denomination banknotes and, as soon as they went out of circulation, stacks of them began appearing in souvenir shops. The tiny, post-revolution one-kip note, barely larger than a business card, was the first to make the transformation from currency to curio. The five-, ten- and twenty-kip notes soon followed. The twenty-kip note is probably the most interesting of this series, having an illustration on the reverse of a tank pointing its big gun across the Mekong towards Thailand.

Coins

Gold and silver shops often have a hoard of old silver **coins**, including French piastres and, to a lesser extent, British-Indian rupees. These are still used as currency by some tribal peoples, such as the Akha and Hmong, who wear the coins as jewellery or ornamentation on clothing and pawn them when necessary. Use caution when buying though, as craftsmen in Thailand are making convincing fakes that invariably find their way into Lao antique shops. Actually it is not so difficult to discern these fake coins as nobody bothers to artificially age them. If the century-old coin looks new then it almost certainly is.

Both the Kingdom of Laos and the Lao Peoples' Democratic Republic issued coins made of a lightweight aluminium alloy that are easily differentiated by their iconography. Coins of the royal government have a hole in the middle and a three-headed elephant. The hammer and sickle embossed coins issued by the PDR lost their value to inflation so quickly that few made it into circulation and they are now quite rare. Both types of coinage are sometimes found in antique shops.

Stamps

Learned philatelists know that Lao **stamps** from the 1950s and early 1960s are some of the most exquisitely designed and coloured stamps ever issued. Of these, the works of French artist Marc Leguay stand out. Printed in Paris, Leguay's scenes of rural Lao life and depictions of characters from Lao mytholo-gy are mini-masterpieces. Most antique shops in Vientiane have a selection of old stamps and at least one shop specializes in philately.

Lao stamps from the early 1970s depicting American astronauts and their achievements in space were replaced in the late 1970s by stamps commemorating the celestial exploits of Soviet cosmonauts. Since the revolution, Lao stamps have been made in Cuba and are not gummed, hence the little glue pots to be found in every Lao post office.

Royalist regalia

With the memories of the war that divided Laos fading, paraphernalia associated with the defunct kingdom are less likely to offend officials of the present régime. This is espe-cially true if the said paraphernalia is being hawked to tourists who will carry their sou-venirs out of sight and out of mind. Brass buttons, badges and medals decorated with the Hindu iconography of the Lao monarchy are sometimes found in gold or silver jew-ellery and antique shops. Royal Lao Army hat devices depicting Shiva's trident super-imposed on Vishnu's discus and brass but-tons decorated with Airavata, the three-headed elephant, are typical finds. Souvenir hunters should keep in mind that attaching medals or badges of the Kingdom of Laos to your clothes and wearing them in public would be considered, in the words of one Louang Phabang antiques merchant, "poor form".

Woodcarving

Until tourism created a demand for sou-venirs, nearly all examples of Lao **wood-carving** were religious in nature. A steady trickle of small, antique, wooden **Buddha images** are finding their way into curio shops (see p.58 for comments on the pur-chase of Buddha images). The Lao, when acquiring a Buddha image, pay particular attention to the expression on the Buddha's face. Does the Buddha look serene? If so it is considered an auspicious image. For those who have bought a stunning, hand-woven textile but are unsure of how to dis-play it, there are ornately **carved hangers** made expressly for this purpose. Workmanship varies, however, so inspect carefully to ensure that there are no splinters or jagged edges which may damage the tex-tile. Keep in mind also that large woodcarv-ings sometimes crack when transported to less humid climes.

Rattan, wicker and bamboo

That **baskets** are an important part of tradi-tional Lao culture is reflected in the lan-guage: Lao has dozens upon dozens of words for them, and they're used in all spheres of everyday life. Many different forms of basket are used as **backpacks**; those made by the Gie-Trieng tribe in Xekong province are probably the most expertly woven. Baskets are also used for serving food, such as sticky rice. These mini baskets come with a long loop of string so they can be slung over the shoulder when hiking, as sticky rice is the perfect snack on long treks, road or boat trips.

Mats made of woven grass or reeds can be found in sizes to accommodate one or two people. The one-person mats are dirt-cheap, easily carried when rolled up and make a lot more sense than foam rubber mattresses. Woven mats are especially handy when taking a slow boat down the Mekong, as the passenger holds are not always the cleanest of places. Ordinary sticky rice baskets and mats can be found at any provincial market and should cost no more than a couple of dollars.

While most **rattan and bamboo furniture** in Laos is much cheaper than at home, the cost of shipping it back tends to equal things out. Recently a couple of companies have begun producing stylish, high-quality rattan and bamboo furniture that is compar-atively pricey. Either way, rattan and bamboo are the favourite food of a tiny, but vora-cious, beetle that commonly infests furniture of this type made in this part of the world. In the end, it's probably not worth the trouble.

Books

English-language books are expensive in Laos. This may be due to the government's ongoing attempts to control information. Reportedly, before a book can be approved for sale in Laos, an official from the Ministry of Culture and Information must give it a thorough reading, which can take up to a year. The hands-down best place to buy books on all subjects Lao is Bangkok.

Cultural tips

While history may have given them ample reason to distrust outsiders, the Lao are a genuinely friendly folk and interacting with them is one of the greatest joys of travelling through Laos. Always remember though that Laos is a Buddhist country and foreigners need to moderate their dress and behaviour appropriately.

Because of the sheer diversity of **ethnic groups** in Laos, it is difficult to generalize when speaking of "Lao" attitudes and behaviour. The dominant group, the so-called "Lao Loum", or **lowland Lao**, who make up the majority in the valleys of the Mekong and its tributaries, are Theravada Buddhists and this has a strong effect on their attitudes and behaviour. Customs among the **hilltribe peoples** are often quite different from those of the lowlanders, but the variety of distinct groups makes it impractical to attempt a list here (see Trekking Etiquette box on p.223). Since visitors are more likely to come into contact with the lowland Lao, it makes sense to focus on the dos and don'ts within that culture.

Travellers who have spent some time in Thailand will note that the Lao and Thai share many of the same cultural traits, so that lessons learned in Thailand can be applied to Laos as well.

Dress and appearance

Appearance is very important in Lao society. **Conservative dress** is always recommended, and visitors should keep in mind that the Lao themselves dislike foreigners who come to their country and dress in what they deem to be

a disrespectful manner. This includes men appearing in public in sleeveless shirts or without a shirt, and women walking around braless. Be aware also that dreadlocks, tattoos and body-piercing are viewed with disfavour by lowland Lao, although hilltribe people are usually more accepting. Dressing too casually (or too outrageously) can also be counterproductive in dealings with Lao authorities, such as when applying for visa extensions at immigration.

When in urban areas or visiting Buddhist monasteries or holy sites, visitors should refrain from outfits that would be more suited to the beach. Women especially should avoid wearing anything that reveals too much skin or could be conceived of as provocative. This includes shorts and sleeveless shirts. Sandals or flip-flops can be worn for all but the most formal occasions; in fact, they are much more practical than shoes since footwear must be removed upon entering private homes or certain Buddhist monastery buildings. Whenever entering any dwelling or living space **always remove your shoes**. The habit of leaving one's footwear outside the threshold is not just a matter of wanting to keep interiors clean, it is a long-standing tradition that will cause offence if flouted.

Behaviour

Lao **social taboos** are sometimes linked to Buddhist beliefs. **Feet** are considered low and unclean and care should be taken not to touch or even point at things with your feet. Be careful not to step over any part of people who are sitting or lying on the floor (or the deck of a boat), as this is also considered rude. If you do accidentally kick or brush someone with your feet, apologise immediately and smile as you do so. That way, even if the words aren't understood, your intent will be. Conversely, people's **heads** are considered sacred and shouldn't be touched. Playful hair tousling is not a sign of adoration among the Lao.

Besides dressing conservatively there are other conventions that must be followed when visiting **Buddhist monasteries**. Women should never touch Buddhist monks or novices, or hand objects directly to them. When giving something to a monk, the object should be placed on a nearby table or passed to a layman who will then hand it to the monk. This is an example of the many precepts that Buddhist monks must adhere to and it applies even when monks are interacting with their own mothers. Before entering monastery buildings such as the *sim* or *wihan*, or if you are invited into monks' living quarters, footwear must be removed. All Buddha images are objects of veneration, and some are also considered to be great works of art, so it should go without saying that touching Buddha images disrespectfully (such as giving them a stiff prod to ascertain what they are made of) is inappropriate. When sitting on the floor of a monastery building that has a Buddha image, never point your feet in the direction of the image. If possible, observe the Lao and imitate the way they sit: in a modified kneeling position with legs pointed away from the image. The same position should be taken when sitting on the floor (or the deck of a boat) near a monk.

The lowland Lao traditionally **greet** each other with a *nop* – bringing their hands together at the chin in a prayer-like gesture. After the revolution the *nop* was discouraged, but it now seems to be making a comeback. This graceful gesture is more difficult to properly execute than it may at first appear, however, as the status of the persons giving and returning the *nop* determines how they will execute it. Most Lao reserve the *nop* greeting for each other, preferring to shake hands with Westerners, and the only time a Westerner is likely to receive a *nop* is from the staff of five-star hotels or fancy restaurants. In any case, if you do receive a *nop* as a gesture of greeting or thank you, it is best to reply with a smile and nod of the head.

As for the **Lao temperament**, most visitors will find it at turns charming, baffling and maddening. With foreign visitors the Lao are almost unfailingly gracious and hospitable, especially in the remoter parts of the country where foreigners are a rarity. The patient and unflappable Lao, however, have found that foreigners can be quick to anger and will vent their spleen in situations where it is clear that losing tempers will get them nowhere. The Lao are likely to find amusement in such situations, smiling or chortling at the foreigner's vein-popping fury. If the foreigner still fails to see the futility of displaying rage, the Lao are likely to flee the scene, giving the hot-head some time to cool. In time the foreigner will learn that, no matter what happens, showing anger is a useless endeavour in Laos.

The Lao have also noticed that many foreign visitors seem to be a bit aloof. They have obviously spent a lot of time and money to get so far from home, but once they get to Laos they walk around briskly, looking at the locals, but rarely bothering to smile or greet those they have come so far to see. The Lao are unsure of what to make of this, for in Laos it is customary for **strangers** to smile at each other to show that they mean well. Foreign visitors who are not grin-stingy will find that a smile and a nod will break the ice of initial reservation some locals may have upon seeing a foreigner, and will invariably bring a smile in response.

The Lao realize that their country is poor and know that foreign visitors might be put off by their rustic lifestyles, particularly in the countryside. Partly to make up for these perceived shortcomings the Lao are very hospitable and enjoy **offering food or drinks** to visitors. This will certainly be the case if visitors are invited into a Lao home. Sadly, some foreigners are not interested in partaking of the humble offerings, declining sometimes to even have a taste. The humiliated host may continue to urge the guests to partake, but will hide any signs of feeling insulted if they flat-out refuse his hospitality. In the future the spurned host will think twice before issuing another such invitation.

Sexual attitudes

As with showing anger, **displaying affection** in public is just not done in Laos. The Lao attitude, which might seem "old-fashioned" to Westerners, is to keep a lid on such passions while in public. What to Westerners are innocent displays of affection, a little hug here, a little kiss there, will be perceived by the Lao as ill-concealed lust. This is not to say that the Lao are prudes. They can be quite forward and frank when discussing sexual matters, but any display of affection in public is considered tasteless.

Particularly disturbing to the Lao are incidents, increasingly common in touristed areas, in which foreign couples are caught having sex in a public or semi-public place. No matter what the foreigners' intentions were, in Lao eyes such behaviour is insulting. The Lao won't see such an act as being the result of two lovers caught up in the moment. Dogs copulate outdoors. People do not. Another growing problem is Western tourists coming to Laos and bringing male or female prostitutes from Thailand with them as travelling companions. The spectacle of Western males parading around traditional rural communities with an Asian prostitute in tow in front of the village children is offensive to the Lao.

Interestingly, while public displays of affection between the sexes is discouraged, Lao friends of the same sex, especially inebriated men, fairly drape themselves around each other. This type of behaviour should not be taken to be homosexual, however. Travellers who have spent some time in Thailand and noted the high number of gays who seem to be out and about there, will notice that the Lao are more conservative in comparison. Unlike Thailand, the **gay scene** in Laos Is very underground. and while foreign gay couples travelling through Laos will never be hassled or threatened, any behaviour that draws attention to one's gayness is likely to instigate mirth among the Lao.

Sexual relations between an unmarried Lao national and a Westerner are officially illegal in Laos. This is partly due to government fears that a Thai-style sex industry could take root in Laos. In Vientiane especially, a law prohibiting Lao nationals from sharing hotel rooms with foreigners is sometimes enforced. Outside the capital the law seems to be much more lax.

Crime and personal safety

Laos is a relatively safe country for travellers, although certain areas remain off-limits because of banditry and unexploded ordnance left over from decades of warfare. The country's recent economic woes have pushed crime rates up slightly in Vientiane, but petty crime remains on a small scale. As a visitor, however, you're an obvious target for thieves (who may include your fellow travellers), so keep your wits about you wherever you go.

Crime and the police

Carry your passport, travellers' cheques and other valuables in a concealed **money belt** and don't leave anything important lying about in your room, particularly when staying in rural bungalows. A few hotels have safes which you may want to use, although you should keep in mind that you never know who has access to the safe. A **padlock** and chain, or a cable lock, is useful for doors and windows at inexpensive guest houses and budget hotels and for securing your pack on buses, where you're often separated from your belongings. It's also a good idea to keep $100, photocopies of the relevant pages of your passport, insurance details and travellers' cheque receipts separate from the rest of your valuables.

On the whole, petty crime is more common in **Vientiane** than anywhere else in the country, and although even here incidents are limited it's best to be on the safe side. Be on your guard in darker streets outside the city centre, and along the river. Motorbike-borne thieves ply the city streets and have been known to snatch bags out of the front basket of other motorbikes that they pass. As tranquil as Laos can seem, petty theft and serious crimes do happen throughout the country – even on seemingly deserted country roads.

If you do have anything stolen, you'll need to get the **police** to write up a report in order to claim on your insurance: bring along a Lao speaker to simplify matters if you can. While police generally keep their distance from foreigners, if you break a law you may be "fined". With a lot of patience, you should be able to resolve most problems, and, if you keep your cool, you may find that you

can bargain down such "fines". It helps to have your passport with you at all times – if you don't, police have greater incentive to ask for more money and may even try to bring you to the station. In some instances police may puzzle over your passport for what seems like an awfully long time. Again, such situations are best handled with an ample dose of patience. If your papers are in order, you shouldn't have anything to worry about.

Banditry

With far more serious consequences than petty theft, **banditry** is a possible threat in Laos, although you can greatly reduce the risks by sticking to the main highways. In the past, buses, motorcyclists and private vehicles on certain highways have been held up, their passengers robbed and, in some instances, killed. Because information in Laos is tightly controlled, no one knows exactly if rumoured bandit attacks have actually occurred or if other incidents have happened and gone unreported. Therefore it's always good to ask at a Western embassy in Vientiane for any **travel advisories** before heading out into remote regions.

Security has improved greatly along **Route 13** between Kasi and Louang Phabang since the mid-1990s when this section of the highway was considered completely unsafe. The insurgent/bandit group generally thought to be responsible for the attacks in this area, the **Chao Fa**, is still active in parts of Xiang Khouang province (see p.197). While bus drivers working this route maintain that the area is now free of such incidents and have stopped carrying guns, as late as 1998 many expatriates working in Laos were still discouraged by their employers from travelling by road between Kasi and Louang Phabang. Since the completion of this stretch of the road, the number of attacks on vehicles has dropped to zero from a decade ago when it is said that ten to twenty people were killed per year.

Another highway with a bad reputation was **Route 7** from Phou Khoun to Phonsavan. Tourists were not allowed to travel it, requiring a long detour through Nam Neun. Today, this highway is upgraded and now opened to traffic and tourists, and is served by daily buses from Vientiane and Louang Phabang.

South of Route 7 lies the **Xaisomboun Special Zone**, an administrative district carved out of Xiang Khouang and Bolikhamxai provinces, parts of which are still considered unsafe. Attacks on local buses have been reported in recent years and four United Nations workers were killed in this area in 1994. The eastern part of this district, where Route 6 connects Muang Khoun with Pakxan, is another troubled area where caution should be exercised.

Another sensitive area is the **far south** along the Cambodian border. Despite increased stability in Cambodia, Laos's southern neighbour remains a volatile country not short on armed thugs who have little regard for life or international borders. There were several incidents of armed thugs holding up buses, firing on tourists and hijacking boats in southern Champasak province in the mid- to late-1990s. Exercise caution when travelling near the border and ask locals for security updates. The most volatile area is unfortunately the section of the Mekong between the Lao island of Don Khon and the Cambodian right bank, waters inhabited by the Irrawaddy dolphin, a popular tourist draw. If you are told that it is unsafe to travel into these areas by boat, heed the warnings.

Unexploded ordnance

The **Second Indochina War** left Laos with the dubious distinction of being the most heavily **bombed** country per capita in the his-

tory of warfare. Not surprisingly, Laos's legacy of bombs, land mines, mortar shells, white phosphorus canisters and anti-personnel bomblets – the leftovers of decades of warfare – is a problem that will haunt the country for decades to come, despite the efforts of de-mining organizations to clear affected areas of the French-, Soviet-, Chinese-, Vietnamese- and American-made ordnance. Fifteen of Laos's eighteen provinces have reported significant problems with **unexploded ordnance (UXO)**. Ten provinces have one or more severely contaminated districts (listed in order of impact they are: Savannakhet, Xiang Khouang, Salavan, Khammouane, Xekong, Champasak, Saisomboun, Houa Phan, Attapu and Louang Phabang), while five provinces have at least one district with significant contamination (Louang Namtha, Phongsali, Bolikhamxai, Vientiane Province, Vientiane Prefecture).

Anti-personnel bomblets, known as *bombi* in Lao, are the most common type of UXO. Dropped from cluster bombs, *bombi* are particularly nasty as these round, tennis-ball sized bombs can easily be mistaken for a toy or a ball by a child. Also common are large bombs – ranging in size from 100kg to 1000kg – an estimated thirty percent of which did not explode on impact.

Although towns and tourist sites are free of UXO, 25 percent of villages remain contaminated and **accidents** continue at a rate of two hundred per year – an average of one accident every other day. As accidents often occur while people are tending their fields, collecting forest products or trying to defuse UXO in order to sell or re-use it, the risk faced by the average visitor is very limited. Nonetheless, it's a good idea to be aware of the dangers of UXO, especially when travelling in the eastern parts of Laos. In such areas, where bombing and ground battles were particularly fierce, stay on well-worn paths and, while it may seem obvious, don't pick up or kick at anything you can't identify. In many towns in these areas, UXO-awareness posters on the walls of local restaurants, hotels and government offices will signal that you have entered a contaminated region.

Spiritual pursuits and alternative therapies

During their period of colonization, the French regarded traditional Lao therapies as quaint and amusing, and this attitude was passed on to the Lao elite who studied in France. In an essay about traditional Lao medicine written in the 1950s by a former Minister of Health, the traditional Lao doctor is repeatedly referred to as "the quack". But renewed interest, partially fuelled by a similar rekindling of enthusiasm in neighbouring China, has seen a resurgence of confidence in traditional techniques.

Recently, a government-sponsored traditional medicine **hospital** opened on the outskirts of Vientiane. Known as the *hong maw pin pua duay ya pheun meuang* in Lao, the founding of this institution is a sign that the Lao are once again taking their traditional healing techniques seriously. Tourism has likewise been partially responsible for renewed interest in traditional massage and herbal sauna, though these alternative therapies are limited to larger towns and cities.

Lao massage

Lao massage owes more to **Chinese** than to Thai schools, utilizing medicated balms and salves which are rubbed into the skin. Muscles are kneaded and joints are flexed while a warm compress of steeped herbs is applied to the area being treated. Besides massage, Lao doctors may utilize other "exotic" treatments that have been borrowed from neighbouring countries. One decidedly Chinese therapy that is sometimes employed in Laos is **acupuncture** (*fang khem*), in which long, thin needles are inserted into special points that correspond to specific organs or parts of the body. Another imported practice is the application of **suction cups** (*kaew dut*), a remedy popular in neighbouring Cambodia. The small glass jars are briefly heated with a flame and applied to bare skin. Air within the cup contracts as it cools, drawing blood under the skin into the mouth of the cup. Theoretically, toxins within the bloodstream are in this way brought to the surface of the skin.

Lao herbal sauna

Before getting a massage, many Lao opt for some time in the **herbal sauna**. Sometimes found in the grounds of monasteries, the set-up usually consists of a rustic wooden shack divided into separate rooms for men and women, and beneath the shack a drum of water sits on a wood fire. Medicinal herbs boiling in the drum release their juices into the water and the resulting steam is carried up into the rooms. The temperature inside is normally quite high and bathers should spend only a few minutes at a time in the sauna, taking frequent breaks to cool off by lounging outside and sipping herbal tea to replace water that the body so profusely sweats out.

The **recipes** of both the saunas and teas are jealously guarded but are known to contain such herbal additives as carambola, tamarind, eucalyptus and citrus leaves. Besides the obvious physical benefits Lao massage and sauna afford the recipient, administering massage and sauna to others is believed to bring spiritual merit to those who perform the labour, making Lao massage and sauna a "win-win" proposition for all involved.

The basi

Visitors to Laos will notice that many lowland Lao wear one or more bracelets of white thread around their wrists. This is a sign that the wearer has recently taken part in a **basi**, the quintessential Lao ceremony of **animist** bent, which is performed throughout the year. Also known as *sukhuan*, the ceremony is supposed to reunite the body's multiple souls, which are thought to succumb to wanderlust and depart from the body every now and again. *Basi* ceremonies are held during Lao New Year as well as being a part of weddings, births and farewell parties. While not believed to be medicinal per se, the *basi* is sometimes performed in addition to other therapies to remedy an affliction. Before the ceremony can be performed, an auspicious time must be gleaned from an astrologer and a *phakhuan* must be prepared. Resembling a miniature Christmas tree made from rolled banana leaves, the *phakhuan* is decorated with marigolds and other flowers and draped with white threads. The arrangement sits in a silver bowl filled with husked rice and is placed in the centre of a mat laid out on the floor. Participants sit in a circle around the *phakhuan* and offerings of food and liquor are placed near it. These will be used to entice the absent souls to return. An animist **priest**, known as a *maw phawn* or "wish-doctor", presides over the ceremony, inviting the souls to return with a mixture of Pali and Lao chants. The white threads that are draped over the *phakhuan* are then removed and tied around the wrists of the participants while blessings are invoked. During the *basi* ceremony performed at Lao New Year, each thread tied around the wrist may be accompanied by a shot of rice liquor and this sometimes leads to an impromptu *lam wong*, or "circle dance", performed by the euphoric participants.

Traditional remedies

In the not-too-distant past Westerners believed that malaria was caused by noxious vapours (indeed *malaria* is Latin for "bad air"). In a similar vein the Lao believed that many illnesses were the result of an offended spirit out to get revenge, or possibly the spell of a hired black magician. To this day many uneducated Lao (the vast majority of the population) still adhere to these beliefs and will seek out **traditional remedies** to cure stricken family members.

Before an illness can be treated it must be **diagnosed**, and the Lao employ an egg as a tool to this end. First the egg is rolled along the affected part of the body and then it is broken and its yolk is examined to determine the source of the illness. If it is determined that the illness was caused by an offended spirit a spirit-doctor will visit the patient, make the appropriate offerings and then call out the names of spirits until the culprit is found. After a discussion with the family of the patient to ascertain what action offended the spirit in the first place, an animal, usually a chicken, is sacrificed and the placated spirit will loosen its grip on the patient. If it is determined that the patient has been stricken by a foreign object (usually a chicken bone or piece of water buffalo skin) that has been projected into the body by a black magician, a doctor will exorcise the object from the victim using deft fingers to pull the object directly from the skin. In some cases incantations and smoke are used to make the victim vomit and expel the foreign object. Often these measures are taken in addition to the administration of Western medicines.

Sports and outdoor adventure

Laos is rapidly taking off as the most exciting outdoor-adventure destination in Southeast Asia: there are amazing trekking opportunities, vast cave systems to be explored and untamed white-water rivers to be rafted. With the emergence of a number of specialized travel companies offering inexpensive, organized, adventure tours in previously remote reaches, it's now easier than ever to experience the wild side of Laos.

Laos is wild country. Over seventy percent of it comprises high terrain with chains of **mountains** reaching heights of over 2800m running its entire length. Covering these ranges are vast expanses of unexplored, virgin **rainforests**. And from these highlands run steep narrow valleys through which **rivers** rush down from the mountain heights to join the "Mother of Waters", the mighty Mekong River, which flows the entire length of the country. Ironically, lack of development and infrastructure has succeeded where conservation efforts in neighbouring countries have failed. Closed to the rest of the world for fifty years by war and self-imposed isolation, Laos today has some of the most pristine wildernesses left in Southeast Asia.

Now re-opened to outside visitors, Laos is paradise for travellers seeking adventure and excitement in the great outdoors. While many visitors are perfectly satisfied to pass their time in the cappuccino bars of Louang Phabang, if you don't mind working up a sweat and getting a bit wet and muddy in the process, there is no end of fun and adventure to be had.

Trekking

The easiest and most popular adventure sport in Laos is **trekking** in the northern provinces. Although trekking in Laos has yet to reach the stage of being an industry as in Nepal or Thailand, there are still rich opportunities for both hiking and multi-day treks, whether you join a guided walk or strike out on your own.

The **far north** has a number of advantages in its favour: mountain scenery, pristine forest areas, and colourful ethnic hill-tribes living in traditional villages. Although there was an initial mad rush in the late Nineties to "see Laos before it's spoiled", the real truth is there has never been a better time to come to Laos to experience the tribal cultures of the north. There are now excellent **tourist facilities** available in many northern towns and **Guide Service Offices** are gradually being opened throughout the north to facilitate tourists who want to take part in guided treks that are both environmentally friendly and have a low impact on the local peoples.

For visitors interested in hilltribes and **organized trekking**, the best towns to head for are Louang Namtha, Muang Sing, Louang Phabang, and Vang Viang, all of which have developed programmes for travellers wanting to make a series of day-trips based out of town or take part in multi-day treks involving camping and village stays. If you want to take a more independent, "do-it-yourself" approach, other towns highly suitable for **independent trekking** opportunities using self-hired local guides include Muang Long, Xieng Kok, Houayxai, Vieng Phoukha, Muang Khoua, and Nong Khiaw, all of which have guest houses and are close to tribal areas.

NBCAs and eco-tours

Another great activity just starting to gain popularity is **eco-tours** to wilderness areas featuring rare and exotic flora and fauna. Here, nature lovers and birdwatchers will find some of the rarest species on the planet and vast forest canopies. Although Laos does not have any national parks in the Western sense, since 1993 the government has established twenty **National**

△ Tuk-tuk

Biodiversity Conservation Areas (NBCAs) and there are another eleven proposed NBCAs awaiting government confirmation. The NBCAs are basically multi-purpose areas, meaning that they are protected but often still have villagers and hilltribes living within their boundaries. The twenty current NBCAs are scattered around the country, often in remote border areas without roads. While many of the parks are inaccessible short of mounting a professional expedition, several have been developed for eco-tourism and have **visitor centres** and **guided walks**. The best developed NBCAs for tourists are Phou Khao Khouay (see p.114), Louang Namtha (see p.218) and Phou Hin Poun (see p.264), all of which can be reached by road.

Water sports

While most river-journey enthusiasts are satisfied with a slow boat down the Mekong between Houayxai and Louang Phabang, many opportunities exist for exploring Laos' faster waterways. If slow cruising down the broad Mekong isn't your style, there are now several companies offering **white-water river rafting** tours on a number of northern rivers including the Nam Ou, the Nam Xuang and the Nam Ming, all based out of Louang Phabang.

Even more popular are **river-kayaking** adventures ranging from easy day-trips for beginners to multi-day adventures down rivers with grade 5 rapids. Professional guided kayaking tours are currently operated on a regular basis on eight northern rivers as well as the Ang Nam Ngum Reservoir. The best bases for kayaking tours are Vientiane, Vang Viang, Louang Phabang and Louang Namtha. Another fantastic region for kayaking, just opening up, is the Khammouane Limestone NBCA (see p.264). Among other scenic wonders, this NBCA features a seven-kilometre-long natural river-tunnel through the heart of a mountain, and is becoming popular for organized tours out of Vientiane.

Caves and rock-climbing

With its great forests of limestone karst scenery receding into the distance like a Chinese scroll painting, Laos is a great destination for cave exploring, spelunkering, and rock-climbing. Prime areas for limestone karst scenery in Laos include Vang Viang, Kasi, Thakhet and Viang Xai. For most tourists, **cave exploring** is limited to climbing up to and wandering around in caves that are fairly touristy and have clearly defined pathways. Serious spelunkers can find vast cave and tunnel systems to explore in the Khammouane Limestone NBCA and the Hin Nam No NBCA, but should seek local permission before launching any major expeditions as many caves have yet to have archeological surveys done. With so many awesome unclimbed and un-named peaks, **rock-climbing** is one sport that seems to have a huge future in Laos. At present the sport is still in its infancy with the country's first bolted cliff face, featuring sixteen routes graded 5b to 8c, recently opened in Vang Viang, but new routes should follow soon.

Mountain biking

With some of the best untamed scenery in Southeast Asia, many unpaved roads, and little traffic, Laos is becoming a very hot destination for **cross-country mountain bike touring**. A lot of independent travellers do self-organized mountain bike touring in Northern Laos – **Route 13** from Louang Phabang to Vientiane seems to be the most popular route. Although the scenery along this route is very beautiful, riders should be warned that it is extremely mountainous and the road crosses several large ranges before reaching the Vientiane Plain. There are much better routes in **Houa Phan and Xiang Khouang provinces** where you'll find fantastic landscapes, plenty of remote villages, and paved roads with very few vehicles on them.

It's a good idea to **plan** carefully. What appear to be very short distances on the map can often take many hours, even in a vehicle. One good thing about bicycle touring in Laos is that should things get too difficult you can always flag down a passing *sawngthaew* and throw the bike on the roof. Another alternative is to join an **organized cycling tour**, of which there are many.

The environment and ethical tourism

Tourism can play an important part in maintaining indigenous cultures, and also provides an invaluable source of foreign currency for many developing countries. Although there are many benefits, there are also some irreversible and detrimental consequences.

The expansion of tourism in **Laos** has been spectacular, growing at around fifty percent per year. While it has been a boon for the economy, it has serious and potentially disruptive effects environmentally, socially, culturally, and economically. The worst example in Laos was the rapid rise of "drug tourism", with many young Westerners coming to the country purely to buy cheap ganja and experiment with opium. Laos is also now established on the backpacker circuit and is experiencing all of the positive and negative effects that can bring on its fragile culture.

Local issues have been covered throughout this book. If you are concerned about the impact of tourism or environmental matters, get in touch with the organizations listed below.

Contacts

Campaign for Environmentally Responsible Tourism (CERT) PO Box 4246, London SE21 7ZE Ⓦ www.c-e-r-t.org. Lobbies to educate tour operators and tourists in a sensitive approach to travel, focusing on immediate practical ways in which the environment can be protected.

EarthWise Journeys PO Box 16177, Portland, OR 97292 Ⓦ www.teleport.com/~earthwyz. American organization promoting environmentally responsible travel.

Partners in Responsible Tourism PO Box 237, San Francisco, CA 94104-0237 ☎ 415/675 0420, Ⓦ www.pirt.org/about.html. An organization of individuals and travel companies promoting responsible tourism to minimize harm to the environment and local cultures. Their website features a "Traveler's Code for Traveling Responsibly."

Tourism Concern Stapleton House, 277-281 Holloway Rd, London N7 8HN ☎ 020/7753 3330, Ⓦ www.tourismconcern.org.uk. Campaigns for the rights of local people to be consulted in tourism developments affecting their lives, and produces a quarterly magazine of news and articles.

Travelling with children

Travelling through Laos with children can be challenging and fun. Children help break the ice with strangers and will be showered with attention. However, it's worth giving some thought as to whether your children – and you – can handle all the additional attention. You'll also need to take extra precautions in light of Laos's poor sanitation, animals and demanding roads.

Bear in mind that Laos lacks adequate **health-care** facilities, worrisome given that children, especially the very young, are more vulnerable to illness. If children do become sick, keep up their fluid intake so as to avoid dehydration. Remember too that diarrhoea can be dangerous for children: rehydration solutions are vital if your child comes down with it. Rabies is a common problem in Laos, so explain to your children the dangers of playing with animals and consider a rabies shot.

In tourist areas it should be no problem finding food that kids will **eat**, although some children may turn up their noses at Lao food. Before leaving for your trip, it might be an idea to take the kids out for a few sample meals at Thai, Lao or Vietnamese restaurants, to help their taste buds adjust.

You'll also want to plan a more comfortable itinerary than you would on your own. Laos's bumpy, windy **roads** and the long distances between tourist centres can be tough on younger children, so take shorter bus journeys and consider renting a van. Bathrooms at the cheapest **guest houses** can be particularly unhygienic, especially if rooms lack en-suite facilities. At more expensive hotels children under 12 can usually stay free of charge in their parents' rooms, while many guest houses and budget hotels have rooms with double beds or can add an extra cot for a small extra cost.

If you're travelling with babies, you'll have difficulty finding **nappies** throughout Laos. For short journeys, you could bring a supply of nappies from home; for longer trips, consider switching over to washables.

For more **advice** on travelling with children in developing countries, consult *Travel with Children* by Maureen Wheeler (Lonely Planet). For specific advice about children's health issues, contact your doctor, or consult one of the travellers' medical services listed on p.29. In the UK, Nomad Medical Centre publishes a special information sheet on keeping kids healthy when abroad (☎020/8889 7014). In the U.S., Travel With Your Children (40 Fifth Ave, New York, NY 10011 ☎212/477 5524 or 1-888/822-4388) publishes a regular newsletter, *Family Travel Times* (✆www.familytraveltimes.com), as well as a series of books on travel with children including *Great Adventure Vacations With Your Kids*.

Travellers with disabilities

Laos makes few provisions for the disabled, so you'll need to be self-reliant. The important thing is to check beforehand with tour companies, hotels and airlines that they can accommodate you specifically. The list below details organizations that can advise you as to which tour operators and airlines are the most reliable.

Public transport will present the biggest challenge: it's difficult to board and cramped inside. In Vientiane and Louang Phabang, wheelchair users may find the uneven pavements, which lack dropped kerbs, difficult to negotiate. Elsewhere there are no pavements and most of the roads are dirt. **Hotels and guest houses** do not have rooms adapted for the needs of the disabled and very few hotels have lifts: the best bet is a ground-floor room.

If you can spare the additional money, the best way to alleviate transport difficulties is to take internal flights and hire a private minibus with a driver. You should also consider hiring a local tour guide to accompany you on sightseeing trips – a Lao speaker can facilitate access to temples and museums. Flying an international carrier whose planes are suited to your needs is also helpful. British Airways, Qantas and Thai International all carry aisle wheelchairs and have at least one toilet adapted for disabled passengers. Keep in mind that airline companies can cope better if they are expecting you, with a wheelchair provided at airports and staff primed to help.

When preparing for your trip, it's a good idea to pack spares of any clothing or equipment that might be hard to find. If you use a wheelchair, you should have it serviced before you go and carry a repair kit. If you do not use a wheelchair all the time but your walking capabilities are limited, remember that you are likely to need to cover greater distances while travelling (often over rougher terrain and in hotter temperatures) than you are used to.

Contacts for travellers with disabilities

UK and Ireland

Holiday Care Service 2nd floor, Imperial Building, Victoria Rd, Horley, Surrey RH6 7PZ ☎01293/774 535, Minicom ☎01293/776 943, ⓦ www.holidaycare.org.uk. Provides information on all aspects of travel, although they have no specific information on Laos.

Irish Wheelchair Association Blackheath Drive, Clontarf, Dublin 3 ☎01/833 8241, ⓕ833 3873, ⓔ iwa@iol.ie. Useful information provided about travelling abroad with a wheelchair.

Tripscope Alexandra House, Albany Rd, Brentford, Middlesex TW8 0NE ☎08457/585 641, ⓦ www.justmobility.co.uk/tripscope, ⓔ tripscope@cableinet.co.uk. This registered charity provides a national telephone information service offering free advice on UK and international transport for those with a mobility problem.

US and Canada

Access-Able ⓦ www.access-able.com. Online resource for travellers with disabilities.

Directions Unlimited,123 Green Lane, Bedford Hills, NY 10507 ☎1-800/533-5343 or 914/241-1700. Tour operator specializing in custom tours for people with disabilities.

Mobility International 451 Broadway, Eugene, OR 97401, voice and TDD ☎541/343-1284, ⓦ www.miusa.org. Information and referral services, access guides, tours and exchange programmes. Annual membership $35 (includes quarterly newsletter).

Society for the Advancement of Travellers with Handicaps (SATH) 347 5th Ave, New York, NY 10016 ☎212/447-7284, ⓦ www.sath.org. Non-profit educational organization that has actively represented travelers with disabilities since 1976.

Travel Information Service ☎215/456-9600. Telephone information and referral service.

Twin Peaks Press Box 129, Vancouver, WA 98661 ☎360/694-2462 or 1-800/637-2256, ⓦ www.twinpeak.virtualave.net. Publisher of the *Directory of Travel Agencies for the Disabled* ($19.95), listing more than 370 agencies worldwide; *Travel for the Disabled* ($19.95); the *Directory of Accessible Van Rentals* ($12.95) and *Wheelchair Vagabond* ($19.95), loaded with personal tips.

Wheels Up! ☎1-888/389-4335, ⓦ www.wheelsup.com. Provides discounted airfare, tour and cruise prices for disabled travelers, also publishes a free monthly newsletter and has a comprehensive website.

Australia and New Zealand

ACROD (Australian Council for Rehabilitation of the Disabled) PO Box 60, Curtin ACT 2605 ☎02/6282 4333; Suite 103, 1st floor, 1–5 Commercial Rd, Kings Grove 2208 ☎02/9554 3666. Provides lists of travel agencies and tour operators for people with disabilities.

Disabled Persons Assembly 4/173-175 Victoria St, Wellington, New Zealand ☎04/801 9100. Resource centre with lists of travel agencies and tour operators for people with disabilities.

Insurance and medication

It's advisable to read your travel **insurance** small print carefully to make sure that people with a pre-existing medical condition are not excluded. A **medical certificate** of your fitness to travel, provided by your doctor, is also extremely useful; some airlines or insurance companies may insist on it. If there's an association representing people with your disability, contact them early in the planning process as they will be able to advise on travel insurance as well as other travel-related issues.

Make sure that you have extra **supplies of medication** – carried with you if you fly – and a prescription including the generic name in case of emergency. As medical facilities in Laos are generally poor, it is unlikely you will be able to find your medication at short notice; indeed you may not be able to find what you need at all. It's a good idea to carry a doctor's letter about your medication prescription with you at all times – particularly when passing through customs at Lao border check points and any Southeast Asian airports that you might be passing through en route to Laos. If your medication has to be kept cool, buy a thermal insulation bag and a couple of freezer blocks before you leave home – that way you can refreeze one of the blocks every day, while the other is in use. You'll also need to adjust your itinerary to suit your needs – some towns in Laos have no electricity, and thus no freezers; it can also be difficult to find ice in many locations.

Directory

Addresses and street names Lao addresses can be terribly confusing, firstly because property is usually numbered twice – when numbered at all – to show which lot it stands in, and then to signify where it is on that lot. To add to the confusion, some cities have several conflicting address systems – Vientiane, for example, has three although no one seems to use any of them. Thus, you won't be able to follow house numbers along a street until you reach your destination. To avoid any unnecessary confusion, numbers have been omitted from addresses given in the Guide, and locations are described as far as possible using landmarks. Only five cities in Laos actually have street names – and that's just the start of the problem. Signs are few and far between and many roads either change names from block to block or have several entirely different names. If you ask for directions, locals most likely won't know the name of a street with the exception of the three or four largest avenues in Vientiane. Use street names to find a hotel on a map in the Guide, but when asking directions or telling a tuk-tuk driver where to go you'll have better luck using a landmark, monasteries or prominent hotels. Fortunately, Lao cities, even Vientiane, are relatively tiny, making it more of a challenge to get lost than it is to figure out where you're going.

Books With only 65 percent of the population literate and surveys showing that only four percent of the people are readers, it should come as no surprise that books keep a relatively low profile in Laos. You'll find a small selection of imported paperbacks and magazines at book stores in Vientiane and Louang Phabang as well as a handful of used titles at guest houses. You may have better luck asking other travellers: bring one book and keep exchanging. See "Contexts", pp.386–390 for recommended reading on Laos and Southeast Asia.

Contraceptives Bring condoms from home rather than relying on those found in Laos. Better quality condoms and birth control are available at pharmacies in Thailand.

Departure tax When leaving Laos by air or via the Friendship Bridge, you'll have to pay a departure tax equivalent to US$10, payable in US dollars, Thai baht or kip. Surprisingly, tax is not yet collected at other border points, although officials may attempt to find other ways to "tax" you – levying small fees for arriving or departing during lunch hour, late in the day or on the weekend seem to be the most popular techniques.

Drugs It's illegal to smoke ganja in Laos although it continues to be widely available. Tourists who buy and smoke ganja risk substantial "fines" if caught by police who do not need a warrant to search you or your room. As in Thailand, there have been many instances of locals selling foreigners marijuana and then telling the police. In Muang Sing police have also been known to go around the guest houses in the evening smelling for hemp. Despite laws against possession, distribution and trafficking of opium, Laos has seen a steady rise in recent years of "drug tourism". Since 2001 there has been a wide-scale government crack-down on such drug tourism and the opium dens in tourist centres like Vang Vieng and Muang Sing have been shut down.

While opium is not as addictive as its derivative, heroin, withdrawal symptoms are similarly painful. Keep in mind that what for travellers may be a brief fling with an overly-romanticized drug leaves a lasting impression on young locals for whom dealing with the attractions of the drug isn't as simple as catching the next flight home. It may also land the Lao citizen with whom one smokes a hefty fine and jail term.

Electricity Supplied at 220 volts AC. Two-pin sockets are the norm. Many smaller towns, including several provincial capitals, have power for only a few hours in the evening or no power at all. Blackouts are not uncommon, so bring a torch. Electrical wiring in budget guest houses is sometimes an accident waiting to happen. Exercising caution when fiddling with light switches and plugging in appliances is advisable.

Laundry Most guest houses and hotels offer same-day laundry service; in larger towns a few shops offer laundry service at prices which can be cheaper than what you'll be charged at your hotel. In either situation, the charge is usually per item. Your clothes will take a beating, so it's best not to entrust prized articles. If you wash your own clothes, small packets of detergent can be found in many general stores and markets around the country. Hang out your underwear discreetly – women should take particular care, as women's undergarments are believed to have the power to render Buddhist tattoos and amulets powerless.

Measurements Laos follows the metric system.

Photography Louang Phabang and the capital are the best places to stock up on film; elsewhere you never know how long the film has been sitting on the shelf in the heat. Lithium batteries can be difficult to find outside of these cities. Developing film is expensive in Laos and the quality isn't top-notch as shops tend to use their chemicals over and over. You'll have better luck

with developing film in Thailand, where photo shops rate fairly well in terms of quality and price; otherwise you might want to wait until you get home – it's always easier to carry film canisters than a bunch of photos anyway.

Showers Bathing takes a bit of finesse in Laos. Traditional Lao showers consist of a large, ceramic jar or a cement tub resembling an oversized bathtub without a drain. Standing next to the tub, you use the plastic scoop provided to sluice water over your body. While it may look tempting on a hot day, don't get into these tubs or try to use them for doing your laundry, as the water has to be used by others. In some towns villagers opt for an even more traditional technique – the river. Men usually bathe in their underwear; women in sarongs.

Tampons Hard to find outside Vientiane's minimarkets, which have a very limited selection. Bring supplies.

Toilets Squat toilets are the norm throughout Laos, although almost all hotels and guest houses have Western-style porcelain thrones. Public toilets are not common in Laos – you'll only find them at airports and some bus stations; at the latter a small fee is usually collected. Carry toilet paper with you – you can buy it in most places – as not every bathroom in Laos is properly outfitted. Most squat toilets require manual flushing – you'll find a bucket of water with a scoop floating on the surface for this purpose. In some small, rural villages people tend to take to the woods because of a lack of plumbing. On long road trips this is also a perfectly acceptable way to relieve yourself and many Lao women usually bring along a sarong (if they're not already wearing one) to lend them a shred of privacy for such occasions. Keep in mind that many parts of Laos have a large amount of UXO, so it's not wise to wade too far into the bush when the bus stops for a bathroom break.

Work Without a prearranged job and work permit, don't count on finding work in Laos, although people have found work by simply showing up in Vientiane and knocking on doors. Vacancies appear from time to time in the *Vientiane Times* and on billboards posted outside of the capital's minimarkets. Teaching English is probably the easiest job to land (a TEFL – Teaching English as a Foreign Language – qualification is useful though not essential) although it's hard to make enough money to live on, and TEFL gigs may be harder to come by given the current economic situation. For long-term volunteer placements, apply to Voluntary Service Overseas, 317 Putney Bridge Rd, London SW15 2PN (℡020/8780 7200, ⓦ www.vso.org.uk.) in the UK.

Useful things to bring

An **internal-frame backpack** is probably the easiest way to lug your things around, with a lightweight daypack for day-trips. A few small padlocks help to keep the curious out of your belongings during those long journeys when your pack is on the roof of the bus.

It's important to bring **clothes** that are comfortable for Laos's hot and humid weather; lightweight cotton garments that are loose-fitting but modest are best. Long-sleeve shirts and pants help to ward off sun and bugs; shorts and a swimsuit are also good to bring, but you should keep in mind the advice given in "Cultural tips", p.61. Be sure to also include one warm sweater if you plan to travel in the north, where it's cold from October to February. Sport sandals, with good traction, are a good choice for footwear, given the long rainy season and the many rivers and streams you're bound to encounter. If you're bringing trainers, you might also consider bringing flip-flops, which are great for slipping out of during temple tours as well as shared showers at guest houses. A sarong doubles as a towel and is useful for maintaining your modesty while changing or bathing in rivers. If you plan on doing your own laundry, bring along a length of cord for drying clothes.

For **protection from the sun**, bring sunscreen, sunglasses and a brimmed hat; an umbrella (available locally) acts as an effective parasol and is a must during the rainy season.

High-strength **mosquito repellent** that contains the chemical compound DEET is another necessity, although bear in mind that prolonged use of DEET may be harmful. A natural alternative is Citronella (called Mosi-guard in the UK), made from a blend of eucalyptus oils. If you plan on travelling in remote areas, you should bring a mosquito net, although most guest houses supply one if they don't have screened windows. Many of the nets supplied at guest houses have some holes, a problem which is easily remedied with a few rubber bands: gather up the offending section of net and twist a rubber band around it. The Australian Embassy Clinic in Vientiane sells mosquito nets treated with mosquito repellent for $20. Another defence against mosquitoes is coils – lit with a match – which can usually be found in most markets or general stores in Laos.

Toiletries are easy to come by in towns, but bring anything out of the ordinary. While you can count on basic medications being available at pharmacies, it's advisable to bring a medical kit (see p.33). If you wear glasses, make sure you bring a spare pair. Those who wear contact lenses should, in addition to bringing a back-up set, bring whatever contact lens solution they require.

Carry your valuables in a **money belt** or neck purse. **Earplugs** come in handy if you plan on travelling by speedboat. **Photos** of home help to break the ice and are a helpful tool in learning a few words of basic Lao. A few other **essentials** include a torch, swiss army knife, a small towel, a sewing kit, a universal sink plug, eye protection for dusty bus trips, sealable zip-lock plastic bags for keeping things separate in your pack and protecting important documents from getting wet, and a travel alarm clock for those early bus departures. Also bring along photocopies of your passport and a few extra passport-size photos.

Guide

Guide

Vientiane and the northwest

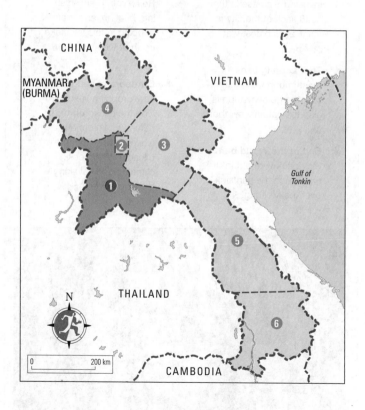

CHAPTER 1 # Highlights

✳ **Lao Revolutionary Museum** Lao history meets Marx in Vientiane's funky relic of the class struggle. See p.96

✳ **Wat Sisaket** The only temple spared by the invading Siamese in their 1828 sack of the city is Vientiane's oldest wat. See p.97

✳ **That Louang** Laos's most important religious site, the golden stupa is also the national symbol. See p.99

✳ **End of the World bars** Kick back with a drink and watch the sun sink over the Mekong. See p.105

✳ **Phou Khao Khouay NBCA** Laos's most accessible wilderness park, home to elephants and tigers, and just two hours from the capital. See p.114

✳ **Ang Nam Ngum Reservoir** There's fishing, boating, and island-hopping in this vast lake north of Vientiane. See p.115

✳ **Outdoors in Vang Viang** Jaw-dropping views provide the backdrop to this natural playground where caving, mountain biking, rafting, rock-climbing and kayaking are all on offer. See p.119

Vientiane and
the northwest

H ugging a bend of the Mekong River on the Vientiane Plain, the low-
rise capital of Laos looks more like a rambling collection of numerous
villages, dotted with a few grandiose monuments, than a capital city.
However, in the mere decade since Laos reopened its doors to foreign
visitors, Vientiane has changed with dizzying rapidity. At the beginning of the
Nineties, the city wallowed in an economic stupor brought about by a fifteen-
year near-ban on free enterprise and a heavy reliance on Soviet aid, but a shift
in policy came with the collapse of the Soviet Union in 1991. Economic
restrictions were relaxed and soon afterwards, Vientiane's collection of billboards
proclaiming the glories of socialism were outnumbered by advertisements for
Pepsi, and the hammer and sickle that had been erected atop the abandoned
French cultural centre was removed. Shop-houses that had long been padlocked
and disused were opened up and transformed into minimarts and video rental
shops. Laos stretched out a conciliatory hand to its neighbour and former
enemy, Thailand, and soon Thai entrepreneurs were arriving in Vientiane to
scout around for economic potential. In the mid-Nineties, the first bridge to
span the Mekong River between Laos and Thailand was constructed outside the
city. Dubbed the "Friendship Bridge", it declares the direction from which most
of Vientiane's foreign investment now comes. In fact, the look and feel of
Vientiane these days is not unlike that of some backward provincial capital in
Thailand rushing to modernize. Some of the city's precious French colonial
mansions have been restored and are being used as places of business, but scores
of venerable old shade trees have been cut down in order to widen roads to
accommodate an ever-multiplying number of cars and motorbikes. Taking their
cue from Thai television, Vientiane's exuberant youth emulate fads and fashions
of the West which have been filtered through the none-too-discerning tastes of
Bangkok. The Revolutionary old-guard, who still run the country, seem unsure
how to react. Official fears of being infected by Thailand's famed social ills occasionally see the police setting up road blocks to snare motorcycle-racing
teenagers or closing nightclubs at midnight, all in the name of preserving Lao
culture. However, the Lao inability to sustain enthusiasm for anything baw muan
("no fun") ensures that crack-downs are short-lived.

The high ratio of foreign expatriate workers posted in Vientiane adds a **cosmopolitan** touch to the city. The expats' numbers and comparative affluence

have led entrepreneurs to open businesses catering specifically to them, providing visitors with a surprisingly wide choice of places to eat. As with other urban centres in the region, the majority of Vientiane's merchant class are ethnic Chinese and Vietnamese, whose forefathers immigrated to Laos during the French era. Despite the changes to their surroundings brought about by the shift to a free market economy, the people of Vientiane have managed to retain their hospitality and sense of humour, and, though rapidly growing, Vientiane is still quaint and easygoing compared to Southeast Asia's other frenetic capital cities.

If the small-town atmosphere of Vientiane gets too claustrophobic, and you start yearning for wide-open spaces, you'll find that escaping this diminutive city is as easy as hopping on a motorbike and driving 20km in any direction. The most popular of the possible **day-trips** is Xiang Khouan or the "**Buddha Park**", a Hindu-Buddhist fantasy in ferro-concrete surrounded by raintrees on the banks of the Mekong. North of Vientiane, the **Ang Nam Ngum Reservoir** attracts locals and foreign visitors alike for relaxing weekend retreats. The lake's tourism and recreational potential has barely been tapped but there is hiking and camping and boat trips to its many small islands. Off the beaten track and a bit more of an effort to reach is the eco-resort of **Lao Pako**, on the banks of the Nam Ngum River, which offers a rural Lao experience within relatively easy distance of the capital.

Slightly further afield but still within day-tripping range of Vientiane is the laid-back resort town of **Vang Viang**. Set amid spectacular scenery on Route 13, the road that connects Vientiane with Laos's other major tourist city, Louang Phabang to the north, Vang Viang is a popular halfway stop and a major recreational region in its own right, with hiking, tubing on the river and cave exploring among the activities on offer. While Route 13 north of Vang Viang winds through spectacular mountain scenery, an alternative route **northwest** to Louang Phabang involves road and river travel through the remote left-bank province of **Xainyabouli**.

The most pleasant time to visit the Vientiane region is November to February, when the **weather** is relatively cool and rain is rare. It's probably best to avoid visiting in the hot season, roughly March to May, when the heat is so oppressive that the local people treat the daylight hours as one long siesta.

Vientiane

Two days is sufficient to see Vientiane's sights. High on your list should be the Buddhist monastery known as **Wat Sisaket**, which offers a good half-day diversion, as does **Wat Simuang**, Vientiane's most popular temple and monastery. Another top attraction is **That Louang**, Laos's most important religious building, best viewed at sundown for the effects of the sunset on its golden surface. Aside from temples and stupas, the **museum of Lao art**, housed in the former royal temple of **Haw Pha Kaew**, and the socialist-era **Lao Revolutionary Museum** are also worth a visit.

Some history

Vientiane's history has been a rather turbulent one, as its meagre collection of structures from the past suggests. An old settlement, possibly dating back to the eighth century, Vientiane had been occupied and subsequently abandoned by the Mon and then the Khmer long before the Lao king Setthathilat moved his **capital** here from Louang Phabang in 1560. Vientiane is actually pronounced "Wiang Jan", the modern romanized spelling being a French transliteration. *Wiang* is Lao for a "settlement with a stockade", a reinforced fence that was built to keep out intruders, while *Jan* means "sandalwood". The wooden ramparts of the "City of Sandalwood" were evidently of little use for repelling invaders, for Vientiane was overrun or **occupied several times** by the Burmese, Chinese and, most spectacularly, by the **Siamese**. During one punitive raid in 1828, the Siamese levelled the entire city. Lao residents who were unable to escape into the jungle were taken prisoner and resettled in areas where they could be controlled and taxed by the victors. To this day, there are pockets of ethnic Lao in the Thai provinces surrounding Bangkok, descendants of Lao who survived the force-marched exile into Siam. For the next four decades, Vientiane was almost completely abandoned.

When **French explorers** arrived in 1867, they found the city all but reclaimed by the jungle. Within a few decades, the French controlled most of what is now Laos, Cambodia and Vietnam. When Vientiane was chosen by the French to be the capital of an administrative division of French Indochina, they rebuilt the city and laid out its system of roads. It is from this period, roughly 1899 to 1945, that the city's crumbling collection of French colonial mansions dates. However, the French presence in Vientiane was never very strong, and this is reflected in the modest number of old French buildings to be found here compared to the other former French Indochinese capital cities of Saigon, Hanoi and Phnom Penh.

1

The end of the First Indochina War between France and Vietnam in 1954 saw a flood of **Vietnamese refugees** from Ho Chi Minh's newly independent Democratic Republic of Vietnam enter Vientiane. As North Vietnamese troops began to infiltrate into South Vietnam while simultaneously occupying large areas of northeastern Laos, the United States started pouring massive amounts of unregulated aid into Vientiane, causing widespread corruption among government and military officials. In August 1960, a disgruntled army captain who resented the vast difference in lifestyles between his high-living superiors and his hard-bitten troops staged a successful **coup d'état**. This was soon followed by the Battle of Vientiane in December of that same year in which two Lao factions, one supplied by the US and the other by the USSR, managed to level whole blocks of the city with mortars and artillery.

As the **war in Vietnam** steadily escalated with growing US involvement, Laos was pulled deeper into the conflict, but while the thunder of bombs shook the countryside, the residents of the capital were relatively unaffected. For most of the war, Vientiane was like an island of calm surrounded by violent seas. A steady influx of refugees, shell-shocked villagers from the outer provinces, arrived in the city seeking sanctuary. The population of the capital swelled and rows of squatters' shanties appeared along the tree-lined avenues, contrasting sharply with the Mercedes-Benz automobiles of wartime profiteers.

When author Paul Theroux passed through Vientiane just before the end of the war he found a morally bankrupt kingdom with "baffling pretensions to Frenchness". After the fall of Saigon in 1975, the **Lao communists** suddenly gained power and, with coaching from the Vietnamese, set out to create the Lao People's Democratic Republic. The princes and prostitutes that Theroux made acquaintance with during his visit either fled or were imprisoned. Undesirables were rounded up and held captive on two small islands in the nearby Ang Nam Ngum Reservoir (see p.115), one for men and the other for women. But, perhaps owing to the Lao temperament, revolutionary fervour never reached the extremes seen in China or Cambodia. Still, a large percentage of the population of Vientiane found it necessary to escape across the Mekong and were replaced by immigrants from the former "liberated zone" in northeastern Laos, further changing Vientiane's ethnic make-up.

The 1980s were a time of quiet stagnation. Soviet aid helped ease the transition to **socialism**, but the majority of Lao with any education were in some form of exile, either "attending seminar" in a re-education camp located in some remote province or squatting in a Thai refugee camp while awaiting resettlement in a third country. Grand plans for progress were announced by the communist government and then promptly forgotten. Not until the collapse of the Soviet Union in 1991 and the suspension of Soviet aid was the government forced to rethink its opinions of capitalism. A number of **economic reforms** were implemented, leading to an explosion of new ventures and businesses. Recent years have also seen a trickle of former refugees, sporting new nationalities, return to Vientiane to visit long-missed relatives and sniff around for business opportunities. However, any accompanying political reforms that might have been expected have not been forthcoming, and the government does not tolerate dissent.

Arrival

Wattay International Airport is Vientiane's main airport as well as the terminus for most internal flights. If you're travelling overland from other regions of Laos or across the Friendship Bridge from Thailand, you'll end up at one of the two main bus stations, both of which are near the city centre. Either way, there's no need to panic to change money for your trip into town, as taxi drivers will happily accept Thai baht or American dollars if you don't have Lao kip.

By plane
Wattay Airport is located on Louang Phabang Avenue, roughly 6km west of downtown Vientiane. Airport facilities include **visa-on-arrival** ($30 plus one passport-sized photograph; see p.18 for more on visas), duty-free, exchange services and an upstairs restaurant. The easiest way to get to the city centre is by taxi ($3) – numerous tuk-tuk and car-taxi drivers will greet you as you emerge from the terminal. A cheaper option is to take a shared taxi in the form of a tuk-tuk or jumbo ($1). If money is really tight, just walk a few hundred metres from the terminal out to Louang Phabang Avenue, and hail a sawngth-aew coming from the north (2000K), which will drop you off at the main bus station next to the Morning Market in the city centre.

Via the Friendship Bridge
Completed in 1994, the **Thai–Lao Friendship Bridge** is the primary land crossing into Laos. The 1240-metre bridge spans the Mekong River at a point 5km west of Nong Khai in Thailand, and 20km east of Vientiane. **Minibuses** (10 baht) shuttle passengers across the bridge and leave every fifteen to twenty minutes between 8am and 7.30pm. The minibuses stop at Thai immigration control at the base of the bridge, where passengers must clear Thai customs before reboarding and continuing on to Lao immigration on the opposite side of the river. At the Lao terminal, you can get a fifteen-day **visa-on-arrival** ($30 plus a passport-sized photo; see p.18 for more on visas), and facilities run to duty-free, banks and a post office. Tuk-tuks ($3) and car-taxis ($4) for the thirty-minute run into the city centre can be found at the terminal, but the cheapest option is to catch the No. 14 bus, which stops at the bridge every forty minutes on its run between Thadua and Vientiane's main bus station next to the Morning Market (1000K). **Motorcycles** may cross the bridge, but you should have the registration papers with you.

By bus
Most **buses from the south** arrive at Vientiane's compact **main bus station**, next to the Morning Market (Talat Sao) on Khou Viang Road, about 1.5km from Nam Phou Place. From here it's only a short tuk-tuk ride to all the central hotels and guest houses. Most **buses from the north**, however, arrive at the **Khoua Louang bus stand** ("Khiw Lot Khua Luang" in Lao), near the Nong Douang Market, about 4km northwest of the city centre. From the Khoua Louang stand there are shared tuk-tuks into the centre (200K). Somewhat typically, other buses from the north may (or may not) stop at the sawngthaew station on Route 13 at the northern edge of town. Either way, the routine is the same with tuk-tuks providing a cheap shuttle service to your destination.

By boat
Speedboats and slow boats from the north arrive at **Tha Hua Kao Liaw pier**, located on the Mekong River 10km west of the centre of Vientiane. The only way to get to the city centre from the landing is by tuk-tuk (10,000K). No regular boat traffic arrives in Vientiane from points south.

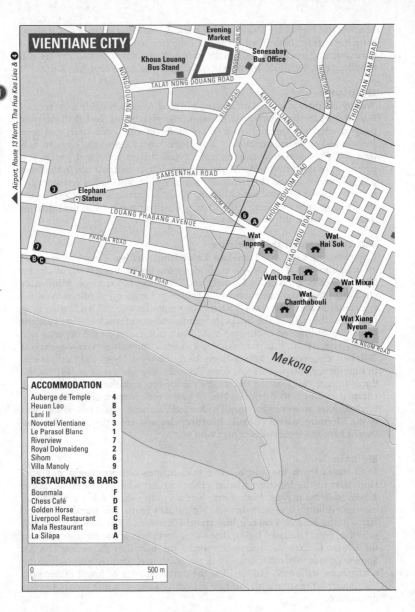

VIENTIANE CITY

Evening Market

Khoua Louang Bus Stand

Senesabay Bus Office

NONGDOUANG ROAD

NONGBOUATHONG RD

TALAT NONG DOUANG ROAD

SILOM ROAD

KHOUA LUANG ROAD

THONG YOM ROAD

THONG KHAN KAM ROAD

SAMSENTHAI ROAD

❸ Elephant Statue

LOUANG PHABANG AVENUE

SILOM ROAD

KHOUN BOULOM ROAD

❻ ❹

PHAGNA ROAD

CHAO ANOU ROAD

Wat Inpeng

Wat Hai Sok

❼

❽❻

FA NGUM ROAD

Wat Ong Teu

Wat Mixai

Wat Chanthabouli

Wat Xiang Nyeun

FA NGUM ROAD

Mekong

ACCOMMODATION

Auberge de Temple	4
Heuan Lao	8
Lani II	5
Novotel Vientiane	3
Le Parasol Blanc	1
Riverview	7
Royal Dokmaideng	2
Sihom	6
Villa Manoly	9

RESTAURANTS & BARS

Bounmala	F
Chess Café	D
Golden Horse	E
Liverpool Restaurant	C
Mala Restaurant	B
La Silapa	A

0   500 m

Information and city transport

The **Lao National Tourism Authority** (NTAL) operates out of an imposing building on Lane Xang Avenue, near the Morning Market (Mon–Fri
8am–5pm; ☎021/212248 or 212251). Apart from a few free pamphlets, however, the office and staff aren't of much assistance to tourists. You'll get better

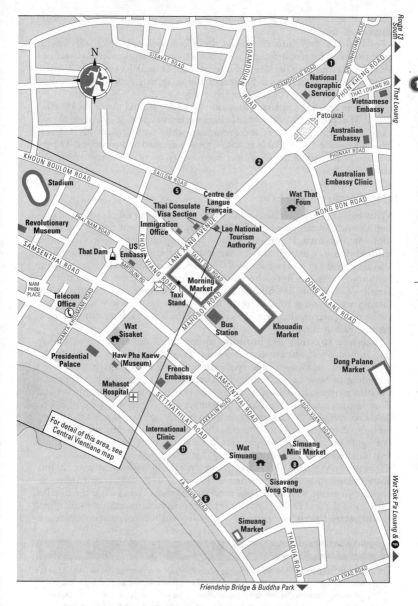

Friendship Bridge & Buddha Park ▼

information from talking to other travellers. For maps and reading material on Laos it's better to stock up in Thailand if possible, but in Vientiane itself the best bet is the Vientiane Book Center at 54/1 Pangkham Road (☎021/212031). Phimphone minimarkets and some of the more popular coffee shops, such as the *Scandinavian Bakery* and *Le Croissant D'Or* maintain noticeboards, displaying information on everything from film festivals, language classes, house rentals and motorbikes for sale to yoga classes and meditation sessions.

For **"what's on" info** check out the *Vientiane Times*, which also carries advertisements for restaurant specials. There's more in-depth information about living in the capital in the Women International Group's *Vientiane Guide* available at the Book Center on Pangkham Road, although it's oriented mainly towards the expatriate community.

There are two free city **maps** sometimes available around town; *The Vientiane Tourist Map*, published by the NTAL, offers a decent citywide orientation, a list of sites and a map of Vientiane Prefecture, while the excellent hand-drawn *Map of Vientiane*, also available at hotels, gives a detailed and accurate 3-D perspective of the city, although it does not identify many of the restaurants and hotels in town.

City transport

Vientiane is a very walkable city but **bicycles** are also an excellent way of getting around and can be rented for $1 per day at many guest houses and rental shops around town. If you don't fancy pedalling about in the tropical heat, **motorbikes** are easy to find and come in handy for exploring the areas around Vientiane; you can rent one for $6–10 per day, depending on the bike and your bargaining skills. You'll also be required to leave your passport as a deposit. Details of recommended **bike** and **motorbike outlets** can be found in the Listings section on p.109. Although travel speeds are relatively slow and the traffic rustic, negotiating Vientiane's cluttered roads at rush hour can take some getting used to at first.

Otherwise, **tuk-tuks** and **jumbos** can be a quick and efficient way of getting around. These often operate as a kind of bus system within the city (picking up people heading in vaguely the same direction), and charge per person according to how far you're going. Shared tuk-tuks generally ply frequently travelled routes, such as Lane Xang Avenue between the Morning Market and That Louang, and Louang Phabang Avenue; they charge a flat fee of 500K. Tuk-tuks can also be flagged down like taxis though you'll need to bargain with the drivers a bit. Many drivers inflate their prices slightly for foreigners, but figure on paying 1000K per person for distances of 1–2km, and adding a few hundred kip per kilometre beyond that.

Downtown Vientiane is too small to support a public transport system, but **bus routes** originating at the main bus station, next to the Morning Market, do connect Vientiane with nearby places on the Vientiane Plain such as the Buddha Park, Lao Pako and Dong Dok University. For destinations further afield, a fleet of **unmetered taxis**, consisting of banged-up old Toyotas, gathers outside the

Vientiane addresses

Finding an **address** in Vientiane can be something of a challenge. Street signs are confined to the centre, road names can bleed into one another and house numbers are generally useless – when asking directions, it helps to know a landmark in addition to the name of the street you're after. As elsewhere in Laos, local inhabitants often use monasteries as landmarks to identify parts of town: for example, Ban Wat Phaxai ("Wat Phaxai district") refers to the area around Wat Phaxai. When showing **addresses in this chapter**, we have given the road name but have generally omitted the house number and instead have given a brief description of location or a nearby landmark.

Morning Market, in the car park on Khou Viang Road. Prices are negotiable and are generally quoted in Thai baht, but drivers will accept Lao kip and American dollars. Hiring a driver for a day tour of sights within the city will cost in the region of $10; for trips out to Ang Nam Ngum (see p.115) expect to pay double that fare.

Accommodation

Vientiane now offers a wide range of tourist **accommodation** from cheap backpacker dives to 4-star hotels like the *Novotel Belvedere*. The majority of the city's seventy hotels and guest houses are located in the centre around Nam Phou Place, within the general area formed by Khoun Boulom Road and Lane Xang Avenue. However, other establishments, especially larger hotels, have opened up beyond this area, particularly along Lane Xang Avenue in the vicinity of Patouxai, as well as on Louang Phabang Avenue, a quick tuk-tuk ride into the centre.

Travellers on a very tight **budget** will find their options somewhat limited. Rooms at any one of the handful of budget standouts such as the *MIC* or *Saybaidee* tend to fill up very quickly, even in low season. There are still a large number of places in the $10 category but the majority of these tend to be extremely poor value with run-down, depressing, old rooms going for as much as $12. Budget hotels in the central area are generally housed in renovated older buildings. As many of them have a wide range of room types, from cheaper fan singles to expansive triples with air con and en-suite bathrooms, it's worth asking to see more than one room and always worth haggling as the price is never really fixed. Prices run from $2 for a dorm bed to between $4 and $8 for a single with fan. The cheaper places fill up fast so if you arrive late in the day you'll probably be looking at $10–12 for a fan room in an old building. It is not an uncommon sight to see late arrivals desperately pounding the pavement around the central district looking for a last-minute reasonably priced budget room. Until more places open up and competition increases, prices are unlikely to drop.

There are much better deals to be found in the **mid-range** establishments. For $15–20 you can buy yourself considerably more comfort, whether it's the luxuries of a standard hotel or the cosiness and hospitality of an upmarket guest house with a garden tucked away in a quiet side street. If you're willing and able to spend the extra money you can actually get something quite luxurious for $25 – worth bearing in mind when you see some of the complete dives that pass for hotels in Vientiane.

Moving further up the scale, a handful of new **expensive hotels** have now appeared on the scene, surpassing that old, three-star socialist gem, the *Lane Xang*. With the existing upmarket hotels struggling to fill their rooms, many managers are amenable to discounts, especially in low season. Before settling on a price at mid-range and high-end hotels, check whether service charge and tax are included in the quoted price. Major **credit cards** are accepted at the more expensive hotels.

Wherever you stay, your case will be helped if you are booking in for a few days and paying in dollars or baht. For **long-stay accommodation** – basically, anything over a few days – you should always push for a discount. Some hotels and guest houses even have set weekly and monthly rates, designed to accommodate expatriates working in Vientiane on short-term projects, and even those that don't will be open to negotiating a long-term room rate. For a list of most of the city's hotels with links to their homepages go to Ⓦ www.laos–hotels.com.

Central Vientiane

Anou Hotel Corner of Heng Boun and Chao Anou rds ☎ 021/213630, ℱ 213635. Forty unremarkable but perfectly decent standard hotel rooms in a quiet but convenient location. Spacious, cool lobby and all the usual facilities. ❺

Chaleunxay Hotel Khou Viang Rd, west of the Morning Market ☎ 021/223407, ℱ 223529. The location of this large business hotel on a big busy street leaves much to be desired, but it's a good deal for Vientiane. The fact that it's mostly Thai businessmen staying here rather than farang tourists makes it a better deal than a lot of tourist hostels in the centre. ❸–❹

Day Inn Hotel 059/3 Pangkham Rd, behind the *Lao Hotel Plaza* ☎ 021/223847, ℱ 222984, ℮ dayinn@laotel.com. Located just a few steps away from the bustle of Samsenthai Rd, the *Day Inn* offers light, airy rooms fitted out with rattan furniture, potted plants, and huge TVs. A well-run, mid-range hotel combining all the mod-cons with a real tropical Fifties ambience. One of the few hotels in the city with a bit of style and attitude and excellent value for money. ❺

Douang Deuane, 6 Nokeo Koummane Rd ☎ 021/222301, ℱ 222300. Standard mid-range hotel rooms with a handful of facilities. Smart, efficient staff, newish gloss and location near the Mekong make this a worthy option, though the windowless first-floor rooms are best avoided. Motorbike and bicycle rental, as well as airport pick-up. ❺

Haysoke I 083/1–2 Hengboon St ☎ 021/219711, ℱ 219755. Chinese-run place with no-nonsense, good value, fairly-priced rooms. *Haysoke II* at 040/20 Chao Anou Rd (☎ 021/240888, ℱ 240889), is of similar good value but caters more for budget travellers. ❸–❹

Hua Guo 359 Samsenthai Rd, opposite the PVO and Boualian Travel. Singles and doubles with air-con, phone, hot water and satellite TV for hostel prices. ❸–❹

Lane Xang Fa Ngum Rd ☎ 021/214102, ℱ 214108. Although the Russians have gone, echoes of the socialist design and aesthetics in Laos' first post-liberalisation hotel remain: huge bathrooms with oceanic sinks, Russian water-heaters and even a beauty-parlour-style hair dryer above the toilet in the executive suite. With its big empty lobby and spacious grounds along the quay, this 109-room hotel maintains the ambience of a socialist hotel built for capitalists. Facilities include badminton courts, snooker parlour, putting green and a kidney-shaped swimming pool. Tremendously good value. ❺

Lani I Setthathilat Rd, opposite Wat Ong Teu ☎ 021/216103, ℱ 215639. Supremely pleasant accommodation in a centrally located house, decorated with antiques and handicrafts, with the added attraction of a terrace dining area. All twelve rooms have air con, hot water and phone, but it's worth the extra $5 to upgrade to the priciest room for that extra bit of space. Reservations recommended. ❻

Lao Hotel Plaza 63 Samsenthai Rd ☎ 021/218800, ℱ 218808, ℮ lph@laoplazahotel.com. Located in the heart of town, this huge luxury hotel is popular with Thai holidaymakers and a good choice if you want something modern. All 142 rooms have air con, hot water, IDD phone, satellite television and refrigerator. Tucked away in the imposing complex are a wide range of facilities: boutique shops, a health club, swimming pool, a decent hair salon, a popular nightclub and an array of restaurants. The hotel has been known to offer substantial discounts. ❻

MIC (Ministry of Information and Culture), Manthatoulat Rd ☎ 021/212362. This cheap, fifteen-room guest house is the budget travellers' perennial favourite. While it's not a dorm, backpackers travelling solo tend to link up to split the cost of the three-bed rooms. The stairwells are still a bit nasty, but the rooms, all with attached bathrooms, are reasonably clean. If it's full you can always try to get in at *Saybaidee* and the *Mixok*, which are both very close by. ❶–❸

Mixay 039 Nokeo Koummane Rd ☎ 021/217023, ℮ mixay039@hotmail.com. Perhaps the cheapest place in town, with spartan but super cheap rooms ranging from fan singles to triples with either attached bathrooms or shared facilities. There's hot water and a reception room with colour TV. Two of the rooms have balconies overlooking the street. Fills up very quickly. ❶–❸

Mixok 188 Setthathilat Rd, next door to ITIC Computer ☎ 021/251606. Very popular backpacker hostel similar to the *Mixay* with singles, doubles, triples, and dorms with shared facilities. Rock-bottom prices and a terrific location on the city's prettiest street. This one has the look and feel of a real hostel. ❶–❸

Orchid Guesthouse 33 Fa Ngum Rd ☎ 021/

△ Wat Simuang

252825, ⓕ021/216588. Given its location right on the main restaurant strip and facing the Mekong, the prices here are extremely reasonable. One of the few budget hotels with a view of the Mekong. ④

Pangkham Hotel 72/6 Pangkham Rd ⓣ021/217053. The *Pangkham* and the *Phone Paseuth* have now merged with the two hotels sharing one lobby and check-in. All the rooms are clean with en-suite bathrooms, hot water, telephone and TV. But air-con rooms cost fifty percent more. Located just north of the Nam Phou Fountain, you can't get more central than this. ④

Praseuth 312 Samsenthai Rd ⓣ021/217932. Old and run-down but cheap, this backpacker establishment offers very basic rooms with shared facilities. The air-con rooms are only $1 more than fan. Think of it as a last-resort option. ③

Santisouk 77/79 Nokeo Koummane Rd ⓣ021/215303. Situated above the *Santisouk Restaurant*, with nine budget air-con rooms and an upstairs balcony. It's run-down and certainly no great shakes but is well known on the backpacker circuit because it's cheap. ②

Saybaidee Setthathilat Rd. One of the top backpacker options and in the same class as *Mixok* and *Mixay*. Very low prices and a great location mean it fills up very quickly. ①–③

Settha Palace Hotel 6 Pang Kham St ⓣ021/217581, ⓕ217583, ⓔsettha@laonet.net, ⓦwww.setthapalace.com. Vientiane is the only Southeast Asian capital without a historic colonial-era hotel. This palatial 1932 building which has just undergone a four-year renovation should go a long way towards filling that gap. Aside from the French period furniture, the hotel's 29 rooms are totally modern with all mod-cons including mini-bars and safes. Beautiful colonial architecture, period furnishings, landscaped gardens. They even pick you up in a London taxi. ⑧

Sihom Sihom Rd, along the dirt alley to the west of *La Silapa* restaurant ⓣ021/214562. Eleven tastefully decorated rooms fitted out with rattan double beds, air-con, refrigerator, and satellite TV. The a/c rooms are only $1 more than fan. Particularly recommended for couples travelling on a budget. ②

Syri Saigon Rd ⓣ021/212682, ⓕ217252. A large house on a quiet lane in the Chao Anou residential district, with spacious double and triple air-con rooms and a nice balcony. Motorbikes and bikes for rent. ④

Tai-Pan 2-12 François Nginn Rd, near the Mekong (ⓣ021/216906–9, ⓕ259-7908). Probably Vientiane's best-value small business hotel.

Rooms, and the array of suites, come with all mod cons. There's also a business centre with email service, sauna and fitness room. ③–④

Thawee 64 Du Puits Rd ⓣ021/217903, ⓕ251609. Comfortable, well-decorated rooms for less money than a lot of the older, run-down places charge. Fan rooms are half the air-con room price. When there's a lull in business they drop their "high season" price by thirty percent, making it about the best deal in town. Because it's good value it's often full, so be sure to book in advance. ③–④

Vannasinh 51 Phnom Penh Rd, near Chao Anou Rd ⓣ021/218707, ⓕ222020. Very well-known backpacker place with fan doubles and more spacious air-con doubles, all en suite. Some of the cheaper fan doubles can feel cramped, despite the high ceilings, but the air-con doubles are okay. With places like the *Thawee* right down the street, this is no longer as good a deal as it once was. ④

Outside the centre

Auberge de Temple Sikhotabong Rd ⓣ021/214844, ⓕ214844. Down a quiet lane off Louang Phabang Ave, this French-owned guest house has eight attractively decorated rooms, some with baths, plus a four-bed dorm. It's west of the city centre, but close to a slew of casual sunset restaurants and bars. Ten percent discount for long-term stays. ③–④

Heuan Lao Off Samsenthai Rd, near Wat Simuang ⓣ021/216258, ⓕ216258. This friendly upmarket guest house is located on a quiet lane opposite a park and offers singles, doubles and triples, all with en-suite bathrooms. ③–④

Lani II off Sailom Rd, near Lane Xang Ave ⓣ021/213022, ⓕ215639. Tucked away on a quiet lane off Sailom Rd, the Lani II has all the mellow atmosphere of the *Lani I* (see p.90) for slightly less money. The veranda, complete with wicker furniture, makes a great spot for a lazy breakfast. Accommodation consists of seven tastefully decorated air-con singles and doubles, the more expensive sporting en-suite bathrooms with hot water. Although it's not so well located as its sister establishment, it's still only a brisk walk to the town centre. ⑤

Le Parasol Blanc Sibounheuang Rd ⓣ021/215090 or 216091, ⓕ222290. Quiet hotel set in a leafy compound just north of Patouxai and popular with French tourists. Swimming pool and a good restaurant serving French, Lao and Thai food, with an outdoor dining area, make this a fine place to relax. Because of the wide verandas some of the rooms are a bit too dark, but all is forgiven after morning coffee under the vines in the garden. ⑥

Novotel Belvedere Vientiane Louang Phabang Ave, Kilometre 2 ☎021/213570–1, ⒻØ213572–3. The best of the modern hotels in Vientiane, the *Novotel* has a wide array of facilities, including a pool, 24-hour business centre with email service, airport reservation desk, French restaurant and tennis courts. If that's not enough, try the beer garden, bar, sauna, health club, snooker hall, game room, Lao massage parlour, bookstore, or disco. Be sure to try out the excellent Sunday brunch as well. All of the two hundred-plus rooms come with the minibar, air con, satellite television and IDD telephone. If you really want to splash out there's a range of suites costing up to $450. ⑧

Riverview corner of Fa Ngum and Sithan Nua ☎021/216231, Ⓕ216232. Located a few kilometres west of the town centre in the middle of the strip of riverside bars, this Thai-owned hotel's quiet rooms are in much better shape than the run-down exterior suggests. Spacious and clean, the rooms have air-con, hot water and phones. An extra $10 will secure a room with a view of the Mekong. ⑤

Royal Dokmaideng Lane Xang Ave, near Patouxai ☎021/214455, Ⓕ214454. Commonly known as the "Royal Hotel", this five-storey three-star hotel is a suitable option for business travellers. There's a business centre with email and a herbal sauna and nightclub for winding down. Quite good if you like big hotels and don't mind being on Lane Xang Avenue. ⑥

Villa Manoly Ban Simuang, next to Honour International School ☎021/212282, Ⓕ218907. East of the city centre, around the corner from Wat Simuang, this attractive villa, with a pleasant upstairs terrace, stands in spacious grounds with a swimming pool just a short walk from the river. The singles and doubles all have high ceilings and en-suite hot showers. ⑤

The City

A humble fountain in the middle of a square marks the heart of **downtown Vientiane**, though grandiose monuments may suggest otherwise. The fountain is the centrepiece of **Nam Phou Place**, though these days, with the increase in traffic, the square looks more like an oddly shaped roundabout. Situated in a quarter built by the French, Nam Phou Place lies at the heart of a cosmopolitan, commercial district now populated by Vietnamese, Chinese and a smattering of Indians, as well as Lao. Here, you'll find the city's greatest concentration of accommodation, restaurants and shops catering to visitors, although you'll have to go a bit further afield to find the capital's hottest nightlife venues, which are discreetly hidden away from centre.

With a few exceptions, most of Vientiane's sights are within comfortable walking distance of Nam Phou Place. Three main streets run parallel to the river to form the backbone of the city centre, cutting across narrower streets to form an easily deciphered grid. Tree-lined **Setthathilat Road**, just south of Nam Phou Place, is unarguably the city's most scenic thoroughfare, particularly the west end, with its four monasteries. Further north runs **Samsenthai Road**, Vientiane's principal commercial district and site of the massive *Lao Hotel Plaza*, as well as the **Lao Revolutionary Museum**, an anachronistic hangover from the days of banner-hoisting socialism. **Fa Ngum Road**, fronting the river, has recently lost some of its behemoth raintrees to the renovation work that is supposedly intended to spruce up the riverfront area. A row of refreshment stands on the bank of the river are favoured vantage points for viewing sunsets. Fa Ngum follows the river as it bends southwest and skirts behind the Presidential Palace. The palace is off-limits to visitors, but the **Haw Pha Kaew**, which occupies the western corner of the palace compound, has been converted into a museum, housing the largest collection of Lao art and antiquities in the country. Roughly opposite the Haw Pha Kaew, across Setthathilat Road, stands **Wat Sisaket**, a picturesque Buddhist

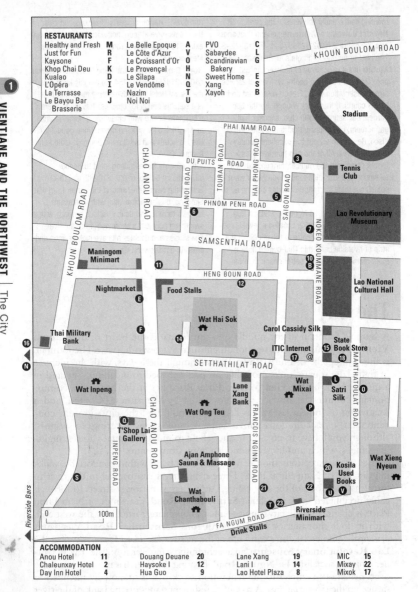

RESTAURANTS

Healthy and Fresh	**M**	Le Belle Epoque	**A**	PVO	**C**
Just for Fun	**R**	Le Côte d'Azur	**V**	Sabaydee	**L**
Kaysone	**F**	Le Croissant d'Or	**O**	Scandinavian	**G**
Khop Chai Deu	**K**	Le Provençal	**H**	Bakery	
Kualao	**D**	Le Silapa	**I**	Sweet Home	**E**
L'Opéra	**P**	Le Vendôme	**N**	Xang	**S**
La Terrasse	**T**	Nazim	**Q**	Xayoh	**B**
Le Bayou Bar	**J**	Noi Noi	**U**		
Brasserie					

KHOUN BOULOM ROAD

Stadium

PHAI NAM ROAD

CHAO ANOU ROAD

DU PUITS ROAD

TOURAN ROAD

HAI PHONG ROAD

HANOI ROAD

SAIGON ROAD

3

Tennis Club

PHNOM PENH ROAD

5

6

Lao Revolutionary Museum

7

NOKEO KOUMMANE ROAD

SAMSENTHAI ROAD

10

B

KHOUN BOULOM ROAD

Maningom Minimart

11

HENG BOUN ROAD

12

Lao National Cultural Hall

Nightmarket

E

Food Stalls

Wat Hai Sok

Carol Cassidy Silk

Thai Military Bank

F

14

J

ITIC Internet

State Book Store

17 @

15

18

SETTHATHILAT ROAD

16

N

Wat Inpeng

CHAO ANOU ROAD

Lane Xang Bank

Wat Mixai

Satri Silk

L

O

Wat Ong Teu

FRANCOIS NGINN ROAD

P

MANTHATOULAT ROAD

Q

T'Shop Lai Gallery

INPENG ROAD

Ajan Amphone Sauna & Massage

20

Kosila Used Books

Wat Xieng Nyeun

S

Wat Chanthabouli

21

22

U

V

Riverside Bars

0   100m

FA NGUM ROAD

T

23

Riverside Minimart

Drink Stalls

ACCOMMODATION

Anou Hotel	**11**	Douang Deuane	**20**	Lane Xang	**19**	MIC	**15**
Chaleunxay Hotel	**2**	Haysoke I	**12**	Lani I	**14**	Mixay	**22**
Day Inn Hotel	**4**	Hua Guo	**9**	Lao Hotel Plaza	**8**	Mixok	**17**

monastery containing what is thought to be the oldest structure in Vientiane.

The eastern edge of the city centre is defined by Vientiane's principal thoroughfare, **Lane Xang Avenue**, which begins at the Presidential Palace and marches away from the river past **Talat Sao** (the Morning Market), a group of buildings with temple-like roofs that shelter numerous shops selling all and

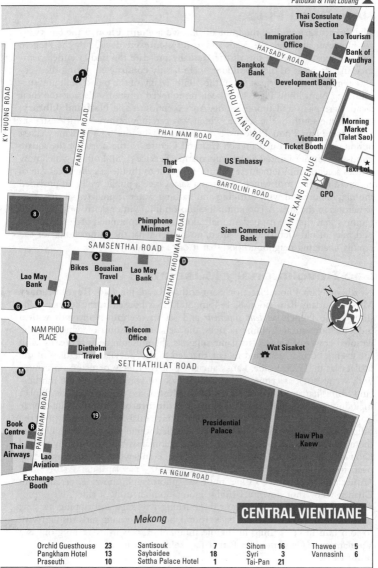

Orchid Guesthouse	23	Santisouk	7	Sihom	16	Thawee	5
Pangkham Hotel	13	Saybaidee	18	Syri	3	Vannasinh	6
Praseuth	10	Settha Palace Hotel	1	Tai-Pan	21		

sundry. The broad avenue terminates at **Patouxai**, a massive victory arch, around which are scattered numerous embassies, international organizations and government buildings. Just beyond the Patouxai monument, the road forks, its right branch leading off towards **That Louang**, the golden-spired Buddhist stupa and national symbol of Laos.

Nam Phou Place

The district surrounding the fountain, known as **Nam Phou**, is the city's oldest. However, although the roads and grid system were devised by the French, few of the structures in this district actually pre-date the mid-twentieth century. In fact, most of these buildings were hastily constructed during the freewheeling days of American aid in the 1950s. Many of the oldest buildings surrounding Nam Phou Place have been remodelled in the last decade and their facades are plain and uninteresting. An exception is the **National Library**, located due south of the square, which was carefully restored with Australian assistance. Nam Phou Place itself is dominated by one of Vientiane's tallest buildings, the abandoned French Cultural Centre. To the north of the square stands the former United States Information Service (USIS) office, which now houses a centre for Vietnamese culture. Adjacent to this lies a cylindrical slab of concrete under a roof which serves as a *sala*. Once a public well that provided the neighbourhood with drinking and bathing water, it predates all the other structures in the area. A Lao cultural taboo on filling in or destroying old wells requires that they be capped and left alone, so the continued presence of this odd relic of old Vientiane is assured, no matter what the future holds for the rapidly changing neighbourhood that it once served.

Lao Revolutionary Museum

North of Nam Phou Place, on Samsenthai Road, the **Lao Revolutionary Museum** (daily 8am–noon & 1–4pm; 3000K) is housed in the former mansion of the French *résident supérieur* and set in overgrown grounds with a hideous fountain and plumeria trees, the delicate blossoms of which are the national flower of Laos. As its name suggests, the museum deals primarily with the events, both ancient and recent, that led to the "inevitable victory" of the proletariat in 1975. Inside, Laos's ancient past is crudely depicted on canvas, with scenes such as crimson-clad Lao patriots of yore liberating the motherland from Thai and Burmese "feudalists". Most of the best artefacts on display, including a wonderfully detailed **Khmer sculpture of Ganesh** and a bronze frog-drum, possibly used in ancient rain-making rituals, don't fit neatly into the official socialist story-line and sadly are labelled vaguely or not at all. Upstairs there are more crude oils: bearded French colonialists bullwhip tightly trussed Lao villagers or toss Lao tots down a well. Black-and-white **photographs** take over to tell the story of the struggle against "the Japanese fascists" and "American imperialists". One must-see photograph shows a certain Thit Chanto who "shot down a F105D fighter-bomber using a rifle". He is pictured, rifle in hand, standing over the burning wreckage and ripping his shirt open in defiance, while in the background, bouquet-waving girls rush forward to join him in celebrating his heroic moment. Also worth checking out is a Vietnamese-made statue of a Pathet Lao soldier cast in fully fledged socialist-realism style.

Setthathilat Road

Running parallel to and one block south of Samsenthai Road, **Setthathilat Road**, with its shady trees and monasteries, is the city's most attractive street. Not all of the monasteries are particularly deserving of attention, however. If time is limited, the four that lie at the street's western end – wats Ong Teu, Mixai, Inpeng and Hai Sok – could be skipped in favour of **Wat Sisaket** and **Wat Simuang** at the eastern end.

The Lao wat

The **wat**, or Buddhist **monastery**, is the centrepiece of most villages populated by ethnic Lao. Here, a contingent of monks and novices lives, providing the laypeople with an outlet for **merit-making** (see p.361). The wat also serves as a hub for social gatherings, and, during annual festivals and Buddhist holy days, a site for entertainment. Sometimes referred to as a "temple" in English, the wat is actually composed of a number of religious and secular structures, some of which could also be described as a temple. The *sim* is usually the grandest structure in the monastery grounds, as it houses the monastery's principal Buddha images, as well as being the place where monks are ordained. The *that*, or **stupa**, is generally a pyramid or bell-shaped structure which contains holy relics: usually a cache of small Buddhas. Occasionally, a Lao *that* will be the reputed repository of a splinter of bone belonging to the historic Buddha himself, while miniature stupas, or *that kaduk*, contain the ashes of deceased adherents. The *haw tai* is a solid structure, usually raised high off the ground, for storing palm-leaf manuscripts, and *kuti* are monks' quarters. Because the latter two buildings are not considered as important as other religious structures in the monastery grounds, they are not as frequently restored, and are thus most likely to exude that "timeless Asia" charm. Minor buildings sometimes found at a wat include a bell tower and a *sala*, or open-air pavilion. Many monasteries have a venerable specimen of a bodhi (*Ficus religiosa*), a wonderfully shady tree of spade-shaped leaves that is said to have sheltered the Buddha while he meditated his way to enlightenment.

Because the wat and resident monks depend on adherents for support, the extravagance of a monastery's **decoration** is directly related to the amount of cashflow in the host village or town. In poor villages, the wat may consist of just a *sim*: a large but simple hut-like structure, raised on stilts without any ornamentation. The only clue to the outsider that this is a monastery will be the freshly laundered monk's robes hanging out to dry alongside a piece of junk metal or war scrap, such as an old artillery-shell casing, which when struck serves as a bell to wake the monks or call them to assemble.

Wat Sisaket

East of Nam Phou Place, on Setthathilat Road, **Wat Sisaket** (daily 8am–noon & 1–4pm; 2000K) is the oldest wat in Vientiane. Constructed by King Anouvong (Chao Anou) in 1818, the monastery was the site of a ceremony in which Lao lords and nobles swore an oath of loyalty to the king. During the 1828 sack of Vientiane by the Siamese, this was the only monastery not put to the torch and, once the smoke had cleared, the Siamese brought the surviving Lao nobility here and made them swear another oath of loyalty, this time to their new overlords. Later, in 1893, the whole ceremony was repeated again before new masters – the French.

Surrounded by a tile-roofed cloister, the *sim* contains some charming, though water-stained, **murals** similar in style to those found at Bangkok's Wat Phra Kaew. The murals, together with the niches in the upper walls containing small Buddha images, and the ornate ceiling, are best taken in while kneeling on the floor (taking care not to point your feet towards the altar – see p.61 for temple etiquette). The Buddha images on the altar are not particularly notable, but a splendidly ornate candle holder of carved wood situated before the altar is an example of nineteenth-century Lao woodcarving at its best.

Outside, the interior walls of the **cloister** echo those of the *sim*, with countless niches from which peer diminutive Buddhas in twos and threes. Lining the galleries are larger images that survived the destruction of 1828 and, in a locker at the western wall, a heap of Buddhas that did not. The shaded galleries are a cool and pleasant place to linger and soak up the atmosphere. Breaching the wall that runs along Lane Xang Avenue, the structure with the multi-tiered roof is the monastery's former **library** (closed to the public), where its palm-leaf manuscripts were once kept.

The Presidential Palace and Haw Pha Kaew

Opposite Wat Sisaket stands the **Presidential Palace**, an impressive French Beaux Arts-style structure, built to house the French colonial governor, and nowadays used mainly for government ceremonies. Just west of the palace, the **Haw Pha Kaew** (daily 8am–noon & 1–4pm; 2000K), once the king's personal Buddhist temple, now functions as a **museum of art and antiquities**. Said to date from the mid-sixteenth century, the structure was destroyed by marauding Siamese during the sack of Vientiane in 1828 and was later earmarked for restoration by the French. The temple is named for the **Emerald Buddha**, or Pha Kaew, which, along with the Pha Bang, the most sacred Buddha image in Laos, was pilfered by the Siamese in 1779 and carried off to their capital. The Pha Bang was eventually returned to Laos and is enshrined in its namesake city of Louang Phabang, but the Pha Kaew remains in Bangkok to this day, much to the resentment of Lao Buddhists.

The museum houses the finest collection of Lao art in the country. Bronze **Buddhas**, many looted of the inlay that once decorated their eyes, line the terrace surrounding the building. Inside are some exquisite works, one of the most striking being a Buddha in the "Calling for Rain" pose (standing with arms to the sides and fingers pointing to the ground) and sporting a jewel-encrusted navel. Also of note are a pair of eighteenth-century terracotta *apsara*, or celestial dancers, and a highly detailed "naga throne" from Xiang Khouang that once served as a pedestal for a Buddha image. Next to the throne stands an elaborate *hao thian*, or candle holder, of ornately carved wood and almost identical to one still in use at Wat Sisaket (see p.97). An arched metal rod attached to the wood is where the lighted candles were placed. On the lawn outside the museum stand outsized bronze **statues** of a kow-towing Lao boy and girl, which were once part of a tableau that included the statue of explorer Auguste Pavie. The Frenchman's statue is now located inside the French embassy compound across the street. Sheltered under an adjacent pavilion is a sample stone urn from the Plain of Jars, but this small, broken jar is a rather poor specimen and not really typical of those at the site.

Wat Simuang

Roughly 1km east of Haw Pha Kaew, down Setthathilat Road, sits **Wat Simuang**. While Vientiane has its share of Buddhist monasteries, this wat stands out in terms of the number of worshippers it receives, the numerous vendors stationed outside the walls giving some indication of its popularity. These pavement stalls sell all the ingredients for a proper tray of offerings: flowers, fruit, incense and candles. The monastery itself was built on an ancient Khmer site, the ruins of which are piled behind the *sim* and consist of laterite bricks with traces of stucco ornamentation. The *sim* of Wat Simuang houses the city's *lak meaung*, a sacred stone pillar. It is believed that the guardian spirit of Vientiane inhabits the pillar, which was consecrated with a human sacrifice at the time of the city's founding. Covered with gold leaf and wrapped in sacred cloth, the pillar is the centrepiece of an altar crowded with Buddha images. That great multitudes of worshippers come here is evident from a glance at the ceiling, coal-black with a thick coating of soot that constantly rises from sputtering candles and smouldering joss sticks.

By quietly taking a seat on the floor you can observe the **rituals** of devotees seeking answers or favours. Two baby-sized, crude images resting on their own pillows are the main focus of the worshippers' attention. After a question is posed or a favour requested, the devotee attempts to lift one of the images while kneeling towards the altar. Being able to lift the image three times over one's head is considered an auspicious sign. Worshippers whose wishes are granted must return and appease the guardian spirit with an offering. Marigolds, coconuts and bananas are particularly popular tokens of gratitude. In the **monastery grounds** surrounding the *sim* are a dozen or so brightly painted sculptures of animals, Buddhist-Hindu deities and mythological figures from Lao legends, making this a favourite playground for local kids.

On a small wedge of land outside the south wall of the monastery towers a monolithic **statue of King Sisavang Vong**, who reigned from 1904 to 1959. The statue survived the revolution, having been executed by a Soviet sculptor and presented to the Lao government in 1972 after a visit to the Soviet Union by King Sisavang Vatthana. Ironically, only a year after the statue was erected in 1974 the royalist government collapsed. A plaque that was once attached to the pedestal has long been missing and, if asked, many locals will only be able to say that the massive statue depicts "an old king".

Patouxai

It has been said that, along with coffee and baguettes, the Lao inherited a taste for pompous town planning from the French. **Lane Xang Avenue**, leading off north from Setthathilat Road, was to be Vientiane's Champs Elysées and **Patouxai** its Arc de Triomphe. While it would be impossible to mistake seedy Lane Xang Avenue for Paris's most famous thoroughfare, if you were to stand at a fair distance and squint, you might be able to convince yourself that Patouxai resembles its Parisian inspiration. Popularly known as *anusawali* (Lao for "monument"), this massive ferro-concrete Arch of Victory (daily 8am–5pm; 1000K), situated in a roundabout at the end of Lane Xang Avenue, 1km from the Presidential Palace, was built in the late 1950s to commemorate casualties of war on the side of the Royal Lao Government. Said to have been completed with concrete donated by the US government for the construction of an airport, the structure has been jokingly referred to as "the vertical runway". If the story is true, then Patouxai is also perhaps the only thing left to show for the unregulated millions of dollars of "aid" that were pumped into Laos during the early years of American involvement in Indochina. After the revolution, the arch was given its current name and partially redecorated so the new government could feel more comfortable with this behemoth reminder of the detested royalists in their midst.

Up close, Patouxai looks somewhat crude and unfinished, but the **view of Vientiane** from the top is worth the climb. A handful of vendors selling souvenirs and refreshments are sheltered by a ceiling adorned with **reliefs** of the Hindu deities – Rahu devouring the sun, Vishnu, Brahma, and Indra on Airavata, the three-headed elephant. Decorating the walls just below the ceiling are characters from the *Ramayana*. Patouxai is best visited in the early morning before the structure has had time to absorb too much heat from the sun's rays.

That Louang

One and a half kilometres east of Patouxai stands the Buddhist stupa, **That Louang**, Laos's most important religious building and its national symbol (daily except Mon & public holidays 8am–noon & 1–4pm; 3000K). The present building dates from the 1930s and is a reconstruction – the original That Louang is thought to have been built by King Setthathilat in the mid-sixteenth century, and it is his statue that is perched jauntily on a pedestal in front of the stupa. Archeological evidence suggests that, like most central and southern Lao Buddhist structures of significance, That Louang was built on top of an ancient Khmer site. What the original Buddhist stupa looked like is a mystery, but a Dutch trader, Gerritt van Wuysthoff, who visited Vientiane in 1641, left an awestruck account of the gold-covered "pyramid" he saw there. Between then and the early nineteenth century, the stupa was embellished and restored periodically, but a punitive raid on Vientiane by the Siamese left the capital deserted after most of its inhabitants fled or were force-marched to Siam. When French explorers Francis Garnier and Louis Delaporte stumbled upon That Louang in 1867, it was overgrown by jungle, but still largely intact. A few years later, Chinese-led bandits plundered the stupa looking for gold, and left it a pile of rubble. A photo on display in the Revolutionary museum, taken in the late 1800s to commemorate the visit of a group of Frenchmen, gives some indication of the extent of the devastation.

A French attempt at **restoration** was made in 1900, after which the stupa was disparagingly referred to as the "Morin Spike", a snipe at the architect, whose idea of a Buddhist stupa resembled a railroad spike turned on its head. Dissatisfaction with the design eventually led to another attempt in the 1930s. Using sketches done by Delaporte as a model, a re-restoration in brick and stucco was carried out over four years. The results of this effort are what you see today. The tapering **golden spire** of the main stupa is 45m tall and rests on a plinth of stylized lotus petals, which crowns a mound reminiscent of the first-century-BC Buddhist stupa at Sanchi, India. The main stupa is surrounded on all sides by a total of thirty short, spiky stupas, which can be reached via any of four gates in the crenellated walls that support the monument. The whole is in turn surrounded by a cloistered wall, vaguely Chinese in style. Within the **cloisters** are a collection of very worn Buddha images, some of which may have been enshrined in the original Khmer temple that once occupied the site. Until just a few years ago, only the stupas' spires were "gilded", but with the passing years, more and more gold paint has been applied, so that now even the inner walls and their crenellations are gold. The effects are best seen just before sunset or during the evenings leading up to the **That Louang Festival** (see Basics, p.56), when the stupa is festooned with strings of lights and moths the size of sparrows circle and cling to its glowing surface.

Wat Sok Pa Louang

Approximately 3km southeast of central Vientiane, **Wat Sok Pa Louang** is mainly of interest to enthusiasts of **herbal sauna** and **traditional massage**. Originally outside the city limits and surrounded by forest, the wat now lies in a suburb of Vientiane that spreads out from the highway south to the village of Thadua. The easiest way to get here is by tuk-tuk (3000K). Wood-fired saunas are started early in the morning and tended all day, enveloping bathers in clouds of healing steam. Impurities are sweated out and the vapours of medicinal herbs soak in. Traditional Lao massage is available as well and is said to interact with the effects of the sauna (see p.66). Visitors are reminded to dress modestly and to bring a sarong to wear into the sauna. A soak in the sauna is 2000K, plus 5000K per forty minutes of massage.

Other temples

The majority of Vientiane's most famous temples are found close to the Mekong – there are twenty temples between the riverbank and the length of Setthathilat Road from Wat Simuong to Wat Tainiai, an area that roughly corresponds to the old city. Most visitors will only have the time and interest to visit the very best of these, such as Wat Sisaket, Wat Simuang, and the Haw Pha Kaew, but there are over a dozen other temples scattered across the city in an east–west arch to the north that seldom see any tourists and which make a great excuse for a bicycle ride through Vientiane's quiet outer neighbourhoods. Once outside of the tourist centre, you'll find a completely different Vientiane that most tourists don't even realise exists, where children play games in the dirt lanes, neighbours casually chat under the palm and banana trees, and saffron-robed monks with shade umbrellas return to their temples after errands.

Eating

The culinary scene in Vientiane has improved remarkably since the early 1990s, when ordering a plate of fried rice usually meant precisely that – fried rice, no meat, no vegetables. The huge rise in tourism and the establishment of a permanent foreign community have given rise to restaurants catering to virtually every taste, from sausage and sauerkraut to Korean BBQ. Vientiane now has a large concentration of French and Italian restaurants, the best of which compare favourably to Bangkok. Although the prices in such restaurants are prohibitive for Lao, foreign visitors will be pleasantly surprised by the comparatively low cost of eating out. If you plan to head out in the provinces for a while, take the opportunity to indulge in the capital's Western culinary offerings before hitting the trail into the provinces where in most towns you'll find yourself eating a lot of fried rice and noodles. Most of the city's **restaurants** are scattered all over centre leading down towards the river. In as much as Vientiane has a main restaurant strip, **Fa Ngum Road** is it.

Food stalls, markets and cheap eateries

For cheap, homely cooking seek out the outdoor food stalls found near any of the city's markets. **Riverside food stalls** can be found along the Mekong on Fa Ngum Road approximately opposite Wat Chanthabouli, with most offering Lao staples like *tam màk hung* (spicy papaya salad), *pîng kai* (grilled chicken) and refreshing fruit shakes from morning until nearly midnight. These stalls also provide an excellent spot to enjoy sunset over the Mekong.

A **night market** offering similar fare, and with tables on the street, sets up on Khoun Boulom Road and along Heng Boun Road in the early evening and stays open till about 10pm. This area is a popular night spot for cheap Chinese, Lao and Vietnamese food with several *fõe* (noodle soup) stalls, *mi pet* restaurants, fruit stands and French bread vendors all nearby and the ice cream and pastry shops of **Bakery Street** just around the corner on Chao Anou Road (the best of the more permanent eateries are listed below). A more extensive night market for good Lao food is at **Dong Palane Market** on Ban Fai Road near Wat Ban Fai – you'll find all the Lao standards on offer. For daytime food, try the **Morning Market stalls** on Lane Xang Avenue near the Lao National Tourism Authority office: here you'll find good Lao-style *khào pûn* (noodles with sauce), *tam màk hung* and more of those excellent shakes. But if it's *khào biak sèn* (rice noodles in .chicken broth) you're after, hop into a tuk-tuk in the afternoon and head straight for Wat Phaxai on That Khao Road, where you'll find noodle shops dishing up bowls of this soup second to none. Crusty **baguettes** (*khào jì*) are a speciality of Vientiane, and vendors selling these French-inspired loaves, plain or filled with Lao-style pâté, can be found around downtown.

Breakfast, bakeries and cafés

The legacy of the French is most deliciously apparent in the range of **cafés** and **bakeries** that crop up all over town. The style of **coffee** served at these places varies, with some offering Lao coffee and some using imported beans. At a nice café on Setthathilat Road you'll pay $2 for a breakfast special such as coffee and a couple of croissants. While places like the *Scandinavian Bakery* charge 7000K for a coffee, the same thing at a Lao café on the river only runs to 2000K, so if you're a coffee fiend on a budget pick up your croissants at *Le Croissant d'Or* then head for *Noi Noi's*. **Brunch buffets** are on offer at the big international-style hotels like *Novotel* and *Lao Hotel Plaza* for roughly $8 – quite expensive for Laos. Cafés and bakeries tend to open early and close by 7pm.

Le Croissant d'Or 78/6 Nokeo Koummane Rd, just around the corner from *Healthy and Fresh* ☎021/223740. The service here is lacklustre but the pastries and croissants are every bit as good as the other "big two" bakeries plus there's never any problem getting a seat. The chocolate croissants and chocolate eclairs filled with cream mousse are to die for.

Healthy and Fresh Setthathilat Rd, just west of Nam Phou Place. Does the best sandwiches in town, great desserts, and good quiches and coffee. Canadian-managed with fast, friendly service. The breakfast sets here are particularly good, especially the egg with ham and melted-cheese sandwich. The baked goods are excellent and worth stocking up on before beginning any long bus journeys.

Scandinavian Bakery Nam Phou Place.

Vientiane's most popular bakery offers sandwiches and a wide selection of pastries and cookies. Despite the recent expansion and outdoor seating this place is completely over-run with tourists and you can forget about getting a seat. Spoiled by its success the coffee is very over-priced for Laos (7000K) and the service is very slow, but the breakfast specials for $1.50 are a good deal, there's CNN, and it's definitely the café to see and been seen in.

Sweet Home Chao Anou Rd, near Setthathilat Rd. A café with a Lao twist – with banquettes and signs featuring a dead ringer for cartoon legend Mighty Mouse on the walls – where you'll find pastries, cheap breakfasts and fine fruit shakes. The pastries lack the flair of those at the foreign bakeries, but the price is right.

Restaurants

Most of Vientiane's **restaurants** open for lunch and then again for dinner; no-frills eateries are usually open throughout the day, closing around 9pm. In most Western restaurants you'll pay on average $3 for each course, and even in more upmarket restaurants you'll rarely spend more than $15 total unless you get into the wine.

Southeast Asian

Bounmala Khou Viang Rd, near Wat Phaxai. Classic, inexpensive Lao-beer-and-roast-chicken joint under a tin roof. Also worth sampling is the roast beef, served with *khào pun* (flour noodles in a sauce), star fruit and lettuce.

Just for Fun Pangkham Rd. Time your meal at this tiny, clean vegetarian-friendly restaurant to avoid the lunchtime crowds, as the tasty over-rice dishes are very good value. Also does some of the

best chocolate cake in town and a great selection of herbal teas. Closed Sun.

Kaysone Chao Anou Rd. A man and his wok still going strong serving *phat thai* and a selection of fine stir-fried dishes and rice for next to nothing out of a small shop-house on Bakery St. Opens early and closes late.

Kualao 111 Samsenthai Rd ☎021/215777. Somewhat over-priced but if you want to have a nice Lao meal with traditional music and dance performances in a beautiful, restored antique house this is the only choice in town. A lot of the dishes are actually Thai and range from $4–5 a dish. Set menus are available for $10 and $15 per person. Tends to cater mostly to large tour groups who come for the atmosphere, traditional music and entertainment.

Nazim Fa Ngum Rd. Inexpensive Indian restaurant facing the river with indoor and outdoor seating. Strong on vegetarian dishes and immensely popular with backpackers. It's so packed most evenings that they the whole pavement is taken over by its tables.

Noi Noi Fa Ngum Rd. Very cheap Lao, Thai and Western dishes at the corner of Fa Ngum and Nokeo Koummane Rd. There's a row of five popular travellers' cafés facing the river here but the *Noi Noi* is the best and also has the cleanest kitchen. The three friendly girls here do everything from sandwiches to stir-fries with most dishes costing under $1. Also serves great Lao coffee for 2000K.

PVO Samsenthai Rd. Fantastic submarine sandwiches, spring rolls, *nâm neuang* and *baw bun* served on the spot or to take out. Great-value, inexpensive and full-flavour food, which you select from a picture menu, wins this shop-front eatery a high recommendation.

Sabaydee Setthathilat Rd, diagonally across from from the Pla-net Internet centre. Lao, Thai, and Chinese dishes served on an outdoor patio setting well-shielded from the traffic of Setthathilat Rd. One of the few places to enjoy Southeast Asian, as opposed to Western, food in the centre of town.

Western

Le Bayou Bar Brasserie Setthathilat Rd, opposite Wat Ong Teu. Reasonable prices with a menu offering pizzas, rôtisserie chicken, pasta, salads, good couscous, as well as terrific flan au caramel and mousse. The quality bar has Beer Lao on tap and you can also sit outside in the narrow outdoor garden.

Le Belle Epoque 6 Pang Kham Rd, in the *Settha Palace Hotel*. Out of the price range of most budget travellers, *Le Belle Epoque* still merits a mention as the classiest act in town serving French food in an elegant dining room. There is nowhere else in Vientiane even remotely like this so it's definitely a stand-out. Even if you don't dine here, you can have a drink at the bar and soak up the colonial atmosphere.

Le Côte d'Azur Fa Ngum Rd, near Nokeo Koummane Rd. This bright, airy place is one of Vientiane's better restaurants and has a good location facing the river. It has terrific service and a

great menu, featuring Provençal-style seafood and pasta, plus a large selection of excellent pizzas. Closed Sun lunchtime.

Golden Horse Fa Ngum Rd, 500m from the eastern end of Fa Ngum Rd. Despite the Chinese-souding name, this patio restaurant is run by an American expat from the south and his Thai wife who specialise in fresh seafood and freshwater-fish dishes. Fish and prawns are imported daily from Thailand and there's also local fish.

L'Opéra Nam Phou Place. Considered *the* place in Vientiane for wining and dining, and then there's the added benefit of excellent Italian food, impeccable service and a selection of Italian coffees and wines, with opera pumping through the sound system. In a word, classy, and a favourite with the diplomatic and business sets.

Le Provençal Nam Phou Place. Lost customers when its chef left and opened *Le Côte D'Azur*, but the menu remains the same and the pizza is still first rate. Closed Sun.

Le Silapa 17/1 Sihom Rd, west of the the Thai Military Bank ✆ 021/219689, ✉ frederic@laonet.net. French-managed restaurant serving French food in a beautifully restored colonial shophouse. The chef is also French and the à la carte menu, while not for budget travellers, is very reasonable at around $5 each for mains and entrèes. The lunchtime $5 set menu is also extremely good value. Open 11.30am–2pm and 6–10pm, closed Sun.

La Terrasse Nokeo Koummane Rd, near Wat Mixai. *La Terrasse* fills its tables nightly by offering outstanding steaks, pizza, Mexican food and salads at prices lower than most of the other Western joints. Seating in a covered courtyard or chic bar/dining area. Highly recommended. Closed Sun.

Le Vendôme Inpeng Rd, near Wat Inpeng. Cosy restaurant in an old house with seating inside or on a pleasant bamboo-curtained terrace. Serving French and Thai food, good pizzas and very tasty calzone. Closed Sat & Sun lunchtime.

Xang Khoun Boulom Rd, near Wat Inpeng. Run by a young Englishman, Xang captures the spirit of a university café, with good coffee, sandwiches, salads and excellent cheeseburgers, plus CNN and sports events. The servings are absolutely huge and reasonably priced. Highly recommended.

Xayoh Corner of Samsenthai and Neokeo Koummane facing the wedding-cake style Lao National Cultural Hall. Vientiane's latest, greatest yuppie-style bistro serving burgers and salads as well as coffees and desserts. There's also a branch in Vang Viang.

Minimarkets and wine shops

For many travellers, especially Europeans, one of the great pleasures of return-ing to Vientiane after a long journey up-country is the availability of cheeses, wine and other imported goods to accompany those crusty baguettes which are a speciality of the capital. There are several **minimarkets** where you can stock up. Mainingom Supermarket (corner of Khoun Boulom and Heng Boun), Riverside Minimarket (Fa Ngum Road near the *Orchid Guesthouse*), and Phimphone minimarkets (with two outlets, both on Samsenthai Road near Chantha Khoumane Road) all have a selection of cheeses, wine, imported beer and chocolate, as well as imported body-care products you won't be able to find elsewhere in Laos. Les Boutiques Scoubidou at the end of Samsenthai Road, near Wat Simuang, boasts the best selection of specialty **gourmet prod-ucts** in town, with French wines, olives, anchovies, pâté, cured meats and sausages. The best selections of **wine** in Laos can be found at Vinothèque La Cave and Le Wine Cellar, both on Samsenthai Road, opposite the *Asia Pavilion Hotel*.

Beer gardens, bars and clubs

Vientiane's location along an east–west stretch of the Mekong makes for spec-tacular sunsets, with the fiery orb lighting up the water before slowly descend-ing into Thailand. Taking advantage of this backdrop, makeshift **stalls** selling bottles of Beer Lao and fruit shakes set up along the sidewalk on Fa Ngum Road opposite Wat Chanthabouli from afternoon till early evening. If you're looking for something even closer to the water and away from the bustle of the city centre, continue west along Fa Ngum Road where for the next 2km you'll find a long row of 35 **beer gardens** with wooden terraces over-hanging the riverbank. The largest and fanciest of these are all in the direct vicinity of the *Riverview Hotel*. These laid-back, open-air venues offering cheap pitchers of golden "Fresh Beer" (*bia sót*) under a thatch roof define the quintessential Vientiane pub experience.

Believe it or not, Vientiane's once notorious **nightlife** helped earn it the name of Wonderland. To hear Paul Theroux tell it in *The Great Railway Bazaar*, opium was easier to find than beer. However, the brothels and strip joints van-ished when the old regime fell in the mid-1970s, and the city's night scene is now just re-emerging after 25 years of puritanical socialism. Many of Vientiane's **nightclubs** are Japanese-style with costumed pop singers, dim lighting, hostesses and deep couches. These places are fairly innocuous – the absurdly overdressed hostesses will only sit with you for a fee – and the cha-cha still rules on the lively dance floors. Many of the city's larger hotels have nightspots like this, and if you want to visit one out of curiosity the nightclub in the *Lang Xang Hotel* is a good choice, although the arrival of foreigners will generate plenty of giggling. As you might expect, many of these clubs also fea-ture **karaoke** lounges.

Of more interest to Western visitors, a number of **dance clubs** playing Thai pop and international dance mixes and catering to well-heeled teenagers have cropped up along Louang Phabang Avenue, just beyond the *Novotel*. Places like *Marina*, *Paradise*, and *Future*, feature DJs playing Western techno music and don't usually get hopping until after 9pm. Smaller, out of the way clubs like *Chess Café* and *Soradith* are able to bend the rules more and go until the wee hours depending on the political climate. There's usually no cover charge, but if there is it will include a bottle of Beer Lao. Sadly, Vientiane's **live music** scene is largely derivative, with popular taste being overwhelmed by a flood of Made-in-Thailand bubble-gum pop churned out by the massive music industry across the river.

City centre bars and clubs

Broadway *Lao Hotel Plaza*, Samsenthai Rd. The dance club in the *Plaza's* basement is considered by some to be the town's most prestigious nightclub. There's deep plush sofas to sink into and you can watch the Lao yuppies and Thai businessmen party, but for real action you'll have to go where the Lao teenagers are.

Chess Café Sakkalin Rd. The happening pick-up bar of the moment where Lao youths, many of whom not too long ago would have been serving time in the Ang Nam Ngum Reservoir, come to shake their post-communist booties. Pumping out deafening European techno and Thai pop, this place really rocks. Bring earplugs.

Gecko Club *Royal Dokmaideng Hotel*, Lane Xang Ave. A very similar scene to the *Lao Plaza Hotel* and popular with the twenty-something expat crowd and children of the new elite. It's an interesting place to just sit with a cocktail and people-watch.

Khop Chai Deu Nam Phou Place. Located in a big French-period house next to Nam Phou Fountain, this is the most popular hang-out for foreign tourists. Downstairs, in the outdoor patio bar, you can get cheap 7000K pitchers of draft beer; up the big spiral staircase you'll find another very pleasant bar on the roof. You can eat inside – the mixed menu has reasonable Lao and Indian dishes, though the farang food is a bit hit and miss. Full of tourists but still the most fun place in town.

Lao Plaza Beer Garden *Lao Hotel Plaza*, 63 Samsenthai Rd. Nowhere near as popular as the *Khop Chai Deu* but still a fine place to sit outside overlooking Samsenthai Rd and have a cold, $1-a-pint draft beer in the evening. Open 6–10pm.

Marina Louang Phabang Ave, 3km west of the centre. The hottest of a number of big discos on the edge of town for Lao teenagers to shake their groove thang and very much in the Thai disco style. Has a good dance floor, separate bar and plenty of couches for breaks between dancing. If you're on a club crawl, other similar venues out this way include *Paradise*, *Blue Star*, *Future*, and *Rainbow*.

Riverside venues

Liverpool Fa Ngum Rd ☏ 020/516800. Just opposite the *Riverview Hotel*, this is one of the larger, better-built riverside restaurants on Fa Ngum Rd and not the only one named after an English football team. Like the *Mala* next door, this place is a lot fancier than the majority of river-view restaurants lining the Mekong here, most of which are just bamboo and thatch affairs.

Mala Restaurant Fa Ngum Rd ☏ 020/215809. Opposite the *Riverview Hotel* and the most upmarket of all the riverside restaurants, with sheets of water cascading down its large plate-glass windows. Inside the decor is very pleasant and comfortable, making this place a top choice for tour group operators.

Sala Sunset Khounta Fa Ngum Rd. Known to some simply as "The End of the World" and others as "The Sunset Bar", this was the original spot for sundowners in Vientiane. It has expanded since the early days, owing to its immense popularity with expats and tour groups, but it still ends up crowded at sunset. Get here early to sample the *tam kûay tani*, a spicy salad of green bananas, eggplant and chillis.

Cultural entertainment

Four hundred and fifty years after superceding Louang Phabang as the centre of political power, Vientiane still lacks the natural **cultural life** of the old royal capital, but it has improved somewhat, largely thanks to the influx of tourists and expats. A few venues now offer a taste of Laos's heritage, even if it is just for the entertainment of foreigners. The *Salongxay Restaurant* in the Lane Xang Hotel, has a good dinner show serving up Lao food accompanied by traditional live music and **classical Lao dancing** from 7–9.45pm daily. There's no expensive set menu here, you can just order some food and enjoy the show. The *Kualao* (see p.102), a dinner-show restaurant housed in a big French-colonial house on Samsenthai Road, mostly caters to package tour groups and is somewhat overpriced, but certainly not beyond the means of most travellers. There's traditional dancing and music – the daily dance show starts at 7pm and lasts two hours.

With Lao singers selling out to demand for Thai music and the capital's cinemas shut since the advent of video, Vientiane's grassroots cultural life really only reawakens during **festivals**. The best time to get a taste of Lao music is in November during the **That Louang Festival** (see p.56), when the nation's best singers and musicians are featured in a string of performances during the two weeks leading up to the festival.

Shopping

Ten years ago, immediately after Laos opened its doors to visitors, bargain-hunting in Vientiane was an experience. Capitalism had been stifled for over a decade, and in the Morning Market and the handful of shops around town, antique textiles and silver could be had for a song, while staples such as rice and cooking oil were unbelievably expensive. The situation has since stabilised and Vientiane's merchants now know the correct value of antiques and handicrafts. In fact, the city's proximity to Thailand tends to keep the price of **Lao handicrafts** higher than they might otherwise be, with Thai buyers regularly snapping up Lao handicrafts for resale in the stores of Bangkok. If you are planning a trip to Louang Phabang, where silver-work and textiles are produced and prices are generally cheaper, you'd be better off doing your shopping there.

Vientiane's **Morning Market** (Talat Sao) is the best place to begin a shopping tour of the capital. While many of the goods on offer will be of little interest to foreigners – Chinese electronics and cheap consumer goods proliferate – there are bargains to be had when it comes to homespun cotton clothing and handicrafts. Besides the Morning Market, most textile, souvenir and antique shops are found on **Samsenthai** and **Setthathilat roads** and along the lanes running between them. As with anywhere else, avoid shops in the lobbies of top-end hotels unless you don't mind paying huge mark-ups. See the Shopping section of Basics (pp.57–61) for further details on what to look out for in the items mentioned below.

Antiques and reproductions

Antique shops can be found in both the Morning Market and the centre of Vientiane. Virtually all metal images or figurines of Buddist or Hindu deities are reproductions from Thailand and Cambodia, though vendors won't admit this. **Opium weights** are usually seen in antique stores but may also be found in upscale textile shops. Prices in Vientiane are way out of line when compared to the rest of Laos with merchants asking two to five times more for weights than their counterparts in Louang Phabang and the other provinces. The authenticity of the "antiques" on sale in Vientiane is also highly suspect. **Opium pipes** can be found in the antique shops on Samsenthai Road – real old pipes may go for $100 or more, but newly-made Vietnamese pipes can be bought for as little as $10. Keep in mind while browsing that, depending on the strictness of anti-narcotics laws, customs officers in your home country may confiscate such a purchase.

Books

The Book Center on Pangkham Road, south of the Nam Phou, has the biggest selection of **English-language books** in the city. On Nokeo Koummane near the river, the new Kosila Books (☎021/241352) has a very good selection of secondhand books. The government-run State Bookstore, on the corner of Manthatoulat and Setthathilat roads, carries just a small selection of English-language books and a few comical, dusty titles from the communist era, including such useful tomes as Lao language guides to the customs and culture of the Soviet Republic of Tajikistan.

Rattan, wicker and bamboo

Check the antique stores of the Morning Market and the downtown area for old or rare **baskets** made by the tribal peoples of Laos. These may sell for as much as $50. Sticky rice baskets and mats costing $1–3 can be found in several shops that line Chao Anou Road beyond the Thong Khan Kham Market. Pai Exclusive, Thong Tum Road (☏021/214804), near the National Circus (*hong kanyasin*), produces chic if pricey designs, and can arrange shipping. They also have a shop in the lobby of the *Lao Hotel Plaza*.

Stamps, coins and banknotes

Most antique and curio shops have a small stash of **stamps, coins** and **banknotes** from present and previous regimes – the shops on Samsenthai and Setthathilat roads are your best bet. A no-name philatelic shop near the corner of Samsenthai and Pangkham roads has a wide selection of stamps, including some designed by the incomparable Marc Leguay.

Textiles

Once a tremendous bargain in Vientiane, antique Lao weavings are now more expensive in Vientiane than in Thailand. If you're determined to buy **old textiles** in Vientiane, the Morning Market is your best bet. **New textiles**, however, are another matter. Lao silk and cotton textiles can be purchased in bolts of plain coloured cloth or as ready-made clothing for $2–5 per item. If you're looking to make a smart purchase without shelling out too much cash, Lao shoulder bags, or *nyam*, are a cheap and functional choice. Hand-woven *pha biang*, a long, scarf-like textile, can be found in a wide variety of colours and patterns, and chequered *pha khao ma*, the knee-length men's sarong, are also good buys. The Morning Market has the best selection and the merchants are used to foreign tourists and enjoy a spirited haggle.

Aside from the markets, Vientiane now boasts an increasing number of up-market **shops** and **boutiques** carrying, and sometimes specializing in, Lao textiles. They often have the best range and most attractively displayed products and, unsurprisingly, the highest prices. Most of these new boutiques and galleries are located **south of Samsenthai Road** between Khoun Bololom and Manthatoulat roads and can be taken in in a single, short walking tour. Perhaps the most impressive of these boutiques is Carol Cassidy Lao Textiles (☏021/212123), housed in a French-era mansion on Nokeo Koummane Road, which produces hand-woven wall hangings tinted with natural dyes under the supervision of an American designer. Other top-drawer places include Satri Lao Silk, 79/4 Setthatilat Rd (☏021/219295, ✉satrilao@hotmail .com), Lao Gallery, Nokeo Koummane Road (☏021/212943), and T'Shop, Wat Inpeng Street (☏021/223178, ✆223178). Not so fancy, but certainly one of the earliest pioneers of traditional textiles, is the Lao Women's Union shop called The Art of Silk, on Manthatoulat Road. This unpretentious shop has good deals on lengths of plain silk and cotton cloth from all over the country, including hard-to-find ethnic textiles from Laos's remote southern provinces.

Woodcarving

Unlike Chiang Mai in Thailand, Vientiane is not a centre of **woodcarving** and the merchandise on offer tends to be crudely carved and garishly lacquered. An exception are the handicrafts of the T'Shop Lai Gallery on Inpeng Road next to *Le Vendôme* restaurant, which specializes in unique mosaics and other handicrafts made from coconut shell. Prices are fixed, though, and certainly not cheap.

Listings

Airlines Lao Aviation, Pangkham Rd ☎ 021/212051, or at Wattay International Airport, Louang Phabang Ave ☎ 021/512000; Thai Airways International, Pangkham Rd ☎ 021/216143; Vietnam Airlines, Samsenthai Rd, mezzanine floor of the *Lao Hotel Plaza* ☎ 021/21756.

American Express Representative agent in Laos is Diethelm Travel, on the corner of Setthathilat Rd and Nam Phou Place ☎ 021/213833.

Banks and exchange Banks, hotels, guest houses, and shop-keepers all over downtown Vientiane will happily exchange foreign currency. Thai and Lao banks, many of which are located along Lane Xang Ave, can cash travellers cheques, but a more convenient option for tourists are bank exchange booths, which can be

Moving on from Vientiane

Vientiane, located at the centre of Laos, is the main hub for all domestic travel. The situation regarding bus stop locations and departure times can only be described as chaotic – there is a system but no one knows what it is. **Buses** go to most major southern towns but for destinations north you'll generally have to go to Louang Phabang for a connection onwards.

Direct **Vietnam buses** leave from the lot at the southwest corner of the Morning Market. A regular boat service from Tha Hua Kao Liaw boat landing connects Vientiane to northern Mekong towns, but there is no longer a boat service to the south. Travellers on the other side of the Friendship Bridge moving on **to Thailand** can get train and bus connections in Nong Khai, while Bangkok-bound flights leave daily.

Sawngthaews

The main staging area for **sawngthaews** and unmetered **taxis** is the big lot at the southeast corner of the Morning Market just opposite the bus station. Here you'll find both shared sawngthaews for towns around the Vientiane Plain, and vehicles for hire or charter. North of town, about 8km up Route 13 there is a second bus lot for sawngthaews heading north towards Vang Viang with departures for Vang Viang every thirty minutes until late afternoon.

Buses

Buses heading to all points **south** leave from the main bus station next to the Morning Market. It's sensible to book a day ahead if you want to take an express, air-con bus to Savannakhet via Pakxan and Thakhek. This private service is operated by Senesabay (☎ 021/218052/217318); their office is next to the Odeon Rama Theatre, near Talat Thong Khan Kham. The bus leaves from a vacant lot opposite the office and stops at the main bus station in Savannakhet. It's also possible to hire a twelve-seater air-con minibus to Savannakhet for $100 from Boualian Travel Company (☎ 021/213061). Buses to the **north** and northeast leave from the Northern Bus Station near Nongduang Market but generally you have to go first to Louang Phabang (see below) and find buses onward from Louang Phabang's Northern Bus Station.

To Bangkok: overnight buses to Bangkok leave between 5pm and 7pm from Nong Khai, Thailand. Take Bus No. 14 or hire a taxi to the Friendship Bridge; once on the Thai side take a shared taxi to the bus station (50–70 baht).

found on Samsenthai Rd as well as on Fa Ngum by the *Lane Xang Hotel*. There are also exchange booths at the Friendship Bridge and Wattay International Airport. Lane Xang Bank is on the corner of Setthathilat and Francois Nginn Rd. Banque pour le Commerce Extérieur Lao (BCEL), Pangkham Rd, has the best exchange rates and the widest range of services, including changing travellers' cheques into US dollars and US-dollar cash advances on Visa; for Mastercard head to Siam Commercial Bank, Lane Xang Ave.

Bicycle rental Bicycles are available at rental shops and some guest houses for $1 per day. There are three bike and motorbike rental outlets in a row on Samsenthai Rd at the corner of Pangkham Rd, including PVO (☎021/214444) and Boualian Lao Travel (☎021/213061, Ⓕ 219649).

Bowling There is a bowling alley on Tha Deua Rd heading east out of town.

Car rental There are a number of places including Asia Vehicle Rental, Lane Xang Ave (☎021/217493, Ⓕ217493) and Khounta Rental, Luang Phabang Rd (☎020/513127) as well as PVO (☎021/214444) and Boualian Lao Travel (☎021/213061, Ⓕ219649) on Samsenthai Rd at the corner of Pangkham Rd. Many guest houses and hotels can make car-rental arrangements that may be cheaper than agencies.

Courier services DHL Worldwide Express ☎021/214868 or 216830; United Parcel Service ☎021/414392.

Embassies and consulates Australia, Nehru Rd ☎021/413610 or 413805; Cambodia, near That Khao, Thadua Rd ☎021/314952 or 315251;

VIENTIANE AND THE NORTHWEST | Listings

To the Friendship Bridge: Bus No. 14 departs every forty minutes from main bus station; a faster alternative is to take a taxi from the lot at the southeast corner of the Morning Market ($4) or hire a tuk-tuk ($3).

To Louang Phabang: Buses north and northeast to Louang Phabang, Phonsavan, and Xam Nua leave from the Northern Bus Station (Khoua Louang Bus Stand) near Nongduang Market (sometimes called the Evening Market or Talat Laeng) on Talat Nongduang Road, 2km northwest of the city centre. There is also now an air-con tourist coach ($10) between Vientiane and Louang Phabang which goes three times a month and can be booked through most guest houses.

To Vang Viang: three blue government buses depart from the main bus station daily; alternatively, sawngthaews leave twice an hour from the bus station on Route 13 and occasionally from the bus lot on Khou Viang Road opposite the main bus station.

To Vietnam: Buses for Hanoi leave from the Vietnam bus booth at the southwest corner of the Morning Market on Mondays, Wednesdays, Fridays, and Saturdays at 6:30pm and should arrive in Hanoi 24 hours later. The fare is $25 and in theory this is supposed to get you a "good" bus. There are two companies providing this service and the size of the bus used depends on the number of advance bookings. There are also buses to Vinh, Hue and Da Nang.

Boats
There are now only boat services to the **northwest** and **north**. Speedboats and slow boats leave from Tha Hua Kao Liaw pier, located on the Mekong River, 10km west of the centre of Vientiane; tuk-tuks cost 15,000K from the centre. Slow boats should leave daily but this is variable. By slow boat it takes three days to get to Louang Phabang ($25 per person); speedboats can make it in a day ($32 per person or $260 to hire the boat). Speedboats to Paklai, 217km upriver from Vientiane, cost $20 per person; or you could hire one for $100.

Trains
To Bangkok: overnight trains to Bangkok leave between 5pm and 7pm from Nong Khai, Thailand. Take Bus No. 14 or hire a taxi to the Friendship Bridge; once on the Thai side, take a shared taxi to the train station (50–70 baht).

China, near Wat Nak Noi, Wat Nak Rd ☎021/315100 or 315103; France, Setthathilat Rd ☎021/215253 or 215257–9; Germany, Sok Pa Louang Rd ☎021/312110–3; India, near Wat Phaxai, That Louang Rd ☎021/413802; Indonesia, Phon Kheng Rd, Ban Phon Sa-at ☎021/413909 or 413910; Malaysia, near Wat Phaxai, That Louang Rd ☎021/414205 or 414206; Myanmar (Burma), Sok Pa Louang Rd ☎021/314910; Philippines, near Wat Nak, Salakoktane Rd ☎021/315179; Sweden, near Wat Nak, Sok Pa Louang Rd ☎021/315018; Thailand (visa section), across from the Lao National Tourism Authority building, Lane Xang Ave ☎021/214582; United States, near That Dam, Bartholonie Rd ☎021/213966 or 212581; Vietnam, near Wat Phaxai, That Louang Rd ☎021/413400–4.

Emergencies Dial ☎190 in case of fire, ☎195 for an ambulance, or ☎191 for police. In the event of an accident dial ☎413306 for the Friendship Hospital Trauma Centre.

Health clubs *Tai-Pan Hotel*, François Nginn Rd ($4 per day).

Hospitals and clinics Australian Clinic, Nehru Rd ☎021/413603, by appointment only, with vaccinations on Thursdays; International Clinic, Mahosot Hospital Compound, Fa Ngum Rd ☎021/214022, open 24hr; Mahosot Hospital, Mahosot Rd ☎021/214018; Setthathilat Hospital, Phon Sa-at Rd ☎021/413783; Swedish Clinic, near Swedish Embassy, near Wat Nak, Sok Pa Louang Rd ☎021/315015.

Immigration department Hatsady Rd near junction with Lane Xang Ave ☎021/212520; open Mon & Wed–Sat 8–11.30am & 2-4.30pm.

Internet access PlaNet CyberCentre, on the corner of Manthatoulat and Setthathilat rds (Mon–Sat 8.30am–10pm & Sun 9am–8pm; ☎021/218972-4; 100K per minute), is the biggest player in town but there are well over a dozen small internet centres scattered around the city centre, all charging 100K an minute and closing at 10pm.

Language courses Centre de Langue Française, Lane Xang Ave ☎021/215764; Lao-American Language Center, Phon Kheng Rd, Ban Phon Sa-at ☎021/414321, ⨍413760. Short-term courses and private tutorials are available.

Laundry Most hotels and guest houses will wash clothes for you; a faster and cheaper alternative is one of the laundries on Heng Boun Rd, near the *Anou Hotel*.

Markets Vientiane has many markets which can either be "wet markets" selling produce, "dry markets" selling manufactured goods, or more commonly a mixture of both. For tourists the best market to visit is the famous Talat Sao, or Morning Market, which has a handicrafts and textiles section. Other significant markets close to the centre include Talat Khuadin, Talat Dongpalan, Talat Nongduang, and Talat Thongkhankham.

Massage and herbal sauna Ajan Amphone, tucked away behind Wat Chanthabouli on Fa Ngum Rd, offers massage at 20,000K per hour, and a sauna for 5000K (Mon–Fri 2–5pm, Sat & Sun 10am–7pm); Hôpital de Médicine Traditionnelle, near Wat Si Amphon, does massage for $1 per hour and sauna for $0.50, and offers acupuncture; Mixay Massage, near Wat Mixai on Nokeo Koummane Rd, offers massage only - $5 per hour; Wat Sok Pa Louang has massage for 10000K per 40min, while the sauna costs 5000K (see also p.100). Mixay Massage on Fa Ngum Rd, 3 doors east of the Riverside Mini-mart.

Meditation An hour of sitting and walking meditation is led by Ajan Paan on Saturday afternoons at 4pm at Wat Sok Pa Louang (see also p.100).

Motorbike rental Rental motorbikes in Vientiane are mostly little 100cc step-throughs like the Honda Dream. Most of the bikes are second-hand, older models imported from Thailand. The asking price is usually $8–10 depending on how new the bike looks, but it's possible to bargin down to $6 a day, especially if you want it for a few days. The *Douang Deuane Hotel*, Nokeo Koummane Rd (☎021/222301–3), PVO, Samsenthai Rd (☎021/214444), and Boualian Lao Travel Company 346 Samsenthai Rd (☎021/213061, ⨍021/219649), all have small fleets of Honda Dreams but PVO is the only place in town with eight proper Yamaha 225cc enduro dirt bikes. These run to $20 a day, about double the price of rental in Thailand.

Newspapers The *Vientiane Times* is sold at the big hotels and most minimarkets; *The Bangkok Post* is sometimes available at the Phimphone minimarket on Samsenthai Rd.

Pharmacies The best pharmacies are on Mahosot Rd north of the main bus station.

Post office The GPO is located on the corner of Khou Viang Rd and Lane Xang Ave opposite the Morning Market. The post restante counter will hold mail for up to three months with a minimal charge. There's also a philatelic counter. Mon–Fri 8am–5pm, Sat 8am–4pm, Sun 8am–noon.

Skating There is a line-skating ring on Tha Deua Rd heading east out of town.

Swimming *Lane Xang Hotel*, Fa Ngum Rd ($2 per day); *Lao Hotel Plaza*, Samsenthai Rd ($5); *Novotel*, Louang Phabang Ave ($5); *Royal*

Dokmaideng Hotel, Lane Xang Ave ($2.50); Sok Pa Louang Swimming Pool, Sok Pa Louang Rd ($0.50).

Telephone services Telecom office, on the corner of Setthathilat and Chantha Khoumane rds, is open daily 7am–10pm and handles international calls and faxes; you can use the operators inside or use their card phones just out front. These days IDD calls can be made from most hotels.

Travel/tour agencies Boualian Lao Travel Company, 346 Samsenthai Rd ☎021/213061; Diethelm, Nam Phou Place ☎021/215920; Inter-Lao Tourisme, Setthathilat Rd ☎021/214832; Lane Xang, Pangkham Rd ☎021/213198; Lao Tourism, Lane Xang Ave ☎021/216671; Lao Travel Service, Lane Xang Ave ☎021/216603-4; Phudoi Travel, Phonxai Rd ☎021/413888; Sodetour, Fa Ngum Rd ☎021/216314, Wildside Adventures, 54 Setthatilat Rd ☎021/223022, ⒺWildside@yahoo.com.

Visa services Boualian Lao Travel Company, 346 Samsenthai Rd (☎021/213061) can arrange visas for Vietnam ($55), Cambodia ($30), Thailand ($16), and China ($45) as well as Lao visa extentions ($2 per day). Express visa service is also avaliable for Chinese ($85, same day) and Vietnamese visas ($95, two days). The proprietor, Mrs. Boualian Dangmani, a Vietnamese–Lao, is sharp as a tack; she speaks fluent English, French, Vietnamese, Thai and Lao.

Around Vientiane

If you need a break from Vientiane or have time to kill while your visa is being processed, it's easy enough to get **out of the city** in under an hour, and shuttle around the expansive Vientiane Plain by public transport or private tour. The most popular destination for a half-day jaunt is Xiang Khouan, the otherworldly **Buddha Park**, southeast of town, while those who have never seen a "Buddha's footprint" might consider travelling further east to **Wat Phabat Phonsan**. North of the capital, the huge **Ang Nam Ngum Reservoir** is a pleasant retreat for boating, fishing and swimming, with scores of islands to explore, as well as a casino for those hoping to earn back that plane ticket. At the southern edge of the Ang Nam Ngum Reservoir is the vast **Phou Khao Khouay NBCA** (National Biodiversity Conservation Area), which can be visited on an adventure tour from the capital. Downstream, **Lao Pako**, an ecotourism lodge on the Nam Ngum River, makes a fine day-trip, though most visitors end up staying on to relax for a few days, visiting country villages and exploring nature trails. Of the two state-sanctioned tourist destinations on the edge of the city, the **National Ethnic Cultural Park** and the **Kaysone Memorial Museum**, the latter is the more worthwhile, making an interesting diversion into the personality cults surrounding communist leaders.

Buddha Park and National Ethnic Cultural Park

Situated some 25km southeast of downtown Vientiane on the Mekong River, Xiang Khouan or the "**Buddha Park**" (daily 8am–6pm; 2000K) is surely Laos's quirkiest attraction – a tacky tourist trap to some travellers; one of the most interesting sights in Vientiane to others.

This collection of massive ferro-concrete sculptures, dotted around a wide riverside meadow, was created under the direction of Louang Pou Bounleua Soulilat, a self-styled holy man who claimed to have been the disciple of a cave-dwelling Hindu hermit in Vietnam. Upon returning to Laos, Bounleua began the sculpture garden in the late 1950s as a means of spreading his philosophy of life and his ideas about the cosmos. Besides the brontosaurian reclining Buddha that dominates the park, there are concrete statues of every conceivable deity in the Hindu-Buddhist pantheon and even a handful of personalities from the old regime.

Near the park's entrance is a strange edifice that resembles a giant pumpkin with a dead tree sprouting from its crown. Entering the structure through the gaping maw of devouring time, you can explore representations of the "three planes of existence": hell, earth and heaven. The crude and cobwebby figures that populate these rooms are reminiscent of a child's nightmare and, although the interior is rigged with electric lights, they aren't always turned on, so bring a torch if you want to see anything. A spiral stairway leads to the roof of the building, which affords a view of the park.

After the revolution, Bounleua was forced to flee across the Mekong to Nong Khai, Thailand, where he established an even more elaborate version of his philosophy in concrete. Ironically, the Lao National Tourism Authority chose Bounleua's sculptures as the symbol of their "Visit Laos Year" campaign, and posters depicting the exiled guru's works can be seen in government offices throughout the country.

To get to the park, just take bus No. 14 from Vientiane's main bus station. Buses leave every forty minutes and stop outside the Buddha Park. Alternatively, get a shared tuk-tuk from the stand near the Morning Market, to Thadua, and then hire a tuk-tuk for the last 3km to the park.

National Ethnic Cultural Park

En route to the Buddha Park, some 18km from the capital, you'll pass the **National Ethnic Cultural Park** (daily 8am–6pm; 2000K), Laos's answer to the tour-the-country-in-one-hour theme park, which almost every Southeast Asian country finds it necessary to construct. Concrete replicas of the traditional dwellings of Laos's ethnic minorities double as snack stands, and there are cement models of dinosaurs. If you're heading for the Buddha Park with a rental car or motorcycle, a swing through here isn't much trouble.

The Kaysone Memorial Museum

Laos's tribute to the man who led the Thirty Year Struggle (see p.270), **The Kaysone Memorial Museum** (Tues–Sun 8–11.30am & 2–4.30pm; 2000K) lies on the edge of Vientiane in the former American compound known during the Second Indochina War as **Six Klicks City** – after its location, 6km from the centre. Once a slice of Americana, with ranch-style homes with swimming pools round the back, nicely paved roads, bars, duty-free booze and stag films, Six Klicks City was an oasis in a quagmire during the years that the US embassy was the seat of power in Vientiane. One month after Saigon and Phnom Penh fell in April 1975, Pathet Lao troops surrounded the barbed-wire-enclosed compound and American residents inside received a phone call telling them not to leave. Three days later, the first busload of Americans headed to Wattay Airport, beginning the end of an era. In December 1975, 264 delegates gathered in the compound's gymnasium and proclaimed the formation of the Lao People's Democratic Republic. Having just emerged from their wartime hide-out in the caves of Viang Xai, the Lao communist party members promptly moved into the American fortress, which was to become Kaysone's headquarters until his death in 1992.

Strikingly modest compared to the mausoleum of Kaysone's Vietnamese counterpart, Ho Chi Minh, the Memorial Museum opened in December 1994 and originally consisted of only Kaysone's residence. A year later, a more conventional museum was opened next door. Visitors are led by a guide, through the tiny **ranch house** where Kaysone lived. You'll be shown his exercise bike and the spot where he used to meditate, as well as cabinets containing Buddha images and bottles of Johnnie Walker scotch – so much for communist austerity, though the guide duly notes that they were gifts of the people. Also on display are gifts given to Kaysone by the leaders of Indonesia, Thailand, Vietnam and China, as well as the books – many of which, ardent Lao nationalists might note, are in Vietnamese – of his well-stocked library. Next door, the later part of the museum contains more conventional exhibits, heavy on the sort of revolutionary photographs common to other Lao museums, but also featuring objects from various stages of Kaysone's life: his desk from his Savannakhet school, the winnowing tray on which he was placed during the first days of his life, and his mother's bed, along with a model of Kaysone's Viang Xai cave, his binoculars, revolver and other items from his time with the resistance movement.

Getting to the museum is easiest by rental motorbike or tuk-tuk. Southbound sawngthaews, departing from the main bus station, pass the road leading to the compound – 6km from the city along Route 13 South. The turn-off is on the left just before the Children's Home. The road leads 300m to the gate of an army outpost, at which point you'll turn left and continue along the road, which curves right, for 1km. The museum entrance is on the right.

Lao Pako Eco-Resort

A journey out to **LAO PAKO**, Laos's first environmentally friendly resort, is perhaps the best quick trip you can make out of the capital. The rustic resort, located on a bend in the Nam Ngum River, 50km northeast of Vientiane, is reached by road and a short river journey. Once there you could easily spend a couple of days soaking up the laid-back atmosphere at this Austro-German-owned woodsy getaway, spread across fifty hectares, and affording ample opportunity for swimming, bird-watching and day hikes to nearby villages. You can also follow a pair of self-guided nature trails, along one of which is a herbal steam bath, modelled on the wood-fired saunas at Wat Sok Pa Louang (see p.100), near a refreshingly cool spring.

An open-air **restaurant** overlooking the Nam Ngum River serves up Lao staples plus a few decent Western dishes, including a very tasty schnitzel. The resort also hosts monthly full moon parties with a BBQ and *lào hai*, traditional rice wine sipped out of reed straws from a large communal stoneware jar.

Accommodation ranges from doubles with en-suite bathroom ($14) or a seven-bed dorm ($4 per person) in a Lao-style longhouse with a huge veranda, to more private detached bungalows also with en-suite facilities and verandas ($18). Rooms are limited, so it's best to call ahead for reservations (☎021/451970 or radio phone ☎451844). **To get there** you first catch the blue government bus to Pakxap from the main bus station at 6.30am, 11am or 3pm to Somsamai (alternatively, a hired tuk-tuk costs about $5), where there's a sign that says, "Boat to LAO PAKO". From here boatmen will ferry you down the tranquil Nam Ngum River to the resort. The boat journey lasts about 25 minutes and costs 8000K. Wildside Adventures in Vientiane (see p.111) does a one day **kayaking** and **trekking tour** near Pak Lao ($35), which includes one night's accommodation at the resort and transfers. The resort can also arrange pick-ups for tours to the nearby Phou Khao Khouay NBCA.

Wat Phabat Phonsan

The somewhat isolated monastery of **WAT PHABAT PHONSAN**, 80km east of Vientiane, is best known for its "**Buddha's footprint**", probably one of the most elaborate of the handful of examples to be found in Laos. As with most so-called footprints of the Buddha, the one at this monastery was originally a larger-than-life recess in stone that vaguely resembled a human footprint. In ancient times, the sandstone bluff upon which the monastery now sits was submerged by the nearby river and, over time, the swirling currents carved deep bowls into its surface. When the water receded, one of these indentations looked enough like a footprint for it to become enshrined as one of those left behind by the historic Buddha during his wanderings through Laos. Never mind that there is no record of Gautama Buddha ever having got this far east, his footprints have been found all over Laos wherever there is a population of Buddhists.

The footprint was embellished with stucco (and later concrete) and the 108 auspicious marks said to be found on the Buddha's foot were carved into the wet stucco. Red paint and gold leaf were then applied to the surface and offerings were made. Nowadays, most pilgrims toss banknotes into the footprint for luck and a wire-mesh cage has been built around it to keep thieves from pocketing the offerings. Still, say resident monks, naughty kids have been known to put blobs of chewing gum on the end of sticks and poke away until their pockets bulge with banknotes.

Next to the building containing the Buddha's footprint is another, housing a concrete **reclining Buddha**. The nearby stupa is said to date from the early twentieth century and is decorated with whimsical motifs reminiscent of Savannakhet's That In Hang (see p.271). Because this monastery is considered to be of high holiness, donations have rolled in from lay Buddhists wishing to dilute some of their sins. These donations have been used to make "improvements" to the wat including new monks' quarters (*kuti*) to replace the charmingly rustic teakwood buildings that date from the French colonial period. Even the river-carved bowls in the sandstone bluff are being filled in with concrete so that the monks don't stumble when traversing the temple compound at night.

The best time to come here is during the annual **temple fair** (*bun*) held during the full moon in July when thousands of pilgrims flock to the monastery to make offerings, play games of chance and dance to *electric lam wong* music until late into the night.

Any **public transport** bound for Savannakhet, Thakhek or Pakxan (see Moving on, p.108) will pass by Wat Phabat Phonsan, which is roughly halfway between Vientiane and Pakxan, about an hour and a half's drive from each. There is no accommodation in the vicinity of Wat Phabat Phonsan, so it's best visited as a day-trip or en route to the south. In the event that you somehow got stuck here overnight it would be possible to get very basic accommodation either at the wat itself or the village across the road.

Phou Khao Khouay NBCA

Located 90km northeast of the city, this huge NBCA (National Biodiversity Conservation Area, see p.70) straddles three different administrative districts and forms the southern edge of the Ang Nam Ngum Reservoir. Within easy striking distance of the capital, **PHOU KHAO KHOUAY** basically is to Vientiane what Khao Yai National Park is to Bangkok. The NBCA features several large ranges and includes two peaks of over 1600m, one of which, Phou Xang, at 1666m, towers over the southern end of the Nam Ngum Lake. There are also several large **waterfalls**, including Tad Xay, Tad Leuk, and Tad Phou Khao Khouay, which can be reached by road, and a smaller dam and reservoir, Nam Luek Reservoir, which can also be reached by motor vehicle from the east. Fauna includes **Asian elephants**, **tigers** and **gibbons**. There is a visitor centre at Tad Leuk. Enquire with Vientiane **tour agencies** about organized packages to Phou Khao Khouay or contact Wildside Adventures (☎021/223022), which offers two-day packages ($50 all inclusive) with hotel pick-up in Vientiane or from the Pak Lao Eco-Resort. There is also a brand new guest house, the *T&M Guesthouse* (❶), in the town of Thabok, where the road into the NBCA meets Route 13.

Ang Nam Ngum Reservoir

Ninety kilometres north of Vientiane, the vast **Ang Nam Ngum Reservoir** sits above the northern edge of the Vientiane Plain, where the rice-growing flatlands surrounding the capital meet the mountainous terrain of the north. Created when the Nam Ngum River was dammed in 1971, the deep green waters of the reservoir are dotted with scores of forest-clad islands stretching to a dramatic horizon lined with mountains, their peaks lost in mist. Foreign travellers, usually in a rush to head up-country, tend to bypass Ang Nam Ngum as they make for nearby Vang Viang, but those who do stop off discover a pretty 250-square kilometre expanse of water with islands, secluded beaches, and swimming spots.

Built with foreign expertise and funding, the Ang Nam Ngum Reservoir – the driving force behind Laos's production of hydroelectricity, the country's largest export earner until the late 1980s – provides electricity for Vientiane and surrounding villages on the Vientiane Plain. Most of the power, however, flows across the Mekong into Thailand, which has an agreement to purchase Laos's surplus electricity. The reservoir is also slowly being developed for tourism and now boasts a two-star hotel on the southern shoreline, the **DanSaVanh Nam Ngum Resort**, complete with casino, golf courses and a marina (see p.117).

At the time the dam was built, the Royalist government had only just plugged Vientiane into the hydroelectric dam before they were forced to cede power to the communist Pathet Lao. In an all too typical example of poor enviromental planning, the builders of the dam had flooded hundreds of hectares of valuable forest fifty metres underwater. The rotting vegetation sucked oxygen out of the water and blocked up the turbines, a problem that was later turned into profit by underwater logging ventures. Still busy recovering the sunken treasure, frogmen drop to the reservoir floor to cut the submerged trees with underwater saws.

Meanwhile, the new communist government found a novel use for the reservoir. After 1975, prostitutes, thieves and teenagers "infected with foreign ideas" were rounded up from the streets of Vientiane, a Lao Sodom in the eyes of the Pathet Lao, and confined on islands in the middle of the lake for "re-education". These days, day-tripping Lao head for Ang Nam Ngum with relaxation in mind, descending on the scenic reservoir in droves on weekends and hiring out wooden boats for picnic cruises. Aside from tourism and timber, the main occupation here is **fishing** – fishermen haul in an annual catch of 850 tonnes of fish, much of which is sold in the markets of Vientiane. Around sunset you'll even see a few of these fishermen heading out to fish for the night, armed with spear guns and crude oxygen machines – so large they nearly overwhelm their slim pirogues – which allow the fishermen to stay underwater for long stretches of time.

There are now a number of convenient options for visiting Ang Nam Ngum either as a day trip from Vientiane or Vang Viang or en route between the two. Short package tours are also available (see Practicalities, p.117). For independent travellers, the most logical base from which to explore the lake is the small town of **Na Nam**, near the dam on the western shore of the reservoir.

Na Nam

NA NAM is easily reached from Vientiane by public transport via Thalat. Although relatively few people live in this port of rickety shacks suspended above the water, Na Nam has a clutch of tourist restaurants, basic accommodation, and a fleet of wooden tourist boats, some seating up to forty passengers, for **lake cruises**. Once in Na Nam, you'll find freelance boatmen down at the waterfront restaurants, who generally ask for $4 per hour but are willing to negotiate day rates in the vicinity of $12. Na Nam guesthouses can also arrange boat tours. Obviously, the more people you have, the more affordable it becomes.

Beyond simply touring the reservoir, possibilities for **boat trips** include Don Dok Khoun Kham, where there's a rustic restaurant, the secluded beach at Don Keng Phou Viang – an hour-long trip which passes the scenic Pha Tao or "star cliff" island – or even down to the *Dan Sa Vanh Nam Ngum Resort*. Some of the islands are quite large, Don 516 for instance, supports a community of five hundred families and is connected to Na Nam by a twice daily passenger ferry which makes the almost three-hour trip out to the island.

If you want **to stay** overnight in Na Nam, a good option is the *Nam Ngum Boat Hotel* (❸). It's often booked by tour groups but independent travellers should have no problems getting a room here during the week. It only leaves its cove if all the rooms have been booked plus an additional $110 has been paid, but the view from the port is scenic. Rooms are not exactly cruise-liner standard, but they come with air-con and hot-water showers and there's also a restaurant on board. **Eating** figures highly in the weekend plans of Lao tourists, and several restaurants have set up shop around Na Nam to cater to this demand. Fish is the obvious dish, and *Nam Ngum*, in the port overlooking the water, delivers with freshly caught reservoir fish cooked in a variety of ways, and has an exceptional view of the lake. Just down the hill, *Boathouse*, a ramshackle barge with pleasant views, does good, moderately priced food. When there's an order, fish kept under the boat are netted and pulled right into the middle of the restaurant.

Don Dok Khoun Kham

Just a ten-minute boat ride from Na Nam, small, densely forested **Don Dok Khoun Kham**, the most accessible of the islands, boasts a pleasant restaurant and a rapidly decaying guest house (❷) that will be a sure hit with horror-film fans. The two-storey house has eight rooms of varying shapes and sizes, all of which are a little the worse for wear. During the week, few guests stay here and the house can at times be without water or electricity, although this is usually only the case if you've arrived after sunset and the caretaker is off spear-fishing for the night. If you don't mind roughing it a bit, the island makes for a pleasant, quiet place to spend an afternoon and a night. You might want to bring added provisions and a deck of cards, although the guest house is well stocked with necessities such as rice, water and Beer Lao, and fresh fish is always on the restaurant menu. Guests are shuttled between the guest house and the restaurant across a small cove by pirogue. The islanders will ferry you back to the mainland for significantly less than what the boatmen in Na Nam will charge to pick you up.

DanSaVanh Nam Ngum Resort

Located on the southwestern shore of the lake, the two-hundred room, $200 million, *DanSaVanh Nam Ngum Resort* (☎021/217594-6; ❺–❻) is the biggest hotel on the lake. Besides the swimming pool, 18-hole golf course, spa and Thai–Chinese restaurant, it also has post-communist Laos's first **casino**, mainly aimed at gamblers from Thailand. While hardly a return to former days when casinos were in full swing in Pakxe and Thakhek, it does signal a slight softening in government attitudes towards this ultimate capitalist pastime. The casino is popular with Thai tourists, and Thai baht is the currency of the tables – kip are not even accepted. The 24-hour gaming centre includes Blackjack, Baccarat and Tai-Sai tables, roulette and Australian slot machines. Other entertainments and activities at this "mega eco-tourism resort" include hang gliding, powerboat cruises, mountain-biking, disco dancing, and, of course, karaoke. After all that activity the hotel website recommends "our cheerful massage girls to pamper your tired body". While you can **get here** via a chartered boat from Na Nam, if you're actually coming to the reservoir for the resort it's more practical to come directly from Vientiane by road. There are free casino shuttle-buses from both the Friendship Bridge and major hotels in the capital.

Practicalities

Getting to Ang Nam Ngum by public transport is easy enough. **From Vientiane**, four blue government buses depart from the main bus station daily for the town of Thalat, from where you can get a shared tuk-tuk for the short run to the reservoir or the regular tuk-tuk shuttle service to Na Nam. Sawngthaews make the trip to Thalat more frequently, and depart from the stand in front of the bus station. A hired taxi costs $20 return – hiring a motorcycle is a cheaper option. With your own transport, you might consider making a scenic detour along the quieter Route 10 via Ban Keun to Thalat. **From Vang Viang**, southbound sawngthaews pass right by the town of Tha Hua at the northern end of the reservoir or you can switch vehicles at the Phonhong junction and cut in to Thalat and Na Nam.

Another option is use the lake as an interesting **alternative route north** to Vang Viang, hiring a boat from Na Nam for the five-hour trip to Tha Hua, on the northern side of Ang Nam Ngum, and then continuing by road to Vang Viang. Or you could catch the Vientiane to Vang Viang "Happy Bus" (☎020/616963), a twelve-seater, air-con minibus that shuttles between the two towns with sightseeing stops at Km 52, Ang Nam Ngum, and Vang Sang (eleventh-century Buddhist reliefs). The bus picks you up from your guest house and departs Vientiane at 9am, returning from Vang Viang at 3pm (daily except Monday; $7 one-way, $12 return). Bookings can be made through your guest house or phone direct.

Out of Vang Viang several travel companies now offer very affordable one-to-three-day **package tours** to the reservoir, which combine hiking, boating and camping. From Vientiane, Wildside Adventures (☎021/223022) has a two-day/one-night hiking and kayaking package ($40), which takes in both the reservoir and the Nam Lik River. They also run the same two-day tours to the reservoir, which start from Vientiane but drop you off in Vang Viang and vice versa for the same price.

Accommodation is available at a few locations around the lake – standards range from grass huts to casino suites. Near the dam itself, there's *EDL Bungalows* (❺), located a few kilometres away from the lake. Built to house Japanese engineers who worked on the dam project, the bungalows have air-con and hot water. To get there, take a shared tuk-tuk from Thalat bound for

Na Nam. The bungalows are about halfway along the route, near the dam, on the left. There's basic accommodation and places to eat in Na Nam (see p.116) or, if you fancy your luck at the gaming tables, you could splash out at the *DanSaVanh Nam Ngum Resort*. Don Dok Khoun Kham offers the most accessible **island-based accommodation** (see p.116), although the views from the run-down guest house and restaurant here are of the dam and less than picturesque port of Na Nam. Further out, better views can be had on Don Mittaphab, but its only hotel (❶) is even more run-down than the one on Don Dok Khoun and has no electricity. Basic food only is available, so it's best to bring extra provisions. A ride out here from Na Nam takes about half an hour. Another paradisical island with extemely basic accomodation is Don Santiphap, a tiny little islet with a simple guest house fit for Robinson Crusoe.

The northwest

Although Vientiane and Louang Phabang are both on the banks of the Mekong River, the land between them is extremely mountainous, while the opposite left bank of the Mekong, composed of huge ranges separating Laos and Thailand, forms its own remote province of Xainyabouli. As almost everyone's itinerary in Laos includes the journey between Vientiane and Louang Phabang, you're highly likely to cross this stunning terrain at some point and there are three main options to choose from for travelling between the two cities.

The first and simpliest option is to follow **Route 13** north from Vientiane through the karst mountains of **Vang Viang**, with its idyllic river and limestone caves, and up the **old Royal Road** through the mountains north of **Kasi**. The breathtaking mountain scenery from Kasi to Louang Phabang makes this one of the most **scenic routes** in all Southeast Asia. If you don't fancy making the ten-hour bus journey from Vientiane to Louang Phabang in one go, Vang Viang makes an ideal stopover and is well worth an extended visit in its own right. From Vientiane, the **Phou Phanang NBCA** runs north alongside Route 13 for 75km. Although there are two tracks going into the reserve off of Route 13, this NBCA is still fairly inaccessible to tourists. However, if you're prepared to rent a 4 wheel-drive vehicle or dirt bike from Vientiane, there is a dirt track running the entire length of the reserve and linking several villages, which forms the western boundary of the NBCA.

The second route, a detour through **Xainyabouli**, the sparsely populated region of rugged valleys and wild elephants on the western side of the Mekong, is more complicated and takes you along a path well off the banana pancake backpacker circuit. Unless you have your own 4-wheel drive vehicle, the Xainyabouli route necessitates travelling at least part of the way by boat along the Mekong – the lack of roads west of the capital makes Xainyabouli much more remote than it appears on maps. The third route is to travel the whole way by **slow boat** (see p.109), an attractive option but requiring at least three days of travel time, although speedboats can make the trip in a day.

Vang Viang

VANG VIANG reclines on the east bank of the Nam Xong River, snugly settled between a spectacular spread of sawtoothed limestone karsts to the west and rolling hills to the east. You could easily spend up to a week here cycling, **cave exploring**, tubing, rafting and hiking, or simply relaxing and enjoying the lazy country atmosphere, good food, and idyllic landscape. With its beautiful caves and nearby **ethnic minority villages**, the town also makes an ideal stopover on the way to or from Louang Phabang.

Vang Viang was already a popular backpacker destination way back in the Seventies when the trip took a full day from the capital. Today, after a 25-year hiatus, the town has quickly responded to the new wave of budget travellers and offers a huge range of backpacker-oriented guest houses and services including internet cafés, corner bars, massage, laundry services, video movies, and pizzerias. Beyond the town, there are a host of outdoor activities to keep you occupied, floating down the Nam Xong on huge tractor inner tubes being among the most popular.

Depending on when you get here the town can be totally packed out or almost empty within a few days as the tourist crowds ebb and flow. But, despite the influx of visitors, Vang Viang feels merely tourist-friendly rather than overrun. Locals call the town "Ban Farang" or "Foreigner's Town" and there is no doubt that with its strategic location close to the capital and mid-way to Louang Phabang, Vang Viang is destined to become Laos's premier resort town. But, for the moment, perhaps because the small and sleepy town itself isn't up to much, it retains its sanity, functioning mainly as a launching point for day-trips into the surrounding countryside. Happily, the townsfolk haven't tired of their town's increased popularity and will gladly point you in the right direction for a day well spent in the countryside.

Arrival, information and getting around

Sawngthaews and buses to and from Vientiane and Louang Phabang arrive at the **bus station** on Route 13 just to the east of town and within walking distance of most accommodation. **Buses** and **sawngthaews** going north and south along Route 13 stop at the bus station with eight buses passing through in each direction daily. If you're heading to Vientiane, sawngthaews are much more convenient, leaving every 20 minutes throughout the day. If you're heading north to Louang Phabang, you'll need to catch one of the buses coming up from the capital sometime after 9am, though it's highly unlikely there will be any empty seats. Sawngthaews to surrounding villages leave from the stand at the central market.

All of Vang Viang's streets are nameless but it's a small town on a square grid so **getting around** is a fairly simple matter. However, the town is rather spread out so a bicycle (6000–8000K per day) can come in handy and is good for excursions into the countryside. Bicycles and motorcycles ($7 per day) can be rented at many places around town. There's a BCEL **bank** (Mon–Sat 8am–noon & 1–4pm) on the main street opposite *the Dok Khoun 1* guest house, a Lang Xang Bank on the town's main north–south road, and an Agricultural Promotion Bank on the same street further south. Diagonally across from the latter is the **telecom office** (Mon–Fri 8am–noon & 1–5pm), which handles international calls; the **post office** is right next to the town

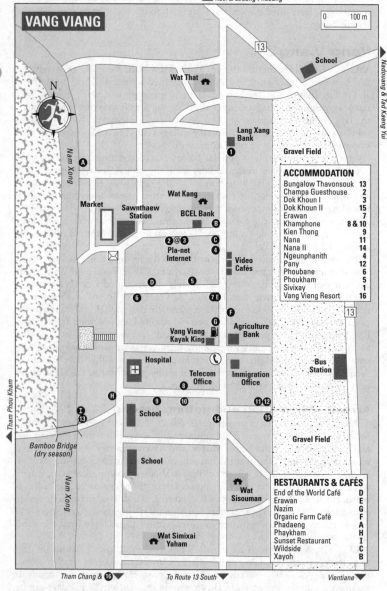

VANG VIANG

Kasi & Louang Phabang

0   100 m

School

Wat That

Lang Xang
Bank
❶

Gravel Field

Nam Xong

ACCOMMODATION

Bungalow Thavonsouk	13
Champa Guesthouse	2
Dok Khoun I	3
Dok Khoun II	15
Erawan	7
Khamphone	8 & 10
Kien Thong	9
Nana	11
Nana II	14
Ngeunphanith	4
Pany	12
Phoubane	6
Phoukham	5
Sivixay	1
Vang Vieng Resort	16

Market

Wat Kang

Sawnthaew
Station

BCEL Bank
Ⓑ

❷@❸   Ⓒ
❹
Pla-net
Internet

Video
Cafés

Ⓓ   ❺

❻   ❼Ⓔ

Ⓕ

Ⓖ

Vang Viang
Kayak King

Agriculture
Bank

13

Hospital

Telecom
Office
❽

Immigration
Office

❾   ❿   ⓫⓬

❶❺

Bus
Station

Ⓗ

Ⓣ
13

School

❶❹

Bamboo Bridge
(dry season)

Nam Xong

School

Gravel Field

Tham Phou Kham

Wat
Sisouman

Wat Simixai
Yaham

RESTAURANTS & CAFÉS

End of the World Café	D
Erawan	E
Nazim	G
Organic Farm Café	F
Phadaeng	A
Phaykham	H
Sunset Restaurant	I
Wildside	C
Xayoh	B

Tham Chang & ⓰   To Route 13 South   Vientiane

market. **Internet** facilities are available at the PlaNet CyberCentre (daily
8.30am–10pm; 250K per minute), next door to the *Champa Guesthouse*, the
friendly A1 Internet (☎023/511296), near the town's main T-junction, or any
of the other half dozen places along the main drag. All the usual services are
also in supply, including herbal sauna, laundry, massage, photo labs, tour agencies, vehicle rental, and video movies.

Accommodation

Despite its small size, Vang Viang is the best-value spot for **accommodation** in the country; it's possible to find a perfectly decent en-suite double here for under $4. On the downside, most of the town's **guest houses** seem to have been built by the same architect, whose forte was huge, concrete monstrosities with Corinthian columns and have absolutely no charm or atmosphere whatsoever. They include *Bounay, Vieng Vilay* by the market, and the three *Dok Khouns*. Despite the huge amount of choice, finding a friendly, family-run guesthouse in Vang Viang is not that easy, and there is already a clear and present danger of Vang Viang turning into a tacky tourist town. At the high end of the spectrum, the choice is limited to the *Vang Vieng Resort* just south of town, the *Nam Song Hotel* and *Bungalow Thavonsouk*, all of which have superb locations on the right bank of the Nam Xong facing the mountains.

Bungalow Thavonsouk At the bamboo bridge. Superbly located deluxe en-suite bungalows with a total of 35 units spread along the banks of the Nam Xong River. Prices depend on the size and quality of bungalow, some of which are quite luxurious and have private balconies facing the karsts. If money isn't an object then Thavonsouk's should be your first and only choice. ❺–❻

Champa Guesthouse Next to PlaNet CyberCentre. Shhhh..... this small, friendly, family-run guesthouse with no sign outside has rooms at half the price of comparable rooms in other guesthouses. ❶

Dok Khoun I, II, & III. Clean, tiled rooms, many en suite and with hot water, in modern, multi-storey buildings at three locations around town. Very popular but so big there's no worries about a lack of vacancies. Reasonably good value and quality but no personality or atmosphere. ❷–❸

Erawan On the main road south of the main T-junction ☎023/511093, ✉erawan-van@hotmail .com. In the back of this very popular restaurant, the Vietnamese–Lao owner and her foreign husband have a handful of double rooms with hot-water en-suite bathrooms for rent. The rooms are quite small but spotlessly clean. ❷

Khamphone On the same street as the *Kien Thong* (☎023/511062). Two big two-storey houses opposite one another. The house on the south side of the road has eighteen spacious, clean, well-lit rooms with tile floors and en-suite bathrooms with hot water. A cut above other similar places and a good choice if you're not on too strict a budget. ❹

Kien Thong On the street with the *Vieng Keo Restaurant* at one end and the *Phaykham* at the other ☎023/511069. Attractive two-storey house with a spiral staircase and a little restaurant downstairs. Has 21 clean doubles, most with en-suite bathrooms and hot water. The air-con rooms, which are double the price of fan rooms, are a cut above with queen-sized bed and a fridge in the room. Good value. ❷–❸

Nana In the alley by the *Vieng Keo Restaurant* ☎023/511036. Fourteen very big, clean, en-suite doubles, in a big house, all with hot water and some with air-con (double the price of fan). The upstairs rooms are by far the better quality and there's also a pleasant terrace on the second floor. Same quality as the *Dok Khoun* next door but with way more personality. ❷–❸

Nana II On the main road south of Vieng Keo restaurant ☎023/511070. Totally different from the original, the *Nana II* is a huge four-storey, L-shaped building more like a hotel than a guest house. The advantage of its 25 rooms, besides being cheap, is that the building is brand new. The corner rooms at the back of the top floor have the best views of the karsts.

Ngeunphanith On the main road between Wildside and the *Sengsavang* restaurant ☎023/511150. Big two-storey guest house with cheap rooms in the front and back. All the rooms here are not created equal so check out a few before deciding. Great location if you want to be right at the main T-junction. ❶

Pany In the alley by the *Vieng Keo Restaurant*. Roomy en-suite doubles in a modern two-storey house on a quiet lane. The upstairs rooms have wood floors and very clean, new bathrooms. More atmosphere than the usual rectangular block guest houses. Above average and an excellent deal for the money. ❷

Phoubane South of the market, just in from the river road ☎023/511037. One of the best deals in town. A pleasant, leafy compound, with decent rooms, some en suite, which are extremely good value for the money. The *Phoubane* also has a Lao herbal sauna that non-residents can use. ❶

Phoukham Directly behind the *Dok Khoun I*. An ugly building with gaudy pillars. The rooms aren't great but, for this style of guest house, they're better value than many similar places. Several of the upstairs rooms have good views of the karsts. ❶

Sivixay On the main road north of the T-junction opposite the *Bounay* ☎ 023/511030. These two modern buildings set in a large compound are not much to look at from the outside but contain 17 very decent, tiled en-suite doubles with fan and hot water at below average prices. ❶

Vang Vieng Resort South end of town ☎ 023/511050. Standard en-suite bungalows with decent facilities and hot shower. A fifteen-minute walk south along the river from the market. Good if you want to get as far away from the hustle and bustle of town as possible. ❻

Eating and drinking

Although a number of foreign-run establishments were recently closed during a visa crack-down, Vang Viang still offers the third best selection of international tourist **restaurants** in the country. It's now possible to get anything from vindaloo to "Israeli Lunch" in Vang Viang. Budget travellers tend to gravitate to the main north–south road where there's a whole strip of **cheap eateries** like *Sengsavang, Sisavang, Saybaydee, Nytuna* and *Phachanh*, offering a choice of Western-style seating or reclining on mats or cushions at low tables and often showing DVD movies. Aside from restaurants in town, there are a few decent places overlooking the river, although local residents on the riverside road have been very slow to realise the tourist potential. Come nightfall, the two hottest bars in town are the *Wildside* and the *Xayoh* at the main T-junction.

End of the World Café Six houses east of the *Phoubane* guest house. Hidden away from both the main tourist drags, this vegetarian restaurant still manages to pull the big crowds, and solely on word-of-mouth. Good tofu dishes and curried veggies, and very popular with the backpacker set.
Erawan Main road south of the main T-junction (☎ 023/511093). Best Western food in town with a pleasant seating area, CNN, and very good mains such as steak with mashed potatoes and steamed vegetables. The fish steak with chips and salad is excellent.
Nazim On the main road next to the gas station (☎ 023/511214). This extremely popular place serves vegetarian and non-vegetarian Indian food. It's absolutely packed most evenings though there have been many next-day reports of the food being a little too authentically Indian.
Organic Farm Café On the main street opposite *Nazim* and *Erawan*. Popular with vegetarians, this restaurant, which is an outlet for a local experimental organic farm, is definitely worth seeking out. The harvest curry with fresh veggies in a creamy curry broth is particularly good.
Phadaeng On the river just north of the market. Terrific little family-run Lao restaurant with extremely cheap prices and 2000K coffee right on the riverbank. The views are priceless and it

makes a very refreshing change from the more tourist-oriented businesses on the main roads.
Phaykham Three houses north of the turn-off to the river-crossing. This old favourite which seves basic Lao grub and sandwiches is currently undergoing a big expansion with the addition of a big, six-metre high deck offering spectacular views over the river and the majestic peaks beyond. Mama-san says the big deck will be finished when she gets more money.
Sunset Restaurant At *Bungalow Thavonsouk* by the bamboo bridge (☎ 023/511096). The best place in town for a sun-downer, boasting a million-dollar view across the Nam Xong. They serve quite good Western and Lao food here and the owner, Alom Thavonsouk, often gets out the guitar and sings a Sixties song or two.
Wildside At the town's main T-junction (☎ 023/511403). Though technically the Vang Viang branch of an adventure tour company, Wildside's open corner-bar is currently the most popular night spot in town, attracting standing-room-only crowds nightly.
Xayoh Opposite Wildside. Not as popular since the new neighbour moved in but still a good place for a drink or meal – fried rice, fried noodles, curry and sandwiches. either inside or on the outdoor patio. There's also an attached internet centre.

Around Vang Viang

The **countryside** surrounding Vang Viang is full of enough day-trip options to easily fill up a week. Scores of **caves** in limestone karst outcrops, tranquil lowland Lao and minority villages, and **Kaeng Yui Waterfall**, all make worthy destinations for a rewarding day's hike, while the Nam Xong River makes for

AROUND VANG VIANG

Tham Hoi
Nadao
Tham Xang
Ban Pha Thao
Tham Pha Thao
Nam Xong
13
Pakpo
Tham Phou Kham
Tham Pha Puak
Nadouang
Tad Kaeng Yui
Naxom
Nathong
Vang Viang
Tham Chang
Namouang
13
Khanmak
Namon
Vang Hua

0   5 km

a fun afternoon of **tubing**, **kayaking** or **rafting** – tubes can be rented at a number of shops on the main street leading to the market. If walking isn't your thing, you can hire bicycles and motorcycles from various outlets around town. Aside from a number of organized tours around Vang Viang itself, there are also one-to-three day excursions to Ang Nam Ngum Reservoir (see p.115) which can be booked through most guest houses.

Organized **day tours**, many of which combine both caving and tubing with lunch in between, are not really necessary but are a fast and convenient way for the uninitiated to get into the Vang Viang groove: once you've done the organized tour you can go back for more on your own. If you do opt to join a tour, be sure to check how many people will be in the group. Some agents have few qualms about stuffing twenty people into a single sawngthaew and too many people not only spoils a good walk but can seriously hasten the onset of claustrophobia when tramping about several hundred metres underground. It's not hard to find a guided tour – just look for signs posted in restaurants and guest houses.

If you decide to visit the caves on your own, it's worth checking out the three colourful, hand-drawn **maps** of the Vang Viang area (2000K each), which show all the **caves** and **trails**; they're available from the *Phaykham* restaurant just north of the turn-off down to the bamboo bridge across the Nam Xong. Otherwise just ask around; everyone in Vang Viang has their favourite cave, swimming hole or countryside getaway. The local people are very friendly and more than happy to point you in the right direction or even lead the way for a small tip and other travellers will also enthusiastically recommend the best places. If you're looking to explore areas north or south of town, there's enough local transport in the form of buses and sawngthaews plying Route 13 to get you up and down the highway cheaply. Or, if you prefer something quick and easy, just hire a tuk-tuk, which will gladly wait for you for the right price. The tuk-tuk stand is at the market.

Most of Vang Viang's attractions lie on the **west bank** of the Nam Xong. There still isn't a permanent bridge (although the subject is already under discussion) so you have to cross via the rickety bamboo bridge (foreigners 500K) by the *Nam Song Hotel*. During the rainy season the bridge is dismantled and you have to cross by pirogue. The village on the west bank across from Vang Viang is called Ban Houay Nye. Once on the other side, Chinese-made tractors trundle along the bumpy paths to nearby villages, acting as makeshift shared taxis that aren't entirely comfortable but are at least faster than walking. These wait at the river's edge or you can simply flag them down as you would a bus or tuk-tuk.

There are now two **kayaking** and **rafting** companies operating in Vang Viang and more are bound to follow. Wildside Adventures (T 023/511403, E wildside-laos.com) has an office at the corner of the main T-junction and offers two different day-trip packages ($8–12) as well as a two-day/one-night hiking and kayaking excursion ($28). Vang Viang Kayaking in the Swiss–Lao looking building opposite the Agricultural Promotion Bank has kayaks for rent but is much less organized.

While **rock-climbing** is well established in Thailand it is still in its infancy in Laos. However, given the stunning karst tower locations all over the country this sport should boom here. In Vang Viang, Wildside has just opened Laos's first fully operational rock climbing site featuring 16 different bolted routes graded from 5b to 8c on the French grading system. A day's climbing costs $20 with equipment, a guide and lunch.

Chang Cave

Vang Viang's best-known cave, **Tham Chang**, has been developed for tourism to such an extent that the proprietors of *Vang Vieng Resort*, whose land you have to cross to get to the cave, levy a fee to enter the resort and again at the cave's entrance (2500K). In the nineteenth century, the cave earned its nom de guerre ("chang" means steadfast) when it was used for defence during an invasion of Chinese Haw from the north. Chinese bandits would have an easy run of the place these days, with steep stairs leading up the side of the cliff to the cave mouth. Inside, gaudy coloured lights illuminate cement pathways leading through the cavern, past rock formations that bear an uncanny resemblance to monkeys, frogs, a white elephant and the three-headed elephant, symbol of Lao royalty. Follow the path to the left and you'll wind up at a second cave mouth which affords a bird's eye view of the valley below. At the base of the cave, cross a stream to find a third cave mouth out of which flows a spring leading into the Nam Xong. It's possible to swim up the stream about fifty metres into this cave, which also has a Buddha image inside. The grassy lawn around the base of the cave is a pleasant spot to catch some rays.

Pha Puak Cave

A little more than 1km north of Ban Houay Nye, lies **Tham Pha Puak**, a cave tucked into a karst encircled by Pha Daeng, or the Red Cliffs. Pha Daeng is considered particularly sacred and some locals even maintain that planes flying over the cliff do so at their peril, no doubt a legend with roots in the Second Indochina War, when Vang Viang was used as an airbase, known to pilots as Lima Site 6. Although in and of itself nothing special, the cave makes a good short walk out of Vang Viang. To get there, cross the river then follow the path through the rice fields north of Ban Houay Nye.

Tubing the Nam Xong

One of Vang Viang's most popular activities, a lazy afternoon floating down the **Nam Xong** on huge tractor inner tubes runs a close second to caving on many travellers' itineraries and some people make several trips. It's a good way to relax, take in the view and just be mellow, with enough rapids and tiny islands to keep things interesting. You can also stop at beaches along the way for a rest or a walk and some enterprising villagers even sell cold soft drinks from the river bank. **Tubes** are available at many shops along the main street leading to the market for 5000K per day.

There's a good **launching point** near the village of Pakpok, roughly 4km north of Vang Viang, which makes for a two- to three-hour trip. If you're in for something longer, jump in at the bend in the river at the Km10 marker, which will have you in the water for at least five hours. Before you grab your tube and head for the river take note that a few foreigners have drowned tubing down the river. If you can't swim or are a weak swimmer, or are drunk or stoned, you should wear a life-jacket while tubing. The river is swift in spots and it's quite easy to become temporarily separated from your tube. You'll also need a good sunblock and a hat if you don't want to come out looking like a lobster. Exercise common sense and ask about river conditions before you float off down the river, and, unless you plan to enter the Mekong 70km east of Vientiane, when you see Vang Viang town to your left, be sure to position yourself towards the east bank so you can get out at the *Nam Song Hotel*.

Phou Kham Cave

Six kilometres west of Vang Viang, **Tham Phou Kham** makes a rewarding half-day trip that takes in some fine scenery and affords the chance to visit a cave and enjoy a good swim along the way. Cross the river by pirogue at the launch near the *Nam Song Hotel* and follow the road through a pretty valley ringed by imposing karsts to Na Thong, 4km west. Hop the fence at the bend in the road just past the village school house and walk through the rice fields towards the cliff face, 1km in the distance. Cross the bizarrely arched bamboo bridge to reach the path leading to the cave. It's a short steep climb to the entrance and the path is extremely slippery in the rainy season, but there's plenty of bamboo to grab onto on the way up. In the main cavern reclines a bronze Buddha, though you'll need a torch if you want to explore the tunnels branching off the main gallery. Outside the cave, the Hollywood-swimming-pool-blue stream is a great spot for a swim, and you can buy cool drinks and fruit nearby. If you've come by bike it's best to leave it at the *tam màk hung* stall across from the above-mentioned village school.

Kaeng Yui Waterfall

While it may seem counterintuitive to turn your back on Vang Viang's majestic karsts, a day out eastward to **Tad Kaeng Yui**, a secluded spot with twin thirty-metre-high waterfalls, is well worth the trip down a rough path. Well off the beaten track, Tad Kaeng Yui nestles in the forest among the hills protecting Vang Viang's eastern flank. It offers a refreshingly cool picnic spot, with small pools of water directly under the falls to lounge in, and rewards the journey with the sense of being smack in the middle of the tropics, miles from anywhere.

To find the falls, first make your way to the village of **Na Douang**, 3km away, by crossing Route 13 just north of the airstrip. Follow this road, flagged by the secondary school on the corner, east to the village. As the waterfall is rarely visited, even by locals, your safest bet is to hire a villager from Na Douang to show you the way. The waterfall, another 3km from the village, is not impossible to find, but as the path nears the falls it can be completely obscured by bamboo owing to lack of traffic. From Na Douang, head southeast towards the hills by cutting through the village rice fields; beyond the fields lies a path leading uphill, through scrub forest, across a number of small streams, and then into the woods. Once you've reached the woods, push on for another 300m. The path turns left and the falls become audible. Plans to exploit the waterfall's tourism potential by building a road out to the falls are a sign that times have changed. If completed, the road will allow visitors to drive in, but will undoubtedly spoil the spot's secluded beauty. At this stage, getting there remains a muddy affair much of the year – even travelling as far as Na Douang. If you plan to do the trip by bicycle, a sit-up-and-beg model risks turning the trip into a Sisyphean feat, but it might be a good splash on a mountain bike.

Pha Thao Cave

A descent into **Tham Pha Thao** is the most satisfying caving trip you can make from Vang Viang. Stretching for more than 2km, the tunnel-like cave is pitch-black and filled with huge and presumably ancient stalactites and stalagmites. It also contains a **swimming hole**, formed in an underground river that winds through the cave. Located in the cliff face behind the Hmong village of Pha Thao, the cave is best visited near the end of the rainy season, when the water level is perfect for a swim in the subterranean swimming pool 800m into the cave. In the height of the dry season, it's possible to go beyond this point and explore the full length of the cave – not an option during the rains when the water level is too high.

En route to the cave, you'll pass through **PHA THAO**, a smallish village populated by former Hmong refugees. The Hmong living here fled the northern mountains of Laos during the post-revolutionary turmoil of the late 1970s and early 1980s and wound up in a Thai refugee camp where they lived until being repatriated in the mid-1990s. Essentially, they are some of the Hmong who were denied visas to the United States and other Western nations and were forced to go "home".

Finding the cave is a matter of getting to Pha Thao, which lies 13km north of Vang Viang. Turn left after the bridge just beyond the Km10 marker on Route 13 – a road sign points the way to the "Nam Xong-Pha Thao Irrigation Project" – and head for the river. Here, you'll have to ford the river or hail a

Dress for success in Vang Viang

The **varied terrain** surrounding Vang Viang can turn treacherous in a hurry, particularly during the rainy season. **Exercise caution** while wandering through caves and scrambling about on the steep slopes of the karst formations, as serious injuries incurred by foolhardy travellers while tramping about in the area are common. Slippery trails demand that proper shoes be worn – Teva-style sandals with good traction are the best for conquering Vang Viang's alternately rocky and muddy trails. Bermuda-type shorts are also a good sartorial choice as you may end up knee-deep in water at some point if you intend to enjoy the countryside to the fullest. A re-sealable plastic bag for valuables such as money and your passport is an excellent idea. Do not leave your valuables with local youths, who may offer to "look after them for you" while you explore a cave.

Finally, while it may be tempting to wander around in your swimming gear – and, it's not uncommon to see travellers sunbathing half-naked on the banks of the Nam Xong – always remember that in Laos gratuitous displays of flesh are considered a form of rudeness and disrespect.

pirogue to take you across for a few thousand kip. This spot also makes a good launching point for tubing (see p.125). Once you've made it across the river, make your way to the village, which lies at the base of the cliff. Here, you'll find a few simple restaurants serving drinks and Hmong food, and the villagers will be happy to point you in the direction of the cave mouth which, obscured by boulders and trees, isn't terribly apparent. If you explore the cave during the rainy season, you'll be up to your chest in water at times – so travel light and don't bring along anything that you don't want to get wet. A waterproof torch and camera are a good idea. Tour groups often pull through this cave during the morning, so you may want to go in the afternoon.

Tham Xang and Tham Hoi

Situated in a karst outcrop that seems to rise from a bed of vibrant-green rice paddies, **Tham Xang** is easily visible from Route 13 about 13km north of Vang Viang. To get there turn left on the dirt road in the village of Sinsomxai, just beyond the Km13 marker, and follow the dirt road to the river. Climb the fence and walk along the paddies downriver, climb a second fence and walk past a sugar cane field and down along the riverbank until you spot a bamboo bridge worthy of an Indiana Jones B-movie. Cross the river here to reach Tham Xang; if you're not feeling acrobatic you can hail a pirogue. Although it's more of an opening than a cave, Tham Xang is roomy enough to house a large Buddha image and is a popular attraction at Lao New Year.

If you've made it to Tham Xang, it's well worth continuing to **Tham Hoi**, a nearby cave as wide as a subway tunnel that reportedly stretches 2–4km into a nearby cliff, although patriotic locals profess it to be 20km deep. In mid-April, New Year revellers take advantage of a makeshift lighting scheme to visit the cave and a few feel the urge to express their inner Michelangelo; suffice to say, the cave isn't unspoilt, yet it's still a treat to visit. To get there, head north from Tham Xang, cross a small footbridge and then zigzag through the rice paddies in a northwesterly direction towards the cliff, 500m from Tham Hoi; a Buddha image stands guard just inside the cave mouth. A caretaker with a torch will lead the way for a small tip and claims that if the water level in the cave is right – usually late in the year – it's possible to make it far enough inside to reach a decent swimming hole.

The Royal Road: Kasi to Louang Phabang

North of **Kasi**, Route 13 embarks on a wild 170-kilometre stretch of highway along steep ridges and around hairpin bends, with headlong views of rugged valleys and remote mountains as far as the eye can see. The Vientiane–Louang Phabang road was first completed by the French in 1943, and although it was improved in the 1960s with American aid, anyone who travelled the road between the Second Indochina War and the mid-1990s, when it was properly sealed, probably wished the Americans had spent less money on bombs and more on asphalt, as this rough track of a road took at best a full 24 hours to traverse, and often as long as three days. The highway was finally completed in 1996 after years of toil by Vietnamese road workers – twenty of whom were killed by guerrillas in the process – at last allowing the route to be travelled in one day.

Kasi

KASI is the last town before Route13 begins its long climb into the Louang Phabang Mountains. The road runs right through the centre of town forming the main street, but the town itself lies in the attractive **Nam Lik river valley** surrounded by rice paddies and low hills, with the occasional karst adding an exotic touch to a pretty landscape. Within easy day-tripping distance of Kasi are numerous vast cave systems rumoured to dwarf anything found at Vang Viang, 60km to the south, and plans are underway to develop the Kasi area into an eco-tourism region. If the rumours of Olympic pool-sized cave lakes and caverns large enough to house cathedrals are only half true, then Kasi's crack at being the next Vang Viang could well become a reality.

Buses plying the road between Vientiane and Louang Phabang usually make a lunch stop here, so there's half a dozen decent **places to eat** up and down the street. There are also three guesthouses, including the comfortable *Vanphisith Guesthouse* (●) near the centre of the strip. If you're staying in Kasi, you might want to go down to the sawmill by the river to watch the elephants that are still used occasionally to haul logs. There are two daily **buses** from Kasi to Vientiane not including the three Vientiane-bound buses coming down from Louang Phabang and additional sawngthaews.

Vieng Kham

Perched on a narrow mountain ridge 39km north of Kasi and just 5km before Phou Khoun, the village of **VIENG KHAM** offers good views to the west of one of Laos's most magnificent **peaks** – a gigantic, lone 2097-metre crag that rises like a giant tooth out of the flatlands below. If you're travelling south, Vieng Kham offers the first view of this breathtaking peak and its more distant companion which stands at an equally impressive 2089m. Just beyond the second peak, out of view, is the Mekong River, and beyond that the distant mountains of Xainyabouli. Whether you're travelling north or south on Route 13, it's well worth getting a window seat on the western side of the bus in order to photograph this spectacular peak. South of Vieng Kham there's a long, slow winding decent towards Kasi that provides good photo opportunities of this unforgettable mountain.

Phou Khoun and Route 7 to Phonsavan

A former French outpost, the mountain village of **PHOU KHOUN**, 44km north of Kasi, is the junction of Route 13 and Route 7 and the largest settlement between Kasi and Xiang Ngeun, 25km south of Louang Phabang. The village has sweeping views of the deep valleys below and is the main market for people living in isolated villages around the area. Given the mountain location, be warned that the weather can get quite chilly here.

From Phou Khoun, **Route 7** branches off of Route 13 and travels due east across the Xiang Khouang Plateau **to Phonsavan** (see p.199) on the Plain of Jars. At the time of writing, the final surfacing of Route 7 was well over a year behind schedule and there was still a 50km stretch of loose dirt road to cross, making the trip to Phonsavan a dusty 10–12 hour run. This last stretch should be paved very soon however, reducing the travelling time by several hours and opening up a whole new route to Phonsavan and Xam Nua. In the meantime, catching the once-daily bus to Phonsavan remains an ordeal. By the time the bus reaches Phou Khoun from Vientiane it is packed, so chances are you'll be standing all the way unless another passanger is prepared to sell you their seat. Should you get stuck at the junction there's a single guesthouse, the *Chiher* (❶), a two-storey shop-house with a green roof, which has no running water and very basic rooms. Once Route 7 is complete you can expect to see more guest houses as well as private sawngthaews doing the Phonsavan run.

Phou Khoun to Xiang Ngeun

Tiny picturesque villages cling to the mountain ridges every 20km or so for the rest of the journey north, none yet offering accommodation and only a few providing a table at which to eat a bowl of *fŏe*. If you're travelling by rented or chartered vehicle, you could try the proper noodle shop at **PHA KENG NOI**, a small village perched on a narrow ridge 15km north of Phou Khoun. **KIOU KA CHAM**, 45km north of Phou Khoun, is an even larger town, populated by **Hmong**, and located high up in the mountains. There are several restaurants, tiny pharmacies and general stores selling basic goods and petrol out of old oil drums, the walls plastered with Vietnamese pin-ups and family snapshots of relatives living abroad: Hmong women dressed to the nines in extravagant traditional garb standing beside their sons and husbands in cheap suits in the living rooms of their suburban American homes. To the north the highway continues to wind through the green-blue mountains, passing ethnic minority villages and swidden fields cutting bare the hillsides, until reaching **XIANG NGEUN**, a large settlement 25km south of Louang Phabang. Xiang Ngeun is another important junction: from here **Route 2** heads southwest 110km to the provincial capital of Xainyabouli, on the western side of the Mekong River.

The Xainyabouli circuit

While the vast majority of visitors use Route 13 between Louang Phabang and the capital, it is possible to swing through Laos's northwestern frontier provided you're willing to allow three to four days for the journey. You can make the entire journey by slow boat, but if you opt for the road-and-river journey, **Paklai** and **Xainyabouli** are the best places to make stopovers. As there are still only rugged tracks between Vientiane and the south of Xainyabouli province, river travel is the best way to do that section of the trip. Route 2, running the length of **XAINYABOULI PROVINCE** between Louang Phabang and Kenthao is especially beautiful, particularly in the rice-growing season (June–November), with the electric-green paddies set against a sea of bluish mountains – some as high as 2000m – receding in waves towards Thailand.

Something of a Lao wild west, this remote, densely forested and mountainous province is home to elephants, tigers and the Sumatran rhino. Recognizing it as the perfect place to disappear, CIA operatives active in the Second Indochina War saw Xainyabouli as the escape route for **Vang Pao** and his band of Hmong irregulars (for more on this see Contexts, pp.348–349) should their "secret war" go wrong. They figured the Hmong would be at home in this province peopled by numerous hilltribes, among them Mien, Khamu and Akha, who migrate freely across the western border with Thailand. The untamed nature of the province is perhaps best illustrated by the traditional lifestyle of the **Mabri**, a tribe of nomadic hunter-gatherers numbering only a few hundred people, who are known to the Lao as *kha tawng leuang* or "slaves of yellow banana leaves" – the name is derived from the tribal custom of moving on as soon as the leaves of their huts turn yellow.

Some of the villages are so **remote** that they hardly feel part of Laos, finding it far more convenient to trade with Thai towns across the border, or to simply exist in relatively isolated self-sufficiency. Seizing upon the Lao government's seeming neglect of its far-flung villages, the Thais claimed three Lao villages near the border as their own in a land grab during the 1980s – an incident that sparked two skirmishes between the historic rivals during the course of four years and highlighted the vagueness of the border.

These days the line separating Laos from its larger neighbour has been sketched somewhat more permanently on the map and it's back to business as usual for traders on either side, with the bustling border town of **Kenthao** functioning as a gateway for goods flowing across the Nam Huang River. A fair number of smuggled cars, sparkling new and without plates, also pass through here and continue on to Vientiane, where they change hands for a fraction of their tax-heavy cost. Amphetamine production is another thorny cross-border issue, with Thai police accusing clandestine factories on the Lao side of producing *ya ma*, or "horse medicine", that ends up on the streets of the Thai capital Bangkok.

A 150-kilometre-long section of the border with Thailand consists of the massive **Nam Phoun NBCA**, Laos's westernmost bio-conservation area. The chain of mountains forming the park's spine includes peaks as high as 1790m. Two significant streams, the Pouy and the Phoun flow down from heights above and cross the width of Xainyabouli Province before flowing into the Mekong. Although the town of Nakong on Route 2 sits right on the edge of the park, the NBCA has yet to be developed for trekking.

As you might expect, getting to Xainyabouli's remotest corners isn't easy. Secluded caves and waterfalls are out there, but none lies on the tourist route at the moment. The region will probably be one of the last places to benefit from the country's rapid improvements in tourist infrastructure, which is inspiration enough to try this route.

The Mekong River: Vientiane to Paklai

Speedboats take about four hours to complete the 217-kilometre journey between Vientiane and the Mekong river-port town of Paklai. The boats depart from Tha Hua Keow Leo pier 10km west of Vientiane (see p.109) – be sure to get to the pier early in the morning, as it's first come first served for space on the speedboat ($20). If there are no other local passengers, it's possible to charter a speedboat for $100. **Slow boats** leave daily and take a full day to reach Paklai.

Upstream from Vientiane, the Mekong forms the Lao–Thai border. Golden stupas dot the banks of Laos's richer cousin, a marked contrast to the shaggy bamboo- and forest-clad hills on the right, many bearing the scars of logging. Further upriver, the Mekong swings north and the Lao tricolour flies from both banks for the first time since Champasak.

Paklai

PAKLAI, a port town 210km south of Louang Phabang, is the best stopover between Xainyabouli and Vientiane. Although not as developed as the border town of Kenthao, 60km to the south, Paklai is bigger, its wooden houses spreading for several kilometres along the riverbank. The town's economic mainstay is timber and timber products, a trade lucrative enough to draw Chinese businessmen from Singapore, Malaysia and China in their land cruisers and banged-up pick-ups to this remote town. Speedboats dock at the **boat landing** on the far southern end of town, 3km from the town square, where you'll find a few restaurants and guest houses. Some captains will take you to Paklai's main port, which lies in the centre of town near the square; failing that, there's usually a tuk-tuk (1000K) at the top of the hill overlooking the pier.

You need look no further than the town square to see that Paklai's not up to much: a scruffy patch of grass with a puny white stupa, crudely crafted from stucco, and topped with a red communist star, which provides a backdrop for schoolchildren to play tag but little else. Here, you'll find the town's main **restaurant**, which serves, among a variety of rice dishes, generous helpings of fried rice with a tasty sauce on the side. Further up the street is a small noodle shop, also nameless, popular for its *fŏe*. The restaurant can also handle a few rice dishes and makes decent Lao coffee. Across the street stands the *Khemekong* (❶), a wooden **guest house** with thirteen rooms, usually reserved for government employees. A better option lies a short walk upriver on the right. The friendly *Ban Na* (❶) has clean rooms and a seating area with a nice view of the river. If you're desperate, a third, government-owned guest house, the *Pak Lay* (❶), lies at the end of this road on the left. Nearly 1km away from the main ferry landing, next to a sawmill, this guest house is a bit run-down and there are no restaurants nearby; the manager does her best, however, and her pet monkey provides entertainment gratis.

Moving on, sawngthaews leave from the market in the morning for the 100-kilometre-journey to Xainyabouli town (10,000K), departing when full. Speedboats and slow boats make the trip up and down the Mekong, but you may have to charter a speedboat if they don't have enough passengers.

Xainyabouli

XAINYABOULI (pronounced "sai NYAboolee"), a dusty, independent-minded town, sits on the Nam Houng River, with the massive grey and white Pha Xang limestone cliffs – so named because they bear a passing resemblance to a herd of elephants in motion – providing a distant backdrop. At the centre of the town, there's a massive thirty-room hotel, an aborted government building begun by a former governor whose political largesse mocks the decidedly country atmosphere of Laos's most remote provincial capital. To add to the incongruity, Xainyabouli is also a training town for budding traffic cops, who are occasionally seen in groups of five or six waving their arms and blowing their whistles at the town's empty roundabout. Unlike the traffic, the town's expat international aid and development community has grown significantly as Xainyabouli province is one of the country's least developed areas.

The bustling **market** is the focus of the town's energies, and manages to maintain a buzz throughout the day. People from the local **hilltribes** often come down to buy and sell, spreading out their weird and wonderful range of produce (roots and forest creatures among other things) on swaths of cloth in neat rows around the fringe of the market proper, while members of the Mien tribe run the more established stalls. Few of the ethnic minorities in the market wear traditional clothes, however, preferring to dress in the style of the low-

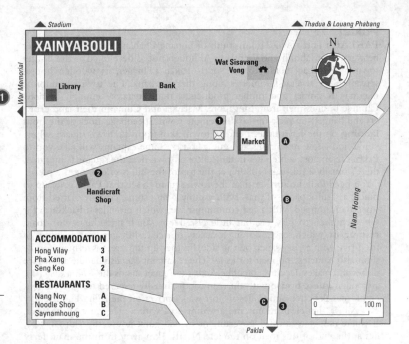

land Lao. The textiles available in this section of the market are mostly from Vientiane so you won't find many treasures here. But east of the market near the *Seng Keo*, there's a small **handicraft shop** selling eye-joltingly colourful Tai Leu textiles, of a style rarely found outside the province, as well as textiles from nearby Tai Dam villages.

Practicalities

Xainyabouli has two **bus stations**, the one at the southern end of town for pick-ups shuttling the 100km all-weather road between Xainyabouli and Paklai and the other at the northern end of town for vehicles making the forty-minute run to the Thadua ferry landing on the Mekong. Tuk-tuks make the trip into town from the bus stations, stopping at the central market (500K). From the northern bus station there are direct sawngthaews to Louang Phabang, though sometimes the trip requires separate sawngthaews for each side of the river.

The *Seng Keo* (❶) a two-storey house with a stone facade set in a grassy compound one block east of the post office, is the best **guest house**, with decent doubles and shared facilities. If the *Seng Keo* is full, try *Pha Xang* (❶), just north of the post office, with sixteen rooms and an attractive courtyard flowing with bougainvillea. The town's disco, complete with the usual hostess scene, sits directly behind the hotel but its throbbing tunes cease at 11.30pm. Next door, the massive government hotel – built by a free-spending former governor and originally slated to be a government office – is the best digs in town. Finally, situated on a riverfront plot, there's the *Hong Vilay* (❶); the lobby and shared facilities are grubby but the double and triple rooms are clean enough.

Along with a smattering of **noodle shops** in and around the market, there are a few good, inexpensive **restaurants**. The well-run *Nang Noy*, across from the market, is the most established – it may not look like much, but it serves good, expensive rice and noodle dishes. A few hundred metres away, the clean, well-lit *Saynamhoung* also serves decent food and has an English-language menu.

Thadua

Slow boats up and down the Mekong usually stop in **THADUA**, 35km north-east of Xainyabouli, making this tiny river port, along with Paklai, one of two towns that travellers wind up visiting in Xainyabouli province. There's little to recommend Thadua, although the aqua-green house at the top of the ferry landing does have a few beds (●). If you find yourself stuck here, a short hike out to **Tad Chao**, a thirty-metre-tall waterfall flowing into the Mekong, makes a pleasant diversion. To get there, turn right after the small market, which sits at the top of the ferry landing ramp, and follow the road until it ends (about 1km) at a small stream on the far side of a wooded ridge. The path leading off to the left climbs a short distance to a pair of unimpressive grottos, containing a *rishi* and a Buddha image. To get to the waterfall, cross the wooden bridge and you'll eventually come to a flight of stairs leading down to the base of the fall. Tad Chao is not Laos's most spectacular fall, but this popular Sunday picnic spot's perch at the side of the Mekong River certainly adds to its appeal.

From Thadua, speedboats make the trip to Louang Phabang regularly, taking about two hours, but unless there are other passengers you'll have to hire the whole boat. Slow boats for Louang Phabang take nearly four times as long. Pirogues skirt across the river regularly, although if you've come by your own transport you're at the mercy of the Thadua ferry, which can take up to an hour. Large pick-up trucks bound for Louang Phabang queue up along the ferry landing ramp on the opposite bank, a gathering of petrol stations and thatch huts known as Pakkhon.

Muang Nan and the road to Louang Phabang

At first glance, **MUANG NAN**, around 20km northeast of Thadua on the road to Louang Phabang, seems little more than a dusty truck-stop whose only saving grace is its location in a slim, pretty valley full of rice fields. But walk off the highway and you'll find a cosy town of traditional homes and old temples hugging the palm-lined banks of the babbling Nan River. The spirited villagers dam up the tiny river annually near the end of the monsoon and hold boat races with long, slender pirogues. While it's difficult to imagine the narrow river offering much sport to a flock of ducks, let alone a fleet of boats, enough city folk from Louang Phabang make the trip down to Nan for the event, held to celebrate Awk Phansa (see p.56), to make it a lively affair.

A newly built government **guest house** stands on a small hill along the highway and has clean doubles and triples with shared facilities. The rate here is per person ($2). The **restaurant** across from the guest house serves *fŏe* with an excellent homemade sauce of tamarind, peanuts and garlic, known as *jaew sakki*, on the side. If you order in advance, they can also prepare vegetable and chicken dishes with a country flair.

Sawngthaews in either direction usually pause briefly on their hourly run through the town. From here, it takes two to three hours to Louang Phabang by sawngthaew, but the gentle rollercoaster of a dirt road is scenic, negotiating uneven hills pocked with remote caves and swinging through narrow valleys of terraced rice fields cut in irregular rectangles, farmed by the hilltribes whose dusty bamboo-and-thatch huts hug the road. A kilometre north out of town, the highway cuts past Muang Nan's school on the right, with the makeshift huts of boarding students from far-flung ethnic minority villages clustered around the wooden school and football pitch along the road. Predominantly Mien, the children live in these temporary huts, as their home villages lack schools and the daily commute is too far – a development dilemma for this mountainous and sparsely populated country.

Travel details

Buses

Pakkhon to: Louang Phabang (5 daily; 3hr); Muang Nan (5 daily; 2hr 30min).

Paklai to: Kenthao (1–2 daily; 1–2hr); Xainyabouli (1–3 daily; 3–4hr).

Vang Viang to: Louang Phabang (5 daily; 6hr); Vientiane (8 daily; 3hr).

Vientiane to: Dong Dok University (8 daily; 30min); Friendship Bridge (every 45min; 45min); Kasi (10 daily; 5hr); Lak Xao (3 daily; 8hr); Lao Pako (3 daily; 1hr); Louang Phabang (5 daily; 10–12hr); Oudomxai (1 daily; 19hr); Pakxan (12 daily; 2hr); Pakxe (3 daily; 14hr); Phonsavan (daily; 18hr); Savannakhet (8 daily; 8 hr); Thakhek (10 daily; 6hr); Thalat (hourly; 2hr); Vang Viang (8 daily; 3hr 30 min); Xam Nua (daily; 30hr).

Xainyabouli to: Paklai (1–3 daily; 3–4hr); Thadua (4 daily; 40min).

Domestic flights

Vientiane to: Houayxai (3 weekly; 1hr 20min); Louang Namtha (3 weekly; 1hr 10min); Louang Phabang (4 daily; 40min); Oudomxai (4 weekly; 50min); Pakxe (1 daily; 1hr 20min); Phonsavan (2 daily; 40min); Savannakhet (1 daily; 1hr 5min); Xainyabouli (1 daily; 45min); Xam Nua (1 daily; 1hr 10min).

International flights

Vientiane to: Bangkok (2 daily; 1hr); Chiang Mai (2 weekly; 2hr); Hanoi (1 daily; 1hr10min); Ho Chi Minh City (1 weekly; 2hr 40min); Kunming (1 weekly; 3hr); Phnom Penh (1 daily; 2hr 30min); Siem Reap (2 weekly; 2 hr 30min).

Slow boats

Thadua to: Louang Phabang (daily; 7–9hr).

Vientiane to: Louang Phabang via Paklai (variable; 3–4 days).

Louang Phabang

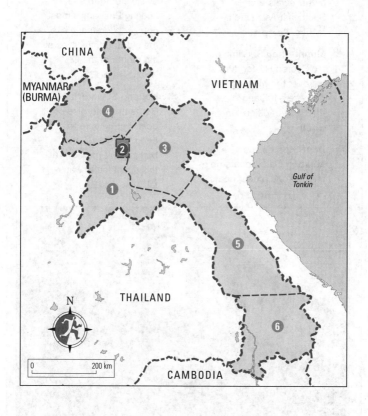

CHAPTER 2

Highlights

* **The Royal Palace** Tour of the French-built palace, once home to the last of the Lao kings. **See p.151**

* **Wat Xiang Thong** Laos's most historic wat is one of the jewels of Southeast Asian architecture. **See p.154**

* **Mount Phou Si** Climbing the Sacred Hill for sunset over the Mekong has become a Louang Phabang tradition. **See p.158**

* **Boat trips on the Mekong** Cargo boats up the Mekong, speedboats up the Nam Ou, or a ferry across the river – you'll find a boat trip for every budget down at the landing. **See p.171**

* **Pak Ou Buddha Caves** Cruise up the Mekong by slow boat to see Louang Phabang's most popular pilgramage site, the old Buddha Caves at the mouth of the Ou River. **See p.173**

* **Kouang Si waterfall** Come by motorbike or boat, but be sure to bring your towel and bathing suit for a day at this spectacular waterfall. **See p.175**

Louang Phabang

estling in a slim valley shaped by lofty, green mountains and cut by the swift Mekong and Khan rivers, **LOUANG PHABANG** – also known as Louang Prabang – exudes remote tranquillity and casual grandeur. A tiny mountain kingdom for more than a thousand years and designated a World Heritage site in 1995, Louang Phabang is endowed with a legacy of ancient red-roofed temples and French-Indochinese architecture, not to mention some of the country's most refined cuisine, its richest culture and its most sacred Buddha image, the Pha Bang. For those familiar with Southeast Asia, the very name Louang Phabang conjures up the classic image of Laos – streets of ochre colonial houses and swaying palms, lines of saffron-robed monks gliding through the morning mist, the sonorous thump of the temple drums hours before dawn, and, of course, long tail-boats racing down the Mekong before the river slips out of view through a seam in the mountains.

It is this heritage of Theravada Buddhist temples, French-Indochinese shophouses and **royal mystique** that lend Louang Phabang a pull unmatched by any other city in Laos. This is where the first proto-Lao nation took root. It's the birthplace of countless Lao rituals and the origin of a line of rulers, including the rulers of Vientiane, Champasak and Lane Xang. Louang Phabang people are tremendously proud of their pivotal role in Lao history. Indeed, they're somewhat known for their cultured ways in the rest of the country; in Lao soap operas, the doctor or the intellectual invariably speaks with a Louang Phabang accent.

Tourist facilities have improved enormously in the last few years, and Louang Phabang now offers decent, inexpensive accommodation, motorbike rental and easier access to surrounding sites and villages. Inevitably, the city has lost some of its sleepy charm and dreamy serenity as a result of the recent influx of tourists, but it's still relatively unspoilt. Moreover, Louang Phabang's strict building code, which passes World Heritage muster, keeps it from becoming another modern architectural nightmare without turning it into a museum.

Most travellers spend only a few days here on a whistlestop tour of Laos, though the city really demands longer. If time is limited, top priority should go to the **old city**, dubbed by the UNESCO World Heritage team as a "historic preservation zone". You can tour the sights from vibrant **Dala Market** along the peninsula to Louang Phabang's most impressive temple, **Wat Xiang Thong**, easily in a day, taking in the **Royal Palace Museum** along the way and still managing to climb up to the golden cone of **Phou Si** for a dazzling sunset perch. The following day, enjoy some of the sights **around Louang Phabang** by taking a boat up the Mekong River and contemplating the hundreds of Buddhas within the holy **Pak Ou caves**, or travelling south through the surrounding hills

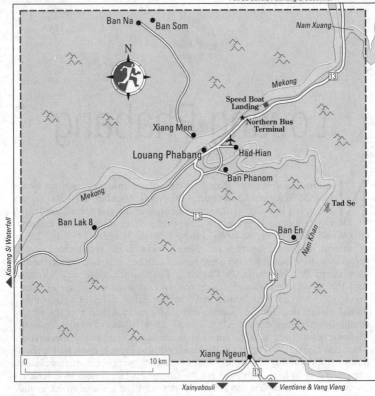

Ban Na ● ● Ban Som
Nam Xuang

N

Mekong

Speed Boat
Landing

Xiang Men ●
Northern Bus
Terminal

Louang Phabang ●
Hãd Hian ●

Ban Phanom ●

Mekong

Tad Se

Ban Lak 8 ●

Ban En ●

Nam Khan

0   10 km

Xiang Ngeun

Xainyabouli ▼   ▼ Vientiane & Vang Viang

to one of the area's two major **waterfalls**, Kouang Si and Tad Se. But whatever you do, be sure you make time to soak up Louang Phabang's languid atmosphere by wandering the streets at dawn, when the town's legion of monks receive alms and life attains all the buzz of a country village, or at dusk, when the air fills with otherworldly chants wafting from the temples.

Louang Phabang's air of serenity is disturbed only at **festival** time. The most famous festivals last for days and inspire a carnival atmosphere that makes it easy to forget that these complex rituals once held the very structure of the kingdom in place for centuries. **Lao New Year** in April is perhaps the town's biggest festival, but two holidays – the boat races and the Festival of Lights – near the end of the monsoon, also bring Louang Phabang to a festive standstill. A visit coinciding with one of these festivals would certainly enhance your stay, though the **most popular time to visit** remains the cooler months of December and January, when the weather is clear and dry.

Some history

Knowledge of Louang Phabang's early **history** is sketchy, at best. The earliest Lao settlers made their way down the Nam Ou Valley, sometime after the tenth century, absorbing the territory on which the city lies. At the time, the area was known as Muang Sawa, a settlement thought to have been peopled by the Austroasiatic ancestors of the Lao Theung. According to folklore, this

The myth of the birth of the Lao

In the early days, when humankind grew unruly and refused to honour the gods, the **chief of the gods** flooded the earth. Three lords managed to survive the flood, floating up to heaven on a raft. They paid homage to the chief of the gods, and once the floods had subsided the lords returned to earth in the vicinity of Dien Bien Phu with a water buffalo, which helped them sow the rice fields in the plain. When the buffalo died, a large vine bearing three gourds grew from its nostrils, and from the gourds came shouts and cries. One of the lords pierced the gourds with a hot poker and a mass of people struggled out of the blackened holes. These were the **Lao Theung**, the Lao of the hillsides. Seeing their plight, a second lord cut more holes with a chisel and from these larger openings emerged the **Lao**. The lords taught the Lao how to grow rice and build homes, but when the population grew too big, the chief of the gods sent his son, **Khoun Borom**, to earth.

Descending to earth on an elephant with crossed tusks, Khoun Borom brought with him teachers and courtiers, teaching the Lao how to make tools and schooling them in the arts of dance and music. After a prosperous reign of 25 years, Khoun Borom sent his seven sons to rule over the Tai–Lao world. The eldest went to **Louang Phabang** and the others to Xiang Khouang, Chiang Mai, Xishuangbanna (in south-western China), Ayuthaya and to regions of lower Myanmar and northern Vietnam.

migration of the Lao to Louang Phabang was led by Khoun Lo, son of Khoun Borom, the legendary first ancestor of the lowland Lao. Khoun Lo, it is said, descended the Nam Ou River, claimed the area for his people and called the settlement **Xiang Dong Xiang Thong**. By the end of the thirteenth century, Xiang Dong Xiang Thong had emerged as one of the chief centres of Lao life in the Upper Mekong region, a principality significant enough to be a vassal state of the great Siamese kingdom of Sukhothai.

However, it wasn't until the legendary Lao warrior **Fa Ngum** swept down the Nam Ou with a Khmer army in 1353 and captured Xiang Dong Xiang Thong that the town emerged as the heart of a thriving, independent kingdom in its own right. Fa Ngum, whose exploits are shrouded in myth, looms large in Lao histories, many of which trace Laos's fragile claims of nationhood to the warrior's rise to power in Louang Phabang. Claiming the throne of his grandfather, Fa Ngum founded the kingdom of **Lane Xang Hom Khao** – the Land of a Million Elephants and the White Parasol – and established the line of kings that was to rule Laos for six centuries.

With Fa Ngum came monks, artisans and learned men from the Khmer court and, according to histories written a century and a half later, a legal code and Theravada Buddhism. Yet Fa Ngum was still very much the fourteenth-century warrior. After his ministers grew weary of his military campaigns and his rather uncivilized habit of taking his subject's wives and daughters as concubines, he was exiled and replaced on the throne by his son, Oun Heuan, in 1373. Oun Heuan is remembered as **Samsenthai** or King of Three Hundred Thousand Tai, a name signifying the number of Lao men that the king of Xiang Dong Xiang Thong could call upon for labour and military service. He's also remembered for his long peaceful reign, during which the city flourished.

Five columns of Vietnamese troops swept through the city in 1478, only to be chased out a few years later by the humiliated Lao king's younger brother. The sacking of the city proved a catalyst for the ushering in of the city's **golden age**: striking temples, including the sim of Wat Xiang Thong, were built, epic poems composed, sacred texts copied and the administration of the kingdom fine-tuned over the next century. Lane Xang was, for the moment, a major power on the Indochinese peninsula. In 1512, King Visoun brought the **Pha Bang**, a sacred Buddha image, to Xiang Dong Xiang Thong, a distinguishing event for the identity of the Lao people and the city itself, and a sign that Theravada Buddhism was flourishing. Visoun's pious son **Phothisalat** helped the faith along by issuing a decree banning worship of spirits, which resulted in animist shrines being torched and their altars thrown into the river. However, King Phothisalat spent much of his time in Vientiane, a more central location for a kingdom whose population had been shifting south along the Mekong. His son, **King Setthathilat**, wary of encroaching Burmese, officially moved the capital to Vientiane in 1563, leaving the Pha Bang behind and renaming the city after the revered image. The Pha Bang may have been known for its protective properties, but they were no match for the might of the Burmese, and Louang Phabang was engulfed by the chaos of successive **Burmese invasions** that swept through the Tai world.

From then on, the city had a roller-coaster ride. With the disintegration of Lane Xang at the turn of the eighteenth century, **Kingkitsalat** became the first king of an independent Louang Phabang. The kingdom was never able to attain Lane Xang's glory but Louang Phabang did manage a semblance of independence by paying tribute to Hué, Bangkok and Beijing, and receiving vassalage from Houa Phan and Xiang Khouang.

When **French explorers** Doudart de Lagrée and Francis Garnier arrived in 1867, they found a busy market and port town of wooden homes situated in parallel rows along streets positioned at right angles, a town that Garnier called "the most eminent Laotian centre in Indochina". With Louang Phabang firmly in Siam's orbit, King Oun Kham scoffed at the French explorers' suggestion that the kingdom would be better off French. The explorers were proved right two decades later when the Siamese left the town virtually undefended and the city was set ablaze by a group of **marauding Haw** led by Deo Van Tri, a White Tai chieftain from Sipsong Chao Tai. Tri was out to avenge himself on the Siamese who had captured his brothers during a mission to subdue unrest on Louang Phabang's frontier. During the siege, French vice-consul Auguste Pavie plucked the ageing Lao king from his burning palace and brought him downriver to safety. From that moment, the king offered tribute to France.

Almost everything was lost during the sacking of the city, but the event provided Pavie with the ammunition he needed to "conquer the hearts" of the Lao and usher in Louang Phabang's **French period**. The town was quickly rebuilt, with the French counting ten thousand people and more than a thousand homes a year after the town's destruction. When the novelty of living in wooden Lao houses on piles finally wore off, the French hired Vietnamese workers to build the homes that lend the city its classic French–Indochinese character, a trend quickly followed by Lao nobility. The city remained remote however: even in 1930 it still took longer to travel by river from Saigon to Louang Phabang than it did to travel from Saigon to France. Louang Phabang's rituals – intertwined with the pomp and ceremony of the kingdom's royal family, by this point the only active royal line left in Laos – continued under the French.

During the two **Indochina wars**, Louang Phabang fared better than most towns in Laos, although the city did play a pivotal role leading up to France's ultimate defeat in Indochina. In early 1953, invading Viet Minh forces nearly reached Louang Phabang, causing the French to hastily reinforce their garrison and the town's Chinese community to board up their shops. Much to the consternation of the French, the town's ethnic Lao majority remained calm, as a blind monk had prophesied that the invaders would not take the city. The king refused to leave his palace, while Crown Prince Sisavang Vatthana cruised

The exile of Fa Ngum

Most histories of Laos trace the origins of the country back to warrior-king **Fa Ngum**, a man whose accomplishments on the throne, the battlefield and in the bedroom are the subject of wild exaggeration and a wealth of legends, perhaps befitting a man touted as the founder of his country and whose exploits were only first recorded more than a century after his death. One of the best-known legends records his **exile** from Louang Phabang and his spectacular **return**.

In the year of the Naga, Fa Ngum was born into the royal house of Xiang Dong Xiang Thong with a set of 33 teeth. Worried that this miraculous abnormality was an **omen** spelling doom for the kingdom, the superstitious royal advisers talked the king into floating the infant prince down the Mekong. A Lao Moses with a crocodile smile, Fa Ngum drifted downstream for a year, his raft heavy with an entourage of advisers, wet nurses and servants – 33 in all – until he reached the Khone Falls. Here, a Buddhist monk found Fa Ngum and took the child to the Khmer court, where he was educated in the manner of a Khmer prince and given a Khmer princess as a bride.

In the many versions of the myth of Fa Ngum's exile there is one detail on which the tales never vary: not long after his expulsion, Fa Ngum returned to Xiang Dong Xiang Thong and fulfilled the omen foretold by his birth. Backed by an army of Khmer soldiers, Fa Ngum forced the king from the throne and established the Kingdom of a Million Elephants and the White Parasol.

confidently around town in his blue Chrysler as preparations for defence of the town gave way to celebrations long before the Viet Minh ran out of supplies and retreated. The French, on the other hand, were somewhat less relaxed about the near-attack upon Laos's royal city. In order to maintain their campaign against the Viet Minh on Vietnamese soil while still protecting northern Laos, the French massed troops in **Dien Bien Phu**, a valley located along the traditional invasion route of Laos. Here France suffered final defeat in her doomed quest to restore the pre-World War II status quo in Indochina.

While Louang Phabang itself remained intact during the fighting that consumed Laos over the next two decades, the Second Indochina War ultimately took its toll on Louang Phabang's ceremonial life, which lost its regal heart when the **Pathet Lao** ended the royal line by forcing King Sisavang Vatthana to abdicate in 1975. Two years later, Louang Phabang and Laos lost the king himself, as the new **communist government**, fearful that the king might become a rallying point for a rebellion, allegedly exiled him to a Houa Phan cave, a journey from which he and his family never returned.

Arrival, information and getting around

Most people arrive in Louang Phabang at the **airport**, just over 2km northeast of the city. It's possible to get a fifteen-day **visa on arrival** here (see p.19) for more information on visas). There are also **exchange** facilities and an **immigration checkpoint**, where you'll need to get your passport stamped. Arrivals on domestic flights don't need to pass immigration. Tuk-tuks (5000K per person) and touts from hotels and guest houses are both on hand to ferry you into the centre.

Louang Phabang has three **bus stations**, all served by tuk-tuks into town. Buses from Vientiane, Vang Viang and other points south along Route 13 stop at the Southern Bus Station, 3km south of the centre. Buses and sawngthaews

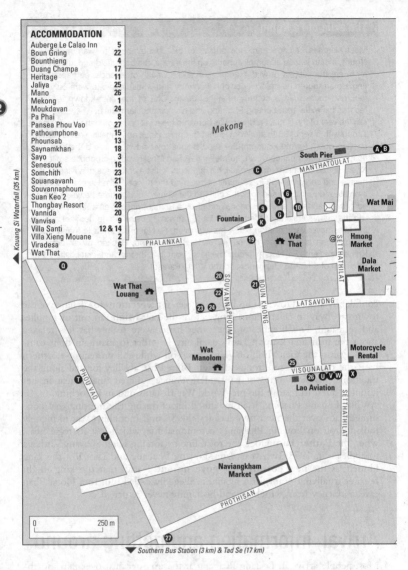

◀ Kouang Si Waterfall (35 km)

ACCOMMODATION

Auberge Le Calao Inn	5
Boun Gning	22
Bounthieng	4
Duang Champa	17
Heritage	11
Jaliya	25
Mano	26
Mekong	1
Moukdavan	24
Pa Phai	8
Pansea Phou Vao	27
Pathoumphone	15
Phounsab	13
Saynamkhan	18
Sayo	3
Senesouk	16
Somchith	23
Souansavanh	21
Souvannaphoum	19
Suan Keo 2	10
Thongbay Resort	28
Vannida	20
Vanvisa	9
Villa Santi	12 & 14
Villa Xieng Mouane	2
Viradesa	6
Wat That	7

Mekong

South Pier

MANTHATOULAT

Wat Mai

Fountain

PHALANXAI

Wat That

Hmong Market

Dala Market

SETTHATHILAT

Wat That Louang

SOUVANNAPHOUMA

BOUN KHONG

LATSAVONG

Wat Manolom

Motorcycle Rental

VISOUNALAT

Lao Aviation

SETTHATHILAT

PHOU VAO

Naviangkham Market

PHOTHISAN

0   250 m

▼ Southern Bus Station (3 km) & Tad Se (17 km)

from the north arrive at the Northern Bus Station, 6km north of town. Buses from Xainyabouli terminate at the Pakkhon depot near to the Southern Bus Station. It's possible to find **shared tuk-tuks** at all three bus stations, which act as shuttles to similar destinations in town (500K). Hiring your own will only cost a bit more (2000K), depending on your haggling skills.

Slow boats dock at the ferry landing directly behind the Palace Museum. From here it's a short walk to old city guest houses on the peninsula and Ban Wat That, a good area for accommodation near the river, although tuk-tuks are usually close at hand should you want one. If you've arrived by speedboat,

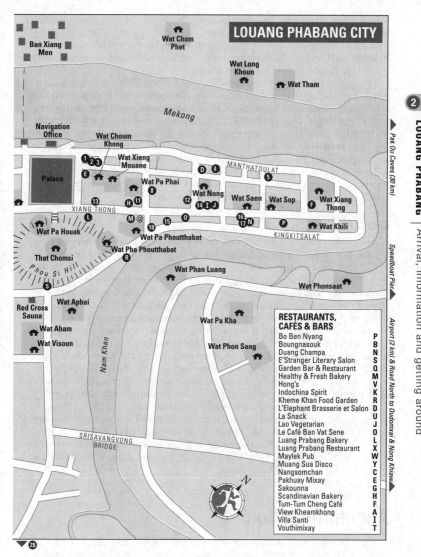

LOUANG PHABANG CITY

Ban Xiang Men

Wat Chom Phet

Wat Long Khoun

Wat Tham

Mekong

Navigation Office

Wat Choum Khong

Wat Xieng Mouane

MANTHATOULAT

Palace

Wat Pa Phai

Wat Nong

Wat Saen

Wat Sop

Wat Xiang Thong

XIANG THONG

Wat Pa Houak

Wat Pa Phouthabat

Wat Khili

KINGKITSALAT

That Chomsi

Wat Pha Phoutthabat

Phou Si Hill

Wat Phan Luang

Wat Phonsaat

Red Cross Sauna

Wat Aphai

Wat Pa Kha

Wat Aham

Wat Phon Sang

Wat Visoun

Nam Khan

SRISAVANGVONG BRIDGE

Pak Ou Caves (30 km)

Speedboat Pier

Airport (2 km) & Road North to Oudomxai & Nong Khiaw

RESTAURANTS, CAFÉS & BARS

Bo Ben Nyang	P
Boungnasouk	B
Duang Champa	N
E'Stranger Literary Salon	S
Garden Bar & Restaurant	Q
Healthy & Fresh Bakery	M
Hong's	V
Indochina Spirit	K
Kheme Khan Food Garden	R
L'Elephant Brasserie et Salon	D
La Snack	U
Lao Vegetarian	J
Le Café Ban Vat Sene	O
Luang Prabang Bakery	L
Luang Prabang Restaurant	X
Maylek Pub	W
Muang Sua Disco	Y
Nangsomchan	C
Pakhuay Mixay	E
Sakounna	G
Scandinavian Bakery	H
Tum-Tum Cheng Café	F
View Kheamkhong	A
Villa Santi	I
Vouthimixay	T

you'll land at the **speedboat pier** 7km northeast of town and will need to hire a tuk-tuk into the centre (5000K) or catch a shared tuk-tuk (1000K).

Information

The National Tourism Authority of Laos (Mon–Fri 8am–5pm; ☎071/212487) maintains a poorly located **tourist office** on Phothisarat Road, about 140m downriver from the Silversmiths' Fountain. It's somewhat more useful than branches elsewhere in Laos, but doesn't have much in the way of in-depth information. While the **maps** included in this guide should be sufficient, the tourist office also stocks the official *Louang Prabang Tourist Map*, which usually sells for 10,000K. A beautiful, hand-drawn free city map, *The 3D Map of Louang Phabang* by Kinnery Advertising, is extremely useful and available at Louang Phabang and Vientiane airports. For local ads and info, check the bulletin board at the *Scandinavian Bakery* on Xiang Thong.

Although there are very few street signs in Louang Phabang, you'll quickly realize by looking at maps and guest-house business cards that the town has made an absolute dog's breakfast of its **street names**. Apart from their very long names (Maha Ouphalathphetsalath Road for example), often with multiple spellings, some roads change names four or five times as they cross the city. For clarity's sake, we've chosen one street name and stuck with it throughout the chapter – not that street names mean much to locals anyway. As elsewhere in Laos, local inhabitants prefer to use landmarks, such as monasteries, to identify parts of town: thus Ban Wat That ("Wat That district") refers to the neighbourhood between Wat That and the Mekong River.

Getting around

Although you can comfortably walk everywhere in the old city, **bicycles** are a great way of getting around the town at large. Heavy Chinese models are available at most budget guest houses and at tourist shops on Xiang Thong Road (10,000K per day). Louang Phabang has no city bus system, so if you don't feel like walking or need to get out to the bus stations, speedboat pier or airport you'll have to rely on the town's fleet of **tuk-tuks** which can be flagged down easily on most busy streets. Typically, a ride anywhere in town is 2000K per person. Trips out to the bus stations cost 3000K; to the airport or speedboat pier it's 5000K. Foreigners generally need to haggle more than locals who know the correct prices, but if you know how much to pay there's rarely a discussion, although a few drivers will refuse to take a Farang anywhere for less than 5000K. Places around town where tuk-tuks tend to congregate include Dala Market, the boat piers, and the three bus stations. In the early morning there are always drivers hanging around guest house areas waiting for foreigners bound for the stations or airport. If you're interested in a trip to the waterfalls or Pak Ou caves, tuk-tuks can easily be arranged. **Motorbikes** – a great way to see out-of-town attractions – are available to rent for $8 a day but must be returned before dark. They can be found for rent at guest houses, rental shops, and along Xiang Thong Road.

Accommodation

Louang Phabang has a wide range of **accommodation** from simple rooms in inexpensive guest houses to five-star luxury resorts. The high season is during the cooler months of December and January but advance bookings are really only necessary if you want to stay in the heart of the old city and have a particular hotel in mind. Otherwise, there's no shortage of rooms at either end of the spectrum. Festivals, such as Lao New Year in April, are also busy times but providing you're flexible, something in your price range will always come up. In low season (May–Oct), most guest houses and hotels are quite open to negotiating their rates. If you're staying in a guest house or small hotel be sure to enquire what time doors are locked at night.

For most people, a location within the **old city** is the first choice. Here you'll find not only most of the city's best attractions but also many shops and restaurants. However, while there's no shortage of charming colonial guest houses in the $20 range, it's becoming increasingly hard to find cheap guest houses in this part of town. One possible compromise if you want to be close to the old city is the **Ban Wat That** neighbourhood, just south of Setthathilat Road, between Wat That and the Mekong River. The area is similar in atmosphere to the old city and has more **budget options**, with four parallel lanes holding a dozen cheap guest houses. Though there are good deals to be had here the area's overblown reputation as a backpacker centre means that many of the guest houses simply aren't good value for money. A better choice for budget travellers, though a bit further from the old city, is the area between the Nam Phou Fountain on **Xiang Thong Road** and **Visounalat Road** to the east. Scattered in this grid of streets, you'll find over a dozen guest houses and inns, many of which are better value than their Ban Wat That rivals. The fourth centre for tourist accommodation is **Phou Vao Road**, which runs from the Kaysone Monument up to Naviengkham Road and forms the southern limit of the new city. Strict controls on building in the old city have resulted in many new hotels springing up here – along the length of this long, wide boulevard, you'll find over a dozen decent hotels and guest houses as well as many restaurants, though the distance from the old city is a drawback.

The Old City

Auberge Le Calao Inn Manthatoulat Rd ☎071/212100, ℱ212085, ℯcalaoinn@laotel.com. An intimate guest house in a beautifully restored Sino-Portuguese mansion dating from 1904, near Wat Xiang Thong. Each of the four tastefully decorated rooms has an arched balcony with a Mekong view that takes in the temples on the opposite bank and beautiful sunsets. An excellent alternative now that the over-hyped *Villa Santi*'s prices have entered the stratosphere, but you'll need to reserve well in advance. The patio restaurant outside overlooking the street is a nice place for a drink but the food is very poor. ❼

Bounthieng Souvannakhamphong Rd ☎071/252488. If you're in the market for a colonial-era guest house facing the Mekong for under $5, this is the place for you. The more expensive upstairs rooms ($10) have hot water en-suite bathrooms and balconies looking right out over the river, a kind of low budget *Auberge Calao* ❷–❸

Duang Champa Kingkitsalat Rd ☎071/212420. An older but nicely done-up two-storey building facing the Nam Khan. Above the very good bar-restaurant are four high-ceilinged rooms, each with four beds and a hot shower. A superior setting near the tip of the peninsula, with views of river life and the mountains beyond. ❹

Heritage Near Wat Pa Phai ☎071/252537. One of the best deals in town, this lovely two-storey colonial house has wooden floorboards, green shutters and a charming little bar downstairs. Doubles and singles are the same price and all the rooms have en-suite facilities. Superbly located just off Xiang Thong Rd. ❸

Mekong Manthatoulat Rd, near the slow-boat pier ☎071/212752. This well-located guest house in a big 1960s building is run by a friendly family and is the pick of the bunch for backpacker digs along the Mekong River. Inside, behind the shop-houses, you'll find seven rooms ranging from doubles with shared bathrooms to the massive upstairs front room, with its two big double beds, balcony and huge en-suite bathroom. ❷–❸

Pa Phai Opposite Wat Pa Phai ☎071/212752. A quirky little guest house with a pleasant patio set up above a quiet street right off Xiang Thong Rd. Has ten decent budget rooms, clean shared facilities and a seating area on the tree-shaded patio. Run by the former Royal Lao Airforce pilot who also owns the *Mekong*. A budget place like this offering simple rooms with shared facilities right in the heart of the old city is a rare find indeed and the *Pa Phai* is often booked out with budget tour groups so book ahead if possible. ❷–❸

Pathoumphone Kingkitsalat Rd ☎071/212946. Run by a friendly couple, the rooms, some with shared facilities, are spread out across three somewhat beat-up old houses. The main draw is the great views from the balconies of the Nam Khan and surrounding mountains. An ideal location if you're in town for the boat races, which take place across the street on the Nam Khan. ❸

Phounsab Xiang Thong Rd ☎071/212595. In a prime location on the old city's restaurant and souvenir strip, this two-storey hotel has high-ceilinged rooms, with or without en-suite facilities. The ground-floor restaurant is a good place for watching the flow of people along Xiang Thong Rd.

Excellent if you want a budget place right in the heart of the café strip. ③

Saynamkhan Kingkitsalat Rd ☏071/212976, F213009. This marvellous re-styled 1939 shop-house next to the Nam Khan and just 40m from the main tourist strip is a top mid-range choice. The interior decor lacks the elegance of the refur-bished exterior, but it's a good spot nonetheless, and there's a pleasant, if narrow, terrace for sun-rise coffees. The rooms come with air con and TV, and a larger corner room has a bathtub. 5

Sayo Facing Wat Xiang Mouan ☏071/252614, ⓔsayo@laotel.com. This grand old colonial man-sion overlooking the Xiang Mouan temple has absolutely enormous rooms with wooden floors and ceilings. Aside from the nicely furnished rooms and modern bathrooms, the building has tons of character and the views over the temple are superb. A great choice and terrific value. ⑤

Senesouk Xiang Thong Rd, opposite Wat Sene ☏071/212074, ⓕ071/212074. Location doesn't get much better than this – right on a quiet stretch of Xiang Thong between the best wats and the restaurant strip. The building itself is a two-storey, colonial-style house. All the rooms are pleasantly done out and have air-con and TV. ⑤

Villa Santi, Xiang Thong Road ☏ & ⓕ071/212267. More than a century old, this villa exudes colonial charm. Formerly known as the *Villa da la Princesse*, the hotel was once home to King Sisavang Vong's wife and took its original name from Princess Manilai, who inherit-ed it. Still run by her family, the hotel was briefly taken over by the communists after the revolu-tion before being returned in 1991. Decorated with antiques, this elegant spot is *the* place to stay in Louang Phabang. Best is a room in the original building; the fourteen-room annexe, around the corner, is nice but it's a newer build-ing. Traditional massage and sauna plus an ele-gant restaurant complete the scene. Reserve well in advance. ⑦

Villa Xieng Mouane Facing Wat Xiang Mouan near the *Sayo* ☏071/252152. Stately rooms with wooden floors in a pretty white colonial-style villa with light-blue trim. The guest house takes its name from the nearby monastery, named after its old temple drum which produces a particularly sonorous thump, "xieng mouane" meaning "pleas-ant-sounding" or "lively". There's a new annexe with very modern rooms in the same colonial style in the back of the building for less money. Family rooms and the grassy lawn between the two build-ings make this a great spot for couples travelling with kids. ⑤

Ban Wat That

Suan Keo 2 Koksak Rd. A backpacker's delight, this is the best of the four budget guest houses in this lane with fifteen rooms starting from $2. The two-storey colonial-style house has blue shutters, tiled floors and a spacious terrace. ①–②

Vanvisa Kokkiang Rd ☏071/212925. Owned by a university professor of French, this yellow Sixties villa on a quiet street in the former silversmithing district is the most charming of the Wat That guest houses. There are just eight rooms, three of which use shared facilities. The leafy front courtyard and ground-floor living room filled with antiques and textiles add to the character. ③

Viradesa Vatthat Rd ☏071/252026. Now under new management, this true backpacker's spot has a wide range of cheap rooms, including dorms (under $1 per bed), in a wooden house with a small front yard facing the lane. The Irish manager can provide lots of info on where to go and what to do. If they're full and you need a cheap dorm, try the concrete *Viradesa 2* down the street. ①–③

Wat That Ban Wat That ☏071/212913. This tiny wooden house contains seven basic rooms, three singles, three doubles and a dorm, with clean shared facilities and hot water. There's a restau-rant in the garden that serves up pancakes, sand-wiches and great fruit shakes. ②–③

East of Nam Phou Fountain

Boun Gning Souvannaphouma Rd ☏071/212274. This is a well-run backpacker's place in an attrac-tive two-storey wooden house on a quiet street. The rooms are reasonable and the management helpful. ②

Jaliya Visounalat Rd ☏071/252154. Across from Lao Aviation, the dozen en-suite rooms tucked away behind this shop-house travel agency are very clean and comfortable and all face onto a pri-vate garden. Cheaper but less attractive rooms are available in the older part of the building. The Lao lady owner organizes everything from postcards and American chocolate bars to motorcycle rentals and day-tours. ②

Mano Visounalat Rd ☏071/253112. Just north of Lao Aviation. This new colonial-style building is an excellent little hotel with comfortable, modern rooms that are very good value for money. ③

Moukdavan Latsavong Rd ☏071/252402. Brand-new, Lao-style, two-storey house with a nice bal-cony and a red-tile roof. Similar to the Somchith. Private bath. Much better value than a lot of the so-called backpacker places in Ban Wat That. ②

Somchith Latsavong Rd ☏071/212522. Wooden house with perfectly decent rooms plus a slim, communal balcony. The bathrooms are a bit run down, but the wooden floors are nice and it's still better value than most Wat That places. ②

Souansavanh Bounkhong Rd ☎071/213020. The *Souansavanh* is the perfect place to try if your first selection is full or you've just arrived and don't feel like tramping around. Set in a huge compound on a quiet street, the hotel consists of three separate buildings, all in the same attractive style, with 27 clean rooms ranging from $3 to $15 depending on how many extra features you need to be comfortable. ①–④

Souvannaphoum Phalanxai Rd ☎071/212200. Two dozen handsomely appointed rooms, all with private balcony, housed in regal white buildings set among spacious gardens. The hotel was once the residence of former neutralist prime minister Prince Souvannaphouma. You can stay in the room he was born in – now the master suite with a deluxe bathtub – which is a relative steal. ⑥

Vannida Souvannaphouma Rd ☎071/212374. This crumbling turn-of-the-century mansion in a hilltop garden on a quiet street is one of the most atmospheric of the inexpensive guest houses in this area. The thirteen rooms are clean but nothing special, though the "special double" with its arched entrance, en-suite bathroom and ceiling fan offers a bit more character. While it's true that it's run down, you're really coming here for the garden and location, and if it was fixed up and renovated you'd pay ten times these prices. ③

Out of the centre

Pansea Phou Vao ☎071/212194, ☞071/212534, ✉phouvao@hotmail.com, ⓦwww.pansea.com. Located on Kite Hill at the eastern end of Phou Vao Rd, the *Pansea Phou Vao* is Louang Phabang's first and only truly five-star hotel. All the rooms here mix Western-style comfort like king-size beds, mini-bar, IDD phones, TV, and air-con with Asian-style design including wood floors, oriental hardwood furniture and wooden blinds. The eighteen superior rooms feature double private balconies and garden-style bathrooms big enough to get lost in. The hotel also has one of the classiest restaurants in town, overlooking an Asian-style outdoor swimming pool. ⑧

Thongbay Resort ☎071/219686, ✉thongbay@laotel.com. Run by two cheerful sisters, this marvellous eco-resort is located on the banks of the Nam Khan river about 2km from the old city. If you don't mind being a bit out of the centre, the eight deluxe Lao-style bungalows here are very well furnished with wood floors, native furnishings, overhead fans and huge garden-style bathrooms. The four choicest units all face out over the river and you could spend hours lying on the balconies watching the villagers tend their vegetable gardens on the opposite bank with Mount Phou Si in the background. A phenomenal deal but don't expect such a cheap price to last once the word gets out. ④

The City

Louang Phabang is the most Lao city in Laos. While other urban centres in the country are heavily populated by ethnic Vietnamese and Chinese, Louang Phabang is the only city in Laos where ethnic Lao are in the majority. The Lao character is particularly stamped on the back streets and cobblestoned lanes of Louang Phabang, which have a distinctly village-like feel, in marked contrast to the shop-houses and commercial scenes that you find on the streets of other Lao cities. One of the joys of a stay in Louang Phabang is simply strolling along these lanes and absorbing the unhurried rhythms of traditional Lao culture.

The **old city** of Louang Phabang is concentrated on a long finger of land, approximately 1km long by 300m wide, created by a long bend in the Nam Khan River which joins the Mekong at the tip of the peninsula. The thicker southern end of the peninsula is dominated by a steep, forested hill, **Phou Si** ("Sacred Hill"), crowned by a Buddhist stupa that can be seen for miles around. As the city grew it expanded outwards from the peninsula to the south and east and continues to do so to this day. The majority of Louang Phabang's architecture of merit – temple monasteries, Asian shop-houses and French-influenced mansions – is found in the old city along the main thoroughfare of **Xiang Thong Road** between the tip of the peninsula and Setthathilat Road.

Setthathilat Road basically divides the old city of Louang Phabang from the newer commercial parts of the city, although there are still plenty of old colonial mansions scattered about in the newer areas to the south and east of Mount Phou Si, as well as a number of other important monasteries including **Wat Ahan** and **Wat Visoun** on the eastern side of Phou Si. The most interesting areas outside the old city for tourists are the **riverbanks**, **Ban Wat That**, the old silversmithing district south of the GPO between Wat That and the Mekong, and **Visounalat Road** which is emerging as a new shopping and accommodation thoroughfare. The boulevard of Phou Vao Road, which has many new hotels and restaurants but little character, forms the southern limit of town, while to the north and west, the **opposite banks of the Mekong and Nam Khan** have nothing in the way of tourist facilities but are extremely charming.

The old city

Louang Phabang's **old city** occupies a long, narrow finger of land created by the confluence of the Nam Khan and the Mekong. There are just four parallel streets running the length of the peninsula but enough cross streets, lanes and dead-ends to keep things interesting. Amazingly, each area seems to exude its own distinct personality. The main thoroughfare is **Xiang Thong** Road along which the bulk of Louang Phabang's tourist restaurants and shops are located. Aside from the main attractions of the **Royal Palace Museum**, **Mt. Phou Si** and **Wat Xiang Thong**, there are a dozen historic wats, or temples, within the old city area, as well as hundreds of turn-of-the-century French colonial shophouses and grand mansions. But the old city is not just about architecture, it's the people who live here and the comings and goings of the townsfolk that give it its charm.

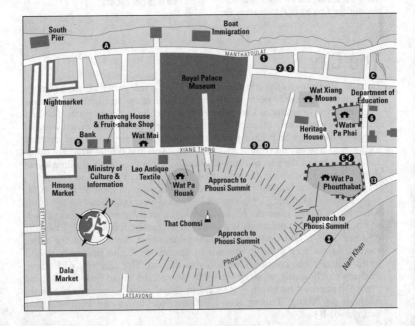

Although it is possible to knock off all the attractions in the old city in a couple of days, it's far more enjoyable to explore it a little at a time, and really soak up the atmosphere. The many **temples** and **monasteries** are certainly too charming be rushed through. An ideal time to visit the temples is around sunset when the atmosphere is considerably enhanced by a contingent of monks and novices chanting in the *sim* before the principal Buddha image. Likewise, early morning around 7am is a good time to watch the ritual of long lines of monks collecting alms along Xiang Thong.

Wat Mai

Just south of the Royal Palace on Xiang Thong Road, Wat Mai Suwannaphumaham, or **Wat Mai** for short, has what must surely be Louang Phabang's most photographed *sim* after that of Wat Xiang Thong. The monastery dates from the late eighteenth or early nineteenth century (depending on whom you believe), but it is the *sim*'s relatively modern facade with its gilt stucco reliefs that forms the main focus of attention. Depicting the second-to-last incarnation of the Buddha set amidst traditional Lao scenes, the facade was created in the 1960s and recently restored, but is already starting to deteriorate. Like most examples of modern Lao temple ornamentation, the facade looks interesting from a distance, but disappointing up close.

It was here at Wat Mai that **Auguste Pavie** and his party resided while trying to establish a foothold in Louang Phabang in the late nineteenth century. Siamese officials, who controlled the Lao court at the time, had billeted the Frenchmen in an isolated hut, hoping this would make them give up and leave, but the abbot of Wat Mai befriended Pavie and invited him to stay at the wat. Soon Pavie and King Oun Kham were communicating via the abbot while the Siamese stood by and watched helplessly. Decades later, France celebrated

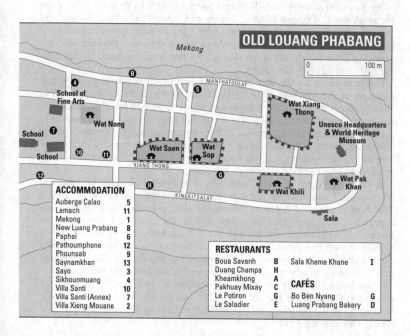

ACCOMMODATION	
Auberge Calao	5
Lamach	11
Mekong	1
New Luang Prabang	8
Paphai	6
Pathoumphone	12
Phounsab	9
Saynamkhan	13
Sayo	3
Sikhounmuang	4
Villa Santi	10
Villa Santi (Annex)	7
Villa Xieng Mouane	2

RESTAURANTS			
Boua Savanh	B	Sala Kheme Khane	I
Duang Champa	H		
Kheamkhong	A		
Pakhuay Mixay	C	**CAFÉS**	
Le Potiron	G	Bo Ben Nyang	G
Le Saladier	E	Luang Prabang Bakery	D

Pavie's contribution to the colonization of Laos by erecting a statue of him where the post office now stands. After the revolution, the statue disappeared, and in the mid-Nineties, Pavie's hometown in France attempted to find it, but without success. During **Lao New Year** festivities, Wat Mai is a hive of activity, as it is here that the Pha Bang (see p.153) is put on display so that the faithful may ritually bathe the image.

Wat Pa Phai to Wat Sop

In the area immediately north of the palace there are three temples of note, **Wat Choum Khong**, **Wat Xiang Mouane** and **Wat Pa Phai**, the Bamboo Forest Monastery. The principal attraction at Wat Pa Phai is the facade of the *sim*, painted and lavishly embellished with stylized *naga* and peacocks. The stucco and mirror work closely resembles that commonly seen on Buddhist structures in Chiang Mai. Directly across from Wat Pa Phai sits a curious old **mansion** which is a fine example of a type of architecture that could be termed "French-Indochinese": the design of the house itself is unmistakably European, but the ornamentation is obviously Asian. The finely carved hardwood doors were almost certainly crafted by Chinese or Vietnamese, and hint at the origin of the curious "Buddha" on the facade posing in a very non-traditional *mudra*.

The whitewashed mansion up the street on the corner of Xiang Thong Road is the former **palace of Crown Prince Vong Savang**. Its proximity to the street makes you wonder at the extraordinary blend of official pomp and casual familiarity that must have existed between the ordinary inhabitants of Louang Phabang and its rulers. To the north stand French-built primary and secondary schools, and every afternoon in the school yard you'll see *kataw* being played. The massive tamarind trees that shade the road in front of the schools once lined the route all the way up to Wat Xiang Thong.

On the next corner is the **Villa Santi**, formerly the Villa de la Princesse, once the residence of Princess Manilai, widow of Crown Prince Vong Savang, and still owned by her family. This charming little palace-turned-hotel caused controversy when it opened in the early Nineties. Government pressure was successful in bringing about a name change, but the hotel continues to thrive on the mystique of erstwhile royalty.

The next block north, **Wat Saen** is the first of a row of monasteries that monopolize the west side of the street for nearly two blocks. Of interest at Wat Saen is an ornate boat shed housing the monastery's two **longboats**, used in the annual boat race festival. Held at the end of the rainy season, the boat races are believed to lure Louang Phabang's fifteen guardian *naga* back into the rivers after high waters and flooded rice paddies have allowed them to escape (see box on p.154). Fittingly, the boathouse is decorated with the carved wooden images of these mythical serpentine creatures.

In 1888, the French counted nearly fifty monasteries in Louang Phabang and its environs. Today, there are just over thirty. Close inspection of the grounds of **Wat Sop**, just beyond Wat Saen, yields some clues as to the reason for their disappearance. The large Buddha image out in the open and the section of unmatched wall in front of it are evidence that this half of the grounds was once the site of a separate monastery. Sometime in the past the *sim* that once sheltered the Buddha was destroyed and the monastery was absorbed by Wat Sop, whose newly restored *that* advertises the growing wealth and prosperity of the city.

Beyond Wat Sop, there are four other temples of note, two on each side of the street: Wat Si Boun Heuang, Wat Khili (see p.158), Wat Pak Kham at the furthest tip of the peninsula, and the greatest of Louang Phabang's temples, Wat Xiang Thong (see p.154).

The Royal Palace Museum

Occupying a fittingly central location in the old city, between Phou Si Hill and the Mekong River, the former **Royal Palace** (Mon–Fri 8.30am–noon & 1–4pm; 10,000K) is now a museum preserving the trappings and paraphernalia of Laos's recently extinguished monarchy. The palace sits at the end of a long drive lined with stately palms. It was constructed in 1904 by the French and replaced an older, smaller palace of teak and rosewood. The new palace was supposed to be crowned by a European-style steeple, but King Sisavang Vong insisted on modifications, and the graceful stupa-like spire that you see today was substituted, resulting in a tasteful fusion of European and Lao design. Another striking feature is the pediment over the main entrance adorned with a gilt rendition of the symbol of the Lao monarchy: Airavata, the three-headed elephant, being sheltered by the sacred white parasol. This is surrounded by the intertwining bodies of the fifteen guardian *naga* (see p.154) of Louang Phabang.

At the far end of the gallery to the right of the main entrance is a small, barred room that once served as the king's personal shrine room. It is here that the **Pha Bang**, the most sacred Buddha image in Laos (see box on p.153), is being kept until the completion of the Haw Pha Bang – the temple in the eastern corner of the palace compound. Flanking the Pha Bang are numerous other Buddha images, including ancient Khmer stone images and several pairs of mounted elephant tusks. One pair, deeply incised with rows of Buddhas, was noted by Francis Garnier on the altar of Wat Visoun in the 1860s. Displayed nearby in richly carved wooden frames are silk panels embroidered with gold and silver thread that depict yet more images of the Buddha.

On entering the palace, visitors are directed through the entry hall to the **king's reception room**, full of huge Gauguinesque canvases portraying what

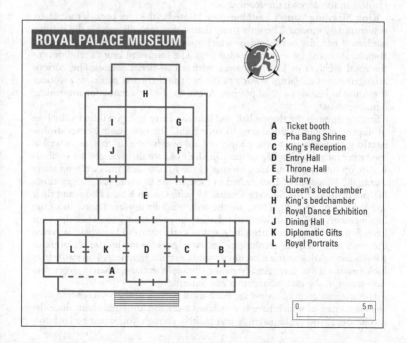

ROYAL PALACE MUSEUM

A	Ticket booth
B	Pha Bang Shrine
C	King's Reception
D	Entry Hall
E	Throne Hall
F	Library
G	Queen's bedchamber
H	King's bedchamber
I	Royal Dance Exhibition
J	Dining Hall
K	Diplomatic Gifts
L	Royal Portraits

0   5 m

appears to be "a day in the life of old Louang Phabang", with scenes of the city as it appeared in the early twentieth century. Painted by Alex de Fautereau in 1930, the paintings are meant to be viewed at different hours of the day when the light from outside is supposed to illuminate the panels depicting the corresponding time of day. An interesting concept, but in practice the lack of sunlight entering this room renders the effect less than stunning.

More impressive is the **Throne Hall**, located just beyond the entry hall. Its high walls spangled with mosaics of multi-coloured mirrors set in a crimson background, the throne hall dazzles even in the dim light. These mosaics, along with others at Wat Xiang Thong, were created in the mid-Fifties to commemorate the 2500th anniversary of the historic Buddha's passing into Nirvana. On display in this room are rare articles of royal regalia: swords with hilts and scabbards of hammered silver and gold, an elaborately decorated fly-whisk and even the king's own howdah (elephant saddle). Also on exhibit are a cache of small Buddha images taken from the inner chamber of the "Watermelon Stupa" at Wat Visoun. Somehow these treasures escaped the plundering gangs of "Black Flag" Chinese who, led by a White Tai warlord, sacked Louang Phabang in 1887. The stupa was destroyed, rebuilt in 1898, but collapsed in 1914. It was then that the crystal, silver and bronze Buddhas were discovered inside.

Leaving the Throne Hall via the door on the right, you come to the **royal library**, which is almost exclusively made up of official archives of the Ming and Ching dynasties, a gift from China during the Cultural Revolution. Succeeding rooms are the **queen's bedchamber**, with a not-so-regal collection of Sixties furniture, and another room filled with glass cabinets containing Royal Lao Government awards, seals and decorations. In a third room is a display of theatrical masks, headdresses and musical instruments used by the **royal dance troupe** in their performances of the Lao version of the ever-popular classical Indian legend, the *Ramayana*.

King Sisavang Vong's bedchamber, located at the very back of the palace, is surprisingly modest. The only thing that looks especially regal is the massive hardwood bed, the headboard of which sports the king's initials and a carved Buddha sheltered by a seven-headed *naga*. The footboard bears a rendition of the royal emblem of Laos, this time with a two-tiered parasol. The curious arrangement of tall lamps at each of the bed's four corners makes you wonder if reading in bed was a royal pastime. Above the bed is a frame for suspending a mosquito net.

Exiting through the throne hall and into the entry hall, you'll find a final set of displays located in the rooms to your right. The near room houses **diplomatic gifts** presented to the people of Laos by a handful of nations, as well as the rather tatty-looking flag of the Kingdom of Laos that was given a symbolic ride up into space and back on one of the Apollo missions. Not long afterwards, the Kingdom of Laos ceased to exist. In the far room hang larger-than-life **portraits** of King Sisavang Vattana, his wife Queen Kham Phoui and their son Prince Vong Savang. These are the only officially displayed portraits of the last members of the 600-year-old dynasty anywhere in Laos. Had they not been painted by a Soviet artist they almost certainly would not have survived the years following the revolution. The same goes for the bronze sculpture of King Sisavang Vong in the museum grounds near the front gate. This statue may look familiar if you have already passed through Vientiane, where a larger version stands in the park adjacent to Wat Simuang.

The artefacts on public view are but a small portion of the royal relics in storage here, many of which have been packed away and forgotten about since the revolution. If you plead patiently and politely enough, you might be let into

The Pha Bang

Much more than an ancient image of the Buddha, the **Pha Bang** is the palladium of Laos. The pursuit and enshrining of palladial images has a long history in Southeast Asia, full of intrigue and Byzantine plotting. Like Thailand's "Phra Kaew" and Myanmar's "Mahamuni" Buddha images, the Pha Bang is believed to possess miraculous powers that safeguard the country in which it is enshrined. Formerly, palladial images were thought to legitimize the sovereignty of a king who had one in his possession. Only a pious king with sufficient religious merit could hope to hold on to such an image, and losing it was thought to be proof that a kingdom and its ruler did not deserve to possess it. Thus the histories of certain palladia read like the itinerary of some much coveted sacred sword or holy grail.

According to Lao legend, the Pha Bang image was cast of gold, silver, copper, iron and precious stones. Overseen by the god Indra, who donated gold for its creation, the image was crafted in the heavens above the Himalayas and then delivered to the capital of Sri Lanka. From there the image made its way to Cambodia and then to the city of Xiang Dong Xiang Thong, later renamed Louang Phabang (the Great Pha Bang) in honour of the image. In the early eighteenth century, the Pha Bang was moved to **Vientiane**, now the capital. Twice the Siamese invaded Vientiane, capturing the image, and twice they returned it to the Lao, believing that the Pha Bang was bad luck for Siam. Since 1867, the Pha Bang has been kept in Louang Phabang, where to this day it is considered the most sacred Buddha image in Laos and centrepiece of the Lao New Year festival. At least, that's the official story. Persistent **rumours** have circulated since the revolution that the authentic Pha Bang was removed from its ornate pedestal and given to the Soviets in return for assistance to the Pathet Lao during the war. The image on display is said to be a copy, while the real Pha Bang is locked away in some vault in Moscow, its powers no longer serving as a talisman for Laos. Whether the story has any truth to it (and it seems highly doubtful), a significant number of Lao believe it, which is perhaps, as one expert on Lao culture pointed out, "a comment on the illegitimacy of the Lao government" in the eyes of the people.

the garage housing the late king's motorpool; here, among other dust-covered classics, you'll see an ivory-coloured 1960 Ford Edsel convertible with royal red upholstery.

Ban Jek

The neighbourhood just north of the former Royal Palace is still known to locals as "**Ban Jek**" or Chinatown, as the rows of shop-houses along Xiang Thong Road were once mostly owned by ethnic Chinese shop-keepers. Here you'll find some fine examples of Louang Phabang **shop-house architecture**, a hybrid of French and Lao features superimposed on the basic South China style that was once the standard throughout urban Southeast Asia. Downstairs was a shop or other place of business, while upstairs the residents lived under a roof of fired-clay shingles supported by brick and stucco walls. This combination kept interior temperatures cool during the hot season and warm during the chilly early morning hours of Louang Phabang's "winter". Shuttered windows, introduced by the French, were coupled with transoms of filigreed wood above doors and windows. This allows air to circulate even when doors and windows are bolted shut. With the number of shops and businesses catering to tourists increasing, many of the original owners have rented their shops out to entrepreneurs from Vientiane. Still, the streets retain much of the charm that they exuded before the outbreak of World Heritage fever even with their inevitable conversion to souvenir and tourist shops.

Naga and ngeuak: water serpents of Lao legend

The ubiquitous **naga** of Lao mythology is sometimes mistaken by visitors for the dragon of China, with which it shares a major characteristic: both are associated with water. For the most part, though, the similarity ends there. The origins of the *naga* are debated. Snake cults are thought to have existed in Southeast Asia long before the arrival of Buddhism in the region, particularly in Cambodia, so it is possible that this snake-like icon is indigenous. Another possibility is that the *naga* is a cultural migrant from Hindu India. In Hindu mythology, the *naga,* Sanskrit for serpent, is sometimes associated with the god Vishnu in his incarnation as Narayana, a cosmic dreamer reclining on the body of a giant *naga* and floating on an endless sea. Buddhism adopted the icon, and a story relates how, while meditating, the historic Buddha was sheltered by a seven-headed *naga* during a violent rainstorm. In Laos, it is probable that the present-day form of the *naga*, called *nak* or *phayanak* in Lao, is a fusion of both indigenous and imported beliefs.

The *naga* is both a symbol of water and its life-giving properties and a protector of the Lao people. An old legend is still related of how a *naga* residing in a hole below Vientiane's That Dam stupa was known to rise up at critical moments and unleash itself upon foreign invaders. While the *naga* is mainly a benign figure, a similar water serpent, the **ngeuak**, is especially feared by Lao fishermen. Believed to devour the flesh of drowning victims, *ngeuak* are said to infest the waters around Si Phan Don. As for the existence of *naga* in modern-day Laos, the Lao point to "proof" that can be seen in a photograph which is sometimes found displayed in homes, eateries and places of business. The photo shows a line of American soldiers displaying a freshly caught deep-sea fish that is several metres long. On some copies of the photograph, the Lao words nang phayanak (Lady Naga) are printed below the scene. Where and when the photo was taken is a mystery, but many Lao believe that the photo depicts a *naga* captured in the Mekong by American soldiers during the Second Indochina War.

Wat Xiang Thong

The most historic and enchanting Buddhist monastery in the entire country, **Wat Xiang Thong**, the Golden City Monastery (daily 8am to dusk; 5000K), near the northernmost tip of the peninsula, should not be missed. The main temple or *sim* was built in 1560 by King Setthathilat, who then promptly moved the capital of the Kingdom of a Million Elephants downriver to Vientiane. It is this wonderfully graceful building that dominates the monastery. Unlike nearly every other temple in Louang Phabang, this *sim* was not razed by Chinese marauders in the nineteenth century or over-enthusiastically restored in the twentieth. Indeed, an old photograph taken under Auguste Pavie's direction shows the temple to have changed little in the last century.

You'll need to stand at a distance to get a view of the **roof**, the temple's most outstanding feature. Elegant lines curve and overlap, sweeping nearly to the ground, and evoke a bird with outstretched wings or, as the locals say, a mother hen sheltering her brood. The **walls** of the *sim* are decorated inside and out with stencilled gold motifs on a black or maroon background. As you enter the dimly lit temple and your eyes adjust to the lack of light, the gold-leaf patterns seem to float on the blackened walls.

Besides stylized floral designs, the motifs depict a variety of tales, including the Lao version of the *Ramayana*, scenes from the *jataka* and stories about the lives of the Buddha, as well as graphic scenes of punishments doled out in the many levels of Buddhist hell. Such depictions were meant to give a basic education in religion to illiterate laypeople. In one of these punishment scenes, on the wall to the right of the main entrance, an adulterous couple is being forced to flee a pack of rabid dogs by climbing a tree studded with wicked thorns. In the branches above perch a flock of crows, awaiting the chance to peck out the sinners' eyes. Other unfortunate souls are being cooked in a copper cauldron of boiling oil (for committing murder) or are suspended by a hook through their tongues (guilty of telling lies).

In the rafters above and to the right of the main entrance runs a long wooden **aqueduct** or trough in the shape of a mythical serpent. During Lao New Year, lustral water is poured into a receptacle in the serpent's tail and spouts from its mouth, bathing a Buddha image housed in a wooden pagoda-like structure situated near the altar. A drain in the floor of the pagoda channels the water through pipes under the floor of the *sim* and the water then pours from the mouth of a mirror-spangled elephant's head located on the exterior wall. The water is considered to be highly sacred and the faithful will use it to anoint themselves or to ritually bathe household Buddhas. A mosaic covers the exterior of the back wall of the sim. Said to depict a legendary flame tree that stood on the site when the city was founded, this particular composition is especially beautiful during the Festival of Lights when the *sim* is decked out with *khom fai dao*, star-shaped lanterns constructed of bamboo and mulberry paper. The flickering candlelight illuminates the tree and animals in the mosaic, making them twinkle magically.

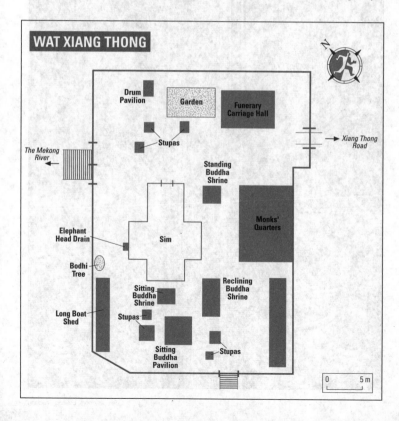

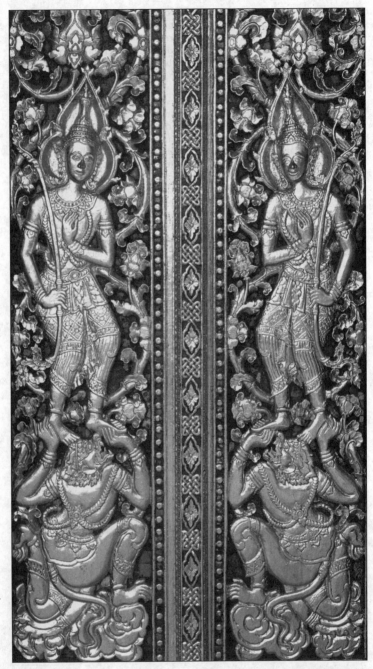

△ Temple doors, Louang Phabang

To the left of the *sim*, as you face it, stands a small brick-and-stucco **shrine** containing a standing Buddha image. The purple and gold mirrored mosaics on the pediments of the structure are especially intricate and probably the country's finest example of this kind of ornamentation, which is thought to have originated in Thailand and spread to Myanmar as well.

Directly behind the shrine is a larger structure known to French art historians as "La Chapelle Rouge", the **Red Chapel**. The red- and gold-coloured reliefs covering this building look modern and uninspiring, but the **reclining Buddha** image enshrined within is one of Laos's greatest sculptures in bronze. The image is thought to date from the sixteenth century and was taken to Europe in 1931 and put on display at the Colonial Exposition in Paris, alongside treasures from Angkor and other sites in France's Indochinese colonies. Adorning the walls of this shrine are countless clay votive tablets stamped with Buddhas. A donation box at the altar is provided for visitors interested in contributing to the upkeep of the monastery. Only fifteen per cent of the admission fee collected at the gate goes to the monastery, however; the remainder is said to go to the government.

On the other side of the monastery grounds is the **Funerary Carriage Hall** (daily 8am to dusk) or *haw latsalot*, a rare example of a modern Lao religious structure that manages to impress. Built in 1962, the hall's wide teakwood panels are deeply carved with depictions of Rama, Sita, Ravana and Hanuman, characters from *Pha Lak Pha Lam*, the Lao version of the *Ramayana*. Check out the carved window shutters on the building's left side where Hanuman, the King of the Monkeys, is depicted in pursuit of the fair sex.

Inside, the principal article on display is the *latsalot*, the royal funerary carriage, used to transport the mortal remains of King Sisavang Vong to cremation. The vehicle is built in the form of several bodies of parallel *naga*, whose jagged fangs and dripping tongues heralded the king's final passage through Louang Phabang. Atop the carriage are three urns of gilded sandalwood. In these ornate containers a royal corpse was kept in an upright foetal position until the cremation. The urns at the front and rear of the carriage held the remains of the king's father and mother respectively. The centre urn contained the remains of the king, which were cremated in April 1961.

Besides protecting these funerary paraphernalia from the elements, the building houses various **religious relics**. Among these are ornate wooden frames containing images of the Buddha that were given to the monastery as offerings. Most on display here feature painted renditions of the Buddha, but more elaborate images, resembling a tapestry of silver or gold thread, are on display with the Pha Bang at the Royal Palace Museum. Supposedly a Japanese tourist recently offered to purchase one of these for US$10,000 cash – and was refused.

A collection of somewhat crude **royal puppets** occupies a wood and glass case. The art of puppetry has all but died out in Laos since the revolution literally killed off royal patronage for this and other vintage forms of entertainment that visitors find quaint and locals less than riveting. Nevertheless, government permission was granted and funding was found for a performance in the mid-Nineties, so perhaps the old tradition will be allowed to make a comeback.

Scores of old and damaged Buddha images, some of which were taken from the altars of defunct monasteries, lean against an unfinished mosaic on the back wall of the hall. The Lao believe that damaged Buddhas are not fit for veneration and some of these images have been retired here, while others end up in the caves across the river. Beside the Funerary Carriage Hall is a leafy **garden** that contains some grand bougainvillea, coconut trees and two grey-green fan palms. It was from this species of palm that traditional **palm-leaf manuscripts** were made. Using a stylus to scratch characters onto the palm leaves, monks wrote down Pali-language chants and recorded historical events that affected the kingdom. Before access to paper and cheap printing made palm-leaf manuscripts obsolete, two or three of these trees could be found growing at every wat.

Wat Khili

On the opposite side of Xiang Thong Road, **Wat Khili** is a rare example of a Xiang Khouang-style temple. Louang Phabang once boasted at least three temples in this low, squat design, which originated on the windy plains of the province and former kingdom after which the style is named. Legend has it that the Chinese "Black Flag" rebels who sacked and looted Louang Phabang in 1887 took special care to destroy Xiang Khouang-style temples because their shape resembled Chinese coffins. It's also said that the Buddha at Wat Khili broke into a cold sweat in 1958, a dark omen signalling the coming war. The province of Xiang Khouang was heavily bombed during the Second Indochina War, leaving no trace of Xiang Khouang-style architecture there and making the *sim* at Wat Khili possibly the last surviving example. The monastery is said to have been founded for the commemoration of the marriage of a Phuan prince from Xiang Khouang to a Louang Phabang princess in the early nineteenth century.

Phou Si

Phou Si (Sacred Hill) is the geographical as well as spiritual centre of the city. Believed to have once harboured a powerful *naga* who dwelt in its bowels, the hill is also seen as a miniature Mount Meru, the Mount Olympus of Hindu–Buddhist cosmology. Though there is nothing to see on the hill itself, save for an ancient-looking *sim* at its foot, and it's not particularly picturesque up close in any case, Phou Si is striking from a distance. Indeed, the golden spires of **That Chomsi** at its summit are the first glimpse of the city that visitors get if they are arriving by boat. Likewise, the peak affords a stunning panorama of the city it crowns, and the shimmering rivers beyond, jungle-clad mountains and moody skies are mesmerizing.

There are **three approaches** to the summit. The first and most straightforward is via the stairway directly opposite the main gate of the Royal Palace Museum. An entrance fee (8000K) must be paid before ascending and this is when you should ask to be let into the adjacent *sim*, which is normally padlocked shut. Known as **Wat Pa Houak**, this fine little temple is exquisitely situated, nestled amid dense foliage and overlooking Xiang Thong Road. A charmingly weathered facade features a rendition of Indra seated on Airavata. The **interior murals**, which French art historian Henri Parmentier once described as "ridiculous", are actually the city's most fascinating, and appear to depict Louang Phabang as a celestial city. Besides Lao characters in classical costumes, there are Chinese, Persians and Europeans in the city, but it is not clear whether they have come as visitors or invaders. After soaking up the murals it is a steep climb through a tunnel of shady plumeria trees to the peak. The second approach, on the other side of the hill, is up a zigzag stairway flanked by whitewashed *naga*, and can be used for descending down to Phousi Road. The third and most rambling approach is via **Wat Pha Phoutthabat** near Phou Si's northern foot (across from the *Saynamkhan Guest House*).

Entering via Wat Pha Phoutthabat affords the most atmosphere. There are actually three monasteries in this compound, one of which is a school for novice monks. The most interesting structure in the compound is the *sim* of **Wat Pa Khe**, a tall, imposing building with an unusual inward-leaning facade. Most noteworthy here are a pair of carved shutters on the window to the left of the main entrance, said to depict seventeenth-century Dutch traders, and a similar if poorly preserved pair of shutters thought to depict Venetians. Why Dutch and Italians are part of the ornamentation on a Buddhist temple in Louang Phabang has been the subject of much conjecture. Perhaps it commemorates the visits of a travelling merchant of the Dutch East India Company who arrived in Vientiane in 1641, and an Italian missionary who arrived soon after, though the penned accounts of neither of these men ever mention reaching Louang Phabang. Perhaps more likely is the theory that these carvings were executed in the mid-nineteenth century and were meant to serve the same function as the images of demons commonly found carved on temple doors and windows: to keep evil spirits at bay.

Behind and to the left of the *sim* is a stairway leading to the "**Buddha's footprint**" after which Wat Pha Phoutthabat was named. The balustrade flanking this shady stairway is decorated by four pairs of curious sandstone carvings. The carvings resemble *somasutra*, found in ancient Khmer temple architecture, which were used to channel lustral water over a phallic stone sacred to the Hindu god Shiva. However, these carvings look distinctly Chinese, and fittings on the rear ends seem to indicate that the carvings were a decorative feature of a large structure before being incorporated into the balustrades of this stairway.

The shrine housing the Buddha's footprint is usually locked. However, if you were to find somebody with a key you would see a larger-than-life stylized footprint complete with the 108 auspicious marks said to be found on the historic Buddha's foot (for more on "Buddha's footprints", see the account of Wat Phabat Phonsan, Vientiane, p.114). On festival days, this shrine is open and pilgrims make offerings by tossing bank notes into the footprint. Adjacent to the shrine is a concrete pavilion where Cambodia's Prince Sihanouk held informal press conferences during the cremation ceremony of King Sisavang Vong.

Continuing up the path, you come to a small concrete grotto with an image of Pha Kajai, the Mahayanist deity most Westerners associate with the Buddha. The path meanders up past stone monks' quarters and the remains of an old anti-aircraft gun, a glowing photo opportunity if you happen to pass by when the resident novice monks are having a spin on the thing. Just beyond the gun is the summit, crowned by the stupa That Chomsi, which looks dented and dull up close.

Viewing the **setting sun** from the summit of Phou Si has become a kind of backpacker ritual so don't expect to enjoy the moment alone. A much quieter spot from which to watch the sunset is Santi Chedi on a hill due east of Phou Si, which affords a marvellous view back towards Phou Si, without the crowds.

Outside the old city

The old city may have the highest concentration of monasteries and old buildings, but there is plenty of interest on and beyond Setthathilat Road including over twenty temples, several markets, and a choice of scenic walks. The most historically important of the temples are **Wat That**, **Wat Visoun**, and **Wat Aham**, although a trip to the **opposite banks of the Mekong and Nam Khan** rivers will reward you with many other venerable riverside temples, as well as a relaxed rural ambience and good views back over the old city. Interesting city **markets** include the Morning Market, Naviengkham Market,

Along the banks of the Mekong and the Nam Khan

Surrounded by **rivers** on three sides, Louang Phabang not surprisingly feels almost waterborne, and the ship-like contour of the peninsula enhances this impression. Numerous stairways, flanked with whimsical guardian images, link palaces, monasteries and homes with nearby rivers and are a statement of the importance of the **Mekong** and the **Nam Khan** in the lives of Louang Phabang's population. The banks along the Mekong side are the more lively, but the Nam Khan side is more evocative of old Louang Phabang, and on either side the show is a never-ending affair.

When the French arrived in Louang Phabang they noted a – "floating suburb" anchored in the shallows on the Mekong's banks. Francis Garnier described how arriving boats and rafts would slowly poke among the houseboats looking for a place to land and discharge their passengers and cargo. With newly paved roads conveying much of the traffic into Louang Phabang, life along the river is less of a circus now, but sights and sounds of riparian commerce linger. Spend enough time **strolling the river road** and you will surely witness the tragi-comic spectacle of a shipment of pigs, squealing like the crack of doom, being manhandled off boats and up steep embankments. On the Nam Khan side, groups of residents tend tidy riverside gardens and make their way down to the river to bathe during dusk's waning light. It is scenes like these, all but vanished and forgotten in more developed countries, that make Louang Phabang such a fascinating place.

On the banks of both rivers can be found huge umbrella-shaped **somsa trees**, easily distinguished by the furry growth of parasitic vegetation that covers the tree's trunk and branches. In the old days, people would plant a somsa tree near their house for its generous shade-producing canopy and also in the hope that a guardian spirit would take up residence in the tree and protect the house.

and Vieng Mai Market, but most visitors stick to **Dala Market** and the nearby **Tribal Market**, both on Setthathilat Road. Although most of the best tourist **shops and boutiques** are on the peninsula there are several good shopping streets beyond the old city; **Phommathat Road** is worth checking out, particularly the junction with Latsavong Road. **Visounalat Road** is also well on its way to becoming the modern town's main commercial street.

Wat That

Wat That, officially known as Wat Pha Mahathat, is situated on a low hill to the south of Mount Phou Si and is reached via a stairway flanked by some impressive and undulating seven-headed *naga* spewing from the mouths of snaggle-toothed *makara*. At the top of the stairs is the most photographed **window** in all of Louang Phabang. Framed in ornately carved teak, the window is a blend of Lao, Chinese and Khmer design. Other elements of the wat suggest influence from northern Thailand, namely the gold-topped *that* after which the monastery was named. The graceful **stupa** is very similar to examples found in Chiang Mai, Thailand. This monastery is also the resting place of Prince Phetsarath and his younger brother Prince Souvanna Phouma; their ashes are interred in a family stupa here.

Dala Market and the Tribal Market

Louang Phabang's main market, **Dala Market** (Talat Dala), is on Setthathilat Road, just east of the GPO. While the usual stacks of toiletries and clothing don't look too exciting, careful inspection of the hardware stalls reveals some interesting items. Wild chicken calls, resembling tin whistles, are on display beside bags of saltpetre and sulphur which, when mixed with ground charcoal, produce homemade gunpowder. A quantity of lead shot completes the kit for a rural hunter. Vials of mercury, utilized by gold-panners to separate gold dust from river silt, are also on sale. Stalls selling gold and silver jewellery double as pawn shops and usually display a selection of royalist regalia – brass buttons, badges and medals decorated with the Hindu iconography of the old kingdom.

Near Dala Market, a small "**Tribal Market**" occupies an old vacant lot on the corner of Setthathilat and Xiang Thong roads diagonally opposite from the GPO. It is known as the Tribal Market because of all the kindly looking Hmong grannies who gather here to sell hats and bags decorated with their trademark geometric designs or animal and human figures. You'll also see the delicately embroidered decorative flaps found on Hmong women's traditional garb. The quality of cloth here is not what you'll find in the old city boutiques but there are many good items and with a bit of bargaining you can get a great deal. Dominating the market, a gigantic billboard extolling socialism and featuring ecstatic factory workers, soldiers and peasants and a giant portrait of Kaysone peels and flakes away in big strips as the grannies in its shadow count their cash.

Wat Visoun and Wat Aham

Wat Visoun and **Wat Aham** (foreign visitors 5000K each) share a parcel of land on the opposite side of Phou Si from the Royal Palace Museum. The *sim* of the former, as seen in a wood-block print executed by French artist Louis Delaporte in 1873, was once a lavishly decorated example of the all-but-extinct Xiang Khouang style. The original *sim* was razed during the sack of Louang Phabang in 1887 by Chinese bandits, and the bulbous, finial-topped stupa, known as *that makmo* – the Watermelon Stupa – was destroyed as well. The looters made off with treasures stored within, but fortunately didn't take everything. What they left behind is now on display in the throne room of the Royal Palace Museum.

Wat Visoun's reconstructed *sim* is an unremarkable mix of Louang Phabang and Vientiane styles, but the Watermelon Stupa is still quite unique. Neighbouring Wat Aham features a delightfully diminutive *sim* and a couple of mould-blackened *that*, one with a picturesque slant. This wat is associated with

---

The founding of Louang Phabang

Louang Phabang's guardian spirits, **Phu Nyoe** and **Nya Nyoe**, emerge annually to participate in the New Year's festival, sharing a place in Lao legend with Khoun Lo, Fa Ngum and assorted betel merchants and hermits, all of whom hold claim to the title of **city founder**, as recounted in this version of the establishment of Louang Phabang. Hacking their way through thick jungle, Phu Nyoe and Nya Nyoe arrived at a hill that resembled a mound of rice, a sign that the settlement was meant for great things. Down the hill, which came to be known as Phou Si, flowed a stream which they followed until they arrived at the confluence of the Mekong and the Khan rivers, where they found a flame tree, hundreds of metres tall and bursting with brilliant red flowers. After vanquishing the evil spirits inhabiting the land with their axes, the ancestors placed a flat rock beneath the great tree, pronouncing it the spot for the palace of the town's future king. They then threw large stones along the banks of the two rivers to mark the boundaries of the town. When they finished, they called forth fifteen *nagas* from the rivers and commanded these water spirits to guard the new city, for which they would receive tribute from the king. From that point forward, the spirits would emerge from the trunks of their banyan trees once a year to participate in the ritual purification of the kingdom.

Phu Nyoe and Nya Nyoe, the shaggy, red-faced spirits that are believed to be the founders and protectors of Louang Phabang (see box on p.161). Effigies of the two deities head the parade during the Lao New Year festivities in April, and they are believed to inhabit the two venerable banyan trees whose shade-giving canopies make this a pleasant place to linger.

Across the Mekong: Xiang Men and around

Surprisingly few tourists bother to cross the Mekong and explore the sleepy village of **XIANG MEN**, but it makes a good half-day trip and gives you a chance to view Louang Phabang from across the river. A passenger ferry operates between Louang Phabang and Xiang Men, leaving from the landing west of the Royal Palace Museum. Alternatively, you could strike a deal with one of the many boats to be found along the riverbank. The short journey should cost around 5000K per person, more if you have the boatman wait for you. You could ask him to let you off at **Wat Xiang Men**, almost directly across from the Royal Palace, or cut across the river to **Wat Tham**, opposite Wat Xiang Thong in the old city, and then walk back to Wat Xiang Men.

Originally built in 1592, Wat Xiang Men has been extensively rebuilt in modern times but retains its beautiful carved doors. The forest behind the wat conceals a royal cemetery for those members of royalty who for religious reasons could not be cremated. An easy climb to the top of the hill north of Wat Xiang Men brings you to the *sim* and stupas of **Wat Chom Phet** (4000K). At dusk the views of the sunset from here are spectacular, further enhanced by the sounds of the city carrying across the water. Walking down the hill to the north brings you to **Wat Long Khoun**, once used by Louang Phabang's kings as a pre-coronation retreat involving ritual baths, meditation and reflection. The wat was sensitively restored in 1995 by the École Française d'Extrême Orient. Of note are the two Chinese door guardians painted either side of the main entrance to the *sim* and the murals within.

The next and final sight to the north is Wat Tham Xiang Maen or **Wat Tham**, which is actually a **cave** repository for old and damaged Buddha images. As with Tham Ting (see p.173) upriver, this cave is a focus of activity during Lao New Year when the residents of Louang Phabang come here to gain merit by ritually bathing the Buddhas.

Santi Chedi

About 3km east of town stands Louang Phabang's largest religious monument. Constructed in 1988 and christened **Santi Chedi**, or "Peace Stupa", this modern, concrete pagoda, is best known for its mural-splashed interior (open Mon–Fri 8–10am & 2–4pm), though its carved windows are great works of art in themselves. However, the main reason to come up here is for the impressive **views** of Phou Si and the Nam Khan River, which needless to say are especially attractive at sunset, as is Santi Chedi itself when its golden surface catches the glow of the setting sun – most impressive from a distance. On the way to Santi Chedi, the road passes the old **French cemetery** but only a few broken tombstones remain. After the revolution the new government used the cemetery as a rubbish dump. Finally, after normalization, the French Government exhumed the bodies and took them back to France.

Across the Nam Khan

Although a long walk along the Mekong foreshore and even around the point and back down Kingkitsalat Road is considered de rigueur on any walking tour of the old city, very few tourists make the short hop across the river to the

north shore of the Nam Khan. Here, facing the old city and running for several kilometres alongside the Nam Khan and the Mekong to the village of Ban Don are a string of old **wats** and **monasteries**, quiet neighbourhoods that rarely see a foreign face, and a few crumbling old French mansions ready to tumble into the Mekong. To reach the north shore, simply cross the Srisavangvong Bridge, and turn left at the first big intersection. This will put you on Maha Ouphalathphetsalath Road, which follows the banks of the Nam Khan all the way to the Mekong and then continues along the Mekong shore through several small villages all the way up to Ban Don where the speedboat landing is located. Along the way you can visit many charming temples like Wat Phan Luang, Wat Pa Kha, or Wat Phonsaat, and take in the superb views back across the Nam Khan towards the old city.

Eating

Louang Phabang is a city that prides itself on its food. Many dishes are unique to the royal city, and others are simply done better – all of which conspires to make it the town in which to dig into Lao food with a sense of mission. Today due to the huge growth in tourism, Louang Phabang boasts more **restaurants** than anywhere else in the country outside of the capital. But, despite the high availability of international cuisine here, you shouldn't miss the chance to try traditional Lao food. At the top of your list should be *aw lam*, a bittersweet soup, heavy on aubergines and mushrooms. Another local speciality, *jaew bong*, a condiment of red chillis, shallots, garlic and dried buffalo skin, makes a nice addition to the pâté sandwiches on sale around town, although it is most commonly eaten with dried beef. You're less likely to use your *jaew bong* as a dipping sauce for *nang nyam*, a local treat consisting of small squares of water buffalo skin left to rot then dried and fried to burn off the hair before being folded over and tied with a slim strip of bamboo. If the sound of that is enough to turn you into a committed veggie, you'll delight in *phak nam*, a type of **watercress** particular to the area and widely used in salads. The most common style of salad appears on menus alternatively as "watercress salad" or "Louang Phabang salad" and is in fact quite similar to a Western salad – a light alternative to the meat salads more commonly served in Lao eateries. Another green delight is *khai paen*, a highly nutritious **river moss** that's usually fried in oil and eaten as patties sprinkled with sesame seeds. Mekong River *khai paen* is chewy, while the moss from the Nam Khan is considered a bit harder in texture.

For other local favourites timing is everything. In July, fried freshwater **prawns**, known as *jeun kung*, with a delicate taste, hit the markets. As the rains ebb, *màk deuy* – one Lao–English dictionary translates this mysterious plant's name as "Job's tears" – in olive-green bouquets, takes the town by storm, appearing in piles on street corners and in the hands of virtually every Lao woman. It's the slightly oily nut at the top of the stem that they're after, a tasty diamond that's a cross between a pea and a peanut. With the arrival of the cooler weather of November, *màk deuy* is supplanted by buttery-tasting papayas. The locals' serious approach to food begins with the way they grow their fruit: Louang Phabang inhabitants shun chemical fertilizers, preferring fruit small in size but large in flavour.

Locals even add a twist to the Lao staple, *tam màk hung*, the **papaya salad**: the distinctive Louang Phabang flavour of this dish comes from the addition of crab juice. It's OK to reach for your chopsticks while munching on this one, as the civilized folk of Louang Phabang shun the fingers-and-sticky rice technique favoured elsewhere in the country.

With so much ado about food, it's only right that Louang Phabang should have its own tipple, and indeed, *lào khào kam*, a dark-red fizzy **wine**, is a welcome respite from *lào-láo*.

Noodles and street stalls

Although basic noodle shops, street stalls and *khào ji pateh* vendors can be found scattered around town offering food for less than $1 from dawn until late at night, Louang Phabang is certainly no centre for street food. A very small **night market** sets up in the evenings between the post office and the river, with vendors selling takeaway Lao standards as well as fresh fruit, but there's nothing even remotely like the kind of food-stall scene you find in Thailand. The vast majority of Louang Phabang residents only eat at home.

Cafés

Bo Ben Nyang Xiang Thong Rd, Ban Khili. Situated in a mulberry paper gallery, *Bo Ben Nyang* serves a range of teas. The narrow upstairs balcony, which affords a wrap-around temple view, is the perfect spot to be at 4pm, when the nearby wats' call to meditation is often transformed into a ten-minute drum-and-gong concert.

Le Cafe Ban Vat Sene Xiang Thong Rd next to the Blue House Gallery. Newly opened by the owners of *L'Elephant*, this is the swankiest coffee shop in town. Housed in a lovely colonial shop-house with a beautiful interior and featuring truly decadent desserts.

E'Stranger Literary Salon Chao Sisouphan at the junction with Phommathat Rd. Get off the "Thang Farang" circuit and come and support the little guys. This two-storey house is the laid-back place for second-hand books, coffee, and world music.

Healthy & Fresh Bakery Xiang Thong Rd. Does the best baked goods in town and excellent set breakfasts. The cinnamon buns and banana breads are top-notch. The bakery is under Canadian management and the service is far superior to the *Scandinavian Bakery*.

Luang Prabang Bakery Xiang Thong Rd. Very tasty "tea-bread" sandwiches and good fruit shakes but the salads and main courses are a hit-and-miss affair, and the service is slow and disorganized.

Scandinavian Bakery Xiang Thong Rd. This Louang Phabang institution is a bit too popular for its own good but a handy spot to catch up on the Bangkok newspapers, read the bulletin boards and get a CNN fix. Free coffee refill.

Restaurants

Most of the city's yuppie tourist eateries are located along a 500-metre strip of **Xiang Thong Road** known as "Thang Farang" or White Man's Way to ex-pats. Here you'll find almost twenty tourist restaurants, most of which serve Western and Lao dishes and almost all of which tend to be pricey by Lao standards. That said, with the exception of upmarket restaurants in fancy hotels like the *Villa Santi*, *Phou Si* (T 071/212292) or the *Souvannaphoum* (T071/212200), a two-course meal in Louang Phabang usually only costs $5 and seldom will you spend more than $10. If you're holidaying in Laos you'll find it really cheap; if you're travelling, the prices will suddenly seem outrageous as it's quite easy to spend as much on a meal as on your hotel room. Much cheaper, and often better, meals can be found at the delightful **riverside restaurants** along Souvanbaniang (Ounkham) Road. Generally, the further you get from "Thang Farang", the cheaper things get, with Lao meals at the opposite end of Xiang Thong Road going for as little as 6000K. Restaurants open daily for lunch and stop serving food by 9pm.

Duang Champa Kingkitsalat Rd facing the Nam Kham ☎071/212420. Lao and French meals served in a spacious, stylishly low-key dining area in a colonial house that's carved with arches and cooled with ceiling fans. To complete the tropical scenario, there's a seriously stocked bar that has enough character to support Bogart's elbows. For French food in a colonial setting, you can't beat the $4 set meals.

L'Elephant Brasserie et Salon Straight towards the Mekong from the *Villa Santi* ☎071/252482; ✉elephant@laotel.com. A cross of Southern California and Casablanca, this is the most chic café in town. With the cane chairs and potted plants you almost expect to see Humphrey Bogart stroll in. A three course meal with dessert and coffee runs to about $20 here but the quality is superb. If you're looking for a major splurge this is the place to spoil yourself with fine quality European food.

Garden Bar & Restaurant *Le Parasol Blanc Hotel*, off Phou Vao Rd ☎071/252124. For a bit of a splurge, the Lao restaurant of the Le Parasol Blanc is really something to behold. Surrounded by the Lao-inspired buildings and a lush tropical garden, this Lao-Thai restaurant is set in a traditional open sala with a huge hardwood deck opening on to a lovely lotus pond. Some nights there's traditional live music. Pricey but worth the experience.

Indochina Spirit Xiang Thong Rd, just north of the Nam Phou Fountain ☎071/252372. The best Lao-Thai restaurant in Louang Phabang, if not Laos, this absolutely charming old house with hardwood floors and Thai and Lao antiques is a gem. Eat inside at a table, or Lao-style on cushions and mats, or al fresco on the lovely brick patio with live, traditional music. This place should be at the very top of anyone's dining list – it's not even expensive.

Lao Vegetarian Xiang Thong Rd. Formerly the *Lamach*, this inexpensive vegetarian restaurant has outdoor tables and a variety of tasty tofu and vegetable dishes. The mango shake here is the dean of Louang Phabang fruit shakes. A convenient spot for a budget meal if you're at this end of Xiang Thong Rd.

Luang Prabang Restaurant Visounalat Rd, just north of the circle ☎071/252981. One of three eateries all using the same monicker, this Luang Phabang restaurant is a very popular traveller's café that caters to the growing crowds staying in the Visounalat Rd area. Best of the seven

places north of the circle and packed most evenings.

Pakhuay Mixay Near Wat Xiang Mouan. The main draw here is the tranquil, garden atmosphere in a quiet residential corner of the old city, near to but worlds away from the bustle and hype of Xiang Thong Rd. A bit off the tourist trail, but many ex-pats and well-heeled locals come for the Lao cuisine, which is worth seeking out on its own merits.

Sakounna Xiang Thong Rd, opposite Wat Ho Xiang. This cream French-colonial building with green shutters and doors makes a good alternative to the tourist restaurants on the opposite side of the palace further north. The menu is pretty standard tourist fare but the price is right and it draws the Ban Wat That dinner crowd in the evenings.

La Snack Visounalat Rd, just south of the *Maylek Pub*. The most popular backpacker restaurant in this up-and-coming budget accommodation area. Good food and very inexpensive set menus at $2.50 and $3 for three courses. Stays open late and plays all kinds of cool music. Worth seeking out if you're in this neighbourhood.

Tum-Tum Cheng Café Sisaleumsak Rd, uphill from Wat Xiang Thong. The new kid on the block serving up Lao food in the downstairs of a cool old colonial building. The food here is generating lots of buzz though the opening hours seem to be highly variable.

Villa Santi Xiang Thong Rd ☎071/212267. One of the classiest places in town to sample Lao cuisine, featuring recipes by the daughter of the legendary Phia Sing, the last chef to cook for the Lao royal family. If you're looking for a romantic meal by candlelight on a balcony overlooking the relaxed evening scene of Xiang Thong Rd it's hard to beat. A drink at the garden bar of this former royal residence is also something of a Louang Phabang tradition. Give the house drink, "Return of the Dragon" a try; it's a mixture of local *lào khào kam* and banana liqueur.

Vouthimixay Phou Vao Rd, next to the *Sanakeo Hotel* ☎071/212888. If you find yourself at this end of town, check out this place – the most atmospheric of the dozen little restaurants along the length of Phou Vao. Set just off the road, the restaurant has a deck and lots of surrounding greenery. A charming spirit house out front completes the picture.

Riverside restaurants

Louang Phabang's numerous outdoor **restaurants along the Mekong** are the perfect spot to be at sunset and after dark for al fresco dining. What's more, the food is not only much cheaper than in places on Xiang Thong but often tastier as well. All of the restaurants along the waterfront offer indoor seating but also set up tables and chairs outside along the riverbank. Don't come here if you're looking for Western food; the house specials are all Lao, Thai and Chinese. Around the point on Kingkitsalat Road there's another good outdoor spot, the *Kheme Khane Food Garden*. In the morning, try the little places up towards the northern end like *Louis Restaurant* and the *Bouasavanh* which serve a full American breakfast with a view of the Mekong for a dollar.

Boungnasouk Souvanbaniang Rd, 20m north of the *View Kheamkhong* ☎071/212726. Excellent views of the Mekong and lovely lamps make this a good place to spend sunset. The fruit shakes are particularly delicious. The menu is mostly Lao–Thai and very inexpensive, with vegetable and meat dishes at $1 and $2 respectively.

Kheme Khan Food Garden Kingkitsalat Rd. High on the bank of the Nam Khan River behind Phou Si, this is a great venue for traditional Lao food with lovely views of the Nam Kham. There's a big wooden deck over the river with wooden tables and chairs so come early enough to enjoy the view. The bird's-eye view of river life also gets a little help from a tidy selection of Western-style cocktails. The *keng kai màk nao*, a soup served with chicken, and the *sai-ua Louang Phabang*, or Lao-style sausages, are standouts on this solid menu of traditional Lao food. An added touch is the substitution of purplish balls of *khào kam* for standard sticky rice.

Nangsomchan Souvanbaniang Rd, straight down from the Nam Phou fountain. This is the last riverside restaurant south and the cheapest too with vegetarian dishes under $1. Wooden chairs and tables with big shade umbrellas set the scene along the bank of the Mekong; you should find plenty to tempt your tastebuds on the eight-page menu.

View Kheamkhong Souvanbaniang Rd ☎071/212726. A lovely outdoor restaurant right on the banks of the Mekong River with candle-lit tables and big white umbrellas. All the dishes here are good but the gongbao-style Cashew Chicken is to die-for. The menu is quite extensive and the food inexpensive and delicious. Probably the best of the riverside options.

Drinking, nightlife and entertainment

In the evening, you might be content to sip a cool drink at one of the town's riverfront restaurants, but if you're looking for something livelier, head over to the popular *Muang Sua* disco (daily 9–11.30pm; 13,000K, ☎071/212263) on Phou Vao Road, a fun **dance club** attached to the hotel of the same name with a laid-back dance floor, where both Lao and foreigner clientele are welcome. All the best places for a drink seem to be French-run, including *Duang Champa* (see p.165), which tends to stay open late at the weekend, the stylish *L'Elephant* (see p.165), and the coolest bar in town, the *Maylek Pub* (⊛www.maylek.multimania.com) at Setthathilat and Visounalat, run by a French-Canadian. Although many of the cocktails at *Maylek* cost more than a hotel room ($8) there's no arguing that the super-modern interiors inside a late French-era building are extremely cool, and the beer at least is not unreasonably priced (9000K). Three doors over from *Maylek*, *Hong's Place* stays open late and has a collection of video movies. Near the Nam Phou Fountain, the very low-key bar at the *Souvannaphoum* hotel, *Le Rendez-Vous*, benefits from the regal atmosphere of a hotel that was once home to former prime minister Prince Souvannaphouma (the hotel name had to lose an "a" to appease Vientiane). If you're looking for a bar on the Lao hipster scene, check out the laid-back *E'Stranger Literary Salon* (see p.164). Most venues close by midnight.

Cultural entertainment

Louang Phabang is the cultural heart of Laos so it's the best place to take in some **traditional music** or **dance**. The *Sin Xay Restaurant* on Phou Vao Road (T071/212587, Esinxay2000@yahoo.com) holds a dinner show with Lao costume dance, music, and traditional folk songs on Mondays, Wednesdays, Fridays and Saturdays, from 7.30 to 9.30pm. The show costs $1 or, for $4, you can tuck into the nine-course buffet dinner as well. Well worth seeing is the live Lao eight-piece traditional orchestra, which plays nightly in the outdoor garden of the *Indochina Spirit* restaurant at 50–51 Chao Fa Ngum Road (T071/252372), near the Nam Phou Fountain. Another atmospheric setting in which to watch a Lao dance performance is the restaurant at the *Villa Santi* hotel on Xiang Thong Road (T071/212267), which puts on its own costume-dance show several nights a week.

Shopping

As the royal capital of Laos, Louang Phabang was traditionally a centre for skilled **artisans** from around the former kingdom. Weavers, gold- and silver-smiths, painters, sculptors of bronze, wood and ivory all held a place of importance in old Louang Phabang and the most gifted artisans were award-ed royal patronage. After the revolution these arts were seen as decadent and officially suppressed, while the artisans associated with the former royalty were shunned. Unable to practise their trade, many drifted to more accept-able occupations or fled the country. Since the easing of restrictions on trav-el, and the subsequent boom in tourism, these traditional arts have been experiencing a revival and there is a wide array of different crafts on sale – as well as the usual selection of tourist junk. **Silver** and **textiles** can be espe-cially good buys in Louang Phabang, but only if you buy from the right peo-ple and haggle.

One of the best places to see everything in one place is the **Pathana Boupha Antique House** (daily 8.30am–7pm; T071/212262), on Chao Xomphou Road, east of That Makmo. This beautiful colonial mansion oper-ates as a private museum and showroom and has a large collection of antique handicrafts and textiles for sale. The ladies of the Boupha family are fascinating to talk to and can show you the family photo albums spanning several gener-ations. Another showroom for Lao handicrafts is the Blue House (T252383, Ebluehouse@lao.tel.com) on Xiang Thong Road next to the *Le Café Ban Vat Sene*. Also housed in a lovely old colonial building, the Blue House acts as a kind of display room and gallery for handicraft artists.

Once you've decided what to buy, there are over twenty **handicraft shops** and **boutiques** located on Xiang Thong Road and plenty of good boutiques in the side streets to check out. Shops selling textiles often hang out their wares in colourful displays to lure the curious. Handicraft and antique shops are also to be found in the old city as well as at Talat Dala, the city's main market, located on Setthathilat Road. Although it's a popular pastime for three-minute experts to decry the commercialization of Louang Phabang, the revival of traditional handicrafts is thanks in no small part to tourist demand, which continues to drive the industry today. See the Shopping section of Basics (pp.57–61) for further details on what to look out for in the items listed below.

Antiques, antiquities and fakes

Instant antiques produced in Thailand, and to a much lesser extent Cambodia, are finding their way back up to Louang Phabang. Buddhist or Hindu figurines cast in any kind of metal are mostly Thai or Cambodian reproductions: a few years back, a Ganesh figurine of the kind that sells in Bangkok for four to six dollars was seen for sale at Ban Phanom for an asking price of $800. **Opium weights** are well represented in the silver shops of Louang Phabang.

Basketry

Baskets made in the nearby hilltribe villages are widely available in Louang Phabang. In fact, it is fairly common to spot groups of villagers tramping from shop to shop with sackloads of baskets and other wares. By greeting them and enquiring politely about what they have for sale you can cut out the middleman and score yourself a beautiful and functional souvenir. If you aren't lucky enough to get baskets direct from the source, try the shops opposite Wat That.

Mulberry paper products

Observant visitors to Louang Phabang may notice the bustling trade in what first appears to be bundles of white garlic. The "garlic" is in fact *Broussonetia papyrifera*, the raw material for **mulberry paper**, known in Lao as *jia sa*. This paper is used throughout Tai cultures, and in Laos is utilized in the construction of *khom fai*, mulberry-paper lanterns that decorate houses and monasteries during the *lai heua fai* festival (see p.55). Notebooks and photo albums made from mulberry paper have found a ready market in the handicraft shops of Louang Phabang. **Ban Khili Gallery** (opposite Wat Sop) offers a good selection of originally designed lanterns, including easily transported collapsible models. This German-run operation also produces tasteful stencil work on mulberry paper featuring traditional Lao–Buddhist motifs inspired by the walls of Louang Phabang's many gaily decorated *sim*. They also now offer DHL shipping.

Royalist regalia

It stands to reason that Louang Phabang, being the former royal capital, should be awash with dusty relics evoking the **monarchy**, and indeed its curio shops have more than anywhere else in Laos, though not as many as you might imagine. Considered a royalist hotbed by suspicious communist officials after the revolution, Louang Phabang and its inhabitants were especially targeted for "re-education". During the early years of the LPDR, royal items were buried, thrown into rivers or melted down by people anxious to forget their own ties to the previous regime. What remained eventually appeared in antique stores, and souvenir-hungry tourists have rid Louang Phabang of these mementos with more thoroughness than the threat of re-education ever did.

Silver

Although Thai antique dealers have made off with quite a bit of old Lao silver (and marketed it in Thailand as old Thai silver), there is still a fair amount of the stuff floating around. Items to look out for include paraphernalia for betel chewing, boxes or bowls and jewellery (see Basics, p.58 for more details). With few exceptions, the **hilltribe jewellery** being peddled in Louang Phabang is the handiwork of the Hmong tribe. All of the articles mentioned above are sold in the shops along Xiang Thong Road or at Talat Dala.

New silver of superior quality can and should be bought directly from Louang Phabang's expert **silversmiths**. The best known of these is Thithpeng Maniphone, whose workshop is located just down the small lane opposite Wat That. As for the quality of the merchandise, suffice to say that when Thailand's Princess Sirindhorn visited Louang Phabang she made a point of patronizing Thithpeng's shop. Other silversmiths are located near the Royal Palace and opposite Wat Aham. New silver for sale at souvenir shops and in the market is less expensive than that of the silversmiths, but the difference in workmanship is quite evident.

Textiles

Traditional **textiles** are practically Louang Phabang's signature product and both antique and new textiles are good value. There are now many upmarket **boutiques** specializing in high-quality Lao textiles. Many of these outlets are every bit as upscale and fashionable as the best quality boutiques in Bangkok or Chiang Mai from which they draw their inspiration. Ock Pop Tok Textiles Gallery and Workshop at 73/5 Ban Wat Nong (☎020/570148, ℮ockpoptok@yahoo.com, ⓦwww.ockpoptok.com), next to *L'Elephant Brasserie*, is typical of the kind of chic shops popping up around this end of town. It is foreign-managed, has knowledgeable sales staff, and is run as a kind of co-op with the villagers who produce the weavings for sale here. Another good boutique is Satri Lao on Siphouthabath Street (☎020/252708), just opposite Pla-net Internet. On the same strip there are two other neighbouring boutiques also selling Lao textiles. Satri Lao has another Louang Phabang branch, Satrilao Deco, located on Ban Vat Sene (☎020/252322), further down Xiang Thong Road.

One of the longest running places in town is **Lao Antique Textiles Collection** on Xiang Thong Road (☎071/212775), next to the *Naunenapha Restaurant*, which has an excellent selection of unusual and antique textiles at reasonable prices. Mr Keomontri, the owner, has been collecting for years and has sold pieces to Australia's National Museum. Prices range from $20 for a hand-woven antique blanket to hundreds of dollars for rare antique *sin* from Muang Houn. Mr Keomontri is very knowledgeable about what he sells and can tell you just which of Laos's many ethnic groups produced a certain piece. There is also a selection of weaving accoutrements, such as hand-carved shuttles and loom pulleys, on offer.

Cheaper, lower quality wares can be found at shops all over town but are cheapest at Talat Dala on Setthathilat Road where *nyam* – shoulder bags – and the all-purpose *pha khao ma*, a chequered, wrap-around sarong that Lao men also use as a turban or scarf, are almost given away. Eye-catching examples of **Hmong embroidery** are sold at the Hmong "Tribal Market" (see p.161). Another good place to look for cheap bolts of Lao fabrics is the T-junction where Phommathay meets Siphouthabath Road on the northern side of Mount Phou Si.

Woodcarving

Lao **woodcarving** is traditionally religious in nature, but the increase in tourism has created a demand for souvenirs and so woodcarvers are now whittling a wide range of objects. These include wooden hangers for displaying textiles, carved with motifs such as the Watermelon Stupa and the three-headed elephant. Small, antique wooden **Buddha images** turn up occasionally in antique stores, but visitors should resist the temptation to purchase, as they are likely to have been pilfered from the caves at Pak Ou. New Buddhas are the better alternative and examples carved in a variety of hardwoods can be found alongside the textiles and old silver in the shops on Xiang Thong Road and in Talat Dala.

Listings

Airlines Lao Aviation's office is located on Visounalat Rd ☎071/212172.

Banks and exchange There are several exchange places along Xiang Thong Rd including the main branch of Lane Xang Bank, opposite the Hmong Market, which changes travellers' cheques and can do cash advances on Visa. Lane Xang Bank also maintains an exchange bureau (daily 8.30am–4pm) on Latsavong Rd; cash and travellers' cheques only. There is no longer a currency black market but some jewellery shops around Dala Market will still give you slightly better than the official rate for cash. The official exchange rates in Louang Phabang are better than anywhere further up-country.

Bicycle rental Numerous shops on Xiang Thong Rd rent out bicycles (10,000K for the day) although mountain bikes are harder to find. Most budget guest houses also rent out bikes. Six different well-planned mountain-bike tours, ranging from beginner to expert, can be booked through the *Indochina Spirit Restaurant* ☎071/252372.

Boat charters Boatmen tend to congregate at the Navigation Office behind the palace or at the nearby "South Pier", just to the south. If you need a boatman who can act as a guide, contact Mr Thongdi at Bouchane Rice Shop, Manthatoulat Rd (☎071/212910), next to the *Auberge Calao*, who speaks excellent English and has two boats.

Hospitals and clinics The main hospital is located on Setthathilat Rd; a new International Clinic (☎071/252049) is around the corner on the hospital's western side. In case of a serious illness, flying direct to Chiang Mai, Thailand, where there are several good hospitals, is the best option.

Internet access Pla-net CyberCentre has two branches, one on Xiang Thong Rd and another on Setthathilat Rd just up from the GPO (both daily 8am–9pm; 200K per min). Several other internet places can be found along Xiang Thong Rd, the cheapest of which is LPB Internet (daily 8am–9pm; 180K per min; ☎071/253444).

Laundry Most hotels and guest houses will wash clothes for you.

Massage and herbal sauna The Red Cross (daily 5–9pm) on Visounalat Rd (☎071/252856 or 212303) has traditional Lao massage at 25,000K per hour (reserve ahead) and an excellent sauna for 10,000K (bring a sarong or pay 1000K to rent one). Proceeds go to help poor villagers. Anoudeth Steambath & Massage (daily 10am–10pm) on Souvanbaniang Rd has a sauna for 6000K an hour and massage for 22,000K an hour.

Minimarkets Small minimarts selling everything from Kodak film to American chocolate bars can be found all along Xiang Thong Rd, especially in the Ban Jek area.

Motorbike rental Motorbikes are unfortunately limited to 100cc step-throughs and are rented out for around $8 per day plus deposit of your passport. Pinekham Service, on the corner of Setthathilat and Visounalat rds, is the biggest motorbike rental in town but many guest houses have motorbikes available.

Pharmacies The best pharmacies are in Dala Market.

Photographic services Lithium batteries are available at VDO, next to the *Luang Prabang Hotel*, on Xiang Thong Rd.

Post office The GPO (Mon–Fri 8am–noon & 1–5pm, Sat 8am–noon) is located on the corner of Xiang Thong and Setthathilat rds. Post restante

Buses and sawngthaews

Buses to Vientiane and Vang Viang and **points south** along Route 13 use the Southern Bus Station, 3km south of the centre, which is best reached by tuk-tuk (3000K). There are five buses a day to Vientiane with the final departure at 5pm. Tickets are sold at the bus station. There is also a thrice monthly air-con **tourist coach to Vientiane** ($10), which can be booked through most guest houses. Southwest-bound **buses to Xainyabouli and Muang Nan** pull out of the Pakkhon depot, near the Southern Bus Station (4000K by tuk-tuk) and depart until mid-afternoon. Buses and sawngthaews to all **points north** use the Northern Bus Station, 6km north of town (3000K by tuk-tuk). Almost all northbound buses depart in the morning; there's no need to buy your ticket in advance.

Boats

Slow boats leave from the Navigation Office landing behind the former Royal Palace in the old city, an easy walk from most guest houses. Departures down to Vientiane or up to Houayxai, as well as up the Nam Ou River, are all posted on a chalk board here, but arrive at the pier early as there are no real fixed departure times. A quick visit to the Navigation Office the day before you plan to depart is prudent. Boats to Xainyabouli may leave from the "South Pier" landing further downriver, at the foot of Setthathilat Road, so make your enquiries beforehand. **Charter boats** to the Buddha Caves, Kouang Si and other nearby destinations are easily found along the riverfront south of the Navigation Office – you'll be approached by boatmen offering a variety of tour options. **Speedboats** leave from a totally separate landing in the suburb of Ban Don, 7km north of the centre on the banks of the Mekong (5000K by tuk-tuk). The eight-seat speedboats travel to points north and south along the Mekong River, as well as destinations along the Nam Ou River. Passengers sign up for their destinations and the boats leave when full. Arrive early to get a seat, although there's no guarantee that every destination is served every day. Alternatively, you can charter a speedboat.

---

services are available free of charge and letters will be kept for three months.

Swimming *Phou Vao Hotel*, Phou Vao Rd ($5).

Telephone services The telecom office (daily 8am–9pm), located behind the GPO, handles international calls and faxes. Collect calls can't be made but a callback service is available (2000K per ten minutes). International direct dial phones are located outside the GPO and phone cards are available at many convenience stores. IDD calls can be made from most hotels. LPB Internet on Xiang Thong Rd (℡071/253444) also offers overseas calls.

Tour agencies Diethlem, Xiang Thong Rd ℡071/212277; Lane Xang, Visounalat Rd ℡071/212793; Lao Travel Service, Xiang Thong Rd ℡071/212725; Lao Youth Travel ℡071/252372, ℮indochina1@yahoo.com, Sodetour, Manthatoulat Rd ℡071/212092.

Around Louang Phabang

Once you've exhausted Louang Phabang's many monasteries and temples, you'll still find many more attractions in the surrounding countryside, all within easy reach of the city. An excursion to the pretty village of **Ban Phanom** will reward you with textiles shopping, together with a look at a traditional lowland Lao village, and can be combined with a pilgrimage to the tomb of French explorer Henri Mouhout and a stop at the Santi Chedi viewpoint (see p.162). The popular **Pak Ou caves** trip gets you out on the water, a wonderful day-trip, especially if you haven't had a chance to travel the Mekong by boat.

There are also two picturesque **waterfalls** nearby, Tad Se and Kouang Si, both of which are good spots for a picnic and splashing around in turquoise waters. All the trips described here can be done in half a day. While it's possible to get to these sites by local public transport, it's much faster and easier to get there on your own by hiring a tuk-tuk with a few fellow travellers or renting a motorbike. The swift rivers, pretty rural areas, and impressive mountains around Louang Phabang also offer many opportunities for **adventure sports** including white-water rafting, mountain-bike touring, kayaking, and trekking tours. Enquires for adventure tours can be made through your guest house or a tour agent like Lao Youth Travel (see Listings, p.171).

Ban Phanom Village

A few hundred metres beyond the golden stupa of Santi Chedi, **BAN PHANOM** attracts its share of the tourist dollar through its pedigree as a former royal weaving village. The palace resettled a Thai Leu community from the northern town of Louang Namtha to provide weavers and dancers for King Sisavang Vong's court. Young girls from Ban Phanom were chosen to be classical dancers and would begin the intensive training regime as young as seven or eight years old – a necessity if they were to learn how to bend their limbs and fingers at the alien angles demanded by Lao classical dancing. The only traces of this tradition left in Ban Phanom lie in the tales woven by older village women who long ago danced for the king. Elsewhere, classical dancing is only a little easier to find, showcased in dinner shows for tourists at restaurants such as the *Kualao* in Vientiane, or for tour groups at upmarket hotels like Louang Phabang's *Souvannaphoum*.

Just off the main road, the Ban Phanom **textile market** is a bit of a tourist trap. You'll find textiles of comparable quality in town for the same prices. The market sells mostly cotton and silk sarongs, as well as a small selection of trousers and shirts in sizes large enough to fit Westerners, plus a sampling of colourful shoulder bags. The main reason for making the trip out to this market is to watch the women work their looms as you browse their wares. If you take the time to wander Ban Phanom's quaint, red-dirt streets you'll find a few independent textile shops as well as women hard at work weaving in the relatively cool space beneath their raised, traditional wooden homes.

Ban Phanom is easily reached by **bicycle** or **motorbike** by following Patoupakmao Road and turning left at the first major intersection beyond *Wiang Mai* restaurant. After 500m, turn right onto a dirt road leading uphill – Ban Phanom is about 300m further. Share tuk-tuks for Ban Phanom (500K) leave Louang Phabang several times throughout the day from Dala Market.

Henri Mouhot's tomb

Four kilometres up the Nam Khan from Ban Phanom is the final resting place of **Henri Mouhot**, the French naturalist and explorer best known as the "discoverer" of Angkor Wat (see box on p.173). A simple memorial, made from stone donated by the Lao king Tiantha and erected by Doudart de Lagrée of the Mekong Commission in 1867, marks the spot, which is easily located by following the yellow signs erected by a French restaurateur in Louang Phabang. As you leave Ban Phanom, follow the right fork 3.7km until you reach a steep dirt path leading down to the bank of the river, a spot favoured by picnicking Lao from Louang Phabang on weekends. The whitewashed memorial lies 200m upriver from the path and about 20m from the river's edge in a dried-up tributary of the Khan.

Henri Mouhout

Although he was the first European to reach the isolated royal city of Louang Phabang, French explorer **Henri Mouhot** was far better known for his nineteenth-century journey to Cambodia which gained him renown as the "discoverer" of **Angkor Wat,** the famed Khmer temple complex built by Suryavarman II. Mouhot was hardly the first to stumble upon Angkor, but the eloquence of his journals, published posthumously in English and French, captured the majesty of the ruins and piqued his European readers' imagination. His writings circulated widely, their influence immediately apparent in such works as *The English Governess at the Siamese Court,* written in 1870 by Anna Leonowens, the governess of *The King and I* fame, and in which certain passages bear remarkable similarity to Mouhot's work. Although less known for his travels in Laos, the final episode in a life of insatiable exploring that took him far from his Jersey home, Mouhot's writings on the country bear the same descriptive flair that brought Angkor to life for his European audience.

Mouhot, who turned to England for sponsorship of his journeys after finding a lack of interest in his native France, spent much of his three years in **Southeast Asia** travelling through the difficult terrain of northeastern Thailand, Cambodia and Laos. In December 1860, Mouhot set off from Bangkok for Laos, aware that no Westerner in recent memory had travelled to the heart of Siam's isolated vassal state and lived. Putting aside premonitions that it was his destiny to die in Laos, he travelled through the Forest of the King of Fire, the present-day Thai provinces of Korat and Loei, and on to Louang Phabang through Paklai, all the while dazzling the Lao with his long red beard and filling his journals with his customarily frank insights on those he encountered, including the children who brought the naturalist insects for his collection in exchange for a bit of brass wire or a "cigarette, for it is a common thing for them to leave their mother's breast to smoke". It took him seven months to reach **Louang Phabang,** a "delightful little town", the setting of which he likened to Geneva. In Louang Phabang, Mouhot was received by King Tiantha, an encounter he described in detail: "After waiting for ten days I have at length been presented to the king with great pomp. The reception room was a shed such as they build in our villages on fête-days, but larger and hung with every possible colour. His Majesty was enthroned at one end of the hall, lazily reclining on a divan, having on his right hand four guards squatting down, and each holding a sabre; behind were the princes all prostrated, and farther off the senators, with their backs to the public and their faces in the dust."

Using Louang Phabang as a base, Mouhot made several exploratory trips in the surrounding countryside, but contracted a fever and, three months after his arrival in the royal city, died at the age of 35, his famously descriptive diary trailing off with the words "Have pity on me, oh my God...!" Mouhot was buried in the shadow of Phou Souwung Mountain, on the banks of the Nam Khan River, his explorations a harbinger of the colonies of France in Laos and Cambodia.

The Pak Ou Buddha Caves

Without a doubt Louang Phabang's most popular day-trip, a river excursion to the **Pak Ou Buddha Caves** 25km north of Louang Phabang at the confluence of the Mekong and Nam Ou rivers, is one of the best quick trips you can make out of the city. Numerous caves punctuate the limestone cliffs on both sides of the Mekong in this vicinity, but the two "Buddha Caves" of **Tham Ting** and **Tham Phoum** are the best known. These caves have been used for centuries as a repository for old Buddha images that can no longer be venerated on an altar, either because they are damaged to the point of disfigurement – termite holes, burn marks, and broken limbs being afflictions common to wooden Buddhas – or simply because newer images have crowded them out. In former times, before the caves became a tourist attraction, the inhabitants of Louang Phabang didn't give much thought to the caves or their contents except during **Lao New Year** when boatloads of townsfolk would make the pilgrimage upriver and ritually bathe the semi-abandoned Buddhas to gain merit. The practice survives to this day and is worth seeing if you happen to be around to catch the spectacle. If not, the caves still deserve an hour or so, if only to gaze at the eerie scene of hundreds upon hundreds of serenely smiling images covered in dust and cobwebs. Tham Ting, the lower cave, just above the water's surface, is more of a large grotto and is light enough to explore without an artificial light source. The upper cave is unlit so bring a torch, or better still, a handful of candles to enhance the spooky effect. An entrance fee of 8000K is collected at the cave.

  Boats to Pak Ou are easily arranged at the "South Pier" landing in Louang Phabang and cost $10 for up to five people to hire for the trip there and back. The ride upriver takes less than an hour. If you want to see the **Whisky Village** (see below) on the opposite side of the Mekong from the Pak Ou Caves, tell the boatman before you leave or you may end up paying more. If you decide to visit the Pak Ou Caves by tuk-tuk from Louang Phabang, the fare is $8 return and 4000K to cross the Mekong.

Whisky Village

Opposite the Buddha Caves on the far side of the Mekong is the "mouth" of the "Ou" River – "Pak Ou" in Lao. The scenery here at the entrance of the Nam Ou is dramatic with a huge limestone peak rising up over the junction of the two rivers. South of Pak Ou, on the banks of the Mekong, is a village that for thousands of years produced stoneware jars but has now forsaken that activity, having found that distilling liquor is more lucrative. The inhabitants of **BAN XANG HAI**, referred to by local boatmen as the "**Whisky Village**", are quite used to thirsty visitors stopping by for a pull on the bamboo straw. The liquor is lào-láo made from fermented sticky rice, and pots filled with the hooch are lined up on the beach awaiting transport up or down the river.

  As it's logical to see the Pak Ou Caves and the Whisky Village on the same trip, most boatmen hired in Louang Phabang are happy to treat it as a package, assuming that after you've seen a cave-full of Buddhas you'll be ready for a good, stiff drink. **Boats** to either or both destinations are easily arranged in Louang Phabang and should cost no more than $10 both ways.

Tad Se

The wide **Tad Se** waterfall wanders down a gradual slope, serenely cascading through trees and easing through a dozen clear blue pools, like some elaborate Zen meditation retreat, until it finally flows into the Nam Khan River. The pools here aren't good for swimming like those at Kouang Si, but are fine for a bit of splashing around. Located south of Louang Phabang, this excursion follows Route 13 south along the beginning of its most dramatically pretty stretch, winding around mountains and past hillside teak plantations, and culminates with a short trip by pirogue downstream to the waterfall. If you've come by your own transport, turn left off Route 13, 17km south of town, and head for Ban En (marked Ban Aine on a blue roadside sign), 2km away. Here you'll need to hire a boat (5000K per person; 10,000K if you're alone) for the short journey to the falls, which are downstream on the opposite bank. The boat cruises downriver for five minutes past tobacco fields and drop-door bamboo fishing traps. You can also get to Ban En very easily by tuk-tuk ($3 return). Alternatively, catch the Vientiane-bound bus, which will let you off on Route 13, and walk the remaining 2km to the village. If you're on a motorbike, be wary of buses and trucks careering through the final turns of the journey up from Vientiane.

Kouang Si

One of the best day-trips from Louang Phabang is **Kouang Si** waterfall (8000K), a picturesque, multi-level fall that tumbles 60m before spilling through a series of crystal-blue pools. The spray from the falls keeps the surrounding grounds cool even at midday. It's a great spot for a picnic and a refreshing swim – there are picnic tables and changing rooms at the site. A large landslide has recently altered the setting somewhat but it shouldn't be long before nature sets things right again. The "no swimming" signs posted at the **upper pool** appear to be intended simply to dissuade you from spoiling photo opportunities – not an issue during the week when the park is free of Lao in their Sunday best out for a picnic. The **lower pool**, the designated swimming zone, is equally good for a swim, although it lacks a direct view of the waterfall. If you didn't pack a lunch, pay a visit to the vendors nearby selling *tam màk hung*, fruit and drinks.

If you're up for some exercise, the steep path on the opposite side of the falls leads to the top and a grassy **meadow** filled with brilliantly coloured butterflies. Tread carefully though, as the path can get quite slippery; more than a few barefoot trampers have slipped and broken a leg here.

There are several options for **getting to the waterfall** which is situated 35km southwest of Louang Phabang. The easiest is to hire a tuk-tuk ($6) or rent a motorcycle in Louang Phabang, but the most scenic is by boat down the Mekong River. If you opt to go by boat, the same boatmen who run the trips to the Pak Ou caves will take you to the falls for $10–12 for a boat. The boat option entails taking a tuk-tuk for the last portion of the journey, something that needs to be established when negotiating the boat fare. The river trip is a pleasant cruise down the Mekong River and the whole trip takes half a day if you don't linger too long at the falls.

The road to Kouang Si follows the Mekong through pretty scenery and villages populated by a variety of different **ethnic groups**, including Hmong. The first village southwest of Louang Phabang is **Ban Lak 8**, settled in the 1960s by Lao Theung fleeing fighting along the Vietnamese border to the north. Three younger villages – the Hmong village of Ban Na Ouane, the Lao Theung village of Ban Nun Sa-at and Ban Thin Keo, a lowland Lao settlement – were resettled here from the mountain near the waterfall by the government, which was fretting that their slash-and-burn methods of farming were affecting the falls. A few kilometres before the idyllic lowland village of **Ban Tha Pene** and the waterfall, a small **elephant camp**, signposted with an advertisement for "elephant service", offers hour-long rides to the waterfall (daily 8am–noon & 2–5pm; 20,000K per hour).

Accommodation near the waterfall is available at a charming, rosewood guest house (❸) in Ban Tha Pene. It's run by the owners of the *Vanvisa* in Louang Phabang and offers six basic rooms with en-suite bathrooms. To find it, turn right before the hill leading out of the village, cross the footbridge over the stream and you'll see it on the left.

Mount Phaban

Phou Phaban, 30km upriver from Xiang Ngeun, is the highest peak in the immediate vicinity of Louang Phabang and, so far, remains well off the beaten tourist track. The Nam Khan River, which empties into the Mekong at Louang Phabang, flows right around the flanks of this 2212-metre peak. To reach the mountain you have to charter a passenger boat to take you up the Nam Khan from Xiang Ngeun, 24km south of Louang Phabang. On the way you can stop at a **cave** and a natural **hot spring** with cold and hot pools. The rapids at the base of the mountain are so turbulent that the boats can't go any further. Upriver, beyond the rapids, the Nam Khan flows through over 100km of unchartered jungle all the way from the Nam Et NBCA.

Adventure tours

Perhaps due to the large number of cultural attractions centred in Louang Phabang, **adventure tours** have gotten off to a much slower start here than in other centres up-country or in Vang Viang to the south. In fact, there is a huge amount of adventure travel possibilities around Louang Phabang including rock-climbing, rafting and kayaking on the Nam Xuang and Nam Khan rivers, and mountain-biking and trekking tours. Currently, the only company actively pushing adventure travel is Lao Youth Travel (☎071/252372, ✉indochina1@yahoo.com) based out of a back office in the *Spirit of Indochina* restaurant opposite Nam Phou fountain. This foreign-run operation (ask for Markus Peschke) offers guided mountain biking and trekking day-trips, as well as rafting and kayaking tours on the Nam Pa, Nam Khan, Nam Ou, Nam Ming and Nam Xuang rivers varying from Grade 1 to Grade 4 in difficulty. There are also multi-day, guided 4-wheel drive tours of the north country. Permission is already pending for a Wildside Adventures office in Louang Phabang but the ubiquitous travel company already does "tours on request" of the Nam Ming and Nam Xuang out of its Vang Viang office.

Travel details

Buses

Louang Phabang to: Muang Nan (5 daily; 3hr); Nam Bak (2 daily; 2hr 10min); Nong Khiaw (2 daily; 2–3hr); Oudomxai (3 daily; 5-6hr); Pakkhon (5 daily; 3hr); Pakmong (5 daily; 2hr); Vang Viang (6 daily; 6–7hr); Viang Kham (1 daily; 4hr 40min); Vientiane (7 daily; 10–12hr).

Slow boats

Louang Phabang to: Nong Khiaw (daily; 7–8hr); Pakbeng (1 daily; 10hr); Thadua (daily; 6–8hr); Vientiane (variable; 3 days).

Flights

Louang Phabang to: Chiang Mai (2 weekly; 2hr); Dien Bien Phu (2 weekly; 1hr); Houayxai (1 daily; 50min); Louang Namtha (4 weekly; 35min); Nan (2 weekly; 1hr 50min); Oudomxai (2 weekly; 35min); Phonsavan (daily; 35min); Vientiane (4 daily; 40min).

The Northeast

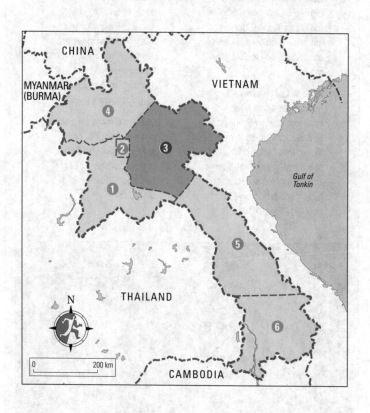

CHAPTER 3   # Highlights

✳ **Route 1** From Nong
Khiaw to Nam Neun
junction, ride across the
rooftop of Indochina to
one of the least-visited
parts of the country.
See p.181

✳ **Suan Hin** These ancient
circles of upright slabs of
rock in a remote forest
still baffle historians and
archeologists today. **See
p.191**

✳ **Pathet Lao caves** A
major Viet Minh head-
quarters during the First
and Second Indochina
Wars, this historic base of
the thirty-year revolutionary struggle also boasts
incredible limestone karst
scenery. **See p.193**

✳ **Plain of Jars** Fields of
ancient giant stone urns
scattered across the
Xiang Khouang Plateau
stand as witnesses to a
vanished civilization. **See
p.203**

✳ **Muang Khoun** Travel
back in time to the
ancient kingdom of
Xiang Khouang where
temple ruins and a giant
Buddha are all that
remains of a once proud
kingdom. **See p.206**

✳ **Muang Kham** Launching
point for caves, hot
springs and visits to
Hmong, Khamu, Black
Tai, and Phuan villages.
See p.207

The northeast

ifficult to reach and short on typical tourist sites, the remote **northeast** is not surprisingly one of the least visited parts of Laos. However, a frontier friendliness among the inhabitants, who come from more than two dozen ethnic groups, and the challenge of tough travel in remote reaches unsullied by tourists, lend the region a certain allure for those who enjoy blazing their own trail. Topographically diverse, the northwest region extends from the towering peaks that border the Vientiane Plain, across the Xiang Khouang Plateau, over the jagged backbone of the Annamite Mountains, and into the Nam Xam River watershed, which flows into Vietnam. The region is bounded by the Vietnamese border to the east and north and by the old Royal Road section of Route 13 to the west. The area encompasses **Houa Phan and Xiang Khouang provinces**, the newly created **Xaisomboun Special Zone** and part of **northern Louang Phabang province**. Historically, this swathe of Laos was the domain of two independent principalities – the Tai federation of Sipsong Chao Tai in Houa Phan and the Phuan Kingdom of Xiang Khouang. Sandwiched between expansive empires to the west and east, both entities struggled to maintain their sovereignty until the late nineteenth century, when the French finally folded most of their territory into unified Laos.

The kings of the defunct royal house of **Xiang Khouang** came from the same family tree as those of Louang Phabang, both kingdoms claiming descent from Khoun Borom, the celebrated first ancestor of numerous Tai–Lao legends. Yet, unlike Louang Phabang, few physical traces of Xiang Khouang's splendour survive. In the place of bejewelled pagodas and distinctive Xiang Khouang-style temples are bomb craters doubling as fishing holes and houses erected on piles crafted from bomb casings – reminders that this was one of the most heavily bombed pieces of real estate in the world, and a testament to the rugged perseverance of the Phuan, Black Tai, Hmong and Khamu peoples who inhabit the province. Much of the bombing was directed at the strategic **Plain of Jars**, which takes its name from the fields of ancient, giant funerary urns that are the northeast's main tourist draw. Indeed, until very recently, for most visitors a trip to the region meant a flying visit to Xiang Khouang's provincial capital **Phonsavan** to see the Jar sites, and a quick sidetrip to nearby **Muang Khoun**, the former royal seat of Xiang Khouang, where a handful of ruins whisper of the kingdom's vanished glory.

Even fewer travellers make the journey to **Houa Phan**, an impenetrable sea of rugged green mountaintops lost in mist and shallow valleys, far from the Mekong River and the traditional centres of lowland Lao life. The only provincial centre in Laos east of the Annamites, Houa Phan's capital **Xam Nua** is a

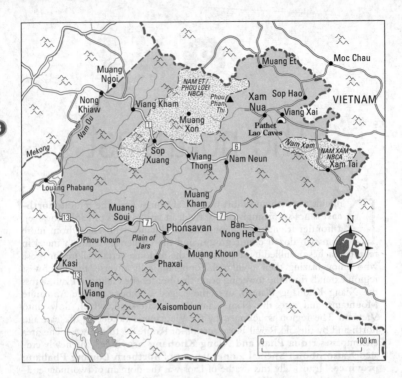

chilly frontier town, closer to Hanoi than Vientiane, a proximity that lends it a distinctly Vietnamese flavour. This lightly populated region is home to more than twenty ethnic groups, most of them Tai, including the Black, Red and White Tai, all of whom share a distinctly Houa Phan character – a fortitude shaped by the remote mountainous terrain and by years spent living in the heart of the **Pathet Lao's liberated zone**. After the Pathet Lao rose to power in 1975, the communists further exploited Houa Phan's isolation by transforming their liberated zone into a massive prison camp. Thousands of former Royal Lao soldiers were interred in the province's notorious re-education camps. Houa Phan's wartime history has been etched into the land at **Viang Xai**, a short ride from Xam Nua. Dozens of **caves** hidden in the sawtoothed limestone karsts of Viang Xai served as the headquarters for the Pathet Lao during their Thirty Year Struggle.

Getting there and around

Poor roads and unreliable **transport** conspire with rugged mountains to keep the northeast remote. As a result, travelling in this part of Laos is still something of an adventure so leave on the earliest possible vehicles, bring some food and bottled water, and be prepared for breakdowns while on the road. At present, the only way to get to the region is to bus in along one of the difficult overland routes (Route 1 and Route 7) from Louang Phabang province, or to fly into Xam Nua or Phonsavan and begin exploring the region from there. Currently none of the northeast's four principal **borders with Vietnam** are open, although there is talk of opening the borders at Nong Het and Pahang to foreigners by 2003. Once the borders through to northern Vietnam open, travel through the northeast is sure to boom.

To get from Louang Phabang to Xam Nua by **Route 1** takes a day by private vehicle or two to three days by public transport so be prepared to overnight in Viang Thong, Viang Kham, or Nam Neun. To get from Vientiane to Phonsavan takes a full day by public bus. The 140-kilometre stretch of **Route 7** from Phou Khoun to Phonsavan is currently being rebuilt. Route 7 is open to foreigners but this section still takes between 8 and 12 hours during the dry season. Once the final 70km is surfaced, the travel times from Louang Phabang and Vientiane to Phonsavan will be dramatically reduced. There is a very basic guest house at the Phou Khoun junction if you get stuck overnight there.

Until the borders with Vietnam open, the most logical route for travellers is the **circle route** through Nong Khiaw, Xam Nua, Phonsavan, and Phou Khoun or vice versa. Owing to a lack of direct transport and long waits in between transfers along Route 1, you should allow two days travel time to get from Nong Khiaw to Xam Nua by road, and then another two days to swing back out to Phou Khoun on Route 13. The worst section is on Route 1 from Sop Xuang to Viang Thong. The situation improves greatly along Route 6 because it's paved and there are direct sawngthaews linking Viang Thong with Xam Nua, Nam Neun and Phonsavan. At some points, you may find sawngthaew drivers unwilling to depart because there aren't enough travellers; passengers are at times asked for more money, or to wait, sometimes for hours. If you have money or enough people you can save hours of endless waiting by **chartering a sawngthaew**. Drivers are usually more than happy to be hired out for the journey, but will still want to pick up passengers en route and collect the extra fares.

Nong Khiaw to Nam Neun

The journey from **Nong Khiaw to Nam Neun** along Route 1 is one of northern Laos's great road journeys, crossing numerous mountain ranges and valleys. It's a very tough trip but the scenery more than makes up for the discomfort. From Nong Khiaw to **Viang Thong** the road is paved but beyond the town of Sop Xuang it becomes progressively worse until finally hitting tarmac again at the Nam Neun junction where paved Route 6 links Xam Nua to Phonsavan and the Plain of Jars. Although it's possible to cover the entire route from Nong Khiaw to Xam Nua or Phonsavan by hired vehicle in a day, the same trip by public transportation usually requires two or even three days. If you're travelling by local sawngthaews you'll probably have to change vehicles at **Viang Kham**, and again at **Viang Thong** (sometimes known as Muang Hiam) the first major town of Houa Phan province. Travellers going east often have to overnight in Viang Thong, while those travelling west may have to break the trip in Viang Kham. Both towns have basic guest houses.

Viang Kham

Roughly 50km from Nong Khiaw, the town of **VIANG KHAM** snakes along Route 1 for several kilometres. Most likely you'll have to change vehicles here for a sawngthaew to Viang Thong. Buses and sawngthaews stop at the **bus stop** on a hill high above the river 3km out on the northeast edge of town. If you're staying overnight you'll have to hike into town or flag down a passing motorcycle. Both of the town's basic **guest houses** are located close to the river, one on each side of the bridge. The guest house on the eastern side of the river – a two-storey concrete house about eight houses before the bridge – is the better of the two (●). There's little to see in the town, which amounts to two rows of wooden houses flanking each side of Route 1, but you'll see many houses with traditional looms for weaving. The river that cleaves the town is the **Nam Xuang**, which eventually winds its way to Louang Phabang. Although highway upgrades have made the river somewhat redundant, intrepid river-riders might find a boatman willing to make the journey south. Lao Youth Travel (see p.171) in Louang Phabang can take you down the Xuang from Viang Kham to Louang Phabang by kayak in dry season and by raft during the rainy season. Wildside Adventures (see p.111) will do the river on a "by request" basis.

Continuing east, Route 1 labours up forested hills and through ethnic minority villages, with their rough huts precariously perched along the ridges above a sea of mountains. The **scenery** is simply spectacular, with rows upon rows of mountain ranges extending into the distance. A chorus line of tall palms on either side of the highway announces **Sop Xuang**, 50km east of Viang Kham. There's nowhere to stay here, but it does have several *fŏe* shops and a solitary *hân kin deum* (an "eat–drink shop"), which can be counted on for noodles and warm beer, though passenger vehicles don't tend to linger here. From here there's one last mountain range to cross before Viang Thong.

Phou Loei NBCA

Phou Loei NBCA, covering an area of 1465 square kilometres, is located in the high, mountainous divide separating Louang Phabang, Houa Phan, and Xiang Khouang provinces. The park consists of north–south ranges – its highest peak, **Phou Soy** at 2257m, is in the northern end of the NBCA. As Route 1 crosses the NBCA between Viang Kham and Viang Thong, the park is easily reached but none of the ridge-top Hmong villages along Route 1 have any formal accommodation and any trekking has to be self-arranged.

Viang Thong

VIANG THONG, more popularly known by its old name Muang Hiam, lies in the upper valley of the Nam Khan River, which sweeps across the wide swathe of rice fields on the town's western flank. The town itself winds along the bottom of the narrow river valley and its main street begs for a high-noon shootout. A pleasant diversion if you find yourself having to hang around for a bus is the thirty-minute walk to the nearby **hot springs**. To get there, cross the bridge and turn right at the *Phu Kae* guest house and walk 1km, past the hill on the left and rice fields on the right. Rising steam and a narrow path on your left mark the way to the swampy clearing where scalding water bubbles up from the ground. While the pools are large enough for a good soak, they're far too hot; a tiny pool near the main road is cooler and a popular spot for villagers to bring their infants for a warm bath.

After the long overland loop to reach Viang Thong, it's strange to think that the swift flowing river through town ends its journey in distant Louang Phabang. Starting from the Nam Et NBCA just north of Viang Thong, the Nam Khan River heads southwest between two ranges of high mountains, over difficult rapids and through dense jungles. The entire area is a big blank on most maps and no passenger boats travel this length of the river. Locals say it's not possible, though it wouldn't take much arm-twisting to get kayaking expedition organizers in Louang Phabang to give it a shot.

Practicalities

The most interesting of Viang Thong's three **accommodation** options are the handful of rooms with shared bathroom at the *Phu Kae* (❶), a white house on a hill just west of the river, which is less convenient but more pleasant for an extended stay. If you're coming in from the west you'll see it to the left before crossing the river-bridge. For those passing through quickly one of the other two options make a better choice as both are near the bus lot. The friendly *Santisouk* (❶), is an extremely basic, rickety two-storey building, just west of the new market, which stuffs truck-drivers and itinerant Chinese merchants into its tiny, thin-walled rooms. The communal bathing facilities at the back, however, are not ideal, with everyone competing for showers just before daybreak, hurrying to get back on the road. There is a very humble restaurant just opposite. The *Souksakhone* (❶), on the same side of the road just to the east of the market, is virtually indistinguishable from the *Santisouk*, with plain, rudimentary rooms and concrete communal facilities.

Don't expect culinary satisfaction in Viang Thong. There's little to choose from among the handful of **restaurants** clustered at the heart of town. *Fõe* is, as usual, easy to come by, and if you're lucky, you may get a simple soup and a plate of boiled chicken to go with some sticky rice. In the mornings though, even a fried egg can be too much to ask for. The **dry goods store** west of the new market does *fõe* and three-minute noodles and directly opposite is a Lao **coffee shack** but be sure to ask the price before you order!

Moving on, it's imperative that you track down a vehicle early, as vehicles for Viang Kham, Xam Nua, Nam Neun and, less frequently, Phonsavan depart from the bus stand next to the market between 6am and 7.30am each morning. If there's no direct transport to Xam Nua or Phonsavan by bus, catch a sawngthaew to Nam Neun – a gruelling two to three hours to the east over a huge mountain range along a rocky, potholed road – from where onward connections to Phonsavan and Xam Nua can be made. A converted Soviet truck leaves daily from Viang Thong for Xam Nua; if you miss this take a sawngthaew to Nam Neun and get a connection north. If you arrive in Nam Neun too late in the morning you may well wind up stuck there overnight as well as vehicles travelling Route 6 leave early.

Nam Neun

From Viang Thong, Route 1 crosses the mountains down to the tiny settlement of Houa Phou (the actual junction of Route 1 and Route 6) before winding a further 6km down into a deep river valley to the village of **NAM NEUN**, which functions as the hub for travel along Routes 1 and 6. Everyone travelling through the northeast by road eventually winds up in Nam Neun, which sits in the centre of the Louang Phabang–Xam Nua–Phonsavan triangle, and is the launching point for buses heading north to Xam Nua or south to Phonsavan. Although it's just fifty tin-roofed shacks around a dirt lot in the middle of nowhere, there is a rugged friendliness about the place. The steep valley walls and churning river make Nam Neun a diamond in the rough, and for many it's a very welcome spot to break the long journey from Nong Khiaw.

The town is set in a steep valley perched above the swift-flowing **Nam Neun River**, which flows out of the Nam Et NBCA and eventually empties into the Gulf of Tonkin at Vinh. A sturdy Russian-built bridge spans the river here making the otherwise tiny town an important stop-over. Travellers moving along Route 6 between Xam Nua and Phonsavan can also break up the long 240-kilometre haul by overnighting here before making the final 140-kilometre run to Phonsavan.

There are only two **guest houses** in town. The extremely basic *Nam Neun* (❶), at the bus lot, is the cheaper. Much better though is the eight-room *Phouchomkub* (❶), a small compound of white-washed, blue-roofed buildings, which has a terrific location right on the river and next door to the town's only wat. The beautiful two-storey house further along the road is part of a Japanese development project. **Food** is available in Nam Neun, but it's fairly elementary: a small selection of grilled meats on bamboo skewers and bags of sticky rice can be bought in the pint-sized market, and two or three restaurants cater to travellers in transit with bowls of instant noodles and warm drinks.

Houa Phan Province

Sometimes known as Xam Nua after the name of its capital city, Laos's sparsely populated northeasternmost province is a sea of misty mountains, dotted with isolated bowl-like valleys. The difficult terrain of **HOUA PHAN** and its proximity to Vietnam, which forms the province's northern and eastern borders, made Houa Phan the perfect headquarters for the Pathet Lao, who operated out of the caves that honeycomb the karst formations in Viang Xai for the better part of their Thirty Year Struggle. Along with Phongsali, Houa Phan was set aside as a regroupment area for the communist forces under the Geneva Agreements of 1954. While the province formed the backbone of the Pathet Lao's liberated zone, not all of Houa Phan was under communist control: for years, the most distinctive peak in Houa Phan's mountains, 1786-metre **Phou Pha Thi** (see box on p.190), was crowned by a "blind bombing" device to guide air raids on Hanoi.

A good neighbour to the Pathet Lao during the war, **Vietnam** retains close ties with Houa Phan, and a steady flow of Vietnamese goods, electricity, merchants and construction workers arrives in the Lao province via three border points – Sop Hao, Na Maew and Xiang Khoun – none of which is currently open to foreign travellers. Travelling beyond Xam Nua town isn't easy. The province only has three roads, Route 6 from Phonsavan, 6A to Hanoi, and 6B to Muang Et. There are plans to open the border crossing to foreigners by early 2003, thus allowing travellers to cross Houa Phan en route between Hanoi and Vientiane.

Houa Phan is predominantly populated by various Tai groups – Red, Black, Neua and White – and migrants from Vietnam and China. With more than twenty **ethnic groups** in the mix, it's perhaps not surprising that even residents from neighbouring Xiang Khouang complain about the difficulty of understanding Houa Phan dialect. During the centuries before French rule, the area was part of a Black Tai principality, known as the Sipsong Chao Tai, which spanned the present-day Lao–Vietnamese border. The principality fell under the sway of the lowland Lao kingdoms of Louang Phabang, Xiang Khouang and Vientiane and under the control of the greater powers that in turn controlled them – Siam and Vietnam. Stone pillars, known as Suan Hin, located several kilometres off Route 6 near Houa Muang and linked by archeologists to the stone funerary urns of the Plain of Jars, suggest that the area was a hub of some forgotten culture long before Tai–Lao and Vietnamese rulers squabbled over this remote region.

Xam Nua

You could be forgiven for thinking that you'd crossed into Vietnam on descending into **XAM NUA**, the provincial capital and the only sizeable Lao town east of the Annamite Mountains. Unlike the rest of Laos, which drains west into the Mekong, all of Houa Phan Province's rivers flow southeast to the Gulf of Tonkin – Xam Nua itself sits in the narrow Nam Xam River valley. If you want to feel like you're in the middle of nowhere, Xam Nua fits the bill, feeling very much like a hill station, sitting in a bowl surrounded by low, pleasant hills with the narrow river rushing through its centre. But things are livening up and the town is currently undergoing a construction boom, with new multi-storey buildings – a mixture of soviet socialist and tacky Thai – springing up everywhere and starting to climb the flanks of the surrounding hills.

Although there's little to see in the town itself, it serves as a comfortable base for the Viang Xai Caves, forests and hilltribe villages, and trips along the Vietnamese frontier. Tellingly, despite the close geographic, historic and economic ties with neighbouring Vietnam, the satellite dishes of this provincial capital still point towards Bangkok, the epicentre of modern-day Tai–Lao life.

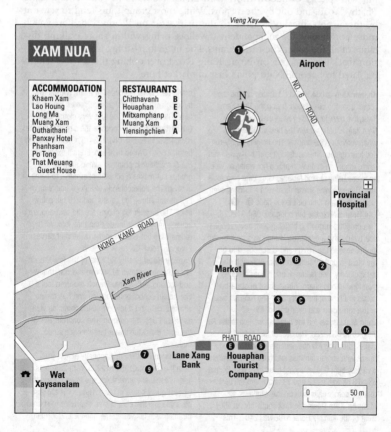

XAM NUA

Vieng Xay

Airport

N

NO. 6 ROAD

Provincial Hospital

ACCOMMODATION
Khaem Xam	2
Lao Houng	5
Long Ma	3
Muang Xam	8
Outhaithani	1
Panxay Hotel	7
Phanhsam	6
Po Tong	4
That Meuang Guest House	9

RESTAURANTS
Chitthavanh	B
Houaphan	E
Mitxamphanp	C
Muang Xam	D
Yiensingchien	A

NONG KANG ROAD

Xam River

Market

PHATI ROAD

Lane Xang Bank

Houaphan Tourist Company

Wat Xaysanalam

0   50 m

Arrival and information

Transport from Nam Nuen and Vieng Thong offloads at the **bus station** on Phathy Road, the town's main street. Across the big bridge over the Nam Xam, Route 6 continues to the airport 3km away. If you've arrived at the **airport**, taxis (5000K) will be on hand to shuttle you to a hotel. There's a **tourist office** (Mon–Fri 8am–noon & 1–4pm), located in the small building at the front of the *Lao Houng Hotel* (☏064/312028; ❶–❷) but the official only speaks Lao and Vietnamese and the ancient looking pamphlets are mostly for other provinces. Better information can be obtained at the Houaphanh Tourism Company, 211 Phathy Rd (☏064/312190, ✆064/312429, ✉hpttourism@hotmail.com), which can organize tours and has rental vehicles. The pastis-drinking owner, Khun Nui, speaks English, French and Thai and has plans to develop trekking and horseback tours in the Houa Long. The *Chittavhan Restaurant* (☏064/312265) also has an eight-seat minivan for rent for $50 a day. **Exchange services** are available at the Lang Xang Bank on the Phathy Road towards Wat Xaysanalam. There is 24-hour electricity in Xan Nua, and telephone but no internet services.

Accommodation

Despite the lack of tourists in Xam Nua, there's certainly no shortage at the inn with plenty of **accommodation** available around the bus station, along Phathy Road, and out by the airport. While most group tours tend to stay out by the airport, the hotels close to the market or on Phathy Road are much more convenient for independent travellers, being within short walking distance of all the town's best restaurants. The huge four-storey, blue-roofed mansion that's just gone up on Nong Kang Road overlooking the town is said to be slated to become Xam Nua's first upmarket hotel.

Khaem Xam ☏064/312111. Located around the corner from the bus station, facing the Nam Xam River, this new, four-storey hotel overlooking the Nam Xam is hands down the best value in town whatever your price bracket. The hotel is family-run and has eighteen immaculately clean, big-windowed rooms, many en-suite with piping hot water, as well as rooms using shared facilities which are also spotless. There's a nice sitting room with a balcony overlooking the Nam Xam on the top floor. ❶–❷

Lao Houng Near the big bridge ☏064/312028. This dreadful sprawling building with several open courtyards and a television lounge was built by the Vietnamese in the 1970s and is supposed to be the most important hotel in town. Although it's dark, gloomy, and falling apart, it does have its own kind of odd charm reminiscent of state-built hotels in China in the early 80s. The rooms however are run-down and over-priced. ❶–❷

Long Ma Just behind the bus station, next to the *Po Tong* ☏064/312230. The best of the under $2 places, the *Long Ma* has perfectly good, big, tiled rooms with shared facilities and hot water. Travellers on a very tight budget should head here first. Rooms 5 and 6 as well as 12 and 13 above, are the best as they are corner units with double windows. ❶

Meuang Xam Down the first south-bound alley west of the *Panxay Hotel* ☏064/312407. This brand-new hotel is housed in a big, two-storey building with a flat roof and balconies facing the lane. The rooms are tiled and very clean. ❷

Outhaithani Directly opposite the airport entrance ☏064/312121, ✆☏064/312415, ✉outhaithani@hotmail.com. Owned by a Lao–French expatriate, the *Outhaithani* is primarily aimed at fly-in tour groups but makes a possible alternative to being in town. The hotel consists of a huge house on a hillside with three log cabins and four bungalow units. The smaller log cabins are the best and are actually much nicer inside than they look. All the rooms have hot water and the restaurant serves European food. ❹

Panxay Hotel Phathy Rd. One of the few French-era buildings in town to survive the war, this very odd-looking, two-storey French mansion looks like an old school house inside and has rooms without bath and a few en-suite rooms, as well as shared accommodation. The concrete *that* in the front indicates that a temple once stood there. ❷

Phanhsam Phathy Rd, diagonally across from from the bus lot ☏064/312255. With 28 rooms and a restaurant downstairs, the *Phanhsam* is the biggest guest house in town. The rooms are just passable and there's a choice of private or shared facilities with hot water. The hotel is under main-

△ The Plain of Jars

land Chinese management and the maids apparently do more than just clean rooms. ❶

Po Tong Right behind the bus lot. Absolutely the cheapest flop-house in town, aimed at Lao truck drivers and travelling Chinese salesmen. While the super-basic, plywood walled rooms with shared cold-water facilities might be cheap, they aren't really good value unless you're counting every 500-kip note. ❶

That Meuang Guesthouse South off Phathy Rd to the rear of the *Phanxay Guesthouse* ☎064/312141. Two connected buildings of a similar quality to the *Khaem Xam* but slightly more expensive and a bit further from the centre. There are thirteen spotlessly clean rooms here, all with tiled floors and en-suite bathrooms. The big draw is the outdoor terrace where you can sit with a beer and take in the view of the surrounding hills. ❷

The Town

There's little to occupy the traveller in Xam Nua, save absorbing the rugged frontier atmosphere of this most un-Lao outpost. Most of the town is on the southern side of the river, although it's now starting to sprawl out towards the airport. However, with the hills pressing in on all sides, there's precious little room for the town to grow. The main street is the 2km-long, four-lane **Phathy Road** – a huge central boulevard lined with institutional-looking government buildings and bearing the unmistakable mark of the Vietnamese, who rebuilt the town after the war. The road has just been completely rebuilt and repaved by Vietnamese road crews.

There are almost no cultural sites but you can walk up Phathy Road to the **victory monument**, an easy climb that affords a good view of the valley, and a bit further on, near the main street's end, there's Wat Xaysanalam (**Wat Phoxai**). Construction of the wat began in 1958 and took nearly a decade to complete, whereupon it was almost immediately destroyed by the bombing. The modest structure that now stands here was completed in the 1980s. It was until very recently the only wat in town and there is only a handful of resident monks. As Christopher Kremmer wrote in *Stalking the Elephant Kings*: "if you're tired of seeing monks in Laos, come to Xam Nua." The town's three other pre-war wats, including the 200-year-old Xiang Khouang-style Wat Inpeng, were never rebuilt. The sad little spires along Phathy Road leading up to the wat indicate where these holy sites once were.

Much more cheerful is the vibrant **market**, on the street running in front of the river, which is a good place to get a feel for the province's character. Vietnamese goods, many of which are bought by merchants at weekend border markets in Xiang Khoun and Na Maew, flood the stalls in a display of vegetables, meats and the occasional severed water-buffalo head. The market buzzes throughout the day, its vendors bundled against the cold with their heads wrapped in colourful scarves, a sartorial twist that most likely lent the province its name – "Houa Phan" means "wrapped head". Sadly, most of the vendor ladies have traded in their traditional turbans for cheap Chinese hand towels.

Behind the wet market is a large, block-long shed housing the **indoor dry market**. Here you'll find all manner of individual wooden stalls selling various goods including Lao **textiles** although much of the best stuff gets sent directly to Louang Phabang or Vientiane. Although a lot of cloth is produced in Houa Phan, it's all made in people's homes, not factories, so it's hard to buy from the source. If you're looking for loom-woven cloth rather than cotton prints it's better to come to the market in the afternoon. The alley behind the dry market houses all kinds of electrical supplies shops bulging with refrigerators, televisions, rice-cookers, bicycles, and home karaoke systems.

Eating and drinking

Xam Nua has several tourist-class **restaurants**. The *Chitthavanh* (☎064/312265), facing the river a few doors down from the *Khaem Xam*, is

Xam Nua textiles

Experts on **Lao textiles** all seem to agree that the most sophisticated pieces, both in design and colour scheme, are produced in the region around **Xam Nua**. Of these, the work of the Tai Daeng and Tai Nua stand out. Classified by ethnologists as "tribal Tai", these ethnic groups are related culturally and linguistically to the lowland Lao. However, unlike the lowland Lao, they are animists for the most part, though Mahayana Buddhist influence can be seen in their textile motifs. These groups believe that death is the most important rite of passage in a person's life, and the funeral ceremony is correspondingly elaborate. To prepare for it, a woman will weave a special skirt to wear to the grave. A geometric design woven into the waistband of the skirt will serve to ward off spirits that might attempt to block her passage into the "Garden of Golden Mangoes". Another significant textile used by the Xam Nua cultures is a "shaman's shawl", worn by spirit mediums while performing healing ceremonies. Symbols on these shawls are remarkably similar to those found on bronze frog-drums of the sixth-century-BC Dong-son culture which was centred in northern Vietnam. Other motifs found on Xam Nua textiles include the swastika, a Hindu symbol that was adopted by Mahayana Buddhism, and the stylized "third eye". Perhaps the most striking and the most "Lao" of the Xam Nua motifs are realistic *naga* woven into textiles using the ikat technique. A fashion revolution followed the political revolution in 1975, when the victorious communists abandoned their headquarters near Xam Nua and moved into Vientiane. The wives of the new leaders enthusiastically sported the Tai Daeng styles of Xam Nua, and it wasn't long before the look caught on. Today the bold, spidery patterns of Xam Nua textiles are a favourite all over Laos.

widely considered the best restaurant in town, with a range of reasonably priced dishes and an English-language menu – all the NGO and foreign engineers eat here. A couple of doors over, the signless *Yiensingchien* is similar and does a good beef noodle soup, good Lao coffees and even sells Lao textiles. In the alley running directly behind the *Yiensingchien*, the *Mitxamphanp* is another above average choice; although it seems to specialise in *foe*, it is nevertheless a proper sit-down restaurant. The *Muang Xam* restaurant, just past the bridge on the road to Nam Neun, is also one of the town's government-recommended tourist restaurants. For Western food, the *Houaphan Restaurant*, 211 Phathy Road (☎064/312190) is exceptionally good, serving up dishes like chicken Kiev and fish with white sauce. In fact, the menu here is one of the most sophisticated you'll see anywhere in Laos, featuring pâté, spare ribs, roast duck and many other delicacies all thanks to Chef Sengmanee, who cooked in Bangkok for two years before recently returning home to Xam Nua. In terms of decor, service and food quality, the *Houaphan* could certainly hold its own even in Louang Phabang. Their Lao food is good too. The town's other Western restaurant is the Lao-French restaurant at the *Outhaithani Guesthouse*, 128 #6, Ban Nathong (☎064/312121), across the street from the airport. This hotel caters almost exclusively to package tour groups and so knows how to fry a buffalo steak with pomme frites. There's also a selection of French wines. As for **drinking**, the two best places in town for a sundowner with a view of the mountains are the terrace at the *That Meuang Guest house* and the patio at the *Outhaithani*.

Around Xam Nua

Houa Phan is one of the most spectacularly beautiful provinces in all of Laos, with some of the north's highest mountains, a large number of diverse ethnic groups, extensive forest cover, and one of Laos's largest NBCAs. There are also enough caves, waterfalls, and limestone karst scenery to give Vang Viang hoteliers sleepless nights: you only need to drive the road in from Nam Neun to realize what amazing tourist potential Houa Phan has. The problem of course is infrastructure – there are at present very few roads. Chinese, Vietnamese, and Lao road crews are currently upgrading the road links to Vietnam and China and hopefully the Vietnamese border will be opened soon. What this means is that to conveniently visit the nearby **hot springs**, **mountains**, **caves**, **waterfalls** and **Hmong villages** you really need to hire transportation. Unfortunately, there's no motorcycle rental in Xam Nua but sawngthaews and a bit of foot power can get the job done. East of Xam Nua, limestone valleys are scooped out with **caves**, which provided a hiding place for the Pathet Lao parallel government.

Phou Pha Thi

Just 20km northwest of Xam Nua, **Phou Pha Thi**, a 1786-metre-high limestone mountain, is the tallest peak in northern Houa Phan and the most distinctive mountain in the province: a broad-based massif, with a near-vertical

The fall of Phou Pha Thi

In a decision that would prove to be the turning point of the war in Laos, US President Lyndon Johnson ordered the installation of a navigational beacon to guide air strikes against the North Vietnamese atop **Phou Pha Thi**. Here, US air force cargo helicopters dropped off the components of the device, code-named Commando Club, which was assembled a few hundred metres from fields growing some of the best opium in Laos. Hmong soliders, not known for their ability to defend fixed positions, were assigned to protect the latest in military wizardry.

A few weeks before Commando Club became operational in late 1967, a couple of monks were caught on the summit of Phou Pha Thi carrying cameras and sketch books; they were Vietnamese spies, and soon after Commando Club began directing its all-weather, high-altitude air strikes on the Hanoi valley, two Soviet-built biplanes, dark-green museum pieces with cloth-covered wings and wooden propellers jury-rigged to fire mortar shells, buzzed the site – the only time during the war that the North Vietnamese attacked a target with biplanes. The planes were shot down, but the Vietnamese, provoked by this high-profile site that threatened their security, moved more troops into Laos. By the time North Vietnamese commandos scaled the summit with grappling hooks and ropes to take the position on March 10, 1968, the nineteen Americans operating Commando Club knew the end was near. The **fall of Phou Pha Thi** was typical of the lack of unified command that plagued the United States' war in Laos. As historian Roger Warner wrote in *Shooting at the Moon*: "The radar installation belonged to the air force, but the CIA was supposed to defend it. The CIA couldn't defend it as it chose, because the ambassador didn't want "unauthorized" weapons on the mountaintop. Kept from direct accountability for its own men, the air force lost interest, even though it had proposed the installation in the first place, and on the mountain itself, nothing held the villagers from wandering where they pleased, including to the little opium patch near the summit, which they harvested just as they always had."

Phou Pha Thi also signalled a shift in the demands the US placed on its Hmong allies: they were no longer being armed to defend their own mountaintops, but were now pawns of the war in Vietnam. Eight Americans were pulled off Phou Pha Thi, leaving eleven dead or missing – the beginning of prolonged confusion, as Warner indicates, over the fate of Americans missing in action in Laos, and for whom the search continues today.

summit. The Nam Xam River, which flows through the centre of Xam Nua and all the way to the Gulf of Tonkin, runs directly down from the peak's cliff on its western flank and a sloping eastern side that leads to a broad plateau southern flanks. Phou Pha Thi is famous for being an important Lima Site during the **Second Indochina War** when the CIA and Special Forces set up a navigation radar tower on the summit to direct all weather bombing runs over Hanoi, 240km to the east. As this secret mountain base, run by the CIA and guarded by 300 Thai mercenaries, was in the very heart of Pathet Lao territory, the story of its eventual capture and destruction is the stuff of local legend (see box on p.190). Visits to Phou Pha Thi are not currently allowed but the situation is set to change very soon. The government is already busy constructing a road to the mountain for the purpose of opening up the site for tourism.

Suan Hin

Located just off Route 6, 50–60km southeast of the town of Houa Muang, the **Suan Hin** or "Stone Garden" is a standard stop on any organized daytrip out of Xam Nua. The megalithic stone gardens surrounded by forest consist of large slabs of rock that have been stood upright and arranged in circles. The age and origin of the sites as well as the culture that created them remain a mystery.

Nam Nua waterfall and the road to Viang Xai

The road heading east out of Xam Nua passes through the Striped Hmong village of **Ban Houa Khang** before descending into a valley of rice fields surrounded by shaggy karsts – the first glimpse of the heart of Pathet Lao territory. Passing through the lowland Lao town of **Ban Muang Liat** and the Hmong village of **Houai Na**, you'll arrive at a fork, 21km from Xam Nua. Bearing left leads to Sop Hao and Xiang Khoun on the old French road to Hanoi, right to **Viang Xai**, 8km away, and eventually the Vietnamese border town of Na Maew. Three kilometres down the Viang Xai road you'll come to a bridge over a swift-flowing stream, and from here a track leads off left to the top of a seventy-metre waterfall, **Tad Nam Nua**. Cutting away from the path, it's possible to scramble along the rocks and riverbank to a viewpoint at the crest of the falls. The classic frontal view is harder to attain: back at the junction, take the Sop Hao road for roughly 2km where you'll find a track leading for over 1km through paddies and eventually across a stream and a sticky thicket of bamboo. An eager local guide, encouraged with the offer of a few kip, is probably in order here.

Nam Et NBCA

Straddling the boundaries of three provinces, the **Nam Et NBCA** is one of the largest in Laos comprising an area of 1915 square kilometres. Linked together with neighbouring Phou Loei NBCA (see p.182), across the provincial border in Louang Phabang province, the two parks total 3400 square kilometres making them the second largest conservation area in the country after the Khammouane NBCAs (see p.264). The terrain here is extremely rugged and mountainous, and from the ridge tops it seems as if the mountains recede into infinity. The highest mountains in the park are along the Vietnam border and the Nam Et River itself flows into the Gulf of Tonkin. The park is very remote and currently has no access roads but can be reached by following the Nam Et River from Muang Et.

Viang Xai

Arriving in **VIANG XAI** ("City of Victory"), you wouldn't know the Pathet Lao and their communist allies in Vietnam had won the Second Indochina War. Sprawled across a valley surrounded by the cave-riddled karst formations used by the Pathet Lao as their wartime headquarters, Viang Xai was cobbled together by comrades from Russia, North Korea and Vietnam as well as labourers from Houa Phan's notorious re-education camps (see box on p.194). In 1973, at the end of the war, there were plans to make Viang Xai the heart of a new socialist nation, but in the end, the Pathet Lao leadership moved out and decided to keep Vientiane as the country's capital. Viang Xai couldn't even compete with nearby Xam Nua as a provincial hub. People moved out and many buildings fell into a state of crumbling decay. Today, a victory arch made of oil drums is the gateway to this wax museum of empty kerbed streets, lined with broken street lamps, and empty, ugly utilitarian structures. A stupa, crowned with a communist star and lost among the weeds, completes the setting. The only sign here that still trumpets the Pathet Lao's triumph with authority is the socialist victory statue that greets visitors as they make their way down the wide main street towards the market. The statue depicts a peasant, a soldier and a worker, one foot atop a bomb inscribed with "USA".

Practicalities

Very few travellers stay in Viang Xai, most preferring to do the caves (see p.193–196) as a **day-trip** from Xam Nua, which has better food and accommodation. However, for those who can afford the time, the scenery, countryside and ambience around Viang Xai deserves further exploration, evoking that of Guilin in China. In fact, if you want to know what Vang Viang was like before it was over-run with trippy backpackers, Viang Xai is the place for you.

There is currently only one **hotel** in Viang Xai – the yellow-fading-to-white, institutional-looking *Viang Xai* (❶) – located about 2km from the market, on the northwestern edge of town. Surrounded by pine trees and karst scenery, the hotel was originally constructed to put up visiting dignitaries. According to Christopher Kremmer's book, *Stalking the Elephant Kings*, when the Lao royal family was sent into internal exile in Houa Phan in 1977, this is the guest house where they lived before they disappeared. Indeed, the guest house seems to have been used as a sort of transit centre for high-ranking officials of the fallen royalist government on their way to the "re-education" camps set up by Chinese and Russian "foreign experts". Today the chipped paint, broken windows and locked banquet room, set for tea, make the *Viang Xai* feel like the set for the Lao version of *The Shining*. But the large rooms have a decaying majesty about them, each kitted out with teetering coat racks and tea sets, and they are outstanding value. Service here is attentive and the staff do their best to keep the shared bathroom clean. Given ample warning, they can also provide meals and drinks (including beer), although food is often limited to sticky rice served with eggs, and plain soup and vegetables.

Aside from the bowls of *fŏe* rustled up in the daytime by the **noodle stalls** in the bare-bones market, satisfying meals can be hard to come by in Viang Xai. If you're planning to stay for more than one night you may want to bring supplies from Xam Nua's market.

Sawngthaews from Xam Nua to Viang Xai (5000K; 30min) leave every hour until mid-afternoon and stop in front of the market. Alternatively, you could charter a sawngthaew for $5 from Xam Nua, which will allow you to stop off at the Nam Nua falls en route. You must **register and pay** a 3000K entrance fee at the Viang Xai **tourist office** (daily 8am–noon & 1–4pm) before you can tour the caves. From the market, bear left at the big stupa, and the tourist office is in the middle of the second block on the right. A guide will be assigned to you here for no extra charge. With the caves, market and guest house all spread out across the valley and no tuk-tuks for hire, you'll end up doing a fair bit of walking in Viang Xai. Be sure not to miss the last sawngthaew back to Xam Nua at about 2pm or you'll have to hitch-hike back.

The Pathet Lao caves

When American air force Chief of Staff General Curtis LeMay jested that the United States would bomb the enemy "back to the stone age", what he hadn't realized was that living like cavemen would prove to be the key to the Pathet Lao's survival of the heaviest aerial bombardment in history. Like Vang Viang in central Laos and Mahaxai in the south, the limestone karst formations in the valleys east of Xam Nua are pockmarked with **caves** and crevices – a perfect hideout for the Pathet Lao's parallel government. **Viet Minh** army units began using the caves and enlarging them in the early 1950s while fighting the French in the days before Dien Bien Phu. Soon, the Lao leftists had joined the Vietnamese underground, and by the middle of the 1960s, Viang Xai and the surrounding area had become a troglodyte city of thousands living in the more than one hundred caves. The caves – some at the foot of hills, others high up, hidden by surrounding escarpments and accessible only by scaling steps cut into sheer rock faces – were an impregnable fortress, but even poking your head outside could prove deadly as craters near the caves attest. Jacques Decornoy, a French journalist and one of the rare Westerners permitted to visit the caves during the war, wrote that his room in a "hotel" grotto was "a dangerous place if one puts one's nose out of the mountain: sometimes one cannot finish shaving because of the jets raiding from Thailand". When Decornoy visited the caves and the grassy fields surrounding them in 1968 he found "a terrain turned over hundreds of times by explosions and no longer resembling anything at all – a chaos of red earth, broken rocks, devastated trees".

The **inhabitants of the caves** followed a routine of sleeping by day and working at night in the fields outside or in the caves themselves: caverns held weaving mills, printing presses and workshops where American bombs and worn-out trucks were upgraded into farming tools and appliances. On Saturdays, adults would take a break and attend **classes**. These classes consisted of professional, cultural and political courses as well as lessons on algebra, geometry and geography. As the liberated zone's director of education explained to Decornoy, "a teacher must be a propagandist of the people. He must know how to run a meeting, how to explain the central political line, he must be a shooting instructor and link manual work with theoretical teaching." The Pathet Lao, however, didn't need propaganda to help Houa Phan's largely rural population understand their point of view – hounded by a barrage of bombs, many did not even know what an aeroplane was until 1964, or for that matter where America was.

The conclusion of the war didn't bring the hardships experienced in the caves to an end: what changed were the inhabitants. After 1975, the caves became a "**re-education camp**" for the soldiers of the Royal Lao government (see box on p.194). For years, the Vientiane government and Houa Phan officials, who regard Viang Xai as a national treasure and a symbol of revolutionary resolve along the lines of Mao's Long March, treated the caves as if they were a military secret. However, following the planning for Visit Lao Year, which began in 1998, they have become more welcoming to foreigners interested in visiting the site. Work has begun on **restoring** the revered caves:

Re-education camps

The first group of prisoners to be transported to **re-education camps** – the Pathet Lao's means of neutralizing its wartime enemies – arrived by invitation in full military dress months before the communist takeover in December 1975. After receiving letters signed by Prince Souvannaphouma, seventy high-ranking Royal Lao Army officers and provincial governors came to what they thought would be an important meeting and were whisked off to the Plain of Jars, where they were fêted with a banquet and a movie. Any hope of a uniquely Lao solution to the Second Indochina War ended there, as these officials were shortly thereafter flown off to Houa Phan, where they were stripped of their rank and separated into small work parties. In the following months, thousands of civil servants and army officers voluntarily entered the re-education centres in Houa Phan, Attapu and Phongsali after being assured the "seminars" would last only a few weeks. With their opponents safely out of the way in the most remote corners of the country – or having opted already to flee to Thailand – the Pathet Lao moved ahead with the final stage of their bloodless takeover virtually unopposed.

Joined later by thousands more who arrived somewhat less willingly, the internees were turned loose in the fenceless camps, which were heavily guarded and hemmed in by the extreme geographical features of the Lao wilderness, and left to forage for food and build their own shelters out of bamboo. Each morning, a bell was rung at 5am and the prisoners were assigned a job for the day – cutting wood in the jungles, building roads, working in the fields. In the evenings, self-criticism and political indoctrination sessions were held. Although there was no physical torture, mindless rules were established in order to control the captives, who were never allowed to settle into one place. The cumulative effect of the "re-education", according to a former Royal Lao Army officer, who spent thirteen years in a Houa Phan camp, was a sort of "brainwashing". Life in the camps was hard – the officer is certain that he only survived because of a Green Beret survival course he attended in the United States – and many ran off or died of malaria. While women were not arrested, wives and families could opt to join their husbands in the camps. Some did, but many more, having lost their principal wage earner, fled to Thailand.

furniture has been removed for restoration, electric lights have been plugged in and the gardens around the cave entrances have been tended.

In the absence of English-speaking guides, brochures and furniture, **what life was like in the caves** is left mostly to the imagination, with occasional prompting by curt signs in French, Lao and English above doorways. At present, only five caves are open to the public, and the tour takes two hours. Each of these caves, named after the Pathet Lao leaders who lived there, had multiple exits, an office and sleeping quarters, as well as an emergency chamber for use in case of chemical weapons attacks. These were kitted out with a Soviet oxygen machine and a metal door of the sort you'd find on an old submarine. After the Paris peace accords were signed in 1973, a few of the leaders built a house outside their cave, where they lived until moving to the former American compound on the outskirts of Vientiane in 1975 in order to take up government office.

Tham Than Kaysone

Tours usually begin with the cave of **Kaysone Phomvihane** (see p.270), who became leader of the Lao communist movement at its formation in 1955, and remained unchallenged in his post as head of the Lao People's Democratic Republic from its inception in 1975 until his death in 1992. Around the corner from the tourist office and to the left, Kaysone's cave now has a large

Drug-addicts, prostitutes and other "anti-social" elements, although considered the least threatening to the new regime, were also rounded up and shuttled off to two islands in **Ang Nam Ngum** (see p.115), where an estimated three thousand people were placed on "Boy Island" and "Girl Island". In 1977, the **royal family** too was arrested and banished to Camp 01 at Sop Hao, in Houa Phan, where the king and crown prince reportedly died of starvation two weeks apart in May 1978. The queen is said to have died in 1981, and like her husband and son before her, was buried in an unmarked grave outside the camp. The only government acknowledgement of their deaths came a decade later, when Party Secretary General Kaysone mentioned in an aside during a visit to Paris that the king had died of old age.

Kept secret from the outside world, there are **no official figures** for the number of people who were interned in the camps, but estimates based on reports by former inmates and their families suggest that at the height of the camps, in 1978–79, the number of internees may have been as high as fifty thousand. Whatever willingness to work with the new government supporters of the Royalist regime originally had quickly evaporated when it became clear that those interned in the camps weren't coming home anytime soon. Confronted with the prospect of being sent off for re-education, more than three hundred thousand people, nearly a tenth of Laos's population, fled the country. According to political scientist Martin Stuart-Fox, this **mass exodus** cost the fledgling government much of its educated class, setting the new Laos back a generation.

The first group of prisoners, low-ranking members of the former regime, was **released** in 1980, and despite finally being deemed fit to live in socialist Laos, many took the first chance they got to cross the Mekong. As the 1980s wore on, more and more prisoners were gradually released under pressure from Western nations and the human rights organization Amnesty International, which reported that in 1985 seven thousand people remained in the camps, a number which had dwindled to 33 by March 1991. The desperately poor Lao government had finally realized that in order to make money, the government needed its educated and professional class. The camps are now empty, but it's worth remembering that in 1999, two political prisoners entered their ninth year of incarceration in a Houa Phan detention centre.

brown house and a meeting hall in front of it, as well as stairs leading to the cave's main entrance – during the war, the cave was accessed by rope. It's one of the larger caves and has an outdoor terrace, which was used for cooking. Born in Savannakhet of a Lao mother and a Vietnamese father, Kaysone spent far more time in Viang Xai than the Pathet Lao's face man, Prince Souphanouvong. While the Red Prince was off playing Vientiane's game of cat-and-mouse politics, Kaysone stayed in Houa Phan, attending frequent meetings in Hanoi – a risky two-day journey from Viang Xai – with North Vietnamese leaders Ho Chi Minh and General Vo Nguyen Giap, the legendary military strategist behind the French defeat at Dien Bien Phu.

Tham Than Nouhak

In the escarpment across the street from Tham Than Kaysone, **Nouhak Phoumsavanh's cave** is tiny compared with those of the other leaders, kitted out with only a bedroom and an emergency room. A peasant's son with only a primary school education, Nouhak was born in Savannakhet in 1916 and was recruited by the Viet Minh while operating a bus line connecting Thakhek, Savannakhet and Vinh in the early 1940s. Nouhak proved himself to be a valuable courier to the Viet Minh and he quickly rose to prominence in the Lao communist movement. Nouhak was Kaysone's right-hand man during the war and the second-ranking member of the party's political bureau for years, eventually becoming chairman of the state assembly and, after Kaysone's death, state president.

Tham Than Souphanouvong

A stand of pomello trees lines the path to **Prince Souphanouvong's cave**, tucked into a narrow indentation in an escarpment northwest of the tourist office. Fit for a prince, the cave has a garage grotto for his car and an outdoor kitchen on a natural patio. Yet reminders of the struggle linger around Souphanouvong's Viang Xai hideaway: a reddish discolouration high up on the cliff face marks the spot where a bomb crashed into the karst. Off to the right, a red stupa bears the ashes of one of the prince's sons who was killed during the war. Considered for years by the West to be the Pathet Lao's most important leader, the Red Prince was one of three remarkable sons of Prince Boun Khong, the viceroy of Louang Phabang. His brothers, Phetsarath and Souvannaphouma, were both former prime ministers, and all three played a major role in shaping twentieth-century Lao history. Souphanouvong lived here with his wife and ten children from 1963 to 1973. In 1975, Souphanouvong became president of the new government, although real power remained with Kaysone.

Tham Than Phoumi

Just west of Souphanouvong's cave is that of **Phoumi Vongvichit**, a cave artificially improved with the aid of dynamite to enlarge the living space and make room for a garage. Phoumi was born the son of a governor of Vientiane province in 1909 and went on to join the Indochinese civil service where he served as secretary to the French resident of Xiang Khouang. As an official in Houa Phan during the Japanese occupation, Phoumi aided Free French guerrillas, but when France reoccupied Laos he joined forces with Souphanouvong in northern Vietnam. Quiet, clerkish Phoumi, who had a knack for communist jargon, became minister of information and culture and, after Souphanouvong became ill, acting president of the Lao PDR before retiring from government in 1991.

Tham Than Khamtay

Beyond the decrepit grandstand and weedy athletic field on the north side of town, you'll come to the cave of **Khamtay Siphandone**. A postman in the former colonial government, Khamtay was born in 1924 into a peasant family in Champasak. As the returning French troops marched on Savannakhet in 1946, Khamtay, then with the Lao Issara, the early Lao independence movement, took with him the entire finances of the province – 150,000K – and ran off to join resistance forces on the Bolaven Plateau. In the grounds are Viang Xai's one mark of modernity – street lamps of the kind you might see in any suburban cul-de-sac, some evidence of the guide's insistence that the current president still pays annual visits to his old haunt. Behind Khamtay's house stands an imposingly thick man-made wall, built to protect the artificially dug cave's entrance from bombing raids. Inside, one doorway once opened onto an added feature of Khamtay's cave, a kilometre-long secret tunnel – now shoulder-deep in water – that leads to a cavernous chamber, formerly used as a meeting hall and, bizarrely, for the odd circus performance.

Nam Xam NBCA

Located to the south of Route 6A, the **Nam Xam NBCA** is the smallest individual NBCA in Laos at just 580 square kilometres. The conservation area basically encompasses a broad bend in the **Nam Xam River** where it makes a lengthy detour around two large mountains within the NBCA, before extending over to the Vietnamese border to the east that comprises the park's eastern boundary. The tallest peak is located in the centre of the park and is 1741m. The eastern area of the park is said to provide a habitat for elephants, bears, tigers, and gibbons. The park can only be reached by four-wheel-drive vehicle; ask about trips with travel agents in Xam Nua.

Xiang Khouang and the Plain of Jars

When the buffalo fight the grass gets flattened

Lao proverb

Xiang Khouang province lies at the crossroads of important trade routes leading north to China, south to Thailand and east to Vietnam, and has been coveted throughout the centuries by rival Southeast Asian empires. Ironically, for all its strategic importance, Xiang Khouang, hemmed in by a ring of dramatic mountains, including the country's tallest peak, Phu Bia, is still difficult to reach by road. Faced with the prospect of a hard road trip via Route 7 or Routes 1 and 6, many visitors opt for a flight into **Phonsavan**, which also gives an unforgettable view of the treeless flatlands and crater-ridden landscape of the **Plain of Jars**.

Xiang Khouang Province is best known for the Plain of Jars, a plateau of grassy meadows and low rolling hills situated at the centre of the province. The Plain takes its name from the clusters of chest-high funerary urns found there. Scattered across the Plain and on the hills beyond, the ancient jars, which are thought to be around two thousand years old, testify to the fact that Xiang Khouang, with its access to key regional trade routes, its wide, flat spaces and temperate climate, has been considered prime real estate in mainland Southeast Asia for centuries.

However, as the flattest area in northern Laos, the Plain of Jars is also a natural gathering point for **armies** – a fact not lost on military commanders of the early kingdoms of Lane Xang, Vietnam and Siam and later the Soviet Union, France and America, the Viet Minh, the Pathet Lao and the Royalists. Fought over dearly in the Second Indochina War, the region was bombed extensively between 1964 and 1973, transforming the Plain into a wasteland, the treeless flatlands and low rolling brown hills pockmarked with craters leaving a lasting impression on those who fly over it into Phonsavan.

Safety in Xiang Khouang

Occasional attacks by mountain **bandits** have given Xiang Khouang province an uncertain reputation. These highwaymen have attacked vehicles, and on one occasion in the mid-1990s even bombed a bus in downtown Phonsavan. Such incidents have been sporadic, the last occurring in 1999, and it is the general consensus that such attacks are the work of bandits rather than insurgency. That said, hundreds of tourists visit the area each month without incident. Of more immediate danger are the **mines**, **bomblets** and **bombs** littering the province. The three main Jar sites have been cleared of Unexploded Ordnance (UXO), but it's advisable to stick to the paths, and don't pick up or kick any object if you don't know what it is. See Basics, pp.64–65 for more details.

Some history

Even the **legends** surrounding the jars reveal how thoroughly life in Xiang Khouang has been overshadowed by **war**, with local lore telling of how the jars were created to hold rice wine by an army of giants to celebrate a military victory. Although the identity of the civilization that built the jars remains a mystery, local folktales telling of the arrival of the Phuan people (see p.371), the lowland Lao group that still dominates the ethnic make-up of the area today, date back as far as the seventh century, when the divine Tai–Lao first ancestor Khoun Borom (see p.139) sent his seventh and youngest son, Chet Chuong, to rule over the Tai peoples of Xiang Khouang. Although the time-frame for this version of events may be a bit premature, Xiang Khouang was nonetheless one of the earlier areas settled by Tai peoples in Laos, and by the fourteenth century, an independent **Phuan principality**, known as Xiang Khouang and centred on modern-day **Muang Khoun**, had already begun to flourish here. While the **Kingdom of Xiang Khouang** had the wealth to build exquisite pagodas, it never amassed the might necessary to become a regional power. Sandwiched between the great empires lying to its east and west, Phuan kings maintained a semblance of independence over the years by offering tribute to Vietnam and Lane Xang and eventually Siam. Whatever price the royal house paid, however, it was not enough to keep Xiang Khouang from being repeatedly annexed, overrun and forcibly depopulated, beginning with the invading armies of the **Vietnamese** on their way back from sacking Louang Phabang in the late 1470s through to the Second Indochina War, when nearly every village in the province was obliterated.

It was a Phuan revolt against Vietnam's attempt to annexe Xiang Khouang, a satellite of the Lane Xang empire, referred to by the Vietnamese as Tran Ninh, that helped provoke Vietnam's invasion of Lane Xang in 1478. Nearly four hundred years later, Vietnam was drawn into another major conflict over Xiang Khouang, but this time it was with Louang Phabang's suzerain, **Siam**. As the nineteenth century progressed, the Kingdom of Xiang Khouang was battered towards extinction. In 1869, warrior horsemen from southern **China** raced across the plain, slaughtering villagers or carrying them off into captivity. These Black Flag bandits pillaged the riches of the kingdom and plundered the contents of the jars. Those that fled didn't get far: Lao and Thai soldiers on their way to Xiang Khouang to quell the invasion rounded up the refugees and frog-marched them through the jungle to the Chao Phraya River Valley in Siam, where they became slaves to Thai lords. The tortuous march lasted over a month, with many dying along the way, lost to sickness and starvation. In two generations, Siamese armies and Chinese bandits reduced the population by three-quarters through death and forced migration. The Phuan state never recovered.

Xiang Khouang enjoyed better protection from its neighbours with the arrival of the **French**, who considered the province's temperate climate – which can be downright cold by any measure for several months of the year – suitable for European settlement and plantation agriculture. The primary cash crop, however, was **opium**, a trade the French quickly moved to control (see p.228). Muang Khoun was chosen as the French provincial capital and the devastated former royal seat of the defunct kingdom was transformed into an architectural gem of French Indochinese villas and shop-houses which might have rivalled the charm of Louang Phabang and Savannakhet had Xiang Khouang not returned to its familiar role as battleground a few decades later.

One hundred years after the carnage of the Chinese bandits, American planes wreaked destruction that was equally undiscriminating, levelling towns and forcing villagers to take to the forest, as the two sides in the **Second Indochina War** waged a bitter battle for control of the Plain of Jars, which represented a back door to northern Vietnam. Throughout much of the 1960s, Xiang Khouang was the site of a see-saw war, with the royalist side led by Hmong General Vang Pao gaining the upper hand in the rainy season and the communist side launching offensives in the dry months. Yet again, Xiang Khouang was caught between superior powers, and once more the refugees flowed south.

Today, villages have been rebuilt and fields replanted. Many of the valley-dwelling, wet-rice farmers, as well as a majority of the townsfolk in Phonsavan, are descendants of the Phuan kingdom. In addition to the Lao, the Phuan are joined by a third lowland group, the Black Tai, and also the Khamu – a Lao Theung group who ruled the lowlands until they were forced into the hills with the arrival of the Tai groups over a thousand years ago – and a significant population of Hmong, who arrived in Laos from China in the nineteenth century and now make up roughly a third of the provincial population. With much of the Phuan kingdom's literature destroyed and many of the customs lost, **Hmong culture** and festivals have come to play an important role in Xiang Khouang life. *Boun Phao Hmong*, or the Festival of the Hmong, celebrated throughout the province in November, draws overseas Hmong back each year for an event featuring water buffalo and bull fights. In December, Hmong New Year, a time for young Hmong to find a husband or wife, is celebrated, as is the lowland Lao festival of *Boun Haw Khao*, a two-day holiday in which food is offered to the dead. It has a distinctly Xiang Khouang flair, however, with the addition of horse races; horses being especially prized by villagers who work Xiang Khouang's far-flung fields.

Phonsavan

The capital of Xiang Khouang province, **PHONSAVAN** has gradually emerged as the most important town on the Plain of Jars since the total devastation of the region in the Second Indochina War. The bomb-casing collections in many guest house lobbies are grim galleries reflecting the area's tragic past when possession of the strategic plain was seen as the key to control of Laos. It was the new communist government that designated Phonsavan the new provincial capital, and parked Laos's fledgling collection of Soviet MiGs nearby, a smug reminder of who won the battle for this bitterly contested area. Hastily rebuilt in the aftermath of decades of fighting, Phonsavan is only now, 25 years after the conflict, just beginning to recover economically, thanks in a large part to international interest in the world-famous Jar sites scattered around the perimeter of the plain. Tourism has given the town new life: bombs at the Jar sites have been cleared away and Khoun Cheuam's jar – the largest of the scores of jars in the area – stares down from tourism posters across the country. Despite the dreadful destruction rained upon the province and its people, the region's future prospects for **tourism** look bright. Although most visitors come only to see the Jar sites, the Xiang Khouang Plateau is a place of great natural beauty and its backroads are well worth exploring.

Arrival, transport and information

Landing at the **airport**, you'll need a tuk-tuk (10,000K) for the four-kilometre ride into town. Alternatively you can get a free lift with one of the hotel reps. Arriving by bus, you'll be dropped at the **bus lot** opposite the dry goods market and the GPO, an easy walk to most guest houses. Vehicles travelling towards Vientiane and Xam Nua all leave from here; those heading for Muang

Khoun and other points south, leave from the Talat Nam Ngum bus station, 3km to the southwest of town on the road to the Jar Sites. The main **tuk-tuk stand** is on the main road just opposite the *Dao Phouan Guesthouse*. For journeys further afield than the town or the jar sites, four-wheel-drives can be hired through most hotels and travel agencies.

Lao Aviation's office is at the airport but most guest houses can handle bookings. There are daily **flights** to Louang Phabang and Vientiane. The Lane Xang Bank (Mon–Fri 8am–noon & 1–4pm) is on the main road, at the south end of town across from the *Phudoi Hotel*, and can **exchange** US dollars travellers' cheques. There is also an exchange kiosk at the airport. There is an **internet shop** next to the *Phonekeo Restaurant* but the lines are usually down. The Telcom is next to the GPO.

Accommodation

Phonsavan has many **guest houses and hotels**, most of which line Route 7, east of the dry goods market. Because Route 7 has only just opened to tourists, Phonsavan has previously catered mostly to fly-in package tour groups. Consequently, the town is not well set up for independent travellers; there are few good restaurants and many guest houses are very overpriced. However, with Route 7 now open and increasing numbers of backpackers making the trip to Phonsavan this situation should correct itself quickly. Also, think twice before shelling out extra money for hot water as electricity still only runs from 6pm to 11pm. If you've got money to spend, two **luxury resorts** sit on the hills to the south overlooking town, both of which offer great views and spacious, charming bungalows with fireplaces, though you will feel cut off from town (and cheaper restaurants) if you've arrived without your own transport. For these two hotels you'll need to reserve beforehand, especially in the high season, as both tend to be booked well in advance by tour groups. Another huge new hotel – the *Hay Hin Hotel* – has also just been built on the hillside just south of town.

Auberge de Plaine de Jarres ☎061/312044. On a hill southeast of town, this very classy lodge has deluxe two-room cabins with fireplaces and private bathrooms, which overlook the town. Spectacular views from the French restaurant and all set in landscaped grounds surrounded by pine trees and bougainvillea. ❻–❼

Daophouan ☎061/312171. Located across from the GPO, this is definitely one of the top choices in town. The eleven rooms in this three-storey building are a notch above others in the same category and all are en suite with hot water. Good quality but a bit pricey even with breakfast included. ❹

Dokkhoun Route 7 east of centre ☎061/312189. Two separate buildings with a lobby full of UXO. The ten rooms in the rear wing are brand new with tiled floors and en-suite bathrooms with hot water. These mid-ranged rooms are much better value than the cheaper ones in the old front building. ❷–❹

Hay Hin Guesthouse Route 7, east of centre ☎061/312252. Not to be confused with the giant new *Hay Hin Hotel* overlooking the town. Super-basic with plywood walls and poor construction,

the *Hay Hin* has two-bed rooms (with or without cold-water bathroom). ❶

Kong Keo ☎061/211354, ✉kingkongjar@hotmail.com. Situated 200m off Route 7 next to the old air strip. Whether you're looking for an inexpensive, clean room with spotless, shared hot-water facilities or a deluxe bungalow with hot water en-suite bathroom in a quiet garden, *Kong's* is simply the best value in town. Kong himself is a real character and his nightly bonfires are legendary. A very good deal – just watch out for that *lào-láo*! ❶–❸

Maly West of the museum ☎061/312156, 🖷312003, ✉sousathp@laotel.com. This guest house has pleasant rooms, hot-water showers and a good restaurant. If you need Western-style comfort, the VIP rooms upstairs in the new building are amongst the nicest in town with wall-to-wall carpeting, television, and huge picture windows. Popular with group tours, it's bit isolated and far from centre. ❺

Phimmahaxay ☎061/312208. On the first corner north of the bus lot, this spanking new, six-room hotel in a modern three-storey building has big rooms with good quality mattresses, but only shared facilities and no hot water (though this may change soon). **2**

Phu Chan ☎061/312264. Sitting on the hillside roughly 2km southeast of town, this friendly, Thai-owned resort has five wooden cabins, each with two large rooms, a roomy common area, a cosy fireplace and striking views of the surrounding landscape. **6**

Vanearoun Route 7 next to the *Phonekeo Restaurant* ☎061/312070. Old and basic but bet-ter value than a lot of other places in the same price range. The bathrooms are tiled and clean but without hot water. The more expensive rooms are a better deal than the cheapest ones. **1**—**2**

Vinhtong ☎061/212622. This place, on Route 7 another block further east of the *Dokkhoun*, is basic but clean with tiled floors, rattan walls, and new en-suite bathrooms with hot water. There are also some bigger units out back for slightly more money. The lobby has a big UXO collection and tourist infor-mation on the surrounding sites. **1**—**2**.

The Town

The original settlement of Phonsavan was, like every other town on the plain, obliterated during the war. The town you see today is a modern **reconstruction** that has largely gone up over the last five years. There is really nothing of note to see, although the town grid is very nicely laid out on a rather grand scale. Indeed, if the length and width of Phonsavan's empty boulevards are anything to go by, local officials have very big plans for this little place. In keeping with this, there are a lot of large new government buildings around town including the **Xiang Khouang Museum**, resembling a step pyramid, at the big intersection by the Lang Xang Bank (now if they'd just get round to naming the streets!). There's also a huge amount of private construction going on, including more than a few gigantic mansions known to the locals as "heroin houses".

Aside from the soon-to-be-opened museum, the only real sights in town are the two main **markets** located on Route 7 at the town's main junction where most of the hotels and restaurants are found. The **wet market** behind the GPO

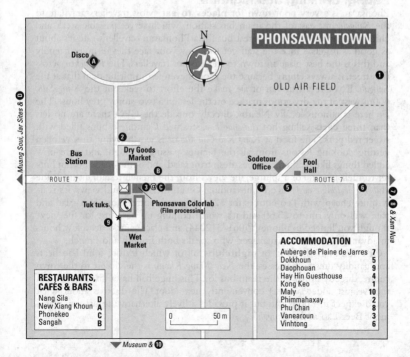

PHONSAVAN TOWN

N

Disco **A**

OLD AIR FIELD **1**

Muang Soui, Jar Sites & **D**

2

Bus Station

Dry Goods Market
B

Sodetour Office

Pool Hall

ROUTE 7

3@C

4 **5** **6**

ROUTE 7

7, 8 & Xam Nua

Tuk tuks

Phonsavan Colorlab
(Film processing)

9

Wet Market

ACCOMMODATION

Auberge de Plaine de Jarres	7
Dokkhoun	5
Daophouan	9
Hay Hin Guesthouse	4
Kong Keo	1
Maly	10
Phimmahaxay	2
Phu Chan	8
Vanearoun	3
Vinhtong	6

RESTAURANTS, CAFES & BARS

Nang Sila	**D**
New Xiang Khoun	**A**
Phonekeo	**C**
Sangah	**B**

0   50 m

▼ *Museum &* **10**

is well worth a wander and the amount and variety of the fresh produce on sale here gives a good indication of just how much people's lives here have improved since the government quietly swept communist economics under the rug. Opposite the GPO on the northern side of the main road (Route 7) is a **dry market** where all manner of consumer durables are sold. Aside from a huge assortment of knick-knacks and everyday items, on the eastern side of the market, you can sometimes find colourful pieces of Xiang Khouang's heritage for sale: small squares of **Hmong textiles**, intricately handwoven in electric greens, oranges and yellows, known as *paj ntaub* (pronounced "pang dao"), and other articles of Hmong traditional clothing. *Paj ntaub* can sell for $100, and hats for $300, a reflection of the intense workmanship that goes into producing the textiles but also indicative of the buying power of Hmong relatives overseas, who send their money from southern California, Minnesota and beyond to keep themselves in the colours of the old country and the family left behind in greenbacks. Another worthwhile souvenir to seek out is the "*khan nyu*" umbrella – beautifully constructed, mulberry-paper umbrellas are an old Xiang Khouang art and require dozens of steps, from crafting the bamboo struts to oiling the hand-made paper. Oil from the fruit of the *mahk nyao* tree produces yellow umbrellas while oil from *mahk bao* roots produces red umbrellas. If you can't find the umbrellas in the market, ask at *Sangah* restaurant or call the folks at NAWACOP (T061/312026, E nawacop@laonet.net).

A huge **new market** is being built by a Chinese construction company on Route 7, about 1km east of the main intersection. Once completed, the government may move the dry market under its roof. There's also talk that the main bus lot might be moved at the same time.

Eating, drinking and nightlife

Phonsavan is a very poor town for **places to eat**. Most travellers gravitate to the *Sangah*, just east of the main bus station, which serves passable steak and chips and Lao dishes. It's not great but for a Phonsavan traveller's café it's about as good as it gets. Once the staff get to know your face they're quite friendly and this is the best place in town to meet other travellers. The *Phonekeo*, across the street, is always empty because the food is even less inspiring than that at the *Sangah*. If you're a true fan of *fŏe*, make the effort to seek out the *Nang Sila*, 600m west of the dry goods market, on the left, in a two-storey grey house. The *fŏe* here is famous locally. Nearby, directly outside the GPO, there are no less than three **carts** selling hot *cha-shao bao*, steamed Cantonese buns filled with sweet red pork. The food at *Kong Keo Guesthouse* is worth trying, they've been getting cooking lessons from all the farangs passing through, and have now added things like mashed potatoes, fresh fruit salad, and home-made peanut butter to their menu. For a splurge, the views from the French restaurant up at the *Auberge de Plaine de Jarres* are outstanding. Given the setting and views, it's really quite cheap with Lao entrees for $2 and French entrees for $5. A salad and pâté will only run to $3.50 and it's worth coming up here just for the view, though you'll need to phone (T061/312044) and place your order a few hours in advance with the Lao manager, who speaks both English and French.

Of Phonsavan's handful of **nightclubs**, all of which feature loud Lao beats and gaudily dressed hostesses, the *New Xiang Khoun* is the closest to the town centre, directly north of the main bus lot. This huge hall has a disco inside and they've just added a hotel conveniently next door. The disco is about what you'd expect in Phonsavan but it provides a lively alternative to drinking late-night Beer Lao at the *Sangah*.

THE NORTHEAST | Xiang Khouang and the Plain of Jars

The Plain of Jars

Many visitors mistake the Jar sites for the **PLAIN OF JARS** and vice versa. The latter is a broad rolling plain covering an area roughly 15km across at the centre of the Xiang Khouang Plateau, which sits high above the Mekong and the Vientiane Plain. The ancient **Jar sites** scattered around the perimeter of the plain led the French to name the region the Plain de Jars – the PDJ to the American pilots who flew over it. Topographically, the plain is something like the hole in a donut with concentric rings of increasingly higher mountain peaks around it. Although the jars are the main tourist attraction of Xiang Khouang Province, there's much more to see here. The Plain of Jars itself offers beautiful scenery, which most visitors, obsessed with seeing the jars, completely overlook. With its bare rolling red, brown, and purple hills, pine trees and eucalyptus, the plain is strongly reminiscent of parts of Southwestern Australia or central British Colombia and would be a paradise for horseback-riding or motorcross riding. For the time being it's well worth **exploring by bicycle or hired motorbike**. Away from the main highway there are countless backroads to explore as well as friendly **Lao Loum and Hmong villages** where it may seem that you're the first foreigner the children have seen. Although the Jar sites scattered around the edge of the plain are probably at least two thousand years old, the story of the plain as a **transit route** for ancient man has yet to be told. As a natural corridor between the coasts of southern China and the vast plains of Korat beyond the Mekong, the Plain of Jars has certainly seen the passage of many tribes and races, perhaps even groups of Homo Erectus, who ranged from northern China to Java between one million and 250,000 years ago.

The Jar Sites

The **Jar sites** are one of the most important prehistoric archeological sites in Southeast Asia. Clusters of stone jars thought to be two thousand years old, along with seemingly older stone pillars, are scattered across the Plain and also in other parts of Xiang Khouang and Houa Phan province. The largest urns measure 2m in height and weigh as much as ten tonnes. Little is known about the **iron-age megalithic civilization** that created these megalithic artefacts; war and revolution kept archeologists from working on the sites for decades. By the time French archeologist Madeleine Colani began excavating at the Jar sites in the 1930s, most of the urns had been looted, although she did find bronze and iron tools as well as coloured glass beads, bronze bracelets and cowrie shells. Colani theorized that the jars were **funerary urns**, originally holding cremated remains. More recent discoveries have revealed underground burial chambers, further supporting Colani's theory. Because of the great age of the jars and the unsolvable mystery of their origin, they have perhaps become famous beyond their aesthetic merits. For people with a very deep interest in archeology and Southeast Asian history the jars are worth making the journey to Xiang Khouang. For most tourists however the jars are something of an anti-climax: if you've come expecting Stonehenge you'll be sorely disappointed. They're best just appreciated for what they are: traces of an ancient, vanished civilization that prospered on the Xiang Khouang Plateau.

Of the dozens of Jar sites, **three main sites** close to Phonsavan have been officially opened for tourists, largely because they are accessible and have a greater concentration of jars. The closest one, known as Site 1, just 2km southwest of town, has over two hundred jars and is the most visited. Sites 2 and 3 are much more scenic and are located about 10km southwest of the village of Lat Houang, which is 10km from Phonsavan, on the road to Muang Khoun.

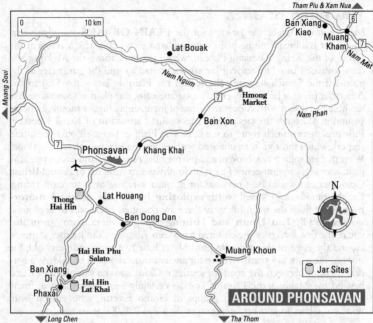

Site 2, with nearly a hundred jars, is located on two adjacent hills called Phou Salato. Site 3, the most atmospheric of the three, lies 4km up the road just beyond the village of Ban Xiang Di where more than a hundred jars dot a hill slope with sweeping views of the plain below.

Site 1

Site 1 or **Thong Hai Hin** ("Stone Jar Plain"), 2km southwest of town, is the most visited site. Unfortunately its proximity to the nearby airbase, which houses the Lao PDR's squadron of ageing MiGs, somewhat mars the surrounding landscape. There's a 4000K entrance fee at the pavilion – built for a visit by the Thai crown prince, a member of Laos's surrogate royalty – where you can also buy drinks. Following the path from the pavilions to the jars, you'll quickly come to **Hai Cheaum** ("Cheaum Jar"), a massive jar 2m high that was named after the Tai–Lao hero of lore who is celebrated in one version of the jar myth as the liberator of the people of the Plain of Jars from a cruel overlord named Chao Angka. Legend has it that the jars were made to ferment rice wine to celebrate the victory; as the jars bear a passing resemblance to *lào hái* jars used today, the boys at the pub in Phonsavan probably didn't have to stretch their imaginations too far to come up with this theory. Walk downhill a little way and you'll find yourself amid another group of jars, one of which has a crude human shape carved onto it. In the hill off to the left is a large **cave** that the Pathet Lao used during the war, and which, according to local legend, was used as a kiln to cast the jars. Erosion has carved two holes in the roof of the cave – natural chimneys that make the cavern a worthy kiln of sorts. Colani suggests that the cave was used as a crematorium: in and around the cave she found the remains of what she believed to be commoners not lucky enough to be interred in the stone funeral urns, which were reserved, she argued, for the ashes of the nobility.

Sites 2 and 3

Back on the Phonsavan–Muang Khoun road, the turn-off for the more scenic **sites 2 and 3** is 3km further on at the market village of Lat Houang. Zipping across the flats surrounding Lat Sen, the town that played host to the old French airstrip, towards Phaxai and the Jar sites, you'll pass narrow dirt runways on the grassy meadows and hillsides. These clearings are used by hunters to trap swallows in nets that they trigger from camouflaged huts at one end of the strip. Smoky fires bring bugs to the surface of the clearing, attracting the swallows. Three to five birds sell for 1000K in Phonsavan's market; the most skilful hunters can catch several hundred birds on a good day, netting a tidy sum.

Ten kilometres on from the turn-off, take a left along a dirt track – a road in slightly worse condition than the Phaxai road – and follow it for 2km through a village just large enough to support a tiny monastery, until you wind up at two adjacent hills, one on either side of the road. Nearly a hundred jars are scattered across the twin hills here, lending the site the name **Hai Hin Phou Salato** ("Salato Hill Stone Jar Site").

The gateway to Site 3, the most atmospheric of these sites, lies in the next village, Ban Xiang Di, 4km up the Phaxai road on the left. Large Lao Phuan houses line the way to Wat Xiang Di, a simple wooden monastery 1km from the turn-off where you'll find the path leading to **Hai Hin Lat Khai**, also known as Hai Hin Xiang Di. There's a depressing, bomb-damaged Buddha here that the guides like to point out. Pick up the path at the back corner of the monastery compound, which hops a stream and cuts uphill through several fields before arriving at a clearing with more than a hundred jars and sweeping views of the surrounding countryside. There's a 4000K entry charge per site at Sites 2 and 3.

Practicalities

Sites 1,2 and 3, together with old Xiang Khouang (see p.206) can be seen in a day, with hotels and tour companies generally pitching the four spots as a package. Lane Xang Travel, Sodetour, Sousath, and Inter-Lao all operate such **day-tours** but, at $50–100 for a van with driver and English-speaking guide, it's the most expensive way of seeing the sites. A much cheaper option is to book a vehicle and guide ($30 for 6 persons) through one of the local guest houses: Mr Manopet, at the *Sangah Restaurant*, or Mr. Boualin Phommasin, at the *Phonekeo Restaurant* (see p.202), can both arrange inexpensive, non-agency tours. Mr. Kong at *Kong Keo* guest house also regularly rounds up foreigners for cut-rate trips out to the Jar sites. Bear in mind when organizing a **non-agency tour** that the price is determined by the type of vehicle used, the itinerary involved, and whether you take just a driver or an English-speaking guide as well, so the cheapest negotiable price might not always be the best deal. As a **guide** can't tell you much more about the jars than a guidebook can, many independent travellers forego them as a way of saving a few dollars. However, a guide is still well worth having, not for information on the jars, but for the incredible and fascinating stories they can tell you about the war and how it affected their families and villages as you travel around the Xiang Khouang countryside.

Guide or no, getting to the Jar sites is easy and can be done for as little as $5 a head. Arranging an even cheaper, do-it-yourself tour is difficult. Tuk-tuks aren't allowed to go there and private taxis and vehicles must be registered for "safety" and have a "special permit" to serve the Jar sites – a system introduced by the big tourist hotels and travel agencies keen to keep this lucrative line of business for themselves.

Muang Khoun (Xiang Khouang)

A ghost of its former self, **MUANG KHOUN**, old Xiang Khouang, 35km southeast of Phonsavan, was once the royal seat of the minor kingdom Xiang Khouang, renowned in the sixteenth century for its 62 opulent stupas, whose sides were said to be covered in treasure. Years of bloody invasions by Thai and Vietnamese soldiers, pillaging by Chinese bandits in the nineteenth century and a monsoon of bombs that lasted nearly a decade during the Second Indochina War taxed this town so heavily that, by the time the air raids stopped, next to nothing was left of the kingdom's exquisite temples. The town was all but abandoned, and centuries of history were drawn to a close. All that remains of the kingdom's former glory is an elegant Buddha image towering over ruined columns of brick at Wat Phia Wat, and That Dam, both of which bear the scars of the events that ended Xiang Khouang's centuries of rich history. Although the town has been rebuilt and renamed, it has taken a back seat to Phonsavan, and, with little in the way of amenities for travellers – there are a few *fòe* shops around the market, but the lone hotel has closed – it's most convenient to visit Muang Khoun as a day-trip.

A long row of low-slung wooden shop-houses, centred on the market, spring up along the road from Phonsavan in the shadow of towering **That Dam**, signalling your arrival in Muang Khoun. A path alongside the market leads up to the blackened hilltop stupa, the base of which has been tunnelled straight through to the other side by treasure seekers hoping to find more than a simple bone of the Enlightened One inside. A British surveyor who travelled through the area in the service of the Siamese king in 1884 – shortly after the invasions by Chinese Haw – surmised that the bandits pillaged the stupa, making off with 7000 rupees' weight of gold. Continuing on the main road beyond the market, you'll pass the ruins of a villa, the only reminder that this town was once a temperate French outpost of ochre colonial villas and shop-houses, and arrive at the ruins of sixteenth-century **Wat Phia Wat**. Brick columns reach skywards around a seated Buddha of impressive size, a mere hint at the temple architecture for which the city was renowned. The only remaining example of Xiang Khouang-style architecture is Wat Khili in Louang Phabang (see p.158), but Wat Khili has been modified so many times that you wouldn't know its link to Xiang Khouang's monasteries unless you viewed it from the back. The recently completed temple at **Wat Siphoum**, the uninspiring structure nearest the market, bears little trace of the old designs for which the city's monasteries were known and serves notice of how much of Xiang Khouang's culture has been lost.

North to Muang Kham

Many of the ethnic groups that populate Xiang Khouang are well represented in the area between Phonsavan and Muang Kham to the northeast, and a trip out to the village of **Muang Kham** and its nearby hot springs by hired car or sawngthaew makes an interesting excursion. Route 7, currently being upgraded by Vietnamese road crews, winds through valleys hemmed by hills bursting with *dok bua khom* – the yellow flowers that are crushed into a natural fertilizer for vegetable gardens – passing dusty Khamu, Black Tai, Phuan and Hmong villages, with their wooden huts. Leaving Phonsavan, you'll first pass through **KHANG KHAI**, the town that became the seat of Prince Souvannaphouma's neutralist government after the Battle of Vientiane in December 1960, before arriving in **BAN XON TAI**, 12km north of Phonsavan, where two village women etched the name of their hometown into Pathet Lao lore when they shot down an American plane during the war. Apparently armed with little more than rifles, the heroines inspired the addition of the adjectives "patriotic" and "brave" to generations-old songs praising the beauty of Xiang Khouang women. Eleven kilometres further along on Route 7, a **Hmong market** sets up weekly on early Sunday mornings, attracting Hmong from numerous villages in the area.

In the hills to the west of the market are the beginnings of the **Nam Ngum River**, one of the Mekong's most important tributaries. Theoretically, it's possible to kayak or raft the Nam Ngum all the way down from the Xiang Khouang Plateau to the Ang Nam Ngum Reservoir. However, the story goes that the last foreigner to try this was arrested en route by overzealous Lao army soldiers unable to figure out why anyone would want to attempt such a thing unless they were a spy. Plans are already well underway to open the river to **rafting operators** and people who have done the river say it's one of Laos's best with world-class white water and huge mountains.

Three kilometres beyond the market you'll pass through the Hmong village of Tha Cho, before arriving in **DAEN THONG**, 12km further on, a village peopled by Khamu, a midland tribe that makes up around seven percent of Xiang Khouang's population. Widely considered to be among the original inhabitants of Laos, the ancestors of the Khamu are thought by some to be the ones who built the funerary urns scattered across the Plain of Jars. The next village, **BAN LAO**, was settled by Black Tai (Tai Dam), who fled to Laos several decades ago from Dien Bien Phu, the Vietnamese valley where the final battle of the First Indochina War was fought. After a further 7km, a dirt track forks off to the east leading to another Black Tai village, Ban Xiang Kiao, while the main road continues over a bridge spanning the Nam Mat stream and winds its way into Muang Kham, a large village formerly known as Chomthong.

Muang Kham and around

Situated in a long flat valley at the northeastern edge of the Plain of Jars, 51km from Phonsavan, **MUANG KHAM** lies at the convergence of the roads to Louang Phabang, Houa Phan and Vietnam and is a pit-stop for trucks ferrying goods between Laos and its eastern neighbour. Other than the drivers of the hulking lorries in the market compound, few travellers stay the night here, preferring to base themselves at Phonsavan, and visit the sights around Muang Kham as a day-trip. Indeed, the town is basically just a T-junction with a small market and the usual Kaysone monument. There are two no-frills **guest houses**, the best being *My Xay Guesthouse* (❶), which occupies a two-storey building directly opposite the market and is usually full of Chinese traders. On the main road (Route 7) that runs in front of the market and the square stand a few **noodle shops**, some of which also serve a selection of *khao keng* dishes (stir fries and curries) to cater to hungry truckers – look for the selection of pots and trays holding lukewarm food set up on tables outside the restaurant. **Buses and sawngthaews** heading north to Nam Neun and Xam Nua, east to Nong Het and south to Phonsavan stop in the market compound.

There are several **sites around Muang Kham** on the itineraries of day-tours out of Phonsavan. None is worth a special journey all the way from Phonsavan in its own right, but collectively they're a good excuse to see more of rural Xiang Khouang province, especially if you're on a flying visit to the Plain of Jars. A sombre pilgrimage to **Tham Piu**, a cave in which hundreds seeking refuge from the wartime bombing were killed when a fighter plane fired a rocket into the grotto, has begun to draw increasing numbers of visitors. The turn-off for the cave lies on the left-hand side of Route 6, 4km north of Muang Kham. Follow the road 1.5km to the foot of the hill and you'll find a steep set of stairs climbing up to the wide mouth of the cave. No memorial has been erected and only blackened rock testifies to the tragic incident.

From Muang Kham, Route 7 east towards the Vietnamese border leads you to two **hot springs**, Baw Nam Hon Lek and Baw Nam Hon Nyai – "Little Hot Spring" and "Big Hot Spring". The smaller of the two lies a little over 3km from town, on an unsignposted road leading off Route 7 to the right, but is usually passed over in favour of the larger spring, which has been converted into a resort of sorts, further east along Route 7. After passing through the tiny Na Ba market and crossing a bridge, turn right at Ban Nam Dien – 16km from Muang Kham – and head for the cliffs to find the spring. The road ends at the resort's gate, 3.5km away from Route 7, where you'll need to pay an entrance fee (5000K). The hot spring fills a swampy green pond of no remarkable beauty, but blooming flowers in the rainy season attract Phonsavan couples, who make the trip out on weekends to picnic and canoodle. A crude piping system draws the spring's steamy water to the site's main attraction: the **hot baths**, which are situated in a long shed among a small cluster of rustic bungalows (❶). A warm bath (5000K) – there are two large tubs per private room – is certainly worth the trip during Xiang Khouang's chilly winters. Kaysone's wife, known for her appreciation of herbal cures, had the bungalow facing the bathing facilities constructed for the use of visiting dignitaries. The bungalows are managed by the proprietors of the small restaurant in the compound. A variety of Lao food is on the menu of this lonely eatery, but you'll most likely end up eating whatever the cook managed to find in the market that day.

The **best way to visit** these sites is to get a group together and hire a car and driver for the day ($40) in Phonsavan, which allows you to stop at the various villages along the way and linger in the hot baths. A cheaper but more difficult alternative is to catch either a sawngthaew to Muang Kham from Phonsavan or a bus going to Nam Neun or Nong Het, both of which will pass Muang Kham. Once in Muang Kham, you can hire a tuk-tuk at the market to take you to Tham Piu, the hot springs, or both.

Nong Het and the Vietnam border

According to local reports, although the deal has not been officially signed, the **Nong Het border crossing to Vietnam** should open to foreigners in 2003. Currently, the border is only open to Lao and Vietnamese and does a booming trade between the Plain of Jars and Nghe An province in Vietnam. Several foreigners have already made the crossing here, but only with special papers issued in Vientiane. Once the border opens, you'll be able to travel from Vientiane across Xiang Khouang province and down to Vinh on the Gulf of Tonkin. It is in fact largely Vietnamese road crews who have rebuilt Route 7 from Muang Kham to Phonsavan as well as the stretch from Phonsavan on to Phoukhoun.

The Nam Ngiap River route to Pakxan

Although long touted plans to rebuild Route 4 from Phonsavan to Pakxe (see p.248) seem to be on permanent hold, plans are currently going ahead to revive the old **river route** from Muang Kham down to Pakxan on the Mekong River east of Vientiane. The **Nam Ngiap** is the largest river in northeastern

Laos and starts its 100km journey to the Mekong just south of Muang Kham. The river is too shallow for boats here so the launching point is the town of Tha Viang, sometimes known as Tha Tom, 50km from Muang Kham. This is very scenic, mountainous country with peaks exceeding 2000m: Mt. Khe just south of Muang Kham stands at 2125m, and Mt. Xao, halfway between Muang Kham and Tha Viang, reaches a height of 2590m. The existing road from Muang Kham to Tha Viang is currently being given a $1.6 million upgrade and is expected to be ready by early 2003. From Tha Viang, **passenger boats** will make their way from the plateau down to the broad plains of the Mekong River. From the town of Thakokkhen it's just a short trip down Route 13 to Pakxan.

West to Muang Soui

From Phonsavan, Route 7 winds west towards the mountainous edge of the the Plain of Jars and then begins working its way through the mountains to the outpost of Muang Phoukhoun on Route 13. This section of the French-built highway – a favourite target of bandits as recently as the 1990s – grinds through pine-topped hills and steep-banked stream beds for 48km to **MUANG SOUI**. Roughly at the halfway mark, the road fords the Nam Ngum River as it builds up steam en route to the Nam Ngum Dam, and then passes a pair of recently settled Hmong villages.

Once a significant village known for its temples, Muang Soui was yet another casualty of the intense fighting in Xiang Khouang province. Rebuilt alongside **Nong Tang**, a pretty lake hemmed in by stubby limestone karsts and praised for its serenity in local folk songs, Muang Soui is a sleepy town of wooden shop-houses and a small market. There isn't any accommodation here yet, but with Route 7 nearly finished and daily buses already passing through, things should start looking up quickly. Aside from the lake, nearby is **Tham Pha**, a forest cave which shelters a Buddha image and a *that*. One kilometre from town, an old 1500-metre-long landing strip, in a state of disuse, cuts across Route 7 as it begins its ninety-kilometre journey towards Muang Phoukhoun.

Long Cheng

Located at the northern edge of the Xaisombioun Special Zone (see box on p.210), just 60km south of Phonsavan, is a mountain famous in the history of the Second Indochina War, known as **Long Cheng** ("Clear Valley"). A remote top-secret mountain-top **airbase** here was the CIA's frontline base for the war in Laos, the headquarters of Vang Pao's anti-communist Hmong army and, for years, one of the best-kept secrets of the Second Indochina War. At an altitude of 960m, Long Cheng occupies a plateau basin, erupting with limestone karsts and surrounded by serrated ridges and imposing peaks. Known to American pilots as simply "Alternate", Long Cheng was outfitted with a 1260-metre-long airfield, capable of handling fast-moving fighters as well as slower moving tactical planes, though the landing strip was often obscured by rain and mist. Although the heavy bombers flew in from bases in Thailand, Long Cheng, heavily defended by ground troops and air-power, was the main staging ground for the "secret war" for the strategic Plain of Jars. Given the huge amount of interest in Long Cheng, caused in no small part by Christopher Robbins' excellent best-selling book, *The Ravens*, the army is currently rebuilding the old road from Phonsavan and plans to **open the site** for tourism in 2003.

Xaisomboun Special Zone

Carved out of parts of Vientiane, Xiang Khouang and Bolikhamxai provinces in 1994, the **Xaisomboun Special Zone**, extending over more than 7000 square kilometres, was created in an effort to quell anti-Vientiane insurgent activities, and has been administered by the Lao military ever since. Much of the southern sector is empty wilderness, but the district is accessible via Route 13B, which runs off of Route 13 just north of Ang Nam Ngum and then branches off at Pha Volo into separate roads north to Phonsavan. Due to improvements in the security situation the military have recently returned two districts to Vientiane Province, however, Xaisomboun is still not considered totally safe for travel. Smack in the middle of the district is **Long Cheng** ("Clear Valley", see p.209) and the district is also home to **Phou Bia**, Laos's tallest mountain at 2819m. Located approximately halfway between Phonsavan and Ang Nam Ngum Reservoir, Phou Bia is closed to tourists as it still has an insurgency problem. It has not yet been designated a national park; at the moment, the closest you can get to seeing it is out of the window on the Phonsavan to Vientiane flight.

As long as remnants of the disbanded Hmong army continue to stage hit and run attacks on civilian and military targets, the new name the communists have chosen for the former Hmong stronghold, Xaisomboun, or "Bountiful Victory", will remain a rather premature one at best, given the government's inability to bring the isolated zone under its control.

Travel details

Buses and sawngthaews

Nam Neun to: Phonsavan (1–2 daily; 6hr); Viang Thong (1 daily; 3hr); Xam Nua (1 daily; 3hr 30 min).
Nong Khiaw to: Nam Bak (hourly; 30min); Viang Kham (2–3 daily; 2hr).
Phonsavan to: Muang Kham (4–5 daily; 1hr 30min); Muang Khoun (2–3 daily; 1hr); Muang Soui (1-2 daily; 2hr); Nam Neun (1–2 daily; 6hr); Nong Het (1 daily; 4hr); Phaxai (2–3 daily; 40min); Xam Nua (1 daily; 6hr).
Viang Kham to: Louang Phabang (1 daily; 4h 40min); Nong Khiaw (2–3 daily; 2hr); Viang Thong (2 daily; 4hr).

Viang Thong to: Nam Neun (1 daily; 3hr); Viang Kham (2 daily; 4hr); Xam Nua (1 daily; 6–7hr).
Xam Nua to: Muang Et (1 daily; 5hr); Nam Neun (1–2 daily; 3hr 30min); Viang Thong (1 daily; 6–7hr); Viang Xai (7 daily; 30min); Vientiane (daily; 30hr).

Flights

Phonsavan to: Louang Phabang (4 weekly; 35min); Vientiane (1–2 daily; 40min).
Xam Nua to: Vientiane (1 daily; 1hr 10min).

The far north

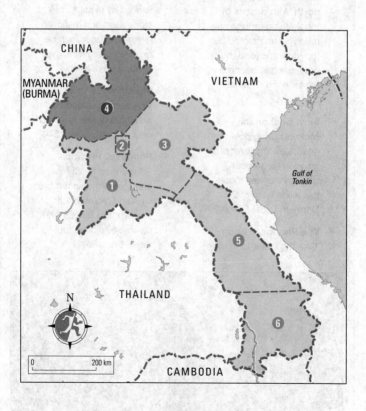

CHAPTER 4 # Highlights

* **Nam Ha NBCA** Hike, kayak or raft, but don't miss this stunning national park near the trekking centre of Louang Namtha. See p.224

* **Hilltribe trekking in the north** With dozens of tribal ethnic groups still relatively unaffected by the modern world, northern Laos has become a big trekking destination. See p.223

* **Slow Boat on the Mekong** Chug down the great Mekong River on a wooden cargo boat through the vast mountain wilderness of Northern Laos. See p.237

* **The Phongsali Loop** Take the week-long loop from Louang Phabang through some of the country's most ethnically diverse regions. See p.241

* **Nam Ou River** The spectacularly scenic Nam Ou, flanked by jagged limestone karst and rustic riverside villages, can be explored using local river boats. See p.244

* **Muang Ngoi** A tiny idyllic village, surrounded by karst peaks and reached only by boat. See p.244

* **Phongsali Province** Surrounded by China and Vietnam, this remote highland region offers vast tropical forests and diverse traditional cultures. See p.241

4

The far north

W hile history has seen the rise and fall of a Lao dynasty enthroned at Louang Phabang, little has changed on the elevated **northern fringes** of the former kingdom. Decades of war and neglect have done their part to keep this isolated region of Southeast Asia from developing and have unwittingly preserved a way of life that has virtually vanished in neighbouring countries. While the fertile valleys of the Upper Mekong and its tributaries have for centuries been the domain of the **Buddhist lowland Lao**, the hills and mountains to the north have been the preserve of a scattering of animist tribal peoples, including the **Hmong**, **Mien** and **Akha**. Gleaning evidence largely from oral tradition, anthropologists speculate that some of these tribal peoples, such as the **Khamu**, were actually here before the lowland Lao migrated onto the scene. Others, such as the Akha, are relative newcomers to the rugged terrain of the north. The highlanders make their living by painstakingly clearing and cultivating the steep slopes while bartering with the lowland Lao for anything that they themselves cannot harvest, hunt or fashion with their own hands. It is largely the chance to experience first-hand these near-pristine cultures that is drawing visitors to the region today.

In the past, visitors only had a few set options for travelling around the far north, considered by many to be the highlight of any trip to Laos. The most popular route was from Louang Phabang up through Muang Sing to Xiang Kok and then back down the Mekong either exiting at Houayxai or returning back down the Mekong to Louang Phabang. Today working out a travel itinerary for a journey through the far north is not so simple since there are now so many different routes and transport options. While the traditional route described above is still very popular, a number of variations on this theme are also possible, with many travellers now using **Routes 2** and **3** to swing up to **Route 1**. Aside from river travel along the Mekong between Louang Phabang and Houayxai, it is also possible to travel up-country by boat along the **Namtha** and **Nam Ou rivers** in season.

Whichever way you choose to go, the two most popular northern towns are the tourist centre of **Louang Namtha**, with its excellent trekking and river trips, and **Muang Sing**, a laid-back Tai Leu town that lies within the borders of the **Golden Triangle**, the world's most notorious opium-producing zone. Both towns have become popular bases for trekking, owing to their comfortable accommodation and easy access to nearby Akha, Mien and Tai Dam villages. Along the Mekong River there are a number of riverport towns with boat traffic, accommodation and roadheads leading up into the interior. These include **Xiang Kok** just a short journey from Muang Sing, **Houayxai**, an

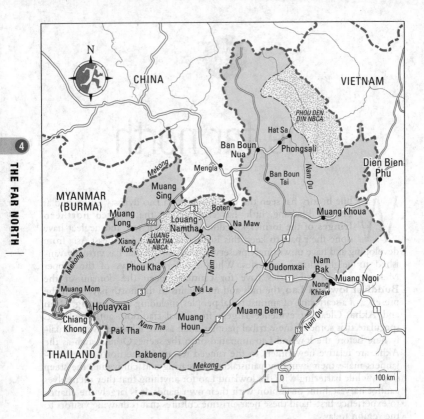

official border-crossing with Thailand, **Pakbeng**, an important stop for slow boats on the Louang Phabang to Houayxai route, and of course, Louang Phabang itself.

Another popular route is the **Phongsali Loop**, which combines both river and road travel and takes nearly a week to complete, passing through the most spectacular scenery in northern Laos. Although the loop can be done in either direction, many travellers opt to begin the loop in Louang Phabang, ascending the **Nam Ou River** by passenger boat with nights spent in **Nong Khiaw**, **Muang Ngoi** and **Muang Khoua**. Leaving the river at the town of **Hat Sa**, you travel by sawngthaew over the mountains to **Phongsali**, a provincial capital situated on a plateau blessed with a year-round temperate climate. Inhabited mainly by the easy-going Phu Noi people, this tidy town is reminiscent of highland towns in southern China's Yunnan province. From Phongsali, you travel by sawngthaew down Route 4 to the city of **Oudomxai**. Although Oudomxai is not a tourist centre, it is the most important road junction in the far north. It can be used as a jumping off point for either of the two main tourist loops described above, or for journeys into China through the border crossing at Boten, or Vietnam via Route 4 at the border crossing to Dien Bien Phu, scheduled to open by the end of 2002.

Oudomxai

Located at the junction of Routes 1, 2 and 4, **OUDOMXAI** is the most important crossroads in northern Laos. Once known as Muang Xai, the town sits in small basin surrounded by mountains: from this high point rivers flow to the north, south, east and west, making it an important trading town. The town also straddles a major trade route to China, and even today it is the most Chinese city in northern Laos. Trucks to and from China pass this way daily and most of the town's hotels, nightclubs and brothels are run by mainland Chinese. There are so many Chinese traders and tourists here that the Chinese yuan is as readily accepted as the US dollar. After the civil war, Muang Xai was renamed Oudomxai which means "Abundant Victory".

Essentially little more than the junction of two roads, there is little to actually see in Oudomxai – in fact it is the least appealing town in all of northern Laos. Although the valley itself is quite pretty, the town has grown up along the two main roads without any planning and is a sprawl of ugly concrete buildings. Even its varied population, including Lao, Chinese and Khamu, is not as colourful as elsewhere in northern Laos. The locals prefer to wear Chinese-made "Western-style" clothing and, except for the occasional Hmong villagers in town for a day of trading, there is no way to tell the ethnic groups apart. However, if you travel around the north long enough there's a very good chance you'll end up having to stop-over here at some point, like it or not. To this end, the town makes a pretty good rest stop. Whether you're on the road between Louang Phabang and Muang Sing, or doing the Phongsali Loop, you'll find that Oudomxai is perfect – there is 24-hour electricity, email, laundry service, hot water and even herbal sauna and massage to be had here.

The only real sight is **Phou Xay Hill** which is located just east of the bridge. On the northern side of the hill just beside the *Dok Boua Daeng* guest house is a long flight of stairs leading to the summit. The top of the hill is crowned by a white stupa with a golden spire which provides good views over the entire valley and is an excellent place to watch the sunset. Near the stupa is a traditional wooden building with a red roof used by monks. The town's main

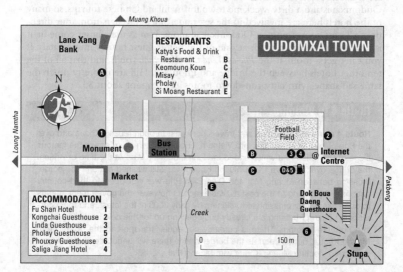

▲ Muang Khoua

Lane Xang Bank

N

Loung Namtha

RESTAURANTS
Katya's Food & Drink
  Restaurant   B
Keomoung Koun   C
Misay   A
Pholay   D
Si Moang Restaurant   E

OUDOMXAI TOWN

Football Field

Monument

Bus Station

Internet Centre

Market

Creek

ACCOMMODATION
Fu Shan Hotel   1
Kongchai Guesthouse   2
Linda Guesthouse   3
Pholay Guesthouse   5
Phouxay Guesthouse   6
Saliga Jiang Hotel   4

Dok Boua Daeng Guesthouse

Pakbeng

0   150 m

Stupa

temple, **Wat Santiphap**, is on a rise just north of town. At sunset you'll often find monks from the wat up at the Phou Xay stupa practising their English with passing visitors.

Practicalities

The **airport** lies 3km east of town; shared tuk-tuks wait there for the town's eight weekly arrivals. From Oudomxai there are flights to Vientiane, Louang Phabang and Houayxai. **Buses** and sawngthaews from all four points on the compass arrive at the town's only bus station, a big dirt lot between the river and the Kaysone monument which stares out from an odd little park on a hill in the centre of town. From here buses leave early in the morning for Louang Namtha, the Chinese border at Boten, Pakbeng, Muang Khua, Phongsali, Vientiane and Louang Phabang. Travellers headed east towards Nong Khiaw should take a sawngthaew to Pakmong and change vehicles there if there is no direct vehicle. The last sawngthaew for Pakmong leaves mid-afternoon.

Lane Xang **bank** is housed in an impressive two-storey house on a hilltop 500m north of the market just past *Misay Restaurant*. There's also a BCEL bank west of the bus station, opposite the Konica Express lab. Both banks exchange foreign currency and travellers' cheques, and accept Visa. Both of Oudomxai's **internet cafés** are located by the hideous *Saliga Jian Jiang Hotel* (℡081/312468) on the main street near the Pholay: Friendship Internet and Oudomxai Internet Café both charge 60K a minute and the latter also does long-distance calls. If you're heading north, Oudomxai is currently the last stop for internet service. For the road-weary, there's a Lao Red Cross **sauna** (daily 4–7pm; ℡081/312391) with traditional massage (20,000K per hour) and a herbal sauna (10,000K; bring a towel and sarong) located behind the stalag-like *Phouxay Hotel*.

Accommodation

There are many **hotels** in Oudomxai but most are dirty and run down, particularly those on the western side of the bus lot. All the newer guest houses are found on the east side of the river on or just off the main road. Although there are a dozen places here, most of them are badly built and poorly maintained. Oudomxai is also a dirty-weekend town for mainland Chinese tourists, so many of the hotels here are involved in the sex trade. Since travellers from four directions all start converging on Oudomxai at about 3pm as their buses come in, it is desirable to secure a room at one of the better guest houses immediately. If you can't get a room at the *Pholay, Linda*, or *Kongchai*, you'll find that all of the ten other hotels between the bridge and Phou Xay Hill are in pretty much the same sad shape, with tatty, run-down rooms all going for about $3.

Route 4 to Vietnam

Route 4 starts in **Oudomxai** and travels northeast through Muang Khoua and over the Phou Den Din Mountains into Vietnam, ending at Dien Bien, site of the famous siege of Dien Bien Phu which ended the First Indochina War. At the time of writing, the bridge over the Nam Ou at Muang Khoua was still washed out and the border crossing between Muang Khoua and Dien Bien Phu was not open to third-country nationals. According to the best available reports however, the government intends to open this border crossing to foreigners by early 2003 at the latest, and tour operators in Louang Phabang are already busy gearing up for this new back-door route into northern Vietnam. There is currently no regular transport to the border from Muang Khoua, but as soon as the border opens there will undoubtedly be sawngthaews connecting Muang Khoua with Muang Mai.

Fu Shan Hotel Just left of the Kaysone monument. Built with mainland Chinese money, the *Fu Shan* (Prosperous Mountain) is a typical communist government-built hotel – a huge three–storey rectangle covered in bathroom tiles. Although it's the biggest hotel in town and boasts a lobby, a Chinese restaurant and a tacky nightclub, its main claim to being the top hotel in town is the presence of TVs in the rooms. The ordinary, run-down rooms are otherwise very poor value. ❸

Kongchai Guest House At the east end of the football field, 20m north up the first alley east of the *Linda* ☎081/211141. Friendly *Kongchai* has simple but clean and reasonably priced rooms with en-suite bathrooms and hot water. The rooms at the front of the building overlook the football field and have views of the mountains. ❶–❷

Linda Guest House East of the bridge ☎081/312147. Despite its ugly facade, the *Linda* has seventeen rooms which are on a par with the *Pholay* in terms of decor and cleanliness (though slightly more expensive), as well as a few VIP rooms at the front which feature air-con and windows facing the street. ❷

Pholay Guest House East of the bridge, before Phou Xay Hill ☎081/312324. The pick of the bunch with clean rooms with fan, en-suite bathrooms and hot water for just 30,000K. *Pholay* is a family-run concern in the old-fashioned Southeast Asian style with inexpensive rooms above and a good traveller's café below. The catch is that there are only six rooms and they fill up very quickly. ❷

Phouxay Hotel At the end of the lane along the west side of Phou Xay. This spooky government-run establishment must rate as one of Laos's most bizarre hotels. Set in a huge compound surrounded by a brick wall topped with barbed wire, the four brick barracks facing a courtyard would make a perfect location for a film about the Cultural Revolution. The ancient-looking rooms are mostly used by transiting civil servants and bureaucrats. There are two private guest houses right outside the main gate and the Lao Red Cross sauna and massage is behind the hotel. ❶

Saliga Jiang Hotel Main street near the *Linda* ☎081/312468. This four-storey Chinese hotel covered in brown bathroom tiles is probably the best of a bad lot if you arrive too late and the *Linda* is full. There's a Chinese restaurant downstairs, karaoke entertainment – and lots of Chinese working girls in and out of the lobby. ❷–❸

The art of sawngthaew travel

Until very recently, transport in northern Laos was limited to its network of rivers, with travellers at the mercy of the water level. Today, with the introduction of four-wheel-drive Toyota **pick-up trucks**, mobility in the mountainous north has greatly improved. Enterprising drivers have converted their pick-ups into buses of sorts, adding two rows of benches bolted to the pick-up's bed and covering the whole affair with a tarpaulin stretched over a steel frame, giving shelter from sun and rain. Unfortunately, long-distance travel on these vehicles can be excruciatingly uncomfortable, especially on yet-to-be sealed roads such as Routes 2, 3 and 4. While there is nothing a passenger can do about the sad state of Lao roads, knowing where to sit in the pick-up can make the trip a bit more tolerable.

The **front seat**, next to the driver, is obviously the best. Everyone knows this and drivers usually charge extra for this choice spot. Being able to speak a bit of Lao may help you secure this seat as drivers enjoy conversing on long hauls and a Lao-speaking foreigner is considered an entertaining diversion. Often though, the driver will bring along a friend or family member and this seat will be reserved. This leaves passengers riding in the bed with a dilemma: relative comfort or a view.

The **innermost seats**, those nearest the cab, are a smoother ride but afford almost no view of the passing scenery. For this reason, non-Lao passengers often try to stake a claim on the seats nearest the tail-gate. Unfortunately, passengers in these seats have to put up with clouds of dust and choking exhaust fumes, as well as amplified jolts and knocks. If the pick-up has a **back bumper** that is wide enough to stand on, adventurous passengers may opt to perch on that while clinging precariously to the tarp-frame. This affords unobstructed views and gusts of fresh air, but watch out for those car-sick Lao passengers who poke their heads out the sides and hurl into the wind.

Eating

Oudomxai has plenty of **restaurants**, particularly Chinese-run places. The restaurant at the *Pholay Guest House* is the best option, serving up good stir-fry dishes – try the pork fried in ginger and the pork fried with basil leaves – and passable European fare. It's also renowned for frozen yoghurt and great fruit smoothies. Three buildings west of the *Pholay* is another traveller's café, *Keomoung Koun*, which isn't as good as the *Pholay* but does passable fried rice or noodles. Directly opposite just inside the alley is *Katya's Food & Drink Restaurant* which is clean and worth trying. For dinner, the *Si Moang Restaurant* is one of the town's better organized establishments. To find it, take the first alley on the right, east of the bridge, cutting through the barracks, then turn right at the T-junction and it's on the first corner. It's a big place with proper tables and seating in a large dining room. The *Misay*, about 400m north past the *Fu Shan Hotel*, is one of Oudomxai's longest-running eateries and worth the short hike. They only serve Lao food but there's a comfortable dining room with good seating and an English menu.

Louang Namtha and around

Straddling Route 3, four hours' drive northwest of Oudomxai, **LOUANG NAMTHA** was heavily contested during Laos's civil war, which is to say that it was razed to the ground. Once the fighting stopped, the surrounding hills were stripped of their trees and the mammoth logs were trucked away to China. Today, the once devastated and depopulated valley is making a comeback as a booming tourist area with rafting, kayaking and trekking. Although the town itself supplies a host of good restaurants, hotels and tourist services, the real reason to come to Louang Namtha is to visit the **Nam Ha NBCA**, walk or cycle to nearby Hmong and Leten villages, take a trek in the hills, or do kayaking or rafting on the Nam Tha and Nam Ha rivers. Louang Namtha is also a launch base for passenger-boat trips down the Nam Tha River to Houayxai.

Arrival, orientation, information and transport

The **airport** and **boat jetty** are both located 7km south of the main town, down Route 3, while the **bus station** sits three streets west of the main street. Situated in a long valley sandwiched between mountain ranges, the town is quite spread out, stretching a good 6km along Route 3: there are no tuk-tuks but shared **sawngthaews** cruise the streets, acting as a kind of bus system. **Bicycles** are available at the Chinese electrical goods shops opposite the GPO among other places for 1500K an hour.

Although Louang Namtha only has electricity from 6–9.30pm there is quite a good range of tourist facilities including two colour photo labs, bicycle rental shops and a travel agency. All of the above are located on or just off the main street. For currency **exchange** there's a BCEL service unit (daily 8.30am–3.30pm) right at the bus station which accepts cash, travellers' cheques and Visa. Lane Xang Bank on the main street just north of Lao Aviation can exchange foreign currency and travellers' cheques, and there's a BCEL branch on the main street almost opposite Lao Tel-com. Louang Namtha already has a branch of Pla-net Computer but they are currently awaiting 24-hr electricity and

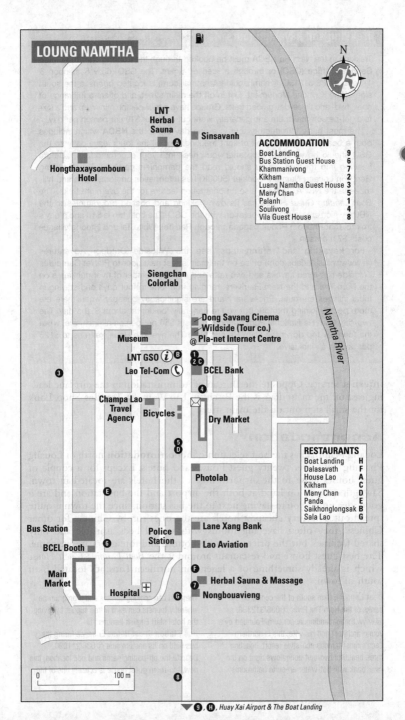

LOUNG NAMTHA

A

Sinsavanh

LNT Herbal Sauna

Hongthaxaysomboun Hotel

ACCOMMODATION
Boat Landing	9
Bus Station Guest House	6
Khammanivong	7
Kikham	2
Luang Namtha Guest House	3
Many Chan	5
Palanh	1
Soulivong	4
Vila Guest House	8

Siengchan Colorlab

Dong Savang Cinema
Wildside (Tour co.)
@ Pla-net Internet Centre

Museum

LNT GSO (i) B
Lao Tel-Com (📞)

1 2 C

BCEL Bank

4

Champa Lao Travel Agency

Bicycles

Dry Market

3

5
D

E

Photolab

RESTAURANTS
Boat Landing	H
Dalasavath	F
House Lao	A
Kikham	C
Many Chan	D
Panda	E
Saikhonglongsak	B
Sala Lao	G

Bus Station

BCEL Booth

G

Police Station

Lane Xang Bank

Lao Aviation

Main Market

Hospital 🏥

G

F
Herbal Sauna & Massage

7
Nongbouavieng

Namtha River

N

0   100 m

8

▼ 9 , H , Huay Xai Airport & The Boat Landing

Trekking and kayaking tours

Trekking in the Nam Ha NBCA must be booked through the **Louang Namtha Guide Services Office** (GSO) or through a licensed agent. The GSO (daily 8am–noon & 1–5pm; ☎086/312150, ✉namhaguides@hotmail.com) is located opposite the south side of the Kaysone Monument, just in off the main street, and offers a full range of one-, two- and three-day guided treks. Groups have a four-person minimum and a six- to eight-person maximum and generally work out at about $10 per person per day.

The most basic introductory tour is a one-day trip to the **NBCA** which includes both a boat journey and a bit of light trekking. Not all the tours leave daily so the GSO should be your first stop after you check into your accommodation. Before heading into the NBCA you should read the pamphlets carefully. The "Trekking Gently in Louang Namtha" booklet (5000K) has information on flora, fauna and hill- tribes in the NBCA. There is also an orientation lecture for the overnight treks. The *Boat Landing Guest House* has its own trekking and boating programmes to the NBCA which are done in cooperation with the GSO. The boat trip is $10 and a day's trek to That Phanom Phouk pagoda through Red Tai, White Tai and Hmong villages costs $7 a person.

For **kayaking** and **rafting** trips, see the Wildside Outdoor Adventures (ⓦwww.wildside/laos.com) office on the main street next door to PlaNet Computer. Wildside has three kayaks and two rafts and offers a number of river packages on the Nam Tha and the Nam Ha rivers, ranging from one to four days and staying in tribal villages en-route. Prices vary and are significantly cheaper when there are more people joining the tour but you're generally looking at about $20 a day. The two-day Nam Ha National Park rafting trip costs $50 per person all-inclusive, while the four-day trip down the Nam Ha and Nam Tha rivers to Houayxai runs to $125 per person all-inclusive.

internet service. Opposite the Bureau of Administration in the dirt lane lead- ing east off the main drag, is the Paseutsin Lao Women's **Textiles** Shop. Look for the small sign out on the main street.

Accommodation

Louang Namtha has the best selection of **accommodation** north of Louang Phabang with over twenty guest houses and hotels. Except for a couple of guest houses close to the airport, most of the hotels are located in town. Sawngthaews are on hand at both the airport and the bus station and are a good idea unless you're staying next to the bus station, since the town is quite spread out. The very cheapest hotels are the ones run by Chinese for other Chinese; they often have big rooms with several beds available and only shared facilities, but the prices are rock-bottom and foreigners are welcome. The best guest house and restaurant around is the *Boat Landing Guest House* which is already something of a legend in northern Laos; it's located 6km south of town.

Boat Landing 6km south of the centre on the banks of the Nam Tha River ☎086/312398, ⓦwww.theboatlanding.laopdr.com. Founded by a young architect and his wife, this is northern Laos's most famous eco-style resort, boasting three beautiful two-unit bungalows right on the river bank with hot-water en-suite bathrooms.

They run Lao cooking classes and a programme whereby tourists can earn a free supper by giving the hotel staff English lessons. ❹
Bus Station Guest House Entrance facing the bus field on its eastern side ☎086/211090. Despite the off-putting name and odd location, this new, ten-room guest house is actually one of the

best deals in town. The attractive, well-constructed building is inside a walled compound so it's quite peaceful. Rooms are clean and have en-suite bathrooms although there's no hot water as yet. ❶

Khammanivong Main road 50m south of Lao Aviation. Ten simple but clean rooms with shared bathrooms in a brand new and attractive wooden house. All the rooms have wood floors, large windows and Lao textile quilts. There are hot showers and the rear balcony has mountain views. An excellent place and one of the best value in town at $2.50 per room. Highly recommended. ❶

Kikham Main road directly across from the Telcom. This Chinese guest house is a backpacker's delight with about the cheapest rooms in town. The singles start from 6000K but are not at all grungy and come with a mozzie net, desk and fan. The more expensive rooms are $1.50. The Chinese restaurant downstairs is a bit loud but if you're on a really tight budget this is the place. ❶

Luang Namtha Guest House Straight north up the road running along the west side of the bus field ☎086/312087. A work in progress with a huge mansion, two nicely built thatched bungalows out back and another concrete building under construction. Both the bungalows overlooking the pond and the main house are very good value for money. ❷

Many Chan Main street opposite the dry market ☎086/312209. Eight simple rooms on the second floor of a wooden house with toilets and hot shower below. The rooms are spartan but very clean. The guest house is run by the friendly and helpful Miss Manychan and her family and it's a fun place to stay. This is the favourite backpacker hotel in town so it fills up very quickly. ❶–❷

Palanh Main street directly opposite *Saikhonglongsak* ☎086/312439. The rooms here, some with shared bath, are about standard quality and slightly more expensive than average, but what sets this place apart is that it's the only hotel in Louang Namtha with 24hr electricity. ❷–❸

Soulivong On the corner one block east of the GPO ☎086/312253. This large, new, three-storey house with a peaked blue roof has clean rooms with tile floors and en-suite bathrooms. The rooms on the 2nd and 3rd floors are the best and there's hot water in the evenings. ❷

Vila Guest House On the main road 1km south of town at Km 2 ☎086/312425. This huge new two-storey mansion has nine rooms, seven with en-suite bathrooms, and an upstairs balcony with mountain views. If you're looking for something clean and modern in town and don't mind paying a bit more then this is your best bet. Behind the main house is a smaller wooden house which has a charming restaurant (breakfast included). ❹

The Town and around

In the main town itself the only formal attraction is the **Louang Namtha Provincial Museum** (Mon–Fri 8.30am–noon & 1–3.30pm; 1000K), housed in a green-roofed building behind the Kaysone monument, where you'll find displays of traditional hilltribe costumes and artefacts, a model depicting battles that took place in the area during the civil war and a rusty collection of weaponry.

The town boasts two traditional **Lao saunas** and massage. The Luang Namtha Herbal Sauna (4.30–7.30pm) is located just west of *House Lao* restaurant. The other sauna is the Herbal Sauna & Massage (sauna $1, massage $1.50 per hr) on the main road between Darasavath and Khammanivong. The latter is a fascinating affair in a traditional grass-roofed building on stilts reached by a thirty-metre-long bamboo bridge. From the deck over a pond you can see the mountains.

The tourist authority has produced an excellent flyer entitled "11 Things to do in Louang Namtha", available around town or at ⓦwww.theboatlanding .laopdr.com. The list includes information on local wats, waterfalls, picnic sites, handicraft co-ops and view points. The GSO has free copies. Otherwise, the most straightforward day-trip consists of renting a bicycle and heading out for the surrounding villages. One good self-organized **day-trip** is to hire a tuk-tuk to take you up the road towards Na Toei, get off with your bicycle where the pavement ends 15km from town, and then coast all the way back down the mountain, a downhill run of about 8km back to the valley floor.

Moving on from Louang Namtha

Sawngthaews for **Muang Sing** and **Oudomxai** leave from Louang Namtha's bus station, a huge empty lot next to and just north of the morning market. Travellers with a valid visa for **China** can take a Chinese-operated bus in the morning from Louang Namtha bus station to the border crossing at Boten and on to Jinghong in China. Sawngthaews only go as far as the border. The road trip down Route 3 to Houayxai is one of those dusty Lao journeys that are fast disappearing with the ongoing road-paving programme. This particular road has been under construction since the mid-Nineties and is still quite bad. The route is plied by sawngthaews, taking between eight and ten hours ($6). During the dry season, passengers eat a lot of dust and during the monsoon season they get wet and the mire is sometimes barely passable. If the ride gets too much, there is a basic guest house in the village of Vieng Phou Kha, 66km south of Louang Namtha. Once the upgrading of the road has been completed the journey should take under six hours.

During the wet season, travellers heading for **Houayxai** have the option of going by passenger boat. The Nam Tha is navigable from about July until January. Unless you have unlimited time to wait around, it's most convenient to hire a boat outright ($80 for a boat that holds up to ten people). If the water levels are high it's a one-day trip but if the water is low it takes one and a half days, with an overnight stop in Na Lae. Boatmen usually only go as far as Paktha, where the Nam Tha meets the Mekong. From there you get a speedboat for the last 36-kilometre stretch along the Mekong from Paktha to Houayxai (1hr; B130 per person). It's very important to strike a clear deal with the boatman as they have been known to re-negotiate the fare once en route if they run into adverse conditions. The GSO office in town has a very useful free flyer explaining the different possible routes and programmes you could negotiate, with approximate prices.

Eating

Louang Namtha's food scene has improved greatly since a few years ago when it was all fried rice and noodle soups. There are now both travellers' cafés and even upmarket **restaurants**. Small food stalls with low tables and chairs sell pre-prepared satay, eggs, cold noodles and spring rolls outside the old Dong Savang cinema opposite the museum near the Pla-net. Plenty of *pho* places are dotted around the bus lot and in the Morning Market.

Boat Landing Restaurant The best food in town is at the hotel of the same name 6km south of the centre. This is a great place to sample quality Lao food and there's a wide choice of northern specialities such as *sa*, *aw lahm*, *moke* and a range of other dishes such as green-pumpkin soup, tofu stuffed with green peppers and "rock algae chips". The spicy Lao purees are particularly worth trying and they also offer multi-course set menus from $6 a head. If you've made it all the way to Louang Namtha, don't miss this wonderful restaurant.

Dalasavath South of Lao Aviation. Belonging to the guest house of the same name, this restaurant is in a nice open sala surrounded by greenery which gives it a bit of local atmosphere. There's good Asian and Western food and their beer garden is a great spot for drinks.

House Lao Restaurant On the main street at the north end of town opposite the *Sinsavanh Guest*

House. This marvellous Lao-style restaurant is the flashest in town. Completely built of wood, the restaurant has a covered deck and there's a bar and a wooden balustrade around the top. A poor location on the main drag, but the atmosphere and the Lao specialities make it a top choice.

Kikham For Chinese food try the restaurant downstairs at the *Kikham*; most of the dishes range from just 6000K up to $1. If the crowds of Chinese diners are any indication, this is the top choice for Chinese although several challengers have opened recently.

Many Chan Main street. The town's most popular travellers' café with inexpensive tasty food including Western and Asian dishes and good coffee.

Panda Restaurant Just north of the bus station. Also worth checking out is the highly popular *Panda* which does very cheap Western dishes and stir-fries out of a tiny shack with plastic chairs and a sandwich board outside. Despite its odd location, the place gets rave reviews and does a roaring business most evenings. Very cheap with most dishes between 5000K and $1.

Saikhonglongsak On the main street. Like the *Many Chan*, this guest house has a very popular travellers' café at street level serving Western and Asian food. The coffee is the best in town and the owner is quite a humorous fellow.

Sala Lao Directly across from the *Nongbouavieng Guest House* on the main road south of the police station. Another interesting spot for authentic Lao cuisine, this no-name place is made of wood, bamboo and nipa with about six tables. It's in a charming traditional Lao house on stilts built over a fish pond. There's no menu but they specialize in fresh fish and Lao specialities such as pungent duck *moke*. A unique experience.

Trekking etiquette

One of the great pleasures of travelling through northern Laos are chance encounters with the region's distinctively dressed hilltribe peoples. **Guided treks**, a popular tourist diversion in neighbouring Thailand, are just getting going in Laos, with Louang Namtha and Muang Sing the two main centres for organized trekking. In fact, self-organized treks are actually discouraged in these two towns where the government, understandably, is trying to regulate the industry. In other northern towns however, it is still possible for travellers to trek independently by simply using a town with accommodation as a base, getting directions and then hiking to a nearby tribal village. Muang Long is currently the most popular base for self-organized trekking, but there are also excellent untapped opportunities to be explored in Phongsali province, particularly in the vicinity of Ban Boun Tai, Muang Khoua and the provincial capital.

While it is possible to organize trekking entirely on your own, if you arrange to be accompanied on your trek by a local who will act as a **guide** and **interpreter**, your experience will be greatly enhanced. A good guide will be able to explain customs and activities that you might otherwise find incomprehensible and can help you to interact with the hill folk who may be unaccustomed to or apprehensive of outsiders. Without a guide, do-it-yourself trekkers often find that their visit to a hilltribe village degenerates into an exercise of mutual gawking. If you do decide to do a trek independently, using a bit of common sense and following a few rules should make for a smooth, memorable visit.

(1) Never trek alone. While Laos is a relatively safe country in terms of violent crime, there have been **robberies** of Western tourists in remote areas. Owing to the Lao government's total control of the Lao media, word of these incidents is suppressed, making it impossible to ascertain just how much risk is involved in solo trekking. Encountering armed men while hiking through the woods does not necessarily mean you are going to be robbed, but it is best to treat all such encounters with caution. If you are approached by armed men and robbery is clearly their intent, do NOT resist.

(2) Most hilltribe peoples are animists. **Offerings** to the spirits, often bits of food, left in what may seem like an odd place, should never be touched or tampered with. The Akha are known for the elaborate gates which they construct at the entrances to their villages. Far from being merely decorative, the gates are designed to demarcate the boundaries between the human and spirit worlds. It goes without saying that climbing onto such a gate to pose for a photograph is poor form.

(3) Many hill folk are willing to be **photographed**, but, just like everyone else, do not appreciate snap-and-run tactics. Old women, particularly of the Hmong and Mien tribes, are not always keen on having their picture taken. It's best to make it clear to a potential subject that you wish to photograph them and to gauge their response before taking a photo.

(4) Passing out sweets to village kids is a sure way to generate mobs of young beggars with rotten teeth. Likewise, the indiscriminate handing out of **medicine**, particularly antibiotics, does more harm than good. Unless you are a trained doctor, you should never attempt to administer medical care to hill people.

Nam Ha NBCA

Established in 1993, the **Nam Ha NBCA** is one of Laos's most convenient and easily accessible conservation areas. Covering 1,470 square kilometres, the park straddles two high mountain chains and boasts two peaks in excess of 2000m. The best-known of the park's rivers are the **Nam Ha** and the **Nam Tha**, both of which are developed for **kayaking** and **rafting** trips. The park is accessible by car, with Route 3 crossing the NBCA in two separate places. Within the NBCA itself there are 25 **hilltribe villages**, the most populous ethnic groups being Akha, Hmong, Khmu and Lantaen, and multi-day trekking tours between these settlements are also possible. Contiguous with the Xiang Yong Protected Area in Yunnan, China, the Nam Ha NBCA is an important biological habitat for many forest creatures including 37 species of large mammals and 288 species of birds. More **information**, as well as bookings for organized tours within the NBCA, can be obtained through the Louang Namtha Guide Services Office (see p.220).

Muang Sing and around

In a short space of time, **MUANG SING**, located some 60km northwest of Louang Namtha, has progressed from a quaint, middle-of-nowhere Tai Leu village to a talked-about-on-three-continents backpacker haven. Ten years ago, barely a trickle of travellers made it to Muang Sing, but since then its residents have opened dozens of guest houses and restaurants to cater to tourists and trekkers in search of **exotic hilltribes** in traditional garb. The town is smaller and more compact than Louang Namtha and the people are friendlier. The valley is also prettier though the **trekking** industry is not yet as well organized.

Lying within the boundaries of the region known as the Golden Triangle, Muang Sing has a long connection with **opium**. Before the construction of the first roads, the town was totally cut off from the outside world. During the late French colonial era, Muang Sing became an important collection point and weigh-station for the French colonial government's opium monopoly. In the post-colonial period, quantities of local opium found their way to RLA-controlled refineries near Houayxai before the communist take-over. After the country re-opened for tourism in the 1990s there was a big tourist rush into Muang Sing to "see it before it's spoiled". Some of these tourists came to seek out and experiment with opium smoking and for a brief period opium dens even reappeared, although these have since been closed down by the authorities. Today the town is chiefly a pleasant little tourist centre with a growing trekking industry, and while it's true that Muang Sing has started attracting increasing numbers of tourists, it is still an agreeable and friendly place where great, sway-backed sows drag their teats down the main road and young novice monks play kataw and ride bicycles around the monastery grounds.

The Town and around

Muang Sing is pretty much a one-street town although the dirt lanes running west of the main road have some quaint neighbourhoods. The town's principal **temple** is the ancient-looking Wat Sing Jai, tucked behind *Muangsing Guest House*, which has a wonderfully rustic *sim* painted in festive Caribbean hues. The monastery is run by a young abbot and adherence to Buddhist precepts is surprisingly relaxed. If you come in the morning there's usually a lot of activ-

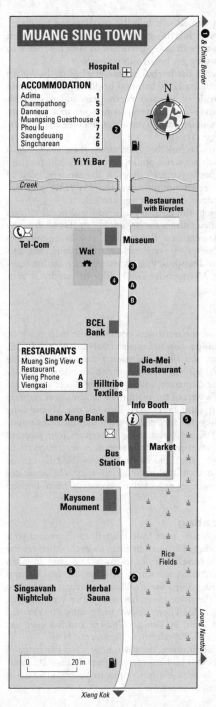

MUANG SING TOWN

1 & China Border

Hospital

ACCOMMODATION
Adima   1
Charmpathong   5
Danneua   3
Muangsing Guesthouse 4
Phou Iu   7
Saengdeuang   2
Singcharean   6

Yi Yi Bar

Creek

Restaurant
with Bicycles

Tel-Com

Wat

Museum

BCEL
Bank

RESTAURANTS
Muang Sing View   C
Restaurant
Vieng Phone   A
Viengxai   B

Jie-Mei
Restaurant

Hilltribe
Textiles

Info Booth

Lane Xang Bank

Market

Bus
Station

Kaysone
Monument

Rice
Fields

Singsavanh
Nightclub

Herbal
Sauna

0   20 m

Loung Namtha

Xieng Kok

ity, mostly the village ladies coming to pray and make offerings.

On the corner of the main road, a few metres from the monastery's main entrance, stands a simple but elegant wooden structure, the former residence of a local lord, which has been converted into a **museum**. Unfortunately, its contents, rumoured to include artefacts from around the district, are a bit of a mystery as the museum is never open and local officials are very reluctant to allow casual visitors to view the displays.

Muang Sing's morning **market** is famous for its colourfully dressed vendors and shoppers, though nowadays camera-toting tourists almost outnumber the locals who these days are more likely to be wearing track suits and Nike knock-offs. If you want to take a photo of a vendor, it's only polite to buy something first and try to have a little conversation. The market convenes very early, just after sunrise, and winds down by about 8am, though goods are on sale all day long. Most of the vendors with fixed stalls are Yunnanese traders who bring essential manufactured goods like cooking oil, trainers, jackets, Western-style clothing and electrical and household goods from factories in China. Local ethnic peoples generally set up a small table and sell vegetables, fruits, herbs and spices. This connection of Chinese lowlanders trading with the mountain peoples of the Yunnan Plateau and culturally absorbing them in the process goes back thousands of years to the Han Dynasty.

To the north, just between the market and the *Jie Mei*

Chinese restaurant there's a shop which sells hilltribe **textiles** and handbags. Many wandering street **vendors** in hilltribe costume hang around the guest houses; they aren't rude but they are extremely persistent so your best bet is to practice your Lao with them till they get bored and go away.

One of the nicest things in town is the **herbal sauna** attached to the *Muang Sing View Restaurant*. It's entered by a rickety bamboo bridge over a creek and has a big open sala restaurant made of bamboo, rattan, grass and wood with potted plants all around. The sauna is a steam room connected to a big drum full of water and herbs with a fire underneath. Come out smelling like lemongrass soup, then go for a **massage** ($1.50).

The Deutsche Gesellschaft für Technische Zusammenarbeit or GTZ, a German federal corporation which helps run opium prevention, reduction and **rehabilitation programmes**, has a project office on the western edge of town. A small but informative free exhibition there (Mon–Fri 9am–4pm) features snapshots and written narratives documenting their efforts.

Outside of town, you can explore the **countryside** and traditional villages on foot or by bicycle. Trips to Ahka villages further afield can also be done by hired tuk-tuk ($5 a day) or by sawngthaew. But the best way to see hilltribes around Muang Sing is to do a one-, two-, or three-day trek through the surrounding mountains to remote and unspoilt villages where daily life has barely changed in centuries. See the Muang Sing GSO office or inquire at your guest house.

Practicalities

There's an **information** booth on the northwest corner of the market which is usually deserted. You can **exchange** cash and travellers' cheques at the BCEL (Mon–Sat 8.30am–3pm) opposite the *Vieng Xai* guest house, or at the Lane Xang Bank service unit (Mon–Sat 8.30am–4pm) on the south side of the market square. The **post office** is the unmarked yellow building directly opposite the market. The **telecom** office is west of the main road, on the street running parallel to the stream. **Trekking** must be booked through the Muang Sing Guide Services Office (GSO). **Bicycles** are available from the restaurant opposite the Exhibition Hall for 5000K a day and at the Mountain Tour postcard shop on the main road, a little further north of the stream. A very good traditional Lao massage (15,000K per hour) and **herbal sauna** (5000K) can be found on the main road, 100m south of the market. Electricity is by generator (6–9pm) but telephone and power is expected to come in from Louang Namtha by 2003.

Accommodation and eating

Food is rather pricey in Muang Sing – your food bill will easily exceed your room bill. The *Vieng Xay* and *Vieng Phone*, right next to each other on the main street, are the most popular travellers' cafés in town. The *Phou Iu Guest House* has the nicest sit-down restaurant and serves fresh fish brought in from fish-farms in nearby China. *Muang Sing View Restaurant*, attached to the Lao sauna place at the south end of the main street, has a very nice covered deck with a superb view over the rice fields. There are two nightclubs, the *Yi Yi Bar* 30m north of the creek which is run by Yunnan Chinese and has beer and karaoke, and the big new *Singsavanh Nightclub* near *Singcharean Hotel*.

Although Muang Sing is still pretty rustic, the town now has a fair range of **hotel** options, from basic old wooden buildings to comfortable en-suite modern places. Electricity is still only available from 6pm to 9pm and none of Muang Sing's hotels has hot running-water.

Pick-ups to Muang Long (2hr), Xiang Kok (2hr 30min) and Louang Namtha (2hr) wait in the station in front of the market and leave when full. The road to Xiang Kok is now fully paved but Route 3 over the mountains through the NBCA to Louang Namtha is still a dusty, bouncy journey along an unpaved road. Most vehicles depart in the morning but it's still possible to find one leaving at around 2pm. The Chinese border north of Muang Sing is not open to Westerners.

Adima 8km north of town on the road to the Chinese frontier. Muang Sing's first eco-tourist resort, featuring bamboo architecture in a rural setting. There is a choice here of rooms in two big thatched bungalows with grass roofs or in two A-frame cabins. The nice bamboo restaurant with a deck overlooking the fields is worth visiting even if you stay in town. You can get a free lift out to the resort daily at 10am from the *Viengxay* guest house in town which is run by the same family. ❷

Charmpathong Northeast corner of the market. The best of the four budget hotels facing the market. Rooms 1, 2 and 3 on the second floor have terrific views over the rice fields towards the mountains. ❶

Danneua Main road just north of the *Muangsing Guest House*. Very big, ugly, concrete building, but the eight upstairs rooms are clean and modern and have en-suite bathrooms. There's a nice wide balcony overlooking the main drag. ❶

Muangsing Guest House Main street near Wat Sing Jai. This very friendly place run by the Kumda family is the backpacker favourite. In the newer, modern building behind the original guest house there are one- and two-bed rooms with shared bath. In winter they'll supply you with a thermos of hot water for bathing. The sitting area on the roof is also good for sunsets and there's a nice little coffee shop downstairs. The mother is a marvellous woman from Louang Phabang who speaks English, Thai and Mandarin. ❶

Phou Iu Main road south of market. The best-built hotel in town with spotlessly clean rooms with high ceilings, tile floors and modern bathrooms. Open less than a year, it's a steal at just over $5 and there's a clean, spacious restaurant downstairs. If you want something clean and modern this is the best option. ❷

Saengdeuang Main road 100m north of the Exhibition building. This large, well-built, two-storey building has eight rooms and a clean restaurant downstairs. But the real draw here are the two traditional thatched bungalows with wood-tile roofs out back. The bungalow rooms have wooden floors, big windows and en-suite bathrooms. ❶

Singcharean West in off the main road, west from the *Phou Iu*. Muang Sing's biggest tourist hotel with 22 rooms aimed at package tour groups from France. Institutional and devoid of atmosphere but if you need something clean and modern with an en-suite bathroom, this fits the bill. ❷

Villages and trekking around Muang Sing

Muang Sing is located in the centre of a flat, triangular plain surrounded on all three sides by high mountains. The Nam Youan River flows down to the plain from China and there are numerous other streams which water the valley. Scores of **hilltribe settlements** are located both in the valley basin and all through the surrounding mountains. Ethnic groups in the region include Tai Leu, Tai Dam, Akha, Mien, Hmong and others. Over the last few years, Muang Sing has slowly started emerging as the premier hilltribe trekking destination in northern Laos.

Until recently, trekking around Muang Sing was a do-it-yourself venture using local youths as guides and hoping for the best. Starting in 2002, however, the Tourist Authority is opening a **GSO** in Muang Sing and will seek to control all trekking in the area. Henceforth, all treks will have to be organized through the GSO as in Louang Namtha, and locals will be fined if caught guiding foreigners on unauthorized treks. This is by no means necessarily a negative development as the local townspeople had made very little progress

A brief history of opium

Opium. The word alone conjures up romantic images of the old Orient. Westerners' glamorization of the drug is based largely upon a thread of memory passed down from the age of European imperialism, when the empires of the British, French, Dutch and Portuguese were built partly upon encouraging and sustaining the opium habits of millions of Asians. In 1773, Britain's East India Company opened a Pandora's box of addiction by targeting China as a market for Indian opium, and by 1900 there were 13.5 million addicts in that country alone. By then, the Chinese were cultivating their own opium crop, and their appetite for the drug had spread to expatriate Chinese settlements throughout Southeast Asia. The governments of Europe's colonies in Asia set up monopolies to regulate and tax opium consumption which in turn enriched and strengthened Europe's grasp on the region.

Opium was introduced to Laos from two directions. Opium cultivation and use was known among **tribal peoples** such as the Hmong and Mien, who brought the poppy's seeds with them as they migrated south into Laos during the nineteenth century. Because the best parcels of arable land in Laos were already occupied by the lowland Lao and Tai Leu, the tribal immigrants were forced to live at high elevations. But the newly arrived tribals soon made an important discovery: opium poppies used up less of the soil's nutrients than other crops, reducing the frequency with which farmers had to perform the labour-intensive slash-and-burn technique. Growing opium and trading it for rice made their lives easier. By the early twentieth century, the **government of French Indochina** began encouraging the migration of Vietnamese and Chinese to Vientiane and the cities of southern Laos, primarily to stimulate trade, and opium addicts among these immigrants created a demand for the drug. Despite these subsequent developments, it is doubtful that the small amounts of opium grown in the hills of northern Laos ever reached the opium dens of the south. Indeed, the French opium monopoly, Opium Régie, suppressed cultivation of the poppy among the tribals in northern Laos in order to tax and control the supply of opium to the licensed dens of Indochina.

By the beginning of World War II, **taxes** on the sale of opium throughout French Indochina made up fifteen percent of the colonial government's revenues. When global war disrupted the traditional maritime route of opium into Indochina, Opium Régie turned to the **Hmong** farmers. Past French attempts to deal with the Hmong on the issue of opium had been disastrous, leading to Hmong uprisings in the

towards developing a local trekking industry on their own and self-proclaimed "guides" were demanding as much as $40 a day without offering any kind of programme or even being able to speak English. If Louang Namtha is anything to go by, the GSO-organized tours will be more professional, more environmentally friendly and cheaper.

Visitors who just want to see some tribal villages without joining a trekking tour can either explore the valley floor by bicycle or charter a sawngthaew for the day. On the main road in Muang Sing, both the photocopy shop opposite the *Phou Iu Guest House* and the Mountain Tour postcard shop north of the stream sell a coloured map of all the hilltribe villages in the area. Approximately 8km northeast of town, on the road to the Chinese border, lie two easily reached hilltribe villages – one Akha and one Mien – which are both well used to receiving foreign visitors. The Mien village is a good place to visit if you're interested in acquiring a pair of fantastically embroidered traditional pantaloons. A good departure point for the villages is the Adima resort which has a pamphlet giving instructions on five do-it-yourself village tours which start and end back at the resort, an excellent introduction to the area.

provinces of Houa Phan and Xiang Khouang. Their fear of provoking the obstinate Hmong led the French to select tribal leaders to act as brokers. The result was an 800 percent increase in Hmong opium production within four years. By the close of World War II, a weakened France had lost control of much of Laos to the Viet Minh and their protégés, the fledgling Pathet Lao. A rivalry formed between two powerful Hmong opium brokers and they took opposing sides, one supporting the colonialist French, the other the communists. The defeat of the French at Dien Bien Phu in 1954 put them out of the picture for good, but the Americans were soon to fill the vacuum.

America's efforts at combating the spread of communism in Southeast Asia created what has been termed a "Cold War opium boom". **US involvement** in the civil war in Vietnam escalated during the 1950s, leading to all-out intervention and the commitment of American troops in the 1960s. In Laos, a similar situation was occurring, but with a crucial difference. Instead of sending military troops into "neutral" Laos, the US sought to preserve the illusion of non-intervention by unconventional means. CIA operatives trained the Hmong guerrillas who had previously sided with the French, using their cash crop to fund their operations. A Byzantine alliance between the Royal Lao Government, opium warlords and the CIA was formed. Utilizing its personal fleet of "Air America" aircraft, the CIA co-ordinated the collection of opium, which was transported to refineries in the **Golden Triangle**, the resulting heroin eventually finding its way to markets all over the globe. By the war's end, the production of opium in the Golden Triangle, which overlaps into Myanmar and Thailand, had reached epic proportions.

While **eradication programmes** in Thailand have had limited success in curtailing cultivation of the opium poppy there, Myanmar and Laos continue to produce significant amounts of the crop. The availability of opium in Laos has been seen as a boon by some travellers who are keen on experimentation. Unfortunately, the recent phenomenon of an ever-increasing stream of foreign visitors intent on sampling the drug is having an effect on internationally funded efforts to detoxify local addicts. A German aid-worker in Muang Sing explained, "Tourists see opium smoking as something from the history books: romantic and mysterious. What they don't see is the other side of the coin: the addict's wife and children. For these people opium addiction means poverty".

The Akha Road (Route 322)

Route 322, the road which links **Muang Sing** and **Xiang Kok**, passes through one of Laos's most remote regions. While the peaceful scenery of forest-covered hills belies it, the history of this region is tied to the production of illicit drugs: opium, heroin and, more recently, amphetamines. It is not certain whether the bulk of amphetamines are produced in labs in Laos or in neighbouring Myanmar, but smugglers use routes through both countries on their way south to Bangkok, a principal market and distribution point for the drug which then finds its way to discos and dance clubs all over Southeast Asia. Travellers are unlikely to see any indication of this activity from the road though.

While the Lao government has mundanely designated this 75-kilometre stretch of road Route 322, a more apt designation might be the **Akha Road**, given the high density of Akha villages through which it passes. The Akha of this isolated region have had little contact with the lowland Lao and this is reflected in their dress. Indeed, the area is one of the few in Laos where you will see Akha men still wearing their traditional headgear: disc-shaped red turbans or tall hats festooned with seed-beads and even the colourful wrappers from cakes of Thai soap – so rare in these parts that they are used for ornamentation. The road is now paved all the way and sawngthaews run in both directions early morning. The main stop between Muang Sing and Xiang Kok is **Muang Long** where there is a guest house and good trekking.

Muang Long and around

Located halfway between Muang Sing and Xiang Kok, **MUANG LONG** is an up-and-coming Tai Leu town surrounded by Akha and Hmong villages. Situated right in the heart of Akha country, the town has long been known as an excellent base for self-organized **trekking**. If you're looking for good trekking in unspoilt areas and don't mind very basic food and facilities, then Muang Long (also called Long) is the place for you.

In Muang Long itself there are a few "sights". At dawn a parade of tribal peoples comes down from the hills to trade at the make-shift **market**. Besides the usual basketloads of peppers, tubers and gourds, villagers bring pieces of rare eaglewood which they gather from the dense forest. This resinous wood, used in Middle Eastern countries in the manufacture of perfumes and incense, is warehoused here before being shipped off to Bangkok where it fetches astonishingly high prices at shops in the small Arab quarter off Sukhumvit Road. There's also a diminutive Tai Leu **stupa** resembling those found in China's Xishuangbanna province which stands a few metres off Muang Long's main road. If you look closely at concrete tablets built into the stupa you'll see examples of the Tai Leu script, which differs greatly from written Lao.

Pick-up trucks going in both directions stop on the main road in the morning before noon. Muang Long has a couple of basic **guest houses**. On the main road, you'll find the *Muang Long* guest house (❶) and the two-storey, wooden *Sysengphet* (❷); a small "restaurant" downstairs from the *Sysengphet* does Lao food and sticky rice.

Around Muang Long

Muang Long lies in a flat narrow valley bottom with the Nam Ma River flowing right down the valley to enter the Mekong at Xiang Kok. Two tributaries intersect the Nam Ma right at the junction of Muang Long: the Nam Dok Long flows down from the north while the larger Nam Louang River enters from deep in the mountains to the south. Together, the two **river valleys**, heavily populated with ethnic tribes, form corridors into the mountains north and south of Muang Long.

There are several easy areas to explore around Long which can be done as **day-trips**. To the south of town, there's a new road under construction up the Nam Louang river valley, which will eventually cross the mountains to connect with Route 3 at Vieng Phoukha. If you follow this road up into the mountains there's a scenic waterfall and tribal villages. To the north of town is another road leading to Ban Jamai which will eventually go all the way to Ban Chak Keun. Another option is to take Route 322 south towards Xiang Kok to the village of Somphammai where you then take a dirt road south into the mountains which leads to a number of **Akha villages**.

Another good location near Long is up Route 322 to the village of **Ban Cha Kham Ping** near Km 35. This is the narrowest section of the Ma River valley and the steep mountains come right to the edge of the road. At Ban Cha Kham Ping there's some amazing pristine sub-tropical **rainforest** which, with a guide, would be well worth the effort of reaching. There's no guest house

231

△ Woman selling ethnic goods

here but a homestay should be possible if you can't get back to Long before dark. Regardless of what routes you take, if you do go for a do-it-yourself trek in this region keep in mind that you should not trekking alone or without a local: wandering around on remote trails in these mountains without a **guide** is foolhardy.

Xiang Kok and around

A rowdy frontier town on a remote stretch of the Mekong, **XIANG KOK** is the last river-town stop before China: the Upper Mekong scenery is fantastic. The river here is narrow, fast and studded with islets of craggy stone, and the region's remoteness gives it a real wilderness feel. Plans are already underway to open the river road from Jinghong in China to Chiang Khong in Thailand to tourists, which should give the town a major boost. Meanwhile, the local economy seems to be based on trade between Thailand and China and smuggling. The town itself is ramshackle. There's a customs post, half a dozen guest houses, a few shops and a brothel. Chinese cargo trucks transfer loads at the boat-landing before heading back to China.

From Xieng Kok you can currently only travel **downriver**. The Xieng Kok boatmen have a bad reputation for extorting money from tourists. They know well that Xieng Kok is the end of the line and many travellers need to get down to Houayxai and exit into Thailand before their visas expire. If there are no other passengers, what should be a $12 per person ride can cost $100 or more and no amount of haggling will bring the price down. Some frustrated travellers have simply returned to Muang Sing. Time, it seems, is on the boatman's side. The best bargaining technique is to pretend you do not want to go downriver at all. Spend some time chatting with the boatmen, share some cigarettes and then rhetorically ask how much it might cost if you did want to go down-river. Locals pay $12 a person but foreigners are routinely expected to pay double that.

Accommodation

Most budget travellers stay at the no-name **guest house** (❶) near the customs office above the boat-landing. The six double rooms here are passable and the toilet and (cold) shower facilities are shared. The best place in town is the *Xieng Kok Resort* (❷) on the embankment overlooking the river and landing. Built by a Thai investor, the resort has twelve comfortable, self-contained bungalows with en-suite bathrooms and charming balconies overlooking the Mekong. On the opposite side of the village are two other tourist guest houses, the somewhat dreary *Sai Thong* (❶) and Xiengkok's newest place, the nearby *Kokbohan Guest House* (❶) on the road to Muang Sing which has $1 bamboo and grass bungalows facing an open court yard. There are also a couple of dirty and dismal Chinese trucker hostels in town. Food is possible at all the guest houses but only the *Xieng Kok Resort* has a proper restaurant. Electricity in Xiang Kok is by private generators and generally runs from dusk until 9.30pm.

Muang Mom

Located on a flat stretch on the banks of the Mekong about an hour's trip north of Houayxai by speedboat, the Lao village of **MUANG MOM** is currently the only Lao town on the Mekong between Xiang Kok and Houayxai which has tourist accommodation. It is also the last town connected by road to Houayxai. There is really no reason to visit here unless you want to experience village life on the Mekong. A tiny little village, Muang Mom slept through the aborted tourist boom which occurred during the late 1990s and

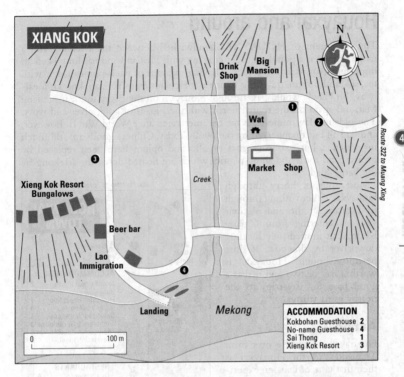

saw the construction of a huge casino on the Burmese bank and the creation of a large, tacky "Golden Triangle" tourist town at Sop Ruak on the Thai bank, where dozens of shopping complexes now stand empty and deserted. Theoretically, Muang Mom is a border crossing for Lao to cross to Burma, presumably to go to the casino. In any case it is not legal for foreigners to cross to Burma here.

Just south of Muang Mom is the village of **BAN KHWAN** on the Lao side. This is the scene of the 1967 "Opium War" fought between the upstart Shan-Chinese drug lord Khun Sa, Chinese Kuomintang opium gangs and the Royal Lao Army which was goaded into action when Khun Sa and the KMT drug barons started a major three-day slug-out at Ban Khwan. Back then, when the Golden Triangle was gaining the infamy that now earns it tourist dollars, the Lao side of the Mekong from Ban Khwan to Houayxai was said to harbour no fewer than six opium refineries.

Practicalities

Muang Mom has a noodle stall and a family-run two-storey **guest house** with twelve basic but passable rooms and shared cold-water facilities (❷). Plenty of **speedboats** are available at the village's landing for journeys upriver to Xieng Kok ($100 per boat) or down to Houayxai. By road, occasional sawngthaews leave from the landing and follow the river 20km to Don Pheung, probably the worst road you'll see in Laos. From Don Pheung there's fairly good gravel road 30km to Nam Keng from where a paved 27-kilometre road leads all the way back to Houayxai. There are speedboat landings in Don Pheung and Nam Keng.

Houayxai and around

The settlement of **HOUAYXAI**, sandwiched between the Mekong and a range of hills, is a popular border crossing with Thailand and has long been an important crossroads for traders. Driving caravans of pack-ponies laden with tea, silk and opium, travelling Chinese merchants from Yunnan, known locally as "Jin Haw", would pass through Houayxai on their way south to Chiang Mai, and again on the return north with their loads of gold, silver and ivory. The old Jin Haw mule caravans became scarce after World War II, however, and had all but disappeared by the 1960s. Today, Chinese goods are still much in evidence, but exotic cargoes of silks and opium have been replaced by greasy hand tools and shiny plastics which are floated down the Mekong by the barge-load.

Most tourists hurry through Houayxai, either rushing through to Thailand at the end of their visas or entering from Chiang Khong but immediately heading downriver by slowboat. If time permits though, Houayxai is worth a day or two and makes a good base for day-trips to the nearby **gem mines**.

Arrival

For travellers crossing over from Thailand's north, Houayxai is their first taste of Laos, an experience that usually begins in **Chiang Khong**, just across the river in Thailand, where you can absorb the sights and sounds of Houayxai from over the sluggish brown river. Aside from boat traffic up and down the Mekong, sawngthaews arrive daily from Louang Namtha.

Accommodation

Houayxai has recently had a **hotel** boom and there are now a dozen choices, all on the main road (Khamkhong Road) which is just uphill from the ferry landing. Since the older hotels haven't lowered their prices, the newer places are ironically actually better value for money. Unfortunately there aren't any really quaint family-run guest houses here, most being modern Thai-style estab-

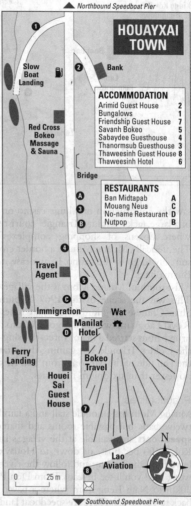

Northbound Speedboat Pier

HOUAYXAI TOWN

Slow Boat Landing

Bank

Red Cross Bokeo Massage & Sauna

Bridge

ACCOMMODATION

Arimid Guest House	2
Bungalows	1
Friendship Guest House	7
Savanh Bokeo	5
Sabaydee Guesthouse	4
Thanormsub Guesthouse	3
Thaweesinh Guest House	8
Thaweesinh Hotel	6

RESTAURANTS

Ban Midtapab	A
Mouang Neua	C
No-name Restaurant	D
Nutpop	B

Travel Agent

Immigration

Wat

Manilat Hotel

Ferry Landing

Bokeo Travel

Houei Sai Guest House

Lao Aviation

N

Southbound Speedboat Pier

0   25 m

Travellers arriving in Houayxai can strike up or down the Mekong by boat, or bus overland up Route 3 to **Louang Namtha**. Lao **visas** can be arranged on the Thai side (see p.19). Those exiting Laos here can obtain a thirty-day visa on arrival from Thai immigration (daily 8am–5.30pm) in Chiang Khong on the Thai side. Once in Chiang Khong, there are direct buses to Chiang Rai or Chiang Mai. The town's immigration station and ferry pier is directly opposite the Chiang Khong ferry pier on the Thai side which also has an immigration post. Boats shuttle you across the river in a minute for 20 Thai baht. From Houayxai there are three different boat piers, one for slow boats approximately 500m north of the ferry pier, and two for speedboats.

Slow boats leave every morning about 9am and stop overnight in Pakbeng. The fares cost $5 to Pakbeng or $10 to Louang Phabang. **Speedboats** (*heua wai*) also make the journey from Houayxai to Pakbeng ($11) and Louang Phabang ($22); crash helmets and life-vests are supposed to be provided. Don't forget to bring earplugs. The southbound speedboat pier is located at Ban Tin That, 2km downriver for boats going south. Speedboats going upriver to Xiang Kok now leave from the northbound speedboat pier at Nam Keng, a ridiculous 27km north of town. The road to Nam Keng is paved and the sawngthaew fare is 10,000K. It's important to arrive at the landings as early as possible in order to get a boat. If there are no other passengers, it may be necessary to hire the boat outright. The speedboats are fast but uncomfortable: the bottom of the boat pounds the river and the noise from the huge engine is truly deafening. Provided you have sunglasses, sunblock and good earplugs the ride is quite fun provided the journey doesn't last more than a few hours.

It's possible to take a daily **truck** up Route 3 all the way to Louang Namtha, but this is a tough trip as the road is unpaved and very dusty and it takes about eight hours. It is possible to break the trip at Vieng Phoukha, 66km short of Louang Namtha, where there is one basic guest house, the *Phongsavath* (❶). Bokeo province's only other road runs alongside the Mekong to Nam Keng (27km), Ton Pheung (57km) and Muang Mom (77km), all of which have speedboat landings. If you're headed for Xiengkok ($12 per person) the landing at Nam Keng is the best since you can always get back to Houayxai if there's no shared boat. At Nam Keng there are a dozen clothing shops and three noodle stands but no accommodation. No regular fixed service runs to Xiengkok so you just have to take your chances or hire your own boat.

lishments. One exception is the small bungalow place right above the slow-boat landing which has thatched cottages with shared facilities overlooking the river (❶).

Arimid Guest House Main road north of the ferry opposite the petrol station. *Arimid* is a collection of thatched cottages on their own small lane running between the main road and bank. The dozen cottages are quite pleasant, if a bit squeezed, with en-suite bathrooms and hot water. The restaurant is also one of the nicest in town. If you're looking for something a bit more Lao-style or are planning on staying in Houayxai a few days this is a good spot to be. ❷

Friendship Guest House Main road south of the ferry landing ☎084/211219. Located 50m south of the landing, the *Friendship* is a multi-storey modern hotel almost identical to the *Thaweesinh*

Hotel in price, standard and appearance. They also have a huge roof where you can enjoy the sunset over the Mekong. Good value. ❷–❸

Sabaydee Guest House Main road north of the ferry. A bit past the *Savanh Bokeo*, this brand-new modern-style hotel boasts spotlessly clean rooms featuring tiled en-suite bathrooms. The four back corner units offer terrific views of the Mekong. The best deal in town. ❷

Savanh Bokeo Main road north of the ferry. Just north of the *Thaweesinh*, the *Savanh Bokeo* offers about the cheapest deal in town, with its large two-, three- and four-bed rooms and shared facilities in a nice old wooden house. ❷

Thanormsub Guest House Main road north of the ferry ☏084/211095. This blue-roofed house just opposite the *Sabaydee* is also a new establishment with very good-value rooms. The house has a central passage leading to fourteen very clean, tiled rooms with en-suite bathrooms and hot water. There are no views here but five corner rooms have windows on two sides. Three rooms are also available with air-con. ❷–❸

Thaweesinh Hotel Main road north of the ferry ☏021/211502. This large, four-storey, concrete building may not have much Lao ambience but it's clean and modern with a nice rooftop patio. The hotel is popular with group tours coming across from Thailand. There's a wide selection of rooms ranging from windowless singles ($2) to air-con doubles with TV ($8). All the rooms have tiled floors and en-suite bathrooms. *Thaweesinh* also has a cheaper guest house of the same name next to the post office. ❷–❸

The Town

Houayxai boasts only two proper "sights" and one of these is best viewed from Chiang Khong across the river: the high, black walls of hilltop **Fort Carnot**, once home to troops of the French Foreign Legion and now a barracks for the Lao army; the fort is not open to visitors. Decidedly more friendly is **Wat Chom Khao Manilat**, also situated atop a hill. The gaudy modern sim is barely worth doing a lap around, but the adjacent, tall, Shan-style building, which was originally a *sim* but is now being used as a classroom for novice monks, is made of picturesquely weathered teakwood. Behind the modern *sim* is a collection of *heuan pha*, literally "cloth houses", built to store belongings of the dead. Originally, these homes for the spirits were fashioned from cloth or mulberry paper, but nowadays many are constructed from plywood – a practice unique to parts of northern Laos and northern Thailand. The top of the stairway leading up to the monastery from Houayxai's main road is a perfect place to watch the sun set. Other wats in town include Vat Keo Phonsavan Thanarom and Wat Khon Keo.

After sundown, there's also a traditional Lao **herbal sauna** run by the Red Cross in Bokeo (daily 5–9pm; sauna 10000K for 3 hr, massage 25,000 per hr) located opposite the Agriculture Forest Office just past the wooden bridge as you go north up the main road. Houayxai's only internet shop (5–9pm; 1000K per minute) is next door to the Savanh Bokeo.

Eating

Mouang Neua **restaurant** opposite the *Thaweesinh Hotel* has an English menu and specializes in tourist fare – the vegetable omelette is a must. Rustic *Nutpop*, near *Thanormsub Guest House*, does stir-fry dishes, cold beer and fruit smoothies in an outdoor setting, while nearby *Ban Midtapab* offers excellent fish and views across the Mekong. *Arimid Guest House* restaurant, opposite the bank at the north end of town, is quite good and is a comfortable place to sit and relax. There are also riverside restaurants overlooking both the ferry landing and the slowboat landing. The most popular place in town though is just a few buildings south of the old *Manilat Hotel*. It's quite large and usually very busy in the evenings so you can't miss it. Avoid the dreadful Lao-Chinese restaurant nearby which is actually a front for a "massage" parlour.

Around Houayxai: the Bokeo gem mines

While not as well known as Mogok in Burma or Pailin in Cambodia, the **gem mines** of Bokeo Province are said by some to be just as rich. Indeed, the name of the province – "baw kaew" – actually means "gem mine" and locals claim that when it rains hard, the sapphires wash right out of the hills.

Slow boats on the Mekong

Slow boats on the Mekong take two days to complete the journey between **Houayxai** and **Louang Phabang**, stopping overnight at the village of **Pakbeng** (see p.238). The boats run in both directions and there are many other private vessels leased by tour companies that do the same trip but won't pick up individual travellers. You can also do the trip by speedboat in just over six hours, but this is much less romantic.

Originally, **slow boats** (*heua sa*) were primarily for cargo and the occasional Lao passengers who relied on them for trade and transport in a part of Laos where roads are sometimes impassable. Since the Lao government eased travel restrictions allowing foreigners to ride the Mekong's antiquated fleet of diesel-powered cargo boats, thousands of tourists have made the two-day journey, most travelling downriver from Houayxai to the old royal capital. Despite the popularity of this conveyance with tourists and the huge amount of money being generated, almost no concessions have been made towards their comfort, save for a ticket booths at each end of the journey. Although this used to be a fun trip with a handful of travellers hopping a ride on the daily cargo boat downriver, in recent years, during high-season, it is not unusual for the boatmen to pack as many as eighty tourists into a single vessel. If this isn't your cup of tea, simply do the trip in reverse, upriver from Louang Phabang to Houayxai, where the same boat returning is virtually empty.

Although there's a general lack of comfort, most travellers agree that the journey is one of those once-in-a-lifetime experiences. The riverbanks along the Mekong are sparsely populated, though the forest is not as pristine as one might imagine. Logging and decades of slash-and-burn agriculture have left their mark, and, on the more accessible slopes and summits, trees have been supplanted by rows of corn stalks and banana trees. Of as much interest are the glimpses into local **village life**. Fisher-folk utilizing bamboo fish-traps and prospectors panning for gold can be seen among the sandbars and jagged rocks that make this stretch of the Mekong a treacherous obstacle course. Along the way, boats also often call briefly at tiny villages situated where tributaries intersect with the river, and villagers take the opportunity to hawk fish, game and other local products to passengers and crew. If you want to help these rural people, buy something from them – even if it's only a bunch of bananas.

Boat **fares** are payable in Thai baht, dollars or kip and the fare from Houayxai is $5.50 to Pakbeng or $11 to Louang Phabang. Once the cargo has been loaded, passengers sit wherever they can find space. Bring along food and bottled water, as none is available on board. Sunblock and an umbrella are also advisable if you plan to sit on the roof. Despite local lore that the roof is supposedly off-limits to women because the guardian spirit of the boat may become offended, the boatmen don't object. A closed-in area on the stern serves as the toilet.

Deposits of corundum (aluminium oxide in its crystalline form, the substance which rubies and sapphires are made of) are plentiful around Houayxai and, when not working their rice fields, farmers take to the gem fields, digging shallow pits into the red earth until the yearly monsoon fills their excavations with rainwater. In 1996, a Danish firm won a contract from the Lao government to mine a 72-square-kilometre tract of land near Houayxai for twenty years. The fenced-off Danish mine is closed to casual visitors, but watching the antics of part-time prospectors, who have turned the land surrounding the mine into a cratered moonscape, is an interesting half-day diversion.

Tuk-tuks can be hired for the half-hour ride to the gem fields for a few dollars per person, or Bokeo Travel, across from the *Houei Sai Hotel*, can arrange the use of a Land Rover for about $20 for half a day. The trip is sometimes combined with a visit to one of the primitive gem-cutting **factories** on the outskirts of town. These small-scale operations depend on part-time prospectors for their supply of rough gemstones and all but shut down during the rainy season. A handful of shops in town by the ferry crossing offer cut gemstones with wide and simple facets. Unlike in Thailand, where most Lao gems are eventually marketed, the gem merchants of Houayxai have so far not succumbed to hard-sell tactics. Prospective buyers can spend time fingering stones and chatting with the merchants and then walk away without making a purchase, and this is probably what you should do unless you are an expert and can discern quality stones from inferior ones.

Pakbeng and around

A single lane dirt road winding up the side of a mountain, the bustling, frontier riverport of **PAKBENG** is the halfway point between Houayxai and Louang Phabang, and the only sizable town or road-head along the 300-kilometre stretch of river between them. As slow boats don't travel the Mekong after dark, a night here is unavoidable if you're travelling this way – a taste of back-country Laos complete with hilltribes and rustic accommodation. Stumbling off the slow boat at the end of a long day, the ramshackle settlement of wood-scrap, corrugated tin and hand-painted signs that constitutes the port area can be a bit of a culture shock. Since Pakbeng is many travellers' first night in Laos, the expression on a lot of faces is "What have I got myself into?".

Don't worry, Pakbeng is only typical of the northern backwoods. Provided you don't miss your morning boat you'll be sipping lattés in Louang Phabang in no time.

The Town

Although first impressions of the town are generally unfavourable, Pakbeng is actually a very interesting town. Once extremely poor, it is now growing rapidly, with even a few big mansions going up. The town's change of fortune is due to its role as an important **trading post** as it's the only road-head leading into the interior in these parts. Goods from Thailand come down the river from Houayxai and then make their way up into the interior from here. Tourism has also been a big boon for the town with the slow boats alone disgorging up to 100 hungry backpackers a day.

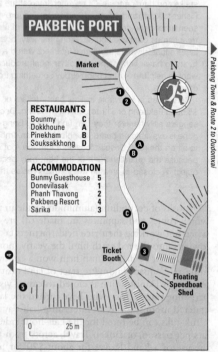

PAKBENG PORT

Market

N

Pakbeng Town & Route 2 to Oudomxai

RESTAURANTS
Bounmy	C
Dokkhoune	A
Pinekham	B
Souksakkhong	D

ACCOMMODATION
Bunmy Guesthouse	5
Donevilasak	1
Phanh Thavong	2
Pakbeng Resort	4
Sarika	3

Ticket Booth

Floating Speedboat Shed

0   25 m

Since most tourists to Pakbeng come by slow boat, arriving late and leaving early, many people think the port area around the landing is Pakbeng. In fact, the real town lies past the top of the hill and stretches for a good kilometre along the main road which follows the Mekong before turning north to Muang Beng and Oudomxai. The town is well worth a wander and has a couple of pleasant **wats** overlooking the Mekong. There's no accommodation or restaurants in the old town although you will find a few noodle ladies and some stalls selling sausages and sticky rice. Along the only street are a shop selling hand-beaten silver jewellery and the "UN Harmony Income Generation Project" – a shack selling handicrafts and nicely made local clothes and purses under the slogan "Be Lao, Buy Lao".

The small **market** is located right at the top of the landing road past the Donevilasak where the road turns sharply right towards the town proper. There's not a lot happening here but it's worth visiting and there are some *pho* stalls. The market convenes every morning and goes most of the day, and is frequented by Hmong women and children, although it appears that traditional dress has gone out of fashion among the Hmong in this vicinity. Heading out of town in either direction will quickly take you to very poor, traditional villages where you'll soon be the centre of attention. The road towards the resort takes you to just such a village in no time.

Pakbeng does not yet have any trekking or organized outdoor-adventure tours but this doesn't mean there's nothing to do in the area. The owner of the *Bunmy* guest house can organize various activities on request, including fishing trips on the Mekong, boat trips to villages and guides for walks to the surrounding ethnic villages and forests.

Practicalities

Slow boats stop at the landing at the bottom of the port road. **Speedboats** pull up to the floating speedboat shed which for some reason is well away from the concrete steps up the embankment, forcing arrivals to climb the muddy hillside instead. **Sawngthaews** from Oudomxai stop first in Pakbeng town and then down at the port area where all the accommodation is.

The town has a lot of small **shops** selling imported foods and household products, since it's an important distribution centre for the interior. There are also several pharmacies. Electricity in Pakbeng is by generator from 6pm until 10pm.

Moving on from Pakbeng

If you're continuing to **Louang Phabang** or **Houayxai** by **slow boat** (see p.237), you should be down at the landing before 8am to avoid being left behind. Going downriver, some captains stop briefly at the caves at **Pak Ou** (see p.173) before Louang Phabang, charging each passenger who disembarks a couple of thousand kip extra. If you're up for it, this does work out cheaper than chartering a boat from Louang Phabang, but it leaves little time to for exploring.

Speedboats leave to go up and down the river throughout the morning. There's a government-run ticket booth above the boat landing that controls all the traffic so it's impossible to bargain your own deal with the boat drivers, as much as they'd be willing. The foreigners' speedboat fare is $12 to either Louang Phabang or Houayxai.

Sawngthaews up Route 2 to Muang Houn, Muang Beng and Oudomxai leave from outside the *Sarika* between 7am and 9am, depending on how many passengers they have.

Accommodation

Once the boat pulls in, don't waste any time securing a **room**. From the landing, the majority of guest houses are just up the hill well before the town itself. Walking up the road you'll find half a dozen guest houses all in the $2 range. They're all pretty much the same: a very basic wooden room with a bed, mosquito net and a fan, and with shared cold-water bathrooms out back.

Bunmy Guest House Turn left from the boat landing and walk about 200m. The only guest house not on the main road, this comprises three big houses right next to the Mekong. The owner is currently replacing the original buildings with better two-storey concrete and wood houses. The newly rebuilt unit has eleven tiled rooms with en-suite bathrooms. There are still cheaper basic rooms with shared facilities in the original buildings and a nice open restaurant with a two-tier deck over the Mekong. ❶–❸

Donevilasak The last place at the top of the hill. Very similar to *Phanh Thavong* next door, but it has the benefit of being a real house rather than just something that was thrown up in a hurry during the tourist boom. ❶

Pakbeng Resort About 800m down the road running west from the landing. The most luxurious place in these parts with eighteen deluxe luxury bungalows on stilts with all mod-cons including

hot water. The Lao-style bungalows are connected by a beautifully built covered walkway which leads to the reception. The resort even has its own boat pier and fancy restaurant with uniformed staff. And you thought this was the middle of nowhere. ❽

Phanh Thavong Next to the *Donevilasak* at the top of the hill. This two-storey house probably has the best atmosphere of any of the cheap guest houses along the main road. The rooms are basic with shared facilities out back but there's a very nice upstairs balcony overlooking the street and a small breakfast place downstairs. ❶

Sarika A big three-storey concrete building right above the landing. This is the largest guest house in town with fifteen rooms all with cold-water en-suite bathrooms. Because the *Sarika* is aimed at package groups who book in large blocks it is rather over-priced and you can't bargain a discount, even when they are empty. ❹

Eating

Because of the fierce competition, many of Pakbeng's **restaurants** now boast tablecloths and even candles, although the most you can expect in these parts is still just a decent stir-fry. The best places are on the eastern side of the street and have Mekong views. *Dokkhoune*, *Pinekham* and *Souksakkhong* are all pleasant, and the *Bounmy* across the street has a bit of candle-lit atmosphere. The restaurant at the *Sarika* is the most formal and has a big balcony overlooking the river. The best option is out at the *Pakbeng Resort*, and the outdoor patio bar there with a view of the Mekong is a great place for a sundowner. In the morning, take-away submarine sandwich makers line the road down to the boat landing – *Pinekham* restaurant also does good take-away sandwiches.

Route 2 – Pakbeng to Oudomxai

Trucks up and down the Nam Beng river valley between Pakbeng and Oudomxai (see p.215) run daily between 8am and 9am, leaving from the foot of the hill. The 150-kilometre-long wreck of a road passes through Hmong and Tai Leu villages, and takes about eight hours. There are two very basic guest houses in **MUANG HOUN**, a small town 52km north of Pakbeng known for its textiles. The inhabitants, perhaps descendants of Tai Yuan who migrated here from what is now northern Thailand, continue to weave in a style that looks remarkably like that of old Chiang Mai. During the Seventies, Muang Houn was the site of a military base that trained and indoctrinated disenfranchised Thai students who would later return to Thailand and take part in the communist insurgency in "red zone" frontier provinces such as

Loei and Nan. Muang Houn may only have very basic accommodation and food, but it can serve as an off-the-beaten track basecamp for self-organized trekking.

The Nam Ou River Valley

After a few days of lounging in Louang Phabang's French bistros, sipping imported wine and munching on watercress salad, it's easy to forget that there are places relatively near which offer very little in the way of creature comforts, no matter how many kip you are willing to spend. The **Nam Ou River** which starts on the China border, drains all of Phongsali province and flows down through western Louang Phabang province to meet the Mekong above Louang Phabang, is just such a place. Much of the Phongsali province watershed is devoid of roads and still well covered with old-growth forests, and the river and its many tributaries remain in many ways as they were when nineteenth-century French explorers passed through.

The river begins its journey on the southern flanks of the mountains separating Laos and Yunnan in China. This northernmost part of Laos, Phongsali province, is hemmed in by high mountains on three sides, and the Ou River is joined by no less than eight major tributaries before entering Louang Phabang province and beginning its final run down to the Mekong. Two of these tributaries, the Nam Khang and the Nam Houn, pass within the **Phou Den Din NBCA**, a huge nature reserve running along the border of Vietnam. The main city of the upper Nam Ou is **Phongsali**, the provincial capital. The town of **Hat Sa** effectively acts as Phongsali's riverport on the Nam Ou. The other two important towns on the Ou River are Muang Khoua and Nong Khiaw, both highway junctions. **Muang Khoua** sits astride the river where **Route 4** continues from Oudomxai to Dien Bien Phu, Vietnam, and **Nong Khiaw** is located where **Route 1** crosses the river on it's way from Oudomxai to Phan Province in the extreme northeast. All of these towns have tourist accommodation and can be reached by road or by river travel along the Ou.

An important Mekong tributary, the Nam Ou holds a cherished place in Lao lore as the original route followed by Louang Phabang's founding father, Khun Lo, and later by Fa Ngum, the warrior-king, as he headed towards Louang Phabang to claim the throne and found the Kingdom of a Million Elephants.

The Phongsali Loop

The **Phongsali Loop** is a popular northern Laos travellers' route which starts and ends at either Louang Phabang or Oudomxai and involves a combination of river travel on the Nam Ou and tough road travel between Phongsali and Oudomxai.

Many travellers do the first part of the loop as far as Phongsali by boat up the Nam Ou River from Louang Phabang, taking in Nong Khiaw, Muang Khoua, Muang Ngoi and Hat Sa en route and then do the return portion by road (the account below follows this sequence). You can also shorten the loop by exiting at either Nong Khiaw or Muang Khoua, both of which have daily sawngthaews returning to Oudomxai. More than a few people never even finish the loop, deciding that the boat journey up the Nam Ou to Hat Sa is so beautiful that they want to return the same way.

Pakmong and Nam Bak

The road route from Louang Phabang to Nong Khiaw takes about two and a half hours. Well-maintained Route 13 takes you north out of Louang Phabang, hugging the Nam Ou River for much of the way. Over halfway along, the road veers away from the river and into a wide valley, passing through **Hmong villages** whose inhabitants have been resettled here from the highlands by the Lao government in an ongoing programme to control and assimilate them (see Contexts, p.374). The majority of villages along this stretch are located far from the road, but periodic glimpses of the people who inhabit them reveal something about the labour-intensive lives they lead. When not engaged in cultivating their teetering hilltop gardens, the highlanders spend daylight hours hunting and gathering in the forest. Women carry firewood using ingeniously designed back-pack baskets fitted with a wooden yoke and head-strap to distribute the weight, and almost every male above the age of 15 can be seen shouldering a firearm of some sort, long-barrelled muzzle-loading rifles and the occasional M1 carbine.

Straddling the junction of Route 1 and Route 13, **PAKMONG** roughly separates the northeast from the northwest. There's no reason to stay in Pakmong, but it's a key spot for bus and sawngthaew transfers – whether you're headed northwest to Oudomxai, east to Viang Thong or south to Louang Phabang. There are direct sawngthaews from Louang Phabang and Oudomxai straight to Nong Khiaw but vehicles that don't turn east often just dump you at the junction town of Pakmong, where you'll have to change vehicles.

Like Pakmong, the quiet settlement of **NAM BAK**, situated in the Nam Bak river valley just a fifteen-minute drive east from the Pakmong junction, loses out to the much more dramatic scenery of its neighbour, Nong Khiaw, further downriver. Despite the fact most travellers head straight for Nong Khiaw or Muang Ngoi, three guest houses line the road – all basic, two-storey buildings. Handiest for the market and onward transport is the *Vanmisay* (❶). Its handful of cramped but clean rooms are up a creaky flight of steps where you'll see a small balcony overlooking the road; the bathroom and basic bathing facilities are around the back. A noodle and coffee shop sits across from the dusty market, where you'll also find the queue for Nong Khiaw-bound sawngthaews. From here it's a quick, thirty-minute ride to Nong Khiaw, via pretty villages with shaggy thatch-roofed houses surrounded by all manner of fruit trees.

Nong Khiaw

Resting at the foot of a striking red-faced cliff, amid towering blue-green limestone escarpments, the dusty town of **NONG KHIAW** on the banks of the Nam Ou River lies smack in the middle of some of the most dramatic scenery in Indochina. Local entrepreneurs are gradually realizing that there's money to be made from the backpackers who use the town as a hub, and it's well on its way to becoming a popular tourist destination on its own merits.

The most scenic route to Nong Khiaw though is the six-hour **boat trip** up the Nam Ou from Louang Phabang, one of the best journeys in Laos. Since most locals now prefer to travel to Nong Khiaw by road (on Route 13), catching a passenger boat on the Nam Ou isn't as easy as it used to be. The best method is get a group of fellow travellers together and hire a passenger boat ($50 for 10 people). Passenger boats going up river to Muang Ngoi (1hr) and Muang Khoua (5hr) also leave from the landing.

There are frequent departures to **Pakmong**, but sawngthaews headed for **Vieng Thong** are very scarce. There's a daily bus that comes through about 10pm from Louang Phabang en route to **Phonsavan** but if you want to make the trip in daylight you have to do it in stages by sawngthaew.

The Town

Although the old town stretches a kilometre along a dirt road parallel to Route 1, all of Nong Khiaw's tourist facilities are located by the big bridge over the Nam Ou. Here, at the western end of the bridge, you'll find the boat mooring, the bus lot and most of the guest houses and restaurants. At the eastern end of the bridge on the opposite bank is **Ban Lao**, a village of about two dozen homes which also has a couple of guest houses and a very popular tourist restaurant. From the western side of the bridge, walking south down the main street takes you west through the old town, its dirt street lined with dusty old wooden buildings, until you emerge back on Route 1 about 2km west of the bridge.

Though there's very little to see in the town itself, Nong Khiaw makes a good base for **day-trips** in the scenic surrounding countryside. Aside from day-trips to Muang Ngoi, there's a cave just 1km to the east along Route 1 which has a big staircase leading up to the entrance and charges 300K. There are also hill-tribe villages in the area including Khammu settlements, but to reach these you'll really need a local guide.

Accommodation and eating

Nong Khiaw now boasts eight simple **guest houses** and several **tourist restaurants**. The *Sunset* is the town's best tourist restaurant with a great sun-deck and lovely views as well as some very good food. A couple of traveller's cafés can be found just west of the *Philasouk*, both of which do passable stir-fries and coffee. The big no-name restaurant right over the water next to the western end of the bridge is a very pleasant spot to sit with a big open deck and good views of the mountains and river.

Manypoon At junction of the main street and Route 1 near the bridge. This rather endearing guest house has seven simple rooms in a lovely house with a small garden, and is arguably the best value in town. The upstairs rooms are the nicest and there's a small balcony with a fine view east and another little balcony looking north. ●

Phayboun Route 1, a short walk to the west of the bridge. Built for group tours, *Phayboun* was originally just a wooden building but a new concrete wing has been added giving it a total of twenty rooms in two buildings. The rooms here are all a cut above the rest, especially those in the new wing which all feature en-suite bathrooms. ●

Philasouk Next to the bridge opposite the bus stop. A good choice with a dozen rooms in a big, old, wooden house. The rooms are basic but comfortable and the shared bathing facilities are tiled and clean. Aside from the good location the house has genuine atmosphere. ●

Sai Nam Ou Right over the river by the boat landing. Favoured by some budget backpackers as it's right next to the river, *Sai Nam Ou* is basically a big shack thrown together out of nipa and bamboo. The deck at least has a million-dollar view of the river and karsts. ●

Somnyot At the corner leading down to the landing. This new building with a tin roof and seven rooms is a good choice if you don't like wooden guest houses: the *Somnyot* has concrete walls. Rooms are clean with big windows and are on par with the *Manypoon*. ●

Sunset Across the river, the *Sunset* is the "in" place with backpackers largely because of its excellent restaurant and lovely two-level sun-deck overlooking the river. Definitely come here to eat but for accommodation you can do a lot better, even at the *Mexay* (●), just 10m up the path. ●

Slow boats on the Nam Ou

Take a boat on the **Nam Ou** and the descriptions of nineteenth-century French explorers spring to life from the pages of their journals. For many people, the inconvenience and unpredictability of the journey is more than made up for by the pristine beauty of the land and the hospitality of the people who inhabit it. The southern leg of the journey is the six-hour ride between Louang Phabang and Nong Khiaw which is wildly scenic, especially the karst forests around Nong Khiaw and Muang Ngoi. Closer to Louang Phabang, where the river follows Route 13, extensive logging and slash-and-burn agriculture have stripped the surrounding mountains: only where the slopes are too rocky or too steep for cultivation have stands of forest been left intact. In an effort at reforestation, however, rows of young teak trees, recognizable by their enormous leaves, have been planted. After the road leaves the river, the scenery takes a turn for the spectacular, with vertical limestone peaks and pristine little white-sand beaches.

Upriver from Nong Khiaw the scenery continues to impress, possibly even surpassing that of the stretch below Nong Khiaw, the river snaking through impenetrable jungle. Because many of the surrounding mountains are simply too steep for slash-and-burn agriculture, the forests have been left virtually untouched. When the river is not too high and fast, this leg is also blessed with shelves of squeaky-clean beach, perfect for taking a lazy swim and admiring the dramatic scenery. However, this primeval landscape lasts only a third of the distance to Muang Khoua and is then replaced by arable hills with a beaten, domesticated air about them. The journey between Nong Khiaw and Muang Khoua takes approximately five hours.

During the **monsoon** season, if the road to Phongsali is washed away, taking a boat up the Nam Ou is the only way to continue north from Muang Khoua. Every rainy season, transport slows to a crawl in the northern province of Phongsali, which is why its rivers are still widely plied by small boats. Beyond Muang Khoua, it's another 100km to Hat Sa, the last town of any size on the Nam Ou until U Thai, far to the northeast. The mountainous scenery on the Muang Khoua–Hat Sa leg doesn't rival the stretch of river on either side of Nong Khiaw, the slopes having long ago been cleared, cultivated and left fallow. Gracefully drooping thickets of bamboo have now replaced all of the old-growth forest, but here and there a solitary behemoth survives, conveying some idea of the majestic heights that the now-vanished canopy must once have reached.

Passenger boats continuing up the Nam Ou River beyond Hat Sa are few and far between, but it is possible to charter a boat to explore Laos's northernmost corner. The going price for an all-day boat trip shouldn't be more than $40. North of Hat Sa there's no formal accommodation but it should be possible to find lodging in any village.

Muang Ngoi

Tiny **MUANG NGOI** on the right bank of the Nam Ou has already surpassed larger Nong Khiaw and Muang Khoua in popularity and is attracting lots of travellers, many of whom are lulled into staying a week or more. Located an hour's boat ride north of Nong Khiaw, Muang Ngoi is a totally idyllic and friendly village set amongst spectacular scenery. Although it's easy enough to just hang out in the village sipping coffee and swinging in a hammock, there are a lot of **activities** to pursue here, including trekking with the local guide to hilltribe villages, canoeing on the river, organized fishing trips, making outings to the caves and waterfall and just generally exploring on the islands and beaches on either side of the river. The scenery is superb, easily rivalling Vang Viang.

Day-trips out of Muang Ngoi are also easy to organize: just ask at your guest house. Fishing- and boat-trips to the waterfall and caves cost about $1 per person. For more serious trekking, the local school teacher, Mr Kongkeo, acts as a guide for interested foreigners and charges about $10 a day per person for multi-day treks which is quite expensive, but his treks get rave reviews.

Accommodation and eating

Muang Ngoi is a one-street village, the main dirt lane running from the landing to the foot of Pha Boom Hill. All of the bungalow places are along the river bank facing west over the Nam Ou. Behind the village is a football field and beyond that the village rice paddies. The main street has a number of restaurants in wooden houses lining the main drag and in the afternoon and evening enterprising locals set up little food stalls selling banana pancakes and Lao snacks such as green crepes with chopped greens and peanut sauce.

Many **accommodation places** only have a grand total of three rooms and none have en-suite bathrooms or hot water. The best are those with large bamboo decks affording a view of the river: five-room *Pha Boom Noi* (❶) at the extreme end of the village has the best views of the valley. If the rooms are all full, *Pha Bou Mai* (❶) right next door will do. Friendly three-room *Khamlak* (❶) is also good with a nice deck and three more units currently under construction, while *Meleka* (❶) has the nicest sundeck in town and three units for rent. *Boupha* (❶) right next door has five rooms and a pleasant deck as well as the town's only free-standing bungalow. If staying in a flimsy nipa bungalow isn't your style, try *Sai Lom* (❶) which features five small rooms in a proper house as well as an excellent sundeck with superb views. *Lattanovongsa* guest house (❶) is also in a two-storey wooden house on the main street just above the landing.

Virtually all of the town's bungalow operations serve **food**, indeed it is their chief money earner. However since most of them are trying to prepare ten different orders at once in a primitive hut with no electric lights and only an open fire to cook over, the service can be pretty slow. If you're in a hurry you'll get faster service at any of the village's proper **restaurants** along the main street. One of the best is *Lattanovongsa* which has a large dining room partially made out of old bombs. The *Ning Ning* right by the landing is one of the biggest and best organized places. There are half a dozen other sit-down restaurants along the main street but the *Khone Sa Vahn* "natural restaurant" around the corner towards the wooden bridge is a cute place also worth seeking out. For al fresco dining, *Sai Lom* and *Meleka* have the nicest sundecks and are glorious places to just sit and take in the views.

Muang Khoua

Located on the left bank of the Nam Ou where Route 4 crosses the river on its way to Vietnam, **MUANG KHOUA** is an important crossroads and outpost in this remote part of Phongsali province. The town itself is built on a steep hillside where the Nam Phak river enters the Nam Ou, and is named for an ancient rust-clad suspension bridge which connects Muang Khoua with the village of Natun. A stroll out onto the high, swaying structure is worth it for the view, but is a stomach-fluttering experience and not for the vertigo-prone. The area around Muang Khoua is rugged and hilly but the surrounding hills have been clear-cut and are covered in bamboo and secondary growth. At one time Route 4 continued across a pontoon-bridge over the Nam Ou here but it has been destroyed. Muang Khoua's principal export is split bamboo shoots, which are laid out in the sun along the steep road leading up from the river. Once dry, the shoots are packed up and trucked to Vietnam. For information on getting to Vietnam from here, see the box below.

Practicalities

Muang Khoua can be reached by road or river. Trucks stop at the town square which is actually a triangle. There's a visitor-information booth here and across the street is a Lane Xang **bank** service unit. Off the main road, a long curving road leads down to the boat landing on the pebble beach along the Nam Ou. The dirt road on the opposite bank is the other half of Route 4.

If you plan to stay in Muang Khoua over a weekend, there are **trekking** possibilities using a local teacher as a guide. Mr Khamman Xayavong teaches English at the local secondary school in Natun and offers guided treks to Phu Noi, Akha, Tai Dam and Khammu villages. He charges $10 per person for his services: ask at the *Nam Ou Guest House* where he posts an advertisement. Muang Khoua has electricity from 6 to 10pm. There are no restaurants in town, but all the guest houses can provide **food**.

Leaving Muang Khoua

Passenger **boats** bound for Hat Sa upriver and Nong Khiaw downriver leave most days. If you miss the boat or want to hire one, there is a choice of fast or slow boats on these legs. While the river is navigable year round by passenger boat, fast boats don't make the journey when the water is low. The fixed passenger rate is around $4 per person either direction. A slow boat (seating twelve) or a speedboat (seating eight) can be hired for $20–25, depending on your bargaining skills. The journey takes five hours by slow boat or less than two hours by fast.

Trucks to Oudomxai ($1.50) leave from in front of the police station early in the morning, the dusty trip taking approximately three hours. At Km 62, the T-junction leading to Oudomxai and Phongsali, is the very busy village of **SIN SAI** where you'll find a decent little guest house over the river which can be used as a base for trekking in this ethnically diverse area. To the east, it had been announced at the time of writing that the Vietnam border was scheduled to open for third-country nationals so there should soon be a service from Muang Khoua to the border at Muang Mai.

Accommodation

Muang Khoua currently has six **guest houses**. At the town square opposite the bank is the two-storey *Sing Savanh* (❶) which is basic but clean and has newly re-fitted bathrooms. To the right, down the path to the suspension bridge over the Nam Phak is *Ketsana* (⊕088/412065; ❶), comprising two houses, one old, one new, which have been joined together. The rooms here are the best and cleanest of the budget guest houses and the location next to the Nam Phak is nice. The most popular backpacker option is the *Guest House Nam Ou* (❶). Like the *Sing Savanh*, the rooms are basic but clean, and you can't beat this funky old guest house's terrific location balanced right on the hillside looking down on the river and landing. The owner, who speaks both English and French, has just built a long wooden staircase down the hillside to the landing road so you no longer need to find your way up the hill. If you've arrived by truck just follow the yellow signs from the square.

If *Nam Ou* is full and you want to be on the river, *Sengali* (❶) just up the landing road has passable if somewhat grungy rooms in a rickety two-storey with a nice new covered verandah. Room #3 has its own balcony with a terrific view of the river. At the very top of the road on the main street is the fanciest place in town, the brand-new *Muang Khoua Hotel* (❷), built by a Chinese-Lao investor. This palatial red-roofed building features a grand spiral staircase outside, huge windows and a terrific rooftop patio with great views of the river. Directly opposite, the far more humble *Manichan* (❶) has very basic but clean rooms with shared facilities for $1 a bed.

Hat Sa

The village of **HAT SA** consists of barely sixty homes, most of which are constructed from the ubiquitous bamboo and palm thatch, although concrete construction has already reached even this remote outpost. Most travellers bypass Hat Sa since they're either in a hurry to start downriver or they've come up from Nong Khiaw and have already had their fill of rustic riverside accommodation. But for those looking to experience the trials, hardships and romance that greeted wayfarers of yesteryear, Hat Sa and the villages further up the Nam Ou are about as far off the beaten track as you can get and worth exploring, especially if you find Nong Khiaw and Muang Ngoi too touristy. Hat Sa is reached in five hours by passenger boat from Muang Khoua ($4): the same trip downriver only takes about four hours. If you're rushed for time, by speedboat it's less than two hours from Muang Khoua, but if you've come to Laos to see and appreciate the country you should really stick to the "slow" passenger boats. Depending on water levels, Hat Sa is about the northernmost Nam Ou town served by speedboats, but it's possible to continue upriver by passenger boat.

Practicalities

Accommodation is very basic although it shouldn't be long before the kind of changes taking place in Muang Khoua reach here. Hat Sa has no electricity yet: the shops near the river sell cheap Chinese torches and batteries. **Food** at Hat Sa consists of fried sticky rice at your guest house or noodles at one of the huts near the river.

Sawngthaews to Phongsali ($1) leave before noon from the landing. Although it's only a twenty-kilometre trip, it takes an hour to reach Phongsali, which is on the other side of the mountains.

Phou Den Din NBCA

Phou Den Din is Laos's northernmost NBCA and runs along the Vietnam border for over 100km. The scenery here is rugged and mountainous, rising up to the peaks in the Phou Den Din range which reach heights of over 1800m and form the border with Vietnam. The 1310-square-kilometre park is said to contain Asian elephant, Asiatic black bear as well as leopards and tigers. This is one of Laos's most inaccessible NBCAs and at present the only way to get in here is by organizing an expedition by pirogue as far up the Nam Ou as possible and then continuing in by foot.

Phongsali

The town of **PHONGSALI**, perched just below the peak of Phou Fa ("Sky Mountain"), looks and feels every bit the capital of Laos's northernmost province. The altitude gained becomes apparent once the sun drops below the horizon and the chill sets in. On clear nights, as soon as the lights go out, the view of the heavens is unparalleled. The crisp air seems to amplify the stellar glow and the Milky Way is splashed across the sky like a giant, luminescent cloud.

After either the three-day river trip from Louang Phabang or the tortuous road from Oudomxai, visitors usually opt to spend a couple of nights in Phongsali to rest up. Happily, it's an engaging place with an invigorating climate and comparatively comfortable accommodation, the perfect antidote for those suffering from travel fatigue.

A wide slice of terrain wedged between China's Yunnan and Vietnam's Lai Chau provinces, Phongsali would surely be a part of China today were it not for the covetous nineteenth-century French. During the Second Indochina War, Phongsali came under heavy Chinese influence, a fact evident in the fortress-like former Chinese consulate, now the *Phou Fa Hotel*. It was during this time also that much of the province was stripped of its hardwood forests, compensation for China's support for the Pathet Lao. The town's inhabitants are made up of the Theravada Buddhist, Tibeto-Burman speaking Phu Noi people and the Chinese Haw, descendants of Yunnanese traders who annually drove caravans of pack-ponies south into old Siam.

The Town

On a slope directly behind the *Phongsali Hotel* is the town's **old quarter**. A wander through these friendly but medieval-looking lanes is like stepping back in time. Phu Noi grannies, wearing their traditional white leggings, sun themselves with one eye shut and the other on the look-out for free-range fowl, lest they pilfer the rice, soybeans and peppers left drying on mats by the roadside. Haw men wearing flappy Chinese trousers lead horses down the broken cobblestone lanes. Interspersed among the squat houses of mud bricks and rough-hewn planks are a few architectural standouts, including one distinctly Chinese building with a beautifully carved **wooden facade** that looks like it belongs on the back streets of Kunming. The quarter's three main streets run parallel for a stretch and then converge at a basketball court-cum-market from which leads Phongsali's main commercial thoroughfare, a tidy street of low shop-houses, some with roofs constructed of oil drums hammered flat and laid out like shingles. Situated on the opposite bank of the town's green bathing pond is **Wat Kaew**, the local monastery. Anyone interested in seeing what Phongsali's ethnic groups dressed like before the influx of cheap "Western-style" clothing from China can pay a visit to Phongsali's **museum**, located across from the *Phongsali Hotel*. The traditional costumes of some of Laos's more obscure groups – the Lolo, the Pala and the Loma among them – are displayed on whimsical wooden mannequins with painted gourds for heads.

Outside of town, it's possible to do a short hike to two **ethnic villages**. Heading west on the track just below the *Phou Fa Hotel* will bring you to two Phu Noi villages of bamboo and thatch huts: Khoun Souk Noi, located about 5km outside Phongsali and, some 4km further, Khoun Souk Louang. Both villages are known locally for their rice-liquor production, and, depending on how you present yourself, you may be invited to partake of a shot or two.

Practicalities

Card-operated long-distance **telephones** are located in front of the post **office**. The bank opposite the post office will exchange US dollars, Thai baht, Chinese yuan and travellers' cheques into kip. There is electricity from 6pm to 10pm.

Passenger vehicles leave at around 7am from the bus lot in front of the museum for the nine-hour journey south to Oudomxai ($4). Pick-ups and sawngthaews to Hat Sa (3000K) leave in the morning and cover the twenty-kilometre distance in an hour. There are north-bound vehicles but the border-crossing to China is not open to third-country nationals. If there's no direct vehicle to go north to U Thai, Ban Pakha or Bosao, it's better to take a vehicle to Ban Boun Nua, 40km southwest of Phongsali, and then get a connection from there.

Accommodation

Laksoun Rustic-looking *Laksoun* catches the overflow of the *Phongsali Hotel* opposite as well as beeping and revving noises from the bus station. Accommodation is in double rooms with shared bath, and the restaurant does Lao food with rare flair. ❶

Phongsali Guest House Located 500m west of the post office, this newish guest house, though somewhat isolated, is much quieter than the competition. Accommodation consists of two- and three-bed rooms with shared bath. Food available on request. ❶

Phongsali Hotel Four-storey block opposite the bus station, which can be noisy early in the morning. The rather tatty rooms come with three or four beds and shared bath. The downstairs restaurant is worth checking out for its good Chinese food, especially the house speciality *phat mi kawp*, crispy fried noodles. ❶

Phou Fa Hotel This renovated former Chinese consulate, near the immigration office, has some atmosphere (including high brick walls and an underground bunker), but is a bit overpriced. Single and double rooms with en-suite bath are small and dank. A "beer garden" on the premises has a view all the way to Oudomxai. ❹

Phongsali to Oudomxai

Regardless of which direction you travel this route, it's a long, hard journey requiring a total of nine gruelling hours in a sawngthaew or truck ($4). This is unfortunate, as the view from inside the covered bed of a sawngthaew is almost zilch, especially when the vehicle is crowded. If you are lucky to get a seat with a clear view, however, you are in for some unforgettable sights. This road passes through some prime **Akha territory**, and the tribal women use the thoroughfare to hike between villages and conduct trade. It's very common in fact to see groups of Akha women parading their wonderful apparel along the roadsides. A few of the villages actually straddle the road and afford fleeting snapshots of Akha life: women displaying glittering headdresses and betel-stained smiles, men shouldering long-barrelled muskets, and gaggles of gaping kids clad only in a layer of ochre-coloured dust. If for the entire ride you are stuffed into the tarp-covered bed of a pick-up, then a tranquillizer is suggested.

Another option is to break the journey at the town of **BAN BOUN TAI** and spend a day trekking through the villages you'd otherwise pass through without seeing. Located 80km (three hours' drive) south of Phongsali, Ban Boun Tai is a large village, often frequented by the inhabitants of nearby Akha villages. Populated by lowland Lao, the village itself is pretty unremarkable but, if you spend a whole day here, it is possible to **trek** into an Akha village on the main road some 15km south. Treks out here can be arranged with the owner of the village's only restaurant. Sawngthaews from Phongsali to Oudomxai arrive at Ban Boun Tai late in the morning and stop at a small store where the proprietor can point you to the no-name **guest house** (❶) that has doubles with mosquito net and shared toilet and bath. A short walk from the store stands the town's only **restaurant**, which serves the usual noodles but can sometimes do fried fish dishes on request. When departing from Ban Boun Tai it is best to park yourself outside the small store (late morning if you're going south, afternoon if going north) and wait. Make sure you flag down the sawngthaew; otherwise it won't stop. Hitching a ride on a passing truck is also possible, but drivers will expect to be paid for the favour. There is no electricity in Ban Boun Tai.

Travel details

Buses and sawngthaews

Hat Sa to: Phongsali (2hr).
Louang Namtha to: Boten (4 daily; 2 hr); Houayxai (8hr); Jinghong, China, via Boten (daily; 11hr); Muang Sing (4 daily; 2hr 30min); Oudomxai (4 daily; 4hr); Xiang Kok (daily; 4hr).
Louang Phabang to: Nam Bak (2 daily; 2hr 10min); Nong Khiaw (2 daily; 2–3hr); Oudomxai (daily; 7hr); Pakmong (5 daily; 2hr).
Muang Sing to: Louang Namtha (4 daily; 2hr 30min); Xiang Kok (2 daily; 2hr 30 min).
Nam Bak to: Nong Khiaw (hourly; 30min); Pakmong (hourly; 10min).
Nong Khiaw to: Viang Kham (2–3 daily; 2hr), Louang Phabang (2 daily; 2-3hr).
Oudomxai to: Boten (4hr); Jinghong, China, via Boten (12hr); Louang Namtha (4hr); Louang Phabang (3 daily; 5hr); Muang Khoua (5hr); Muang Sing (6hr); Pakbeng (8hr); Phongsali (11hr), Vientiane (daily; 19hr).
Pakmong to: Louang Phabang (5 daily; 2hr); Nam Bak (hourly; 10min); Oudomxai (3 daily; 3hr).
Phongsali to: Hat Sa (2hr); Oudomxai (11hr).

Flights

Houayxai (HOE) to: Louang Namtha (2 weekly; 25min); Oudomxai (2 weekly; 30min); Vientiane (3 weekly; 1hr 20min).
Louang Namtha to: Houayxai (2 weekly; 25min); Louang Phabang (4 weekly; 35min); Vientiane (3 weekly; 1hr 10min).
Louang Phabang (LPQ) to: Houayxai (1 daily; 50min); Louang Namtha (4 weekly; 35min); Oudomxai (2 weekly; 35min).
Oudomxai to: Houayxai (2 weekly; 30min); Louang Phabang (2 weekly; 35min); Vientiane (4 weekly; 50min).
Vientiane to: Houayxai (3 weekly; 1hr 20min); Louang Namtha (3 weekly; 1hr 10min); Oudomxai (4 weekly; 50min).

Boats

Houayxai to: Louang Namtha (passenger boat 1–2 days); Louang Phabang (slow boat 2 days; speedboat 6hr); Pakbeng (slow boat 1 day; speedboat 3hr); Xiang Kok (speedboat: 4hr).
Louang Namtha to: Houayxai (passenger boat 1–2 days); Pak Tha (passenger boat 1–2 days).
Louang Phabang to: Houayxai (slow boat 2–3 days; speedboat 6hr); Nong Khiaw (passenger boat daily; 8hr); Pakbeng (slow boat 1 day; speedboat 3hr); Vientiane (slow boat variable; 3 days).
Muang Khoua: to Hat Sa (slow boat 6hr; speedboat: 2hr).
Nong Khiaw: to Muang Khoua (4hr).

South central Laos

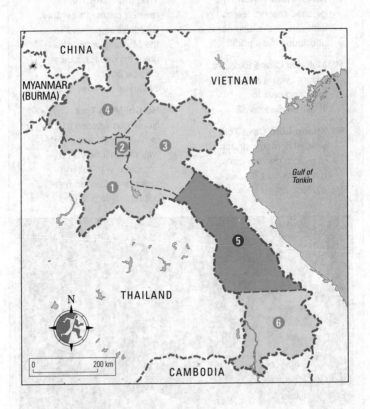

* **Nam Kading NBCA** An impressive mountain range and pristine rivers falling from a 400-metre plateau make this a prime hiking destination. **See p.255**

* **Nakai-Nam Theun** This gigantic reserve teems with rare and exotic flora and fauna. **See p.258**

* **Mahaxai Caves** Excellent hiking, cycling and cave-exploring near to Thakhek. **See p.262**

* **Khong Lore Cave** This seven-kilometre stretch of river is one of Asia's top kayaking sites. **See p.264**

* **Savannakhet** The French-Indochinese shop-houses and easy-going ways of this colonial gem have won it a reputation as the south's Louang Prabang. **See p.264**

* **That Ing Hang** This revered sixteenth-century Buddhist stupa next to the Mekong provides a great excuse for a bicy-cle ride out of Savannakhet. **See p.271**

* **Ho Chi Minh Trail** Numerous arteries of the famous clandestine high-way can still be visited – complete with rusting tanks and downed heli-copters. **See p.276**

5

South central Laos

Many travellers see very little of **south central Laos**, spending just a night or two in the principal towns of **Thakhek** or **Savannakhet** before pressing on to the far south or crossing the border into Vietnam. However, those willing to take time out from the more popular north and south of the country will find that there is much more to the region than the main Mekong towns, not least the otherworldly beauty of the Mahaxai stone formations at the edge of the **Khammouane Limestone NBCA** near Thakhek, and the largest of all Laos's conservation areas, massive **Nakai–Nam Theun (NNT) NBCA** to the northeast.

The three narrow provinces that make up south central Laos, **Bolikhamxai**, **Khammouane** and **Savannakhet**, are squeezed between mainland Southeast Asia's two most formidable geographical barriers: the Mekong River and the Annamite Mountains. The mighty **Mekong** has long served as a lifeline for the inhabitants of this stretch of the interior, providing food and a thoroughfare for trade and transport. In the late nineteenth century, European colonialism turned the life-giving "Mother of Waters" into a political boundary, and the Lao on its west bank were incorporated into Siam. More recently, the river became a further political and economic divide, when short-lived but draconian post-revolutionary policies forced large numbers of the inhabitants of the towns along this stretch of the Mekong, primarily ethnic Vietnamese and Chinese, to flee across the river into Thailand.

East of the river, the elevation gradually increases, culminating in the rugged **Annamite Mountains**, which, throughout much of recorded history, have divided Indochina culturally into two camps: Indian influence prevailing west of the chain and that of China dominating the east. These mountains make up one of the region's least inhabited areas and are teeming with wildlife, including some of Asia's rarest and most endangered species, such as the tiger, Javan rhinoceros and elephant, though a lack of roads makes much of this wild region virtually inaccessible to visitors.

As might be expected, the three principal settlements and provincial capitals of south central Laos – Pakxan, Thakhek and Savannakhet – are all on the Mekong. **Pakxan** is the smallest of these cities and lies at the mouth of the Xan River which flows down from the 2620-metre Mount Phou Xaxum on the Xieng Khouang Plateau. **Thakhek**, capital of Khammouane province, leads something of a double life. By day, the town is somnolent, its inhabitants shunning the heat behind brick and stucco walls. Come sundown, the local youth kick their motorbikes to life and roar around the local nightspots. East of Thakhek is a dramatic landscape of imposing and impossibly vertical mountains of the kind often depicted in old Chinese scroll paintings, which forms

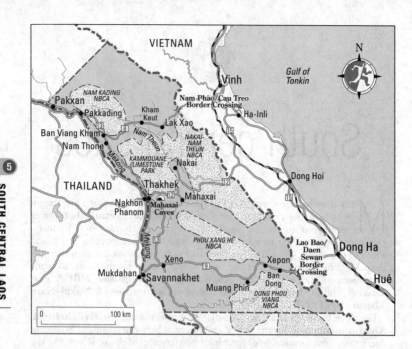

the southern boundary of the **Khammouane Limestone NBCA**. Easily visited on a day-trip from Thakhek, these awesome limestone formations are riddled with labyrinthine tunnels and caverns. **Savannakhet**, the capital of the province of the same name, has been described as southern Laos's equivalent of Louang Phabang, its inhabitants living comfortably among architectural heirlooms handed down by the French. Situated at the junction of two ancient trade routes, the town also displays evidence of other cultures – Vietnamese, Thai and Chinese – that have left their mark while passing through.

Aside from the main north–south artery of **Route 13**, central Laos has three other important highways which cross the region horizontally from east to west. The three roads – Routes 8, 12 and 9 – connect the Mekong River Valley with the provincial interior, beyond into Vietnam and eventually over to the Vietnam coast. After leaving Route 13, the northernmost highway, **Route 8** – paved and served by daily buses from Vientiane – snakes up through mountains, rainforests and the Phu Pha Maan "stone forest" before winding down to the city of Vinh on the Gulf of Tonkin. The main Lao town along this route is Lak Xao and the border is known as the **Nam Phao/Cau Treo** border crossing. The middle route, **Route 12**, begins at Thakhek and crosses the Annamites, connecting with Vietnam's Highway 15. This route is not served by public transport, and, in any case, the border crossing is not open to foreigners. The southernmost route, **Route 9**, is not paved but is served by daily buses connecting Savannakhet to coastal Vietnam. The road starts in Savannakhet, crosses the Annamites and ends in the city of Dong Ha on the coast of Vietnam. The main town along this route is **Xepon** and the border is known as the **Lao Bao/Daen Sawan** crossing.

Near Xepon, Route 9 bisects another route of more recent vintage: the **Ho Chi Minh Trail**. Actually a network of parallel roads and paths, the trail was used by the North Vietnamese Army to infiltrate and finally subdue its southern neighbour. The area is still littered with lots of war junk, some of it dangerous. The best way to view these rusting relics is to use Xepon as a base, making trips to nearby Muang Phin and Ban Dong.

Pakxan and around

Route 13 passes through **PAKXAN**, the first major settlement on the narrow neck of Laos, but few travellers actually stop over in this small and sleepy Mekong town. There is a ferry crossing here to Beung Kan in Thailand, but it is open only to Thai and Lao citizens. Reportedly, there are plans to upgrade Route 4 from Phonsavan to Pakxan, making it possible for northbound travellers from Savannakhet to head straight to the Plain of Jars without having to make a detour to Vientiane. When and if this happens, it will make spending a night in Pakxan a more tempting option than it is at present. The town is growing, however, and a number of guesthouses and restaurants have opened. Pakxan town officials have also tried to boost tourism by staggering the timing of its annual **boat racing festival**, which usually takes place sometime in October, so as not to conflict with the much larger races in the capital. One advantage of attending the races here is that you don't have to contend with the heaving crowds that pack the riverbank in Vientiane.

Practicalities

Buses stop at the town's only bus station, on Route 13 next to the local Lane Xang **bank** where you can change money. The most centrally located **guest house** is the *Phatana* (❶) with fan rooms and shared facilities. Where the Xan crosses Route 13 there is a very nice no-name **restaurant** with a big wooden deck over the river. On the opposite side of the river is the *BK Guest House* and north up the same road which leads down to the river you'll find *Hongxakham Guest House* (☎054/212362; ❶). On the east side of town is the *Liangvay Guest House*, on the north side of Route 13, which has fan and air-con rooms (☎054/212634; ❷), and around the corner is the *Phavisouk* (☎054/212768; ❶). All of these guest houses are small family-run operations offering simple rooms with shared facilities.

Nam Kading NBCA

Forty kilometres southeast of Pakxan, **Nam Kading NBCA** is Bolikhamxai province's largest conservation area and a place of dramatic scenic beauty. Running parallel to the Mekong and encompassing 1740 square kilometres, the park's chief feature is a chain of mountains down its length. The highest peak is the 1588-metre **Mount Pha Pet** which can clearly be viewed as you travel Route 13. Behind the ridge, on the eastern boundary of the NBCA, the **Nam Mouan** and **Nam Theun** rivers converge to form the **Nam Kading** which then flows out through a gap in the mountains to join the Mekong at the village of **PAKKADING**, or Mouth of the Kading.

Despite its proximity to both Route 13 and Route 8, the park has yet to be developed for tourism and the best base of operations for Nam Kading is still Pakxan. Although Pakkading sits in a crook of the Mekong at the point where the river is joined by the Nam Kading, it is simply a through-point with no accommodation. There are however a number of good fish **restaurants** along the highway at Pakkading and it is a favourite lunch spot for truckers and travellers plying Route 13. To the east of town, the highway crosses a Russian-built bridge and goes south out of Pakkading. Drivers often pause to light a cigarette before crossing the bridge and then respectfully toss the lit cigarette into the swift waters below: an offering to appease the feisty water serpent believed to live at the river's mouth. Nam Kading gets its name because as the Nam Theun spills off the plateau the waterfalls make a "kading" sound – the sound of a water buffalo's bell. Every year a buffalo is sacrificed to the water serpent, though the offering wasn't enough to spare the lives of a Russian engineer and several Lao workers who died during construction of the bridge.

East to Lak Xao and the Vietnam border

At the tiny junction town of **BAN VIANG KHAM**, 47km south of Pakkading, Route 8 begins its journey over the Annamite Mountains to Vietnam. These days the majority of travellers pass through here on direct, aircon buses running the Vientiane/Vinh route, but the newly paved road traces a centuries' old trading route to Vietnam, running through ruggedly beautiful countryside, and the frontier town of Lak Xao can be used as a base for trips to both the Ho Chi Minh Trail and the Nakai-Nam Theun NBCA. Travellers doing Route 8 in stages can overnight in either Ban Viang Kham or the tiny town of **NAM THONE**, a leafy village set amid rice fields and sheltered by blue mountains, on Route 13 4km south of Ban Viang Kham. Basic *Phimachak* (❶) is easy to find in the town centre.

East of Ban Viang Kham, Route 8 zigzags through hilly countryside, dotted with woods and tiny stream valleys, the southern horizon punctuated by blacktopped limestone pillars draped in lush vegetation. An hour's drive along this route takes you to the village of **NA HIN**, which sprang up during the construction of the Theun-Hin Boun Dam, completed in 1998. The hydroelectric potential of the area is vigorously demonstrated during the monsoon season, when the rains recharge a medley of waterfalls on the surrounding hillsides. The densely forested hill guarding the valley's southeastern side supports as many as six sizeable waterfalls, all visible from the highway. Today Ban Na Hin has found a new lease of life as a gateway into the Phou Hin Poun NBCA, more popularly known as the **Khammouane Limestone NBCA**. The village boasts a guest house, and from the bus station there are direct daily connections to both Vientiane and Thakhek. The best **accommodation** in the area, however, is *L'Auberge Sala Hine Boun* (☎031/212725, ☎031/213110, ✉salalao@laonet; ❺), an eco-resort located on the banks of the Nam Hin Poun River inside the NBCA. To reach the resort you need to take a tuk-tuk to Ban Na Phouak and then go two hours by boat ($15) up the Nam Hin Poun. The resort features deluxe bungalows and is within easy day-hiking distance of a number of hilltribe villages, Tham Thieng cave and the famous seven-kilometre Khong Lor underground river, best seen by kayak.

Continuing east on Route 8, you pass **Ban Phonhong** and cross a toll bridge spanning the Nam Theun, the river which powers the Theun-Hin Boun Dam. The road then reaches **KAM KEUT**, a quaint, shady village of traditional homes, set in an expansive valley of rice fields hemmed in by a low wall of hills. It was once the principal settlement in the area, but has seen its guest house close and the population diminish in recent years, as Lak Xao has emerged as the regional hub.

Lak Xao

The sprawling boom town of **LAK XAO** is something of a disappointing sight after the stunning journey east, but is spared from being a complete blot on the landscape by the impressive limestone escarpment which stands sentinel on the outskirts of town. Carved out of the hills by the logging company, Phudoi, in the 1980s, Lak Xao facilitates border trade with Vietnam, as well as providing a base for conservationists tending to the rare wildlife and pristine forests along the Lao-Vietnamese divide, and employees of the Nam Theun II dam project. Few travellers pass through Lak Xao, and for most, it's little more than a launch pad for trips into Vietnam, 35km to the east. The town's **logging industry** continues to thrive, as the continual buzz of chainsaws and roar of trucks testify. Helicopters haul the logs out of the forests, with some of the priciest wood – that of the coniferous Mai Long Len trees – finding its way to the Tokyo bedrooms of wealthy Japanese. It is thought that this durable wood possesses the ability to heal respiratory ailments and it's prized by Chinese and Japanese alike. The wealth tapped from the surrounding forests is reflected in the town **temple** – located next to the hotel. Lavish by a country town's standards, the wat has been embellished by merit-making donations from Phudoi company officials.

Once known for selling exotic wildlife, Lak Xao's **market** has largely cleaned up its act since recent scientific discoveries heaped international attention on the nearby conservation zone. With representatives of international environmental organizations regularly passing through, mouse-deer and other goodies are no longer available. The market does however have some interesting stalls, selling **silver jewellery** from minority tribes and old silver bars etched with Chinese characters. You might also see villagers from **remote hilltribes**, some of whom, dressed in their finest traditional clothes, are so timid in their dealings with traders that it's clear they're making a rare foray into town.

Another market is held from the 15th to the 20th of each month about 35km to the east just inside the Lao border. **Vietnamese traders** come here to hawk everyday goods such as spanners, mouse traps, Hanoi beers and pharmaceuticals. The market may not be of great interest in itself, beyond offering an insight into cross-border trade, but the journey out is scenic, passing through wide valleys and vibrant green fields. Shared tuk-tuks leave from the market in Lak Xao.

Practicalities

Buses that make the trip to Lak Xao stop in the lot outside the market, 3km from the town's main hotel, the *Phudoi* (❷): tuk-tuks (2000K) are on hand to ferry you down there. On either side of the A-frame building are a disco-restaurant and a quirky, grey concrete building with clean rooms which come with towels and a complimentary bar of Parrot-brand soap – believed by the lowland Lao to ward off hilltribe black magic. Much newer is the *Souriya Guest House* (❶) near the market which has clean rooms with en-suite bathrooms. Across from the market, *Only One Restaurant* serves steamboats while *Thiphavongsay* nearby has a range of traditional Lao dishes. The bank next door to *Thiphavongsay* can **exchange** dollars and Vietnamese dong.

The Nam Phao/Cau Treo border crossing

The **Nam Phao/Cau Treo** border crossing into Vietnam is 35km from Lak Xao and best reached by hiring a tuk-tuk (20,000K) from the market. Shared

Nakai-Nam Theun NBCA

Running almost the entire length of Khammouane Province, the **Nakai-Nam Theun** (NNT) NBCA is Laos's largest conservation area and one of the last great wildernesses of Southeast Asia. Encompassing 3710 square kilometres, the park begins on the 500-metre-high Nakai Plateau and then extends eastward right up to the backbone of the mighty Annamite Mountains which form the border with Vietnam, and include some of the highest mountain peaks in Laos.

Covered by a vast forest and encompassing a wide range of elevations and habitats, the NBCA almost defies superlatives in terms of the diversity of its **flora** and **fauna**. Over 400 bird species, many threatened, have already been identified. The park is even more biologically important in terms of the large and small **mammals** found within its boundaries. Tigers, Asian elephants, leopards, gibbons and monkeys are only amongst the more high-profile animals in the park. No less than nine species of **primates** occur in the NBCA including pygmy loris, douc langur, and pale-cheeked gibbons. Small **carnivores** include clouded leopards, marbled cats and Asiatic golden cats, making the NBCA the most important area in the world for small carnivores outside Madagascar. So rich is the park in wildlife that both new and previously believed extinct animals continue to be discovered today, including the saola, giant muntjac and Indochinese warty pig.

The recent addition of an extension or **corridor** westward across the Nam Theun River valley now links the NNT NBCA to the 1580 square-kilometre **Phou Hin Poun** or **Khammouane Limestone NBCA** which is composed of a large, highly scenic range of mountains running between the Nakai Plateau and the plains of the Mekong river valley. This, linked together with the NNT NBCA and the spectacular limestone karst forest of **Hin Nam No NBCA** to the south, now form a connected unit of over 6000 square kilometres of protected conservation area.

tuk-tuks (3000K) can be had, but are often overcrowded and leave infrequently – except when the border market's open (from the 15th to the 20th of each month). For those crossing into Laos from Vietnam, there's usually a tuk-tuk on hand for hire into Lak Xao.

Crossing the border (daily 7.30am–5pm) is generally hassle-free, but start your journey early to ensure you don't end up stuck at the border: transport on both sides is sparse and neither immigration post is near a town of any size. A small exchange kiosk sits in the Lao terminal, but don't expect to get a decent rate. The settlement on the Vietnamese side of the border is **Cau Treo**, 105km west of Vinh on Highway 8.

Thakhek and around

Less visited than Savannakhet to the south, **THAKHEK**, capital of Khammouane province, is gradually gaining popularity as the best base to explore the nearby **Mahaxai Caves** and karst formations and the massive **Khammouane Limestone NBCA**. It is also an entry point into Laos from Nakhon Phanom in Thailand, as well as being a good place to break the long journey down Route 13 to Savannakhet.

Thakhek's roots date back to the Chenla and Funan empires. The name Thakhek, which means "Visitor's Landing", is relatively new, but is a reference to the town's importance as a trading centre as far back as the eighth century. As Sikhotabong, and later Lakhon, the principality spanned both banks of the Mekong and was a hub for trade routes connecting civilizations in Vietnam,

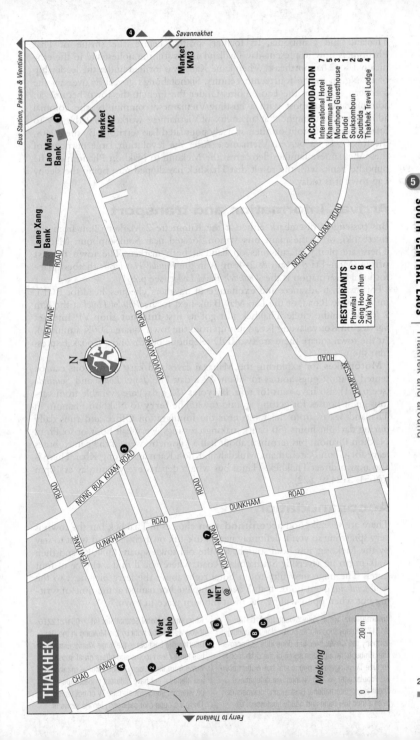

THAKHEK

ACCOMMODATION
International Hotel   7
Khammuan Hotel   5
Mouthong Guesthouse   3
Phudoi   1
Souksomboun   2
Southida   6
Thakhek Travel Lodge   4

RESTAURANTS
Phawilai   C
Seng Hoon Hun   B
Zuki Yaky   A

Bus Station, Paksan & Vientiane

Savannakhet

Market KM3

Market KM2

Lao May Bank

Lane Xang Bank

VIENTIANE ROAD

NONG BUA KHAM ROAD

NONG BUA KHAM ROAD

KOUVOLAVONG ROAD

CHAMPASAK ROAD

OUNKHAM ROAD

OUNKHAM ROAD

KOUVOLAVONG ROAD

VIENTIANE ROAD

N

Wat Nabo

VP INET @

CHAO ANOU

Mekong

Ferry to Thailand

0   200 m

259

Thailand and Cambodia. Its former spiritual centre, the shrine of That Phanom, is now in present-day Thailand and is still the holiest site in the ethnically Lao–Thai northeast. When Lane Xang was formed under the leadership of Fa Ngum in the fourteenth century, Sikhotabong's governor oversaw the southern extent of the Lao empire. Under the French, the town became an administrative outpost with a bustling Vietnamese community: the colonial administration thought that an influx of Vietnamese workers was the key to finally turning a profit on their sparsely populated Lao territory. By the 1940s, the town was 85 percent Vietnamese. After the revolution, large numbers of these Vietnamese families fled across the Mekong to Nakhon Phanom on the opposite bank, with the result that Thakhek has slipped into being the sleepy Lao town it is today.

Arrival, information and transport

Bus passengers disembark either at the Kilometre 2 Market (2km from the riverbank), or at the main **bus** station, located near Souksomboun Market. There are plenty of tuk-tuks on hand at both markets. The town **tourist office** (Mon–Fri 8–11am & 2–4pm) is in the *Phudoi Hotel*, but the best place for local information is the *Thakhek Travel Lodge* (see p.261).

For Visa cash advances and **exchange** of travellers' cheques, head for BCEL on Vientiane Road, or the Lao May Bank next to the *Phudoi Hotel* at the Km 2 Market traffic circle. Thakhek just got its first **internet** shop, VP Internet Service on Kouvolavong Road just up from the town square (300K a minute). At the town square there are two IDD telephone booths and a Kodak Express film shop.

Motorbikes for exploring the Mahaxai caves and karst formations can be rented at most guesthouses for about $8 a day. The *Travel Lodge* and *Southida* (see p.261) also have vans for rent. **Bicycles** ($2 a day) are available from various guest houses for getting around town. The **ferry** to Nakhon Phanom in Thailand, leaves from the ramp near the Immigration Office and runs daily during daylight hours (50 baht), making crossings every half hour or so. From Nakhon Phanom bus terminal, about half a kilometre west of the centre, buses leave for Ubon Ratchathani, Mukdahan, Khon Kaen and Nong Khai. There is also now a direct Thakhek–Hanoi bus which departs every Saturday at 10pm (℡051/212439; $22).

Accommodation

There are several good **accommodation** choices in Thakhek but the town is very sprawling so you'll definitely need a tuk-tuk on arrival. If you want to stay by the Mekong, just head straight for the old town square (3000K) and then walk north up riverside Setthathilat Road, where you'll find a choice of four hotels. The huge new fifty-room hotel right above the ferry pier next to the *Souksomboun* guest house hadn't been completed or named at the time of writing but when open will be the most modern place in town.

International Hotel Kouvolavong Rd ℡051/212171. Renovation of this post-colonial building, formerly the *Chaleunxai*, has done little to improve the atmosphere, although some of the drab rooms include TV, refrigerator, phone and hot-water shower. Popular with visiting Vietnamese delegations, there is an "International Restaurant" downstairs with a loud live band and gaudy hostesses. ❷

Khammuan Hotel Setthathilat Rd ℡051/212216. If you want to be right by the Mekong in the Old Quarter, the best bet is the huge *Khammuan* which has large clean rooms and offers great sunset views from the balcony. Good value – the rooms are identical but have different prices depending on whether you want air-con, TV or hot water. There's a huge roof patio with terrific views of both the Mekong and the mountains. **①**–**③**

Mouthong Guest House Nongphuakham Rd between the radio tower on Kouvolavong Road and Vientiane Road ☎051/212387. This huge two-storey, modern mansion is a bit out of the way but a very good choice. The building is new and the rooms come with hot-water en-suites, TV and air-con. **③**

Phudoi Kilometre 2 Market Circle ☎051/212048. The only reason to stay here is if you've arrived late by public transport and are leaving early, otherwise the location halfway between the bus stations and the square makes little sense. Owned by the Phudoi company, this drab modern hotel has twelve air-con rooms and a disco. **④**

Souksomboun Setthathilat Rd ☎051/212225. Formerly the *Sikhot*, this priceless old French colonial police station right on the riverfront mow sadly features bizarre, tacky 70s interior decor that is more Las Vegas than Lao. In the ugly motel annex off to the side, there are equally spacious and cheaper fan rooms but without any atmosphere. Behind the hotel is the loud Disco 2002, where hordes of young Thakhek youths on motorbikes hang out. **③**

Southida Chao Anou Rd ☎051/212568. Travellers looking for a bit of quality should try this new hotel just around the corner from the *Khammuan*, which has eight clean, tiled-floored, air-con rooms and en-suite bathrooms with hot water in a new three-storey building. There's a good restaurant downstairs and they rent mini-vans, 50cc motorcycles and bicycles. **③**

Thakhek Travel Lodge ☎020/515137, ⓔ travel@laotel.com. The most popular budget option is this new three-storey guest house located up a side road halfway between the Km 2 and Km 3 markets. Features dormitories and fan rooms with shared facilities as well as air-con rooms with en-suite bathrooms, all reasonably priced. They also rent bicycles, motorbikes, and vans. **①**–**③**

The Town

These days, Thakhek has a deserted feel. A wander round the streets leading out from the tiny **town square** reveals French villas and shop-houses, crumbling into overgrown gardens, and too-wide dirt streets contribute to the town's sleepy, almost haunted atmosphere. Aside from a few old French-era shop-houses and mansions, there is little to see around the square except the pot-holed dirt road running south along the Mekong to a big concrete sala. In houses just a block from the main square locals cook their suppers over open fires in their backyards and cows graze on the verge. This tranquil air of neglect is shattered nightly by club-hopping teenagers who keep the city vibrant until after midnight, buzzing around on brand-new motorcycles, the inheritors of a tradition only half buried by the revolution in 1975. During the Second Indochina War, Thakhek was a sort of Havana on the Mekong, with visiting Thais flocking to its riverbank casino. These days, it's Nakhon Phanom on the opposite bank that's the big metropolis, while sleepy Thakhek slumbers. Separated only by the Mekong River, the two Lao peoples living on each bank couldn't have a more different way of life.

Recently however, Thakhek has begun to show signs of finally stirring. Vientiane Road, the main boulevard leading to the pier, has just been widened and paved, and a huge new V-shaped tourist hotel is under construction at the ferry landing. There are a few nice colonial-era buildings around the town square and on **Chao Anou Road**, north of the square, is a fine row of 1920s shop-houses featuring interlocking swastika designs of moulded stucco (although this Hindu motif appears in Lao weaving it is rare in Lao architecture). Between Chao Anou and Setthatilat is a large temple, Wat Nabo.

Thakhek's main attraction however is outside of the centre. Known locally as Muang Kao, **Wat Pha That Sikhotabong**, 6km to the south and easily reached by tuk-tuk, is one of the country's holiest pilgrimage sites and a great scenic spot, especially at sunset. The golden Lao-style stupa occupies spacious grounds on the banks of the Mekong, a prominent position that makes it visible from the opposite bank. The stupa, which has been restored three times in the past fifty years, was built in the nineteenth century under the orders of Chao Anou, the revered Lao king, who tried in vain to throw off the yoke of

Thai control and reunify the once-powerful Lao kingdom of Lane Xang. Ruins in the immediate vicinity of the stupa suggest that this site has been sacred for centuries; they are said to be all that remains of a shrine erected during the reign of King Nanthasen in the tenth century. A pair of whitewashed sandstone nagas, pilfered from some Khmer temple, are arranged symmetrically near a small altar, where pilgrims leave offerings of candles and incense. The third lunar month, which usually falls in July, is the best time to visit, when the temple celebrates its annual *bun* and a carnival-like atmosphere prevails. Walking out of the south gate, you'll find an excellent open-air restaurant – more of a large shelter with a corrugated tin roof, really – where you can order up Lao mainstays such as roast chicken, *tam màk hung* and sticky rice.

Eating and drinking

Many of Thakhek's best local **restaurants** are far out on the outskirts of town. Closer to centre, most of the eateries are located on or close to the town square. The most popular place with local expats is the humble *Seng Hoon Hun* (no English sign) under the huge tree at the west side of the town square. Aside from decent stir-fries they have an ice cream freezer with imported Magnum bars. Nearby, at the southwest corner of the square, is *Phawilai*, which serves up noodles, grilled chicken, and *mu yáw*, a local sausage, all washed down with cold beer. North of the square is a large, clean stall with tables and seating outside the nightclub of the *Khammuan Hotel*, but they only do noodle soups. For a proper sit-down meal, the restaurant at the *Southida* is the best bet in the **old quarter** and specialises in "suki" steamboats. Five doors up Vientiane Road is another steamboat place called *Zuki Yaky*. If when leaving town you get stuck waiting for a bus at the main **bus station** on Route 13, there's a decent little restaurant in the white building with the red metal roof across from the station, which has seating and a clean toilet out back.

Mahaxai Caves

East of Thakhek, potholed Route 12 is swallowed up by a surreal landscape of karst formations. Hidden among the sea of jagged limestone hills are the **Mahaxai caves**, many of which lie within the Khammouane Limestone NBCA. A number of the more easily accessible caves are well-known local spots, popular with both Lao families on a weekend picnic and foreign tourists. Readily accessible, these more popular caves line the Thakhek–Mahaxai road, with the furthest one only about 20km from Thakhek. Not all of these caves are worth visiting, but the ones that are make a day-trip through the strange beauty of this area a must if you're passing through Thakhek.

A good point to start a **walking tour** of the caves is Tham Ban Tham, 7km from Thakhek, on the road to Mahaxai. From here you can walk to **Tham En**, taking in other caves en route, a twelve-kilometre walk in all. To find the first cave, turn south down the dirt road that turns off Route 12 towards **BAN THAM**, a small village nestling at the base of the first limestone escarpment. The gaping mouth of the tautologically named **Tham Ban Tham** ("tham" meaning "cave") should be visible from the highway. Cut through the village to find the concrete stairs leading up to the cave, which contains a shrine, centred around a sizeable Buddha image. Perched partway up the side of the hill, Tham Ban Tham offers a commanding view of the surroundings, and is particularly pretty at sunset. If you've come with a local, ask to see the shrine to Ganesh, an elephantine rock hidden in a tunnel within the main cavern. From Ban Tham, follow the road cutting north to get back on the main road.

Just before the second wooden bridge along this road, roughly 17km from Thakhek, a dirt path on the right leads to **Tham Xiang Liap**. After 300m the trail reaches a stream, which flows into the entrance of the cave on the opposite bank. While not the most inspiring cave, Tham Xiang Liap is a pleasant stop chiefly for its seclusion and the novelty of scrambling across a stream full of rocks into the half-submerged cave mouth. During the monsoon, the water level may be too high to enter the cave. Nearby is the disappointing **Tha Falang**, reputedly a favourite spot during colonial times with Thakhek's French residents, who would come here to picnic by a stream among the hills. To get here, continue east along the main road, crossing the second wooden bridge. A sign reading "Limestone NBCA" in English accompanied by a crudely drawn district map marks a sandy turn-off on the northern side of the road, a few hundred metres from the bridge. Bearing right, you'll reach a small clearing 1km away on the left and here on the bank is the *tha*, or landing. It's a pretty unexceptional spot though, and it's not clear what drew Laos's former colonial masters: the area only musters some charm during the rainy season when the water-sculpted rocks are submerged and the hills a vibrant green. During the dry season, the brackish water stagnates against the rocks.

Drink vendors set up shop in the recesses of two cliffs 100m beyond the turn-off for Tha Falang, signposting the path leading to **Tham Sa Pha In**, which is without question the best of the caves. A small sign on the left points towards the path leading to the cave, a short walk from the main road. Look for the bamboo gate to find the cave entrance. The cave was renamed for the Hindu god Indra after the Second Indochina War, when villagers claimed to see the Hindu deity's image reflected in the pool. Illuminated by an inaccessible opening in the ceiling of the cave, the pool glows emerald green, the colour of Indra's skin. You can pause to light a candle by the shrine in the back of the cave before clambering down to sit by the pool, where swifts dive-bombing the surface and the drone of insects conspire to give the deep cavern an otherworldly atmosphere. A sign at the mouth of the cave asks visitors not to touch the water, which is considered sacred.

The most visited of Mahaxai's caves, **Tham En**, named for the large number of sparrows that are said to inhabit the cave and popular for what the Lao call its natural air conditioning, lies another 4km up the road and is easily located by the gate, where an official collects 2000K per visitor plus a vehicle fee. A concrete stairway takes you deep into the tunnel mouth, but there is still plenty of room to clamber around on the rocks and climb up to one of the several cave mouths that offer commanding views of the forest outside. Pint-sized bungalows, designed to provide tourist accommodation, were started here but never finished, and it's hard to see how this mini-resort could offer much more than an emergency bed between Mahaxai and Savannakhet. On weekends, the cave is packed with day-tripping locals snacking on roast chicken, playing cards and picnicking.

The easiest way to reach the caves is by hiring a motorbike ($8 per day) or tuk-tuk from Thakhek, but some visitors prefer to cycle out or catch a Mahaxai-bound bus to the caves and then explore on foot. Public transport can be tricky, however: pick-ups and buses travel the road frequently enough in the morning but aren't so reliable late in the afternoon. To get back, you'll have to flag down one of the buses or pick-ups coming from Mahaxai – of which there are several a day – although again, you can't count on catching one late in the afternoon.

Mahaxai

Fifty kilometres east of the Mahaxai Caves lies the beautifully situated town of **MAHAXAI**, engulfed in limestone karst formations, on the banks of the Xe Bang Fai River. A bumpy fifty-kilometre drive from Thakhek through the Khammouane Limestone NBCA, this lively little town lacks sights of its own but is never the less a charming place offering visitors enchanted by the strange beauty of Khammouane's karst formations a chance to soak up the surroundings at a more measured pace. Buses and pick-ups grind to a halt at the central market, next to an old tin-roofed temple. You'll find just one **hotel**, with huge rooms (❷), as well as several noodle shops and *tam màk hung* vendors, all just steps away. Hiring a boat to cruise the river, which stretches from the mountainous Vietnamese border to the Mekong, can be a bit of a chore – ask by the river or around town – but, if you can swing it, a two-hour round-trip by motorized pirogue in either direction is scenic, with the upstream route taking in stunning cliffs and the downstream option skimming through gentle rapids, past submerged water buffalo and villagers catching fish. Most cave touring originates in Thakhek, but the area surrounding Mahaxai is also honeycombed with caves – ask the villagers.

Khammouane Limestone NBCA

The most accessible of Khammouane province's three NBCAs is the Phou Hin Poun NBCA, more popularly known as the **Khammouane Limestone NBCA**. Unlike the neighbouring Nakai-Nam Theun and Hin Nam No NBCAs to the east, the Khammouane Limestone NBCA can be accessed by road or river from a number of approaches, making it the most practical and affordable of the three NBCAs to visit. The best way to experience the park is on an organized tour which will generally include kayaking, hiking and **village stays**. Within Laos, a number of tour companies now operate guided **expeditions** into the park. Wildside Adventures in Vientiane offers a "Khong Lore Cave and Khammuane Exploration" out of the capital for $120 per person all inclusive (see p.111 for contact details). Organized tours are best booked out of Vientiane from where they depart rather than Thakhek, although it is still possible to link up with tours from Thakhek provided you make arrangements with the tour operator by phone or fax. The chief highlight of many of the tours is the journey by kayak through the wonderfully dramatic **Khong Lore Cave**, a natural seven-kilometre river tunnel through a limestone karst mountain into a hidden valley

Although it will not allow you penetrate the interior of the park to the degree a professionally organized expedition can, a **do-it-yourself-tour** from Thakhek is also easily arranged and affordable. There's an **eco-resort** within the park (see p.256) on the **Nam Hinboun River** which is accessible via Route 8. Given the remoteness of the area, advance booking is advised.

Savannakhet and around

The town of **SAVANNAKHET** (known locally as "Sawanh") is southern Laos's most visited provincial capital. Its popularity is due in part to its central location on the overland route between Vientiane and Pakxe and Thailand and Vietnam, linked to each other by a 240-kilometre-long road carved by the

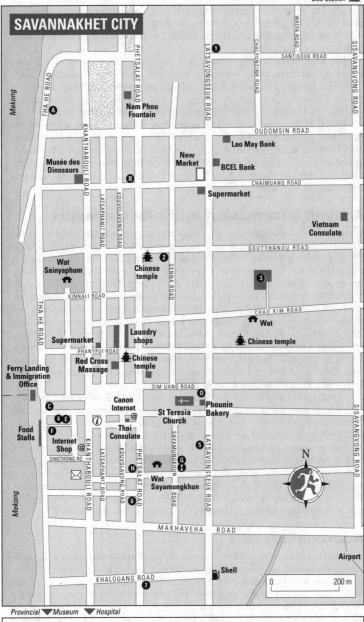

SAVANNAKHET CITY

Bus Station ▲

Mekong

Tha He Road

Phetsalat Road

Khanthabouli Road

Latsavongseuk Road

Chaleunsinh Road

Waifa Road

Sisavangvong Road

Santisouk Road

Nam Phou Fountain

Oudomsin Road

Lao May Bank

BCEL Bank

New Market

Chaimuang Road

Supermarket

Musée des Dinosaurs

Latsaphanit Road

Kouvolavong Road

Vietnam Consulate

Southanou Road

Wat Sainyaphum

Senna Road

Chinese temple

Kinnali Road

Chao Kim Road

Wat

Chinese temple

Supermarket

Laundry shops

Phanypui Road

Red Cross Massage

Chinese temple

Sim Uang Road

Ferry Landing & Immigration Office

Canon Internet

St Teresa Church

Phounin Bakery

Food Stalls

Internet Shop

Thai Consulate

Sayamungkhun Road

Phetsalat Road

Latsaphani Road

Kouvolavong Road

Singthong Rd

Khanthabouli Road

Wat Sayamungkhun

Mekong

Makhaveha Road

N

Airport

Khalouang Road

Shell

0   200 m

Provincial ▼ Museum ▼ Hospital

5

SOUTH CENTRAL LAOS | Savannakhet and around

265

ACCOMMODATION

Leena Guesthouse	**3**	
Nanhai	**1**	
Phonevilay	**7**	
Saisouk Guesthouse	**6**	
Santyphab	**4**	
Savanbanhao	**2**	
Sayamungkhun	**5**	

RESTAURANTS

Baw Bun Shop	**F**
Hoongthip Garden Restaurant	**B**
Lao-Paris 4 Seasons Café	**C**
Mekong Riverside	**A**
Rendezvous	**D**
Sakura Korean BBQ	**G**
Sensabay	**E**
Starlite Restaurant	**I**
Tommy Corner	**H**

French. The surrounding area that makes up Savannakhet province, stretching from the Mekong River to the Annamite Mountains, is Laos's most populous region: for centuries the inhabitants fought off designs on their territory from both Vietnam and Thailand.

Aside from being an important junction, Savannakhet also possesses very impressive **architecture**, which includes the St Teresia Catholic Church from the French colonial period and narrow streets and shop-houses of ochre-coloured stucco that are reminiscent of parts of Hanoi. Savannakhet's inhabitants, however, as travellers who have recently arrived from Vietnam are quick to note, are much mellower than their neighbours east of the Annamite Mountains, despite the fact that a large percentage of the town's population is ethnic Vietnamese, descendants of entrepreneurs who immigrated to Laos during French rule. Most have been living here for generations and consider themselves to be more Lao than Vietnamese in habit and temperament.

Arrival, information and city transport

Buses offload at the station on the north side of the town (air-con buses from Vientiane disgorge passengers at a separate stand nearby, known locally as Khiw Sensabai), with **tuk-tuks** on hand to make the two-kilometre run into the city centre (3000K). The passenger **ferry** from Mukdahan, Thailand (50 baht), arrives at the Immigration Office in the town centre. The ferry departs roughly every thirty minutes on weekdays, less frequently on weekends. The airport, serving Lao Aviation flights, is on the southeastern side of the town, a few blocks from the centre, off Makaweha Road. There is no longer a slow-boat service between Savannakhet and Vientiane, now that Route 13 has been upgraded. Travellers doing the "**Indochina loop**" through Cambodia, Vietnam, Laos and Thailand have the option of the 240-kilometre-long Route 9 on their way between Laos's two neighbours, hence the presence of both a Thai and a Vietnamese consulate in the town.

As Savannakhet is incredibly spread out, you may find **tuk-tuks** easier than trying to walk the long blocks outside the old quarter, especially in summer. Tuk-tuks can be flagged down around town and cost 1000K for short distances within the centre. Bicycles ($1 per day) are another excellent way of seeing the town and can be rented at *Santiphab Hotel* near the square and at some guesthouses. Both Savanbanhao Tourism (℡041/212202) on Senna Road, three blocks north of the church, and the *Nanhai Hotel* have vans with drivers for hire. Self-drive at either place is not an option and there are no rental motorcycles in Savannakhet. The Tourism Authority office (℡041/212755), which seems to move frequently, is currently located on Latsaphanit Road just south of the square.

Accommodation

Savannakhet has a very good choice and range of **accommodation**. If you're staying on to soak up the town's atmosphere or are stuck waiting for a Thai or Vietnamese visa, you'll find a wide range of hotels and guest houses to choose from. Generally, the most atmospheric and convenient area to stay is in the old city, but don't expect to find charming guesthouses in colonial buildings as you do in Louang Prabang. Savannakhet's priceless colonial architecture is largely overlooked and there aren't even any hotels or guesthouses facing the Mekong River (except for the *Mekong Hotel* which serves as a Vietnamese brothel). Outside of the immediate vicinity of the old city are a handful of more modern options, catering to Thai business travellers and international aid workers;

these hotels lie scattered on the wide streets on the fringe of the old city but can be inconvenient for those without their own car.

Leena Guest house Chao Kim Rd, walk 200m east off Latsavongseuk Rd and follow the signs ☎041/212404. This huge, two-storey house in a quiet residential area has twelve spotlessly clean en-suite rooms, some with air-con. No hot water yet but the owner plans to start installing water heaters soon. There's also a pleasant breakfast restaurant downstairs in the next building. Brand new, great value, and sure to be popular. A bit out of the old town but there's a huge wat and a Chinese temple nearby. ❷

Nanhai Santisouk Rd ☎041/212371. This modern five-storey hotel is the biggest in town. Built and owned by mainland Chinese investors, the rooms come with TV, air con and refrigerators. The presence of a pool, a Chinese restaurant, a lobby and a lift on the premises make this the top hotel in town but it's characterless and too far from the old town to be useful for most Western tourists. ❺

Phonevilay Phetsalat Rd ☎041/212284. At the corner of Khalouang Rd. Three big buildings on a corner lot. Aside from the two-storey house here, there are six simple but clean air-con rooms with en-suite bathrooms and hot water. The rooms are decent but the staff a little unfriendly. ❸

Saisouk Guest house Phetsalat Rd, at the corner of Makhaveha St a block south of Wat Sayamungkhun ☎041/212207. New, home-stay style guest house in a lovely wooden house in a quiet area. Shared facilities and no hot water but if you're looking for a friendly, relaxed atmosphere with genuinely nice people, this is the place for you. The rooms, some with air-con, are big and well-lit with wooden floors, and the toilets are very clean. There's a big tiled balcony overlooking a local school yard and palm trees all around. ❶

Santyphab Between the square and the river ☎041/212277. Dingy rooms which are strictly for those on a very tight budget: cheap and central but grungy, and not really good value for money. They have dollar-a-day bicycles for rent. ❶

Savanbanhao Senna Rd, four blocks north of church ☎041/212202. Four large houses set in a big walled compound, each with six units inside. There are also two one-storey buildings around back with cheaper non-air-con rooms. Unfriendly service and no atmosphere at all, but a wide range of clean, good-value rooms, all with en-suite bathrooms and hot water. In the unlikely event it's full, the ugly *Savanphathana* (❷) right next door has plenty of cheap rooms. ❷–❸

Sayamungkhun Latsavongseuk Rd ☎041/212426. A large, lovely colonial-era house on the main street easy walking distance to the old quarter: if you're looking for atmosphere this is the place to come. The building is in the style popular with successful Chinese merchants of the time being: Western but with some Oriental motifs and features. Excellent value and one of the only guesthouses in a heritage building. ❷

The Town

Savannakhet is Laos's third largest city after Vientiane and Louang Prabang. The town square was the heart of the **French settlement**, the surrounding streets reserved for the villas of French officials and the shop-houses of Vietnamese merchants. Yet only a kilometre or two away from this bastion of French civilization, the paved roads became dirt paths meandering through traditional Lao villages which were largely unaffected by French rule and remain culturally pristine to this day.

French Quarter

Roads laid out on a neat grid surrounding the town square constitute the **Old French Quarter**, and are lined with some fine examples of European-inspired architecture, most of which looks much more ancient than it really is. Indeed, it is doubtful that any of these crumbling structures predate the early twentieth century. Vietnamese and Chinese joss houses and schools attest to the wealth and influence of Savannakhet's merchant class. Gravitating towards urban areas and searching for business opportunities, the Chinese found their way to Savannakhet in small numbers before the arrival of the French. But the Vietnamese came for the most part at the encouragement of the French, who doubted the business acumen of ethnic Lao. After the revolution, most of Savannakhet's ethnic Vietnamese and Chinese fled across the Mekong into Thailand, taking their capital and entrepreneurial skills with them. Even today, 25 years after the revolution, much of Savannakhet is empty of people, its shops shuttered, and packs of stray dogs roaming the streets. Only recently have the Chinese and Vietnamese started coming back in any numbers to invest. They have gradually reclaimed many of the old French-era shop-houses and are opening up a few businesses on the ground floors. The Thai Consulate, housed in a 1926 mansion, is a fine example of how beautiful the French-era buildings can be when properly restored. One of the best areas for a stroll or spin on a bicycle to see old buildings is the district of tree-lined streets and former French administrative offices south of the post office. The old town also has several pleasant wats and a few Chinese temples worth a wander.

St Teresia Catholic Church

Savannakhet's main square is dominated by the octagonal spire of **St Teresia Catholic Church**. Built in 1930, the thick masonry walls keep the interior blessedly cool, even on the hottest of days. Objects of interest include an old teakwood confessional and, high up on the walls, a set of hardwood plaques, with Vietnamese mother-of-pearl inlay, depicting the fourteen stations of the cross. Not surprisingly, the biblical characters have distinctly Asian faces: Christ resembles a Confucian sage, while the Roman soldiers look more like turban-wearing Mongols. On Saturday and Sunday mornings, mass is said in Lao to an overwhelmingly ethnic-Vietnamese congregation.

Wat Sainyaphum

Just north of the ferry landing, on the road running along the Mekong, sits **Wat Sainyaphum**, Savannakhet's largest Buddhist monastery. Nearly all the structures at this wat, save for the school building in the northwest corner of the compound, have been recently restored in garish, circus-like hues. It is still worth a visit, however, especially if you are looking for a serene, shady spot to catch up on your postcard writing.

Musee Des Dinosaurs

The new **Musee Des Dinosaurs** (daily 9am–noon & 1–4pm; free) on Khanthabouli Road north of Wat Sainyaphum was set up with some help from French paleontologists, and is meant to showcase finds from the five digs going on in the countryside around Savannakhet. Aside from a few old bones and photos of the digs, it is not really very interesting except for the opportunity to chat with the friendly curators, who appreciate foreign visitors and a chance to talk in English.

Provincial Museum

Housed in a peeling colonial-era mansion, 1km south of the ferry landing, the unkempt **Provincial Museum** (daily 8am–noon & 2–4pm; 5000K) is mostly given over to old photographs of Kaysone, Savannakhet's most revered native son (see box on p.270), and the events leading up to the communist takeover in 1975. There's a giant bust of the great leader and pictures of him bear-hugging a variety of dictators including Ho Chi Minh, Fidel Castro, Hun Sen and Jiang Zemin. In a sign of the times, the collection of captured RLA light artillery pieces formerly lined up in the weedy yard in front of the museum and pointed at Thailand has been discreetly removed.

△ Village houses with water urns

Kaysone: the man behind the bamboo curtain

When the leaders of Laos set about honouring their prime minister and communist party leader **Kaysone Phomvihane** on his death in 1992, they turned to North Korea. Experts at producing bronze work in the heroes-of-socialism style, North Korean sculptors executed 150 bronze busts of Kaysone, which have since been erected in pavilions throughout Laos. Whether these bronzes are a faithful portrayal of Kaysone is a matter of irrelevance to most Lao, since from 1958 until 1975, the man who led the Lao People's Revolutionary Party from its inception in 1955 was rarely seen in public. Only now that the state has begun remaking itself in his image is the cloud of secrecy surrounding the man dissipating, but the lack of biographical details about his life makes it difficult to discern the private Kaysone from the state-cultivated one.

What is known is that Kaysone was born in Savannakhet in 1920, the only son of a Vietnamese civil servant father and a Lao mother. As a teenager he left for Hanoi, where he studied at a law school under the name of Nguyen Tri Quoc before dropping out to devote himself to the life of a revolutionary. By 1945, he had attracted the attention of the great North Vietnamese leader Ho Chi Minh, who sent Kaysone back to his hometown, instructing him to infiltrate a Lao nationalist movement supported by the American Office of Strategic Services, a forerunner of the Central Intelligence Agency. Kaysone would later match his wits against the CIA as commander of the communist forces during the Second Indochina War.

When Souphanouvong arrived on the scene in Savannakhet later on in 1945, Kaysone and his followers deferred to the leadership of the prince, whom Kaysone followed to Bangkok after the French returned to power in 1946. Soon after, Kaysone became a member of the newly formed Committee for Resistance in the East, chaired by Nouhak Phoumsavanh, coordinating anti-French guerrilla raids along the Lao-Vietnamese border and responsible for liaisons with the Viet Minh, a tie which was to earn him the trust of the North Vietnamese, who eventually recruited him into the Indochinese Communist Party (ICP). After training at the Viet Minh's military academy, Kaysone became commander of the Latsavong brigade, the guerrilla unit in southeastern Laos which marked the beginnings of the Lao People's Liberation Army. Although unknown in national circles (it would take years for the international press to recognize him), Kaysone was already a force to be reckoned with, and, in 1950, when Souphanouvong formed the national resistance government that came to be known as the Pathet Lao, Kaysone was named defence minister. In this capacity, Kaysone spent the next four years recruiting and

Around Savannakhet

A **bicycle ride** out in any direction from the centre of town gives you an opportunity to view the difference in lifestyles between the ethnic Vietnamese of the town and the ethnic Lao in the countryside. Brick and stucco give way to teak and bamboo, while rows of shade trees come to an abrupt halt and fruit trees – mango, guava and papaya – begin to appear in every yard. Children walking to and from school carry small cylindrical baskets showing a preference for sticky rice over steamed rice, and older Lao men favour a sarong in traditional shades of purple, orange and black over the shorts or trousers worn in urban areas. Depending on the season, **rice fields** are either being ploughed, planted, weeded or harvested by hand. Farmers are busiest in the hours just after dawn and before dusk, wisely spending the hottest time of the day snoozing in hammocks suspended in the shade.

training members for the Pathet Lao's fighting force, of which he formally became commander in 1954. On the formation of the Lao People's Party the following year, Kaysone became secretary general – a post he would hold for the next 37 years. His control of the revolutionary movement was further solidified in 1959 when Souphanouvong and other Pathet Lao leaders were jailed in Vientiane. Though Kaysone relinquished his post as commander of the army to Khamtay Siphandone in 1962, he continued to direct military strategy until the end of the Thirty Year Struggle in 1975. He also led several delegations over these years to the Soviet Union, where he was received with all the honours accorded a communist party leader.

It was only fitting that Kaysone – a man who disdained the perquisites of military rank, indeed who was never even referred to by rank, and adopted the atypical surname of Phomvihane, the Lao word for the Sanskrit brahmavihara, or "Four Principles of Great Leadership" (kindness, mercy, sympathy and impartiality) – should emerge as the first prime minister of the Lao People's Democratic Republic in December 1975. For the next seventeen years, Kaysone firmly held the reins of power in Laos and, among diplomats, earned a reputation as a clever man, eager to learn and willing to acknowledge his mistakes. He has also been called the most pragmatic of Southeast Asia's socialist leaders, praise he earned after he ditched the botched socialist economic policies of the late 1970s and initiated reforms – long before change took root in the Soviet Union and Vietnam, Laos's socialist backers. Indeed, Kaysone's Laos hardly fitted the mould of a typical socialist country at all by the time of his death at the age of 72 in 1992, when Buddhist monks from wats around the capital chanted funeral incantations and received alms during a seven-day period of mourning in his honour. Until Kaysone's death the country's leadership rarely presented itself to the public as anything but a group, but the former prime minister's greying hair and full face has since become the image employed by a party reaching out for symbols of nationalism, his name invoked in speeches and the source of inspiration for a museum erected at his former Vientiane home (see p.112). But what is perhaps more striking than the party's decision to transform Kaysone into a "man of the people", who relished simple food and knew all the country songs by heart, are the pedestals upon which his bust has been placed – shaded by red and gold pavilions topped by tiered parasols, Kaysone's monuments exude something of the regal splendour once reserved for the Theravada Buddhist monarchs who ruled over the kingdom of Lane Xang.

That Ing Hang

A much revered Buddhist stupa dating from the sixteenth century, **That Ing Hang** is located just outside Savannakhet and can be reached by bicycle or motorcycle: follow Route 13 north for 13km until you see a sign on the right and follow this road for a further 3km. The stucco work which covers the stupa is crude yet appealing, especially the whimsical rosettes which dot the uppermost spire. Off to one side of the stupa stands an amusing sandstone sculpture of a lion, grinning like a Cheshire cat, which could only have been hauled here from one of the Khmer ruins downriver. The stupa is best visited during its annual festival in February when thousands make the pilgrimage, camping in the walled courtyard that surrounds the stupa. During the celebrations, the door to a small chamber at the base of the stupa is opened, and male devotees queue up to make offerings to the Buddha images inside. By custom, women are prohibited from entering this inner sanctum.

Eating and drinking

The food and service at all of Savannakhet's **travellers' cafés** is notably poor, but the town does have some good local **restaurants** if you know where to look. Two famous local noodle dishes worth seeking out are *baw bun* (Vietnamese rice noodles served with chopped-up spring rolls and beef) and *ap-jao* (a Chinese dish loaded with stir-fried veggies and slices of beef, served in a tangy sauce). Other local delights include bamboo shoots and watermelon and *Sin Savannakhet* – sweet, dried, roasted beef. There are a few local Lao restaurants such as *Xokxay* and *Savanhlath* on and around the town square. In the evenings, shops selling soft drinks – the fruit shakes are in a class of their own – and a few *tam màk* hung vendors crop up on the riverbank in front of Wat Sainyaphum, a pleasant spot to catch the sunset over Thailand and mingle with the locals.

Baw Bun Shop Fourth shop-house from the river, in the alley behind *Santyphab Hotel*. Nothing in Savannakhet is easy. Not only is this place hard to find (no English sign) but it's only open in the morning. Still, if it's *baw bun* you're after, this is the place.

Hoongthip Garden Restaurant 79 Phetsarath Rd ☎041/212262. This is the nicest restaurant in town, housed in a big wood building with open sala-style seating under a green roof in Thai-Lao style. If you're after a good meal in pleasant surrounds with some atmosphere, look no further.

Lao-Paris 4 Seasons Café 30 Chaleunmoung Rd, near the river. For lack of a better alternative, all the travellers seem to end up at this Vietnamese shop-house near the river, which is the closest thing Savannakhet has to a travellers' café. Alright for sandwiches and coffee but the service is incredibly slow and they play the same Seventies hits tape day in and day out.

Mekong Riverside North end of Tha He Rd. Tables on a wooden terrace outside a big house supply an excellent sunset view. For some unfathomable reason, this is the only restaurant in town to take advantage of the view across the Mekong. Not to be confused with the nicely restored but honkey-tonk *Mekong Hotel* just down the street.

Rendezvous 179 Latsavongseuk Rd at the corner of Simuang Rd. This is a travellers' café with an English menu and a few Western dishes like eggs and chips, but service is poor. Much better is the no-name place directly across the street which is very local and hasn't any sign but can whip up a strong, steaming Lao coffee in a few seconds.

Sakura Korean BBQ Sayamungkhun Rd behind Wat Sayamungkhun. Very good Korean BBQ steamboat with a choice of beef or fish and lots of fresh veggies and glass noodles. Cheap, delicious and highly recommended.

Sensabay Next to *Santyphab Hotel*. Popular backpacker spot with quite tasty Western and Asian food but slow service. However, it's the best backpacker place, with inexpensive food and good stir-fries, and the fish'n'chips is well worth trying.

Starlite Restaurant Sayamungkhun Rd behind Wat Sayamungkhun. Like the *Sakura BBQ* right next door, this place serves $2 "suki" steamboats and is very popular with young locals. Cheap and delicious and a lot more fun than the travellers' cafés.

Tommy Corner Phetsalat Rd, directly opposite Wat Sayamungkhun. Very nice two-storey white house with an outdoor patio right on a quiet corner. A very pleasant place to stop by and have a cool drink or a meal.

Listings

Airlines Lao Aviation, at the airport, southeast of the city centre ☎041/212140.

Banks and exchange There are two banks near the intersection of Latsavongseuk and Oudomsin roads. The Lao May Bank faces Oudomsin Road and the BCEL faces Latsavongseuk Road.

Consulates Thailand: On Kouvolavong Road on block south of the square (Mon–Fri 8.30am–noon & 2–3.30pm; ☎041/212373); tourist visas cost just $7, an amazing deal, and require two photos.

Provided you apply before noon, the visa is ready the next afternoon. Vietnam: on Sisavang Vong Road (Mon–Fri 7.30–11am & 1.30–4.30pm; ☎041/212418); visas cost $50, require two photos and take five working days.

Hospitals and clinics The biggest hospital is located on Khanthabouli Road, near the provincial museum; a 24hr clinic operates on Phetsalat Road, a block south of the Hoongthip Hotel. The biggest pharmacy is on the corner of Oudomsin and Senna roads.

Moving on to Vietnam and Thailand

To Vietnam

A daily bus to **Vietnam** leaves at 10pm. Different cities are served, including Hué, Da Nang, and Hanoi ($8–10), depending on which day of the week you travel. Buses to Hué go on Mondays, Thursdays and Sundays. Buses to Da Nang depart on Tuesdays, Wednesdays, Fridays and Saturdays. Since the Da Nang bus passes through Hué anyway, this effectively means there are daily buses to Hué. There is also a Hanoi bus on weekends. In any case, all the Vietnam buses necessarily stop in Dong Ha where Route 9 meets Vietnam's Highway 1, so you can always transfer there for other cities in Vietnam.

To Thailand

The passenger **ferry** that runs across the Mekong between Savannakhet and Mukdahan in Thailand (50 baht) docks at the Immigration Office on Tha He Road. The ferry departs 6 times daily on weekdays at 9.10am, 10.10am, 11.10am, 1.30pm, 2.15pm and 4pm. At weekends there are departures just 3 times a day at 10.30am, 2.15pm and 4pm. You'll find an exchange kiosk in the Ferry terminal. On the Thai side frequent buses leave for That Phanom and Ubon Ratchathani.

Internet access Canon Internet on the southeast corner of the town square (daily 8am–9pm; 200K per minute or 10,000k per hr); a second internet shop with the same prices is on Khanthabouli Road 100m north of the GPO.

Laundry Fast and cheap at the laundry shops along Kouvolavong Road, north of the town square.

Markets Talat Nyai (main market), at the north end of town towards the bus station has four levels of goods. A new market has just been constructed on Latsavongseuk at the corner of Chaimuang Road. Stalls selling fresh fruit daily are on Latsavongseuk at the corner of Soutthanou Road.

Massage There's a Red Cross traditional massage on Kouvolavong Road across from the Chinese temple.

Newspapers A few copies of the *Bangkok Post* arrive at the minimart, next to the *Santyphab Hotel*, daily around 5pm, and there's a free reading copy at the *Lao-Paris* café (see p.272).

Post and telephone The GPO is on Khanthabouli Road, a few blocks south of the town square (Mon–Fri 8am–noon & 1–5pm, Sat & Sun 8–11am). The Telcom building with overseas phone and fax service building (daily 8am–10pm) is just behind it.

Swimming *Phonepaseud Hotel*, Santisouk Road, has a 25-metre-pool which is open to non-guests for a small fee.

East to Xepon and the Vietnam border

Running from east to west from Savannakhet to Dong Ha, pot-holed **Route 9** links Thailand and Vietnam and is currently the southernmost road link between the two neighbours. From Savannakhet on the banks of the Mekong, the yet to be repaved highway heads east through a series of drab and dusty towns, passing Muang Phin and then Xepon, where it begins its climb up into the Annamite Mountains. The road ends its Lao journey at the **Lao Bao pass**, before crossing into Vietnam and continuing down to Dong Ha, where it joins Highway 1.

The French completed the road in 1930, as part of an Indochinese road network intended to link Mekong towns with the Vietnamese coast, bringing in Vietnamese migrants and trucking out Lao produce. Today, the Thais have shown an interest in Route 9 as a possible trade corridor, linking their poor northeastern provinces with the port of Danang in Vietnam. It was a project which was strongly supported by the Lao government, but plans for upgrading the route were checked by the Asian financial crisis.

For the time being, Route 9 is a bumpy, dusty track, and a very tough trip, despite direct bus services between Savannakhet and Dong Ha. While most travellers barrel through on the direct buses, the frontier is not without sites of interest. As you approach Muang Phin, Route 9 begins to cross the north–south arteries of the **Ho Chi Minh Trail**, a network of dirt paths and roads which spread throughout southeastern Laos, running from the Mu Gia Pass in Bolikhamxai province south through Attapu and into Cambodia. While much of the debris from the war lies off the beaten track, some of these war relics, such as a downed American helicopter in **Muang Phin** and bombed-out US tanks at Ban Dong, are easily accessible. Muang Phin can also be used as a base for the Dong Phou Viang NBCA. Another place worth stopping off in to explore the surrounding area is the recently rebuilt market town of Xepon. Xepon and its neighbouring towns are populated predominantly by Phu Tai people, a lowland Lao group. To the west, the valleys have long been inhabited by Lao, drawn south centuries ago by the prospect of river valleys ripe for wet-rice cultivation. They also benefited from their proximity to the trading route from Hué, the ancient Vietnamese royal seat, to Savannakhet and on to Siam.

Xeno and Muang Phin

East of Savannakhet, Route 9 heads past teak plantations until it reaches the **XENO** junction, 35km away, at the intersection of Route 9 and the country's north–south axis, Route 13. Once a French military outpost and later a Royal Lao airfield, Xeno these days is known mostly for its gypsum quarries. There is no reason to stop here but should you find yourself stuck for the night, air-conditioned rooms are available at the town's sole hotel, the multi-storey *Pounlaodi* (❶–❷), across from the market.

You'll know you've reached **MUANG PHIN**, roughly 100km east of Xeno, when your bus halts right in front of the massive Vietnamese-Lao friendship monument, a testament to communist cooperation during the Second Indochina War, and exuding far more revolutionary zeal than anything found in Vientiane. The golden rendering of a Pathet Lao and North Vietnamese soldier

The Vietnamese influence

A planned link to the Vietnamese power grid reflects the continuing influence exerted by **Vietnam** in this area. Indeed, ties between Muang Phin and Vietnam go back a long way: the area's Phu Tai inhabitants paid tribute to the court in Hué during much of the eighteenth and nineteenth centuries. In the middle of the nineteenth century, however, the Vietnamese rulers, having just wrapped up a war with Siam, were content to exact a light tribute of wax and elephant tusks from the Phu Tai, preferring to leave the Tai minority's territory as a loose buffer zone between regional powers. By this point, Vietnamese merchants, following the traditional trading route across the Lao Bao pass, were already arriving in Muang Phin with cooking pans, iron, salt and fish sauce, and returning east with cows and water buffaloes in tow. A story told by an early French visitor to the town attests to the business acumen of one of these merchants. Upon arriving in town, he found prices too high, but was reluctant to return home without making a good profit. With a quick conversion to Buddhism the merchant's problem was solved: he shaved his head and shacked up in the local temple where he could defray his expenses until prices dropped, at which point the merchant donned a wig, bought up a few buffalo and hightailed it back to Hué.

dwarfs the town, whose rundown appearance bears testament to Muang Phin's unfortunate position on one of the fronts during the war. There's little to recommend Muang Phin as a stopover, but if you're here you may opt for a quick trip to check out what's left of a downed American helicopter, one of the more easily accessible **war relics** on the Ho Chi Minh Trail. Follow the road that strikes south from the friendship monument for 30m and you'll find it on your left.

If and when **Route 23** is reconnected to Toumlan, Muang Phin will become a convenient hub for travellers wanting to cut down directly to Salavan, as well as a base for visiting the huge Dong Phou Viang NBCA just south of town. But these days, the town is little more than a through point on the road to the border. There are now two new private **guest houses** here; *Sikham* (❶) just west of the bus station is new and clean, and a little further down the street there's also the new *Sysamphone* (❶).

Xepon

A picturesque village in the foothills of the Annamite Mountains, 40km from the Vietnamese border, **XEPON** is a pleasant rural stopover for those in transit on the route to Vietnam or Savannakhet. Cows and water buffalo meander along red dirt roads, pausing to graze in the fields that separate the village's wooden homes, and flame trees add a splash of fire to the misty green hills surrounding the settlement. To look at the crumbling, custard-coloured school building, perched on a hill overlooking the market, you'd think Xepon was much older than it is. In fact, the original town of Xepon was destroyed during the war – along with every house of the district's two hundred villages – and was later rebuilt here 6km west of its original location, on the opposite bank of the Xe Banghiang River. The old city (written as "Tchepone" on some old maps) had been captured by communist forces in 1960 and became an important outpost on the Ho Chi Minh Trail. As such it was the target of a joint South Vietnamese and American invasion in 1971 (see p.276), aimed at disrupting the flow of troops and supplies headed for communist forces in South Vietnam.

Practicalities

Xepon is such a small town that even the **market** fails to generate much of a buzz, despite being the hub of everyday life. After the bus drops you off in front of the market, it's a short walk uphill to the government **guest house** (❶), a long wooden structure with blue trim, which offers dormitory-style accommodation and an outdoor pump for a shower. The caretaker drops by once or twice a day to check for new arrivals and clean up the rooms. If you've come by your own transport or don't mind the brisk 1.5-kilometre walk, the forestry department runs a somewhat nicer guest house (❶) at the edge of town, also featuring dormitory-style rooms. There's no water, so be prepared to bathe in the nearby stream. To get here, take a left at the second road west of the market and follow the road to the foot of the hill.

There's an excellent **noodle shop** on the western side of the market complex, popular with locals. Run by a family from Vientiane, the shop makes a hearty bowl of *fõe*, loaded with chunks of roasted chicken and garlic. A second option is the small **restaurant** (across from the market and marked by an English sign) run by a chatty Phu Tai woman. Noodles, omelettes and stir-fried vegetables can be selected from an English-language menu scrawled on a chalk board, although the innards mingled into the *làp sin* may not appeal to all. There are no official exchange services in Xepon, but cash can always be exchanged. From Xepon, sawngthaews run up to Ban Dong as well as the border town of Daen Sawan where you can continue by motorcycle taxi to the Lao Bao border post.

The Ho Chi Minh Trail at Ban Dong

Halfway between Xepon and the Vietnam border is the town of **BAN DONG**, the site of one of America's most ignominious defeats during the war, and a popular stop on tours of the **Ho Chi Minh Trail**. East out of Xepon, you'll cross a Russian bridge, built to replace the destroyed French one, the shrapnel-riddled remains of which lie in the river below. The highway gradually climbs through the foothills of the Annamite chain, passing bomb craters – often obscured by brush – and unexploded ordnance, dragged to the roadside by villagers clearing their land. Women squat by the road with their intricately woven baskets, selling bamboo shoots – a local speciality. The area's abundant bamboo crop is in fact partially a by-product of the spraying of defoliants by American forces who hoped to expose the arteries of the Ho Chi Minh Trail: hardy bamboo is quick to take root in areas of deforestation, whether it is caused by swidden agriculture or chemical defoliants. Rows of bamboo-and-thatch drink shops, competing to quench the thirst of Vietnamese truckers, signal your arrival in Ban Dong, and are the only feature that distinguish this seemingly unremarkable village from the handful of other villages on this stretch of Route 9. However, Ban Dong is a **popular stop** on any tour of the Ho Chi Minh Trail, and villagers are slowly growing accustomed to tourists poking around for a glimpse of the American tanks left over from the battle, known as **Lam Son 719**.

Operation Lam Son 719

On the outskirts of the village of Ban Dong on Route 9, sit two rusting American tanks, all that remains of a massive invasion and series of battles that have become a mere footnote in the history of the decade-long American military debacle in Indochina. In 1971, US President Nixon, anticipating a massive campaign by North Vietnamese troops against South Vietnam the following year (which happened to be an election year), ordered an attack on the Ho Chi Minh Trail to cut off supplies to communist forces. Although a congressional amendment had been passed the previous year prohibiting US ground troops from crossing the border from Vietnam into Laos and Cambodia, the US command saw it as an opportunity to test the strengths of Vietnamization, the policy of turning the ground war over to the South Vietnamese. For the operation, code-named **Lam Son 719**, it was decided that ARVN (Army of the Republic of Vietnam) troops were to invade Laos and block the trail with the backing of US air support. The objective was Xepon, a town straddled by the Trail, which was some 30–40km wide at this point. Nixon's national security adviser, Henry Kissinger, was later to lament that "the operation, conceived in doubt and assailed by scepticism, proceeded in confusion". In early February 1971, ARVN troops and tanks pushed across the border at Lao Bao and followed Route 9 into Laos. Like a caterpillar trying to ford a column of red ants, the South Vietnamese troops were soon engulfed by superior numbers of North Vietnamese (NVA) regulars. Ordered by President Thieu of South Vietnam to halt if there were more than 3000 casualties, ARVN officers stopped halfway to Xepon and engaged the NVA in a series of battles that lasted over a month. US air support proved ineffectual, and by mid-March scenes of frightened ARVN troops drastically retreating were being broadcast around the world. In an official Lao account of the battle, a list of "units of Saigon puppet troops wiped out on Highway 9" included four regiments of armoured cavalry destroyed between the Vietnam border and Ban Dong.

The tank that's easiest to find lies five minutes' walk off the road that cuts south out of town towards Taoy, and which was once a crucial artery of the Ho Chi Minh Trail. Shaded by a grove of jackfruit trees, it rests atop a small hill east of the road, partially dismantled for its valuable steel. Someone has since scrawled a message in red paint on the iron carcass, warning locals that they should leave the rest of the tank intact as a monument to Pathet Lao military triumph. In truth, the tanks speak of the might of the North Vietnamese Army, which routed ARVN troops in their attempted invasion of Laos (see box on p.276). As of 1998, UXO-Lao (the Lao National Unexploded Ordnance Programme) has cleared Ban Dong of unexploded war debris, but it's still a good idea to ask a villager to show you the way, as you should always take extra care when leaving a well-worn path, and vegetation in the rainy season can obscure the tank's location. If you're travelling by public transport, the best time to visit Ban Dong is in the morning, as there are no late-afternoon buses plying this stretch of highway, and Ban Dong has no accommodation. For getting back in the afternoon, check to see if another bus will swing through town to pick you up; otherwise you'll have to rely on flagging down a ride.

Daen Sawan

The quality of the road takes a dive as it makes its final push towards the mountain pass of Lao Bao which leads to Vietnam. After passing through many small ethnic minority villages, the last town on the Lao side of the pass is **DAEN SAWAN**. For a remote border town, Daen Sawan is quite tourist-friendly with food, accommodation and exchange services. Travellers not using the direct express buses can find accommodation at the *Friendly* **guest house** (❶) which has basic rooms with shared bathrooms and a helpful owner who speaks fairly good English. Attached to the guest house is the *Loung Aloune* **restaurant** which can muster up a tasty plate of fried rice, along with the usual smattering of Lao dishes. Baguettes are on offer at another shop nearby. Even if you are on the direct bus you may have to wait a couple of hours in Daen Sawan. There is a Lao May Bank in town as well as a branch at the Lao Immigration Office on the border. The rates are not good so only change what you need: $20 is more than enough to get you to Savannakhet. From Daen Sawan, you can hire a motorcycle taxi for the final one-kilometre ride to the Lao immigration post. If you've entered Laos from Vietnam, there are two buses a day to Savannakhet from Daen Sawan leaving in the morning, the last at 10am. There's also an early afternoon bus to Xepon.

The Daen Sawan/Lao Bao border crossing

A short distance from the Lao immigration post is the **Daen Sawan/Lao Bao** border crossing into Vietnam. Travellers into Vietnam must have a valid visa and the crossing is not always hassle-free. Vietnamese officials may send you back if your visa is not stamped for "Lao Bao", and motorcyclists have also reported problems, with officials sometimes unwilling to allow larger bikes to enter. On the Vietnamese side, there are motorcycle taxis to take you down the hill to Lao Bao town where buses leave for the twenty-kilometre journey to Khe Sanh every thirty minutes, with some going straight through to Dong Ha on Route 1, where bus or train connections can be made to Hanoi and Hué.

If you've entered Laos from Vietnam and are not on a through bus, you'll have to get a motorbike 1km down to **Daen Sawan** town where there are buses to Xepon and Savannakhet. **Accommodation** is available on both sides of the pass for those who miss their bus connections or have visa problems.

Travel details

Buses

Daen Sawan/Lao Bao to: Muang Phin (3 daily; 2hr 30min); Savannakhet (2 daily; 7hr 30min); Xepon (4 daily; 1hr 15min).

Lak Xao to: Thakhek (1 daily; 5hr); Vientiane (3 daily; 8hr).

Muang Phin to: Daen Sawan/Lao Bao (3 daily; 2hr 30min); Savannakhet (3 daily; 5hr); Xepon (3 daily; 1hr 15min).

Savannakhet to: Daen Sawan/Lao Bao (2 daily; 8hr); Danang (4 weekly; 15hr); Hanoi (weekly; 24hr); Hué (3 weekly; 15hr); Muang Phin (3 daily; 5hr); Pakxe (3 daily; 6hr); Thakhek (9 daily; 2hr);

Vientiane (6 daily; 12hr); Xepon (2 daily; 6hr).

Thakhek to: Hanoi (weekly; 24 hrs); Lak Xao (3 daily; 4hr); Mahaxai (5 daily; 2hr 30min); Pakxe (3 daily; 9hr); Savannakhet (9 daily; 4hr); Vientiane (10 daily; 8hr).

Xepon to: Daen Sawan/Lao Bao (4 daily; 1hr 15min); Muang Phin (3 daily; 1hr 15min); Savannakhet (2 daily; 6hr 15min).

Flights

Savannakhet (ZVK) to: Pakxe (4 weekly; 45min); Vientiane (1 daily; 1hr 5min).

6

The far south

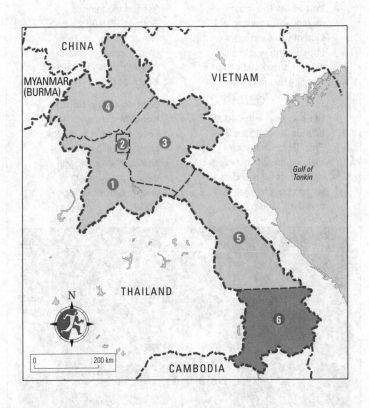

CHAPTER 6

Highlights

✴ **Watch the river flow** Kick back for a day or three in the laid-back backpacker town of Champasak, amongst temples, sacred mountains and Khmer ruins. See p.292

✴ **Wat Phou** The most harmonious Khmer ruin outside of Cambodia, this fifteen-century-old hillside landmark exudes a serenity lost in overrun Siem Reap. See p.295

✴ **Si Phan Don – the 4000 Islands** Travel to the Si Phan Don, where the Mekong creates hundreds of idyllic small islands and life has not changed in centuries. See p.301

✴ **Dolphin-watching at Khon Island** See the rare and endangered Irrawaddy fresh-water dolphins in one of their last surviving habitats. See p.308

✴ **Explore the Bolaven** Ascend the famous Bolaven Plateau for cool breezes, crashing hundred-metre falls and the freshest coffee around. See p.311

✴ **Boat down the Nam Xe Kong** Would-be Huck Finns shouldn't resist the chance to slip down the Xe Kong River through the country's most remote provinces. See p.319

6

The Far South

he tail-end of Laos is anchored by the provinces of **Champasak**, **Xekong**, **Attapu** and **Salavan**, a region which lay at the crossroads of the great empires that ruled Southeast Asia centuries ago – Champa, Chenla and Angkor. Bordered by Thailand, Cambodia and Vietnam, the **far south** conveniently divides into two sections, dictated primarily by topography, with **Pakxe**, the region's most important market town, as the hub. In the west, the **Mekong River** cuts Champasak province roughly in half, while further east, the fertile highlands of the **Bolaven Plateau** separate the Mekong corridor from the rugged Annamite Mountains that form Laos's border with Vietnam.

The dozens of ancient Khmer temples scattered throughout the lush tropical forests and jade rice paddies on either bank of the Mekong hold mysteries yet to be unravelled by today's archeologists. Pilgrims from the lowland Lao communities that dominate the Mekong River Valley of the far south gather relics from these sites, ignorant of the gods that inspired them, and place them upon their gaudy, modern Theravada Buddhist temples. In the last years of the monarchy, even members of the royal family had the audacity to plunder statues of deities to decorate their modern villas, as if proclaiming a rightful link to the *devaraja*, the god-kings who ruled over Angkorian Cambodia. The most famous of these temples, **Wat Phou**, is the spiritual centre of the region and the main tourist attraction in southern Laos. An imposing reminder of the Angkorian empire that once dominated much of Southeast Asia, Wat Phou is one of the most impressive Khmer ruins outside Cambodia, and lies a few kilometres from the town of **Champasak**, the former royal seat of the defunct Lao kingdom of the same name.

From here it makes sense to go with the flow of the river south to **Si Phan Don**, where the Mekong's 1993-kilometre-journey through Laos rushes to a thundering conclusion in the series of waterfalls that hindered French attempts to connect Saigon with the hidden riches of inner China. The region's name means "Four Thousand Islands", a reference to the vast number of land masses dotted with long-established ethnic Lao villages and rice paddies, which the Mekong, stretched to its maximum width of 14km, wraps around before spilling over the Khone Falls – Khon Phapheng and Somphamit – into Cambodia. These waters support some of the most important freshwater fisheries in Southeast Asia.

Much of the area east of the Mekong lies off the beaten track and is likely to appeal most to the intrepid and those who relish a dose of "real travelling". Typically, travel in this region involves journeying on hard wooden seats along bumpy roads to remote towns or out-of-the-way spots of raw natural beauty.

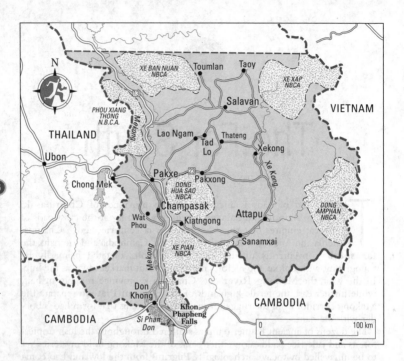

Just east of Pakxe, the **Bolaven Plateau**, with its rich agricultural bounty and crashing waterfalls, straddles the provincial borders of the remote provinces of Salavan, Xekong and Attapu, an area with a long history of settlement by midland Mon-Khmer groups, whose names – Laven, Taoy, Alak, Katang, Ngae – are seldom heard outside Laos. The isolation of the thickly forested hills in this region has made it an ideal place for insurgents throughout the ages to hide out – from anti-French rebels to the North Vietnamese in the Second Indochina War. The latter transformed trails and roads along Laos's eastern edge into the Ho Chi Minh Trail, a thoroughfare along which supplies and troops made their way into Cambodia and South Vietnam. American forces and their allies, the Royalist Lao and the Thai, subjected the area to some of the most intensive bombing in history, a campaign which included the use of chemical defoliants such as the notorious Agent Orange. By braving the primitive transport linking the far-flung villages of Salavan, Xekong and Attapu, you'll witness the resilience of the land, still home to a diverse variety of wildlife, and travel among peoples as cut off from the rest of Laos as they have ever been.

Pakxe, the region's commercial and transport hub, provides the most convenient **gateway to the far south**, with travellers arriving either from Savannakhet or from Thailand via the Chong Mek border crossing. From the south, the border with Cambodia is now open and a growing stream of intrepid backpackers are using it. Getting around in the deep south can be exhausting, as transport is limited to slow, crowded buses navigating poorly paved roads, some of which are impassable in the rainy season. Another drawback to the network stitching together the southern provinces is that it can be difficult to avoid backtracking, but, on the bright side, several significant towns can be reached by river, providing a more comfortable, if time-consuming, mode of travel. The most pleasant **time of year** to visit the region is during the cool season (Nov–Feb), when the rivers and waterfalls are in full spate and the scenery greenest.

Some history

The **early history** of the far south remains a hot topic of debate among archeologists. Although the ruins of an ancient city buried near the town of Champasak and not far from the region's most significant religious site, Wat Phou, indicate that the area was the centre of a thriving civilization as early as the fifth century, no one seems sure if the town was part of Champa, a Hinduized kingdom that ruled parts of central Vietnam for more than fourteen centuries, or the Chenla kingdom, which is thought to have been located near the Mekong River in present-day northern Cambodia, extending through what is now southern Laos. The **Khmer** were the first people to leave a clear imprint on the area, and the temple ruins that survive throughout the far south along the Mekong River suggest the region was an important part of the Khmer empire from the eighth to the twelfth century, when the Angkor empire was at its height. It is also thought that the better part of southern Laos was dominated by ethnic Khmer, in particular the **Mon-Khmer ethnic groups** that still inhabit the Bolaven Plateau region and the rugged mountains of the Annamite Mountains beyond.

The **ethnic Lao** are relative newcomers to the region, having made their way slowly south along the Mekong from the Lao heartland of the Upper Mekong, as Angkor's power, and its hold over present-day southern Laos, waned. By the early sixteenth century, the centre of the ethnic Lao world was shifting steadily south, and King Phothisalat spent much of his time in Vientiane. Eventually, his son and successor Setthathilat officially transferred the capital of Lane Xang from Louang Phabang to Vientiane in 1563. While the origins of the first ethnic Lao principality in the Champasak region are unclear, legends trace the roots of the **Lao kingdom of Champasak** back to Nang Pao, a queen said to have ruled during the mid-seventeenth century. The story goes that **Nang Pao** was seduced by a prince from a nearby kingdom and gave birth out of wedlock, initiating a sex scandal for which she has been remembered ever since. The queen is said to have acknowledged her mistake by decreeing that every unwed mother must pay for her sin by sacrificing a buffalo to appease the spirits, a tradition continued into the late 1980s by unwed mothers, known as "Nang Pao's daughters", from some of the ethnic groups in the area. Legend has it that Nang Pao's actual daughter, Nang Peng, ceded rule over the kingdom to a holy man, who in turn sought out Soi Sisamouth, a descendant of Souligna Vongsa, the last great king of Lane Xang, and made him king.

The origins of the Champasak kingdom come into sharper focus with the crowning of **Soi Sisamouth** in 1713. Soi Sisamouth ascended the throne of an independent southern kingdom in the wake of the dissolution of Lane Xang at the turn of the eighteenth century. With his royal seat centred on present-day Champasak, near Wat Phou, Soi Sisamouth extended the new kingdom's influence to include part of present-day Thailand, as well as Salavan and Attapu. But the king, and his successor Sainyakuman, only managed to maintain a tenuous independence and, after its capital was captured by Siamese forces in 1778, Champasak was reduced to being a **vassal of Siam**, and so it remained until the French arrived more than one hundred years later. King Yo made a gambit to regain independence for Champasak when he joined forces in 1827 with his father Anou, Vientiane's legendary last king, in an ill-fated fight to throw off the yoke of Siamese domination. The botched rebellion had disastrous consequences for both kingdoms – the kingdom of Vientiane was left to ruin while Champasak was drastically reduced in size.

Siam gobbled up so much of Champasak's territory that there was little left for the **French** when they arrived late in the nineteenth century and claimed all territory east of the Mekong River. Caught between French ambition and a still-powerful Siam, Champasak was split in half, and its king, Kam Souk, was forced to rule from the left bank, severed from a large number of his subjects. Champasak's meagre territory was reunited by the Franco-Siamese treaty of 1904, but Kam Souk had to travel to Pakxe to swear his allegiance to France and was treated as little more than a civil servant, stripped of the royal privileges that the kings of Louang Phabang and Cambodia were permitted to keep.

Although Kam Souk's son, **Prince Boun Oum na Champasak**, successfully parlayed his birthright into a prime spot in the national limelight, it seems Nang Pao's kiss of death was reserved especially for him. In exchange for the title of Inspector General for life, Prince Boun Oum renounced his claim to the throne of a sovereign Champasak in 1946 and recognized the king of Louang Phabang as the royal head of a unified Laos, effectively ending the Champasak royal line. Although Boun Oum continued to perform the ritual duties that lent legitimacy to his princely title until the early 1970s, when the right-leaning prince fled the country after the Communist takeover, he spoke of the kingdom as being doomed from the start on account of Nang Pao's misdemeanour: "With an unmarried mother as queen, everything started so badly that the game was lost before it began."

Pakxe

Capitalizing on its location at the confluence of the Xe Don and the Mekong rivers, roughly halfway between the Thai border and the fertile Bolaven Plateau, **PAKXE** is the far south's biggest city, and its commercial and transport hub. For travellers, it is mostly a convenient stopover en route to Si Phan Don and Cambodia, though it makes a more comfortable base than Pakxong for exploration of the Bolaven Plateau and nearby NBCAs. There is also a border crossing to Thailand just west of Pakxe at Chong Mek making it a logical entry or exit point for travellers doing a north–south tour of Laos. Unlike other major Mekong towns however, Pakxe is not an old city. Rather it has risen in prominence from relatively recent beginnings a hundred years ago as a French administrative centre, to being the region's most important market town, attracting traders from Salavan, Attapu, Xekong and Si Phan Don, as well as from Thailand. The diverse population of Vietnamese, Lao and Chinese today numbers 60,000 and the growing city makes a very convenient staging post or basecamp for travel in Laos's far south.

Arrival and city transport

Pakxe has a lot of transport options and is served by an airport, two bus stations, a sawngthaew station, and a passenger boat landing. **Buses** to and from the north use the Northern Bus Station, 7km north of the city on Route 13. Buses to and from points south and east use the Southern Bus Station, 8km southeast of town on Route 13 at the big T-junction. Tuk-tuks to either station are 3000K and can be flagged down in town or taken from the stand near

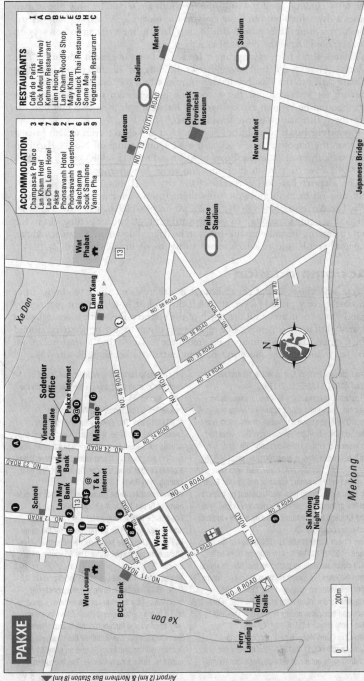

PAKXE

ACCOMMODATION
Champasak Palace   3
Lan Kham Hotel   4
Lao Cha Leun Hotel   7
Pakse   8
Phonsavanh Hotel   2
Phonsavanh Guesthouse   1
Salachampa   6
Souk Samlane   5
Vanna Pha   9

RESTAURANTS
Café de Paris   I
Dok Meui (Mei Hwa)   A
Ketmany Restaurant   D
Lien Huong   B
Lan Kham Noodle Shop   F
May Kham   E
Seneluck Thai Restaurant   G
Some Mai   H
Vegetarian Restaurant   C

Xe Don

Market

Stadium

Stadium

Museum

NO. 13 SOUTH ROAD

Champask Provincial Museum

New Market

Japanese Bridge

THE FAR SOUTH | Pakse

6

Wat Phabat

13

Palace Stadium

Lane Xang Bank

NO. 38 ROAD

NO. 37 ROAD

NO. 36 ROAD

NO. 35 ROAD

NO. 34 ROAD

NO. 41 RD

N

Sodetour Office

Vietnam Consulate

Pakse Internet

C G D

Massage   G

NO. 46 ROAD

NO. 1 ROAD

NO. 24 ROAD

H

A

NO. 23 ROAD

School

Lao May Bank

Lao Viet Bank

T & K @ Internet

13

4 & F

E

B

2

1

NO. 12 ROAD

NO. 11 ROAD

6

5

8 7

West Market

Mekong

NO. 10 ROAD

NO. 9 ROAD

Sai Khong Night Club

9

Wat Louang

BCEL Bank

NO. 11 ROAD

NO. 8 ROAD

Drink Stalls

Ferry Landing

Xe Don

0   200m

the ferry landing. Most towns in the far south are served by only one or two buses a day, which tend to leave early in the morning. An express van departs for Attapu from the Southern Bus Station daily in the early afternoon – guest houses should have the details of exactly when.

There is also a huge **sawngthaew lot** located on the eastern side of the East Market. Here you'll find sawngthaews heading in all directions, including Champasak and the Thai border. If you miss a bus, you can always come here and try for a sawngthaew. Just to confuse matters even more, there are also northbound buses from the sawngthaew lot, although these also pull into the Northern Bus Station before leaving town.

Passenger boats to and from Si Phan Don as well as ferries to Ban Muang Kao, on the opposite bank, dock at the Xe Don landing off No. 11 Road, an easy walk from most hotels. Boats to Si Phan Don (15,000K) via Champasak (5000K) leave daily in the mornings and arrive late afternoon.

The **airport** lies 2km northeast of the city on Route 13, and is served by tuk-tuks on hand to greet the daily flights from Vientiane and Savannakhet. The Lao Aviation office (☎031/212252) is on No. 11 Road, near BCEL bank.

Pakxe is compact enough to **get around** on foot, but for getting out to the bus stations or the museum tuk-tuks can be flagged down just about anywhere, especially on Route 13 which serves as the town's main boulevard.

Accommodation

Pakxe isn't chock-full of cheap **hotels**, but there's something to choose from in nearly every price bracket, although the budget hotels are not particularly good value compared with the north of the country; the south is generally less touristy but more expensive. The majority of places to stay are scattered around the Central Market (currently being rebuilt following a fire), a short walk from the ferry landing, and also north of the Central Market along Route 13.

Champasak Palace Cnr of Route 13 and No. 1 Road ☎031/212263, ☎212781, ☎palace@cscoms.com, ☎www.champasakhotel.com. Though he didn't actually take up residence here, the town's fanciest, ninety-room hotel was a palace built for Prince Boun Oum who fled to France after the 1975 revolution. Fit for a prince, if not a king, it is an absolute steal at $25 for a double. Royal-sized rooms lead onto wide terraces with sweeping views of the Xe Don River and the surrounding hills, and a decent restaurant on the ground floor serves moderately priced Thai and Chinese food, accompanied by a fully stocked but overpriced bar. ❻

Lan Kham Hotel Route 13, 150m east of No. 12 Road ☎031/213314. A new, modern-style hotel with clean, reasonably priced rooms. Rooms range from two-bed fan rooms right up to air-con rooms with hot water en-suite and TVs. Downstairs attached to the lobby is an internet centre (500K/1 min) and a popular noodle restaurant. The hotel also rents bicycles ($2 a day). ❷–❸

Lao Cha Leun Hotel Directly opposite the Salachampa ☎031/251333. This brand-new, modern-style hotel has very clean air-con rooms with en-suite bathrooms with hot water and is centrally located right around the corner from the West Market. ❸

Pakse No. 5 Road, near the West Market ☎031/212131. The Pakse was once the city's favourite budget hotel. It has been closed for renovations for almost four years now but it looks like work is progressing. If and when it re-opens it has a great central location near the market, the boat landing, and Route 13.

Phonesavanh Guest House No. 12 Road a block north of Route 13. Just a short walk down No. 12 Road the Phonesavanh Hotel now has a brand-new annex which has newer rooms for the same low price. There are seven rooms all with en-suite bathrooms but no hot water. The $5 rooms have air-con. ❷

Phonesavanh Hotel Cnr of Route 13 and No. 12 Road ☎031/202842. Budget travellers should head here – it's a dump but the location's good and it has a certain seedy charm. The rooms are very spartan and the shared toilets and showers are not great but it is definitely the cheapest place in town with rooms from $2 and an extra $1 for ensuites. There's no hot water. The friendly staff maintain a useful information board in the lobby with travellers' postings from all over the south. ➊

Salachampa No. 10 Road, near the market ☎031/212273. If you're looking for a colonial-era hotel, the *Salachampa* has spacious rooms with high ceilings in this elegant restored French villa, with teak floors and breezy verandas. Spurn the cheaper modern cottages on offer. ➌

Souk Samlane No. 10 Road, behind the Chinese Society Building ☎031/212002. Uninspiring but sanitary rooms, some with attached bathrooms and balconies. The cheaper rooms also have an attached bathroom but at half the price have no hot water or air-con. This is a favourite with budget backpackers. ➊–➌

VannaPha No. 9 Road ☎031/212502. A bit of a walk south of the centre, but one of the best value in town. Set in a quiet compound, the *VannaPha* has clean, air-con rooms with wood floors and newly refurbished en-suite bathrooms with hot water. Given the quality of the rooms, this is the best value in town but it's a bit far from the restaurants. ➌

The Town

Nestling between the Mekong and a bend of the Xe Don River, Pakxe's city centre, where you'll find the market and most of the hotels and restaurants, is surrounded by water on three sides. Along No. 11 Road, the street that follows the Xe Don, are a few remaining examples of crumbling Franco-Chinese shop-houses and the town's main temple, Wat Luang. Turning away from the river here, you'll soon find yourself by the big new **West Market**. The old market here was destroyed in a fire in 1998 and this new multi-storey market should open soon. Indeed, much of the centre of Pakxe is currently a work in progress. All the centre's roads are being rebuilt and paved and this is perhaps why most of the city's hotels, restaurants, and shops are currently scattered along Route 13 rather than around the market area. For some reason the streets in the centre of the city have all been laid out diagonally, but it's such a small place that finding your way around isn't a problem.

Although many travellers just over-night here, with its good choice of hotels and restaurants Pakxe is also a suitable base for a number of good day-trips including Wat Phou and the Bolaven Plateau. Should you find yourself stuck in town for a couple of days there are a number of things to do to kill some time.

The **Champasak Provincial Museum** (Mon–Fri 8–11.30am & 2–4pm; 1000K), 1.5km east of the town centre on Route 13, houses some fine examples of ornately carved pre-Angkorian sandstone **lintels** taken from sites around the province, situated in the rear gallery. A dusty selection of costumes and jewellery from tribal peoples, and a small display of antique ethnic clothing are found in the upper gallery. The rest of the museum is given over to the obligatory display of photographs and artefacts of the long Lao struggle to establish a worker's paradise on earth.

Also on Route 13 is **Wat Pha Baht**, just east of the bridge that crosses north over the Xe Don. The wat features a stylized Buddha's footprint, but like the rest of Pakxe's monasteries, the architecture doesn't reflect much divine inspiration.

On a low hill west of Wat Pha Baht stands the **Champasak Palace Hotel** (see p.286 for details), a majestic eyesore resembling a giant cement wedding cake, and one of the few prominent reminders of the late Prince Boun Oum na Champasak, a colourful character who was the heir to the Champasak kingdom and one of the most influential southerners of the twentieth century. Legend has it that Boun Oum needed a palace this size so that he could accommodate his many concubines. The palace, left incomplete after the one-time prime minister wound up on the wrong side of history and left for France in the 1970s, was converted into a hotel by Thai investors, who retained its original wooden fittings, tiled pillars and high ceilings. The stucco motifs on the gables depicting the country's post-revolutionary zeal were not in the prince's original plans.

For one of the few surviving examples of colonial architecture in the far south, be sure to check out the **Chinese Society House**, on No. 5 Road near the *Hotel Salachampa*, yet another French-era building. With many of the town's French-influenced buildings in disrepair or already replaced by modern shop-houses, the Society House, beautifully renovated in 1998, is an elegant example of a style on the way out in rapidly modernizing Pakxe.

After the market fire in 1998 the town's market vendors all moved out to a new venue located east along Route 13, the **East Market.** Since the vendors are all settled into this new market, it remains to be seen what will happen when the downtown market eventually opens. Some locals say there will just be two competing markets but no one is sure. On some maps the as yet unfinished West Market is referred to as the "Morning Market" while the East Market is called the "New Market". In the meantime, the East Market is well worth a visit and is certainly big enough to remind you of Vientiane's Morning Market. Along with the usual array of mounds of tobacco, plastic ware and live chickens, local specialities available at the market include tea, coffee and a variety of fruit and vegetables from the fecund Bolaven Plateau, as well as fish from the islands of Si Phan Don, including gigantic golden carp featherbacks, and the fermented fish paste known as *pa dàek* sold out of ceramic jars.

Eating and drinking

Pakxe has the best range of restaurants south of Savannakhet, not just because of its size but because of the number of foreigners working here and its mix of ethnic Vietnamese, Chinese and Lao communities. Most of the town's better restaurants are found either on Route 13 between No. 12 and No. 24 Roads, or on No. 46 Road just east of No. 24 Road. Aside from restaurants, there are also two bars in the town proper – *Sai Khong*, on No. 9 Road near the Mekong River, and *Sengtawan Cabaret*, above the ferry landing – both of which offer bad bands and taxi dancers. More peaceful spots for a cold beer are the cheap drink stalls under the shady trees directly above the ferry landing, where you can look out over the Mekong and Xe Don rivers.

Café De Paris Off the western side of the East Market. While it's nothing to write home about, this little ice cream parlour is clean, comfortable and well lit, which is something in these parts. Aside from sundaes and imported ice cream bars they also serve decent 2000K Lao coffee and all types of burgers (6000K) which they painstakingly construct piece by piece. Clean and tasty.

Dok Meui (Mei Hwa) No. 24 Road, north of the Vietnamese Consulate. This is the town's fanciest Chinese restaurant, housed in a huge two-storey modern house. The menu is very extensive and has photographs of all the elaborate dishes but no prices. The Chinese-Lao family that runs the restaurant speak some Mandarin. If you do seek them out don't be surprised if you're the only diners as they usually only cater to big Chinese and Thai tour groups.

Ketmany Restaurant Route 13, right next door to

Pakxe Internet. Aside from Thai-Lao food they also have ice cream, cakes and coffee.

Korean BBQ No. 46 Road just east of No. 24 Road. For a more lively atmosphere, this is Pakxe's most popular restaurant, serving very tasty, inexpensive, BBQ meat steamboats and always crowded to capacity. Absolutely great with cold beer.

Lien Huong Directly across the street from the May Kham. A small Vietnamese place with cheap spring rolls and *foe*. A good spot for a 2000K Lao coffee.

Lan Kham Noodle Shop Route 13 below the hotel of the same name. This very clean noodle shop is immensely popular and only open at lunchtime, when it's packed.

May Kham On the corner of Route 13 and No. 12 Road. Offers an extensive array of Chinese dishes in a proper sit-down setting. The stewed duck with black mushrooms is outstanding.

The Lao-Thai border crossing at Chong Mek

To get to the **Lao-Thai border crossing** at Chong Mek, go to the East Market and catch a sawngthaew for the forty-kilometre trip to the border crossing (daily 8.30am–4pm), which takes around one hour. The fare is 5000K and drivers will accept Thai baht as well as kip. The expansive market that straddles the border thrives at weekends. After crossing into Thailand, sawngthaews will be waiting to shuttle you to the town of Phibun Mangsahan, where you can transfer to buses to Ubon Ratchathani, which has plentiful road and rail links. There are also two direct Chong Mek-to-Bangkok air-conditioned buses that leave from the market at 4pm and 5pm respectively.

Seneluck Thai Restaurant Route 13 opposite Pakxe Internet. Run by a marvellous bunch of Laos who have lived and worked in Thailand. In the evenings, it's also something of a hang-out for a less conventional Lao crowd.

Some Mai No. 46 Road just east of No. 24 Road. Almost across the street from the Korean BBQ, the *Some Mai* is also a steamboat place where you pay just $1 per meat platter and get all the veggies, noodles and broth included.

Vegetarian Restaurant Route 13, next door to Pakxe Internet. Various veggie stir-fries, curries, and tofu dishes.

Listings

Airlines Lao Aviation's booking office (☎031/212252) is on No. 11 Road, near BCEL bank.

Banks and exchange BCEL is on No. 11 Road, Lao May Bank and Lao Viet Bank are on Route 13 opposite the *Lan Kham Hotel*, and Lane Xang Bank is on Route 13 opposite the *Champasak Palace Hotel*.

Consulates Vietnam, on No. 24 Road (Mon–Fri 8–11am & 2–4.30pm; ☎031/212058); visas cost $50, require two photos and take five working days.

Hospital South of the market on No. 9 Road.

Internet access Lan Kham Internet (☎031/213314), T&K Canon Centre Service (☎031/214542), and Pakxe Internet (☎031/213435) all on Route 13 between No. 12 and No. 35 Roads.

Massage Route 13, opposite Pakxe Internet. Massage for $2 an hour. Open Mon–Fri 4–8pm and weekends 2–8pm.

Post Office At the corner of No. 8 Road and No. 1 Road (daily 7.30am–9pm).

Telephone services International calls and faxes at Telecom, on the corner of No. 1 and No. 38 roads (daily 8am–9pm).

Tour agencies Sodetour, corner of Route 13 and No. 24 Road ☎031/212122; Lane Xang Travel, Route 13, below the *Phonesavanh Hotel* ☎031/212002; Inter-Lao Tourisme, in the lobby of the *Champasak Palace Hotel* ☎031/212778.

Around Pakxe

As more and more tourists make their way south to Pakxe, the number of **day-trip options** has begun to grow. **Ban Saphai**, a silk-weaving village north of the city, offers the chance to see villagers weaving *sin* according to age-old practices, and experience life in a traditional town on the island of **Don Kho** in the middle of the Mekong. In the hills south of the city, the villagers of **Kiatngong** raise elephants, which can be hired for trekking, while nearby **Ban Phapho** presents the opportunity to observe elephants being trained for work in the forest. Other sights, such as the coffee plantations and waterfalls of **Bolaven Plateau** (see p.311) and the **Khmer ruins** near Champasak (see p.295), can also be taken in on day-trips.

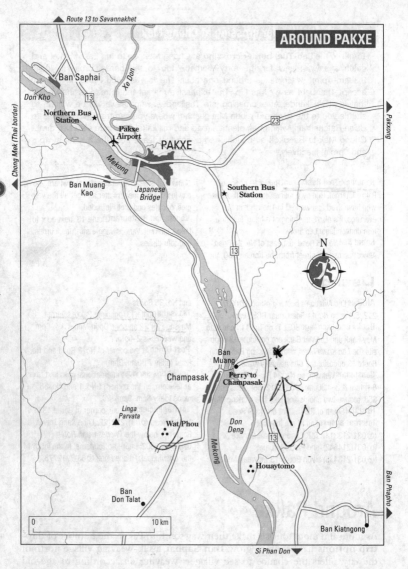

AROUND PAKXE

Route 13 to Savannakhet

Ban Saphai

Don Kho

Xe Don

Chong Mek (Thai border)

Northern Bus Station

Pakxe Airport

PAKXE

23

Pakxong

Ban Muang Kao

Japanese Bridge

Mekong

Southern Bus Station

13

N

Ban Muang

Champasak

Ferry to Champasak

Linga Parvata

Wat Phou

Don Deng

13

Houaytomo

Ban Don Talat

0   10 km

Mekong

Ban Kiatngong

Ban Phapho

Si Phan Don

Ban Saphai and Don Kho

Sawngthaews leave regularly from the sawngthaew lot near Pakxe's Eastern Market to make the fifteen-kilometre trip north to the cluster of villages known locally for their **silk weaving**. Of these, **BAN SAPHAI**, a sizeable village on the left bank of the Mekong River, a few kilometres west of Route 13, has become increasingly popular with tourists keen on seeing women weaving on traditional hand looms, set up in the shade under the family house. Their textiles are sold in one or two shops in the village's market, or, if you prefer, you can negotiate with one of the weavers directly, although there's nothing here that you won't find in Pakxe. Sawngthaews stop at the market in the centre of town and visitors should check to see when the pick-up is returning to Pakxe, as transport along the route is rather limited.

The villagers of **DON KHO**, a shady island located directly across the river from Ban Saphai, are also known for their talent at the loom. In fact, you might well opt to head straight here, as the friendliness of the villagers and the meandering dirt paths along the Mekong make for a pleasant visit. You should be able to hire a boat from the riverbank (if there aren't any, the attendant at the riverside petrol station can scare up a boatman) to ferry you across and back (5000K).

Kiatngong, Phou Asa and Ban Phapho

Located approximately 50km southeast of Pakxe, **KIATNGONG** is one of several villages in the area whose inhabitants keep elephants. Recently, it has started hiring out elephants to tourists for treks up nearby **Phou Asa**. A jungle-clad hill with some **mysterious ruins** atop its summit, Phou Asa is thought to date back to the nineteenth century. The site's layout suggests it was possibly used as a fort, though archeologists admit that the crudely stacked stone walls and pillars are an enigma. Local villagers, believing the ruins to be the remains of an ancient Buddhist monastery, periodically make pilgrimages to the site to leave offerings at a "Buddha's footprint" carved into a low cliff below the ruins. From the summit, commanding views of the surrounding dense jungle, rice fields and villages lend credence to the fort hypothesis.

Elephants have been traditionally used by the people of Kiatngong to haul timber and rice. Villages located far in the interior used to hire Kiatngong's elephants and mahouts to carry their rice harvest to main roads, where it could be transferred to trucks. Recently, though, new roads have made this mode of transport obsolete and mahouts have begun selling off their elephants. The last time villagers organized a hunt to round up wild elephants was in 1988, and many are turning to water buffalo as a more practical beast of burden. A steady stream of potential elephant trekkers, however, will ensure that at least for the time being, villagers here will continue to keep elephants as their ancestors did for centuries.

The **best way to get here** is by your own transport; Sodetour in Pakxe (see p.289 for address) rents out vans – or pick-ups in the rainy season – to the village, charging $50 for the round trip, but it's much cheaper to rent a sawngthaew from the East Market. Once there hiring elephants is about $5 for half a day. The trek takes in Phou Asa and the ruins on its summit. The best time to come is at dusk, when spectacular sunsets can be enjoyed from the top of the hill. It's also possible to get here by bus from Pakxe in less than two hours, but you may have to flag down a passing ride to return to Pakxe at the end of the day.

Another elephant village located some 20km from Kiatngong, **BAN PHAPHO** is involved in the training of elephants for the timber trade. As in Kiatngong, elephant trekking can be arranged at the village, although Ban Phapho lacks the picturesque ruins and views that make Kiatngong the more popular destination of the two. Both villages can be visited in one day if you rent a vehicle from Pakxe.

The legacy of the Angkorian empire

In the mid-nineteenth century, French explorers began stumbling across the **monumental ruins** of a centuries-dead empire that had once blanketed mainland Southeast Asia. Soon word of these "lost cities" reached Europe and an intrigued populace groped for theories to explain such grandeur amidst the sparsely inhabited jungles of an "uncivilized" corner of Asia. Surely, they mused, these monuments were the work of expatriate Romans or perhaps some far-wandering tribe of Israelites. Further exploration and the subsequent colonization of much of Indochina by France brought these mysterious monuments to the attention of French scholars and archeologists, some of whom were to dedicate their entire careers to unravelling the secrets of these tantalizing remnants of an empire.

In time, the **Khmer**, the inhabitants of modern-day **Cambodia**, were rightfully acknowledged to be the descendants of the founders of a highly sophisticated culture, whose influence stretched north to Vientiane in Laos and as far west as the present-day border of Thailand and Burma. From its capital, located at Angkor in what is now northwestern Cambodia, a long line of kings reigned with absolute authority, each striving to build a monument to his own greatness which would outdo all previous monarchs. With cultural trappings inherited from earlier Khmer kingdoms, which in turn had borrowed heavily from Indian merchants that once dominated trade throughout Southeast Asia, the Khmer rulers at Angkor venerated deities from the **Hindu** and **Buddhist** pantheons. Eventually, a new and uniquely Khmer cult was born, the *devaraja* or god-king, which propagated the belief that a Khmer king was actually an incarnation of a certain Hindu deity on earth. Most of the Khmer kings of Angkor identified with the god Shiva, although Suryavarman II, builder of **Angkor Wat**, the most magnificent of all Khmer monuments, fancied himself an earthly incarnation of Vishnu. An intriguing account of life at Angkor was penned by Chou Ta-Kuan, a Chinese traveller who visited the capital in the thirteenth century. In it he tells of imposing stone temples stunningly sheathed in gold and a king loyally guarded by an army of spear-wielding amazons.

Champasak, Wat Phou and the Khmer temples

From Pakxe, daily passenger boats ply the forty-kilometre stretch of the Mekong south, past misty green mountains and riverbanks loaded with palm trees, to the charming riverside town of **Champasak**. An up-and-coming backpacker resort, Champasak also serves as the gateway to **Wat Phou** and other **Khmer ruins**. Although it is easily possible to use Pakxe as a base and visit Wat Phou as a day-trip from there, there is plenty of accommodation available in Champasak, and it is recommended as an attraction in its own right, allowing you to take in the sights at a leisurely pace. With its old wooden houses, three temples, Khmer ruins, mountains and river boat trips, plus cheap guest houses and good food, it's easy to imagine this place becoming another Muang Ngoi in no time.

It's not hard to see why this lush river valley, dominated by an imposing 1500-metre-tall mountain, has been considered prime real estate for nearly two thousand years by a variety of peoples, in particular the Khmer. On the slopes of the mountain overlooking Champasak, historically known as Lingaparvata and considered holy for centuries, resides the pre-Angkorian temple of Wat Phou. The surrounding forests are rich with wildlife, including the rare Asiatic black bear. The pristine state of the environment – it is without question one

In 1177, armies from the rival kingdom of Champa, taking advantage of a period of political instability, were able to sack Angkor, leaving the empire in disarray. After some years of chaos, **Jayavarman VII** took control of the leaderless Khmer people. Convinced that the old state religion had somehow failed to protect the kingdom from misfortune, Jayavarman VII embraced Mahayana Buddhism and went on to expand his empire to include much of present-day Thailand, Vietnam and Laos. But the days of Khmer glory were numbered. Soon after the death of Jayavarman VII the empire began to decline and by 1432 was so weak that the **Siamese**, who had previously served as mercenaries for the Khmer in their campaigns against Champa, were also able to give Angkor a thorough sacking. The Siamese pillaged the great stone temples of the Angkorian god-kings and force-marched members of the royal Khmer court, including the king's personal retinue of classical dancers, musicians, artisans and astrologers, back to Ayuthaya, then the capital of Siam. To this day, much of what Thais perceive as Thai culture, from the sinuous moves of classical dancers to the flowery language of the royal Thai court, was actually acquired from the Khmer. After the collapse of the Angkorian empire, Siam moved in to fill the power vacuum and much of the Khmer culture absorbed by the Siamese was passed on to the Lao.

Following the **revolution in 1975**, the communist leaders of Laos, who identified with the newly reunified Vietnam and saw Thailand and its culture as decadent and Americanized, made a vigorous attempt to cleanse the new Laos of "reactionary" culture and iconography. Casualties of these purges include former royal Lao icons such as the image of the Hindu deity Airavata, and the **three-headed elephant**, formerly found on the Lao flag and on all Lao currency. Despite revolutionist efforts to revise the past, you don't have to look very hard to find major evidence of the legacy of the ancient Khmer in modern-day Laos. **Written Lao**, with its gracefully curving lines, was adapted from a script developed by the Siamese, who had borrowed heavily from an alphabet devised by the ancient Khmer.

of the most scenic landscapes chosen by the Khmer for any of their temples – was a major factor in UNESCO's decision to propose the area as a World Heritage site. A few kilometres up the road, an ancient buried city, with ruins dating back to the fifth century, is currently the object of intense archeological interest. Experts are unable to agree on who the inhabitants of this city were, with some calling it a western outpost of the Champa kingdom and others celebrating it as the cradle of Khmer civilization.

Another famous Khmer ruin in the area is **Houaytomo** which lies on the opposite, eastern bank of the Mekong. To get there you can hire a low-lying pirogue to zip you south along the river, skimming the surface, past Lao children at their favourite swimming holes. If you're travelling in the hot season, when the river level lowers and the water turns a sparkling blue-green, you can also combine this trip with a visit to the stretch of pristine beaches on **Don Deng**, the river island opposite Champasak where the sandy bank provides an excellent place for a swim.

Champasak Town

Meandering for 4km along the right bank of the Mekong, **CHAMPASAK** is an unassuming town of wooden shop-houses and two red dirt roads with a pace so decidedly leisurely that it's difficult to imagine it as the capital of a once bustling kingdom, whose territory stretched from the Annamite Mountains into present-day Thailand. However, when France's Mekong expedition, led by

Doudart de Lagrée and Francis Garnier, arrived in 1866, they found a city which was the most important in the south, a status later usurped by Pakxe when it became a French administrative centre.

These days, the quiet cluster of ten villages that constitutes Champasak makes Pakxe seem like a pulsing metropolis. On the main road, downstream from what is arguably the most under-used roundabout in Laos, two elegant **French mansions**, tanned a pale yellow by the tropical sun, stand out from the traditional wooden shop-houses. The first mansion belonged to the former **palace of Prince Boun Oum na Champasak**, the scion of the royal family of Champasak and a one-time prime minister. Although in 1946 he renounced claims to sovereignty in the former kingdom, Boun Oum retained his royal title and continued to perform his ritual duties as a Buddhist monarch until he fled the country prior to the Pathet Lao takeover; he died in France in 1980. During Lao New Year, Boun Oum performed purification rites at the town's temples to expel evil spirits and on the final day of celebrations he would preside over ceremonies at this palace, in which a *maw thiam*, or medium, called the spirits of Champasak's past rulers, and a *basi* ceremony was held. Since the advent of the new government, however, the pageantry has been abandoned and New Year ceremonies in this former royal seat have become a strictly family affair.

As is the case with the *nagas* in front of Boun Oum's house, which were taken from Wat Phou, the area's most exquisite **pre-Angkorian relics** have unfortunately wound up in the late prince's private collection. One local villager working with a team of archeologists in the ancient city is old enough to remember Boun Oum looting one site. Some experts even believe that many of the pieces in his collection are fake, implying that the prince sold off the originals. Whatever the case, there is talk of incorporating the collection, now in the care of a local official, into a public exhibition in the near future.

Practicalities

Buses and **sawngthaews** (7000K **from Pakxe**) will let you off at Champasak's tiny roundabout, where you'll find almost everything you need, including a **post office** (open until 9pm weekdays for phone calls), and a tiny wooden bank, which can exchange cash and travellers' cheques. The **boat and ferry dock** is about 2km north of the roundabout; tuk-tuks are available at the dock.

There aren't **any proper hotels** in town, but the *Saythong* (❶), just south of the roundabout, has basic rooms with shared facilities in an old wooden house, above a restaurant overlooking the Mekong. Across the street, *Kham Phou* (❶) has roomy doubles and triples and wooden en-suite bungalows in the garden. Fifty metres south, just opposite a stunning colonial mansion, the *Souchittra Guest House* (❶) has basic rooms in the old house with a clean, shared bath or self-contained bungalows on the lawn overlooking the Mekong. The town's most sophisticated guest house is *Kham Khong* (❷), 2km south of the roundabout, which has en-suite bungalows and a restaurant with a nice deck overlooking the Mekong. To **eat**, *Dok Champa GH & Restaurant*, on the roundabout, offers the best selection of Lao dishes in town and also rents bicycles (5000K per day). Most guest houses have some bikes for rent (5000K a day).

Tuk-tuks can be hired for the eight-kilometre journey to Wat Phou. The drivers charge 30,000K for up to six passengers, and wait for you while you visit the ruins. When it comes to moving on, three buses pass through Champasak each morning en route to Pakxe (1hr 30min) and can be hailed from the town's main road. It's also possible to cross the river to Ban Muang and then get a shared sawngthaew. For **bus connections** to Si Phan Don you have to cross the river to Ban Muang and wait for a bus heading south on Route 13, or alternatively take the daily **boat** from Pakxe which calls in at the Ban Phapin ferry landing, located at the northernmost end of Champasak, around 9am in the morning. Boats to Houaytomo ($6) can be arranged through your guest house or directly with the boatmen who hang out at the Ban Phapin landing.

Wat Phou and around

One of the most evocative Khmer ruins outside Cambodian borders, **Wat Phou** (daily 8.30am–4.30pm; 5000K), 8km southwest of Champasak, should be at the top of your southern Laos must-see list. A romantic and rambling complex of temples dating from the sixth to the twelfth centuries, Wat Phou occupies a setting of unparalleled beauty. Unlike ancient Khmer sites of equal size or importance found in neighbouring Thailand, Wat Phou has yet to be restored and landscaped according to modern tastes. There are no paved walkways, rolling green lawns or fastidiously groomed bits of topiary here. Walking among the scattered and half-buried pieces of sculpted sandstone gives an idea of what major Khmer sites in the region looked like before long-venerated stone images were carted off to museums.

Wat Phou, which in Lao means "Mountain Monastery", is actually a series of ruined temples and shrines at the foot of Lingaparvata Mountain. Although the site is now associated with Theravada Buddhism, sandstone reliefs indicate that the ruins were once a **Hindu place of worship**. When viewed from the Mekong, it's clear why the site was chosen. A phallic stone outcropping is easily seen among the range's line of forested peaks: this would have made the site especially auspicious to worshippers of Shiva, a Hindu god that is often symbolized by a phallus.

Archeologists tend to disagree on who the original founders of the site were and when it was first consecrated. The oldest parts of the ruins are thought to date back to the sixth century and were most likely built by the **ancient Khmer**, although some experts claim to see a connection to Champa, a Hinduized kingdom once centred in what is now south-central Vietnam. Whatever the case, the site is still considered highly sacred to the ethnic Lao who inhabit the region today, and is the focus of a festival that attracts thousands of pilgrims annually.

Approaching from the east, visitors come first to the dilapidated shell of a building that was erected in the 1950s for Prince Boun Oum and served as his residence during the annual festival. Nowadays UNESCO is trying to decide whether or not to tear it down. Needless to say, some locals are opposed to the idea of tearing down a former royal residence, and it looks quite picturesque from a distance. Save your film, though, as the real ruins are further up the hill.

The **stone causeway** leading from the prince's former residence up to the first set of ruins was once lined with low stone pillars, the tips of which were formed into a stylized lotus bud. Stone pedestals along the way indicate that a few statues may have lined this path as well. On either side of the causeway there would have been reservoirs known in Khmer as *baray*. As ancient Khmer architecture is rich in symbols, it is surmised that these pools represented the oceans that surrounded the mythical Mount Meru, home of the gods of the Hindu pantheon.

Just beyond the causeway, on either side of the path, two megalithic structures of sandstone and laterite mirror each other. According to local lore, they are

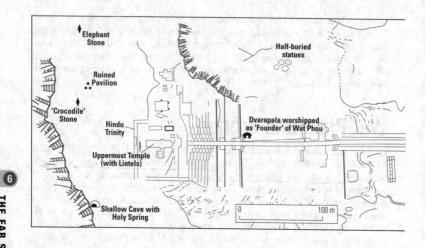

Elephant
Stone

Half-buried
statues

Ruined
Pavilion

'Crocodile'
Stone

Hindu
Trinity

Dvarapala worshipped
as 'Founder' of Wat Phou

Uppermost Temple
(with Lintels)

Shallow Cave with
Holy Spring

0   100 m

segregated **palaces**, one for men and the other for women. Archeologists are
sceptical though, pointing out that stone was reserved for constructing places
of worship, and, even if this hadn't been the case, the vast interiors of both
buildings were roofless and would have afforded little shelter. The structure on
your right, as you approach, is the best preserved. Its carved relief of Shiva and
his consort Uma riding the sacred bull Nandi is the best to be found on either
of these two buildings. As with much of the architecture of the pharaohs of
ancient Egypt, that of the Khmer kings of Angkor was monumental and sym-
metrical. Even in their ruined state, you can imagine the awe these stacked and
carved stones must have inspired, especially with the spectacle of a majestic
royal procession passing through their midst.

As the path begins to climb, you come upon jagged stairways of sandstone
blocks. Plumeria trees line the way, giving welcome shade and littering the
worn stones with delicate blooms. Known in Lao as *dawk jampa*, they are the
national flower of Laos. At the foot of the second stairway is a shrine to the
legendary founder of Wat Phou. The statue is much venerated and, during the
annual pilgrimage, is bedecked with offerings of flowers, incense and candles.
Once again though, local folklore and archeological record diverge. According
to archeologists, the statue is actually that of a *dvarapala*, or temple guardian. In
the field behind this statue, half buried in the ground, lie the headless torsos of
two similar statues. When and why this one statue has come to be venerated in
such a fashion is unknown.

Continuing up the stairs, you come upon the final set of ruins, surrounded
by mammoth mango trees. This uppermost temple contains the finest examples of **decorative stone lintels** (see box, p.298) in Laos. Although much has
been damaged or is missing, sketches done by Georges Traipont, a French surveyor who visited the temple complex in the waning years of the nineteenth
century, show the temple to have changed little since then. On the exterior
walls flanking the east entrance are the images of *dvarapalas* and *devatas*, or
female divinities, in high relief. On the altar, inside the sanctuary, stand **four
Buddha images**, looking like a congress of benevolent space aliens.
Originally, this altar would have supported a *Shivalinga*, or phallic stone, representing Shiva. Today, it is crowded with a collection of ancient odds and ends
gathered from the surrounding area. Doorways on each side of the altar lead to

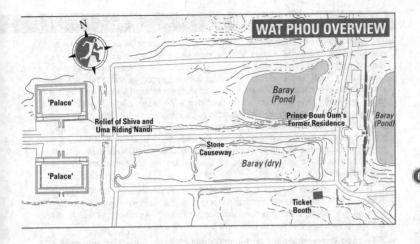

'Palace'

Relief of Shiva and
Uma Riding Nandi

Baray
(Pond)

Prince Boun Oum's
Former Residence

Baray
(Pond)

Stone
Causeway

Baray (dry)

'Palace'

Ticket
Booth

an empty room with walls of brick. It is surmised that these walls constitute the oldest structure on the site, thought to date back to the sixth century.

To the right of the temple is a Lao Buddha of comparatively modern vintage, and just behind the temple is a relief carved into a half-buried slab of stone depicting the Hindu trinity. A multi-armed, multi-headed Shiva (standing) is flanked by Brahma (left) and Vishnu (right). Continuing up the hill behind the temple you'll come to a **shallow cave**, the floor of which is muddy from the constant drip of water that collects on its ceiling. This water is considered highly sacred, as it has trickled down from the peak of Lingaparvata. In former times, a system of stone pipes directed the run-off to the temple, where it bathed the enshrined *Shivalinga*. By tradition, this water was utilized in ceremonies for the coronation of Khmer kings and later the kings of Siam. Even today, Lao pilgrims will dip their fingers into a cistern located in the cave and ritually anoint themselves. Foreign visitors should resist the temptation to use this water to scrub off some trail-dust – indeed, doing so would be extremely poor form, not so different from going into a church and washing your face in the baptismal font.

If you follow the base of the cliff in a northerly direction, a bit of sleuthing will lead you to the enigmatic **crocodile stone**, which may have been used as an altar for pre-Angkor period human sacrifices. Although it's a juicy story, there is no hard evidence that ritual sacrifice was a part of the ceremonial rites that took place here. Nearby is a pile of sandstone rubble that once formed a pavilion and is thought by archeologists to be one of the oldest structures on the site. A few metres away to the north is the **elephant stone**, a huge, moss-covered boulder carved with the face of an elephant. This carving is relatively recent, probably dating from the nineteenth century.

If you were to hike straight up the mountain to the **summit of Lingaparvata**, it would take two days of rigorous climbing over vertical cliff-faces and dense forest. Recently, an Italian team of archeologists did just that. On the very tip of the natural phallic outcropping that is the peak of the mountain, they discovered a small *Shivalinga* of carved stone. Sadly, the archeologists found it necessary to remove this artefact which had crowned the sacred mountain for untold centuries, catching raindrops that would eventually filter down to the cave of lustral waters at the foot of the mountain. The trophy now rests on a dusty shelf in the UNESCO headquarters in Champasak.

Decorative lintels at Wat Phou

The importance of the **decorative lintel** in Khmer art cannot be overstated. Here, more than anywhere else, Khmer artisans were free to display their superb stone-carving skills. Their imaginative depictions of deities, divinities, characters and events from Hindu and Buddhist mythology are recognized as some of the most exquisite art ever created. Early examples date from the seventh century, and as the styles and motifs have evolved over the centuries, experts are able to date lintels by comparing them to known works. This does not necessarily fix the date of the host temple though, as the Khmer were known to remove or replace lintels while restoring or constructing new temples. Among the decorative lintels at **Wat Phou** are some particularly fine examples which compare favourably with those found in temples at Angkor. The lintels at Wat Phou are listed below; the numbers correspond to those on the map on p.300.

1) The god Krishna defeats the naga Kaliya In this story from the Bhagavad Purana, Krishna answers the pleas of villagers to rid the nearby river of a water serpent, known as Kaliya, that has been terrorizing the village. A similar lintel was found at Muang Tam, a Khmer ruin in Thailand's Buriram province.

2) The god Vishnu riding the bird-man Garuda Although Vishnu on Garuda was a common theme in Khmer art, images of the two were rarely depicted on lintels. After conquering the Khmer in 1432, the Siamese adopted the Garuda to symbolize their own monarchy – hence an image of Garuda is found on all Thai banknotes and official documents.

3) The god Indra riding the three-headed elephant Airavata Despite being a Hindu god, Indra holds a significant place in Theravada Buddhist mythology. Until the Lao revolution, Airavata was the official symbol of the Lao monarchy. The image of the three-headed elephant was formerly found on the Lao flag and Lao currency and can still be seen on the facade of the former royal palace in Louang Phabang.

4) Indra on Airavata A larger and more detailed depiction of #3.

5) Deity atop Kala Although this deity is very commonly depicted on lintels, it is

Hong Nang Sida Temple

Situated about 1km south of Wat Phou, **Hong Nang Sida** is a small twelfth-century Khmer temple, built on an ancient thoroughfare that once stretched from Wat Phou to Angkor Wat. The trail leading south to the temple from Wat Phou through the rice paddies is easy to locate during the dry season, but you may have to ask the guards at the entrance to Wat Phou for directions once the rains have started and the trail becomes obscured by weeds. This little-visited ruin is overgrown with brambles which make it difficult to explore, and the possibility of poisonous snakes should also be considered, but the site has an alluring air of mystery about it. The dimensions of Hong Nang Sida are modest compared to those of Wat Phou, and very few of the sandstone blocks from which it was constructed are adorned with carvings. Still, as with Wat Phou, the warm light on the venerable stone walls is particularly magical during sunrise and sunset.

Houaytomo Temple

If your thirst for Khmer temples has yet to be quenched, a visit to **Houaytomo**, a tenth-century temple, is an option. Best visited as a day-trip from Champasak, this ruin is set in the midst of a lush forest on the banks of a

uncertain just who it is supposed to be. As the deity is holding a mace and sitting in the "royal ease" pose, perhaps it depicts a generic king or ruler. Kala, a temple guardian also commonly found on Khmer lintels, is sometimes confused with Rahu, who is believed to devour the sun and moon during eclipses. Kala is usually depicted with two stylized garlands spewing from the corners of his mouth.

6) Deity atop Kala (see #5) On the portico above the lintel is what is left of a scene from the Churning of the Sea of Milk myth, a contest between gods and demons for possession of the elixir of immortality. This scene is depicted most spectacularly on the bas-reliefs at Angkor Wat in Cambodia.

7) Krishna killing Kamsa From the Bhagavad Purana, this lintel is a gruesome depiction of Krishna tearing his uncle in half. According to this myth, it was foretold that King Kamsa's death would come at the hands of one of his own family members. This prophecy launched the king on an orgy of killing which was only halted when his nephew put him to death.

8) Deity atop Kala (see #5)

9) Deity atop Kala (see #5) On the ruined portico above this lintel are the remains of a depiction of the god Vishnu in his incarnation as Narayana, reclining in cosmic slumber as he floats atop a naga on the waters of a vast primordial ocean.

10) Shiva asa rishi atop Kala A unique lintel depicting Shiva as a rishi, or wandering ascetic, perched above Kala. The image of the Hindu sage, usually dressed in a tiger skin and sitting in an attitude of meditation, has been adopted by Buddhism in Laos and Thailand, and is the object of veneration at numerous small monastery shrines in both countries.

11) Deity atop Kala (see #5) Sadly, this lintel has been badly damaged, possibly by looters trying to remove part of the sculpture for the thriving stolen-antiquities trade in Thailand.

12) Deity atop Kala (see #5)

stream, for which it is named. Also known by various other names, including Oum Muang, the temple is thought to have been dedicated to the consort of Shiva in her form as Rudani and was "discovered" by Frenchman Etienne Edmond Lunet de Lajonquière early in the twentieth century. Although much of the structure has collapsed and some of the lintels have been removed, a couple of interesting pieces of sculpture remain *in situ*, most notably an unusual stone pillar located inside the laterite sanctuary. The pillar is crudely carved with the moustached faces of a mysterious deity, perhaps Shiva. Archeologists working for UNESCO speculate that it is a *mukhalinga*, literally "phallus with face", and that it dates from the seventh century. Lined up outside the walls of the temple are a collection of lintels, obscured by a thick layer of moss. As the whole area is shaded by the forest's thick canopy, it is cool and pleasant even at high noon.

The best way to reach Houaytomo is to hire a **pirogue** in Champasak ($6). When the river is high enough, the boat will be able to navigate the Houaytomo Stream and dock at the ruins. During the dry season you'll have to disembark on the banks of the Mekong and walk a couple of kilometres. The journey by boat takes about two hours. When the river is low, a trip to Houaytomo can be combined with a stop at the beaches of Don Deng for a lazy afternoon of sunbathing.

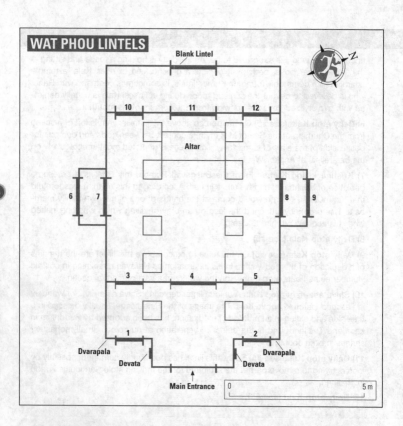

WAT PHOU LINTELS

Blank Lintel

10   11   12

Altar

6   7   8   9

3   4   5

1   2

Dvarapala   Dvarapala
Devata   Devata

Main Entrance   0   5 m

Xe Pian NBCA

Just southeast of Houaytomo and running the entire length of Route 13 all the way to Si Phan Don is the **Xe Pian NBCA**. Although many tourists travel right alongside it for almost 150km on route to Don Khong, few are aware they are right next to Laos's southernmost NBCA and one of the country's largest (2665 square kilometres) nature reserves. Roughly triangular in shape, Xe Pian is bounded by Routes 13 and 18 to the west and north and extends southward all the way to the Cambodian border. The terrain here is mostly flat plains although there are mixed deciduous forests and several peaks between 300m and 800m. In the east, the **Xe Kong River** enters Cambodia through the park, and tigers, elephants, leopards and **rhinoceros** may survive here. The best way to visit the NBCA is from Pakxe, where travel companies can organize four-wheel drive trips through the north of the park.

Si Phan Don

In Laos's deepest south, just above the border with Cambodia, the muddy stream of the Mekong is shattered into a fourteen-kilometre-wide web of rivulets, creating a landlocked archipelago. Known as **Si Phan Don**, or Four Thousand Islands, this labyrinth of islets, rocks and sandbars has acted as a kind of bell jar, preserving traditional southern lowland Lao culture from outside influences. Island villages were largely unaffected by the French or American wars, and the islanders' customs and folk ways have been passed down uninterrupted since ancient times. As might be expected, the Mekong River plays a vital role in the lives of local inhabitants, with 95 percent of island families fishing for a living and catching an average of 355 kilograms of fish per family per year. Ecological awareness among locals is high, with nearly half of the villages in the district participating in voluntary fisheries conservation programmes. The archipelago is also home to rare wetland flora and fauna, includ-

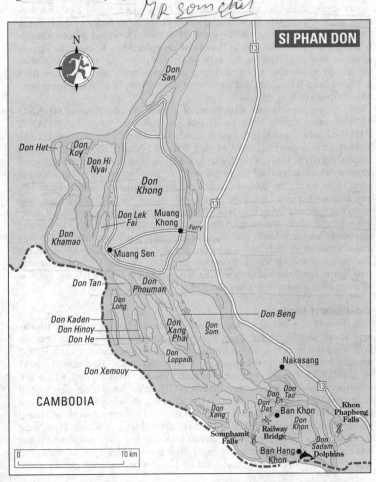

ing a species of freshwater dolphin, and during the dry season it is sometimes possible to catch a glimpse of these endangered mammals. Southeast Asia's largest, and what many consider to be most spectacular, waterfalls are also located here. The area's biggest sight-seeing attractions, the **Khon Phapheng** and **Somphamit** waterfalls dashed nineteenth-century French hopes of using the Mekong as a trade artery into China. The remnants of a French-built railroad, constructed to carry passengers and cargo past these roaring obstacles, can still be seen on the islands of **Don Khon** and **Don Det**, along with a rusting locomotive and other ghosts of the French presence. The most developed place to base yourself is the popular island of **Don Khong**, with its collection of quaint villages and ancient temples but there's also plenty of accommodation on Don Khon and Don Det.

Don Khong

The largest of the Four Thousand Islands group, **DON KHONG** draws a steady stream of visitors, most of whom use it as a base to explore other attractions in Si Phan Don. Don Khong is surprisingly wide for a river island, though, and has a few interesting sights of its own. The island is known locally for its venerable collection of **Buddhist temples**, some with visible signs of a history stretching back to the sixth or seventh century. These, together with the island's good-value accommodation and interesting cuisine, based on fresh fish from the Mekong, make Don Khong the perfect place for indulging both adventurous and lazy moods.

Don Khong has only two settlements of any size, the port town of **MUANG SEN** on the island's west coast, and the east-coast town of **MUANG KHONG**, where most of the accommodation and cafés are situated. Like all Si Phan Don settlements, both Muang Sen's and Muang Khong's homes and shops cling to the bank of the Mekong for kilometres, but barely penetrate the interior, which is reserved for rice fields. The islanders are an amiable lot and seem to be taking the mini-onslaught of foreign travellers in their stride. The best way to explore Don Khong and experience the traditional sights and sounds of riverside living is to rent a **bicycle or motorcycle** and set off along the road that circles the island. Don Khong's flat terrain and almost complete absence of motor vehicles make for ideal cycling conditions. Muang Khong's guest houses offer bicycles for rent ($1 per day): try *Villa Kang Khong*, which also rents out motorbikes. For touring, the island can be neatly divided into **two loops**: southern and northern, each beginning at Muang Khong, or done all in one big loop which takes about three hours without stops.

Southern loop

The chain of picturesque villages which line the south coast make the **southern loop**, roughly 20km long, the more popular of the two itineraries. Following the river road south from Muang Khong, you soon cross a rotting wooden bridge, with an inscription indicating that it was constructed in 1963 by USAID (United States Agency for International Development), which was sometimes used as a front for shadowy CIA activities during the Second Indochina War. Take care to stick to the narrow path along the river, and not the road that parallels it slightly inland. A couple of kilometres south of Muang Khong lies the village of **BAN NA**, where the real scenery begins. Navigating the trail as it snakes between thickets of bamboo, you come upon traditional southern Lao wooden houses trimmed with painted highlights of white and royal blue. The homes are surrounded by plots of barren, hard-packed earth,

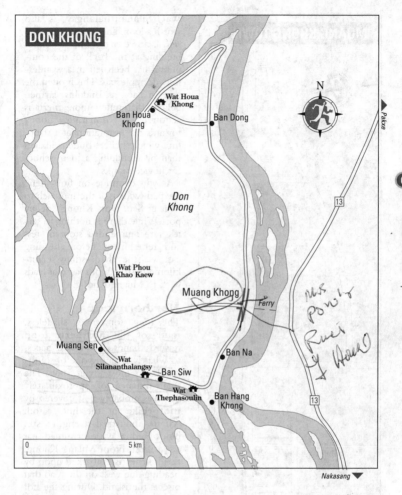

kept tidy by frequent sweeping with a stiff coconut-frond broom and enclosed by low fences of split bamboo.

Near the tail of the island the path forks: a veer to the left will lead you to the tiny village of **BAN HANG KHONG** and a dead end. Keeping to the right will put you at the gates of **Wat Thephasourin**, parts of which were constructed in 1883. The *sala* and monks' quarters, composed of teak-plank walls and terracotta tile roofs, are particularly pleasing to the eye, making this a good place for a breather and a swig on the water bottle. From here the path soon skirts the edge of a high riverbank, at intervals opening up views of the muddy Mekong flowing sluggishly southwards. The dense canopy of foliage overhead provides welcome shade as you pass through **BAN SIW**, whose quaint gingerbread houses, decorated with wood filigree, look invitingly cosy. The bamboo-and-thatch drink shops that line this section of the path are a good place to linger while enjoying a rejuvenating sip of coconut milk. The village monastery,

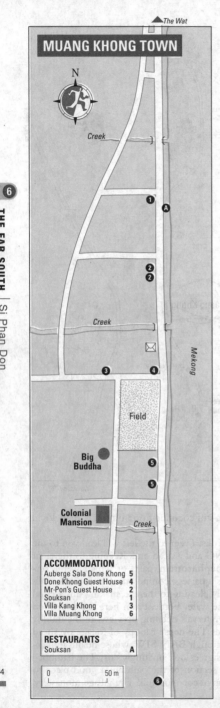

Wat Silananthalangsy, is also worth a look. The recently restored *sim* lacks charm, but a school building at the back of the compound has been left in a wonderfully decrepit state. This is often the case in Laos, as Buddhist laymen believe that much more merit is acquired by donating money towards the restoration of a structure which shelters Buddha images than by rebuilding a mere school for novice monks.

As you continue on from here, the path widens at the approach to Muang Sen, Don Khong's sleepy port. While there is nothing to see, it's a recommended stop for rest and refreshment before heading east via the shade-stingy eight-kilometre stretch of road that leads back to Muang Khong.

Northern loop

The long, sometimes shadeless, route of the **northern loop** rewards handsomely with access to what is certainly one of southern Laos's most idyllic spots. The total distance of approximately 35km is probably best covered by **motorbike** in the hot season, when industrial-strength sun block and a wide-brimmed hat are a must. From Muang Khong, this journey is embarked upon by heading due west on the road that bisects the island. During the hot season the plain of rice paddies that makes up much of the interior of the island looks and feels like a stretch of the Kalahari. After the rains break and rice paddies are planted, the scenery is actually quite beautiful.

Just before reaching the town of Muang Sen on the western side of the island, turn right at the crossroads and head north. Follow this road up and over a low grade and after about 4km you'll cross a bridge. Keep going another 1.5km and you'll notice large black boulders beginning to appear off to the left. Keeping your eyes left, you'll see a narrow trail which leads up to a ridge of the same black stone. Park your bike at the foot of the ridge, and, following the trail up another 200m to the right, you'll spot a cluster of monks' quarters constructed of weathered teak.

These structures belong to **Wat Phou Khao Kaew**, an evocative little forest monastery situated atop a river-sculpted stone bluff overlooking the Mekong. Until a recently built *sala* constructed of modern materials added a bit of the late twentieth century to the landscape, you could wander the grounds of this wat and almost believe that the clock had been turned back a hundred or so years. The centrepiece of this monastery is a crumbling **brick stupa** crowned with a clump of grass. A fractured pre-Angkorian stone lintel sits at the base of the stupa and, assuming it was once fixed to it, would date the structure to the middle of the seventh century.

Nearby sits a charming miniature *sim*, flanked by plumeria trees. A curious collection of carved wooden deities, which somehow found their way downriver from Burma, decorate the ledges running around the building. In 1998, a life-sized **bronze Buddha** image was stolen from the altar, only to turn up hidden under a hastily made tent of branches in an isolated stretch of forest on the mainland. The antique image's *ushnisha* (flame-like finial on the crown of the head) was missing, but the Buddha was otherwise intact. Undoubtedly it had been destined for Thailand's black market in plundered antiquities. At present, the image is stored at the police station in Muang Khong. If you want to have a look at the inside of the *sim*, ask one of the resident monks to unlock the door for you, or you can peer through the windows on either side of the main entrance, which faces the river.

If, after a look round Wat Phou Khao Kaew, you're still feeling energetic, you can continue another 6km north to **BAN HOUA KHONG**. On the outskirts of this village stands the modest **residence of Khamtay Siphandone**, former revolutionary and current prime minister of Laos. Not far away is a **monastery** which has been restored to reflect the status of the village's most important part-time inhabitant. The wat is not all that remarkable, except perhaps for the collection of artefacts in the main temple. Sharing the altar with rows of Buddha images is a *somasutra* from an ancient Khmer temple: while it looks somewhat like a gargoyle, it would actually have been used to channel lustral water onto an enshrined *Shivalinga*. It is possible that the artefact was brought here from Wat Phou Khao Kaew. Next to the altar is a display case filled with small Buddha images and other dusty relics.

Pushing on from Ban Houa Khong, you follow the road east to Ban Dong and then south to Muang Khong. If you choose the latter, this last leg of the journey is approximately 13km.

On arriving at the northern outskirts of Muang Khong, just before reaching the high school, you will pass a trail bordered with white stones which leads to **Tham Phou Khiaw**, or Green Mountain Cave. Although it has gained quite a reputation among travellers, based no doubt on the obscurity of its location, the cave is no Lost City of Gold: actually, it's a shallow grotto sheltering one termite-riddled Buddha and a number of clay pots containing crude votive tablets, each with an image of the Buddha pressed into it. Unless you're here during the Lao New Year celebrations, when islanders visit the site to make offerings and ritually bathe the images, or the Bun Bang Fai festival, a month later, when bamboo skyrockets are launched in a rain-making ritual, it's not really worth the effort; the trail leading up to the cave is overgrown at other times of the year and you'll have to hire a local guide.

Practicalities

A total of seven **buses to Don Khong** leave from Pakxe's bus station daily. Two of these go directly to Muang Khong, crossing the Mekong by ferry from Ban Hat Xai Khoun. The other five pass through Ban Hat Xai Khoun on their way to Nakasang.

Boats to Don Khong leave daily from Pakxe around 8am. The trip downriver takes eight hours or longer, depending on how many stops are made en route, and costs $3. These boats make a stop at Champasak around 10am, so it's possible to take a boat to Si Phan Don from there as well. It's advisable to bring water and food along; otherwise your only chance of refreshment is from the snack vendors who converge on the boat during stops. On reaching Don Khong in the late afternoon, boats will dock at either Ban Houa Khong or Muang Sen, both on Don Khong's west coast. From here you'll need to hire a tuk-tuk ($1.50) or motorcycle for the eight-kilometre trip across the island to Muang Khong, where the best selection of food and accommodation is located.

Boats going to Pakxe from Don Khong ($3) usually leave from Muang Sen daily but the only way to know for sure is to ask at your guest house. If by chance there is no boat that day, a Pakxe-bound bus leaves Muang Sen around 8am and passes through Muang Khong before boarding the ferry to Ban Hat Xai Khoun and heading north up Route 13. It is possible to get a ride to Pakxe by private vehicle every morning at 7am at *Mr Pon's Restaurant* for $1 (2hr 30 min).

In Muang Khong you'll find the island's only **post office**, just south of the bridge, and a telecom office, about 200m west of the ferry landing, where international calls can be made (Mon–Fri 8am–noon & 1-4pm; Sat 8am–noon). There is also a small Agricultural Promotion Bank. Several of the guest houses and shops facing the Mekong offer **bicycles** for rent ($1 per day). Don Khong has 24-hour electricity.

Accommodation

Most of the island's accommodation – and all that listed below – is concentrated in Muang Khong, which is on the quieter side of the island and provides a good launching point for excursions around the Si Phan Don area. Over in Muang Sen there are only two guest houses: *Say Khong* (❷), directly above the ferry landing, has spacious doubles and triples with fans and a balcony; and *Muong Sene Guest House* (❶), situated a little further east, on the road to Muang Khong. Since Muang Sen has the island's main pier it tends to be a bit noisier than Muang Khong. The majority of travellers, however, head for Muang Khong.

Auberge Sala Done Khong 100m south of the ferry landing ☎031/212077. A nicely restored French-era villa with air con and hot water, catering largely to package-tour clientele. ❺

Done Khong Guest House Adjacent to the ferry landing ☎031/214010. Basic rooms with shared facilities, popular restaurant and friendly staff. ❷

Done Khong II 300m from the ferry landing on the road to Muang Sen. Set in an airy teak house with verandas offering commanding views of the countryside, its accommodation ranges from dorm beds (15,000K) to comfortable en-suite doubles. ❷

Mr Pon's Guest House 150m north of the ferry landing. *Mr Pon's* is a great place to stay offering clean rooms in a wood house with private or shared facilities, hot water, and a very popular restaurant downstairs. Mr Pon has also just built a new building right next door so there'll be more room at the inn. ❶

Souksan 300m north of the ferry landing ☎031/212071. Chinese-Lao-owned establishment with river-view Chinese restaurant and accommodation ranging from dormitory beds to fairly luxurious bungalows, priced according to whether or not you switch on the air con. ❶–❻

Villa Kang Khong 100m west of the ferry landing ⊕ 031/213539. Helpful, French-speaking owner, Mr Thongleuam, offers five-star service at budget prices, making the spacious, comfortable rooms in this French-colonial-era teak house excellent value. Highly recommended. ❷

Villa Muang Khong 300m south of the ferry landing ⊕ 031/213011. Smallish, but modern, bungalows with fan and attached toilet. The restaurant on the premises needs to be warned one day in advance if meals are expected. ❺

Eating

All of Don Khong's guest houses serve food, and as you might expect, fish is the island's staple. The islanders have dozens of recipes, all worthy of a place on your plate – from the traditional **làp pa** (a Lao-style salad of minced fish mixed with garlic, chillies, shallots and fish sauce) to the tropical fish steamed in coconut milk – but whatever you do, be sure to try the island speciality, **mók pa**. Steamed in banana leaves, this sublime fish dish has the consistency of custard and takes an hour to prepare.

For this and just about anything else, *Mr Pon's* stands out as the best **restaurant** in Muang Khong, serving tasty, plentiful dishes at the guest house of the same name 150m north of the ferry landing. If it's Chinese food and a perfect river view you're after, head for *Souksan* restaurant, which stands on stilts above the Mekong. *Done Khong Guest House*, once the only place to eat in town, remains popular and its banana crêpe is divine. If you're staying at the *Villa Kang Khong*, don't miss out on the immaculately served breakfast, consisting of eggs, sliced and toasted baguettes and Lao coffee.

The people of Si Phan Don are very proud of their *lào-láo*, which has gained a reputation nationally as one of the best **rice whiskies** in Laos. For those who haven't taken a liking to Lao white lightning, you're in luck: Muang Khong has devised a gentler blend known as the "Lao cocktail", a mix of wild honey and *lào-láo* served over ice with a dash of lime.

Don Khon and Don Det

Tropical islands in the classic sense, **DON KHON** and **DON DET** are fringed with swaying coconut palms and inhabited by easygoing, sarong-clad villagers. Located south of Don Khong, the islands are especially stunning during the rainy season when rice paddies in the interior have been ploughed and planted in soothing hues of jade and emerald. Besides being a picturesque little haven to while away a few days, the islands provide opportunities for some leisurely trekking. Linked by a bridge and traversed by a trail, Don Khon and Don Det can be easily explored on foot. In fact, there are as yet no motor vehicles on the islands, making them one of the precious few places in Southeast Asia not harried by the growl and whine of motorbikes. There is, however, a fee of 5000K for a day pass or 9000K for ten days **to be on the islands**.

A delightfully sleepy place with a timeless feel about it, **BAN KHON**, located on Don Khon at the eastern end of the bridge, is the two islands' largest settlement and has the most upmarket accommodation (see p.310). A handful of quaintly decrepit French-era buildings with terracotta tile roofs adds some colonial colour to the village's collection of rustic homes of wood, bamboo and thatch. A short walk west of the old railroad bridge, past the ticket booth, stands the village monastery, **Wat Khon Tai**. Just behind the newly built *sim* is the laterite foundation of what was once a Khmer temple dedicated to the god Shiva. As with several Buddhist temples in southern Laos, this one was built upon the ruins of an ancient Hindu holy site, suggesting that this otherwise humble settlement of Ban Khon is around one thousand years old. On a pedestal nearby stands a *Shivalinga*, which was probably enshrined in the original Khmer temple. In southern Laos it isn't too uncommon to find a *Shivalinga* on the altar of a Buddhist temple or lying about somewhere in the monastery grounds. Because Khmer *Shivalinga* are usually simple and lack the intricate carving for which Khmer art is famous, they are rarely the target of art thieves and so stand a better chance of remaining on or near their original place of enshrinement.

Taking the southwestern path behind the wat, you'll soon be aware of a low, almost inaudible purr which gradually becomes a roar the further you proceed. After following the path for 1.5km, you'll come to a low cliff overlooking **Somphamit Falls**, a series of high rapids that crashes through a jagged gorge. Fishermen can sometimes be seen carefully negotiating rickety bamboo catwalks suspended above the violently churning waters.

To see the remnants of Laos's **old French railroad**, follow the trail south from the old railroad bridge. A short distance back from the bridge lies the rusting toy locomotive that once hauled French goods and passengers between piers on Don Khon and Don Det, bypassing the falls and rapids that block this stretch of the river. Nearby, behind thick brush bordering rice fields, is an overgrown **Christian cemetery** which includes the neglected tomb of a long-forgotten French family that died on the same day in 1922 – some say murdered by their Vietnamese domestics. It is actually possible to follow the former railroad all the way across both islands; however, with the exception of two alarmingly precarious bridges constructed from railroad scrap and lengths of rail recycled as fences, there are few signs that a railway ever existed. A similar but shorter walk is from Don Khon to Don Det across the bridge and along the three-kilometre elevated trail to the small village at the northern end of the island where a Stonehenge-like structure that was used for hoisting cargo from the train onto awaiting boats is all that remains of the railroad's northern terminus.

Dolphin-spotting

Don Khon's most popular attraction are the dolphins which can be spotted off the southern side of the island. To get there, take the railroad trail for 4km through rice paddies and thick forest to the village of **BAN HANG KHON**, the jumping-off point for **dolphin-spotting** excursions. The April–May dry season, when the Mekong is at its lowest, is the best time of year to catch a glimpse of this highly endangered species. They tend to congregate in a deep-water pool, and boats can be hired out from the village to see them. During the rest of the year, chances of seeing the dolphins decrease, as deeper water allows them more range. Visitors should also bear in mind that the **security situation** on the Cambodian side of the river is variable. If boatmen refuse to shuttle you out to see the dolphins, don't insist as they will know what the current situation is as to whether it's safe to venture in that direction. Dolphin-watching boats cost $5 and you are understandably obliged to pay for the boat regardless of whether you see any dolphins. Sadly, however, if current trends continue, dolphin-spotting off Don Khon may soon be a thing of the past. The present dolphin population here is only ten, down from thirty in 1993.

Communities that live beside waters inhabited by dolphins often spin legendary tales of the bond that links man and beast. The distant stretches of southern Laos, where the rare **Irrawaddy dolphin** cruises the Mekong and its tributaries, are no exception. Indeed, this freshwater dolphin holds a unique place among the Lao: they are the one creature exempt from a Lao diet famous for consuming everything that hops, flies, swims or crawls. The bluish-grey dolphin (*orcaella brevirostris*), known as *pa kha* in Lao, grows to a length of 2.5m and is distinguished from its dolphin relatives by a blunted beak. It lives in coastal waters stretching from the Bay of Bengal to the northern Australian coast, and inhabits the Irrawaddy River in Burma, the Mahakam in Kalimantan and the Ganges in India. The dolphins are rare in Lao waters, as most are unable to swim beyond the Khone Falls near the Lao-Cambodian border. Those that do make it this far upstream favour a fifty-metre-deep pool off the southern tip of Don Khon, but have also been seen in the Xe Kong, Xe Kaman and Xe Pian Mekong tributaries in the southeastern province of Attapu (see p.309 and box on p.323).

Villagers from Si Phan Don tell of dolphins saving people from drowning and pulling them from the jaws of crocodiles. They are thought to be reincarnated humans, to possess a human spirit, and are even said by some to have breasts like a woman. That the dolphins are a "human fish" is etched into local lore in the *Lam Si Phan Don*, a traditional folk song from the area. In one version of the lam, the raft of Nang Sida – the wife of Rama whose kidnapping sets the *Pha Lam Pha Lak* (the Lao version of the *Ramayana*) in motion – plunges over the Khone Falls, killing her and her loyal boatman. She is reborn as a river tern (*nok sida* in Lao), he as a dolphin; it is a relationship played out daily in the river, with the dolphin leading the tern to its meals.

But the dolphins may soon be no more than legend. Over the past century their **numbers** in the Mekong have dwindled dramatically, from thousands to little more than one hundred today. Gill-net fishing and, across the border, the use of poison, electricity and explosives have cut into their numbers. In the past, fishermen were reluctant to cut costly nets to free entangled dolphins, causing them to drown, but this no longer happens, as Lao villagers are now compensated for their nets – part of an initiative begun by the **Lao Community Fisheries and Dolphin Protection Project**. The use of explosives, however, remains common across the border. Khmer soldiers began the practice of tossing hand grenades into the river and scooping up the fish which floated to the surface. Some shot the dolphins for sport, and the Khmer Rouge, during its 1970s reign of terror, reputedly killed them by the hundreds in the Tonle Sap, extracting oil from their skins.

Fortunately, the grassroots fisheries conservation effort, of which the dolphin is the most visible symbol, is meeting with success, and villagers from nearly half of Khong District's villages voluntarily participate in the **Si Phan Don Wetlands Project**, which encourages communities to set aside conservation zones and establish laws to regulate how and when fish are caught, a step towards protecting one of the world's most ecologically diverse river systems. Participating fishermen say the changes have already registered improvements, with catches larger outside the zones than they were in those areas in previous years. A few villagers have even claimed that *ngeuak* – mythological water serpents – have returned to Lao waters.

Practicalities

It is possible to do both Don Khon and Don Det plus the waterfall at Khon Phapheng as a **day-trip** from Don Khong, although ideally Don Khon on its own is worth a few days visit. If time is very limited, a Don Khon plus falls day-trip can be done as a day-package from Muang Khong; ask at any of the guest houses or restaurants. The boat for the day trip costs 10,000K per person, and you can see both waterfalls and the defunct railroad in one day. The boat can't go directly to Khon Phapheng Falls, so the boatman will take you to the right bank, where a sawngthaew (another 10,000K per person) will be waiting to take the passengers on the thirty-kilometre round-trip to the falls (9000K admission). Afterwards, your boatman will be waiting to take you back to Don Khong.

If you intend to spend some time on Don Khon or Don Det, the cheapest option of **getting to the islands** from Muang Khong is to take the ferry (1000K) across the river to Ban Hat Xai Khoun and then get a bus to **NAKASANG** where you can get a boat to Don Khon or Don Det ($1–2). The boats depart from the landing, a short walk from the market. Alternatively, you can join a Don Khon day-trip and negotiate a one-way, discounted price for the boat trip to Don Khon.

Although Don Khon was the first island to take off with travellers, Don Det has already surpassed its larger neighbour in popularity. On Don Khon, most of the bungalows are located near the village of Ban Khon on the north end of the island. On Don Det, there are now bungalow places scattered all the way around the island, but the largest concentration is at the north side. There's not a huge difference in the two islands, and **where you stay** is largely a matter of finding a bungalow to suit your taste and budget; the best option is to shop around for your own ideal piece of paradise. If you're arriving by boat you should specify if you want to disembark at Don Khon or Don Det.

On Don Khon is *Pon's River Resort* (●), a collection of stilted bamboo huts with shared facilities and a decent restaurant. *Mr Bounh's* (●) offers simple bungalows with clean shared facilities in a quiet compound close to the river. Next door is the fanciest place on Don Khon, the *Sala Don Khone* (☎031/251461; ●), which is east of the railway bridge near the Don Khon landing. The rooms in this converted French-era bungalow, which was once a hospital, feature air conditioning and hot-water showers. There are also free-standing Lao-style wooden bungalows and a nice riverside restaurant.

On Don Det, *Santiphab* (●) next to the railroad bridge is popular with backpackers. About 2km further up the trail from the bridge, *Mr Tho's Bungalows* (●) are basic bamboo-and-thatch huts and hammocks from which you can idly watch river life passing by. If they're full try *Souksan Bungalow* (●), on the northern tip of the island. Regardless of where you stay, never leave any valuables unattended in your bungalow.

Every bungalow place on the islands have **restaurants** serving Lao food and the usual traveller's fare. Remember that food, not accommodation, is the real money earner here, so do take at least some meals at the bungalow you stay at.

From the southern end of Don Khon it is possible to hire a boat down the river to Veunkam where there is a Lao Immigration office and a **border crossing** into Cambodia. The asking price is $4 for up to three passengers.

Khon Phapheng Falls

Despite technically being the largest waterfall in Southeast Asia, **Khon Phapheng**, to the east of Don Khon, is not all that spectacular. Indeed, it's best described as a low but wide rock shelf that just happens to have a huge volume of water running over it. The vertical drop is highest during the March–May dry season and becomes much less spectacular when the river level rises during the rainy season. Still, the sight of all that water crashing down on its way to Cambodia is quite mesmerizing and a well-built tourist pavilion above the falls provides an ideal place to sit and enjoy the view. There's also no shortage of food shacks serving *som tom*. Most tourists do the falls as a package from Don Khong (see p.302) but it is also possible to get there by sawngthaew from Ban Hat Xai Khoun (opposite Muang Khong) or Nakasang (5000K). There is a 9000K admission fee for foreigners and 1000K extra for a motorcycle.

Bolaven Plateau

High above the hot Mekong River Valley stands the natural citadel of the **Bolaven Plateau**, dominating eastern Champasak Province and overlooking the provinces of Salavan, Xekong, and Attapu to the east. As gradual as Route 23's eastwardly climb out of Pakxe is, there's no mistaking when you've reached the Bolaven Plateau, roughly 30km from Pakxe. The suffocating heat of the Mekong Valley yields to a refreshingly cool breeze, and coffee and tea plantations, exulting in the nutrient-rich soil, begin cropping up along either side of the highway. Hilly, roughly circular in shape, and with an average altitude of 600m, the high plateau has rivers running off in all directions and then plunging out of lush forests along the Bolaven's edges in a series of spectacular waterfalls, some more than 100m high, before eventually finding their way to the Mekong. The provincial capitals of Pakxe, Salavan, Xekong, and Attapu all surround the Bolaven, but the main settlement on the plateau itself is the town of Pakxong. South of Route 23 between Pakxe and Pakxong is the **Dong Hua Sao NBCA.**

The French, recognizing the fertility of the terrain, cleared wide swathes of forests and planted strawberries, coffee, tea and cardamom. Although it was cardamom that provided the south's chief export during colonial times, coffee is the crop that dominates the plateau these days, earning the well-paved highway that links Pakxe with Pakxong the moniker the **Coffee Road**. Introduced to the area by the French in the 1920s, coffee plants are now crammed into every spare centimetre of land, with villagers hoping to earn extra kip by hawking their private crop to brokers, who sell the roasted beans upcountry and around the world. Long before the French planted their first coffee crop, midland hilltribes were practising swidden agriculture on the plateau. Today, twelve ethnic groups, including lowland Lao, Laven, Alak, Suay and Taoy, live in the area. Given that ethnic minorities are in the majority here, it's only fitting that the plateau takes its name from one of these groups, the Laven.

Historically, the Bolaven has yielded more than just rich agricultural pickings. For the French, controlling the area was a headache during the early years of their rule. An Alak holy man, believed to possess supernatural powers, sparked a rebellion against the land's new colonial masters, and, fuelled by anger at the disruption of established political and economic relationships in the area, the revolt (see p.339) spilled into the Mekong basin and into neighbouring Thailand. This rebel spirit was later co-opted by the Pathet Lao in their attempt to create a nationalist history of rebellion against foreign powers. During the Second Indochina War, the plateau's elevated terrain provided a strategic military position as well as access to the far-flung outposts of Salavan and Attapu. **Pakxong**, one of the Bolaven's principal towns, was levelled in bombing raids during the war and has not been able to rekindle the charm it once possessed. The legacy of decades of battle still haunts the people of the plateau, with farmers tending to their crops amid fields laden with unexploded bombs.

One of the easiest waterfalls to access is **Tad Lo** on the forested northwestern edge of the plateau, a popular spot with travellers looking for somewhere pleasant to relax for a few days and enjoy the plateau's cool climate. You can lounge in the pools of the Xe Set River below the waterfall and do some elephant trekking to nearby tribal villages.

Banana Junction

The tiny village, nicknamed **BANANA JUNCTION** but properly known as Lak 21 and located, as its name indicates, 21km from Pakxe, is an important junction for **bus transfers**. There are connections here for Tad Lo and Salavan in the northeast or Pakxong and beyond. It's the blur of sun-yellowed bunches of bananas, suspended from bamboo poles in makeshift thatch lean-to's, that lends this three-way intersection its nickname. When bananas are out of season, pineapples and durians find their way onto the stands. If durian – that spiky oblong fruit whose foul stench resembles that of a backed-up bog – is your thing, those on sale here are fresh off the fertile Bolaven Plateau and are known for their exceptional creaminess.

Dong Hua Sao NBCA

Located in the southwest quarter of the Bolaven Plateau, **Dong Hua Sao** is currently the first and only **NBCA** up on the plateau itself. The most important features of Dong Hua Sao are the **Tad Fan Waterfall** and a 1300-metre peak in the west of the 900 square-kilometre NBCA. Two of eleven areas currently under consideration for NBCA status are also located on the **Bolaven** and are designated Bolavens Northeast and Bolavens Southwest. Assuming the proposals go through, the three protected areas would merge into a single conservation area totalling 2465 square kilometres and covering the greater part of the outer Bolaven Plateau.

Tad Fan Waterfall

Falling water enthusiasts will get a kick out of **Tad Fan**, a cascade some 100m high set amidst primeval jungle as far as the eye can see. Of several waterfalls in the area, this one is the easiest to locate. Travelling east on Route 23 to Pakxong, turn right at the kilometre 38 marker. The dirt road leads through a coffee plantation and then forks; take the branch to the left and you will end up at the edge of a cliff overlooking the falls. A trail leads down to a better vantage point, but it's not advisable to attempt this slippery path during the rainy season, as it's a long drop down into the abyss.

There is an eco-resort located out at the falls, the *Tad Fane Resort* (T021/350160; **③–④**) which has a restaurant and ten nicely built Lao-style bungalows near the falls.

Pakxong

Laos's famed coffee capital, **PAKXONG**, some 60km east of Pakxe, was rebuilt after the war and is just now beginning to find a market for its traditional cash crop. Those searching for some epicentre of coffee culture will be disappointed, but arriving on the plateau from the baking lowlands, especially during the torrid March–May hot season, will make you wonder how a bit of altitude can turn the cruel midday sun into a shoulder-warming friend. The vast majority of Pakxong's inhabitants are **Laven**, an ethnic group that has almost completely assimilated with the ethnic Lao. About the only trait that differentiates the Laven from the lowland Lao, besides language, is their hospitality which,

Lao Java

In the early twentieth century, the French were looking for ways to make their newest chunk of Indochina profitable. Laos had become a disappointment when the grand scheme of using the Mekong as a trade link to China turned out to be impractical, but the French soon had other plans. Would **coffee**, which had been successfully introduced to Vietnam, also thrive in Laos? It seemed worth a try. Saplings were brought from the orchards around Buon Me Thuot in Vietnam and planted at varying degrees of elevation. From the banks of the Mekong on up to the Bolaven Plateau, rows of arabica and robusta were carefully nursed. After four years, the first harvest saw mixed results: coffee at lower elevations failed to fruit, but planters on the Bolaven were rewarded for their patience.

By the 1940s, **coffee plantations** covered the plateau and the future looked bright until a bout of the blight caused the arabica trees to wither and die. Next, war and revolution intervened, and by the 1980s, the once painstakingly tended trees had gone wild. However, interest in Lao coffee has been rekindled over the last decade and the old plantations have benefited from a certain amount of foreign investment. A blight-resistant strain of arabica was recently introduced from Costa Rica, and the "Association des Exportateurs du Café Lao" is hoping to increase annual coffee production to 20,000 tonnes by the year 2000. Planters are also optimistic, citing tales of recent harvests so bountiful that branches snapped under the weight of the clusters of beans.

Although coffee made its way to Laos via Vietnam, the **coffee-drinking etiquette** and accoutrements of Laos have a flavour all their own. The tin-drip, used in Vietnam to filter coffee into a glass, is rare in Laos. The Lao favour pouring hot water through a sock-like bag filled with ground coffee. As in Vietnam, an order of hot coffee, or *kafeh hawn*, will come in a glass half-filled with sweetened-condensed milk. Perhaps more in step with the climate is *kafeh yén*, in which the same concoction is mixed and poured into a mug of crushed ice, the perfect pick-me-up after a long afternoon siesta.

believe it or not, actually exceeds that of the lowlanders. This is especially apparent during Lao New Year, when foreign guests are sure to be welcomed with prodigious amounts of potent rice liquor.

The temperate weather and amiable locals notwithstanding, Pakxong's sites are almost nil. The **town** itself is a small collection of mould-blackened concrete shop-houses lining wide, dust-scoured streets, which wouldn't look out of place on the set of a spaghetti Western. A gatepost at the entrance of the market is possibly the only structure in town to have survived the war. Beyond it is a depressing block of ramshackle shops and noodle stands. Perhaps noting the lack of ambience, some of Pakxong's residents have begun exploring the decorative possibilities of unexploded ordnance (UXO). If you are looking for a cheap thrill you will find one at the Shell service station on Route 23 just west of town. There, a 250-pound bomb and other sundry bits of ordnance, all of it presumably still live, have been painted and neatly arranged in a garden near the petrol pumps. Despite the bleakness of the town, the surrounding countryside and **coffee plantations** provide some diverting scenery, especially during March and April when the coffee trees are covered with intoxicatingly fragrant white blossoms.

Practicalities

If only Pakxong boasted a cosy guest house surrounded by gardens where you could enjoy the invigorating climate. Sadly, it does not. The town's only **place to stay**, *Pakxong* (❶), 500m beyond the market, is dingy and uncomfortable.

Moving on, buses headed for Xekong and Attapu pass the town, and hourly sawngthaews leave from the market for Pakxe.

Tad Lo Waterfall

The ten-metre-high **Tad Lo Waterfall**, on the banks of the Xe Set River, draws a steady stream of foreign visitors, providing the perfect setting for a few days' relaxation and the opportunity to ride an elephant along the breezy western flank of the fertile Bolaven Plateau. In the hot season, the pools surrounding Tad Hang, the lower falls, are a refreshing escape from the heat: large boulders in the river shade a few surprisingly deep swimming holes and are perfect spots for lounging in the sun. Just be sure to clear the water before 8pm, however, when the floodgates of a dam upstream unleash a torrent of water without warning.

The Bolaven revolt

A chanting mob, two thousand-strong, descended on Savannakhet in April 1902, convinced by a holy man that any bullets fired at them would be miraculously transformed into frangipani flowers. Three times they attacked, and each time they were mown down by troops from France's "Garde Indigène". The rout, which left 150 dead, marked the climax of the so-called **Holy Man's Revolt**, which had its origins with the arrival of the French in 1893 and simmered on for many years afterwards in the highlands of the south.

The French brought with them administrative changes, increased taxation and reshuffled the traditional relationships which had guided life in Laos for generations. At first, resistance was textbook Lao. Villagers avoided direct confrontation, preferring to make their displeasure about the new order known through passive means: villages undercounted their populations, adapted a generally uncooperative attitude, or simply left. The first serious opposition didn't arise until eight years after the French employed gunboat diplomacy to wrest control of Lao territory from Siam.

When **Ong Kaew**, an Alak tribesman believed to possess supernatural powers, prophesied that "the end of the world as we know it" was nigh, he found willing listeners among midland tribes living along the plateau, chafing under increased taxes and *corvée* labour demands instituted by the French commissioner of Salavan. Sensing that Ong Kaew was gaining too much influence, the commissioner ordered the burning of a pagoda erected in the holy man's honour. This only served to increase support for Ong Kaew, and in April 1901, he and a band of rebels attacked the commissioner and his guard. Soon after, nearly all of the Bolaven region was in revolt.

By 1902, the revolt had spilled across the Mekong and briefly gained the support of older lowland Lao families, who felt threatened by the collapse of the social and economic order to which they were accustomed. After the disastrous march on Savannakhet, Ong Kaew and another Lao Theung leader, **Ong Kommadam**, whose son would later continue to resist the French and ultimately become a Pathet Lao leader, retreated across the Xe Kong River as villages were burned and less fortunate leaders rounded up and executed. But the defeat at Savannakhet and renewed attempts by France to pacify the Bolaven region did little to dispel the holy man's popularity, and it took a new commissioner at Salavan, **Jean Dauplay**, to force Ong Kaew to surrender in 1907. Three years later, with the holy man's influence over the Bolaven inhabitants as strong as ever, Dauplay arrested Ong Kaew, who died "during a jail break" the next day. The revolt was effectively over.

Not all was lost during the insurrection. French authorities were careful to place more of the burden on lowland Lao when they raised taxes in 1914, and Ong Kaew had unwittingly sown the seeds for what the Pathet Lao would later claim to be the stirrings of Lao nationalism.

Elephant treks ($4 for 2hr) through the forested hills around Tad Lo are easy to arrange through any of the guest houses. Sitting high up in the howdah, you get some sense of the grace of these regal beasts, which for centuries were cherished by Lao and French travellers alike for their ability to glide through tricky terrain. A ride typically takes two hours round-trip from Tad Lo Resort, and involves a short stop at Tad Lo, 500m upstream, before pulling through a nearby village inhabited by midlanders of Alak ethnicity, who have a long history of settlement on the plateau.

Practicalities

The Tad Lo falls are just two hours northeast of Pakxe by **bus** and about 30km southwest of Salavan. The road is mostly dirt but is flat and in good condition. The turn-off for Tad Lo is 88km northeast of Pakxe, just beyond the village of Lao Ngam; buses will drop you at the turn-off where a congregation of restaurants and general stores crowds the mouth of the one-and-a-half kilometre long dirt road that leads to Tad Hang, the lower falls. From here it's a 1.5-kilometre tuk-tuk ride (2000K per person) along a dirt road to Tad Hang. When leaving, find a driver to take you back to the highway, where you can pick up a morning bus to Salavan or Pakxe.

High on a hill overlooking Tad Hang perches the *Tad Lo Resort* (T031/212105 ext 3325; ❺–❻), with thirteen rooms in an assortment of **bungalows** ranging from very basic to well-appointed structures at the river's edge. Across the river, *Saise* **guest house** has a handful of cheaper rooms with shared facilities in a raised house (❷), plus some very pleasant en-suite ones in a "green house", a few hundred metres upstream (❷). The six rooms – four are en-suite – are the best deal to be found in the area, especially the VIP rooms which have balconies overlooking the river. Beds fill up quickly at both establishments, so reserve ahead; the Sodetour office in Pakxe (see p.289) can do this.

Choices for **eating** are limited, but the *Tad Lo Resort* has a relaxed open-air restaurant, with rattan furniture and commanding views of the Xe Set, where you can choose from a range of moderately priced French and Lao dishes. Be sure to try the fish with chillies steamed in banana leaves, a southern speciality. For cheaper fare, head down the hill to the *Little Shop*. **Moving on** from Tad Lo, it's a hike back to the highway, where buses en route to Salavan and Pakxe can be flagged down in the morning.

The remote provinces

Salavan, **Xekong** and **Attapu**, cut off from the Mekong River Valley by the Bolaven Plateau and made remote by the rugged jigsaw of the Annamite Mountains, are some of the least visited provinces in Laos. Poor infrastructure and the scars of war conspire to keep the region as isolated as it's ever been. With the Ho Chi Minh Trail streaming across their borders, these provinces were victims of some of the heaviest bombing during the Second Indochina War. Villages were decimated, roads destroyed – some are still impassable today – and the dangerous litter of battle still lies about. The densely forested mountains of Attapu and Xekong, however, are still home to a rich variety of wildlife and numerous ethnic minority villages.

Arcing around the **Bolaven Plateau**, these provinces can be seen in a convenient clockwise loop from Pakxe. From Banana Junction (see p.312), 21km east of Pakxe, head northeast for roughly 100km along well-maintained Route 20 towards Salavan, where bus connections are available for the bumpy ninety-kilometre trip to **Xekong** via **Thateng**, the dusty northern gateway to the Bolaven Plateau. Just east of the plateau, uninspiring Xekong provides a jumping-off point for the pretty five hour boat trip along the babbling Xe Kong River to **Attapu**, capital of Laos's southeasternmost province. Miraculously unscathed by the American bombing raids, the serene city of Attapu, known throughout southern Laos as the "garden city", is one of the gems of the far south. From Attapu, it can be a rough haul back to Pakxe up the eastern flank of the Bolaven and through the coffee plantations surrounding Pakxong, as the steep, poorly engineered Attapu–Pakxong road, a seasonal route cut by a South Korean hydroelectric company working in the area, becomes nearly impassable in the rainy season. At the moment, no public buses and very few private vehicles travel Route 18, the shortcut to Si Phan Don, which shadows the southern edge of the Bolaven, although the Asian Development Bank once had plans to upgrade the road as far as Vietnam.

Salavan

North of the Bolaven Plateau, the provincial capital of **SALAVAN** is only just beginning to recover from the effects of the war. In recent years new buildings of more permanent materials have begun slowly replacing the rickety wooden structures, but a walk around town still reveals evidence of Salavan's tumultuous history. The ruins of **Wat Phon Kaew**, located in the grounds of the provincial hospital, consist of a shrapnel-pocked gateway and a ruined stupa. At the nearby army base a rusting anti-aircraft gun sits in a weedy field, and the observant visitor will note the presence of more than a few bomb craters.

Located on a flank of the former Ho Chi Minh Trail, Salavan was held by the Royal Lao government until 1970, when an NVA (North Vietnamese Army) push to consolidate control over the Trail drove the Royalists out. The town then became a target for American B-52s, employing Arclight strikes, in which the bombers flew at such high altitudes that they were neither visible nor audible from the ground. The effects of such tactics are not hard to imagine. One minute you are going about your business and then, without warning, the ground begins to erupt deafeningly all around you. As with other towns subjected to carpet bombing, those who were not killed, fled, and Salavan was not repopulated until after the war.

In the 1980s, scrap dealers set up shop in Salavan, giving monetary worth to the twisted chunks of metal that littered the area. Today, nearly all of the war scrap has gone and it is conceivable that you could wander around here without ever catching on to Salavan's tragic past.

Practicalities

The daily buses that pull into Salavan's **bus station** connect the town with Pakxe, Xekong and Pakxong, with smaller buses and pick-up trucks heading off from here to the province's interior. Overly optimistic maps suggest the possibility of travelling north to Savannakhet province (through Toumlan to Muang Phin and through Taoy on to Ban Dong), but these roads, effectively taken out during the war, are now overgrown and lacking key bridges.

If you're interested in travelling to the outer districts of the province, seek out the helpful provincial **tourism officer**, Mr Bounthone, whose office is located at the *Saise guest house*: he'll be able to update you on the progress of road and bridge repairs in the surrounding area and point you in the direction of any interesting festivals taking place in nearby ethnic minority villages.

Accommodation Salavan now has three guest houses. *Silsamai* (❷), just north of *Vilaivane Restaurant*, has rooms with fans or air-con. The *Thipphaphone*

(❷) and the *Chindavone* (❷) are the other choices in town.

Aside from the adjoining Lao restaurant, the **market** offers a group of stalls selling pre-made Lao food and sticky rice. Also in the vicinity, the *Vilaivane*, a tidy little **restaurant** with bamboo interior, has a dusty rack of foreign liquor and an English-language menu with a short list of inexpensive Lao, Chinese and Vietnamese food. In the immediate vicinity of the market you'll find the **post office** as well as a branch of Phak Tai **bank**, where you can exchange US dollars and Thai baht in cash only.

Thateng

From Salavan it's a laborious climb southeast through rich jungle and midland tribal villages up the steep curves of the Bolaven Plateau to **THATENG**, 40km away. A dusty, ramshackle congregation of threadbare markets and crooked wooden houses with thatch roofs, Thateng was where the French commissioner to Salavan, Jean Dauplay, "the father of Lao coffee", chose to settle in the 1920s. Sadly, Thateng's strategic location as the gateway to the plateau made it a prime target for American bombs as it was thought that control of the plateau was the key to controlling the bulk of the far south. The town was basically wiped out, and although villagers returned after the war, the place is nowadays little more than an unappealing through-point.

UXO

For the visitor to Laos, knowledge of and a healthy respect for **unexploded ordnance (UXO)** is a must. There are very few places in Laos that are unaffected by UXO. Besides the mind-boggling number of bombs dropped on Laos by the United States during the decade-long "secret war" (see p.352), intense ground battles were waged between several factions using weapons from myriad sources. The deadly remnants of clashes between the Pathet Lao, Viet Cong and North Vietnamese Army on one side and the Royal Lao Army, South Vietnamese Army and French and American armed forces on the other still blanket the ground. Ordnance from the US, China, Russia, France and even Great Britain has been found by disposal experts in Laos. They estimate that as much as thirty percent of weapons that were meant to explode on impact didn't. These include bombs, rockets, mortar rounds, grenades and artillery shells. Of course, this figure does not take into account the countless number of mines planted and then forgotten.

Despite all this, the average traveller to Laos has little to worry about if a few **simple rules** are followed. Although it may seem obvious, the number one rule is: don't be a trailblazer. When in rural areas, always stay on well-worn paths, even when passing through a village. In certain parts of Laos, rare is the village that doesn't have at least one untouched piece of UXO rusting away in the very spot it was dropped decades ago. Locals will all know where the danger is located, but may neglect to warn visitors. In areas that are known to be heavily contaminated with UXO, such as the districts surrounding the former Ho Chi Minh Trail, you'll need to take special care, as unexploded devices can be anywhere. When taking a toilet break during long-distance bus journeys, it's not a good idea to penetrate too deeply into the bush looking for privacy. UXO unearthed during road construction is often pushed onto the shoulder, where it becomes overgrown with weeds and forgotten. Disposal experts say that fast-growing bamboo has been known to unearth UXO, lifting it aloft as the stalk grows and then letting it fall onto a trail that was previously clean. An innocent gesture, such as pausing during a hike to kick at something that caught the eye, can lead to tragedy. For more information on the UXO situation in Laos see the excellent ⓦ www.uxolao.org.

The Xekong River Valley

The **Xekong** is one of Laos's great rivers, starting high in the Annamite Mountains from the eastern flanks of the 2500-metre high Mount Atouat and flowing southwestward around the southern edge of the Bolaven Plateau and across the plains of Cambodia to join the Mekong at Stung Treng. The main towns along the Xekong in Laos are **Xekong** and **Attapu** which are linked by a paved road. Roads into the vast forest interior are still extremely poor but various tributaries link the Xekong to no less than four of Laos's most pristine NBCAs, and organized kayaking tours are starting to take-off.

Xekong

In 1984, a wide expanse of jungle was cleared of trees and graded flat and the town of **XEKONG** was born. Founded partly because the nearby town of Ban Phon was deemed no longer habitable owing to unexploded ordnance (UXO), Xekong, some 50km east of Thateng, is now the capital of a new province, created when Attapu was divided in half. This town has something of a frontier feel about it and admittedly, there is not much of interest in the town itself, but intrepid travellers may be attracted by the prospect of a scenic journey downriver from here to Attapu.

Three major branches of the **Ho Chi Minh Trail** snaked through the jungle surrounding Xekong, making this area one of the most heavily bombed in Laos. Animist tribal peoples living in the adjacent hills, under constant threat of attack from the sky, erected talismans above their huts to ward off falling bombs. Some of these strange war relics are still in place: rusting tail-fins from dud bombs have been arranged to form a protective X over thatched roofs, and, in at least one village, carved wooden miniatures of "Huey" helicopters, looking like militaristic weather vanes, are mounted above the tribal meeting house. Some of these tribes also produce **hand-woven textiles** which are highly sought after by collectors. Decorative patterns feature traditional motifs such as animals and plants, alongside stylized fighter planes and bombs of obvious inspiration. Despite the massive destruction caused to Xekong's ecosystem caused by the dropping of bombs and defoliants, the area is host to a surprisingly large and varied wildlife population. Herds of wild elephants regularly raid village rice barns, and tigers have been seen lapping at the pools below Tad Xe Noi falls, just 25km south of the provincial capital. Other rare species known to inhabit the wilds of Xekong include the Siamese crocodile and pygmy slow loris. There is even thought to be a small population of Sumatran rhinos deep in these jungled hills.

If you're ready to devote half your visa time to Xekong, prepare yourself for this cruel hitch: the astonishing amount of **UXO** that blankets this province makes exploration extremely dicey (see box on p.317). UXO disposal teams assigned to the province conclude that, like parts of Europe that were heavily fought over during both world wars, Xekong will be losing victims to UXO for decades to come.

As if the danger of UXO weren't enough, there is a disturbing beasty lurking in Xekong's waterways: the *pa pao* is an innocuous-looking blowfish with a piranha-like appetite and, according to locals, a particular fondness for lopping off the tip of the male member. The risk of losing a plug of flesh to a ravenous blowfish notwithstanding, the journey by pirogue down the stretch of river between Xekong and Attapu is undoubtedly the best way to view this most inaccessible corner of southern Laos.

Practicalities

Buses to and from Pakxe operate from the lot outside the morning market, about 1km from the main market. A handful of tuk-tuks await arriving buses and will ferry you into the centre for 2000K. Heading into town, you'll pass a branch of the Lao May bank where you can **exchange cash** and traveller's cheques, and the **post office** and telecom building where international calls can be made. A daily bus plies the paved route which follows the Xe Kong River south to Attapu; it leaves the morning market at 7am, arriving in Attapu about two hours later, and departs for the trip back to Xekong at noon. A pleasant alternative is to hire a boat to Attapu (see below). Daily buses also go to Salavan on a recently paved road.

Sekong Souksamlane (☎031/212022; ❷), 500m downriver from the market, has decent, if somewhat over-priced **rooms**. A cluster of cheap places to eat surrounds the hotel, but the hotel **restaurant** cooks rather good Thai food at reasonable rates. The array of handicrafts that line the establishment's walls are for sale, including intricately woven rattan quivers from local ethnic groups such as the Katu and Alak. If you're in the market for a bit of shopping, however, head over to the Lao Women's Union in the governor's office, where the prices are better.

Xe Kong River to Attapu

If you've made it as far as Xekong, the scenic **Xe Kong River**, which meanders through little-visited countryside, provides a strong incentive to hire a boat for the journey south to **Attapu**. At around $20 per boat, it's not cheap but well worth the trip. To find a boat, follow the road that passes in front of the *Sekong Souksamlane* hotel south for 1km until you reach a boat landing on the riverbank where you'll find the boatmen and then have to bargain the price.

Emerging from the mountains of Vietnam, the Xe Kong meanders south by southwest entering Cambodia via the Xe Pian NBCA then eventually joining the Mekong River north of Stung Treng in Cambodia. Motorized pirogues make the four-hour journey through gentle rapids and past lushly forested riverbanks, where people living in the surrounding hills come to catch fish and bathe. Late in the dry season, the trip can take seven hours, and the shallow waters require passengers to walk short stretches of the journey along the bank. Although the fare doesn't rise at this time of year, captains limit the number of passengers to two, thereby increasing the price per person.

During the Second Indochina War, US aircraft struck at the threads of the Ho Chi Minh Trail running parallel to the Xe Kong, hoping to disrupt the endless tide of men and supplies streaming southwards. Bombs invariably wound up in the river and the resulting explosions sent scores of fish floating belly-up to the surface, unintentional war reparations quickly collected by villagers living amid a battlefield. Today's depleted fish catches are still blamed on the war, but more modern fishing equipment has surely had an impact, as has the use of explosives for catching fish, a technique that was utilized by Vietnamese soldiers during the war and remains part of the Cambodian fisherman's arsenal along some stretches of the river. One victim of such high-impact methods, the Irrawaddy dolphin, until a decade ago a frequent visitor to Attapu's maze of rivers in the rainy season, now rarely visits these waters (see box on p.309).

Attapu

A cosy settlement of almost 20,000 people, most of whom are Vietnamese, Chinese or Lao Loum, remote **ATTAPU**, the capital of Laos's southeastern-most province, occupies a bend in the **Xe Kong River** just south of where it is joined by the **Xe Kaman River**. Reliant on the poorly engineered roads from Pakxong and Xekong, Attapu can be difficult to reach, especially in the rainy season, but it's well worth the journey.

It was near this distant outpost that the Ho Chi Minh Trail diverged, with one artery running south towards Cambodia and the other into South Vietnam. But despite its role as the final staging point in Laos for North Vietnamese supplies, Attapu somehow eluded the grave effects of war that wiped other southern cities off the map. Coconut palms and banana trees, their leaves shining jade in the sunlight, shade spacious wooden houses with gener-ous balconies, high on stilts, lending the city a quiet urban splendour.

That the town remains an oasis among rugged mountains perhaps reflects what some American military advisors mocked as the reluctance of the Royal Lao Army, who controlled Attapu in the late 1960s, to engage their opponents in battle – a trait which prompted the Americans to nickname the Royalist troops "the Fastest Army Running", a moniker derived from the army's old French acronym FAR. When the Pathet Lao announced that they intended to take the city in April 1970, Royal Lao troops lived up to their reputation and fled. Five years later, the Pathet Lao made the entire province a **re-education camp** (see p.356), resettling political enemies and forbidding them to leave the province for years. The Pathet Lao perhaps thought it only fitting to punish

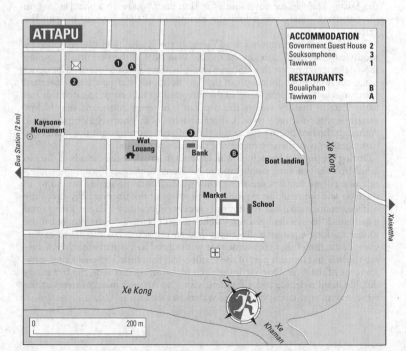

opponents with a dose of what they had had to endure, living in the country's remotest areas during their Thirty Year Struggle; what better place than one which, even by nineteenth-century Lao standards, was known for its "extreme unhealthiness", as reported by French explorer François Jules Harmand, who visited Attapu in 1877. This reputation festers to this day, with Attapu registering the country's highest rate of malaria (appropriate precautions are described on p.31). Such tumultuous history lends new currency to the old legend surrounding Attapu's name. When the first lowland Lao immigrants to the region asked the indigenous people what the name of their town was, the latter thought the Lao were pointing to a pile of water buffalo dung, or itkapu in their language, and responded accordingly. With a slight change in pronunciation to accommodate the Lao accent, the town of "buffalo shit" was born. Attapu has no warehouse of tourist attractions: the way to enjoy this town is by leisurely wandering in its rambling red-dirt lanes, absorbing the easygoing pace and chatting with the genial residents. In the evening, head to the southern end of town, where the Xe Kong pauses to flow east to west, and the high riverbank invites you to catch a sunset over the river. If it's sights you crave, walk over to the town's main **wat**, which occupies a massive block in the heart of town. On the northern side of the compound, standing out among the gaudy modern temple architecture, you'll find a handsome French-style monastery school building, the monks gazing through weathered wooden windowsills and igniting the cool yellows of the stucco walls with the saffron of their holy robes.

Practicalities

Arriving in Attapu by **bus**, you'll wind up in a dirt field on the southwestern outskirts of the city, 2km from the centre. If you're on the **express bus** from Pakxe, don't get off here, as the bus may continue into town. Attapu's other point of arrival is the **ferry landing**, where the car ferry and boats from Xekong dock. From here walk up the ramp scaling the riverbank and follow the road into town to Attapu's only **bank**, a branch of Lao May, which is a good point of orientation.

Attapu has two **guest houses**. The better of the pair is the family-run *Souksomphone* (❶), which has seven clean, spacious rooms, most with expansive double beds; look for the modern building opposite the bank. Near the post office, *Tawiwan* (❷), formerly the official guest house, has rooms with creaky wooden floors and shared bathrooms in a cluster of two-storey houses set back from the road. At the eastern end of this compound is the town's most popular **restaurant**, which government officials and foreign residents frequent daily. Here you'll find good, moderately priced noodle and rice dishes, some of which taste of Indian spices – the legacy of a South Asian doctor who recently worked in the area. Service, however, is so slow that you may be convinced that you've found the epicentre of lazy Laos. Walking two blocks towards the ferry landing from the bank, and turning right, you'll find *Boualipham*, a shop-house restaurant that serves frosty 333 beers from Vietnam and an inexpensive range of fruit and rice dishes. The main area for **food stalls** lies along the same east–west road that the *Souksomphone* is on, with hawkers setting up between the bank and the wat.

Moving on from Attapu, the bus to Xekong leaves at noon and arrives at Xekong's morning market at around 2pm. The **express bus** leaves Attapu for Pakxe at 6am, making the non-stop trip in a lightning-quick four hours. Otherwise you're stuck with the gruelling regular bus, which can take twice as long. In the rainy season, getting to and from Attapu becomes something of a

△ Temple door, Don Khong

challenge, and you may well find yourself getting out to push a bus axle-deep in mud. Route 18 to Si Phan Don via Route 13 is still unpaved and there is no public transportation across, although there are plans to eventually upgrade this road as far as Vietnam in the future. **Boats** up the Xe Kong River to Xekong can be arranged through the owner of the *Souksomphone*; for more on this route, see p.319.

Across the river from Attapu

When François Jules Harmand asked about **crossing to the left bank** of the Xe Kong River during his visit in the late 1870s, the village chief answered each question about the possibility of such a trip with *baw dai* ("No can do") – a refrain the French explorer heard so often he was pressed to consider whether the Lao language possessed any other words than these. Visitors today still get much the same response, with locals pointing out that while Attapu's densely forested mountains conceal rare spots of natural beauty, they are very difficult to reach – a fact not lost on the Lao Theung leader, Kommadam, who hid here for decades after he took part in a rebellion against the French (see box on p.314).

It's hard to imagine that **getting around** the rugged peaks has become any easier since Harmand's visit. Transport is nearly nonexistent – a lone pick-up truck operates on the opposite bank – and the area is poorly mapped, leaving most travellers, many quite happily, confined to the provincial capital. Since the province is littered with **minefields** (one of which lies 3km west of the town centre) and deadly UXO (Attapu has two of the most heavily bombed districts in the country), the best way to see the area is to hire a local guide, though this is difficult since there are no tour agencies in town. You may be able to find someone by asking at the *Souksomphone*. If you're determined to go it alone, you're bound to come to the attention of local authorities, so it's wise to check in at district offices. With travelling around the province so difficult, many visitors opt for a **boat trip**, an easy way to get a taste of the area's rural charm. You should be able to hire boats by asking at the boat landing or at your guest house.

Attapu shares neighbouring Xekong's rich variety of wildlife. Lured by this abundance, Suay villagers arrived here several centuries ago to capture wild elephants still plentiful in this part of the Annamite Mountains. Although the Suay migrated west in the eighteenth century, poachers in these hills still hunt exotic animals, which they sell off to buyers from Vietnam. The fact that such work has become quite lucrative gives villagers added incentive to continue this practice, and those that do are not keen on individuals seen to be poking around.

Around a dozen ethnic minorities live in these hills and, with many of the same groups living on the Vietnamese side of the mountains, these peoples reflect the porous nature of many of the borders in Southeast Asia. As the indigenous people of this area, these groups are considered by lowland Lao to be close to the spirits of the land, a belief that inspires some superstitious ethnic Lao to fill their pockets with Parrot Brand soap – the garlic of toiletries, believed to ward off black magic – before entering tribal villages.

In the late nineteenth century, when the region was in Bangkok's sphere of influence, some of these midland villages paid tribute to Siam, usually in the form of **gold dust** stored in the quill of a large bird's feather, in order to hedge their bets against being captured in a slave hunt, a practice abolished by the French. The sight of these flecks of gold convinced French explorers that hidden riches might lie in the mountains, and they dug mines, but the colonial administration saw little profit from these ventures. Indeed, a brief visit to the villages outside Attapu is evidence enough that the area is no goldmine.

Dong Amphan NBCA

Wedged against Vietnam and Cambodia in the extreme southeast corner of the country, **Dong Amphan** is one of Laos's most enticing NBCAs as well as one of the most inaccessible. The **Xe Kaman** River forms the northwestern boundary of the park and is a habitat for Irrawaddy **dolphins**. Parallel to the river is a large range of mountains rising to over 1400 metres, and the peaks on the eastern boundary of the park bordering Vietnam are also impressive, rising to 2052m. The park is well forested with both mixed deciduous forests and evergreen forests at higher altitudes and mammals are said to include elephant, black bear, leopard, and tigers. Attapu is the best base for accessing the park by boat but this will still require a fair bit of money and determination.

Travel details

Buses

Attapu to: Pakxe (3 daily; 4–7hr) via Pakxong (2 daily; 5hr).
Champasak to: Pakxe (3 daily; 2hr 30min).
Pakxe to: Attapu (2 daily; 4–7hr); Ban Phapho (3 daily; 3hr); Ban Saphai (hourly; 30min); Champasak (3 daily; 1hr); Chong Mek (every 30min; 45min); Don Khong (4 daily; 5hr); Kiatngong (3 daily; 2hr 30min); Muang Sen (2 daily; 5hr 30min); Nakasang (5 daily; 3hr); Pakxong (hourly; 2hr); Salavan (5 daily; 3hr); Savannakhet (3 daily; 6–8hr); Thakhek (3 daily; 8–10hr); Vientiane (3 daily; 12–15hr); Xekong (2 daily; 4–5hr).
Pakxong to: Attapu (2 daily; 5hr); Pakxe (hourly; 2hr).

Salavan to: Pakxe (5 daily; 3hr); Taoy (1 daily; 5hr); Toumlan (1 daily; 2hr); Xekong (2 daily; 4hr).
Xekong to: Pakxe (2 daily; 4–5hr); Salavan (2 daily; 4hr).

Flights

Pakxe to: Savannakhet (4 weekly; 45min); Vientiane (1 daily; 1hr 20min).

Boats

Pakxe to: Champasak (1–2 daily; 1hr 30min); Muang Sen (1–2 daily; 8–10hr).

Contexts

Contexts

History

Laos as a unified state within its present geographical boundaries has only existed for little more than one hundred years. Its national history stretches back six centuries to the legendary kingdom of Lane Xang, a rival to the empires of mainland Southeast Asia until it splintered into a cluster of weak principalities dominated by their more powerful neighbours.

The beginnings

As long as forty thousand years ago, Laos was inhabited by **hunter-gatherers** who lived in relatively permanent sites and used tools made of stone, wood and bamboo, not terribly different from many of those still in use in rural Lao villages today. By 8000 BC, these peoples had become **farmers**, growing beans, peas and rice and domesticating animals such as chickens, swine and cattle. Excavations at a site in present-day northeastern Thailand reveal that copper and bronze work in the region dates back four thousand years – as early as anywhere in the world. **Ironworking** was the next step forward, and by 500 BC the inhabitants of the Khorat Plateau in northeastern Thailand were using ploughs with iron tips, pulled by water buffalo, to cultivate wet rice. The sophistication of the metallurgy of the region is perhaps best indicated by the bronze drums crafted by the Lac Viet people of northern Vietnam in the first millennium BC, ritualistic artefacts discovered in 1920 near Dong Son in Vietnam and later at several sites in Laos.

The **earliest indigenous culture** to have been investigated by archeologists in Laos was an iron-age megalithic people that lived in what is now Xiang Khouang province on the Plain of Jars. This people built stone pillars which were positioned next to underground burial chambers, and large stone funerary urns to hold the ashes of their dead. The civilization is thought to have progressed from crafting the three-metre tall stone slabs to the massive jars after the development of iron tools. Bronze objects, resembling artefacts from Dong Son and northeastern Thailand, as well as beads foreign to the region suggest that the civilization was a wealthy one and lay at the centre of trade routes to China, Vietnam and points south. However, very little else is known about this people and what became of them.

By this time, broad linguistic and cultural groups were beginning to emerge in Southeast Asia. Small villages were developing and between them there was regular communication and trade in such items as pottery, salt and metal tools. The early inhabitants of Laos and the surrounding parts of central and southern Indochina spoke Austroasiatic languages such as Mon and Khmer, while the ancestors of the lowland Lao spoke proto-Tai languages, and were still living in the river valleys of southeastern China.

What is known about this group of **Tai** people comes mostly from documents written by their neighbours. Tai peoples described in early Chinese documents were valley- and lowland-dwelling subsistence farmers who typically cultivated wet rice and vegetables and, unlike the Chinese and Vietnamese, lived in houses built on piles. They reared water buffalo less for use as beasts of burden than as symbols of wealth and status or for use in ritual.

The **Tai villages** of the first millennium AD were probably much like the villages of rural Laos today, and would have consisted of a small cluster of households sharing labour during harvests. A need for mutual protection against outside forces most likely drove such villages together into larger units known as *muang* – a term which refers to both a group of villages and the central town in a network of villages. The leader of a *muang*, the *chao*, employed his own resources to arm and supply the villagers in defence of their *muang*, and in return he received labour service or produce.

With the lowlands to the east and northeast densely settled by Vietnamese and Chinese populations, the Tai peoples slowly migrated west and southwest into northern Laos and southern Yunnan, and eventually as far as Assam in northeastern India, displacing the sparse indigenous population of Austronesian and Austroasiatic groups and forcing them into the less desirable upland areas – where their descendants still live today.

This **migration of the Tai** and the displacement of indigenous peoples that accompanied it is reflected in the Lao legend of Khoun Borom (see box on p.139), the story of the heavenly first ancestor – Khoun Borom – which bears similarities to folk tales of other Tai groups. Khoun Borom is said to have arrived on earth in the vicinity of Dien Bien Phu, in northwestern Vietnam, before sending his seven sons to rule over the Tai world – to Louang Phabang; Xiang Khouang; Xishuangbanna in southern Yunnan; Hamsavati, the Mon state of Pegu in Burma; Ayuthaya, in the lower Chao Phraya River Valley; Chiang Mai in northern Thailand; and an area in central Vietnam. A version of this tale from Xiang Khouang dates this event in 698 AD.

By the ninth century, the Tai were spread across upland Southeast Asia and surrounded by Nanchao, a well-organized military state located in southwestern China; a Vietnamese state on the verge of independence from China; Champa, an Indianized kingdom on the coast of Vietnam; Angkorian Cambodia; and the Mon and Pyu kingdoms of Burma.

Indianized influences

The cultural roots of the present-day Lao lie in **Indian civilization**, not Chinese. From the first century AD, Indian traders made their way east through Southeast Asia by land and by sea en route to China. Hinduized enclaves sprang up along the routes they travelled. The first of these to emerge were along the coast of Indochina, and included the Funan empire, a Mekong Delta state with trading links as far as Persia, and Champa, which was centred near Danang. Later, inland civilizations developed in Burma, Cambodia and Thailand. It was these classical Indianized civilizations along with individual Indian traders and travelling monks, rather than Chinese culture, that would shape the identity of the Lao, an influence evident today in the sharp difference between the Tai groups who underwent Indianization, became Buddhist and incorporated Pali and Sanskrit words into their languages, and those that did not.

The Dvaravati

The foundation of Buddhist civilization in Thailand and Laos was laid by a unique Theravada Buddhist cultural complex identified with the Mon people and known as **Dvaravati**. Although its history is obscure, it is clear this civilization grew up around the overland trade route stretching from the Indian Ocean to the Gulf of Thailand. It dominated the Central Plain of Thailand for several centuries, although more as a cultural influence than an empire. Monastery boundary stones, clay votive tablets, Indian-influenced Buddhist statuary and objects foreign to Southeast Asia such as coins and lamps found at sites across Thailand and parts of Laos suggest that Dvaravati was a prosperous, expansive civilization that flourished between the sixth and ninth centuries.

Although no definitive capital has been established, Dvaravati sites appear to have been most densely clustered around the lower Chao Phraya River Valley, extending westwards towards Burma, eastwards towards Cambodia and the Khorat Plateau of northeastern Thailand and northwards towards Chiang Mai and upper Laos – along what were regular routes of communication and trade. These lines of contact were significant for the Tai *muang* that were to emerge in Laos, as they contributed to the spread of Buddhism in the area. This is evidenced by the discovery of eleventh- and twelfth-century relics in Louang Phabang and near Phonhong on the Vientiane Plain, the earliest Buddhist statuary yet discovered in these parts of Laos.

As the ninth century drew to a close, Dvaravati's influence over central Southeast Asia was rapidly being eclipsed by the Khmer Empire of Angkor, with its god-kings Suryavaraman I, Suryavaraman II and Jayavarman VII, who built Angkor Wat and countless other massive monuments.

The Khmer

The first references to the **Khmer** of Chenla appear in Chinese texts with Chenla's conquering of Funan. Khmer Chenla appears to have been located near the Mekong River in northern Cambodia and extended through present-day southern Laos, where the Khmer built temples on Don Khong, at Wat Phou and at other sites.

It was Jayavarman II who established the Khmer capital at Angkor in northwestern Cambodia, where he and later kings erected the series of massive religious monuments for which the ancient Khmer are best known, and established the foundation of an empire that rapidly grew into the most powerful force in the region.

The Khmer empire was ruled by kings who were usually identified with the Hindu gods Shiva or Vishnu, although Mahayana Buddhism later came into vogue at the Khmer court. At its height, the empire extended from its core of Cambodia and the sourthern half of northeastern Thailand into Vietnam, central Thailand and Laos, where the Khmer built dozens of Angkor-style temple complexes, and embellished older Chenla sites, as seen today at Wat Phou. As a result of this expansion, the Khmer gained control over important trade routes between India and China from which they derived their wealth and strength. The empire was held together by an extensive network of communications and institutions, as well as a system of highways linking key centres of the empire, traces of which are visible between Wat Phou and Angkor. As the empire grew, Khmer governors, who were sometimes princes with ties to the royal house at Angkor, were placed in control of newly acquired areas, bringing with them tax collectors, judges, scribes and monks and ordering the construction of enormous religious monuments.

The people then living in what is now southern Laos were probably pre-dominantly Khmer as far north as Savannakhet, although by the eleventh and twelfth centuries, ethnic Tai made up a significant portion of the population on the fringes of the Angkor empire.

Early Tai and Lao principalities

The first record of contact between the Khmer empire and a Tai state occurred sometime after the seventh century near Chiang Saen, where a Tai state known as **Yonok** emerged along the Mekong River in the vicinity of Bokeo province. By the late tenth century, Buddhism was blossoming in Yonok, transforming the localized Buddhism in practice into an institutionalized religious tradition with ties to the civilizations of the Mon and Ceylon. It was around this time that the Tai were beginning to move onto the lowland plains, suitable for extensive cultivation of rice, and develop into organized states, although none was yet large enough to dominate their non-Tai neighbours.

Though the origin of the first Lao principalities is ill defined to say the least, it appears that the first significant Tai centres in what is now Laos took root in the north, at Louang Phabang and Xiang Khouang, both of which are identified in legends as areas ruled by the sons of Khoun Borom.

By the thirteenth century, Louang Phabang, along with Chiang Saen, Jinghong (the Tai Leu capital located in Yunnan) and a Black Tai centre near the Black River, had emerged as one of the chief Tai centres of the Upper Mekong, an area settled by people who called themselves **Lao** and lived under the threat of invasion from Nanchao and Vietnam. A century later, though still significant, Louang Phabang, then known as Xiang Dong Xiang Thong, had become but one of many small Lao principalities that existed on the fringes of two larger Tai states that had emerged: **Lan Na**, centred on Chiang Mai, and **Sukhothai**, the principality which is viewed as the cornerstone in Thailand's development. These states had capitalized on the collapse of the region's classical Indianized empires, Angkor and Pagan, their growth fuelled by large bases of rice land and manpower. Inscriptions from the Siamese *muang* of Sukhothai indicate that Lao rulers from Xiang Dong Xiang Thong were paying tribute to the Siamese state of Sukhothai by the late thirteenth century.

Yet even as the sun began to set on Angkor in the thirteenth century, the Khmer empire's most lasting impact on its still nebulous northern neighbour was to come in the form of a helping hand to the young exile who was to transform the petty Lao principalities scattered across Laos and portions of Thailand into a power in mainland Southeast Asia.

The rise of Lane Xang

Lao legends tell of a young prince belonging to the ruling family of Xiang Dong Xiang Thong who was cast out of the fledgling Lao principality, only to wind up in the Khmer court at Angkor where he was taken in, educated and married to a Khmer princess (see p.141). The generosity of Angkor, by that point on the verge of collapse and perhaps desperate for an ally, didn't stop there. Provided with an army by the Khmer king, this prince, **Fa Ngum**, fought his way up the Mekong valley atop a war elephant in 1351 – subduing first the principalities of the lower Mekong valley, Sikhotabong (present-day Thakhek) and Kham Keut (near Lak Xao), before proceeding to the Plain of Jars where, with the aid of an exiled Phuan prince, he captured Muang Phuan, the capital of the principality of Xiang Khouang.

Descending the Nam Ou River, Fa Ngum finally reached Xiang Dong Xiang Thong, where he ascended the throne in 1353 and began the reign that is popularly considered the cornerstone in Laos's development. Fa Ngum called his new kingdom **Lane Xang Hom Khao**, the Kingdom of a Million Elephants and the White Parasol, a name signifying military might and royal prestige. In the ensuing two decades of his reign, Fa Ngum expanded Lane Xang south through the Vientiane Plain into northeastern Thailand, northeast to the Black Tai area west of the Black River and north into Sipsong Pan Na (present-day Xishuangbanna in China).

Lane Xang was a decentralized state. Its three principal hubs, Xiang Khouang, Sikhotabong and Vientiane, were virtually autonomous. Their main contribution to Xiang Dong Xiang Thong was a share of their revenue and manpower – the greatest asset in a sparsely populated land – in deference to the greater reserves of men and prestige of that city's ruling line. These three *muang* in turn claimed a share of the income and manpower of smaller towns surrounding them. Given the ever-shifting balance of power in the region over the course of the next few centuries and because these and other smaller *muang* remained virtually autonomous, Lane Xang's frontiers were fluid, with *muang* often shifting allegiances or even paying tribute to two empires at once.

With Fa Ngum and his Khmer queen, Kaew Keng Nya, came Cambodian monks and artisans, a new civil administrative system and a code of laws. Although Fa Ngum and his Khmer retinue are also attributed with introducing Buddhism to Lane Xang, it seems more likely that the religion was already a presence in the area, as suggested by the discovery of Buddhist statuary dating from the eleventh and twelfth centuries. Closely related in style to relics found in the Central Plain of Thailand, these artefacts most likely arrived via Dvaravati. One thing that seems fairly certain is that Buddhism flourished with the arrival of Fa Ngum and probably grew further with the arrival of Fa Ngum's second queen, Kaew Lot Fa. Kaew Lot Fa came from the Siamese Kingdom of Ayuthaya, another neighbouring state with a strong Buddhist tradition and elaborate court rituals.

Though Fa Ngum was a strong leader, there was a fair amount of internal strife. After twenty years on the throne, Fa Ngum was ousted by his ministers, who had grown weary of years of warfare and the king's conscription of the wives and daughters of the elite into his personal service. He was succeeded by his only son, Oun Heuan (1373–1417), who ascended to the throne in 1373 and ruled for 43 years, ushering in an era of peace during which the city flourished. This period of stability was due in part to his marriage into the ruling houses of both Ayuthaya and Lan Na, his more powerful neighbours to the south and west. Oun Heuan is remembered as Samsenthai or King of Three Hundred Thousand Tai, a name signifying the number of Lao men available to Lane Xang for labour and military service. After Oun Heuan's death, a period of bitter political infighting began – with eight kings in 22 years – which left the kingdom severely weakened.

The leading ministers of the town restored stability to Lane Xang by offering the throne to the ruler of Vientiane, Vangburi (1438–79), the only surviving son of Oun Heuan. Whereas Fa Ngum had merely tipped his hat to Theravada Buddhism, Vangburi was a devout Buddhist, taking the name

Sainyachakkaphat Phaen Phaew (a name derived from the Pali term for "Universal Buddhist Monarch") upon his coronation and promptly appointing new abbots in key monasteries. Theravada Buddhism, slower to take hold east of the Mekong at first, now served to legitimize the rule of the kings of Lane Xang. In return for the king's patronage the monks taught that the king ruled because he possessed superior moral merit.

Sainyachakkaphat took pains to heal the rifts wrought by two decades of struggle over the throne and tried to return Lane Xang to its former glory. However, his rule was not to last. Vietnam – angered by Lane Xang's betrayal of the Vietnamese struggle against the occupying forces of China's Ming Dynasty and further provoked by a Phuan revolt against Vietnamese control over Muang Phuan – invaded Lane Xang in 1479. Lao chronicles record the causes behind the attack somewhat differently, however, noting that Emperor Le Thanh Tong had been offended, not by the massacre of his mandarins and soldiers, but by the fact that the Lao's response to his request for hair from a recently captured white elephant, an animal revered by the Lao, was to send him a box full of dung.

Whatever the cause, five columns of **Vietnamese troops** swept through Xiang Dong Xiang Thong a year after the revolt in Muang Phuan, and Sainyachakkaphat, humiliated, abdicated and fled. The Lao king's younger brother, Souvanna Banlang (1479–85), regrouped the Lao troops and eventually chased off the Vietnamese troops, whose final retort was the sacking of Muang Phuan on their way home.

Yet Xiang Dong Xiang Thong's destruction proved to be a catalyst for Lane Xang's first golden age, a century when the civil administration was fine tuned, striking temples were built and epic poems composed.

The kingdom of the Pha Bang

Souvanna Banlang's three successors – La Saen Thai (1486–96), Somphou (1496–1500), and Visoun (1500–20) – ruled over a peaceful and prosperous Lane Xang, their reigns marked by strengthened ties with Ayuthaya and an upswing in trade across the Khorat Plateau. The wealth generated by trade went into the adornment of Xiang Dong Xiang Thong. These rulers also reorganized the government, appointing ministers to oversee specific departments, establishing an extensive hierarchy among government officials and dividing the capital into districts and sub-districts, all of which served to make the kingdom more stable than it had ever been before. Buddhism flourished, under Visoun in particular, as monks took up residence in the city and the monasteries became centres of literary culture, where sacred Pali texts were studied.

It was during the reign of **Visoun** that the Lao Buddhist world view came together. Visoun ordered the composition of the *Nithan Khoun Borom,* which brought together legends concerning the origin of the Lao, Khoun Borom and the founding of Xiang Dong Xiang Thong, complete with grand stories of Fa Ngum's deeds, and placed these myths and legends within the framework of Theravada Buddhism. Arguably, Visoun's most important act was bringing the **Pha Bang** to Xiang Dong Xiang Thong from Vientiane in 1512, a defining event in the development of Lao identity and one which reinforced the institution of Buddhist kingship. The golden Buddha image, which was installed at Wat Visoun, became the palladium of the ruling dynasty and the symbol of unity and power of the kingdom itself.

Whereas Visoun and his immediate predecessors had ruled over a peaceful state concerned primarily with domestic affairs, Visoun's son Phothisalat (1520–47), and grandson Setthathilat (1548–71), had major state ambitions for Lane Xang, which they saw as being the equal of its neighbour and rival, Ayuthaya. In pursuit of his expansionist aspirations, **Phothisalat** established a wide network of regional relations, which included taking a Lan Na princess as his queen. He chose to reside at Vientiane, which had the advantage of being closer to the trade routes linking Lane Xang with Vietnam, Ayuthaya and Cambodia. Vientiane was also closer to the population centre of the expanding Lao world: with the downfall of Angkor in the previous century, the Lao had begun to shift south into the middle Mekong Valley and onto the Khorat Plateau where the land was flatter and more fertile.

Phothisalat was a man driven by his profound piety. He gave generously to the monastic order or *Sangha*, and recorded his gifts in stone – the earliest Lao king to do so. In one significant gesture, he made an endowment to Sikhotabong's religious centre, and is credited with raising the shrine of That Phanom to a primary position in the religious life of the Mekong area south of Vientiane, a place it still holds today among the Buddhists of south central Laos and the ethnic Lao of northeastern Thailand. Phothisalat also left his mark on the spiritual life of Xiang Dong Xiang Thong, when, in 1527, he broke with local traditions and banned the practice of animism, ordering the destruction of the religious buildings associated with such beliefs.

Phothisalat's aggressiveness contributed to the souring of relations with Ayuthaya. Tensions between the neighbours flared up over the now weakened state of Lan Na; Lane Xang prevailed, and Phothisalat's son **Setthathilat** assumed the throne at Chiang Mai in 1546. He quickly hurried home, however, after the death of his father, who was crushed beneath his elephant during a display of his riding skills. In his hasty departure, Setthathilat nonetheless managed to pilfer Lan Na's talismanic Emerald Buddha, the sacred Pha Kaew that today is the palladium of the ruling line in Bangkok.

Setthathilat was only fourteen when, in 1548, he assumed the throne of Lane Xang. The young king's hold over Lan Na gradually slipped away, as internal disputes in Chiang Mai and the rise of a powerful Burmese kingdom in the west dashed hopes of a greater Lao state, one that would unify Lane Xang and Lan Na.

The Burmese invasions

Wary of the growing **Burmese threat**, Setthathilat reacted defensively. In 1563, he officially moved his capital to Vientiane and quickly set about building brick ramparts around the city. In deference to Xiang Dong Xiang Thong, the Pha Bang was left behind and the city was renamed after the revered image, while the Emerald Buddha was placed in the newly constructed Haw Pha Kaew in Vientiane.

Lane Xang managed to forge an alliance with Ayuthaya, but the Tai states would prove no match for the armies of the Burmese warrior-kings who reduced Lan Na, Ayuthaya and Lane Xang to vassalage in a matter of a decade. Setthathilat's strategic shift of the capital seemed to pay off at first, but the Burmese sacked the town in 1565. The invaders were eventually repelled by a guerrilla campaign led by the king. After reclaiming Vientiane, Setthathilat renovated That Phanom in Sikhotabong and built That Louang in the capital in an effort to lift the morale of his vassals in the central Mekong area who had misgivings about being ruled by a royal line whose roots were in Louang Phabang, especially one that was taxing their resources by waging a costly war.

By the end of 1569, Lane Xang was the only Tai power remaining. Burma once again set its sights on Vientiane, which fell for the second time, and once again Setthathilat regained his capital – but this time the heavy demands on the *muang* of the central Mekong brought resentment to boiling point. Lured into a campaign against the mountain peoples of the south by the powerful ruler of Sikhotabong, Setthathilat was never seen again. The king's downfall revealed a major weakness in the power structure of Lane Xang: the monarchy still depended on the loyalty of its vassals, but the latter no longer felt any strong allegiance to the king or to Lane Xang as a state.

With the death of Setthathilat, Lane Xang plunged into turmoil as the Burmese retook Vientiane and extended their rule to the Vietnamese frontier. By the early 1580s the kingdom was in such disarray that no king sat on the throne for nearly a decade. It would take half a century for Lane Xang to recover.

Sourinyavongsa and the Golden Age

The decisive character who returned stability to Lane Xang and eventually ushered in its **Golden Age** was Sourinyavongsa (1637–94). Although he was rarely seen in public, Sourinyavongsa was a popular king, known for his firm administration of justice, who ruled over a peaceful and prosperous kingdom.

A mission from the Dutch East India Company led by Gerritt van Wuysthoff and a party of Jesuits, **the first Europeans** to reach Lane Xang, arrived during Sourinyavongsa's reign to find a flourishing Buddhist kingdom whose wealth was poured into the construction of religious monuments and the monastic order. Monks – more numerous than the soldiers of Germany, as one visitor observed – came from as far as Cambodia and Burma to Vientiane, which had emerged as a regional centre of Buddhist studies.

Sourinyavongsa ensured that his reign was a peaceful one by aligning Lane Xang through marriage with neighbouring powers, although he did not hesitate to resort to force when necessary – after all it was a violent struggle among relatives that won him the throne in the first place. When the ruler of Xiang Khouang refused to offer his daughter in marriage to Sourinyavongsa, Lane Xang invaded Xiang Khouang, seizing the woman in question and taking several thousand captives, who were resettled near the capital. Thereafter Xiang Khouang paid regular tribute to Vientiane and was forced to break off its relationship with Vietnam. Sourinyavongsa took the daughter of the Vietnamese emperor as a concubine and established the boundaries between the two states in a treaty with Vietnam which identified all people living in houses on piles as Lao subjects and all living in homes that rested on the ground as Vietnamese. The frontier with Ayuthaya remained unchanged, with both countries respecting the watershed line between the Mekong and the Chao Phraya rivers, a border established by Setthathilat. Lane Xang was left holding sway over the northern and eastern portions of the Khorat Plateau.

Closer to home, Sourinyavongsa avoided the bitter rivalries that contributed to the downfall of Setthathilat, by striking a balance between the regional interests of the kingdom. He appeased the powerful families of the central Mekong by dividing the powers of state among three chief ministers – the minister of the palace conducted foreign relations and ran the royal secretariat; a second commanded the army and oversaw Vientiane; and a third, the viceroy, the powerful ruler of Sikhotabong, ruled the south.

While the new balance of power provided the stability Lane Xang needed to flourish, no provisions were made to maintain that stability after the king's death. In the end, the kingdom paid the price for Sourinyavongsa's stern brand of justice: the king had executed his only son for adultery, leaving no obvious heir to the throne when he died in 1694. Once again royal succession turned into a political crisis; this time around, however, the country's three regions went their separate ways.

The division of Lane Xang

Vientiane was taken over by a Lane Xang prince who returned from exile in Vietnam to establish a new kingdom there, although Vietnam exacted a heavy price in silver bars, elephants and rhinoceros horns for their assistance in the endeavour. Very soon, however, **Setthathilat II** (1698–1735), as this king chose to call himself, had trouble on his northern flank. Sourinyavongsa's grandsons – Kingkitsalat and Inthasom – had fled Vientiane to Chiang Hung (present-day Jinghong) some years before and sought assistance from their mother's relatives in Sipsong Pa Na. With the aid of a cousin, the princes raised an army, captured Louang Phabang in 1706 and soon after marched on Vientiane. Setthathilat appealed for help from Ayuthaya. The king of Ayuthaya negotiated a division of the territory at the bend in the Mekong, south of Paklai, making Kingkitsalat the first ruler of an independent Louang Phabang kingdom, and leaving Setthathilat II to rule over Vientiane.

Meanwhile, in the south, a new ruling house had emerged at **Champasak**, dividing the kingdom further. Little is known of the origins of this *muang*, although legends trace its roots to a holy man who, ruling the kingdom as a regent for an unmarried queen, sought out a young prince to take the throne. The prince, sometimes said to be a long lost son of Sourinyavongsa, assumed the throne as King Soi Sisamouth in 1713. Thus the new ruling lines of each of the three major principalities, Louang Phabang, Vientiane and Champasak, could claim, however tenuously, some link to Fa Ngum and, by extension, to Khoun Borom. Family ties notwithstanding, it didn't take long for these isolated principalities of inland Southeast Asia to be at each other's throats, making these weak states easy prey for their larger neighbours. The rivalry between Louang Phabang and Vientiane was particularly bitter, deteriorating further when a second wave of Burmese invasions swept across the Tai world in the 1760s and forces from Vientiane aligned with the invaders and helped sack Louang Phabang.

Ayuthaya, which had flourished since the last wave of Burmese invasions, was next. The Burmese breached the walls of Ayuthaya and took the city in 1767, razing everything to the ground and hauling off tens of thousands of prisoners. The city was abandoned, but with remarkable speed the Siamese built a new kingdom, one that was to succeed at the expense of the Lao states.

The rise of Siam

Under the charismatic leadership of King Taksin, a military genius, the **Siamese** quickly rebuilt their kingdom downriver from Ayuthaya near Bangkok, and within a decade had retaken its territory, conquered Lan Na, and were prepared to expand to the east to secure its perimeter. Taking advantage of a peaceful Burma and a distracted Vietnam, 20,000 Siamese soldiers set out towards Vientiane in 1778 – less than a decade after Ayuthaya's devastating collapse.

A second army of 10,000 soldiers swept east through Cambodia and, after conquering first Champasak and then Sikhotabong, this smaller force turned north and marched on Vientiane. Here, the two Siamese forces met before the ramparts of Vientiane and were joined by a battalion from Louang Phabang bent on revenge. The city fell, and hundreds of prisoners, including the royal family, were dragged back to Siam and forcibly resettled on the plains north of the Siamese capital. The two Buddha image palladia of Lane Xang, the Pha Bang – which had been relocated to Vientiane by Setthathilat II in 1705 – and the Pha Kaew, were hauled off by the victors as well and enshrined in Thonburi. By reducing Champasak and Vientiane to vassal states and bringing Louang Phabang into an unequal alliance, Siam had extended its empire to the Annamite Mountains and forced the Lao world to adjust to a predominantly Bangkok-centred existence for the next century.

Anou's rebellion

The captured Lao princes returned to Vientiane as vassal kings, beginning with Nanthasen (1782–92). He brought with him the Pha Bang, which the Siamese king had decided was bad luck for his kingdom. Nanthasen didn't waste time in rekindling the old conflict with Louang Phabang, which his forces conquered in 1792. But Siam, preferring to divide and rule, was wary of allowing any of the Lao vassal states to improve their position at the expense of another, and so recalled Nanthasen. He was replaced by Inthavong (1792–1804), the elder brother of the accomplished general Anou, who served as viceroy and led Lao armies to fight in the name of Siam in battles with Burma. By the time of Inthavong's death at the turn of the century, Vientiane had already begun to pay tribute to Vietnam and was sufficiently within the Vietnamese orbit for **Anou** (1804–28), when chosen to ascend to the throne, to immediately notify Hué.

Siam became increasingly alarmed by Vietnam's growing influence, and, worried that Vietnam had its eye on Champasak, decided to run the risk of turning Anou into a powerful, and potentially dangerous, vassal by appointing Yo (1819–27), Anou's son, to the Champasak throne. Anou, who envisioned restoring Lane Xang to its former glory by unifying the disparate Lao states and repatriating Lao captives resettled by Siam, made good on Bangkok's fears. On the pretence of coming to Siam's aid in the event of an attack by the British, who had by this time established a presence in Burma, Anou's and Yo's troops advanced across the Khorat Plateau early in 1827, and by late February had come within a few days' march of Bangkok. However, Anou had seriously misjudged the strength of the Siamese, who struck back fiercely, capturing Yo and sacking Vientiane. Anou fled to Vietnam.

When he returned to Vientiane with a small force several months later, fighting broke out which resulted in Anou's capture. According to some accounts, he was betrayed by Chao Noi, the ruler of Xiang Khouang. Siamese forces destroyed every building in the capital, save for one monastery, Wat Sisaket, and dragged the entire population back to Thailand, where they were resettled. Vientiane was abandoned to the jungle; it was still in ruins when French explorers arrived four decades later. The Lao king was placed in an iron cage and exposed to the sweltering heat of Bangkok, where he died, an example to Siam's vassals of the price of rebellion. Anou was the last Lao ruler to attempt to liberate the former territories of Lane Xang.

Although the primary source of tension between them lay to the south, in Cambodia, Siam and Vietnam jockeyed for control over the fragmented Lao *muang* during the decades that followed Anou's defeat. Siam undertook a massive, systematic programme of resettlement of the Lao population to the Khorat Plateau, swelling the population of this thinly populated area. In fact, the cities and villages in this area remain predominantly Lao today. By force and diplomacy, Siam depopulated the area east of the Mekong, particularly in south central Laos, leaving a wasteland of burned villages and rice fields. Only Louang Phabang managed to stay intact. Vietnam countered by formally incorporating Lane Xang's eastern territory back into the organization of its state.

Xiang Khouang represented the greatest source of conflict in the struggle. Situated on the Plain of Jars, the Phuan principality occupied an area that was effectively a back door for a military invasion of Vietnam. In the aftermath of Anou's defeat, the Vietnamese emperor executed Noi, the Phuan ruler, allegedly for his treachery against Anou, and the area was made a province known to the Vietnamese as Tran Ninh. Siam, with the assistance of Louang Phabang, quickly moved to retake the principality, and when it did, much of the Phuan population was forcibly resettled to the south.

By the middle of the nineteenth century, an equilibrium had been reached, and the Lao territories became a buffer zone between the two powers. Siam was dominant in the Mekong valley, the Vietnamese held sway in the east; joint control was exercised over what was left of Muang Phuan. This balancing act was soon upset, however, by **marauding Chinese**, who swept through the northern Lao territories on horseback in the 1870s and 1880s. The remnants of Chinese rebellions, these raiders, known as "Haw", gathered in bands identifiable by the colour of their battle flags.

Obliged as suzerain to assist Xiang Khouang and Louang Phabang, Siam, its position in Laos endangered by the incursions, launched a series of military expeditions. The last of these campaigns – which extended well north of Louang Phabang – backfired when the Siamese commander angered a White Tai chief, leading to the sacking of Louang Phabang and eventually to Siam's loss of Laos to the French.

French conquest

France's initial interest in Laos stemmed from a belief that the Mekong River would provide a backdoor route to China. As the nineteenth century wore on, French governments became increasingly imperialistic. In the Far East, with Britain threatening to dominate trade with China, France saw Vietnam, and by extension Laos, as a potential route into the resource-rich Yunnan region.

France acquired her Indochina colonies in a rather haphazard fashion, often through the exploits of individual adventurers or the unilateral action of French officials. By the time the Mekong Exploration Commission of 1867–68 set off from Saigon for Laos and Yunnan, **Cochinchina** (present-day southern Vietnam) was already a French possession. Interest in Laos, however, quickly waned after the explorers, led by Doudart de Lagrée and the charismatic Francis Garnier, found that significant stretches of the river were unnavigable.

Interest in Laos was rekindled by French explorer **Auguste Pavie**, who conducted a "conquest of hearts" in the name of France in the 1880s and 1890s while trekking across Laos in search of political alliances and trade routes. As vice-consul in Louang Phabang, Pavie was the chief advocate of France's extension of the Indochina empire to the banks of the Mekong River. He won an important ally for France by rescuing the northern kingdom's ageing ruler King Oun Kham almost singlehandedly when the city, left virtually undefended by the Siamese, was torched in 1887 by a White Tai leader from Sipsong Chao Tai, out for revenge against Siam. Pavie's effort led the king to state: "[Louang Phabang] is not a conquest of Siam. Louang Phabang, wanting protection against all attacks, voluntarily offered its tribute. Now through Siam's interference, our ruin is complete…we will offer tribute to France…".

The relentless efforts of Pavie, coupled with gunboat diplomacy in Bangkok, eventually forced Siam to relinquish its claim to all territory east of the Mekong in 1893, although not before nearly sparking a war between Siam, Britain and France. Britain and France eventually settled on the Mekong River as the boundary between British Burma and French Laos and agreed to guarantee Siamese independence in the Chao Phraya River Valley in order to ensure a buffer zone between the two Western powers.

French rule

For half a century, Laos was ruled as a **French colony**, but for all Pavie's determination, Laos was regarded as little more than the remote hinterland of Vietnam, the least important of the five components of **French Indochina** – Annam (central Vietnam), Tonkin (the north), Cochinchina (the south), Cambodia and Laos.

The boundaries with Burma, China, and Vietnam that were adopted by France – essentially the limits of the Mekong watershed – were carved with indifference to the complex existing political structures and ethnic groupings. In short, the borders meant nothing to the peoples of Laos. In the south, the kingdom of Champasak was split in two (a situation remedied by subsequent Franco–Siamese treaties which added land west of the Mekong in the south and in Xainyabouli, and roughly established the border Laos shares with Thailand today). In the north, two Tai Leu *muang* were severed from Sipsong Pa Na, an act which served to foster political instability in that region.

After initially dividing the Lao territories into three regions which were administered from Vietnam, the French eventually settled on **Vientiane** as their administrative capital and split the country up into eleven provinces, with the kingdom of Louang Phabang existing as a nominal protectorate.

After France realized that the Mekong was a poor transport route and that explorers' claims of an Eldorado were but a pipe dream, Laos became the neglected backwater of the European nation's Southeast Asian acquisitions. Accordingly, French presence in Laos was minimal. Whereas 40,000 French competed for civil service jobs in Saigon and the Mekong Delta, only a hundred such jobs were available in Laos. The French, who found the Lao work ethic suspect and regarded the hill peoples with disdain, brought in **Vietnamese** to fill most of the upper and middle ranks of the civil service (Lao occupied lower positions such as junior clerks and translators) and the bulk of the spots in the Garde Indigène, the paramilitary police force established to maintain law and order in the colonies.

The French made do with limited administrative manpower by simply floating their **administration** on top of existing feudal court structures. The royal houses of Xiang Khouang, Champasak and Louang Phabang – Vientiane's ruling line had been eliminated after Anou's defeat – were preserved, although France reduced the status of the rulers of Xiang Khouang and Champasak to that of governors and reserved the right to approve the successors to all three houses. Outside the cities, the French established an administrative system that pitted various ethnic groups against one another, effectively cutting administrative costs at the same time as they deflected resentment – and at times violence – away from themselves.

In order to cover the cost of administration, France imposed heavy **taxes** on opium, alcohol and salt, levied a head tax on males between 18 and 60, and required all adult males to perform unpaid corvée labour. Often required to walk days to work sites far from their villages, while supplying their own food, villagers sometimes responded by simply clearing out of an area altogether, returning once the project was completed.

Such measures also provoked several **revolts**, some led by messianic religious figures, in the late nineteenth and early twentieth centuries, with the first large uprising beginning on the Bolaven Plateau in 1901 (see box on p.314). As similar disturbances also occurred around the same time across the Mekong, it seems they were more in response to central government intrusion into rural life and the disruption of old social, economic and political orders throughout the region than they were specifically anti-French. However, the fact that such uprisings occurred largely among upland peoples, upon whom the French made harsher demands and for whose customs they showed less respect, suggests that the methods employed by France's colonial administration didn't lie too far away from the cause. These revolts, though at times extreme in their violence, were often localized affairs, but they were later construed as forerunners of the nationalist movements of the Lao Issara and Pathet Lao.

While explorers' reports that Laos was teeming with **natural resources** proved overly optimistic, the French did manage to exploit, among other things, tin deposits near Thakhek and teak trees, which were cut and floated down the Mekong, and introduced coffee. France's chief agricultural exports were cardamom from the Bolaven Plateau area and, from the highlands of Xiang Khouang, **opium**, a product that was later allegedly used by the CIA and the Pathet Lao to finance their respective war efforts. For its part, the French Indochina Government established a monopoly over opium, which accounted for one-seventh of its total budgetary receipts and brought the Hmong of Xiang Khouang into the money economy faster than most other groups in Laos.

Trade was in the hands of Chinese merchants, as it had been for centuries. Goods followed traditional routes from Laos and the west bank of the Mekong across the Khorat Plateau towards Bangkok and away from French Vietnam. The same Chinese merchants who exported cardamom, sticklac and benzoin, skins and ivory to the trading houses of the Siamese capital were already importing cheap British and German products by the time the French established themselves in Laos.

With trade flowing towards Bangkok, minimal exports and a depleted population providing an insufficient tax base, the colony remained dependent on **federal subsidies**. The French hoped to remedy these problems by building roads and, eventually, a railway from the Vietnamese coast – a project derailed first by the Great Depression and then by World War ll – and by encouraging mass Vietnamese migration, in order to tackle the age-old problem of too much land and too few people. Although relatively few Vietnamese wound up settling west of the Annamites, Vientiane and southern Mekong towns such as Thakhek and Savannakhet had substantial Vietnamese populations. And had it not been for World War II, the French may well have succeeded in making the Lao a minority in their own land, in which case Laos might not exist today.

For all its talk of the "civilizing mission" of their particular brand of imperialism, France actually appeared to have no mission in Laos, other than to deny territory to the British. Although the French did construct a skeletal highway system linking Laos with Vietnam and rebuilt monuments destroyed by the Siamese in the early 1800s, few improvements were made to the educational system – not a single high school was built, and by 1940 there were fewer than 10,000 primary-school students in a colony of one million – and the health care system seemed concerned with little more than preventing the spread of diseases that might threaten the cities. Elsewhere in Indochina, the French built schools, universities, a railway network and an extensive highway system. It would take a world war to make the French pay more attention to Laos.

World War II

The fall of France to Germany in 1940 changed everything for Laos. Most importantly, perhaps, it demonstrated to the Lao the vulnerability of the French. It also planted the seeds for the development of Lao nationalism. The initial fallout from events in Europe was the **Japanese occupation** of Laos. Vichy France was left responsible for the administration of Indochina and gave the Japanese the right to move and station troops throughout the region. Sensing an opportunity to avenge its defeat of 1893, Siam, renamed **Thailand** in 1939, seized the west-bank territories of Xainyabouli and Champasak, leaving the Lao angry with both the Thai for encroaching on their territory and the French for failing to defend the country.

To counter the appeal of Thai nationalist propaganda, the French encouraged a weak **nationalism** among the Lao elite. This movement was spearheaded by Charles Rochet, a colonial official whose affection for the people of Laos had left him embittered at France's neglect of the colony. Rochet, who saw the movement as a last-ditch effort to save Laos from being wiped off the map, met with movement leaders weekly, devising ways to generate Lao pride through a cultural renaissance of literature, theatre, music and dance, patriotic rallies and the creation of a national development programme. Schools were built, the health care system improved and the first Lao newspaper was published. And, in a sign that Lao nationalism was coming of age, a suggestion to romanize the Lao language was stymied by the viceroy of the royal house of Louang Phabang, Prince Phetsarath. Rochet's efforts met with the criticism of conservative colonial officials who felt that he was arousing dangerous sentiments. They were to be proved right, although it would be left to the Japanese to shatter the illusion of French power and provide the spark for Lao independence.

In March 1945, the Japanese staged a pre-emptive strike to neutralize French forces in Indochina, imprisoning French soldiers and civil servants. In a major blow to French prestige, Japan proclaimed an end to France's colonial regimes. In northern Vietnam and Laos, a few French soldiers managed to escape and survive in the jungle, with the help of loyal Lao and ethnic minorities. Japanese forces reached Louang Phabang by the following month and forced Sisavang Vong, the pro-French king, to declare independence, forcing his hand by hauling off the crown prince to Saigon. Somewhat less reluctantly, **Phetsarath**, who could trace his family line back to Anou, the last king of Vientiane, became prime minister. The eldest of three remarkable brothers who would have a profound impact on Lao history, Phetsarath was now the second most powerful political figure after King Sisavang Vong. Then, in August, the United States dropped the first atom bomb on Japan. Soon after, Japan surrendered.

Free Laos

Nationalists across Indochina moved to take advantage of the power vacuum created by **Japan's surrender**. In Laos, an independent-minded Lao elite formed a government which became known as the Lao Issara, literally "**Free Laos**", while next door the Viet Minh seized power and Ho Chi Minh proclaimed the establishment of the Democratic Republic of Vietnam.

The rapid awakening of the Lao elite after years of French rule left them factionalized, with support split between opposition to the Japanese and opposition to the French. A power struggle ensued as King Sisavang Vong welcomed the return of the French and Phetsarath reaffirmed the independence of Laos and declared the union of the Kingdom of Louang Phabang and the territory of Champasak in a single, independent Kingdom of Laos. The king repudiated Phetsarath by dismissing him as prime minister and viceroy on October 10. In response, the newly constituted **Lao Issara government** deposed the king two days later, on October 12.

This new government, which based itself in Vientiane, contained some of the key figures who would dominate politics in Laos over the course of the next few decades, including Phetsarath's younger brothers Souvannaphouma and Souphanouvong, both of whom were educated in Paris. Before joining the new government in Vientiane as Minister of Foreign Affairs and Chief of the Liberation Army, **Souphanouvong**, already in Vinh when the Japanese surrendered, was flown to Hanoi by an American general to meet Ho Chi Minh. After winning the North Vietnamese leader's support he returned to Laos on foot with a contingent of Viet Minh soldiers – the first instance of Vietnamese armed support for a Lao nationalist movement. As the group crossed the Annamite Mountains, Souphanouvong took a solemn oath to continue the struggle until an independent Laos had been won.

The **Potsdam Agreement**, which marked the end of World War II, failed to recognize the Lao Issara government. Under the terms of the agreement, the Japanese surrender was accepted by the Chinese Nationalists north of the Sixteenth Parallel and by the British to the south, where French reoccupation forces were gathering steam in southern Laos, their return facilitated by the

British. In March 1946, the French forces, along with their Lao allies, made their way slowly up the Mekong Valley. Lao Issara volunteers, led by Souphanouvong and assisted by the Viet Minh, resisted the French forces near Thakhek, but the French successfully reoccupied Vientiane in April 1946 and three weeks later they reclaimed Louang Phabang. Thousands of Lao Issara supporters and Vietnamese fled to Thailand, where Prince Phetsarath established a government-in-exile in Bangkok, as the French reasserted their control over Laos.

Although the Western community readily donated blood to help heal Prince Souphanouvong from the wounds he suffered at Thakhek, the United States and Britain did not respond to Lao Issara appeals for support, even as Souphanouvong repeated US President Franklin Roosevelt's statement that the French should not be allowed to return to Indochina.

The Kingdom of Laos

In 1947, the newly constituted **Kingdom of Laos** began to take shape. Prince Boun Oum of Champasak, who had helped the French in the south, renounced his claim to a separate southern kingdom, strengthening the French position in Vientiane and paving the way for Laos to be unified under the royal house of Louang Phabang. The territories west of the Mekong were restored, elections for a Constituent Assembly were held and a new constitution proclaimed.

The nominally independent kingdom was included in the French Union, but France still maintained political, military and economic control of the country. The members of the new government, which was a conservative and decidedly pro-French body, were drawn from the elite families that had benefited from the French presence all along. The government lacked cohesion, however, with loyalties to leading families and regional factions counting for more than national unity. Furthermore, the king opted to remain in Louang Phabang, rather than move to the seat of power, Vientiane, leaving the royal and administrative capitals separate.

The French by now were increasingly bogged down in their struggle with the **Viet Minh** which had erupted in December 1946 and would become known as the First Indochina War. What had begun as a police action had rapidly become a costly "war without borders" that was to last eight years and cost the lives of 93,000 on the French side and an estimated 200,000 Viet Minh supporters.

The Viet Minh did not confine their efforts to Vietnam, however, with the Vietnamese nationalists coordinating and participating in Lao Issara guerrilla raids, led by Souphanouvong, on French convoys and garrisons. The Viet Minh's influence over Souphanouvong took its toll on the unity of purpose within the Lao Issara. By May 1949 the rift had become irreparable and Souphanouvong, determined to go it alone, was removed from his post.

In July, France appealed to the more moderate elements of the Lao Issara by conceding greater authority and independence to the Vientiane government. The Lao Issara announced its dissolution. As Souvannaphouma, along with two dozen moderate Lao Issara leaders, returned to Vientiane on board a French transport plane, Souphanouvong set out from Bangkok on foot for Viet Minh headquarters in Tonkin. Meanwhile, the leader of the movement, Phetsarath, remained behind, refusing to return to Laos until 1957, when his title of viceroy was finally restored by the king.

The Pathet Lao

When Souphanouvong arrived at Viet Minh headquarters in late 1949, he was warmly welcomed by Ho Chi Minh, who had ambitious plans for the Lao prince. Souphanouvong, who sought only arms and money from the Viet Minh, also received some advice from Vo Nguyen Giap, the legendary Vietnamese general who in a matter of a few years would win glory by defeating the French at Dien Bien Phu. In the course of the meeting, Giap told the Lao prince to keep away from towns, saying "Remember, those who rule the countryside rule the country."

While the moderate members of the dissolved Lao Issara joined the new **Royal Lao Government** (RLG) in 1950, Souphanouvong founded his own government, which saw itself as the successor to the Lao Issara. In August 1950, in a far corner of northern Laos, Souphanouvong presided over the **First Resistance Congress**, which was supervised by the Viet Minh and attended by a number of other Lao who had already made independent contact with the Viet Minh. The Congress adopted a twelve-point manifesto, at the bottom of which appeared the notation "**Pathet Lao**", literally "the Land of the Lao". This became the name by which Souphanouvang's resistance group was to be known.

The **manifesto** called for a truly independent and unified Laos to be governed by a coalition government with the RLG; for democracy and freedom; equality of ethnic groups; eradication of illiteracy; and the reduction of taxes. The Pathet Lao also pledged cooperation with the Vietnamese and Khmer in the common struggle against the French. The committee selected to lead the organization included many of the men who would lead the Pathet Lao through the Thirty Year Struggle.

In the years immediately following the congress, the Pathet Lao focused on recruiting members in northern and eastern Laos for the Lao People's Party and the Liberation Army. Kaysone Phomvihane directed the Committee for the Organization of the Party, which recruited new cadres, until the **Lao People's Party** was formally established in 1955. The Pathet Lao cadres moved into remote villages, teaching literacy, building schools and organizing village militias. Like the Viet Minh before them, village by village the Pathet Lao expanded their influence.

The Pathet Lao had more success appealing to highland minorities than they did to the lowland Lao. The Royal Lao Government already controlled the major population centres and, for some ethnic Lao, the Pathet Lao alliance with the Viet Minh carried with it the threat of Vietnamese domination. Unlike the Royal Lao Government, the Pathet Lao confronted issues concerning national identity head on – anyone who fought the French was a true Lao patriot. The resistance government sought to organize itself as an umbrella organization for all anti-French resistance, including that of minority groups. Minority cadres were offered a chance to play a part in the national struggle, as displayed by the inclusion of two tribal resistance leaders, Faydang Lobliayao, a Hmong from the important Lo clan of Nong Het, and Sithone Kommadam, the son of the great Laven leader of the Bolaven Revolt.

The First Indochina War

By the early 1950s, the **First Indochina War** had engulfed the region. Chinese military aid flowed to the Viet Minh, while the United States, smarting from the fall of China to the communists, supported France. After the routing of the nationalists in China and the outbreak of the Korean War, the French could portray, with greater success, their struggle against the Viet Minh not as a colonial war but as a fight in defence of the "Free World".

For the Viet Minh, Laos was an extension of their battle against the French, a way of forcing the French to spread their resources thinly. Twice in 1953 they staged major invasions of Laos. In their first attack, the Viet Minh nearly reached Louang Phabang, causing panic to sweep through Vientiane and people to flee across the Mekong. In Louang Phabang all was calm, however, as a blind monk had prophesied that the invaders would not take the city and battle preparations had given way to celebrations long before the Viet Minh ran out of supplies, leaving the French baffled. The Viet Minh seized large areas of the country during the offensives and turned them over to the Pathet Lao.

By this point, Souphanouvong had formally established the headquarters of the resistance government in **Xam Nua**, which lay at the heart of an extensive "liberated zone"; meanwhile in Paris, Souvannaphouma was pressing the French for complete independence. By the time full independence was granted in October 1953, however, Laos was a divided country, with large areas controlled by the Pathet Lao and the rest of the country under the Royal Lao Government.

Taunted by the Viet Minh invasions of Laos, which France was obliged by treaty to defend, the French Commander-in-Chief in Indochina General Henri Navarre ordered the French Expeditionary Force's parachute battalion to establish a base in **Dien Bien Phu** in November 1953. Navarre reasoned that by establishing a massive base camp in this isolated valley along the traditional invasion route of Laos, he could force the Viet Minh into an open battle – while at the same time protecting Laos – and end the war in eighteen months. The war did end, but not quite as he expected. The Viet Minh encircled the valley and began a bloody assault that lasted 59 days and cost the lives of 20,000 Viet Minh soldiers. The French were forced to surrender on May 7, 1954, a day before talks to end the conflict were scheduled to start in Geneva. France's effort to restore the pre-World War II status quo in Indochina had collapsed.

The Geneva Conference

On May 8, the nine delegations attending the **Geneva Conference**, which had gathered to discuss the situation in Korea, shifted their focus to Indochina. The government in Vientiane was represented by Phoui Sananikone, the scion of Vientiane's leading family and a leader of the anti-Japanese resistance in northern Laos during World War II. The Viet Minh arrived with a young Lao by the name of Nouhak Phoumsavanh, a member of the Pathet Lao resistance government who was travelling on a Vietnamese passport, and proposed that Laos's resistance government be represented as well. Phoui was left to defend the sovereignty of the Vientiane government and the proposal was rejected.

Laos was an independent country, Phoui argued, and the resistance government was a fabrication of the Viet Minh, representing "absolutely nothing". The conference's final declaration included Phoui's proclamation that the Royal Lao Government would not pursue a policy of aggression nor would it allow a foreign power to use its soil for hostile purposes.

The **Agreement on the Cessation of Hostilities** was signed on July 20 – by the Viet Minh and France – which in addition to a ceasefire also called for a regrouping of opposing forces, leading to elections in two years.

Although Laos was reaffirmed as a unitary, independent state with a single government, the Pathet Lao did manage to win de facto recognition as an insurgency group and were allotted the provinces of Phongsali and Houa Phan in which to regroup.

Meanwhile, Vietnam was divided at the Seventeenth Parallel and the stage was set for a widening of the conflict into an ideological battle between the superpowers.

America intervenes

The **United States** had since 1950 been funding an estimated seventy percent of the French war effort in Indochina. In 1951, the US signed an economic aid agreement with the government of Phoui Sananikone which aimed to speed up the development of a free and independent Laos. After the 1954 Geneva Accords, which the US did not sign, considering them a sell-out to international communism, strengthening the anti-communist governments of Indochina became a priority for President Dwight Eisenhower's administration. The withdrawal of the French military left a power vacuum on the edge of a historically expansionist state, a worrisome state of affairs in the eyes of the United States.

As of 1955, the US was financing most of the **Lao government budget** and completely bankrolling the Royal Lao Army, countering the Viet Minh, which was shouldering the entire cost of the Pathet Lao's army. Feeling that the French were not taking their responsibility of training the Lao army seriously enough, the US skirted the terms of the Geneva agreement by training select officers in Thailand and by equipping and expanding the police force. Other funds went into churning out propaganda, building roads and communications networks, and propping up the kip. The Americans bought truckloads of the local currency above the black market rate, burned the notes and gave the government US dollars in exchange. Merchants exploited the programme by trading in bags of kip for dollars. They then bought luxury goods which they subsequently sold to Thailand for a profit.

For the next eight years, the US spent more on foreign aid to Laos per capita than it did on any other Southeast Asian country, including South Vietnam. US aid worked out to around $150 per person, twice the average person's annual income and five times the amount that Thailand received per capita, though the overwhelming majority of the aid was military and the average citizen didn't see any of it. The fat cats in Vientiane got fatter, especially the army commanders who routinely claimed salaries for non-existent soldiers.

In the United States' thinking, it was Laos – and not South Vietnam – that was the key to Indochina. Fretting over recent communist takeovers around the world and dogged by the argument that China might have been saved with adequate aid, the United States' policies were motivated by the fear of the chain reaction that could follow in Southeast Asia were Laos to be overrun by communism – the so-called **Domino Effect**.

As US dollars poured into the country, the army grew increasingly independent and powerful and existing rivalries between leading families were reinforced, with the powerful clans more concerned with improving their social standing than exercising responsible political power. After only a few years of independence from France, key players in the Vientiane government were rapidly developing a neo-colonial state of mind.

Back in Washington, the government's feelings about Laos were clear. As President Eisenhower prepared to turn over the helm to John F. Kennedy, he told his successor: "If Laos is lost to the free world, in the long run we will lose all of Southeast Asia."

Quest for unity and neutrality

After Geneva, the priority of the Royal Lao Government was to regain control of the two Pathet Lao provinces so that elections could be held in accordance with the peace settlement. But when elections finally went ahead in December 1955, it was without the Pathet Lao, disgruntled at being refused its demands for changes to the electoral law and freedom for its front organization, the Lao Patriotic Front (behind which stood the Lao People's Party), to operate as a political party. The elections resulted in the formation of a government led by **Prince Souvannaphouma**, who entered into negotiations with his half-brother Souphanouvong in the belief that **national unity and neutrality** were the key to the preservation of the state. The two sides cut a deal in November 1957 to include two Pathet Lao members in a coalition government in exchange for the reintegration of Houa Phan and Phongsali into the rest of Laos.

Left alone, it seemed, the people of Laos could work out their problems on their own, or so Souvannaphouma thought. However, when elections the following May gave leftist candidates 21 seats in the National Assembly, the United States felt otherwise. Fearful of "losing Laos", the US embassy and the CIA got down to business, actively promoting the creation of the right-wing Committee for the Defence of National Interests, known as the CDNI, and withholding aid from Souvannaphouma's government, forcing its collapse in July. Power in Vientiane had shifted from the National Assembly to the American Embassy.

With the collapse of the First Coalition Government, any hope for a neutral, united Laos was rapidly disintegrating. After a right-wing government – led by **Phoui Sananikone** – took charge in August, the tentative truce put in place by the Geneva Accords began to unravel. Civil war seemed inevitable. In January, claiming that a North Vietnamese invasion was imminent, Phoui demanded and received emergency powers for a year, effectively shutting the Pathet Lao out of Vientiane's political arena and opening the door for the Royal Lao Army to gain control of the Ministry of Defence. A ruthless and powerful military figure, **General Phoumi Nosavan**, assumed the post of vice minister of defence. The story goes that he originally chose between staying on with Prince Souphanouvong in his alliance with the Viet Minh or travelling to Vientiane to cooperate with French forces in 1949 by drawing matchsticks. A decade later, no such indecision hampered Phoumi as he eagerly auditioned for the role of strongman. Immediately stepping up harassment of the Pathet Lao's political front, he did not disappoint the Americans.

After negotiations to integrate two Pathet Lao battalions into the Royal Lao Army stalled, one battalion slipped back to Houa Phan, where the communist forces were preparing to resume their insurgency. The government considered the leftist troops to be in rebellion and responded by arresting Pathet Lao leaders in Vientiane, including Souphanouvong. As skirmishes signalled a return to the battlefield, the lost opportunity for peace was underscored by the passing of the country's most powerful political figures, Prince Phetsarath and King Sisavang Vong, who died within two weeks of each other in October.

Phoumi's coup and the growth of the Pathet Lao

Phoui's failure to rein in the increasingly powerful military had sown the seeds for his ousting. With a helping hand from the vehemently anti-communist CDNI, General Phoumi, by now in charge of the ministry of defence, staged a **coup** in December. His troops took to the streets of Vientiane under the false pretext, yet again, of a Pathet Lao attack. Although Phoumi failed in his bid to lead the newly formed government, it was nonetheless controlled by the military and staunchly aligned with the United States and Thailand. New elections were held in April and a rigged ballot left the leftists without a seat, much to the satisfaction of the United States.

The **corruption** of the generals and politicians in Vientiane and the purge of communist cadres in the countryside gave the Pathet Lao propaganda machine ample material with which to win the hearts and minds of the people. As Souphanouvong bided his time reading Greek classics in jail, Kaysone Phomvihane, as head of Pathet Lao military operations, expanded his control over the organization's leadership. Communist forces were active throughout most of the country, and by 1960, roughly twenty percent of the population, spread over half the country, was no longer under government control.

Although the RLA generals were far too concerned with vying for influence to worry about the communists' successes in indoctrinating the rural population, the men they assigned to guard Souphanouvong and his comrades certainly took note. As the new government – one which was set on a show trial for the Red Prince – was taking shape, all fifteen Pathet Lao prisoners, along with their guards, slipped off in the night. Souphanouvong began his now legendary five-hundred-kilometre march to Pathet Lao headquarters in Houa Phan.

The Laotian crisis

The Pathet Lao weren't the only ones fed up with the self-serving politicians and generals in Vientiane. In August 1960, a disgruntled 26-year-old army captain named **Kong Le** seized control of Vientiane, much to the surprise of the United States and the Cabinet, whose ministers were away in Louang Phabang.

Vang Po and the CIA's secret Hmong army

Soon after Soviet aircraft began dropping weapons and supplies by parachute to Pathet Lao and Neutralist forces stationed on the Plain of Jars in December 1960, an undercover Central Intelligence Agency operative by the name of Bill Lair boarded an H-34 helicopter in Vientiane and flew off into the soaring mountains of Xiang Khouang in search of **Vang Pao**, a little-known Royal Lao Army lieutenant-colonel. With Laos in the midst of a crisis that held the rapt attention of the world's superpowers, the thirty-year-old Hmong officer was holding out against the communist forces who had taken over the Plain of Jars and the surrounding hillsides, an area heavily populated by Hmong.

Lair and Vang Pao had been preparing for this meeting, albeit unknowingly, for a decade. The Texan had spent the better part of the 1950s training members of Thailand's national police in the ways of guerrilla warfare, a measure taken against the perceived threat of an invasion by communist China. Vang Pao, meanwhile, had been earning his reputation as a ruthless and clever soldier by leading daredevil raids against North Vietnamese forces stationed in Laos, first as a police officer and later as a member of a group of French-trained hilltribe irregulars. As retold in Second Indochina War correspondent Jane Hamilton-Merritt's *Tragic Mountains*, Vang Pao made it clear in his meeting with Lair that the Hmong and the United States shared a common enemy: "For me, I can't live with communism. I must either leave or fight. I prefer to fight."

In the cool of a hillside thatch hut, the seeds of the CIA's so-called **secret army** had been sown. To Lair and Vang Pao, American and Hmong needs were a perfect fit. The United States provided weapons and training for the indigenous population, who were led by one of their own in a fight for their own cause.

The **Hmong** were naturals as guerrilla soldiers. Determined to defend their homeland, they knew the terrain and were adept at hiking long distances in rugged mountains. They could run circles around the Pathet Lao and the North Vietnamese. After a three-day crash course in the weapons of modern warfare, Vang Pao's initial force of several hundred soldiers won their first battle, ambushing a curious band of Pathet Lao who had tracked the supplies descending from Air America planes by

Proclaiming himself a neutralist, Kong Le called for an end to "Lao killing Lao" and an end to foreign interference in the affairs of the country. He then invited Souvannaphouma to lead a new government.

Laos began to split apart. As the Pathet Lao took advantage of the confusion and seized more territory, Phoumi, who refused to join Souvannaphouma's government, regrouped what troops he could in Savannakhet, where he gained the backing of the CIA. Planes belonging to Air America, a civilian contract airline operating in Asia which was later revealed to be a front for the CIA, began flying into the Mekong River town with arms and bundles of money.

In November, Phoumi's men, coordinated by American advisors and assisted by a group of crack Thai troops, began a march on Vientiane, as Moscow and Washington – both of whom saw Laos as an excellent place from which to control Southeast Asia – looked on. The Soviet Union, aware that the US had supplied the rightists with arms and equipment, began airlifting supplies to Kong Le's neutralist forces in the capital. Laos was now at the heart of an **international crisis**, the centre of a Cold War showdown.

By the time Phoumi's troops reached Vientiane in December, the neutralists had allied themselves with the Pathet Lao and the Viet Minh. With both sides reluctant to spill Lao blood, a sloppy battle ensued which was won by the rightists. The neutralists retreated north to eventually join Pathet Lao forces on the Plain of Jars. Souvannaphouma, who fled for Phnom Penh before the bat-

parachute. Operation Momentum, as the project was known, was a success.

Hmong recruits swelled the ranks of this band of hilltribe irregulars by the thousands as the clandestine army developed into an effective **guerrilla fighting force**. As their numbers approached twenty thousand over the course of the decade, Hmong soldiers rescued downed American pilots, learned to fly fighter planes and bravely marched into battle, often trailed by their wives and children. Most importantly, Vang Pao's slapdash band of irregulars were all that stood between the Mekong and the North Vietnamese.

At first, American involvement remained minimal: costs were low and Americans few and far between, a far cry from the battle next door in Vietnam where the United States threw increasing amounts of money and troops at the problem with little to show for it. But a low-cost, home-grown war run out of the hip pocket of a lone CIA agent wasn't what the United States military had in mind for Laos. As the 1960s progressed, the war in Laos escalated, advisors flooded the American ranks, and the role of air power grew to criminal proportions, and with it the role of the Hmong. Although they were best at guerrilla warfare, the Hmong were often called upon to fight conventional battles and defend high-profile sites, such as a key bombing beacon atop **Phou Pha Thi** in Houa Phan province. Casualties soared, as the troops were increasingly involved in set-piece battles with a seemingly more and more determined North Vietnamese force. An estimated 25 percent of the Hmong who enlisted to fight were killed in battle.

By 1968, Vang Pao's forces were no longer fighting for their homeland, they were fighting for the United States, pawns of the **war in Vietnam**. The institutionalization of the Laos war had reduced Operation Momentum to a bloated recruitment programme churning out war-weary Hmong mercenaries. Half a world away in Washington DC, former ambassador to Vientiane William Sullivan, questioned in Senate hearings as to whether the US had any responsibility for the well-being of Vang Pao and his people, made it painfully clear where the Hmong stood: "No formal obligation upon the United States; no."

tle, was formally ousted by King Sisavang Vatthana as prime minister and replaced by Prince Boun Oum of Champasak. The United States increased its aid to Phoumi's forces, while the Soviet Union countered by airlifting fifty tonnes of supplies a day to the Plain of Jars, which the neutralists and Pathet Lao had captured in January.

By March 1961, the Americans had decided Laos wasn't worth fighting over after all. As a neutralist–Pathet Lao offensive got underway, President Kennedy announced American support for a **political settlement** involving the neutralization of Laos, an unspoken acknowledgement that America saw military victory unlikely given the incompetence and reluctance to fight on the part of the Royal Lao Army, something that Kennedy sensed when he first met the diminutive Phoumi and commented, "if that's our strongman, we're in trouble". A draw was preferable to losing Laos. With Cuba, Berlin and numerous other hotspots on the radar, Washington worried about spreading itself too thinly. Carefully pronouncing the country's name as "Lay-oss" – figuring that it might prove rather difficult to rally support for action in a country called "Louse", the president concluded his March 23rd speech on the "Laotian Crisis" saying: "All we want in Laos is peace, not war; a truly neutral government, not a Cold War pawn; a settlement concluded at the conference table and not on the battlefield."

The United States had already begun to hedge its bets, however. Lao army troops were training in Thailand, US army advisors had arrived with new weapons and a handful of planes, and the CIA launched Operation Momentum, which established a **clandestine army** recruited from the Hmong ethnic minority and under the command of Vang Pao, a Hmong lieutenant-colonel, whose military brilliance would earn him the rank of general in the Royal Lao Army by the end of the Second Indochina War.

The second Geneva conference

Two months after Kennedy's speech, a **second conference** was convened at **Geneva**, but despite the determination of the Soviet Union and the US to neutralize tensions over Laos, it took a year and a decisive defeat for the royalist army at Louang Namtha before the feuding Lao factions reached an agreement on the formation of a **second coalition government**. Under the terms of the settlement, reached in July 1962, Souvannaphouma would again become prime minister, the three factions – neutralist, Pathet Lao and royalist – would gain cabinet portfolios and all foreign military personnel would leave Laos.

The second coalition, however, was a failure: it didn't reunify the country nor did it shield Laos from the escalating war in Vietnam. While the rightists and the Pathet Lao enjoyed military and economic support from their backers, the neutralists were weak. With only diplomatic support (principally from France), the neutralist forces were reliant on the forces of the right and left for supplies. Divisions among the moderate elements developed, as the two other factions attempted to absorb their troops. The coalition – which quickly became little more than a façade – lasted less than a year, dissolving after the April 1963 assassination of a neutralist cabinet member. Fearing arrest or assassination, Pathet Lao ministers fled the capital. Laos was being drawn increasingly into the **Second Indochina War**, as North Vietnam and the United States undermined the country's neutrality in the pursuit of their agendas in Vietnam.

Following the second round in Geneva, Washington's priority was South Vietnam, where, by 1962, it already had ten thousand military advisors and support troops. The Geneva Accords, as far as Washington was concerned, had fixed the Laos problem and so the country once poised to become a battleground for the superpowers began to fade into the background, becoming, in the words of President Kennedy's Secretary of State Dean Rusk, "the wart on the hog of Vietnam".

By October 1962 American and Soviet military personnel had withdrawn from Laos, but only forty North Vietnamese had cleared the checkpoints, leaving an estimated five thousand troops in Laos.

Soon the United States – which had continued to support its Hmong allies all along – realized that there were advantages to pretending to adhere to the Geneva Accords while quietly supporting a small war in Laos, just as the North Vietnamese were doing.

The tacit agreement

Lao territory was a crucial part of the North Vietnamese war effort. They could not risk allowing the United States to use northern Laos, in particular the Plain of Jars, to threaten North Vietnam and they needed to control the mountainous eastern corridor of southern Laos in order to move soldiers and supplies to South Vietnam along the Ho Chi Minh Trail (see p.274). The US saw no option but to challenge North Vietnam's strategy.

Eventually, all sides with a stake in Laos came to the same conclusion about the Geneva Accords: while they would have loved to point an accusing finger at the opposition's violations of the agreement they had much more to gain by quietly pursuing their own agendas. So the right-wing Lao, the Americans and the Thais on the one side and the Pathet Lao, the North Vietnamese and their Chinese and Soviet backers on the other all tacitly agreed to pretend to abide by the accords, guaranteeing Laos's neutrality while keeping the country at war.

Even after the de facto collapse of the Second Coalition Government in 1963, patriotic Souvannaphouma was determined to keep the vision of a neutral Laos alive. He first flew to Beijing and Hanoi to seek support for extricating Laos from the war in Vietnam. Next he travelled to the Plain of Jars for a three-way meeting with his half-brother Souphanouvong, whom he refused to believe was really a committed communist, and Defence Minister Phoumi, who had already asked Saigon to send troops into Laos in pursuit of communist soldiers there. After the negotiations proved futile, an exhausted Souvannaphouma returned to Vientiane and, on April 18, 1964, with tears rolling down his cheeks, he announced his plans to resign, prompting Phoumi's rightist rivals to launch a surprise coup the next day. Under house arrest, Souvannaphouma appeared on his balcony, as US Ambassador Leonard Unger shouted encouragement to the embattled prime minister from the garden next door – an event which the French ambassador, present at the time, dubbed "la diplomatie à la Roméo et Juliette". Within a matter of days, the prince was back in power and the generals were out. The US had decided that they liked the neutralist prince after all.

Excluded from the new government, the Pathet Lao went on the offensive, chasing Kong Le's remaining neutralists off the Plain of Jars and into an alliance with Vang Pao and his Hmong army. The communist offensive fitted neatly into what would become the standard seesaw pattern of fighting in northern Laos, in which each side went on the offensive when the season best suited them. As the rains drew to a close in October and the roads dried up, the communists would begin their attacks, concluding their operations by the monsoons, during which time they would try to hold their newly won territory, while the rightists – with US air support and better supply lines favouring them during the rains – would go on the offensive. Pushing out from the Mekong Valley, the royalist and Hmong forces would usually retake what was lost, with the end result that neither side wound up controlling more than they had at the beginning.

But as the communists pressed on in the spring of 1964, they came up against a whole new enemy: **airpower**. Single-prop T-28 aircraft hammered at communist positions, scaring off their soldiers who had never faced aeroplanes before. Within a matter of weeks, T-28 bombing runs were joined by US jets, which took off from bases around Asia. Not intended specifically for Laos, the jets were sent over Laos as they happened to be in the neighbourhood.

Once the bombing began, Washington apparently decided it wasn't such a bad idea. News reports produced by the few journalists in Laos could be controlled, the US reasoned. They were right: although the bombing campaign would be reported for years by Pathet Lao and North Vietnamese radio, it would take five years before the United States public heard anything about it.

Escalation

Souvannaphouma initially gave his permission for US flights over Laos, but after two American jets were downed over northern Laos the prime minister had second thoughts and once again threatened to resign unless the bombing raids ceased. However, Souvannaphouma was in no position to argue. The US had restored him to power and paid his government's budget. And it would be only thanks to US backing that Souvannaphouma, trying to preserve a minimum of freedom of action, would remain in power for the next decade in the face of successive right-wing coups.

In 1964, a new phase of the war in Laos began. With the US pushing hard for an **escalation of the bombing** in the summer, Souvannaphouma, prodded by the US embassy, declared that the North Vietnamese were using the eastern flank of Laos to send combatants and supplies to South Vietnam along what would become known as the **Ho Chi Minh Trail**. He then gave the go-ahead for what were euphemistically known as "armed reconnaissance" flights over Laos, permission that essentially became a blank cheque for the US to bomb wherever it pleased.

The war was intensifying next door in **Vietnam**, too. Whatever misgivings US President Lyndon B. Johnson had about the Southeast Asia problem he had inherited from his predecessors, he was determined not to go down as the president who lost to the communists. Although Johnson, facing an election in November 1964, initially decided to keep his plans for the escalation of the war in Vietnam secret from voters and from Capitol Hill, he was able to make his stand against communism more public in August when the *USS Maddox* came under attack off the coast of North Vietnam. In response to the incident, US senators passed the **Gulf of Tonkin Resolution**, which became Johnson's justification for the Vietnam War. No such resolution was passed regarding Laos; after all, the country was "neutral".

When Ambassador William Sullivan assumed his post in Vientiane his assignment was to wage war while maintaining the fiction of the Geneva Accords, which he had personally helped to negotiate. He came to the Lao capital near the end of 1964, aware of US plans for Operation Rolling Thunder – a sustained carpet-bombing campaign against North Vietnam designed to go "after the manure pile" rather than simply swatting flies, as the Commander of the US Air Force, General Curtis Le May, eloquently put it. Even before the Vietnam operation began, Sullivan established his own programmes for Laos, called **Operation Barrel Roll** in the north and **Operation Steel Tiger** in the south.

Sullivan set the tone for the US campaign in Laos – ground troops (with the exception of reconnaissance missions and raids on the Ho Chi Minh Trail area) were kept out and military planes had to take off outside the country. The war took place in total secrecy. As British journalist Christopher Robbins wrote in *The Ravens,* based on interviews with pilots who fought in "the Other Theatre", "There was another war even nastier than the one in Vietnam, and so secret that the location of the country in which it was being fought was classified....The men who chose to fight in it were handpicked volunteers, and anyone accepted for a tour seemed to disappear as if from the face of the earth."

From 1964 until the ceasefire of February 1973, United States planes flew 580,944 sorties – or 177 a day – over Laos and dropped 2,093,100 tonnes of bombs – equivalent to one planeload of bombs every eight minutes around the clock for nine years – making Laos the most heavily bombed country per capita in the history of warfare.

The turning point: 1968

On March 10, 1968, communist forces overran a strategic limestone massif in Houa Phan which the US had crowned with a high-tech bombing guidance device that directed attacks on Hanoi and was guarded by Hmong troops. The **fall of Phou Pha Thi** (see box, p.190) underscored the lack of unified command that plagued the various US factions – the embassy, the CIA and the air force – responsible for fighting the Laos War.

According to Roger Warner in his book *Shooting at the Moon*, while some involved in directing the US war effort thought the US had erred by provoking the North Vietnamese with the installation of this direct threat to Hanoi's security, others argued that the North Vietnamese escalation in Laos was simply a part of the same intensive effort that produced the January 31 **Tet Offensive**, in which a combined force of 70,000 communists violated a truce to launch attacks on more than a hundred cities across South Vietnam. Forty thousand North Vietnamese troops were estimated to be in Laos at the time, pushing with a new sense of determination towards the Plain of Jars and on to Long Cheng, the nerve centre of Vang Pao's army, high up in the hills.

In a Washington reeling from Tet, which brought with it the popular perception that the communists were winning the war in Vietnam, President Johnson vetoed requests for a massive troop expansion, and on March 31 he suspended bombing north of the Twentieth Parallel to jump-start the peace talks in Paris that would grind on for five years. By the year's end the bombing had completely ended.

The suspension of bombing in Vietnam was terrible news for Laos, as the US Air Force's reaction was to send more planes over Laos than ever before. Swarms of planes circled the country, zeroing in on their targets with the help of a new breed of forward air controllers known as Ravens, introduced in the wake of the Phou Pha Thi disaster. These pilots, "sheep-dipped" in civilian clothes, flew single-engine Cessna propeller planes, with a hilltribe translator in the backseat to communicate with ground forces, guiding up to three hundred American sorties per day. The early days of Operation Momentum, when the CIA quietly waged a grassroots guerrilla war, were a distant memory.

Nixon's presidency

President **Nixon** began his term in office in January 1969, promising to "end the war and win the peace". In order to facilitate pulling out of Southeast Asia while saving face for the United States, Nixon initiated a policy of **"Vietnamization"**. This involved a gradual withdrawal of US forces coupled with an intensification of the air war and more matériel support, as well as pursuing communist sanctuaries with greater intensity in the hope that South Vietnam could hold its own against the North.

From a peak of 540,000 in early 1969, the number of US troops had shrunk to nearly half that figure by the end of 1970, while during the same period, South Vietnamese forces jumped to more than a million from 640,000. Despite the gradual withdrawal of US troops, Nixon's effort to Vietnamize the war ironically ended up appearing to the American public as a widening of the conflict.

The first major test of this strategy was the United States' **invasion of Cambodia**, which lay at the end of the Ho Chi Minh Trail. Until 1970, Cambodia, under the leadership of Prince Norodom Sihanouk, had stayed neutral in the war. Neutrality for Sihanouk, however, meant allowing the North Vietnamese to operate on Cambodian soil and the United States to bomb the North Vietnamese with B-52s. On March 18, 1970, a right-wing pro-US general named Lon Nol replaced Sihanouk in a coup and, two weeks later, US and South Vietnamese troops invaded the regions of the country nearest South Vietnam.

The operation set off a political uproar in the US. Massive **anti-war demonstrations** spread across America after four National Guardsmen opened fire on demonstrators at Kent State University in Ohio, killing four. Politically, the Cambodian "incursion", as it was termed, and subsequent protests prompted the US Congress to pass a measure forbidding the use of American ground troops in Cambodia and Laos. Had they not, US ground troops might have taken part in **Lam Son 719** (see p.276) – one of the most disastrous operations undertaken by the United States in the whole of the war – in which South Vietnamese troops attempted to sever the Ho Chi Minh Trail in southeastern Laos, a communist stronghold.

In February 1971, nearly 20,000 South Vietnamese troops, backed by American air power, drove across the Annamite Mountains, in the hope of cutting North Vietnamese supply lines in the vicinity of Xepon, 40km west of the border. The operation represented new tactics by the Pentagon. After years of strategically bombing the veins of the Ho Chi Minh Trail, Washington appeared to recognize that aeroplanes can't stop people. The move proved catastrophic. Five thousand South Vietnamese were killed or wounded, 176 Americans died and more than one hundred US army helicopters were shot down, with an estimated six hundred more damaged. Images of South Vietnamese troops clinging to the skids of American helicopters in a desperate bid to flee the massacre carried the message that even with massive US air and matériel support the South Vietnamese didn't stand a chance, pushing US policymakers closer to the realization that the war was a lost cause.

Peace at hand

Washington had begun to realize that Southeast Asia was merely a small part in the Cold War, and that as long as the US continued to fight in Indochina, it would continue to give the Soviet Union and China – the two communist giants, whose border forces had clashed in March 1969 – a reason to cooperate. By the time Nixon announced that his national security advisor, Henry Kissinger, had secretly visited China in July 1971 and that he would soon visit China himself, the president seemed ready to sacrifice South Vietnam – and by extension Laos and Cambodia – in order to create an opening with China.

With **peace talks** deadlocked in Paris, Nixon sent Kissinger, with former Laos ambassador Sullivan at his side, to take charge. After the Americans flexed their muscles in Vietnam one last time with the Christmas bombings of Hanoi in late 1972, the United States, North Vietnam, South Vietnam and the Viet Cong at last signed the **Paris Accords** on January 27, 1973. Under the terms of the agreement, a ceasefire was established and all remaining American troops were repatriated by April. In reality the accords would accomplish little more than smoothing the US withdrawal from Indochina.

While the US saw an agreement on Laos as an afterthought that would be quickly resolved, Souvannaphouma held out against a settlement, wanting assurances from the Americans that the North Vietnamese would pull their troops out of Laos. But the Vietnamese had never acknowledged having troops in Laos in the first place and, with the US already committed to a withdrawal, there was little Washington could do for Vientiane. The North Vietnamese knew this and took the position that they would only withdraw from Laos and Cambodia after a new government had been put in place. Late in February, the Vientiane government and the Pathet Lao signed an Agreement of the Restoration of Peace and Reconciliation, which neither the US nor the North Vietnamese signed – as if they had never been in Laos in the first place.

The Pathet Lao takeover

Continued negotiations resulted in the formation of a **third coalition government** in April 1974, with leftists taking half the ministerial portfolios and the remainder going to the right. Souvannaphouma once again presided as prime minister and Souphanouvong headed the policy-making National Political Consultative Council, which met in Louang Phabang.

When Phnom Penh and then Saigon fell to communist forces in April 1975, a complete communist takeover in Laos appeared a foregone conclusion. "Liberating" towns as they went, Pathet Lao forces gradually closed in on Vientiane, where demonstrations were held in the capital against the continuing US presence and right-wing political and military figures. A Pathet Lao force of fifty women soldiers symbolically "liberated" Vientiane on August 23. Power was slowly but surely shifting to the Pathet Lao.

Relieved of his RLA command by Souvannaphouma after refusing to stop fighting, Vang Pao was finally persuaded to leave Laos in May by the US, whose representatives were pulling out as well. A mass exodus of Hmong towards Thailand followed. An estimated thirty thousand Hmong – nearly a tenth of the tribe's entire population within the borders of Laos – had died during the war. As thousands fled, their suffering continued, as many were robbed and shot while trying to flee to Thailand.

Lowland Lao generals of the royalist side were more willing to try to cooperate with the new government. Although large numbers fled the country, many more chose to stay and serve the new government. Thousands of civil servants and military officers went willingly to re-education camps (see pp.194–195) in the remote northeast and southeast of the country after being told these "seminars" would only last a few weeks.

The absence of right-wing figures opened the door to further Pathet Lao advances which culminated in a **National Congress of People's Representatives** on December 2, 1975, when the congress proclaimed the Lao People's Democratic Republic and accepted the abdication of King Sisavang Vatthana.

The Lao People's Democratic Republic

The **Thirty Year Struggle**, with its roots in the short-lived Lao Issara government, was over. The man in charge was the little-known party secretary-general **Kaysone**, who was named prime minister. When Kaysone appeared at a reception on December 5 it was the first time he had been seen in public in seventeen years. The man who had been the face of the Pathet Lao all along, Souphanouvong, assumed the role of president. The prince essentially became a figurehead – after all, it wouldn't do to have a communist country run by a French-educated prince.

Unlike their comrades in Vietnam and Cambodia, the Pathet Lao took power in a **bloodless coup**. After overthrowing the government of Souvannaphouma and abolishing royalty, the Pathet Lao named the prince and the king as advisors to the new government and demonstrated further flexibility by inviting the United States to maintain its embassy in Vientiane.

The Pathet Lao's flexibility ended there, however, as they continued to round up civil servants and military personnel with ties to the royalists until as many as fifty thousand people were in **re-education camps**, which turned out to be malaria-ridden labour camps, heavy on self-criticism sessions. Whatever willingness to cooperate with the new regime there was left among the lowland Lao quickly evaporated as the government refused to allow the return of people in camps. Many, on their release, left the country. By the mid-1980s Laos had lost ten percent of its population – including an overwhelming majority of its educated class, setting the country back a generation in its development, according to political scientist Martin Stuart-Fox.

Considerable problems faced the new government, which took over a country stripped of money and resources. Very little economic development had taken place since the departure of the French, who themselves had done little to promote development. The **economy**, which had only been kept afloat by a massive influx of US funds, was now a shambles, crippled by the termination of US aid, runaway inflation and the closure of the border with Thailand – the country's primary source of imports, which resulted in severe shortages of basic foods. The Pathet Lao's decision to consolidate their grip on power by shipping off potential opponents hurt the country further by incarcerating or scaring off valuable human resources, people who took their capital with them. Thirty-five thousand ethnic Vietnamese and Chinese – the traditional merchants of the country – boarded up their shops in Vientiane and crossed the Mekong.

Intent on ushering in a socialist state, the Pathet Lao followed **Eastern bloc models**: they collectivized farms, centralized control of prices and nationalized what little industry there was in the country. The revolution was extended to the personal sphere as well. The government required long-haired teenagers to get haircuts and women to wear traditional skirts in an effort to develop Lao socialist men and women. Prostitutes and petty thieves were shipped off to re-education camps of their own on islands in the middle of Ang Nam Ngum.

As living standards declined within Laos and the number of refugees swelled in camps in Thailand, **opponents of the regime** found ready recruits to strike back against the new government. The Thailand-based Lao National Revolutionary Front produced anti-government propaganda and sent sabotage teams into Laos, while remnants of the Hmong secret army went on the offensive in northern Laos, capturing a town on the outskirts of Louang Phabang in March 1977. Fearing that opponents might rally around the figure of the king, the government arrested the royal family and banished them to Houa Phan, where the king, queen and crown prince died, something which the government only officially acknowledged in 1990.

Vietnamese forces helped quell the Hmong revolt, and in July, Vientiane and Hanoi signed a 25-year **Treaty of Friendship and Cooperation** which formalized Vietnamese political, economic and military assistance, including the stationing of more than 30,000 Vietnamese troops in Laos over the next decade. Relations were also close with the Soviet Union, which sent hundreds of technicians and advisors to Laos, drawing it firmly within the Soviet sphere of influence.

By 1979, external and internal difficulties facing the new government forced it to re-evaluate its policies; as a result, its agricultural cooperative programme was suspended and a less rigid form of socialism was adopted.

The new thinking

Despite the changes, little had been accomplished by the time the Pathet Lao celebrated its tenth anniversary in power and the completion of its first five-year plan in December 1985. Heavily dependent on foreign aid, Laos remained one of the world's poorest countries, with a per capita income of $100. The time had come, in the eyes of Kaysone, for a change.

After overcoming opponents of reform, Kaysone was able to implement the **New Economic Mechanism**, approved by the Fourth Party Congress in November 1986, which essentially introduced a market economy. Without an upheaval among the party's leaders – many of whom had worked together since their days in the Indochinese Communist Party in the 1940s – the ageing hardliners of the Pathet Lao embarked on a series of reforms, generally known as *jintannakan mai* or the New Thinking, which was as thorough as anything to be found in Eastern Europe at the time. By the late 1980s, the centralized socialist economy had been largely dismantled. Farmers could own their own land and sell their crops at free-market prices, state-owned businesses had to make a profit or close their doors and wholly owned foreign investment projects, protected against nationalization, were authorized.

Political changes did not accompany the economic reforms, however. Local elections held in 1988 – the first since 1975 – and subsequent national elections in 1989 did provide some popular legitimacy for the government at a time when anti-communist opposition had increased, but candidates were approved by the party prior to polls. And although the re-education camps wound down, the government showed in 1990 that it would deal strictly with **dissent** when it arrested three critics whom it accused of "activities aimed at overthrowing the regime". The three, former government officials who called for democracy and the creation of a multiparty system, were sent off to Houa Phan where, according to Amnesty International, one has since died in prison and two are still being held.

For many, less government intrusion in people's lives and an abundance of material goods flooding the markets, brought on by the opening up of the economy, went a long way towards smoothing over discontent. Of course, the discontented could also vote with their feet – crossing the Mekong and blending in with the ethnic Lao population of northeastern Thailand. But by the late 1980s, the Mekong had once again become a two-way street, as Lao refugees were invited to return, and Western tourists began to visit the country.

In 1991, the Fifth Party Congress endorsed the long-awaited **Constitution**, which guaranteed basic freedoms and the right to private ownership of property. The congress served to indicate that the party was no longer above the law when one member of the politburo was demoted for corruption. Economic reform also received an endorsement, with the party replacing the communist red star in the national crest with the That Louang stupa and eliminating the word "socialism" from the national motto.

The 1992 death of Kaysone, who had led the communist movement since the inception of the Lao People's Party in 1955, presented a serious challenge to the regime, but a smooth transition, resulting in the appointment of Nouhak Phoumsavanh as state president and Khamtay Siphandone, the prime minister, as president of the party, ensured the government's political stability.

Regional integration

As communism began to collapse in Eastern Europe and Vietnam began to withdraw its forces from Laos, the government improved ties with Thailand – but only after a nasty little border war erupted in 1988 in Xainyabouli province – and with other capitalist countries, notably Japan, Australia and Sweden. Cooperation with the United States in the search for missing US servicemen on Lao soil and control of the opium trade (Washington regards Laos as the number three producer of the world's opium supply) improved ties with the United States, culminating in the 1992 re-establishment of full ambassadorial relations.

With the collapse of the Soviet Union in 1991, Laos also began to smooth over difficulties with China which had arisen as a result of Vientiane's alliance with the USSR and Vietnam. China has in fact emerged as Laos's most important foreign military ally, a major source of military equipment and a powerful economic force on Laos's northern border.

Thus, by the early 1990s, Laos enjoyed relatively good relations with all its border countries, allowing it to slip back into its familiar role of a crossroads between contending regional powers. The Australian-financed **Friendship Bridge** – opened in 1994 outside Vientiane – as well as membership in the **Association of Southeast Asian Nations** in July 1997 were two important signs that Laos had finally begun to shake off decades of isolation.

For the **Sixth Party Congress**, the bridge to Thailand symbolized the way in which the New Thinking was being corrupted, as economic reforms brought a host of new problems, including corruption, gambling dens, brothels and increased crime. The conservative policies introduced by the congress indicated the party intended to slow the pace of reforms and would attempt to contain the fallout from "socially evil outside influences", in part by appealing to traditional Lao values. (While Lao newspapers routinely pummelled the sleazy side of the Thai economic miracle – as well as the Thai inclination to "look down on Lao people" – in the press, *The Far Eastern Economic Review* indicates that the government didn't allow such frictions to interfere with the generous helpings of Thai aid, trade and investment upon which it has relied in recent years.)

Although the party was firmly in charge, the reforms, with the accompanying social problems, increased official corruption and growing income disparity, represented the greatest challenge to internal order in the eyes of the party, more so than the **continuing insurgency** in Hmong-dominated areas in the north. Nonetheless, a slight upswing in insurgent activities, reportedly by the group known as the Chao Fa occurred in the mid-1990s, perhaps owing to government plans for **resettlement** of highland groups. The official reason for resettlement was to put an end to opium cultivation and slash-and-burn agriculture, and bring farflung villagers closer to hospitals and schools. The consequences in some cases have proved fatal for the highlanders, who have contracted valley-related diseases such as malaria.

Laos today

The 1997 **Asian economic crisis** provided a harsh illustration of the downside of regional integration and proved a major setback for the country's economy. The Lao currency – among the hardest hit of the region's battered currencies – lost eighty percent of its value between June 1997 and the beginning of 1999; annual inflation soared to 170 percent; direct investment plummeted from $1.2 billion in 1995 to $150 million two years later; and civil servants saw the value of their salaries drop from around $50 a month to one-tenth that figure. Meanwhile, aid from regional powers – many of whom were undergoing serious problems of their own – slowed to a trickle. The crisis brought many of the weaknesses of the Lao economy to the surface, in particular the country's heavy reliance on foreign aid, which accounts for roughly fifteen percent of GDP, a level at which self-sufficiency is difficult to achieve.

Although its economy has since begun to show signs of improvement, Laos continues to rank among the world's poorest, least developed countries. Indeed, the World Bank has said that Laos's social indicators are more akin to those of sub-Saharan Africa than they are to the rest of Southeast Asia. Roughly half the adult population is illiterate, some forty percent lack access to safe drinking water and the country continues to be mired at the bottom of World Health Organization rankings. And, as *The Economist* points out, half of the country's people live below Vientiane's own poverty line.

As the ruling communist party slumbered toward the 25th anniversary of its hold on power in 2000, a **bombing campaign** shook the sleepy Lao capital. Beginning in March, a series of bombs exploded around Vientiane, leaving at least one dead and many more injured. More than a dozen small bombs were planted during the year, with the airport, a central market and a bus among the targets. While theories abounded as to who the bombers might be – royalists, insurgent Hmong and a pro-China government clique were among the leading suspects – no one laid claim to the attacks, which ended as unexpectedly as they began, not long after the party's December 2 anniversary. Meanwhile, in July, a group of sixty rebels attacked a Lao border post at Ban Vang Tao, opposite Chong Mek, engaging soldiers in a gun battle before retreating into Thailand. Five rebels died in the raid, which appeared to have been launched from Laos's neighbour.

Not all of the unrest in recent years has been violent in nature. In October 1999, a rare **anti-government demonstration** by the Lao Students Movement for Democracy was held to publicly call for human rights and political change, but it was quickly quelled. Five students were arrested and their whereabouts remain unknown. A second demonstration, in Champasak province in late 2000, is thought to have been dealt with in similar fashion.

If the acts of 2000 were meant to spark widespread unrest that would topple the government, the effort seems to have failed. While success at economic planning continues to elude the current leadership, the regime appears to have the political arena well in hand. At the **Seventh Party Congress** in 2001, all eight of the surviving nine politburo members appointed at the previous congress five years earlier were retained, with Khamtay Siphandone, who also serves as Laos's president, reappointed party secretary. The party remains the only legal political organization, a fact which made for few surprises at national assembly elections in February 2002. As president Khamtay Siphandone reportedly said before casting his vote, "There won't be any change." With resistance groups pursuing their own disparate agendas and the people too poor to worry about politics, he may well be right.

Religion and belief systems

The multiplicity of belief systems in Laos mirrors the complexity of its mulligan stew of ethnicities. Theravada Buddhism is the majority religion, practised by approximately two thirds of the total population, followed by animism and ancestor worship. The remainder practise Mahayana Buddhism and Taoism, and a small percentage of the population follow Christianity or Islam.

The vast majority of lowland-dwelling ethnic Lao, whose numbers make up over half of the population of Laos, are adherents of **Theravada Buddhism**. Sometimes referred to as the "southern school" of Buddhism owing to its geographic spread, Theravada Buddhism is prevalent in Sri Lanka, Myanmar (Burma), Thailand and Cambodia as well. However, to say that Theravada Buddhism is the professed religion of the majority of the population is an oversimplification. As with many Buddhists of Southeast Asia, most Lao adherents also involve themselves in the regular propagation of animist spirits and may even make offerings to certain Hindu deities. Other ethnic groups such as the Tai Leu, Phuan and Phu Noi also practise Theravada Buddhism, as do a fraction of the tribal Tai groups such as the Phu Tai, Tai Daeng and Tai Dam. Some ethnic-Chinese and Vietnamese are adherents of **Mahayana Buddhism**, the so-called "northern school" of Buddhism. The ideological rift between the two schools is as vast as the one that divides Catholicism and Protestantism. Theravada Buddhism is the more austere of the two and has been described as having an "every man for himself" philosophy, that is to say, each individual adherent is believed to be responsible for his or her own accumulation of merit or sin. Mahayana Buddhism is more of a "group effort", with adherents praying for divine assistance from *bodhisattva*, near-Buddhas who have postponed their enlightenment in order to serve as the compassionate protectors of all mankind.

Lao-style Theravada Buddhism is a fascinating blend of indigenous and borrowed beliefs and rituals that owes much to the practices of neighbouring Thailand. During Laos's many years of vassaldom to the various kingdoms made up of lands that now lie within Thai borders, many outside religious beliefs and customs found their way into the royal courts of the Lao kingdoms at Louang Phabang, Vientiane and Champasak and, from there, into the valleys of the interior via the tributaries of the Mekong River. The Hindu customs and beliefs that were adopted by the Thai after their sack of Angkor, in what is now Cambodia, were also passed on, in diluted form, to Laos. Later, Chinese and Vietnamese immigrants brought Mahayana Buddhism with them and, as the immigrants prospered and assimilated, the images of their gods found their way into urban monasteries. Go into one of these monasteries today and you may well see alongside images of the Buddha a representation of a Hindu god such as Ganesh or a Mahayana Buddhist deity such as Kuan Yin.

For most Lao Buddhists, religion in everyday life revolves around the all-important practice of **making merit**, or *het bun*. This accumulation of merit is paramount to a Theravada Buddhist's spiritual strategy, a way to dilute the destructive effects of any sin that may have been warranted by the performance of bad deeds, while at the same time ensuring that the next incarnation will be better than the present one. Making merit is accomplished most readily by giving alms to Buddhist monks and novices. This enchanting practice can be witnessed just after dawn, when barefoot monks solemnly walk through the neighbourhood or village surrounding their monasteries in order to collect offerings of food from laypeople. Merit thus acquired is believed to bring the giver good fortune in this life and the next, and also to dilute the destructive effects of sin that may have been accumulated. Male adherents may also make merit for themselves and their families by taking vows and becoming a novice monk for a limited period of time. Even more merit may be acquired by becoming an ordained disciple of the Buddha. Most ethnic Lao men do become novices at some time in their lives, usually before marriage. Interestingly, a man who has yet to do time in a monastery is referred to as *dip* or "unripe", alluding to the fact that many Lao don't consider a man complete without some time spent in the monastery. For most Lao males, the time spent wearing a robe is short, usually no more than three months or so during the rainy season. Before the advent of public schools, lessons in reading and writing learned at the monastery were about all the education the average Lao could hope for. Many of the holidays in the Lao calendar are associated with Buddhist festivals and give the visitor a chance to observe the practice of merit-making, whether it be ritually bathing Buddha images or donating new robes to monks.

The monks themselves take **vows** to uphold no less than 227 precepts. These range from abstinence from sexual relations, alcohol and the wearing of any sort of ornamentation to more arcane rules such as a prohibition on urinating while standing upright (so as not to soil robes). Laos's history of social upheaval and a generally relaxed attitude towards rules, however, have meant that, especially in rural monasteries, not all of the precepts are strictly adhered to.

Lao legend has it that Buddhism came to Laos in the fourteenth century, but archeological evidence suggests that Buddhism existed in parts of what is now Laos as early as the eighth century. As the state religion, Buddhism enjoyed royal patronage up until the time of the revolution. In the years leading up to the revolution, the communists cleverly used Buddhist monks, many of whom were unhappy with widespread government corruption, as instruments for diffusing propaganda. Once the cause had been won, however, the communists moved to gain total control, banning the practice of alms-giving. This effectively made it impossible to remain a monk, as it is against Buddhist precepts for monks to cultivate plants or raise animals for food. The move backfired, however, as laypeople were shocked at the new régime's heavy-handed treatment of the monkhood and resented the fact that they were being deprived of any opportunity to make merit. Popular outcry forced the government to rescind the draconian measures, but only after large numbers of monks fled to Thailand or abandoned their robes and became laymen. Today, the study of Marxist–Leninist theory is still mandatory for all monks, but Lao Buddhism has made a strong comeback and economic reforms and liberalization have helped to increase the numbers of men in the monkhood to pre-revolution levels.

Animism, the belief that natural objects are inhabited by spiritual entities or possess supernatural powers, predates Buddhism in Laos. While the Buddhist Lao still harbour vestiges of these beliefs, some midland and highland tribal peoples are exclusively animist. An easily recognized example of animism among Buddhists is the practice of erecting a "spirit house" on plots of land. These are ordinarily found in a corner of a piece of property and resemble a miniature house or sometimes a model of Mount Meru, the Hindu Mount Olympus, atop a pedestal. The spirit house is the customary abode of the *jao* *bawn*, or spirit of the site. Since long before ever having contact with Buddhism, the Lao have believed that certain spirits inhabit natural landmarks such as hills, trees, large rocks or plots of land. Building structures and cultivating land are believed to displace the spirits and so an alternative home must be provided. The idea is to make the spirit house a more habitable place than the dwellings for humans located on the same plot of land. Naturally, if the *jao bawn* is comfortable in its digs, it is less likely to cause trouble for people living in the vicinity. Offerings to keep the spirit of the site propitiated may include flowers, incense, candles or sweets. A much simpler offering to *jao bawn* that visitors may note is the practice of pressing spirit offerings of sticky rice against trees or rocks.

Animism among the midlanders and highlanders is more prevalent. One manifestation of animism that can be readily seen at all elevations is the *talaew*, a six-pointed star made from strips of bamboo and placed over doors and gates or in rice fields. The device is thought to bar evil spirits from entering and doing harm. After the revolution, the communists discouraged many animist practices, such as the annual sacrifice of water buffalo in tribal villages in the south, believing that such worship wasted resources and held back the progress of the nation. As with Buddhism, animism quickly revived once official suppression was relaxed.

Ancestor worship in different forms is also practised by many of the highland tribes that migrated to Laos from China, including the Akha, Hmong and Mien. Practices vary, but all believe that the spirits of deceased ancestors have the ability to affect the lives of their living descendants. Like babies, the ancestors are thought to be rather helpless and dependent on the living for earthly comforts. The ancestors reward descendants who remember them with offerings, but can become harmful if neglected. The Mien also worship **Taoist** deities, and are known for the crude but charming painted images of these deities which are traditionally displayed on the Mien altar.

Hinduism, or Braminism, was first introduced to what is now southern and central Laos by the Khmer, who adopted many Hindu traditions and beliefs from Indian traders who began arriving in the ports of Southeast Asia in the first century AD. Some elements of the annual ceremonies at Wat Phou, the ancient Khmer site in Champasak province, reflect Hindu rituals handed down to the Lao from the days when the Khmer kings at Angkor ruled much of Southeast Asia. While the Laos' recognition of Hindu divinities is minimal compared with that of their Thai cousins, two such deities, namely the multi-armed, four-faced Brahma and the green-skinned Indra, have become icons in the Theravada Buddhist pantheon and so are commonly depicted in Lao monasteries. Images of Ganesh, the so-called elephant god, can be found on the premises of some Buddhist monasteries and shrines, particularly in the south. The *shivalinga*, or stone phallus symbolizing the god Shiva, was commonly enshrined at ancient Khmer temples and, because many Lao Buddhist monasteries were built on top of ancient Khmer sites, the *shivalinga* and other bits of Khmer statuary are often found on Buddhist altars, particularly in the south.

Christianity arrived in Laos in 1642 in the form of an Italian Jesuit missionary but, according to his journal, he was far from successful. Not until the French colonial period did Christian missionaries scramble to make converts throughout Laos. While they had little success with the Buddhist Lao, a number of the animist highlanders were converted. A significant number of Laos's ethnic-Vietnamese population is Catholic and the largest concentration of Catholics is found in southern Laos, particularly Savannakhet, which boasts the country's most elaborate Catholic church. Lao Christians also fared badly after the revolution. Because the communists saw Christianity as a "Western", and therefore potentially subversive religion, missionaries were expelled and churches throughout the country were closed. An example of one such church is located near Kilometre Five on Tha Dua road outside of Vientiane. The former Methodist church is now a garage for fire engines.

Followers of **Islam** are found mainly in Vientiane, where a small community of Cham Muslims, refugees from the Khmer Rouge reign of terror in Cambodia, reside in the vicinity of a mosque located near the Nam Phou (fountain). In northern Laos, small pockets of Chinese Muslims (known locally as *jin haw*), descendants of mule-caravan traders from Yunnan, can be found in Phongsali and other highland towns.

The arts

The vast majority of works of art created in Laos – sculpture, painting, architecture, even decorative motifs on jewellery – are inspired by Buddhism. With the important exception of Lao textiles, nearly all Lao works of art are designed with veneration of the Buddha in mind. The motivation behind much Theravada Buddhist art relies heavily on the concept of making merit. Wealthy patrons looking to acquire religious merit and dilute an accumulation of sins can do so by commissioning the crafting of an image of the Buddha or by financing the building or restoration of any of the structures found in monastery grounds.

Owing to Laos's distance from lucrative trade routes and its tumultuous history, prosperity and the subsequent patronage of the religious arts never reached the heights that were attained in neighbouring Cambodia, Thailand and Myanmar (Burma). Nevertheless, a style did develop that is distinctively Lao and, although the number of works which exhibit a high degree of refinement and sophistication is rather small, Lao art makes up for it with a crude vigour and whimsy that rarely fails to charm.

Sculpture

The historic Buddha was a prince who gave up his wealth and birthright in order to pursue the "middle path" – a philosophy of moderation – towards enlightenment. Just before his death, the Buddha was said to have discouraged his followers from making images of him, saying that it was his teachings that should be worshipped, not a likeness of him. For a time after the Buddha's passing, Buddhists used **symbolic imagery** to recall the enlightened one. An empty throne or a royal parasol was sometimes depicted commemorating the Buddha's decision to abandon his life of luxury and seek the path to enlightenment. However, human nature being what it is, adherents needed something more concrete. The **first images of the Buddha** were probably made several centuries after the Buddha's death. By that time, no living artist had actually seen the Buddha, but a list of physical traits said to be unique to the Buddha had been passed down. The result of this list of fairly rigid attributes is that Buddha images from all over Asia share much the same characteristics. Lao images are no different and many of their seemingly bizarre features, toes of equal length for instance, are due to the strictness with which the aesthetic canon has been followed. In much the same vein, the attitude of the Buddha's arms and hands, or *mudra*, are rich with **symbolism** and must be depicted accurately if they are to be understood. Most of these gestures correspond to Buddhist theory or to events that occurred during the Buddha's lifetime. Besides the standard gestures and poses, the Lao have invented a couple of their own. One is a standing Buddha with arms to its sides and fingers pointing downwards, known as the "Beckoning Rain" pose. Buddhas with this *mudra* are found only in Laos and parts of northern Thailand. A similar standing Buddha with arms crossed at the wrists is also a Lao-invented *mudra*, known as "Contemplating the Tree of Enlightenment". The most sacred Buddha image in the country, the Pha Bang (see p.153), is also a standing Buddha, this time with arms held out in a blocking gesture, known as the "Dispelling Fear" pose.

Observant visitors will notice that one *mudra* in particular is especially popular with the Lao. This is found on Buddhas sitting in a half-lotus position, with the left hand resting palm-upward on the image's lap and the right hand extended down and touching the earth with the fingertips. Known as "Victory Over Mara", this pose commemorates the historic Buddha's triumph over Mara the Tempter, a Satan-like figure that tried unsuccessfully to distract the Buddha from his path to enlightenment.

The best place to see sculpted images of the Buddha is on an altar in a Buddhist monastery. Typically, a massive central image, usually constructed of brick and stucco, is flanked by numerous smaller images cast from bronze or carved from hardwood. Caves are a less obvious venue for admiring Lao Buddhas, though by the time an image is deposited in a cavern, it is usually damaged. The caves at Pak Ou near Louang Phabang surely house the largest concentration of Lao Buddhas on earth. In Louang Phabang itself, the Pha Bang undeniably gets the most attention, but the superb reclining Buddha enshrined in a small "chapel" at Wat Xiang Thong is perhaps the best example of Lao sculpture to be found in the country. Lastly, the Haw Pha Kaew, a museum in Vientiane with a small but outstanding collection, is a must-see for those interested in more sophisticated examples of Lao sculpture.

Architecture

Of all Lao architectural elements, the *that*, or **stupa**, is probably easiest for the visitor to appreciate. This is due mainly to the fact that it is at once readily recognizable and varied in design. The concept of the stupa – a monument atop a reliquary containing sacred relics of the Buddha – originated in India and spread throughout Asia. In each country where Buddhism took root, the local architects and artisans put their own ideas to work when designing a stupa, thus the bell-shaped stupas of Sri Lanka have little in common stylistically with the multi-storied "pagoda" stupas found in China and Japan. The That Louang stupa, located in Vientiane and the national symbol of Laos, is a fusion of aggressive angles and graceful curves that make it quite different from designs predominant in neighbouring countries (although stupas in this style can also be found in the northeast of Thailand where ethnic Lao predominate). This design of stupa is probably the greatest single Lao contribution to Buddhist architecture.

Within a typical Lao wat there are a number of buildings serving different functions, but it is the **sim**, a structure in which the monastery's principal Buddha image is enshrined, that gets the most attention from Lao architects and artisans. Lao *sim* have two main styles: Vientiane and Louang Phabang. The Vientiane style owes much to the Bangkok school of architecture, while the style of Louang Phabang shares characteristics with that of Chiang Mai in northern Thailand. From a distance, the difference between these two styles can easily be discerned. The roof of the Vientiane-style *sim* is high and steep, while the Louang Phabang-style roof gently slopes nearly to the ground.

Variations on *sim* design were produced by the Phuan and Tai Leu ethnic groups. The rare **Xiang Khouang style**, once found in the province of the same name, is low and squat, designed to withstand the weather of the

△ Pagoda detail

windswept Plain of Jars. The handiwork of the Phuan people, this style did not survive Laos's violent history, and the only remaining example is at Louang Phabang's Wat Khili (see p.158). Examples of architecture produced by the Tai Leu are very similar to that found in China's Xishuangbanna region. The *sim* at Muang Sing's Wat Sing Jai is a picturesque example of the Tai Leu style.

Decorative features on the *sim* and other structures found at a Lao *wat* are in a variety of mediums. Carved wood, moulded stucco and, to a lesser extent, mirrored-glass mosaics typically ornament the exterior while inside, detailed murals cover entire walls. Doors and windows of the *sim* are often made from teakwood, ornately carved with the figures of celestial beings or demons upon a background of stylized flames or floral forms know as *lai lao* – "Lao pattern". The structure's wooden pediments – triangular segments of the upper facade that support the roof – are another place to look for pleasing examples of *lai lao*, along with carved depictions of Hindu deities such as Kala and Indra atop Airavata. Many of these motifs have origins in ancient Khmer ornamentation, such as that found at Wat Phou in Champasak province. Lao stucco-work is sometimes gilt-covered and almost always looks better from a distance. The use of stucco for ornamentation was introduced to Laos by the Khmer or possibly the Mon, but the methods and designs of Lao stucco-work owe more to the Tai Yuan of what is now northern Thailand. Likewise, the use of mirrored glass also came to Laos via Thailand. The mosaics at Wat Xiang Thong are Laos's most famous example of ornamentation using this medium but the works are modern, having been created in the late 1950s. Lao murals are meant to be read like a story and those found on the walls of the *sim* usually depict one of the *jataka* tales, the Lao version of the *Ramayana* (see p.384), or scenes of local life. The Lao belief that religious merit can be made by restoring old monastery buildings ensures that nearly all Lao *sim* are restored every fifty years or so. The artisans who restore these buildings are under little pressure to be true to an earlier design. Indeed, it is believed that the more lavish the new design, the more merit is likely to be made by the patron who commissioned the restoration. The result is that much of the decoration on Buddhist buildings in Laos is nowhere near as old as the structure it adorns.

Textiles

An art historian once described Lao art as a provincial version of the art of Thailand. He was obviously quite ignorant of the existence of **Lao textiles**. Indeed, in discussions about art, Lao textiles are often overlooked or relegated to the level of "handicraft". Recently, though, Lao textiles have begun enjoying the attention and recognition that they deserve.

The matrilineal society of the lowland Lao and tribal Tai meant that when a man married, he immediately set up house on the property of his new bride's parents. Sometimes this entailed leaving his home village and subsequently, when this couple's son came of age, he would do the same. With such a custom, men's roots in a village were never deep and this was reflected by their simple dress: it told almost nothing of a man's background. Women, on the other hand, were the heirs to a weaving tradition. Techniques improved with each new generation and were passed on. Each **ethnic group** had its own particular patterns and colours, which varied from village to village but were still recognizable as belonging to that group. Sometimes, as with the Tai Daeng, these variations were great – indeed, one could fill a hefty book with the myriad designs found in Tai Daeng weaving. According to experts, the "grammar" of a textile can be read to reveal not only the ethnicity of the wearer, but also her marital and financial status. Because all women in a village wove and wore similar patterns and a woman normally wore only what she herself had made, it was apparent at a glance who had mastered the art of weaving – a highly desirable skill in the eyes of young men looking for a prospective bride. Not surprisingly, a woman's most striking apparel was saved for festival days when all the young men from the village and beyond would be in attendance.

The many years of war in Laos had a predictable effect on textile weaving. Quality weaving requires peace and stability. Refugees fleeing a war are unlikely to take their looms along with them, especially the heavy bed-sized looms of the lowland Lao. Looms can be rebuilt once conditions improve but, by sad coincidence, peace in Laos was accompanied by the introduction of inexpensive, mass-produced textiles. The importance that Lao mothers once placed on teaching their daughters the secrets of the loom rapidly faded. As a result, however, antique pieces have become highly sought-after collectables, and museums as far afield as Australia have hired textile experts to scour Lao villages for examples of nineteenth- and early twentieth-century Lao weaving.

Laos's ethnic mosaic

While many of Southeast Asia's nations are ethnically diverse, Laos is one of the few that is still visibly so. That is to say, it is one of the last countries whose minorities have not been totally assimilated into the culture of the majority. This is partially because the majority is only in the majority by a thin margin and partially due to the relatively short period of time that the majority has had to reshape the country in its own image.

In an effort at categorization, the Lao government officially divides the population into **three groups**. Which group an ethnicity fits into is determined by the elevation at which that ethnicity dwells. These categorizations are not based on how the members of a group are related to one another; indeed, many unrelated ethnic groups may reside at any one elevation. Instead, this method of categorization may be seen as a tenuous majority's subtle means of proclaiming cultural superiority over its sizeable population of minorities while at the same time trying to bring them into the fold.

The lowland Lao

The so-called **Lao Loum** (or lowland Lao) live at the lowest elevations and on the land best suited for cultivation. For the most part, they are the **ethnic Lao**, a people related to the Thai of Thailand and the Shan of Burma. The lowland Lao make up the majority in Laos, between 50 percent and 60 percent, and are the group for which the country is named. They, like their Thai and Shan cousins, prefer to inhabit river valleys, live in dwellings that are raised above the ground, and are adherents of Theravada Buddhism. Of all the ethnicities found in Laos, the culture of the lowland Lao is dominant, mainly because it is they who hold political power. Their language is the official language, their religion is the state religion and their holy days are the official holidays. As access to a reliable water source is key to survival and water is abundant in the river valleys, the ethnic Lao have prospered. They have been able to devote their free time – that time not spent securing food – to the arts and entertainment, and their culture has become richer for it. Among the cultural traits by which the Lao define themselves are the cultivation and consumption of sticky rice as a staple, the taking part in the animist ceremony known as *basi* (see p.61), and the playing of the reed instrument called the *khaen*. Laos is by no means the only place where ethnic Lao dwell. Most of Thailand's northeastern region is populated with ethnic Lao and, owing to internal migration patterns caused by economic factors, Bangkok has the largest concentration of ethnic Lao anywhere. This fact is not lost on the Lao of Laos who feel that history has deprived them of much of their original territory.

Akin to the ethnic Lao are the Tai Leu, Phuan and Phu Tai, found in the northwest, the northeast and mid-south respectively. The **Tai Leu** of Laos are originally from China's Xishuangbanna region in southern Yunnan, where nowadays they are known as the "Dai minority". In Laos, their settlements stretch from the Chinese border with Louang Namtha province, through Oudomxai and into Xainyabouli. They are Theravada Buddhists and, like the Lao, also placate animist spirits. They are known to perform a ceremony similar to the *basi* ceremony which is supposed to reunite the wayward souls of their water buffalo. The Tai Leu are skilled weavers whose work is in demand from other groups that do not weave, such as the Khamu. Among foreign visitors, the best known Tai Leu settlement is Muang Sing.

The **Phuan** are in the same historical predicament as such Southeast Asian peoples as the Mon and Cham: they were once a recognized kingdom, but are now largely forgotten. Formerly located in the province of Xiang Khouang (the capital of which was formerly known as Muang Phuan), the kingdom's territory was at once coveted by the Siamese and Vietnamese. Aggression from both sides as well as from Chinese "Haw" bandits left the kingdom in ruins and the populace scattered. A British surveyor in the employ of a Siamese king reached Muang Phuan in the 1880s and remarked that the Phuan "exhibited refinement in all they did, but their elegant taste was of no avail against the rude barbarian". To this day, there are villages of Phuan as far afield as central Thailand, the descendants of Phuan villagers who were taken captive by the Siamese during military campaigns over a hundred years ago.

The Phuan are Theravada Buddhists, but once observed an impromptu holy day known as *kam fa*. When the first thunder of the season was heard, all labours ceased and villagers avoided any activity that might cause even the slightest noise. The village's fortune was then divined based on the direction from which the thunder was heard.

The **Phu Tai** of Savannakhet and Khammouane provinces are also found in the northeast of Thailand. They are Theravada Buddhists and have assimilated into Lao culture to a high degree, although it is still possible to recognize them by their dress on festival days. The predominant colour of the Phu Tai shawls and skirts are an electric purple and orange with yellow and lime-green highlights.

Other Tai peoples related to the Lao are the so-called "**tribal Tai**", who live in river valleys at slightly higher elevations and are mostly animists. These include the rather mysteriously named Tai Daeng (Red Tai), Tai Khao (White Tai) and Tai Dam (Black Tai). Theories about nomenclature vary. It is commonly surmised that the names were derived from the predominant colour of the womenfolk's dress, but others have suggested that the groups were named after the river valleys in northern Vietnam where they were thought to have originated. These Tai groups were once loosely united in a political alliance called the Sipsong Chao Tai or the Twelve Tai Principalities, spread over an area that covers parts of northwestern Vietnam and northeastern Laos. The traditional centre was present-day **Dien Bien Phu**, known to the Tai as Muang Theng. When the French returned to Indochina after World War II, they attempted to establish a "Tai Federation" encompassing the area of the old Principalities. The plan was short-circuited by Ho Chi Minh, who, after defeating the French, was able to manipulate divisions between the Tai groups in order to gain total control. The **Tai Dam** are found in large numbers in Houa Phan and Xiang Khouang provinces, but also inhabit northern Laos as far west as Louang Namtha. This ethnic group are principally animists and have a system of Vietnamese-influenced surnames that indicate political and social status. The women are easily recognized by their distinctive dress: long-sleeved, tight-fitting blouses in bright, solid colours with a row of butterfly-shaped silver buttons down the front and a long, indigo-coloured skirt. The outfit is completed with a bonnet-like headcloth of indigo with red trim.

Mon–Khmer groups

The ethnic Lao believe themselves and their ethnic kin to have originally inhabited an area that is present-day Dien Bien Phu in Vietnam before migrating into what is now Laos. Interestingly, there is historical evidence to support their legends. As the Lao moved southwards they displaced the original inhabitants of the region. Known officially as the **Lao Theung** (*theung* is Lao for "above"), but colloquially known as the *kha* ("slaves"), these peoples were forced to resettle at higher elevations where water was more scarce and life decidedly more difficult.

The **Khamu** of northern Laos, speakers of a Mon–Khmer language, are the most numerous of the indigenes, but have assimilated to a high degree and are practically indistinguishable from the ethnic Lao to outsiders. The Khamu are thought to number around 350,000, making them one of the largest minority groups in Laos. Their origins are obscure. Some theorize that the Khamu originally inhabited China's Xishuangbanna region in southern Yunnan and migrated south into northern Laos long before the arrival of the Lao. The Khamu themselves tell legends of their being northern Laos's first inhabitants and of having founded Louang Phabang. Interestingly, royal ceremonies once performed annually by the Lao king at Louang Phabang symbolically acknowledged the Khamu's original ownership of the land. The Khamu are known for their honesty and diligence, though in the past were easily duped by the lowland Lao into performing menial labour for little compensation. Their lack of sophistication in business matters and seeming complacency with their lot in life probably led to their being referred to as "slaves" by the lowland Lao. Unlike other groups in Laos, the Khamu are not known for their weaving skills and so customarily traded labour for cloth. The traditional Khamu village has four cemeteries: one for adults who died normal deaths, one for those who died violent or unnatural deaths, one for children and one for mutes.

A large spirit house located outside the village gate attests to the Khamu belief in animism. Spirits are thought to inhabit animals, rice and even money. Visitors to the village must call from outside the village gate, enquiring whether or not a temporary village taboo is in place. If so, then a visitor may not enter and water, food and a mat to rest on will be brought out by the villagers. If there is no taboo in effect a visitor will be told so and may enter. Male visitors may lodge in the village common-house if an overnight stay is planned, but may not sleep in the house of another family unless a blood sacrifice is made to the ancestors. The Khamu household is thought to be the property of the women residents and therefore, there is no ban on women visitors staying the night. The village common-house also serves as a home for adolescent boys and it is there that they learn how to weave baskets and make animal traps as well as become familiar with the village folklore and taboos. The boys may learn that the sound of the barking deer is an ill omen when a man is gathering materials with which to build a house or that it is wrong to bring meat into the village from an animal that has been killed by tiger or has died on its own. Young Khamu men seem to be prone to wanderlust, often leaving their villages to seek work in the lowlands. Their high rate of intermarriage with other groups during their forays for employment has contributed to their assimilation.

Another Mon–Khmer-speaking group which inhabits the north, particularly Xainyabouli province, are the **Htin**. Owing to a partial cultural ban on the use of any kind of metal, the Htin excel at fashioning household implements from bamboo, particularly baskets and fish traps, and are known for their vast knowledge of the different species of bamboo and what they can be used for.

Linguistically related to the Khamu and Htin are the **Mabri**, Laos's least numerous and least developed minority. Thought to number less than one hundred, the Mabri have a taboo on tilling the soil which has kept them seminomadic and impoverished. Half a century ago the Mabri were nomadic hunter-gatherers who customarily moved camp as soon as the leaves on the branches that comprised their temporary shelters began to turn yellow. Known to the Lao as *kha tawng leuang* ("slaves of the yellow banana leaves") or simply *khon pa* ("jungle people"), the Mabri were thought by some to be naked savages or even ghosts, and wild tales were circulated about their fantastic hunting skills and ability to vanish into the forest without a trace. The Mabri were said to worship their long spears, making offerings and performing dances for their weapons to bring luck with the hunt. Within the last few decades, however, they have given up their nomadic lifestyle and now work for other groups, performing menial tasks in exchange for food or clothing.

The Bolaven Plateau in southern Laos is named for the **Laven** people, yet another Mon–Khmer-speaking group whose presence predates that of the Lao. The Laven were very quick to assimilate the ways of the southern Lao, so much so that a French expansionist and amateur ethnologist who explored the plateau in the 1870s found it difficult to tell the two apart. Besides the Laven, other Mon–Khmer-speaking minorities are found in the south, particularly in Savannakhet, Salavan and Xekong provinces. Among these are the **Bru**, who have raised the level of building animal traps and snares to a fine art. The Bru have devised traps to catch, and sometimes kill, everything from mice to elephants, including a booby-trap that thrusts a spear into the victim.

The **Gie-Trieng** of Xekong are one of the most isolated of all the tribal peoples, having been pushed deep into the bush by the rival Sedang tribe. The Gie-Trieng are expert basket weavers and their tightly woven quivers, smoked a deep mahogany colour, are highly prized by collectors. The **Nge**, also of Xekong, produce textiles bearing a legacy of the Ho Chi Minh Trail that snaked through their territory and of American efforts to bomb it out of existence. Designs on woven shoulder bags feature stylized bombs and fighter planes, and men's loincloths are decorated with rows of tiny lead beads, fashioned from the munitions junk that litters the region.

The **Alak** and **Katu** have of late been brought to the attention of outsiders by Lao tour agencies who are eager to cash in on the tribal custom of sacrificing water buffalo in a ceremony reminiscent of the final scene in the film *Apocalypse Now*. The Katu are said to be a very warlike people and until as late as the 1950s carried out human sacrifices to placate spirits and ensure a good harvest. The ethnic Lao firmly believe that these southern Mon–Khmer groups are adept at black magic, and advise visitors to keep a cake of fragrant soap on their person to foil the sorcery of tribal witchdoctors.

Highland groups

The third official category, the **Lao Soung** (literally the "high Lao"), live at the highest elevations. They are comparative newcomers to Laos, having migrated from China at the beginning of the nineteenth century and settling on the only land available to them, at elevations over 1000m above sea level. This group includes Laos's most colourfully dressed ethnic groups, such as the Hmong, Mien, Lahu and Akha. Of these the **Hmong** are the most numerous, with a population of approximately 200,000. The Hmong are a highly independent-minded people who migrated south from China to escape persecution. In Laos they found relative freedom at the loftier elevations until the arrival of the French, who sought to tax them. This led to a number of bloody revolts. Later, an incident caused a schism between two Hmong clans, and the French backed one side, causing the other side to become allied with the fledgling Lao communist movement. The communists promised the Hmong their own independent state if they were victorious. After the French defeat, their Hmong allies were recruited by the CIA to form a "secret army" which used opium grown by the Hmong to finance the continued fight against the communists. With the communist victory in 1975, the promise of an independent homeland was conveniently forgotten and many Hmong, whether they had opposed the victors or not, were severely persecuted. Pogroms, including the alleged use of chemical weapons, caused tens of thousands of Hmong to flee to refugee camps in Thailand for eventual resettlement in the United States and France. Today, the remaining Hmong continue to be perceived by the Lao government as a liability. Hmong bandits (or patriots, depending on whom you talk to) continue to make some routes in northeastern Laos dangerous to traverse. The Hmong farmers' use of the slash-and-burn method of agriculture has given the government reason to put resettlement programmes into effect that bring Hmong villages down to lower elevations. The long-term impact that these programmes will have on Hmong culture is as yet unclear, however.

The Hmong are divided into several sub-groups, named for the predominant colour of their costumes. These include the White Hmong, Red Hmong, Blue Hmong and Striped Hmong. Their apparel is among the most colourful to be found in Laos and their silver jewellery is prized by collectors. Hmong babies receive their first silver necklace at the age of one month. By the time they are adults they will have several kilogrammes of silver jewellery, most of which is cached until special occasions such as Hmong New Year. Their written language uses Roman letters and was devised by Western missionaries.

The **Mien** are linguistically related to the Hmong and also immigrated into Laos from China, but their culture is much more Sinicized. The Mien use Chinese characters to write their documents and worship Taoist deities. Like the Hmong, they cultivate opium, which they trade for salt and other necessities that are not easily obtained at high elevations, and are known to be astute traders. The Mien women's costume is perhaps Laos's most exotic. Intricately embroidered pantaloons are worn with a coat and turban of indigo blue. The most striking feature is a woolly red boa, attached to the collar and running down the front of their coat. It is estimated that nearly half the population of Mien fled Laos after the communist victory.

The **Akha** are another of the highlands' stunning dressers. They believe that art is more appropriately displayed on one's body, as opposed to hanging it on walls. Catching a first glimpse of the Akha women's distinctive headgear – covered with rows of silver baubles and coins – is surely one of the highlights of many a Lao visit. Speakers of a Tibeto–Burman language, the Akha began migrating south from China's Yunnan province to escape the mayhem of the mid-nineteenth century Muslim Rebellion. This was followed by another exodus after the Chinese communist victory in 1949 and again during the Cultural Revolution. They now inhabit parts of Vietnam, Myanmar (Burma) and Thailand as well as Laos, where they are found mainly in Phongsali and

Louang Namtha provinces. Their villages are easily distinguished by the elaborate "spirit gate" leading into the village. This gate is hung with woven bamboo "stars" that block spirits as well as talismanic carvings of helicopters, aeroplanes and even grenades, as well as crude male and female effigies with exaggerated genitalia. The Akha are animists and, like the Hmong, rely on a village shaman and his rituals to help solve problems of health, fertility or protection against malevolent spirits. Chickens and pigs are sometimes sacrificed and chicken bones are utilized to divine the future. As with the Hmong and Mien, the Akha use opium to soothe the day's aches and pains, and some Akha also utilize massage to the same effect. The Akha raise dogs as pets as well as for food, but they do not eat their own pets. Dogs that will be slaughtered for their meat are bought or traded from another village. The Akha are fond of singing and often do so while on long walks to the fields or while working. Some songs are specially sung for fieldwork but love ballads are also popular. There is even a sort of "Akha blues": songs about poor Akha villagers struggling through life while surrounded by rich neighbours.

The **Lahu** inhabit areas of northwestern Laos, as well as Thailand and Burma. A branch of the Lahu tribe known as the Lahu Na, or Black Lahu, are known first and foremost for their hunting skills. Formerly they used crossbows but now manufacture their own muzzle-loading rifles which they use to hunt birds and rodents. Old American M1 carbines and Chinese-made Kalashnikov rifles are used to bring down larger game, and Lahu hunters are sometimes seen at the side of the road displaying a freshly bagged deer or boar for sale.

The environment

Laos is a land of pristine forests, formidable mountains and swift rivers. A landlocked state in the heart of tropical Southeast Asia, it covers a land area of nearly 237,000 square kilometres, a size comparable to that of England. Bordered by China to the north, Vietnam to the east, Cambodia to the south, Thailand to the west and Myanmar (Burma) to the northwest, Laos is dominated by rugged highlands cut by narrow river valleys and shares in two of Southeast Asia's most prominent geographical features: the Annamite Mountains and the Mekong River, with the Mekong picking up more than half of its water flow during its nearly two thousand-kilometre journey through Laos. With a heat and humidity typical of a tropical region, Laos's climate nourishes a natural wealth of wildlife that not only includes numerous rare or endangered species, but also continues to surprise the scientific world as new species of plant and animal life are discovered or rediscovered in the country's forests and rivers.

Early French explorers marvelled at the sheer beauty of Laos's landscape, as they dodged tigers and collected samples of strange and wonderful insects. Indeed, the country's former name, the Kingdom of a Million Elephants, boasts of these tropical riches. But Laos's natural wonders have been greatly diminished since the late nineteenth century – there are at most a few thousand elephants roaming the country's frontiers today, and the forest has shrunk by at least twenty percent during the past five decades alone. A recent push by the government, in conjunction with a handful of concerned international groups, towards **conservation** offers some hope that Laos's significant habitats and the wildlife populations found there will be spared the harsh realities all too common in a poor nation struggling to develop.

There is certainly much worth conserving: of the more than 1200 species of wildlife reviewed by the International Union for the Conservation of Nature in 1993, 247 have been identified as having regional or global significance, accounting for nearly forty percent of the mammals; twenty percent of the birds and reptiles; five percent of the fish; and well over fifty-five percent of the amphibians. If the impressive recent discoveries of new mammal species in the Nakai–Nam Theun biodiversity conservation area are anything to go on, future studies of Laos's little documented environment promises to yield further discoveries and rediscoveries, particularly in the areas of fish, reptiles, amphibians and plant life.

Climate and geography

Laos has a **tropical monsoon climate**, with a rainy season extending from May to October, a cool dry season from November to February and an at times excruciatingly hot dry season in March and April. Although the rainy season occurs at roughly the same time throughout the country, rainfall varies significantly from place to place, with the highest amounts – 3700mm – soaking the Bolaven Plateau in the far south, and considerably less falling in Mekong River cities such as Savannakhet (1440mm), Vientiane (1700mm) and Louang

Phabang (1360mm). Such high average rainfalls fail to reveal the fact that in some years precipitation is not enough in parts of the country, causing droughts which severely affect **rice** yields. The grain, as the cornerstone of the Lao diet, accounts for eighty percent of agricultural land.

Agriculture plays a significant role in Laos's economy as the vast majority of people in Laos live off the land. Besides rice, other crops include cardamom, coffee, corn, cotton, fruit, peanuts, soybeans, mung beans, sugarcane, sweet potatoes, tobacco and various vegetables. For the most part, farmers employ one of two cultivation systems when growing rice. In the lowlands, farmers generally practice the wet-field paddy system, while swidden cultivation (sometimes known as shifting or slash-and-burn agriculture) is primarily employed in the highlands. Large level areas along the Vientiane Plain, in Savannakhet and in Champasak are perhaps the areas best suited for extensive paddy rice cultivation in the country, and these places have not surprisingly emerged as the country's population centres.

Swidden cultivation techniques practised by the Lao Theung and Lao Soung date back thousands of years and vary from group to group, with some peoples living in permanent villages around which they rotate cultivation within a large swathe of forest, and others shifting their settlements from hill-side to hillside. Nearly all midland and upland groups rely on swidden rice cultivation. A debate over the practice rages among environmentalists, with some charging that the technique is highly destructive to the forest and others arguing that, when practised correctly in a sparsely populated environment, such as is found throughout many parts of Laos, swidden cultivation is sustainable and keeps the soil fertile and the forests in balance.

The Lao government, deciding that shifting agriculture is a major cause of deforestation, has committed itself to a policy which seeks to bring an end to swidden cultivation within the near future. As part of this policy, the government has begun a massive **resettlement** programme, which seeks to preserve valuable hardwoods for commercial use while protecting forest habitats and also aims to bring hill peoples closer to community resources such as hospitals and schools. The programme is bound to put increasing pressure on Laos's already limited amount of arable land – only four percent of Laos's total land area according to the United Nations Development Programme. While Laos's overall population density is nineteen people per square kilometre, the population density of cultivated cropland rises to 350 per square kilometre – a situation that could become critical given the country's steadily growing population. Thus, as the International Union for the Conservation of Nature puts it, it's clear that the future wealth of Laos is unlikely to be supported by agricultural activities.

Rivers and forests

With such a limited land base for agriculture, it's no surprise that **freshwater ecosystems** are of massive importance to Laos. The heart and soul of Laos's freshwater ecosystems is the **Mekong River**, the longest river in Southeast Asia, and, in terms of volume, the tenth largest in the world, carrying 475,000 million cubic metres to the sea each year. With the beginnings of its 4180-kilometre journey in a frozen stream high up in the Plateau of Tibet, the Mekong travels the entire length of Laos before slipping through Cambodia and fanning out into the "Nine Dragons" that constitute the river's delta in Vietnam. The Mekong is joined by fourteen major tributaries during the course of its 1993-kilometre journey through Laos. Nearly all the rivers and mountain streams in the country eventually find their way into the Mekong, as ninety percent of Laos drains into the river.

Rural life revolves around the Mekong River System, which encompasses everything from the myriad mountain streams to the flooded rice paddies to the river itself. It generates power, waters crops, provides a place to bathe and is an all-important source of fish. In most of lowland Laos, as well as in many parts of the highlands, fish and other aquatic animals provide more than seventy percent of the animal protein in people's diet. Nowhere in Laos is this more evident than in the country's southernmost tip, where every family fishes and every meal includes something from the Mother of Waters. It is in this region that the Mekong expands to attain its greatest width – fourteen kilometres at the height of the rainy season – and journeys through the country's best known **wetlands**: Si Phan Don and the Khone Falls. These wetlands are of regional importance, as a nesting ground for birds and a spawning ground for fish, and are home to the rare Irrawaddy dolphin, the "human fish" whose numbers are in a drastic state of decline (see p.309).

To know the Mekong, as *Mekong Currency* author Liesbeth Sluiter says, one must meet the **forests**, which possess an intimate relationship with the river and its tributaries. Guardians of Laos's water, forests soak up the rains of the monsoon, slowly releasing the water into streams and back into the air. Laos has one of the highest percentages of intact forest cover in the world, at more than forty percent. With natural, unmanaged vegetation covering more than eighty percent of the country, Laos contains a variety of forest types. The country is dominated by mixed **deciduous forests**, in which trees survive lengthy periods of minimal rainfall by shedding their leaves in order to conserve water. Tall, pale-barked dipterocarps, a group of tropical hardwoods prized for their timber, tower over these monsoon forests, ranging in height from ten to forty metres. Natural stands of teak, rosewood and mahogany were once common features of Laos's deciduous forests, though these much sought-after hardwoods, considered ideal material for building everything from furniture to the decks of tony yachts, have been substantially reduced in number. Hardly in short supply, **bamboo** thrives in Laos's monsoon climate and appears in more varieties in Laos than in any other country with the exception of two of Laos's neighbours, China and Thailand. Growing at astonishing rates during the rainy season, bamboo rules the understorey of the deciduous forests, surviving in soils too poor for many other types of vegetation and dominating secondary forests – those areas where a new generation of plants has grown up after forest has been stripped bare by swidden agriculture, rampant logging or the harsh excesses of chemical defoliants. Flexible bamboo is used by the Lao for making everything from houses to Laos's national musical instrument, the *khaen*, while bamboo shoots find their way into a variety of Lao dishes. Other, less common forest types in Laos include dry dipterocarp forests, noteworthy for their more open canopies and found along the arid plateaus of southern Laos, rare old growth pine forests and semi-evergreen and hill evergreen forests, the latter soaked by frequent rainfall and possessing moss-covered forest floors and dense undergrowth.

Conservation zones and wetlands

In the early 1990s, the government of Laos established a system of **National Biodiversity Conservation Areas** throughout the country, which put under protection more than twelve percent of the country's total land area, one of the highest ratios in the world. There are now nearly two dozen of these NBCAs around the country, home to a stunning variety of endangered animals and encompassing a wide range of habitats and landscapes from the mixed deciduous forests and dry sandstone bluffs found along the Thai border in Champasak province to the wet forests and savannah grasslands of the Nakai Plateau and the limestone mountains of Khammouane.

Even as new areas are under consideration for inclusion in the programme, the existing system is still being fine-tuned, with the International Union for the Conservation of Nature drafting regulations for the management of the protected areas that aims to translate the broad policies governing the NBCAs into a workable system. Logging, runaway swidden agriculture and poaching are serious problems in some protected areas, while one, the Nakai–Nam Theun somewhat ironically finds itself the proposed site of a massive dam project. Thus, the term "conservation zone" may appear a misnomer at first, but under the existing system, the NBCAs are divided into zones for production, protection and conservation. Therefore hydropower projects, logging or the collection of non-timber forest products by villagers are not out of the question. While some parts of the conservation areas are accessible and open for tourism, such as the caves of the Khammouane Limestone NBCA near Thakhek, most are well-off the beaten track. A survey of some of the more interesting areas follows.

Southern Laos

Flush against the Vietnam border in Khammouane and Bolikhamxai provinces and to the south of Lak Xao, the **Nakai–Nam Theun** is without question one of the world's more important biodiversity areas. Indeed, three of the last five large mammals to be discovered or rediscovered worldwide inhabit this area. A lost world of evergreen forests, savannah grasslands and jagged, mist-shrouded peaks, the Nakai–Nam Theun is one of the richest wildlife and forest areas remaining in Southeast Asia. It is best known for the recent discovery of the saola, a large mammal resembling a shaggy brown and white deer with spindly horns, the giant-antlered muntjak and the black muntjack as well as the rediscovery of the Indochinese warty pig, which had been described a century ago – by a Jesuit priest in Shanghai who purchased a few skulls of the creature from southern Vietnam in 1892 – before being lost to science. Once a royal hunting reserve, this area is now the largest single protected area in Laos, extending over 3700 square kilometres, with an elevation ranging from 500m on the Nakai Plateau to mountain peaks of well over 2000m, and is home to at least eleven globally threatened large mammal species. Its forests provide habitat for most of the mainland Southeast Asia fauna, including such rare animals as tiger, lesser slow loris, clouded leopard – a small tree-dwelling cat which hunts birds and monkeys by night – Asiatic black bear and elephant, whose numbers in this area have been reduced by poachers to an estimated three hundred. More than four hundred bird species, among them the endangered white-winged duck, crested argus, beautiful nuthatch and greater spotted eagle, have been recorded here, the highest diversity of any site surveyed in Laos. The area is also noteworthy for its forests, composed of pristine stands of wet and dry evergreen, cypress forest, old growth pine, found only in parts of Southeast Asia, and riverside forest – all of which are regionally threatened habitats. Nakai–Nam Theun is also treasured for its four river systems which have figured in national development plans, specifically the recently completed Theun–Hin Boun Dam, west of the NBCA, and the massive Nam Theun II, still in the pipeline, the entire catchment of which lies within the protected area.

Further south, spectacular waterfalls plunge from soaring escarpments cloaked with pristine evergreen forests in **Dong Houa Xao**, a 910-square-kilometre zone to the east of Pakxe and the south of Pakxong, which encompasses a flat, upland area along the Bolaven – of immense floral and faunal interest – and the lowlands along the Plateau's southern flank. With its habitat further diversified by the presence of sandstone flats and wetlands, Dong Houa Xao is home to nearly 250 species of birds, including the rare Siamese fireback, green peafowl and red-collared woodpecker as well as primates, including the endangered douc langur and gibbons, sun bear and the world's largest species of wild cattle, the gaur, once a prized trophy among big game hunters during colonial times.

Shadowing the Laos–Cambodia border and spanning the southern stretches of Attapu and Champasak provinces, the **Xe Pian** is for the most part covered by dense semi-evergreen forest, interspersed with tracts of dry dipterocarp forest. Wetlands and riverine systems are also an important feature of the Xe Pian, which takes its name from the snaking Xe Pian River that bisects the reserve's eastern and southern flatlands. As home to eight threatened bird species, the protected area is of global significance for wildlife conservation and supports numerous lowland bird species as well as a wealth of migrants. Woolly-necked storks and nesting sarus cranes are both thought to inhabit the wetlands of the Xe Pian. A large number of gibbons fill the central forests of the Xe Pian with their unmistakable hooting, and villagers have reported seeing kouprey, the elusive grey forest ox whose global population is thought to number no more than three hundred, hog deer and Eld's deer, as well as wild water buffalo and rhinoceros. Rhino horns are prized by the Lao, who believe them to possess magical properties, and the Chinese, who consider them a useful ingredient in aphrodisiacs. Black bears, sun bears, peacocks, leopards and otters, hunted for their skins which are sold to Cambodians, have also been spotted in the area, as have two rare river creatures: the Irrawaddy dolphin, which is said to still pay seasonal visits to the Xe Pian, and the Siamese crocodile, already extinct in most Southeast Asian rivers.

Just west of the Xe Pian lie two **wetlands** of regional significance, Si Phan Don and the Khone Falls. Here, the Mekong concludes its journey through Laos, swirling past the countless outcroppings of soil and rocks that constitute the "Four Thousand Islands" of the region's name. Considered the richest fishing grounds in Laos, Si Phan Don possesses large tracts of seasonally flooded forest, along the banks of the Mekong and on the dots of land in between, which constitute a crucial spawning ground for the unknown number of fish species inhabiting this portion of the river. At the southern tip of Si Phan Don – and the entire country for that matter – lie the Khone Falls, an eight-kilometre wide series of channels composed of waterfalls and rapids flowing between rocky islands. The falls, which begin 5km north of the Cambodian border, are a vital passageway for the Mekong's many species of migratory fish.

The seasonally flooded islands here are also an important sanctuary for **birds** and represent one of the last nesting areas of the river tern, greater thick-knees and river lapwing, all of which appear as the water level begins to recede in January. The trees of the wetlands' flooded forests also provide perches for thick-billed pigeons, pied hornbills and green imperial pigeons and offer a welcome spot for blue-tailed bee-eaters to rest after one of their aerial insect chases. The area is also one of the rare places in Southeast Asia visited by red-headed and white-rumped vultures, whose numbers are on the decline owing to hunting and a shortage of food, caused partly by the fact that Laos now has fewer tigers, whose leftovers make a favourite vulture snack. Other rare or endangered birds making the rounds in the area are the grey-headed fish eagle, the woolly-necked stork and the giant ibis.

Beneath the surface, Laos's lower Mekong area possesses a stunning array of **fish species**, including giant golden carp, featherbacks, eels and fresh-water rays that grow well over a metre in length, fish that climb the Khone Falls by sucking their way up the rocks with their lips and the mysterious *ba leum,* a fish weighing 200kg that fishermen attempt to snare with the entrails of dogs attached to a hook at the end of a thirty-metre length of rope. But the jewel of the Mekong is without a doubt the blunt-nosed Irrawaddy dolphin, a handful of which still frolic in the waters between Laos and Cambodia.

Central and northern Laos

East of Ang Nam Ngum and less than two hours' drive from Vientiane, centrally located **Phou Khao Khouai** is perhaps the most accessible of the conservation zones and as such must balance its role as a recreational site for Vientiane residents intent on picnicking near its waterfalls and as a preserve for endangered species such as tiger, Asiatic black bear and green peafowl. In this often steep upland area large tracts of evergreen forests dominate the valleys and hillsides, while coniferous and scrub forests flourish in the thin soils masking sandstone bedrock formations at higher elevation.

In the far northern corner of northeastern Houa Phan province, elephants roam the bamboo forests of **Nam Et** protected area, more than half of which lies 1000m above sea level. Nam Et has been severely affected by shifting cultivation which has left the area with relatively little dense forest. As such it may find itself reduced in size in the near future, but nonetheless remains an important refuge for bears, endangered cats, such as the clouded leopard and tiger, wild cattle, and dhole, the rare, reddish wild dogs that hunt in packs. To the southwest of Nam Et, **Phou Loei**, occupying more than 1400 square kilometres in Louang Phabang and Houa Phan provinces, is one of the most important wildlife and evergreen forest conservation areas in northern Laos. Composed of rugged highlands, most of which are well over 1000m, and cut by the Nam Khan and Nam Xuang rivers, Phou Loei has a significant amount of bamboo forests and grasslands resulting from swidden cultivation – still the primary form of agriculture among villagers living in the area. Hunting and fishing with poison present further challenges to managing this NBCA, whose wildlife includes silver pheasants, banteng, hog deer, bears and cats, as do the creation of new settlements in farflung areas noted for their pristine forests.

Environmental issues

In its rush to develop by capitalizing on key natural resources, primarily its wetlands and forests, Laos must come to terms with a number of critical, often interrelated, **environmental issues**. Perhaps the greatest source of concern for conservationists is Laos's many **hydroelectric dam** projects. It is no secret that dams have the potential to cause a serious negative impact on the environment, yet for Laos, the Mekong and its tributaries, with an estimated hydroelectric potential of more than 18,000 megawatts – more than half the river's total estimated potential – represent an alluring means for generating much-needed foreign exchange. Dams, in the view of the International Union for the Conservation of Nature, are not necessarily incompatible with conservation goals; instead, they represent a critical challenge to the integration of conservation and development objectives. No project better illustrates this than the proposed $1.2 billion, 600 megawatt Nam Theun II dam, which, if built, will directly affect the Nakai–Nam Theun conservation zone, an area along the Laos–Vietnam border that has emerged as a biodiversity hotspot of global significance.

Laos's potential for hydropower development is inextricably linked to its forests, which protect the catchments that provide the water that ultimately generate the energy. Although Laos boasts a very high proportion of forest cover, **deforestation** is a major problem, with the country's forest cover having steadily declined over the past five decades from an estimated seventy percent at the time of the French withdrawal from Indochina to roughly forty percent today. Laos's forests are threatened by the clearing of lowland forest for permanent agriculture, the use of chemical defoliants during the Second Indochina War, infrastructure development, shifting agriculture, new settlements and logging, which continues at a steady pace despite the institution of a nationwide logging ban in 1991 by the Vientiane government. Large companies from Asian countries continue to win logging concessions from the government. An estimate by Laos's ministry of science and technology suggests that in the early 1990s, more than one third of the government's foreign currency revenues came from the sale of timber.

According to an environmental impact report, not only does the government need to improve the effectiveness of plantation forestry and reforestation programmes currently underway, but Vientiane also needs to improve its overall forest management and develop and enforce a set of regulations governing logging, a difficult task given the government's limited resources and the vast tracts of forest spread through the country. Simply designating biodiversity conservation zones isn't enough to preserve the country's natural wealth. One positive development occurred in 1995, when the governor of Attapu and six other officials from the southeastern province were convicted of timber smuggling in a case illustrating that the Vientiane government is prepared to take action to protect its natural resources. Nonetheless, the case also demonstrates that some of the very people who should be protecting this natural resource are abusing their power by exploiting the forests for their personal gain.

Deforestation places increasing pressure on Laos's rural population, who rely on the forest for food, firewood, construction materials, herbs, medicine and a host of other things. The declining forests also threaten Laos's wildlife, which is already struggling to survive other intense pressures, including **hunting and the wildlife trade**. Despite the country's relatively low human population density, the level of hunting has increased in recent decades, the result of the increased availability of guns and explosives, improved access to previously remote areas via newly cut logging roads and the exorbitant prices that rare and endangered species fetch on international markets. Hunting and the gathering of forest products is also on the rise, given increased demand for consumer goods. While much of the wildlife trade is for local food consumption and use in traditional medicine, large quantities of wildlife and wildlife products are sold to Thailand, Vietnam and China. Thus, while posters and pamphlets warning villagers against hunting vulnerable species are visible in government offices and noodle shops throughout the country, elephant ivory, bear paws, pangolin scales, turtle shells, rare types of orchids, tiger parts and bird bills – all highly valued items in this cross-border trade – continue to find their way onto restaurant tables in Hanoi and into traditional medicines in Bangkok and Hong Kong.

River life is also at risk. Dams and other high-impact development projects threaten the sustainability of the **fisheries** of Laos's wetlands at the same time that these are being adversely affected by modern fishing techniques, overfishing and the use of destructive techniques involving poison and explosives. A grassroots fisheries conservation effort in Si Phan Don offers a glimmer of hope for Champasak province's wetlands and for sustainable development all over Laos. The programme encourages villages to set aside conservation zones and establish laws to regulate how, when and where fish can be caught, a step towards protecting one of the world's most ecologically diverse river systems which participating fishermen claim is already improving fish catches in the river. While the Canadian biologist spearheading the project says that positive results won't be measurable for years and that there are many natural and human factors, such as dams, pollution and floods, beyond the villagers' control, the programme, a mixture of cooperation, education and reliance upon local knowledge of the land and water, shows promise.

While it is unclear if such a grassroots initiative, were it to be embraced by the millions of rural people whose daily survival depends on the country's forests and rivers, could be an effective guard against large-scale degradation of Laos's environment, the government of Laos, with precious few resources to squander in its quest for development, could do worse than follow its lead. The danger for Laos, according to the International Union for the Conservation of Nature, is allowing excessive exploitation of its natural resource base before its human resources are developed through better education and the country's economic base diversified. Yet if Laos acts now and works towards using its natural resources in a sustainable manner, it still has a chance to avoid the levels of environmental degradation and deforestation found in many of its neighbours.

Literature and myths

Classical Lao literature has its roots in the *jataka* tales, a collection of 547 stories about the Buddha's previous lives. The tales recount the events and experiences which led to his incarnation as Siddhartha Gautama, the prince who sought the meaning of life and attained enlightenment. Penned in India and Sri Lanka, they spread with Buddhism to Southeast Asia.

Of more direct impact on Lao literature were an additional fifty tales that employed the same basic theme as the *jataka*. Known as the **panyasa jataka**, these were perhaps composed by the Mon and abridged by the Tai Yuan of Lan Na, a kingdom centred around Chiang Mai in what is now northern Thailand. Contacts between Chiang Mai and Louang Phabang resulted in the *panyasa jataka* arriving in Laos where the stories were modified further and expanded upon. Eventually the Lao versions came to differ significantly from the Tai Yuan versions, in that the former deviated from strict religious themes and became more entertaining, even to the point of having some sexual content. Two types of story emerged: prose and poetic. Prose stories contained much Pali, the language of the Theravada Buddhist scriptures, and were written in a script called *phasa tham*, or Dharma language. These would have only been comprehensible to monks who had studied the language. Much more popular with lay people were the poetic stories. These were written using the Lao script and contained mostly Lao vocabulary. As Lao is a tonal language, these poems did not rhyme as poetry composed in English sometimes does. Instead, tones and alliteration were used to produce a rhythm. Both types of stories were recorded by writing on the fronds of a certain kind of palm with a stylus, and some of the longer versions made use of hundreds of palm leaves. These surprisingly durable palm-leaf manuscripts were kept in a special library in the monastery grounds or sometimes in private homes. Occasionally, the stories were copied anew, but there was no pressure on the scrivener, usually a monk, to remain true to the original. The result was literally hundreds of versions and variations of these stories that not only taught values but also contained a wealth of information about traditional Lao society. During certain festivals, villagers would gather at the local monastery or in a private home to hear the stories read aloud and in this way some favourites eventually emerged. The **Sang Sin Sai** in particular is felt by many Lao to be the pinnacle of Lao literature. As with all of these stories, the plot takes a back seat to the poetry itself and the author is obscure. Attributed to "Pangkham", the story is almost certainly the product of many authors and editors. Today, with the rapid spread of electrical power to all parts of Laos, the novelty of television has meant that the reading of the old stories is not quite the event that it once was. Still, the fact that most ethnic Lao men spend some time in the monastery as a monk or novice ensures that the stories are in no immediate danger of being forgotten.

Of the Indian literature to become established in Southeast Asia, the Hindu **Ramayana** is by far the best known. This epic poem, with its host of vivid characters possessing comic-book hero attributes, arrived in Southeast Asia during its "Indianization" at the hands of Hindu traders. In the original, Hanuman, the King of the Monkeys, assists the god Rama in rescuing his wife Sita from the many-headed, multi-armed demon Ravana. Once the *Ramayana* became established in Southeast Asia, however, it didn't take long for local variations to emerge. The inhabitants of Java, Bali, Burma, Cambodia and Thailand all composed their own distinct versions and eventually the story spread from coastal areas into the Indochinese hinterland. Although a version of the poem was well known to the Khmer who once inhabited what is now southern Laos, the *Ramayana*'s introduction to the ethnic Lao came much later via Siam. Suitably modified to suit Lao tastes, the Lao version, known as **Pha Lak Pha Lam**, became a favourite of the Lao court. This popularity is reflected in depictions of the *Ramayana* in murals and reliefs found at Buddhist monasteries, especially those that were patronized by the monarchy. French colonization brought scholars, some of whom had studied the Khmer version of the poem. The French, perhaps because they were already familiar with it, tended to overemphasize the *Ramayana*'s significance to Lao literature, proclaiming it Laos's most important work. Later, Indian scholars, eager to aggrandize the influence of Indian culture in a country they considered an outpost of "Greater India", echoed French opinions. In fact, the *Ramayana* was an elitist indulgence that was never popular at the village level.

Much more popular was a tradition of oral folk tales that were eventually transcribed as both poetry and prose. Known as **Xiang Miang**, the name of the central character, the stories seem to be almost the opposite of the *jataka*-style morality tales. Xiang Miang is a lazy but clever trickster who enjoys outwitting authority figures, especially the king. In a typical exploit he covets the king's prized cat and so decides to kidnap it. Once he has the cat safely home, Xiang Miang teaches it to shun the fresh fish it is accustomed to by beating the cat every time it nears a fish placed on the floor. The cat soon learns to eat rice and when the king arrives to claim his cat, Xiang Miang "proves" it doesn't belong to the king by letting the cat choose between a plate of rice and plate of fish. Knowing that going near the fish will bring on a beating, the cat chooses the rice and the king goes home empty handed.

Modern Lao literature began in the 1940s when Lao writers began experimenting with Western-style novels and short stories. The first Lao novel, *Phaphutthahup Saksit* (*The Sacred Buddha Image*), was a detective story with a half-French, half-Lao protagonist. When Laos became divided after the French defeat, Lao literature split into two camps: writers under the Royal Lao Government continued to produce works in traditional Lao, Western and Thai styles, while in the Pathet Lao camp, works imitating Soviet literature were churned out. After the revolution, those writers who had been published under the old regime either fled or were "re-educated". One of the few to make the transition was Outhine Bounyavong, who survived the change in government by quickly adapting his style to meet the communists' demands. Another noted writer to come onto the scene since the revolution is Bounthanong Somsaiphon, who is known for his novels and short stories. One of his stories, *Kaduk Amerikan* (*American Bones*), concerns a man's conflicting emotions about the arrival of American "bone hunters" – teams trying to recover the remains of American soldiers missing in action in Laos.

The present climate for Lao writers living in Laos has been described as "tricky". Laos is still rather **restrictive** in what it will allow to be published, but a few Lao writers manage to make social commentary without the government's approval by publishing in Thailand in the Thai language.

Books

As Laos is one of the least-known countries in Southeast Asia, it should be no surprise to find that books about it are hard to come by, to say nothing of quality works on the country. With the demand very limited, you're likely to have more luck searching for many of the titles listed below at an online bookstore such as *www.amazon.com* or *www.powells.com* than you would wandering the aisles of your local bookshop. You may find that some books will need to be specially ordered, even at online stores, while others, such as those published by White Lotus, will be easier to find, and sometimes cheaper, to find at bookshops in Bangkok or Vientiane. The abbreviation o/p, which appears after some of the titles below, means "out of print". Titles marked ⊡ are particularly recommended.

Culture, society and environment

Tom Butcher and Dawn Ellis *Laos* (Pallas Athene). A rambling wrap-up of the country's customs, religion and history. At its best when using Lao legends and customs as a way into understanding the country and its people.

Sucheng Chan (ed) *Hmong Means Free* (Temple University Press). Fascinating personal narratives by three generations of Hmong refugees from five different families, which describe their lives as farmers on the hilltops of Laos, as refugees in the camps of Thailand and as immigrants in the United States.

⊡ **Grant Evans** *The Politics of Ritual and Remembrance: Laos Since 1975* (University of Hawaii Press). A provocative collection of anthropological essays focusing on the rituals and social structures of Laos yesterday and today and the attempts by the post-1975 government to reinvent "Laos".

⊡ **Anne Fadiman** *The Spirit Catches You and You Fall Down: A Hmong Child, Her American Doctors, and the Collision of Two Cultures* (Noonday Press). An excellent exploration of the sad, absorbing tale of Lia Lee, a severely epileptic child, born to a family of Hmong refugees living in California who clash with their daughter's Western doctors over how to treat the child's condition.

Betty Gosling *Old Luang Prabang* (Oxford University Press). A description of the history, geography and culture of the former royal capital which explores the relationship between royalty, mythology, religion and ritual.

Stephen Mansfield *Culture Shock! Laos* (Times Books International, Singapore). A cultural starter kit detailing how to avoid such faux pas as touching your spouse in public, pointing your foot at someone and eating your sticky rice with chopsticks. A helpful introduction if you're off to work in Laos and interesting even if you're only planning an extended visit.

Patricia Cheesman Naenna *Costume and Culture: Vanishing Textiles of Some of the Tai Groups in Lao PDR* (published by the author). A breakdown of the myriad textiles to be found in Laos including detailed descriptions of Lao weaving and dyeing techniques. The text is a bit academic, but colourful photographs make it of interest to the casual reader.

Mayoury Ngaosyvathn *Lao Women: Yesterday and Today* (Lao State Publishing Enterprise, Vientiane). A pioneering study about women in Laos that examines the status of women with regard to family, religion and society. While dissecting Lao women's portrayal in myths, legends and court chronicles, this insightful case also assesses the obstacles preventing women from becoming equal partners in socialist Laos.

Henri Parmentier *L'Art du Laos* (o/p). An excellent source, if it can be tracked down, of rare photographs of Lao temple architecture and art published by the Ecole Française d'Extrême-Orient in the early 1950s. The text, in French,

should be taken with a grain of salt, however, given the overly condescending tone of the author.

Phia Sing et al, *Traditional Recipes of Laos* (Prospect Books). Not only is this one of the rare books explaining how to prepare Lao cuisine, it's the only book containing the recipes of the former royal chef and master of ceremonies of Louang Phabang.

Liesbeth Sluiter *The Mekong Currency* (International Books). An earthy account of green issues along the Mekong corridor, in Laos, Cambodia and Thailand, Sluiter's book does an excellent job of presenting environmental concerns from the perspective of the fishers and farmers whose livelihoods are sustained by the Mekong and its tributaries.

Travellers' accounts

★ **Marthe Bassenne** *In Laos and Siam* (White Lotus, Bangkok). The evocative account of a French expatriate woman's 1909 journey up the Mekong River to Louang Phabang.

Louis Delaporte *A Pictorial Journey on the Old Mekong* (White Lotus, Bangkok). Volume three of the Mekong Exploration Commission's report is devoted to the exquisite illustrations of the artist who accompanied French explorers Francis Garnier and Doudart de Lagrée during their 1866–68 expedition.

Francis Garnier *Travels in Cambodia and Part of Laos* (White Lotus, Bangkok). The English translation of the first volume of the report by France's Mekong Exploration Commission, which set out from Saigon to find a backdoor route to China via the Mekong, details the

group's travels from Cambodia to Louang Phabang.

Francis Garnier *Further Travels in Laos and in Yunnan* (White Lotus, Bangkok). Volume two of the Mekong Exploration Commission's report focuses on the weary explorers' travels in Upper Laos and Yunnan, with entries on a Muslim uprising in China and Garnier's explorations of alternative trade routes.

★ **F.J. Harmand** *Laos and the Hilltribes of Indochina* (White Lotus, Bangkok). A cultural barbarian by today's standards, the French explorer's report on his late-nineteenth-century journey through southern Laos nevertheless is a valuable record of funerary and religious customs of the tribal highland minorities of the Bolaven Plateau. The account, which also focuses on his encounters with the Phu Tai people of the Savannakhet region, is liberally sprinkled with amusing and insightful anecdotes from his travels while he was researching the region's natural history and searching for an overland route from Champasak to Hué.

Harry Hervey *King Cobra: An Autobiography of Travel in French Indo-China* (o/p). An American writer's account of his journey from Saigon to Vientiane, where he mingles with French expatriates and Lao royalty. Although his historical facts are often quite askew, Hervey, who sought to unlock the mysteries of the Angkorian empire, is a rare traveller for the early twentieth century, offering open-minded observations recorded in lush, detailed prose.

 Christopher Kremmer *Stalking the Elephant Kings: In Search of Laos* (University of Hawaii Press). It's worth struggling through the at times self-righteous attitude of this book, which tracks the journalist's journey into remote Laos in search of the monarch who went missing shortly after the communists assumed power in 1975, as it's the only work to seriously examine the fate of the royal family.

Henri Mouhot *Travels in Siam, Cambodia, and Laos* (White Lotus, Bangkok). The account of the final journey of the legendary "discoverer of Angkor Wat", filled with his characteristically blunt observations of the people of Laos, from the tobacco-hungry infants to the uncouth court officials that he encountered on his journey to Upper Laos which resulted in his death outside Louang Phabang.

History

Nina S. Adams and Alfred W. McCoy (eds) *Laos: War and Revolution* (o/p). A collection of political speeches, historical essays on subjects from Air America to the ancient Thai–Vietnamese struggle over the country, interviews with Lao politicians and refugees, and essays by French journalists and Vietnamese soldiers, this gem of a book, albeit a dated one that comes from the academic leftist point of view, arose out of the desire of the Committee of Concerned Asian Scholars to remedy the lack of information regarding Laos available during the United States' "bitter war against the people of Laos".

Area Handbook Series *Laos: a country study* (Federal Research Division, Washington DC). One in a continuing series of books prepared by the Federal Research Division of the United States Library of Congress, this comprehensive (though somewhat outdated) study provides in-depth background and analysis of Laos's economic, social and political institutions, as well as the cultural and historical factors shaping them. Also available online.

Kennon Breazeale and Snit Smuckarn *A Culture in Search of Survival: The Phuan of Thailand and Laos* (Yale University Press, New Haven). An impressive history tracing the migrations and forced resettlements during the nineteenth century of the Phuan people of Xiang Khouang.

 Jane Hamilton-Merritt *Tragic Mountains: the Hmong, the Americans, and the Secret Wars for Laos, 1942–1992* (Indiana University Press). This impressive account of the Hmong written by Hamilton-Merritt, a Pulitzer Prize-nominated correspondent during the Second Indochina War, ranges from the personal to the political as it follows the Hmong from the battlefields to life after the war.

Victor T. King *Explorers of Southeast Asia: Six Lives* (Oxford University Press). Six different authors examine the journeys of various nineteenth-century European explorers, including Frenchmen Henri Mouhot and Francis Garnier.

⭐ **Alfred W. McCoy** *The Politics of Heroin: CIA Complicity in the Global Drug Trade* (Lawrence Hill Books). Laos, not surprisingly, figures prominently in this exhaustively researched, revised and expanded version of McCoy's landmark *The Politics of Heroin in Southeast Asia*.

Mayoury Ngaosyvathn and Pheuiphanh Ngaosyvathn *Paths of Conflagration: Fifty Years of Diplomacy and Warfare (1778–1828)* (Ithaca). A re-examination of the relationship between Laos and Thailand which draws on a wealth of new source material in examining Chao Anou, the Lao king who rebelled against Siamese suzerainty during the early nineteenth century.

⭐ **Christopher Robbins** *The Ravens: Pilots of the Secret War of Laos* (o/p). Although difficult to find, this book on America's secret war is well worth reading. Many of the details of America's secretive Laos operations during the Second Indochina War didn't come out until this gripping work by Robbins, a British journalist, was published in 1987. Based on interviews with American pilots who fought in Laos, this hard-to-find book is well worth tracking down.

⭐ **Stan Sesser** *The Lands of Charm and Cruelty: Travels in Southeast Asia* (Picador/Vintage Departures). Among the five insightful essays in this superb book is a 53-page segment on Laos during the late 1980s and early 1990s. In presenting a well-observed account of the country as it struggles to rebuild itself after the war, Sesser mixes reflections on Laos's recent history with insights into the country's political leadership, culture and economic reforms. The book builds on articles Stesser originally wrote for *The New Yorker*.

⭐ **Martin Stuart-Fox** *A History of Laos* (Cambridge University Press). Written by an Australian scholar who covered the Second Indochina War as a foreign correspondent, this work represents the best available overview of Laos's history, although it's extremely light on the country's early history.

Martin Stuart-Fox *The Lao Kingdom of Lane Xang: Rise and Decline* (White Lotus, Bangkok). For a thorough account of pre-colonial history, this somewhat muddled account digs up information about the country's early years hard to find elsewhere and fills out portraits of the Lane Xang rulers who get short shrift in *A History of Laos*.

Martin Stuart-Fox *Buddhist Kingdom Marxist State* (White Lotus, Bangkok). Fox outlines the history and politics of modern Laos from French rule to the present, with particular emphasis on the Lao PDR during the Pathet Lao's first two decades in power.

Martin Stuart-Fox and Mary Kooyman *Historical Dictionary of Laos* (Scarecrow Press). A encyclopedia of key people and events in the history of Laos which, though expensive and difficult to find, is worthwhile for the many insightful nuggets of information tracked down by the authors, and the extensive bibliography.

John Tenhula *Voices from Southeast Asia: The Refugee Experience in the*

United States (Holmes & Meier). A moving collection of oral histories, told through narrative, dialogue and poetry, of Indochinese refugees, many of whom have relocated to the United States.

★ **Roger Warner** *Shooting at the Moon: The Story of America's Clandestine War in Laos* (Steerforth Press). Winner of the Overseas Press Club's award for the best book on foreign affairs, Warner's thoroughly researched and crisply written account of American involvement reads like an adventure novel. Letting tragic events speak for themselves, Warner brings to life the key players and significant events as he follows the secret war from its origins at the end of World War II to the American withdrawal from Indochina. (An earlier version of this book was published as *Back Fire* by Simon & Schuster.)

Language

Language

Language

L ao belongs to the Tai family of languages, which includes Thai; Shan (Tai Yai), spoken in Myanmar (Burma); Phuan, spoken in Laos and parts of Thailand; and Tai Leu, spoken by the Dai minority of southern China's Yunnan province. Besides Lao and its "cousin" languages, such as Tai Leu and Phuan, sundry other languages are spoken within the borders of Laos. These include tongues belonging to the Mon–Khmer and Tibeto–Burman families of languages which are spoken by upland tribal peoples, as well as Vietnamese and Chinese spoken by immigrants from Laos's neighbouring countries.

French was once the second language of the educated and elite classes, but it has fallen out of favour with the younger generation who are convinced that learning English is the key to obtaining a high-paying job. Still, fluent French-speakers may be found among the over-fifties, usually an indication that they were once functionaries of the old royal regime. During the 1980s, Lao students were sent to study abroad in fellow Soviet-block countries such as Poland, East Germany and Cuba, and hence it is sometimes possible to find a Polish-, German- or Spanish-speaking Lao, though they will be the first to admit that their language ability has become rusty with years of disuse. Since economic liberalization came into effect, **English** has become the preferred foreign tongue, and travellers will find that getting around in urban areas can be done using basic English. Once out in the countryside, however, the situation changes, and visitors will have to make an effort to learn some Lao phrases to get by. Travellers shouldn't feel too put out if they consider that urban Lao sometimes experience similar problems when travelling in rural areas.

One of the greatest obstacles to building a nation that successive Lao governments have had to deal with is language. While Lao as it is spoken in Vientiane has official language status, there are pockets of Laos where no dialect of Lao, much less the Vientiane version, will be heard. With little money or resources to post qualified teachers to isolated villages, **Vientiane Lao** is simply not being learned in these areas. At present, the Lao government is experimenting with the somewhat drastic step of relocating tribal children to lowland towns where they live in huts in the school grounds and, theoretically, are exposed to language and lifestyles that will help them assimilate and become more "Lao". In the meantime, many of the non-Lao-speaking ethnic groups in rural areas will continue to live as they always have done, speaking their own tongue amongst themselves while maintaining a handful of Lao phrases to conduct trade or other dealings with the lowland Lao.

To fully understand the contemporary state of the Lao language in urban areas, it is necessary to look at how it relates to **Thai**, to which it is closely linked. The spoken Thai of Bangkok and the spoken Lao of Vientiane are very similar, as akin as Spanish is to Portuguese. As vassals of the Thai, the Lao absorbed a fair amount of Thai vocabulary, mainly through the Buddhist monkhood and channels between the royal courts. This shared vocabulary was, for the most part, taken from **Pali**, in which the scriptures of Theravada

Buddhism were written. During the Lao civil war, Thailand sided with the Lao royalists. The communist victory and death of the Lao monarchy saw the end of flowery court language, but although the communist government temporarily suppressed Lao Buddhism, no direct attacks on Pali-derived vocabulary were mounted. Some aspects of everyday spoken and written Lao were targeted, however. In an effort to erase class divisions, the communist government discouraged the use of personal pronouns that flaunted status or begged servitude. A typical banned pronoun was "*doi kha noi*", which translates into English as "I" but which literally means "I, small slave". Such a personal pronoun would have been used in the old days by a commoner speaking to a superior of noble rank.

After the revolution the Lao government also made official changes to the **Lao alphabet** in order to simplify it, as well as purge it of aspects that the communists felt were too similar to Thai. The Lao government's policies had, for a time anyway, the desired effect of levelling class divisions, and the simplified alphabet has no doubt made teaching the illiterate to read an easier task. However, the changes and simplifications have had an unforeseen effect on the Lao language. What the Lao government didn't anticipate was the growing sophistication of the **Thai media** and subsequent boom in popularity of Thai films, television and popular music in Laos. Every day, tens of thousands of Lao tune in to receive a dose of Thai, with its stratified personal pronouns and honorifics. Even broadcasts of the Thai royal language, almost identical to the extinct Lao royal language, can be heard daily on the Thai television news. These factors have conspired to give the Lao something of an inferiority complex about their own language, and they often compare it unfavourably to Thai by saying that Thai sounds more "beautiful" and "polite" than Lao.

Visitors who travel between Laos and Thailand may notice the similarity in the scripts of the two countries. This is because the Lao script was actually based on an early version of written Thai. During colonial times, the French considered replacing the **Lao script** with an alphabet similar to *quoc ngu*, the Romanized script now used to write Vietnamese. The project was never implemented, as French influence was waning at the time, but devising the system presented quite a challenge. The Lao language contains sounds that don't exist in French, or any other Western European language for that matter, making transliteration an inexact exercise at best.

Imperfect as it was, the fledgling **French transliteration system** has had some staying power. The Lao seem comfortable with the French system, and many educated Lao prefer to have their names transliterated in the French manner, which serves to differentiate them from the Thai, who use a different system. **Official maps of Laos** produced by the Lao government use a modified form of the old French system. This can create problems for English speakers who assume that the system was created for them. But if you keep in mind, for example, that the Lao "ou" rhymes with the French "vous" not the English "noun" – reading Lao place names shouldn't be a problem. The transliteration of place names in this book follows the modified French system used by the Lao National Geographic Service. For the transliteration of Lao words in the following section, a simplified version of the same system is used. This is not to say that travellers will find exactly the system in use throughout Laos: the Lao are quite cavalier when it comes to **consistency** in transliteration. In Vientiane, for instance, it is possible to see the Arch of Victory monument transliterated as "Patouxai", "Patousai", "Patuxai" and "Patusai".

Key to pronunciation

Consonants

b as in "big"	sometimes appears at the beginning of a word)
d as in "dog"	
f as in "fun"	ny as in the Russian "nyet"
h as in "hello"	p as in "speak" (unaspirated)
j (or CH) as in "jar"	ph as the P in "pill"
k as in "skin" (unaspirated)	s (or X) as in "same"
kh as the K in "kiss"	t as in "stop" (unaspirated)
l as in "luck"	th as the T in "tin"
m as in "more"	w (or V) as in "wish"
n as in "now"	y as in "yes"
ng as in "singer" (this combination	

Vowels

a as the AH in "autobahn"	i as in "mimi"
ae as the A in "cat"	ia as in "India"
ai as in "Thai"	o as in "flow"
aw as in "jaw"	oe as in "Goethe"
ao as in "Lao"	u (or OU) as the OU in "you"
e as in "pen"	ua (or OUA) as the UA in "truant"
eu as in French "fleur"	

Tones and markers

Lao is a **tonal language**, which means that the tone a speaker gives to a word will determine its meaning. While the tone system may make some visitors despair of ever learning any Lao, mastering a handful of simple phrases will greatly enhance your travels in Laos. The Lao are always delighted by foreigners who make the effort to converse with them in their own language and will reciprocate with more than the usual graciousness. The dialect of Lao spoken in Vientiane, which has been deemed the official language of Laos, has **six tones**. Thus a Lao word such as *sang* can have six different meanings. Depending on its tone, *sang* can mean either "elephant", "craftsman", "granary", "laryngitis", a species of bamboo, or "to build". This is not quite as impossibly complicated as it sounds. Speakers of English use tones as well, though in a different way. In English, tones are used to express emotion or differentiate between a question, statement or exclamation. For example, the word "really" can mean different things depending on the tone in which it is spoken. "Really?" sounds quite different from "Really!" Lao in fact uses these same tones to differentiate between meaning. The Lao word *sang* spoken like a question ("Sang?") means "granary" but if spoken as an exclamation ("Sang!") it means "elephant". As with most tonal languages, many Lao words are just one syllable. Originally, all Lao words were monosyllabic, but with the introduction of Buddhism to Laos, the language began to absorb polysyllabic words from the

Indian languages Pali and Sanskrit. Speakers of non-tonal languages generally find these polysyllabic loan words easier to understand and say than the monosyllabic words that rely mostly on tone to be understood. Since it is impossible to learn the six tones properly without actually hearing them, try getting a speaker of Vientiane Lao to recite **numbers one to nine in Lao** to you, since all six tones feature in these numbers (shown on p.399). Number one is a mid tone (unmarked) and since the mid and low tones are so similar, the beginner may pronounce these two tones identically. Number two is a rising tone (~), number five is a low-falling tone (`), number six is a high tone (´), and number nine is a high-falling tone (^).

Words and phrases in Lao

As a stranger you should remember to utter a greeting first. Questions the Lao commonly ask in conversation may seem personal to Westerners ("Are you married?") but this is simply an indication of the importance of the family in Lao culture. Questions in Lao are not normally answered with a yes or no. Instead the verb used in the question is repeated for the answer. For example: "Do you have a room?" would be answered "Have" in the affirmative or "No have" in the negative.

Greetings and small talk

Hello - sabai di (said with a smile)
How are you? - sabai di baw
I'm fine - sabai di
Can you speak English? - jâo wâo phasã angkit dâi baw
No I can't - wâo baw dâi
I only speak a little Lao - khói wâo phasã láo dâi nói neung
Do you understand? - jâo khào jai baw
I don't understand - khói baw khào jai
Where are you from? - jâo má tae sãi
I'm from England/ America/Australia/ New Zealand - khói má tae angkit/amelika/ awstelin/nyu silaen
What's your name? - jâo seu nyãng
My name is.... - khói seu

How old are you? - jâo anyu ják pi
How many brothers and sisters do you have?
 - jâo mí âi nâwng ják khón
Are you married yet? - jâo taeng ngan léu baw
Yes, I'm married - taeng ngan lâew
No, I'm not married - yáng baw taeng ngan
How many kids do you have? - jâo mí lûk ják khón
I've got two kids - mí lûk sãwng khón
I don't have any kids - yáng baw mí lûk
Are you enjoying Laos? - thiàw méuang láo muan baw
I'm enjoying it very much - muan lãi
Goodbye - lá kawn
Goodbye (in reply) - sok di

Getting around

Where are you going? - pai sãi (often used as a familiar greeting)
To the market - pai talat
To the guest house - pai bân phak
To the Mixai hotel - pai hong haem misai
To the boat launch/pier - pai thà heuá
To the bus station - pai khiw lot
Will you go? - pai baw
How much will you go - pai thao dai for?
One thousand kip per person - phù la phán kip

Where is the......? - ....yu sãi
Where is the guest house? - bân phak yu sãi
Where is the boat launch/pier? - thà heuá yu sãi
Drugstore - hân kãi ya
Post office - paisani
Police station - sathani tamluat
Museum - phiphithaphan
Thai embassy - sathanthut thai
Chinese embassy - sathanthut jin

Vietnamese embassy – **sathanthut wiatnam**
Is the .... far away? – **...... yu kai baw**
Is the airport far away? – **doen bin yu kai baw**
It's far – **kai**

It's not far – **baw kai**
Go straight – **pai sêu sêu**
Turn right – **lîaw khwã**
Turn left – **lîaw sâi**

Accommodation

Do you have a room? – **mí hàwng wàng baw**
Do you have a double room? – **mí hàwng sãwng tiang baw**
Does the room have a fan? – **hàwng mí phat lóm baw**
Mosquito net – **mûng**
Bathroom – **hàwng nâm**
Toilet – **suam**
Air conditioning – **ae yen**
Blankets – **phà hom**
Hot water – **nâm hâwn**
Can I see the room? – **khãw beung hàwng kawn dâi baw**
How much per night? – **khéun la thao dai**
Seven thousand kip per night – **khéun la jét phán kip**
Can you discount the price? – **lút lakha dâi baw**

Where is the toilet? – **hàwng suam yu sãi**
How many nights will you stay? – **si phak ják khéun**
I will stay two nights – **si phak sãwng khéun**
Sorry, no discounts – **lút lakha baw dâi**
Can you clean the room? – **het anamai hàwng dâi baw**
Can I have the room key? – **khãw kajae dae**
Can I move to another room? – **yâi hàwng dâi baw**
This room is full of mosquitoes – **hàwng nî mí nyung lãi**
This room is too noisy – **hàwng nî siãng dang**
Do you have a laundry service? – **mí bawlikan sak phà baw**
Do you have bicycles for rent? – **mí lot thip hài sao baw**

Eating

Useful phrases

Where can I buy ....? – **êu .... dâi bawn nãi**
Where can I buy food? – **sêu ahãn dâi bawn nãi**
Where is a restaurant? – **hàwng ahãn yu sãi**
Do you have a menu? – **khãw laikan ahãn dae?**
Do you have...? – **mi...baw?**
Not spicy.... – **baw phét**
I am vegetarian – **khói kin te phák**
I would like... – **khói ao...**
Can I have the bill? – **khãw sék dae?**
I didn't order this – **khói baw dâi sang náew nî**
What's this? – **nî nyãng?**
With/without – **sai/baw sai**
Without fish sauce – **baw sai nâm pa**
I'd like a plate of that – **khãw baep nân ján neung**
I can't eat meat – **khói kin sîn baw dâi**
No sugar – **baw sai nâm tan**
No ice – **baw sai nâm kâwn**
Bon appétit – **soen sàep**
Bottle – **kâew**

Chopsticks – **mâi thu**
Cup/glass – **jawk**
Delicious – **sàep**
Fork – **sawm**
Noodle shop – **hãn kãi fõe**
Spoon – **buang**
Restaurant – **hân ahãn**

Staples

bai hóhlapha – basil
boe – butter
hét – mushroom
hua phák bua – onion
hua phák thiam – garlic
jaew – sauce
jeun khai – omelette
kai – chicken
kha – galingale
khai dao – egg, fried
khào jâo – rice, steamed
khào ji – bread
khào niaw – rice, sticky
khing – ginger
kûng – shrimp

màk kheua - aubergine
màk len - tomato
màk phét - chilli
mu - pork
nâm kat - coconut milk
nâm pa - fish sauce
nâm tan - ugar
naw mâi - bamboo shoots
nok - bird
nóm sòm - yoghurt
pa - fish
pa dàek - fish paste
pét - duck
phák - vegetables
phák nâm - watercress
phák salat - lettuce
phõng sú lot - MSG
pu - crab
sìn ngúa - beef
tâo hû - bean curd
tôm khai - egg, boiled

Noodles

fõe - rice noodle soup
fõe hàeng - rice noodle soup without broth
fõe khùa - fried rice noodles
khào piak sèn - rice noodle soup, served in chicken broth
khào pûn - flour noodles with sauce
mi hàeng - yellow wheat noodles without broth
mi nâm - yellow wheat noodles

Everyday dishes and "drinking food"

kaeng jèut - mild soup with pork and vegetables
khào ji pateh - bread with Lao-style paté and vegetables
khào ji sai boe - bread with butter
khào khùa or khào phát - fried rice
khào khùa sai kai - fried rice with chicken
khùa khing kai - chicken with ginger
khùa phák baw sai sìn - stir-fried

bia - beer
bia sót - beer, draught

kafeh - coffee
kafeh dam - black coffee
kafeh net - instant coffee
kafeh nóm hawn - hot Lao coffee (with milk and sugar)

vegetables without meat
làp mu - minced pork
man falang jeun - chips
m u phát bai hólapha - pork with basil over rice
pîng kai - grilled chicken
pîng pa or jeun pa - grilled fish
tam màk hung - spicy papaya salad
tôm yam pa - spicy fish soup with lemongrass
yam sìn ngúa - spicy beef salad
yáw díp - spring rolls, fresh
yáw jeun - spring rolls, fried

Fruit

lamut - sapodilla
màk hung - papaya
màk kîang - orange
màk kiang - rose apple
màk kûay - banana
màk lînji - lychee
màk mángkhut - mangosteen
màk mî - jackfruit
màk mo - watermelon
màk muang - mango
màk náo - lime/lemon
màk nat - pineapple
màk ngaw - rambutan
màk nyám nyái - longan
màk phom - apple
màk sida - guava
thulian - durian

Sweets

kalaem - ice cream
khào lãm - sticky rice in coconut milk cooked in bamboo
khào niaw màk muang - sticky rice with mango
nâm wãn - sweets in coconut milk
nâm wãn màk kûay - banana in coconut milk

Drinks

kafeh nóm yén - iced coffee (with milk and sugar)
lào-láo - rice whisky
màk kuay pan - banana shake
màk mai pan - fruit shake

nâm deum – water
nâm hâwn – water, hot
nâm kâwn – ice
nâm màk phâo – coconut juice
nâm sá – tea
nâm soda – soda water
nâm tâo hû – soy milk

nâm yén – water, cold
nóm – milk
owantin – Ovaltine
sá jin – tea, Chinese
sá yén – tea, iced

Shopping

Is this for sale? – an nî khãi baw
How much? – thao dai
How much is this? – an nî thao dai
I'd like to buy .... – khói yak sêu.....
Cigarettes – ya sùp
Medicine – ya
Antiques – khãwng kao
Souvenirs – khãwng thilaleuk
Clothes – seuà phà
Silk cloth – phà mãi
Do you have ......? – mí ...... baw
Do you have soap? – mí sabu baw
Toothpaste – yã si khâew

Washing powder – sabu fun
Toilet paper – jîa hàwng nâm
Candles – thian
Mosquito coils – ya kan nyung baep jút
Flip-flops – koep tae
How much is this? – an nî thao dai
How much is it in dollars? – ngóen dawn
  khit thao dai
I only have kip – khói mí tae ngóen kip
It's very expensive – phaeng lãi
How much of a discount can you give? – lút
  lakha dãi thao dai

On the road

Does this vehicle go to .....? – lot nî pai .....
  baw
How much is it to go to.....? – pai ..... thao
  dai
How many hours will it take? – sai wela ják
  sua móng
What time will the bus depart? – lot si awk
  ják móng
What time will we arrive? – si hâwt ják
  móng
Is this seat vacant? – bawn nang nî wàng
  baw
It's vacant – wàng
It's taken – baw wàng
Can I hire the vehicle/boat outright? – mão
  lot/heuá dâi baw

How much to hire the vehicle/boat outright? –
  mão lot/héua thao dai
Don't pick up any other passengers – baw
  tâwng hap phù doi sãn khon eun
Do you agree to the price? – tók lóng lakha
  baw
I agree – tók lóng
I don't agree – baw tók lóng
Please stop here – jàwt nî dae
Please stop so I can urinate – jàwt thai bao
  dae
What's wrong with the vehicle? – lot pen
  nyãng
Will we be parked – jàwt yu nî don baw
  here for long?

Numbers

0 sun	8 pàet	16 síp hók
1 neung	9 kâo	17 síp jét
2 sãwng	10 síp	18 síp pàet
3 sãm	11 síp ét	19 síp kâo
4 si	12 síp sãwng	20 sao
5 hà	13 síp sãm	21 sao ét
6 hók	14 síp si	22 sao sãwng
7 jét	15 síp hà	30 sãm síp

31 săm síp ét	80 pàet síp	10,000 síp phán
32 săm síp săwng	90 kâo síp	50,000 hà síp phán
40 si síp	100 hôi	100,000 săen
50 hà sip	200 săwng hôi	200,000 săwng săen
60 hók síp	1000 phán	1,000,000 lân
70 jét síp	2000 săwng phán	2,000,000 săwng lân

Days of the week and time

Sunday – **wán thít**
Monday – **wán jan**
Tuesday – **wán angkhán**
Wednesday – **wán phut**
Thursday – **wan phahát**
Friday – **wán súk**
Saturday – **wán săo**
Today – **mêu nî**
Yesterday – **mêu wan nî**
Tomorrow – **mêu eun**
Morning – **tawn sâo**
Noon – **thiang wán**
Afternoon – **tawn bai**

Early evening – **tawn láeng**
Late evening – **tawn khám**
Midnight – **thiang khéun**
Next week – **athit nà**
Last week – **athit thi lâew**
Next month – **deuan nà**
Last month – **deuan thi lâew**
Next year – **pi nà**
Last year – **pi thi lâew**
Now – **tawn nî**
Later – **theua nà**
Just now – **ta kî**

Emergencies and health

Help! – **suay dae**
Can you help me? – **jâo suay khói dâi baw**
There's been an accident – **mí ubatihet**
I need a doctor – **khói tâwng kan hă măw**
I'm not well – **khói baw sabai**
I have a fever – **khói pen khai**
I have diarrhoea – **thâwng khói baw di**
I'm in a lot of pain – **khói jép nák**

Please take me to the hospital – **song khói pai hong măw dae**
I've been bitten by a dog/snake – **khói theuk mă/ngu kát**
Where is the toilet? – **hàwng suam yu săi**
I lost my passport – **pâm doen thang khăwng khói siă hăi**
My pack is missing – **kheuang khăwng khói siă hăi**

Common answers to questions

I don't know – **baw hû**
There isn't/aren't any – **baw mí**

It cannot be done – **baw dâi**
It's uncertain – **baw nàe**

Glossary

Akha highland ethnic group

ARVN Army of Republic of Vietnam, the defunct South Vietnamese Army

baht Thai currency, also a unit for measuring gold

ban house or village

basi animist Lao ceremony

bia sot draught beer

bombi type of anti-personnel bomb which explodes when touched

Brahma Hindu god

bun (or boun) festival

dawk jampa plumeria blossom, the national flower of Laos

devaraja god-king A Khmer concept of divine kingship

devata female divinity

don (or dawn) island

dvarapala guardian divinities at doors and gateways of Khmer ruins

falang white person, person of European descent

fōe Vietnamese noodle dish ("pho" in Vietnamese) found throughout Laos

hân kin deum casual eating and drinking spot

HCMT Ho Chi Minh Trail, series of trails used by the NVA to infiltrate South Vietnam

heua sa slow boat

heua wai speed boat

Hmong highland ethnic group

Indra Hindu god

jataka mythological tales of the Buddha's previous lives

jumbo three-wheeled motorized taxi

kafeh hawn hot coffee

kafeh yén iced coffee

kha slave. Formerly used as a pejorative for hilltribes

Khamu an upland ethnic group

khào rice

khào ji French bread

khào niaw sticky rice

khiw lot bus stand

Khmer Cambodian

khwaeng province

kip Lao currency

lak kilometre, often used in place names

lam wong traditional dance

Lane Xang ancient Lao kingdom

lào hái rice wine sipped from straws out of a large stoneware jar

lào-láo strong alcoholic drink made from sticky rice

làp minced meat dish

lintel horizontal beam or stone over a door or window

lustral water holy water used to bathe a Buddha image

makara mythical water monster

maw thiam spirit medium

Mien a highland ethnic group

muan fun, enjoyable

muang (or meuang) city or town

mukhalinga phallic-shaped stone symbolic of Shiva with an image of the god's face carved into it

naga benevolent mythical water serpent (pronounced "nak" in Lao).

nam phu (or nam phou) fountain

ngeuak malevolent mythical water serpent

NTAL National Tourism Authority of Laos

NVA North Vietnamese Army

pa dàek fermented fish paste, used as seasoning

pa kha Irrawaddy dolphin

pa pao blowfish with a vicious bite found in southern Laos

pak mouth of a river

Pathet Lao communist guerrilla movement which gained control of Laos in 1975

Patouxai monument in Vientiane

Pha Bang a Buddha image belived by many to be the talismanic protector of the Lao nation

Pha In Hindu god Indra

Pha Lak Pha Lam Lao version of the Ramayana

Pha Phut the Buddha

Pha Phutthahup Buddha image

phi spirit or ghost

phu (or phou) hill or mountain

Phuan lowland ethnic group

pirogue narrow dug-out canoe

Ramayana epic poem of Indian origin (Pha Lak Pha Lam in Lao)

rishi hermitic ascetic

Royal Lao Army (RLA) army of the defunct Kingdom of Laos

sala pavilion with a raised floor and roof but no walls

samana re-education camp, derived from the word "seminar"

sawngthaew pick-up truck used for public transport

Shiva Hindu god

Shivalinga phallic-shaped stone symbolic of Shiva

sim building in a monastery housing the main Buddha image

sin women's wrap-around skirt

soi lane or alley

somasutra stone pipe for channelling lustral water

stupa Buddhist structure built to contain holy relics ("that" in Lao)

tad (or tat) waterfall

talat market

Talat Sao Vientiane's Morning Market

tam màk hung spicy papaya salad

thanon road or street

that Lao word for Buddhist stupa

tuk-tuk three-wheeled motorized taxi

ushnisha finial symbolizing enlightenment found on the crown of the head of Buddha images

UXO unexploded ordnance

Vishnu a Hindu god

wat Buddhist monastery

wiang (or viang) town surrounded by wooden palisades

xiang town surrounded by brick or earthen ramparts

Index

and small print

Index

Map entries are in colour

Twenty Years of Rough Guides

In the summer of 1981, Mark Ellingham, Rough Guides' founder, knocked out the first guide on a typewriter, with a group of friends. Mark had been travelling in Greece after university, and couldn't find a guidebook that really answered his needs. There were heavyweight cultural guides on the one hand – good on museums and classical sites but not on beaches and tavernas – and on the other hand student manuals that were so caught up with how to save money that they lost sight of the country's significance beyond its role as a place for a cool vacation. None of the guides began to address Greece as a country, with its natural and human environment, its politics and its contemporary life.

Having no urgent reason to return home, Mark decided to write his own guide. It was a guide to Greece that tried to combine some erudition and insight with a thoroughly practical approach to travellers' needs. Scrupulously researched listings of places to stay, eat and drink were matched by careful attention to detail on everything from Homer to Greek music, from classical sites to national parks and from nude beaches to monasteries. Back in London, Mark and his friends got their Rough Guide accepted by a farsighted commissioning editor at the publisher Routledge and it came out in 1982.

The Rough Guide to Greece was a student scheme that became a publishing phenomenon. The immediate success of the book – shortlisted for the Thomas Cook award – spawned a series that rapidly covered dozens of countries. The Rough Guides found a ready market among backpackers and budget travellers, but soon acquired a much broader readership that included older and less impecunious visitors. Readers relished the guides' wit and inquisitiveness as much as the enthusiastic, critical approach that acknowledges everyone wants value for money – but not at any price.

Rough Guides soon began supplementing the "rougher" information – the hostel and low-budget listings – with the kind of detail that independent-minded travellers on any budget might expect. These days, the guides – distributed worldwide by the Penguin Group – include recommendations spanning the range from shoestring to luxury, and cover more than 200 destinations around the globe. Our growing team of authors, many of whom come to Rough Guides initially as outstandingly good letter-writers telling us about their travels, are spread all over the world, particularly in Europe, the USA and Australia. As well as the travel guides, Rough Guides publishes a series of dictionary phrasebooks covering two dozen major languages, an acclaimed series of music guides running the gamut from Classical to World Music, a series of music CDs in association with World Music Network, and a range of reference books on topics as diverse as the Internet, Pregnancy and Unexplained Phenomena. Visit **www.roughguides.com** to see what's cooking.

Rough Guide Credits

Text editors: Helena Smith and Caroline Osbourne
Series editor: Mark Ellingham
Editorial: Martin Dunford, Jonathan Buckley, Kate Berens, Ann-Marie Shaw, Olivia Swift, Ruth Blackmore, Geoff Howard, Claire Saunders, Gavin Thomas, Alexander Mark Rogers, Polly Thomas, Joe Staines, Richard Lim, Duncan Clark, Peter Buckley, Lucy Ratcliffe, Clifton Wilkinson, Alison Murchie, Matthew Teller, Andrew Dickson, Fran Sandham (UK); Andrew Rosenberg, Stephen Timblin, Yuki Takagaki, Richard Koss, Hunter Slaton, Julie Feiner (US)
Production: Susanne Hillen, Andy Hilliard, Link Hall, Helen Prior, Julia Bovis, Michelle Draycott, Katie Pringle, Zoë Nobes,

Rachel Holmes, Andy Turner.
Cartography: Melissa Baker, Maxine Repath, Ed Wright, Katie Lloyd-Jones
Cover art direction: Louise Boulton
Picture research: Sharon Martins, Mark Thomas
Online: Kelly Cross, Anja Mutic-Blessing, Jennifer Gold, Audra Epstein, Suzanne Welles, Cree Lawson (US)
Finance: John Fisher, Gary Singh, Edward Downey, Mark Hall, Tim Bill
Marketing & Publicity: Richard Trillo, Niki Smith, David Wearn, Chloë Roberts, Demelza Dallow, Claire Southern (UK); Simon Carloss, David Wechsler, Megan Kennedy (US)
Administration: Tania Hummel, Julie Sanderson

Publishing information

This second edition published October 2002 by **Rough Guides Ltd**,
62–70 Shorts Gardens, London WC2H 9AH
Penguin Putnam Inc., 375 Hudson Street, NY 10014, USA
Distributed by the Penguin Group
Penguin Books Ltd,
80 Strand, London WC2R ORL
Penguin Putnam Inc.,
375 Hudson Street, NY 10014, USA
Penguin Books Australia Ltd,
487 Maroondah Highway, PO Box 257, Ringwood, Victoria 3134, Australia.
Penguin Books Canada Ltd,
10 Alcorn Avenue, Toronto, Ontario M4V 1E4 Canada
Penguin Books (NZ) Ltd,
182–190 Wairau Road, Auckland 10, New Zealand
Typeset in Bembo and Helvetica to an original design by Henry Iles.

Printed in Italy by LegoPrint S.p.A

© Jeff Cranmer and Steven Martin 2002

440pp includes index
A catalogue record for this book is available from the British Library
ISBN 1-85828-905-X

Help us update

We've gone to a lot of effort to ensure that the second edition of **The Rough Guide to Laos** is accurate and up-to-date. However, things change – places get "discovered", opening hours are notoriously fickle, restaurants and rooms raise prices or lower standards. If you feel we've got it wrong or left something out, we'd like to know, and if you can remember the address, the price, the time, the phone number, so much the better.

We'll credit all contributions, and send a copy of the next edition (or any other Rough

Guide if you prefer) for the best letters. Everyone who writes to us and isn't already a subscriber will receive a copy of our full-colour thrice-yearly newsletter. Please mark letters: "**Rough Guide Laos Update**" and send to: Rough Guides, 62–70 Shorts Gardens, London WC2H 9AH, or Rough Guides, 4th Floor, 345 Hudson St, New York, NY 10014. Or send an email to **mail@roughguides.com**.

Have your questions answered and tell others about your trip at **www.roughguides.atinfopop.com**.

Acknowledgements

The **authors** would like to thank Kirby Coxon for an excellent job updating this edition of the guide and Helena Smith for keeping everything running smoothly along the way. Thanks also to Peter Koret, whose insights proved invaluable in writing the section on Lao literature.

The **editor** thanks Alison for editorial help; Rachel for typesetting; Katie for the colour section; Louise for the cover; Mark for the inside photos; Sam Kirby for maps; Antonia Hebbert for proofreading; and Jo Mead for indexing.

Readers' letters

Thanks to all the readers who took the trouble to write in with their comments and suggestions (and apologies to anyone whose name we've misspelt or omitted):
Anja Balfour; D. Dubbin; Meg Fearns; John Garratt; Garth Gilmer; H.M. Graham; S. Greenwood; Audrey Knight; Monica Mackaness; Mark Mills; Chris Mosley; Anja Mutic; Terry Nakazono; Patrick Wildisen; Anne Wheeler.

Photo credits

SMALL PRINT

Cover credits

Main front picture Buddha Park, Vientiane © Image Bank
Small front top image Laotian textile © J.Jones/Ffotograff
Back lower image Plain of Jars © M.Greenslade/Ffotograff
Back top image Mekong River © A.Gasson/Trip
Back lower image Wat Xieng Thong, Louang Phabang © M.Greenslade/Ffotograff

Colour introduction

Wat Xiang Thong © Gavin Hellier/Robert Harding
Fishing in the Mekong River at sunset © Steve Davey/La Belle Aurore
Dyed silk © Tim Hall/Robert Harding
Morning market, Pakse © Tim Hall/Axiom
Hmong tribeswoman © T. Lester/Trip
Monks collecting alms, Mekong riverfront © Steve Davey/La Belle Aurore
Kayaking on the Nam Xong river, Vang Viang © Steve Davey/La Belle Aurore
Limestone karst cliffs © Steve Davey/La Belle Aurore
Pile of ordnance © Martyn Evans/Travel Ink
Flock of white geese © Martyn Evans/Travel Ink
Toys depicting mythical animals © Jim Holmes/Axiom

Things not to miss

Buddha image, Wat Sisaket © Tim Hall/Robert Harding
Sacred Hill, Louang Phabang © Trip/Ask Images
Trekking © Steve Davey/La Belle Aurore
Villa Santi © Steve Davey/La Belle Aurore
Long-boat races on the Mekong © Jim Holmes/Axiom
Kouang Si Falls © Martyn Evans/Travel Ink
Mekong River sunset © Martyn Evans/Travel Ink
The former Royal Palace, Louang Phabang © Jim Holmes/Axiom
Plain of Jars © Steve Davey/La Belle Aurore
Colonial houses © Alain Evrard/Robert Harding
Wat Xiang Thong © Gavin Hellier/Robert Harding
Lao woman weighing greens © Steve Davey/La Belle Aurore
Traditional cloth-making © Jim Holmes/Axiom
Sunset behind limestone karst cliffs © Steve Davey/La Belle Aurore
That Chomsi © T. Bognar/Trip
Drinking tea at the herbal sauna © Steve Davey/La Belle Aurore
That Louang Festival © T. Lester/Trip
Passenger boat heading up the Nam Ou river © Steve Davey/La Belle Aurore
Champasak © Charlie Marsden/Travel Ink
Haw Pha Kaew © B. Vikander/Trip
Patouxai © Tim Hall/Robert Harding
Buddha caves © B. Vikander/Trip

Black and whites

Tuk-tuk © Travel Ink
Wat Sisaket © T. Bognar/Trip
Wat Simuang © Rolf Richardson/Robert Harding
Louang Phabang © Robert Harding
Temple doors, Louang Phabang © Martyn Evans/Travel Ink
Bomb casings © Jim Holmes/Axiom
Plain of Jars © Steve Davey/La Belle Aurore

Trekking en route to an Akha village © Steve Davey/La Belle Aurore

Hmong woman selling goods © Charlie Marsden/Travel Ink

Mekong Valley, village house © Tony Waltham/Robert Harding

That Ing Hang ©Tony Waltham/Robert Harding

French-style house, Pakse © Tim Hall/Robert Harding

Temple door © Robert McLeod/Robert Harding

Pagoda detail © Jim Holmes/Axiom

SMALL PRINT

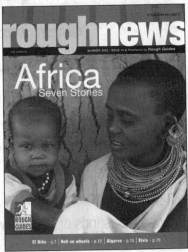

Don't bury your head in the sand!

Take cover!

with Rough Guide Travel Insurance

Worldwide cover, for Rough Guide readers worldwide

UK Freefone **0800 015 09 06**
US Freefone **1 866 220 5588**
Worldwide **(+44) 1243 621 046**
Check the web at
www.roughguides.com/insurance

ROUGH GUIDES